The Macintosh Bible guide to Word 6

Maria Langer

Peachpit Press

The Macintosh Bible Guide to Word 6
Maria Langer

Peachpit Press
2414 Sixth Street
Berkeley, CA 94710
510/548-4393
510/548-5991 (fax)

Peachpit Press is a division of Addison-Wesley Publishing Company.

Cover design: YO, San Francisco
Cover illustration: John Grimes

ISBN 1-56609-073-3

9 8 7 6 5 4 3 2 1

Printed and bound in the United States of America

Printed on recycled paper

Dedication

To Mike

Acknowledgments

I'd like to thank the following individuals, who made writing this book possible — or at least a bit easier to do.

My first thanks goes to Ken Brown, who brought me to Peachpit. Without Ken, I probably would not have been involved in this project at all.

Next, I'd like to thank Jeremy Judson at Peachpit for his patience, understanding, and unfailing ability to listen to my long distance, off-topic telephone chatter. I'd also like to thank him for reminding me that it's okay to say no once in a while.

I'd like to thank Ted Nace for proving, to my delight, that all publishers are *not* the same. I'd also like to thank the rest of the folks at Peachpit for being so darn nice and making me feel like part of the Peachpit family. That means a lot more to me (and probably to other authors) than they might think.

Next, I'd like to thank Joanne Davis and David Carson at Microsoft. Their prompt responses to my technical support questions helped make this book accurate. I'd like to thank the folks on the Beta Administrative Support team for getting betas to me on a timely basis. Finally, I'd like to thank the rest of the folks at Microsoft for putting together such powerful and flexible software products and for including the kinds of features in Word 6 that a writer can really use.

There are a few other folks on the thank you list: Alex Miloradovich for his kinder, gentler editing; Mark Budzyn for providing a screen shot I could not produce and for telling me about the file hierarchy tree; and the Peachpit design and layout team for putting together a great looking book.

Finally, I'd like to thank my significant other, Mike, for putting up with my wildly swinging moods during the months I worked on this book. How he can continue to live with me after six books in two and a half years is a mystery to me.

Table of Contents

Introduction

CONGRATULATIONS! YOU'VE MADE TWO VERY SMART DECISIONS.

The first decision was to make Microsoft Word your word processor. Well, maybe that wasn't *your* decision, but it was a smart decision nonetheless. Word is a powerful, feature-packed program that can handle your word processing needs, no matter how basic or demanding they are. As you work with Word, you'll find that it's easy to learn — you'll be creating dynamite-looking documents in no time at all. Unlike other, more simple word processing applications, you're not likely to run into Word's limitations. Why? Because Word does just about everything you'll ever need a word processor to do — and more.

The other smart decision was buying this book. Good work! But if you haven't bought it yet, what are you waiting for? Stop browsing! *This* is the one! Read on and I'll explain why.

About this Book

In this book I show you how you can use Microsoft Word to create, edit, format, save, and print documents you can be proud of. But I go far beyond the basics. I'll also show you how you can tap the power of Word to make your work easier or faster to do. After all, no matter how good a program is, no one wants to spend all their time working with it.

Written in plain English (my favorite language), this book provides important background information, step-by-step instructions, screen illustrations, and real-life examples to:

- **Explain why things work the way they do.** Understanding the logic of how a program works gives you insight that'll help you get your work done without a lot of time-consuming experimentation. That's what background information is all about.
- **Tell you what you need to do to get the job done.** To turn your ideas into a printed document, you must complete a number of small tasks. This book uses a task-oriented approach that provides detailed steps for completing each little job you need to do to get the big job done.
- **Show you what your Mac's screen looks like as you work.** There's no need to wonder whether you're doing something right as you follow the instructions in this book. There are plenty of illustrations to keep you on track.
- **Tell you how other Word users use Word.** I've been teaching people how to use Microsoft Word for over four years now. In this book, I'll tell you about some of the things my students use Word for, both at home and in the workplace. I'm willing to bet you'll learn a lot from us!

And, if you haven't caught on yet, I'm a firm believer that humor makes it easier and a heck of a lot more fun to learn. I've written this book the way I teach a class, complete with jokes and little stories. The only things you'll find in my classes that you won't find in this book are my run-on sentences (fortunately for you, I write better than I speak) and my New Jersey accent. If you ask me, you're not missing much.

Whom is this Book For?

This book is for just about anyone who wants to learn how to use Microsoft Word:

- **New Word Users.** If you've never used Word before, this book is for you. I explain Word from the ground up, beginning with the basics and moving on to more advanced topics. Even if you've never used a word processor before, I'll have you up and running with Word before you can say "Microsoft" backwards.
- **Experienced Word Users.** Word has been around for a while. If you've used previous versions of Word (most recently 5.1, 5.0, and 4.0) this book will help you move on to Word 6 by drawing your attention to brand new features. Just don't be surprised if you also learn about old features of Word that you never knew about.

What's Inside

This is a big book. Don't let that scare you. It's big because it's got a lot of information in it. Fortunately, it's organized in a way that makes it easy to find, understand, and use the information you need.

This book has five main parts. Each part contains several chapters. Here's a rundown of the parts and the chapters within them:

Part 1: Getting Started with Word

This part covers Word's basics, launching Word, Word's environment, and creating, editing, saving, and printing a Word document. If you've never used Word before, be sure to pay close attention to this part of the book since it'll provide basic information you need to get started, and then move on to more advanced topics. If you're an experienced Word user, at least browse through this part to identify new features in Word version 6 (there are lots of them!) as well as tips and tricks that can make even basic tasks easier to do.

The chapters are as follows:

Chapter 1: Windows, Menus, and Toolbars

Chapter 2: Working with Text

Chapter 3: Working with Files

Chapter 4: Printing Documents

Part 2: Formatting

This part of the book explains character, paragraph, section, and document formatting options. You'll learn how to use Word's menu commands, toolbars, rulers, and styles feature to format your documents so they appear just the way you want.

The chapters are:

Chapter 5: Font Formatting

Chapter 6: Paragraph Formatting

Chapter 7: Paragraph and Character Styles

Chapter 8: Section and Document Formatting

Chapter 9: Templates and Automatic Formatting

Part 3: Special Text and Graphics Formatting

This part of the book will show you some of the special text and graphics formatting features available in Word. These go beyond basic formatting to meet special word processing needs.

The chapters are as follows:

Chapter 10: Headers, Footers, Footnotes, and Endnotes

Chapter 11: Tables

Chapter 12: Graphics and Objects

Chapter 13: Frames, Borders, and Shading

Chapter 14: Bookmarks, Captions, and Cross-references

Chapter 15: Lists, Outlines, and Master Documents

Part 4: Putting Word's Features to Work

This part of the book shows you how to take advantage of some of the productivity features and tools Word offers. These features make it easy to perform both basic and advanced word processing tasks.

The chapters are:

Chapter 16: Text Editing with Find, Replace, AutoText, and AutoCorrect

Chapter 17: Proofing Tools

Chapter 18: Annotations and Revisions

Chapter 19: Envelopes and Labels

Chapter 20: Indexes and Tables

Chapter 21: Mail Merge

Chapter 22: Forms

Part 5: Advanced Features

This part of the book is for power users. It introduces you to advanced tasks and features that let you use Word the way you want to get your work done.

The chapters are:

Chapter 23: Customizing Word Options

Chapter 24: Customizing Toolbars, Menus, and Shortcut Keys

Chapter 25: Sharing Information

Chapter 26: Automation with Wizards and Macros

But Wait! There's More!

That's just what you'll find inside the numbered chapters. But that's not all there is.

Before We Start: Word Processing Basics

If you've never used a word processor before, all this talk about documents and saving and editing might be getting you nervous. Calm down. There's a whole section of the book, right near the beginning, just for you. It'll teach you the very basics of word processing, including the concepts of on-screen editing and formatting, scrolling windows, and storing documents on disk. You'll even learn some word processing terms you can use to impress your typewriter-stricken friends.

Appendix A: Installing Word

As software becomes more and more complex, so does its installation. Word is no different. Appendix A will walk you through the installation of Word 6.

If you haven't installed Word yet, read Appendix A first. If you have installed it and didn't really know what you were doing, read Appendix A to find out what you did.

Appendix B: Cross-Platform Considerations

If this were a perfect world, all computers would be Macintoshes. Unfortunately, this is not a perfect world. And sometimes — maybe more often than you like — you have to exchange document files with people who aren't lucky enough to have Macintoshes on their desks. This Appendix discusses some important considerations when the same Word files are accessed by Macintosh or Windows version users.

Appendix C: Keyboard Shortcuts

You want shortcuts? This book has 'em. It includes all the Word keyboard shortcuts you'll ever want to use — and then some.

What's Not Inside

This book might be fat but it doesn't include everything you need to know to use Microsoft Word on your Macintosh. For example, this book won't tell you how to use a mouse. It won't tell you how to turn your Macintosh on. It won't even tell you how to format a disk. You can find that kind of information in the manuals that came with your Macintosh.

If you're brand new to the Macintosh and are reading this book to learn how to use Word, that's fine. But you may have to do a little preliminary work first. If words like *point*, *click*, *drag*, and *icon* seem like random ravings of a lunatic, go through the program called Macintosh Basics. This program, which comes with every new Macintosh, teaches some important concepts you simply must know before you begin reading this book. Or sit down with the manuals that came with your Macintosh and read up.

How to Use this Book

You can use this book as either a tutorial or a reference book. Use it for both, for that matter. Read through it — I promise to be entertaining. Or use the table of contents and index to find exactly the piece of information you're looking for to get the job done.

What the Icons are For

Throughout this book, you'll see icons. They haven't been thrown in for decoration. They're designed to draw your attention to various bits of information that I think are important — or at least interesting.

New in Word 6

This icon appears in the margin beside the discussion of any brand new Word 6 feature. It's there for the benefit of folks who have used previous versions of Microsoft Word, just to make sure they don't miss something new and exciting.

Tip/Trick

This icon appears beside any little tips or tricks I think you might be interested in. You'll find it beside shortcuts and other useful tidbits of information.

Important Note

This icon appears beside any very important or potentially dangerous instructions. Pay attention to these icons — they may save you a lot of grief.

What the Sidebars are For

This book also includes a number of sidebars. I use sidebars in three ways:

FYI

These sidebars provide additional information that is not vital to using Word, but can be helpful to you. Sometimes I'll use these sidebars to tell you stories. Other times I'll use them to explain why a certain feature of Word might be useful. You can read them or skip them — your choice.

For Example

These sidebars provide examples of how other Word users take advantage of Word's features. Look for these sidebars to find all kinds of real-life ideas for using Word.

Try This!

These sidebars provide numbered step-by-step instructions for performing a specific task. Use these as tutorials to learn by trying things for yourself.

Tell Me What You Think

I love getting feedback from people who read my books (especially *good* feedback). After you've had this book for a while, why not show off your Microsoft Word skills by writing me a little note to let me know what you thought of it? I promise to read it (good or bad), although I can't promise to respond. You can send it to me at:

Maria Langer
P.O. Box 212
Harrington Park, NJ 07640-0212

If you've got a modem, you might prefer reaching me via one of the online services. I'm on a bunch of them:

America Online: MariaL1
CompuServe: 70461,1663
AppleLink: MLANGER
Internet: marial1@aol.com
Fidonet: Maria Langer, 1:2605/157
OneNet: Maria Langer,Electronic Pen

If I left anything out or wasn't clear on something, please be sure to scold me so I can fix it when the next version of Word (and this book) comes out.

Let's Get Started

That's enough information about the book. Let's get to it and let it speak for itself.

Before You Start: Word Processing Basics

NOT LONG AGO, BACK WHEN I WAS IN COLLEGE, I DREADED doing term papers. It wasn't the writing that scared me. It was the typing. Back then, people didn't have word processors or computers. They had typewriters.

I was lucky enough to have a portable electric typewriter — a big monster that weighed about forty pounds and vibrated my desk when I turned it on. Because it was electric, I didn't have to pound on the keys with my fingertips to get letters on the paper. I had to slide in the paper, being sure to line it up properly. I had to make sure the first line on each page started at about the same place. I had to type carefully to avoid mistakes. When the bell rang, I had to remember to press the Return key to slide the paper back and start a new line.

That wasn't so bad. What was bad was when I made a mistake and had to take out the correction fluid — foul-smelling stuff that never seemed to dry within a reasonable amount of time. Or when a mistake was so bad that I had to tear out a half-finished page and retype it. Or when I forgot to leave enough room at the bottom of the page for footnotes and then had to retype *the entire page*. I can remember retyping pages three or four times until I got it just right. Honestly, I think a portion of the term paper grade should have been based on how well it was typed.

Nowadays, we've got computers and word processors that make it almost pleasant to create documents — even documents with footnotes! In this part of the book, I'll explain the differences between word processing and typing and introduce some word processing concepts you should know about when using Microsoft Word. I'll also tell you about a few Macintosh keyboard keys you won't find on a typewriter keyboard. If Word is your first exposure to word processing after setting aside your typewriter, this section is for you.

What's the Difference?

While a computer keyboard and a typewriter keyboard might look very similar, using a word processor on a computer is very different from typing on a typewriter. Sure, they both put words on paper, but a word processor gives you far more control over the way you can enter, edit, and format your documents. It even gives you the ability to save the work you've "typed" so you can work with it again another time.

Let's take a closer look at some of the differences between word processing and typing.

Entering and editing text

On a typewriter, you type. On a word processor, you enter text. What's the difference? Good question.

When typing on a typewriter, you must type words in the order they must appear. Words make sentences, sentences make paragraphs, paragraphs make finished pages. If you decide that you want to add something to a sentence you've already typed, you must retype the page it appears on. To be productive, you must know exactly what you want to type, in the order you want to type it, *before* you begin typing.

Not so with word processing. You can enter text in any order you like. While it certainly is easier to enter text in sentences and paragraphs, there's nothing to stop you from adding, removing, or rearranging something you've already entered. Of course, this makes editing a lot easier, too. If you find a mistake in the middle of your document, no problem. Just fix it.

FYI: Linear vs. Nonlinear Thinking

Typing versus word processing brings up the concept of linear versus nonlinear thinking. If you're using a typewriter to write — as opposed to using it to type something you've already written out by hand — you must create a document from start to finish. This is *linear* (in a line). If you're using a word processor, on the other hand, you can create a document in any order you wish. If you're like me and find it difficult to write the beginning and ending of a piece, write the middle first, then do the beginning, and finally, write the end. And change any part of it along the way. This is *nonlinear*.

Although this certainly makes a writer's life easier, after a while, it also tends to make it difficult for a writer to think linearly. After all, why dream up a letter, story, report, or book in the order it finally appears in when you can write it in any order you like? Still, I wouldn't have it any other way. If I had to write books on my old college typewriter, I would have remained an accountant forever. (And if I ever write a spreadsheet book, I'll tell you what spreadsheets have done for the accounting field.)

Character formatting

On a typewriter, your character formatting or style options are limited to bold and underline. On my college typewriter, if I wanted to make something bold, I had to type it once, then use the Backspace key to go back to the beginning of it and type it again. By typing it twice, it *looked* bold. If I wanted to make something underlined, I had to type it, then use the Backspace key to go back to the beginning, hold down the Shift key, and press the Hyphen/Underscore key until it was underlined. I couldn't do italics, although some typewriters can. They require that the typist stop typing, remove the type element (usually an inky ball), and replace it with another to type in the italicized word. Then remove the italic type element and put the original back in to continue typing plain text. It really doesn't seem worth the bother, does it?

Macintosh word processors give you access to multiple formatting options that you can combine to make thousands — if not millions — of character formatting combinations. Make text bold, underlined, italic, shadowed, outlined, strikethru, all caps, small caps, hidden, superscript, subscript, condensed, expanded, or even colored! Change the *font* or typeface. Make characters as large or small as you like. All of these changes are only a few mouse clicks and menu choices away. And if you decide you don't like the changes you've made, you can revert to the normal style of your document and start all over again.

FYI: Why Use Character Formatting?

What's the benefit of formatting text in your document? Well, by careful use of character formatting, you can make your document more effective as a communication tool. Imagine what this book would be like if all the text, including the section headings, appeared in the same exact size and style of text. Would it be as easy to find information? Of course not. Character formatting helps you communicate. Just don't get carried away.

Document formatting

On a typewriter, most document formatting is done manually. You determine the top margin by where you position the paper to start typing. You determine the bottom margin and page breaks by where you stop typing on a page. Right and left margins are determined by where you position those little thingamabobs on the carriage — you know, those margin setting things. Still, you have to tell the typewriter when you've finished typing a line of text by manually sliding the carriage holding the paper (on a manual typewriter) or pressing the Return key (on an electric typewriter).

Word processors handle most of these things automatically for you for every page. *Default* or standard settings determine margins and page breaks for the entire document or just portions of it. You can change these settings and the word processor will format the document the way you specified. Text automatically continues on the next line when you reach the end of a line. (This is called *word wrap* — more on that in a while.) Page break markers automatically appear when you've reached the limit of what can appear on a page. But don't worry, you can override page the automatic page breaks on any page. There's no need to tell the machine when you're done typing a line. There's no need to stop typing and insert a fresh sheet of paper to start a new page. Just enter text and let the word processor take care of the page formatting details for you.

Saving

When you type, the only record of what you're typing is on the paper in your typewriter. Unless you have one of those really fancy electronic typewriters with a memory feature, your keystrokes are not saved. So if you type a document and, a week later, realize that you need to make some changes to it, you have to type the whole thing again, incorporating the changes into the new copy.

This isn't the case with word processors. Word processors let you save your documents as files on your computer's disk. Once saved, you can open, edit, and print a document whenever you like. The only typing you'll have to do is to make changes. The original document is stored in its entirety for you to work with. I'll tell you more about saving files in Chapter 3.

Printing

On a typewriter, you print as you type. This is probably the biggest drawback to typing. Each time you press a keyboard key other than [Shift], [Spacebar], [Tab], [Backspace], or [Return], a character appears on a piece of paper. To change something, you must remove what's already on the paper. That's where smelly correction fluids and sticky correction tapes come in. Good luck using them if you're typing on colored paper.

Word processors, however, don't print until you tell them to. You can write an entire 600-page book without printing a single word until after you type the words "The End" on what will be the last page. When you're ready to print, print whatever pages you like. Print two or three copies if you feel like it. There's very little extra effort required on your part.

FYI: What Will it Look Like?

If you're concerned about what each page of your document will look like when you print it, word processors like Word give you a Print Preview command that shows you exactly how your document will look on paper, page by page. The really great thing about this is that if you don't like the way something appears in Print Preview, you can go into your document and change it. All without wasting a single sheet of paper. Imagine how many trees you can save!

More than just typing

These are just a few of the differences between typewriters and word processors. You'll find these differences when you compare a typewriter to just about any word processor.

But there are other differences, too. Most of them are things a word processor can do that a typewriter simply can't. Things like checking spelling and grammar, offering synonyms, storing often-used words and phrases for future use, automatically hyphenating, and counting characters, words, lines, and paragraphs. These features (or the lack of them) are what distinguish one word processor from another. As you'll see throughout this book, Microsoft Word has one of the most complete feature sets available among Macintosh word processors.

Word Processing Concepts

Now that you know some of the differences between typing and word processing, I'll discuss some word processing concepts.

Insertion Point

The *insertion point* is the place where text appears when you type. In Word, it appears as a blinking vertical bar, as shown in the following illustration:

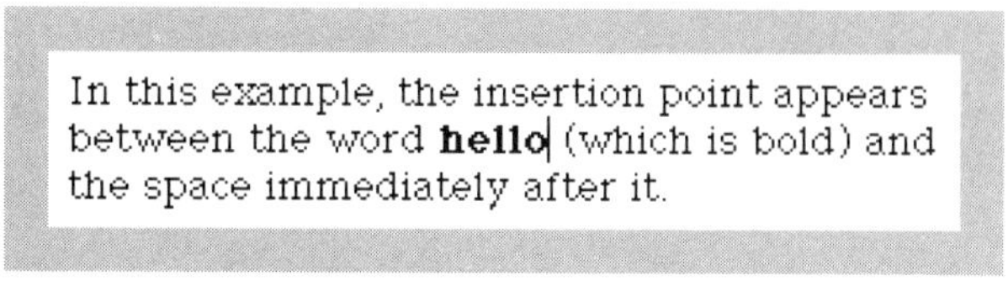

It's called the insertion point because text is inserted at the point it appears. (Clever, huh?) That means that if the insertion point is in the middle of a word and you start typing, whatever you type will go into the middle of that word. Everything after the insertion point will be pushed to the right to make room for whatever you're typing.

Word wrap

Word wrap, which I mentioned briefly earlier, refers to the way text automatically begins a new line when nothing more can fit on the current line. Text flows from line to line as you type. You do not need to do anything special for a word processor to do this. In fact, if you *do* try to help out a word processor by pressing Return at the end of each line, you're defeating the purpose of word wrap, which is to make sure text flows naturally.

Pressing Return at the end of each line makes it impossible for the word processor to automatically adjust the way words flow from line to line when you insert or delete text. Use the Return key only to begin a new paragraph.

IMPORTANT NOTE

Nonprinting characters

This brings up the topic of *nonprinting* characters. When you press Return, you're doing more than telling Word to start a new paragraph. You're actually typing in a Return character. The Return character is only one example of an invisible character. The Space and Tab characters are two others. None of these characters show in a printed document, but Word treats them as it does any other character. You can insert, delete, and even format them — although why you'd want to format an invisible character is beyond me.

What does this mean to you? It means you can't use Return, Spacebar, or Tab to move around within your document unless you really do want to insert a Return, Space, or Tab character. In Chapter 2, I'll tell you more about the right way to move around in your documents.

FYI: Viewing Nonprinting Characters

Word gives you the ability to display nonprinting characters. They appear as gray backwards Ps (for Returns), elevated dots (for Spaces), and arrows (for Tabs). There are others, as well. To display them, click the Show/Hide ¶ button on the Standard toolbar along the top of the screen. In Chapter 2, I tell you more about showing nonprinting characters and why you might want to do it.

Scrolling

Unless your document is very short, you probably won't be able to see the whole thing on your screen at once. That's where *scrolling* comes in. As you type, your document *scrolls* away off the top of the screen.

What does this mean? Well, think of your document as a long, continuous sheet of paper. Think of the Word document window as a picture frame that the paper can't fit into. As you enter text, the long sheet of paper moves up so that the place you're typing always appears in the frame, which remains motionless on your screen.

Word's document windows provide standard Macintosh scroll bars that you can use to scroll through your document. In Chapter 1, I tell you more about how you can use them to see various parts of your document.

WYSIWYG

WYSIWYG, which is pronounced "wizzy-wig," is an acronym for "What You See Is What You Get." This means that the way your document appears on the screen is the way it will print. This isn't always true, as you'll discover later in this book, but it is true for most character and paragraph formatting. Make a word bold and it appears bold on your screen. Make a word larger and italic and it appears larger and italic. Double-space a paragraph and it appears double-spaced. This is what WYSIWYG is all about.

The main benefit of WYSIWYG, at least as far as I'm concerned, is that there are no surprises when it comes time to print your document. The formatting you included in your document is there for you to see as you work with it. You can see character styles, sizes, and fonts. You can see line spacing, word wrap, and page breaks. There are no complex formatting codes to remember and decipher. You don't have to wonder about how something is formatted.

Experienced Macintosh users have come to take WYSIWYG for granted. After all, it's a built-in feature of most Macintosh programs. But in the early days of word processing — and still today on some non-Macintosh word processing systems — WYSIWYG was not available. You never knew what your document would look like until you printed it. So be thankful you've got it!

Keys You Won't Find on a Typewriter

Now that we've covered the main differences between typewriters and word processors and discussed some word processing concepts, let's take a closer look at the Macintosh keyboard. There are a few keys there that you won't find on a typewriter keyboard.

Delete (and Del)

The [Delete] key deletes text. It either deletes the character immediately before the insertion point or it deletes selected text. I'll tell you more about using [Delete] and selecting text in Chapter 2.

On extended keyboards, there's also a [Del] key, which appears right beneath the [Help] key. This key deletes the character immediately after the insertion point or deletes selected text. I'll also tell you more about this key in Chapter 2.

Command

The [⌘] key is used in combination with other keys to access Word's menu commands. A *shortcut key* is a keyboard combination you can use instead of choosing a command from a menu with your mouse. For example, [⌘][S] is the shortcut key to save a document. To use this shortcut, hold down [⌘] and press [S]. This is the same as choosing Save from the File menu.

Option

The [Option] key is also used in conjunction with other keys. But rather than just providing shortcuts for menu commands, [Option] enables you to type in special characters available in most Macintosh fonts. I'll tell you more about special characters in Chapter 5.

Control

The [Control] key, like the [⌘] key, can be used in combination with other keys to perform commands. Because it is seldom assigned to a command, it's a good choice when setting up your own shortcut keys. I'll tell you how you can customize shortcut keys in Chapter 24.

Enter

On the Macintosh keyboard, there's a [Return] key *and* an [Enter] key. [Enter] appears on the numeric keypad on the far right side of most keyboards. The [Return] and [Enter] keys are different, although in many situations, they perform the same functions. Still, to perform some commands, you must use one key or the other. When it really does matter, I'll be sure to point it out for you. [Enter] is most often used to select the default button — the one with the dark border around it — in a dialog box without using the mouse. I'll talk more about dialog boxes in Chapter 1.

Escape

The [Esc] key is most often used to select the Cancel button in a dialog box without using the mouse. I'll talk more about dialog boxes in Chapter 1.

Function Keys

If you have an extended keyboard, you have a row of 15 *function keys* across the top of your keyboard. These keys are used as shortcut keys, both alone and in combination with ⌘, Option, and Shift.

Other Keys

Extended keyboards also have keys labeled Home, End, Pg Up, and Pg Dn, as well as keys with arrows on them. These keys let you move the insertion point around your document. I'll discuss them in Chapter 2. The Help key, which also appears on extended keyboards, gives you quick access to Microsoft's Help feature, which I'll discuss in Chapter 1.

Summary

Word processing differs from typing, and, hopefully, you agree that word processing is a lot better. You learned about some important word processing concepts and word processor features, and took a look at the Macintosh keyboard and learned about some keys that don't appear on a typewriter. This basic background information is enough to get started with Microsoft Word.

Now on to the first part of the book, where I'll guide you through the processes of creating, editing, saving, and printing a Word document. In Chapter 1, you'll get started with a close look at Word's windows, menus, and commands.

P A R T

1

Getting Started with Word

THIS FIRST PART OF THE BOOK GUIDES READERS AS THEY launch Microsoft Word, review the parts of the document window, and create, edit, save, and print a Word document. Although written primarily for raw beginners, the next four chapters identify and discuss many brand new Word version 6 features. Even experienced Word users can find a lot of valuable information within these chapters.

Chapter 1: Windows, Menus and Toolbars

Chapter 2: Working with Text

Chapter 3: Working with Files

Chapter 4: Printing Documents

1

Chapter 1: Windows, Menus and Commands

IN THIS CHAPTER, YOU'LL GET STARTED BY LAUNCHING Microsoft Word and taking a close look at its window, menus, and toolbars. Word's document window combines standard Macintosh window elements with a few elements you'll only find in Word. Its menus are chock full of commands logically grouped by function. Its toolbars put a wide variety of often-used commands well within mouse pointer reach. Since you'll be working with these things every time you use Word, it's a good idea to get to know them.

If you're brand new to Word, don't skip this chapter! It'll provide a good foundation for what's to come. If you've used Word before, you may want to browse through this chapter to learn more about commands and buttons you're unfamiliar with, including those that are new to Word version 6.

Launching Word

There are several ways to *launch* or start Microsoft Word.

Word's Application Icon

The Word installation procedure, which is covered in Appendix A, puts several folders and files on the hard disk of your Mac. One of these folders is the Microsoft Word folder. When you open it, you should see a number of files and folders. One of them is the Word application icon, which looks like this:

To launch Microsoft Word, open its application icon. You can open the icon by either double-clicking it (my preferred method) or by clicking it once to select it and then choosing Open from the Finder's File menu. If you've done it right, your mouse pointer turns into a watch cursor, telling you that your Macintosh is working. A moment later, Word's splash screen, which is full of version and copyright information, appears. Finally, Word displays the Tip of the Day, which is discussed a little later in this chapter.

Word Document Icons

You can also launch Microsoft Word by opening a Word document icon, which looks like this:

Simply double-click the icon or click it once to select it and choose Open from the File menu. This is a quick way to launch Word and have it automatically display a specific document.

Try This! Launching Word by Opening a Word Document Icon

Microsoft Word comes with a Word document you can open — in fact you *should* open — and read. It's called "Read Me Before Installation" and it contains information about Microsoft Word that didn't make it into the Word manual.

1. Insert Disk 1 of the Microsoft Word application disks. If necessary, double-click the Install Disk 1 disk icon on your desktop to open the disk's window..
2. Locate the document icon called "Read Me Before Installation" and open it by either double-clicking it or clicking it once to select it and choosing Open from the File menu.

This launches Word and displays the "Read Me Before Installation" file.

Alias Icons

System 7 gives you the ability to create aliases of applications or documents. An alias is a special file that you can put anywhere on your hard disk or on the Desktop on screen. It acts as a pointer for your Macintosh. Its icon looks just like the original file's icon, but the alias's name, which can be anything you like, shows in italics. When you open an alias, your Macintosh looks for the original file and opens that. You can make an alias of the Word application icon or any Word document icon and open the alias to launch Word.

For Example: Using Word Aliases

TIP/TRICK

Want some ideas for where you can put a Word alias icon? Some people place a Word alias on their Desktop so they don't need to dig through folders to find and launch Word. I put a Word alias icon in the Apple Menu Items folder inside my System Folder, so Word is available under my Apple menu. This makes launching Word convenient without cluttering up my

Continued

Desktop. If you always use Word when you use your Macintosh, you might consider placing it in the Startup Items folder inside your System Folder. Then your Macintosh will automatically launch Word every time you start up.

Drag and Drop

You can also open a document with Word by dragging the document icon onto the Word application icon (or an alias of it) and letting go.

This technique is called *drag and drop* and is a built-in feature of System 7. The main benefit of using this method is that it enables you to quickly and easily open non-Word documents with Word, right from the Finder. Keep in mind, however, that Word can't open all documents, so your results may vary. I'll tell you more about using Word with documents created by other applications in Chapter 24.

Tip of the Day

NEW IN WORD 6

Microsoft Word version 6 includes a brand new Tip of the Day feature. Every time you start Word by opening the Word application icon (or an alias of it), a Tip of the Day dialog box appears, displaying a productivity tip for Word. By reading what's in this box, you can learn new things about Word every day.

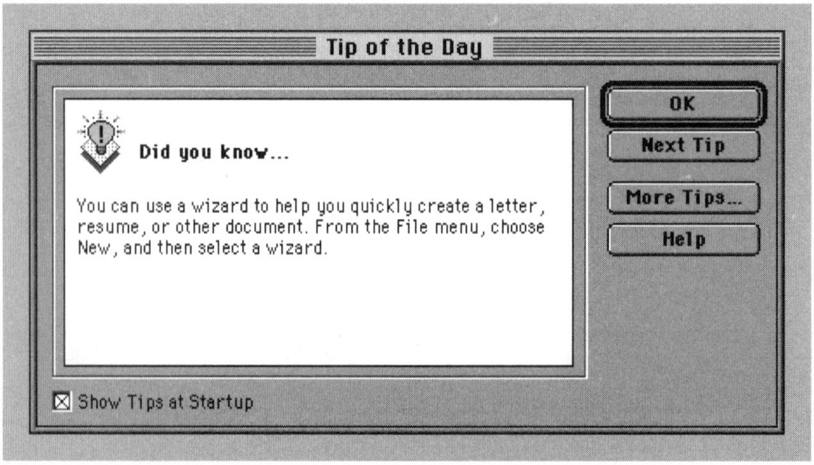

When you're finished reading the Tip of the Day, click OK to close the dialog box and get to work. If you want to read more tips, click the Next Tip or More Tips button. The More Tips button displays the Tip of the Day Contents in Word's Help window. I'll tell you more about Word's help feature later in this chapter.

If you prefer never to see tips when you start Word, turn off the check box beside Show Tips at Startup. You can always display this dialog box by choosing Tip of the Day from the Help menu.

Word's Window

When you launch Word by opening its application icon (or an alias of its application icon), it displays an empty document window called "Document1." When you launch it by opening a document icon (or an alias of a document icon), it displays a document window containing the document you opened. Either way, the window has the same components. Some of these are standard Macintosh window elements while others are found only within Word.

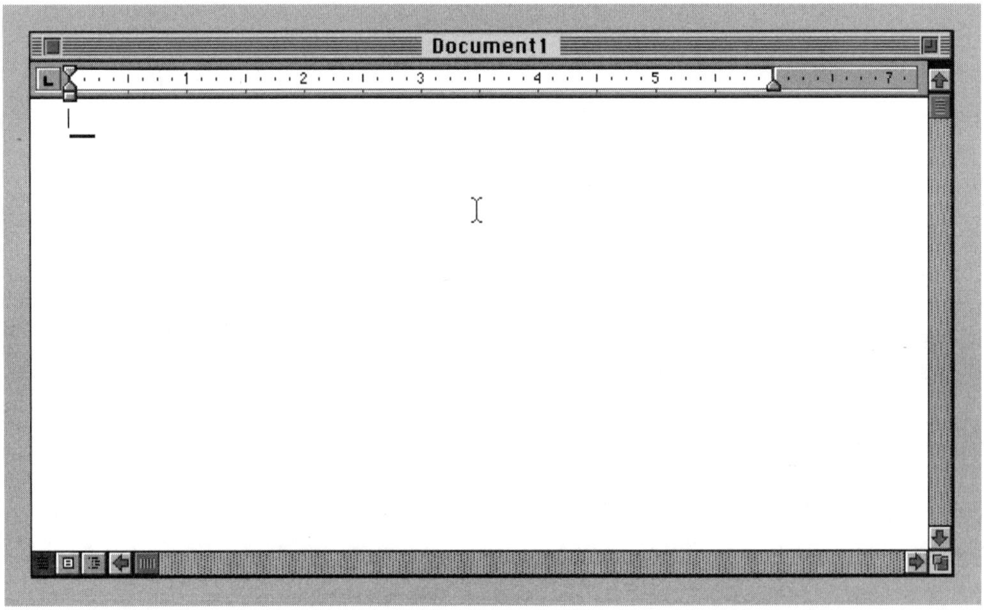

Title Bar

The title bar displays the name of the current document. If your document has not yet been saved, the title bar displays the word "Document" followed by a number. The number begins with 1 and increments each time you create a new document. When you quit Word and relaunch it, the numbers start at 1 all over again. If the title bar has horizontal lines running through it like the one in the previous illustration, the window is active.

You can use the title bar to move a window. Put your mouse pointer anywhere in the title bar except in the close or zoom boxes, press your mouse button down, and drag the title bar. You'll see an outline of the window move. When you let go of the mouse button, the window moves to its new position.

Close Box

The close box provides a quick way to close a window. Just click in the close box and the window disappears. I'll tell you more about closing windows later in this chapter.

Zoom Box

The zoom box lets you toggle the window between two sizes: full size and a custom size you can create with the size box.

Size Box

The size box lets you specify a custom window size. To use it, put your mouse pointer inside the size box, press your mouse button down, and drag the corner of the window. You'll see an outline of the edges of the window move. When you let go of the mouse button, the window is resized.

Split Box

The split box lets you divide the window into two parts. Double-click it to split the window. You can then view your document in both the top or bottom part of the window.

Since each part of a split window has its own vertical scroll bar, you can scroll within either part. To remove the split, double-click the split box again.

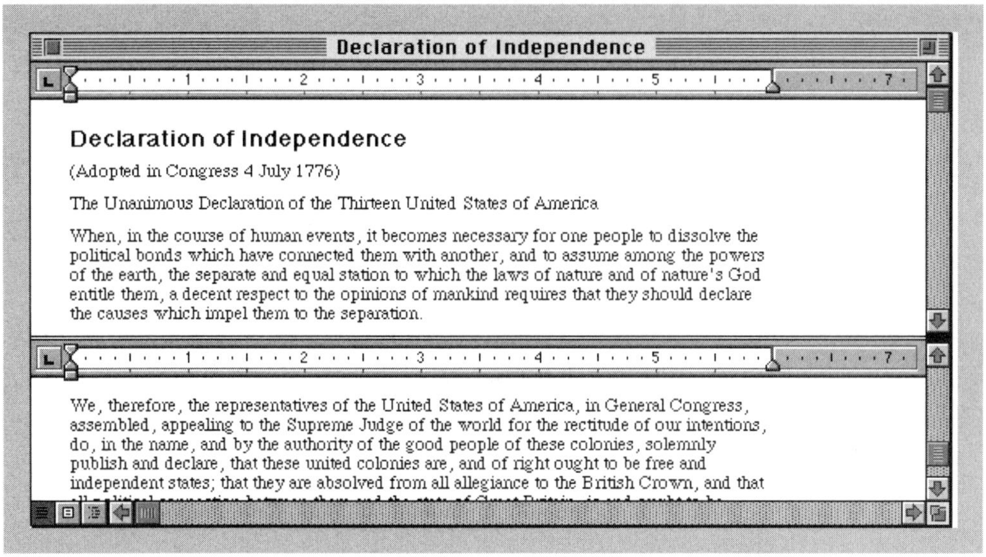

You can also split a window by choosing Split from the Window menu. To remove the split, choose Remove Split from the Window menu. I'll tell you more about Word's menus later in this chapter.

FYI: Why Split a Window?

Using the split box to split a window into two parts makes it possible to view text at the beginning and end of a document at the same time. This is useful if you need to consult something written elsewhere in the document while working.

Scroll Bars

The two scroll bars let you scroll through documents that don't fit inside the window. In most cases, you'll use the vertical scroll bar to scroll up and down in a long document. You can also use the horizontal scroll bar to scroll right and left in a wide document.

If you're unfamiliar with the concept of scrolling, consult the first part of this book titled "Before You Begin: Word Processing Basics."

Each scroll bar has three parts that can be used for scrolling:

- **Scroll Arrow —** There's a scroll arrow at either end of each of the scroll bars. Each time you click one of the arrows on the vertical scroll bar, the document scrolls one line at a time. Click on the up arrow of the scroll bar to scroll the document down so you can see the beginning of it. Click on the down arrow of the scroll bar to scroll the document up so you can see the end of it. The scroll arrows on the horizontal scroll bar work much the same way but shift the contents of the window to the right or left.

  Does this sound confusing? Well, think of it this way: Click up to see up. Click down to see down. Click right to see right. Click left to see left. That's a lot easier to remember, isn't it?

- **Scroll Box —** Each scroll bar has a scroll box within it. The scroll box indicates your relative position within the document. For example, if the scroll box is at the very top of the vertical scroll bar, you're viewing the very beginning of the document. If it's in the middle, you're viewing the middle of the document. To scroll quickly within a document, drag the scroll box up or down (or right or left) in the scroll bar to change your view of the document.

- **Scroll Bar —** The rest of the scroll bar — the gray bar itself — can also be used for scrolling. Just click in the bar to move one screenful at a time. For example, if you click in the scroll bar above the scroll box, the contents of the window will shift down so you can see the screenful above it. It sounds complicated, but it's not. It's also a fast way to scroll a document.

NEW IN WORD 6

View Buttons

Word offers several ways to view a document. In version 6, Microsoft added three View buttons at the bottom of the document window to make it easy to switch from view to view. Just click a button to change to that view.

- **Normal View Button —** Normal view is the standard view in Microsoft Word. It displays the document as one long scrolling sheet. Although it doesn't offer true WYSIWYG (what you see is what you get) formatting of each page, it does show most character and paragraph formatting. It's the best view for entering, editing, and formatting text because it's the fastest for Word to display on your Macintosh. I'll be working in Normal view for most of this book.

- **Page Layout View Button —** Page Layout view provides true WYSIWYG display of each page. That means it displays each page exactly the way it will print. It's useful for checking the positioning of graphics and framed text, as you'll see in Chapters 12 and 13. Unfortunately, because Word has to work so much harder to display each page in Page Layout view, it may be too slow for entering, editing, and formatting text. In fact, when displaying a complex document in Page Layout view on a slow Macintosh, the average person can probably type faster than Word can display the new text.

- **Outline View Button —** Outline view is great for creating outlines and working with documents with headings. It lets you collapse an outline to show only headings. It also makes it easy to reorganize a document by moving headings and changing heading levels. I'll tell you all about Outline view in Chapter 15.

Word offers other views of a document. I'll discuss them later in this book.

Inside the Window

Now let's take a look inside the window at a few things that are very important — and not so important — to Word users.

Rulers

NEW IN WORD 6

Word has always had a ruler, but in version 6, Word's ruler got a face lift. Well, maybe it was more like a crash diet. It certainly is a lot smaller. And now, in Page Layout view, there are two rulers. To show or hide the rulers, choose Ruler from the View menu.

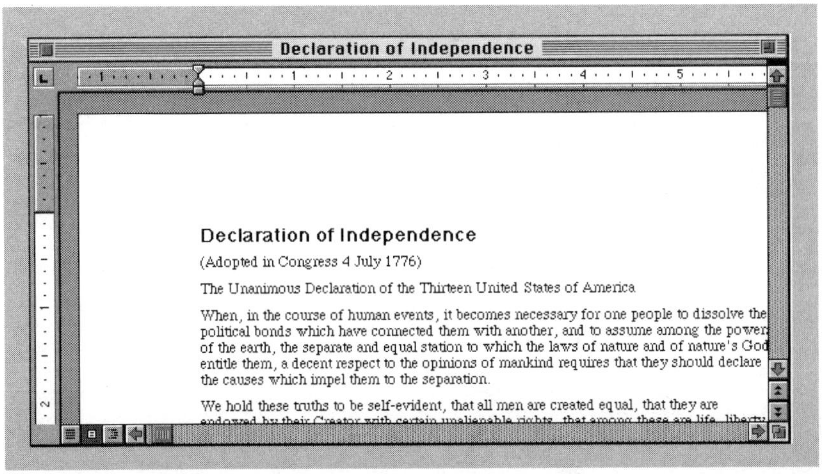

- **Horizontal Ruler —** This ruler is used to set tab stops and indents for paragraphs. I'll tell you more about that in Chapter 6. You can also use it to adjust the width of columns in multiple column text, which you'll learn more about in Chapter 8.
- **Vertical Ruler —** This ruler can be displayed only in Page Layout view or Print Preview. Use it, along with the horizontal ruler, to change margins and position items on the page. I'll tell you more about how you can use the rulers for doing this in Chapters 8 and 13.

Insertion Point

The insertion point appears as a blinking vertical bar. This is a very important part of the window since it indicates where the text you type will appear. In Chapter 2, I'll tell you more about the insertion point, including how you can move it.

Paragraph Mark

Each time you press the return key, Word inserts a nonprinting character called a paragraph mark. You can show or hide paragraph marks by clicking the Show/Hide ¶ button on the Standard toolbar, which I'll discuss briefly later in this chapter and in more detail throughout this book. When displayed, the paragraph mark looks like a backwards P. I'll tell you why it's a good idea to show these and other nonprinting characters in Chapter 6.

End Mark

The end mark appears as a dark horizontal line beneath the last line of your document in Normal and Outline views. The only important thing to know about it is that you can't type anything below it.

Mouse Pointer

The way your mouse pointer appears on your screen depends on where it is. When the mouse pointer is in the middle of the document window, it looks like an I-beam pointer. If you move the mouse pointer to a menu, it turns into an arrow for selecting menus and commands. It turns into other things in other places. Throughout this book, you'll see how the mouse pointer changes as you work with Word.

Menus and Commands

Like just about all Macintosh applications, Word has a menu bar running across the top of the screen. Each menu on the menu bar contains a series of commands you can use with Word. In this section, I'll show you the kinds of commands you can expect to find under each of Word's menus. I'll also discuss how to use Word's menus — including the brand new shortcut menus — and the dialog boxes that appear when you choose some commands.

Word's Menus

Microsoft Word has hundreds of commands. Fortunately, by default, they're not all on the menus. If they were, Word's menus would be very long indeed. In Chapter 24, I'll show you how to add and remove menu commands and specify your own shortcut keys. For now, let's look at Word's default menus.

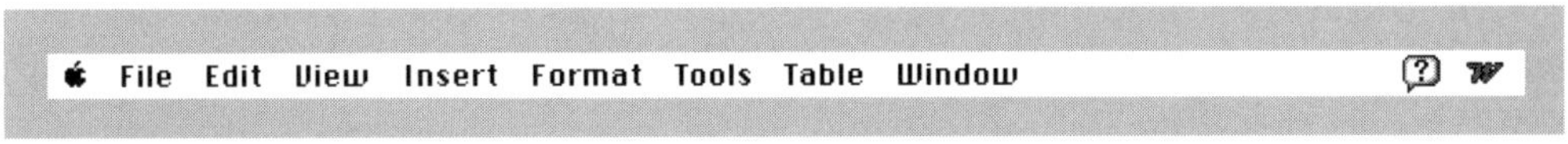

The File Menu

The File menu gives you access to file-related commands, like those to open and close files, create new files, save files, and print files. A list of the most recently opened documents also appears, making it easy to reopen a document that you recently worked with. And of course, the Quit command is in its usual position at the bottom of the menu.

The Edit Menu

The Edit menu offers document editing commands, including the standard Undo, Cut, Copy, and Paste commands. It also offers Find, Replace, and Go To commands, access to Word's AutoText feature, and System 7 publish and subscribe commands.

The View Menu

The View menu lets you change the view of your document. It also lets you view or hide various window and document elements.

The Insert Menu

The Insert menu lets you insert various things into your documents, including page and section breaks, the date, symbols, an index, table of contents, files, pictures — you name it. If you can put something into a Word document, you can use the Insert menu to do the job.

The Format Menu

The Format menu offers a variety of formatting commands. You can access dialog boxes to format fonts and paragraphs, work with borders and frames, and create and remove styles. The commands you need to make your document picture perfect are under the Format menu.

The Tools Menu

The Tools menu gives you access to a variety of utilities that come with Word. If you did a complete installation of the Word program, you can use several powerful utilities, including a spelling checker, grammar checker, and thesaurus. Other Tool menu commands include Hyphenation, Word Count, Mail Merge, and Envelopes and Labels. This menu also offers commands to create macros and customize Word.

The Table Menu

NEW IN WORD 6

The brand new Table menu includes commands for formatting and working with cell tables.

The Window Menu

The Window menu lets you display and arrange windows, including the Clipboard and other open Word documents.

The Help Menu

NEW IN WORD 6

The System 7 Help menu gives you access to Word's greatly improved Help feature. I'll tell you more about using commands on the Help menu later in this chapter.

Other Menus

The menu bar includes two additional menus. Let's take a brief look at them as well.

The Apple Menu

The Apple menu traditionally contains the desk accessories installed in your Macintosh. Under System 7, however, the Apple menu can include any application, desk accessory, control panel, document, or folder you like. The Apple menu does not change from application to application, so it will contain the same items no matter which program you're using. You can choose an option from the Apple menu at almost any time, even while working with Word.

The Application Menu

The icon at the far right side of the menu bar is a menu, too. Pull it down to display or hide application windows or make another open application active. The appearance of the icon in the menu bar depends on which application is currently active. If Word is the active application, you'll see a tiny Word application icon. If the Finder is the active application, you'll see a tiny Finder icon — it looks like a compact Mac. You can always tell what the active application is just by looking at this icon.

Using Menus

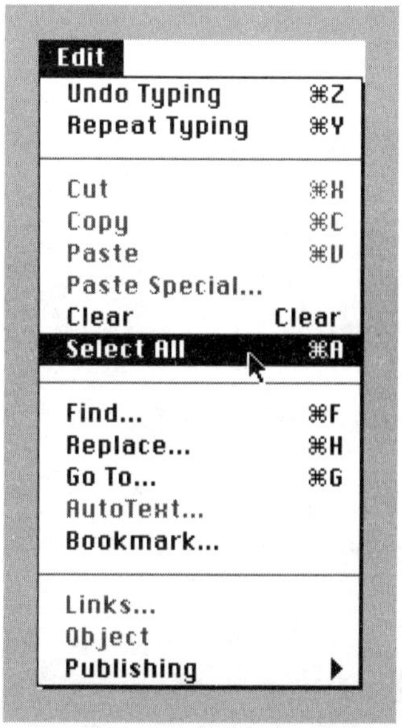

Word's menus work like any other Macintosh application's menus. To choose a command, move your mouse to the name of the menu, press and hold your mouse button down, and drag down until the command you want becomes selected. Let go of the mouse to choose the selected command.

You may notice that some menu commands are gray or are followed by an ellipsis (...). Other menu commands may have a check mark in front of them. All this means something.

If a Menu Command is Gray

Menu commands can be available or unavailable depending on a variety of factors. For example, if you don't have any text selected, you cannot choose the Copy command from the Edit menu. If a command is unavailable when you pull down its menu, it will appear in gray and you will not be able to choose it. Word knows what it can and can't do. It won't frustrate you by letting you use commands that won't work.

If a Menu Command is Followed by an Ellipsis

Menu commands followed by an ellipsis display a dialog box of additional options. The Open, Save As, and Print commands are three examples under the File menu. I'll tell you more about dialog boxes later in this chapter.

If a Menu Command has a Check Mark Before It

Menu commands with check marks in front of them indicate that the option is turned on. You can usually turn off an option by selecting it again. The check mark disappears.

Try This! Mouseless Menus

Yes, it is possible to use Word's menus without touching your mouse. And I'm not talking about shortcut keys, which I'll cover later in this chapter.

1. Press [F10] (on an extended keyboard) or hold down [⌘] and press [Tab] (on any keyboard) to activate the menu bar. The Apple menu becomes highlighted and underscores appear under a character in each menu name.
2. Press the key corresponding to the underlined letter in a menu name. That menu drops down. You can also use the [←] or [→] keys to change active menus.
3. Press the letter or number corresponding to the underlined letter or number in the name of the command you want. You can also use the [↑] or [↓] keys to move from command to command and then press [Return] when you've highlighted the command you want. That command is chosen and the menu disappears.

Continued

4. If you decide you don't want to choose a command after all, press [Esc]. This deactivates the menu bar.

What is the benefit of this? Well, the only thing I can think of is that it makes it possible to use Word when your mouse isn't working right — or if you really do hate to use a mouse.

Using Shortcut Menus

Word 6 also offers shortcut menus, special menus that apply only to selected items. To display and use a shortcut menu, position the mouse pointer on the text or item you want to work with, hold down [Control], and press your mouse button down. The shortcut menu for that item appears.

NEW IN WORD 6

To choose an item from the menu, drag to select the command you want. Then let go of the mouse button. If you decide you don't want to choose a command on the menu after all, simply let go of the mouse when none of the commands are selected.

You can also display a shortcut menu by pressing [Shift][F10] (on an extended keyboard only) while pointing to the item you want to work with. The shortcut menu appears and remains in place. Click a command to select it or click elsewhere in the document window to dismiss the menu.

TIP/TRICK

FYI: Is This Really a "Shortcut?"

I've been using shortcut menus since they appeared in Microsoft Excel 4.0 and I'm not convinced that they're really "shortcuts." After all, do they really save any time? All they're doing is giving you a menu with just the commands you can use on a selected item. They're not making it quicker to choose a menu command. They're just narrowing down your options. If you already know where a command is on Word's menus, isn't it just as quick to pull down that menu and choose that command?

Continued

But that's just my opinion. For what it's worth.

Now shortcut keys — that's a different story. They really do save time. Read about them in the next section.

Using Shortcut Keys

Shortcut keys make it possible to choose menu commands without using a mouse. Instead, you press a combination of keyboard keys.

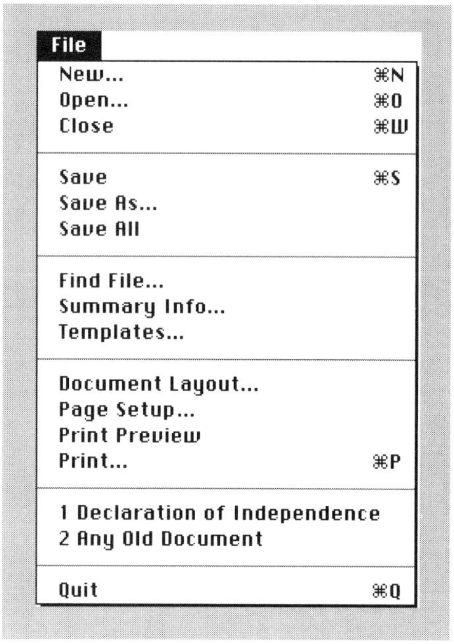

Word displays available shortcut keys to the right of the command names on its menus. For example, pull down the File menu and look at the Save command. Notice the cloverleaf, which is the Command key symbol, and letter S to the right of the command?

This means that pressing [⌘][S] is the same as choosing the Save command from the menu. To use this shortcut, hold down the [⌘] key and press the [S] key.

Some shortcut keys work with other keys, like [Shift] or [Option]. For example, [⌘][Shift][S] activates Word's Style command and [⌘][Option][L] activates Word's spelling checker.

Appendix C has a complete list of all the standard shortcut keys available in Word. In Chapter 24, I'll tell you how you can change shortcut keys and add your own.

Using Dialog Boxes

Word makes extensive use of dialog boxes. It has to put all those commands somewhere! Its dialog boxes have the same standard parts you'll find in the dialog boxes of other programs, along with a brand new part called a tab.

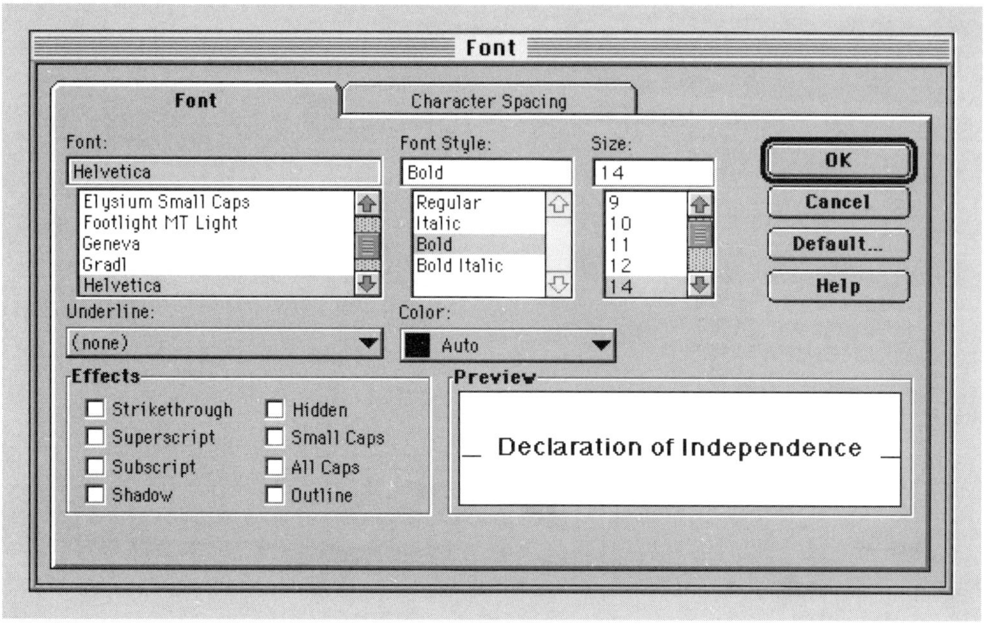

Let's take a closer look at the Font dialog box, which provides a sample of nearly every kind of part there is.

Push Buttons

Push buttons let you work with the values in a dialog box. To use a push button, click it with your mouse. (One click will do it — no need to double-click a button!) If a button is gray, it cannot be clicked. If a button has an extra dark border around it, it's called the *default button*. If a button includes an ellipsis, clicking it will display another dialog box.

Most dialog boxes offer several standard push buttons.

- **OK** — normally accepts the settings in the dialog box and dismisses it, completing the command. This button could also be labeled Save, Print, Open, or Apply, depending on the dialog box it appears in. It is often the default button.
- **Cancel** — tells Word not to do the command at all. I sometimes think of the Cancel button as the "forget it" button. The Cancel button sometimes turns into a Close button, depending on changes you made in the dialog box. The Close button simply closes the dialog box. It's the same as clicking the dialog box's close box, if it has one.

NEW IN WORD 6

Here are three useful shortcuts for selecting push buttons in a dialog box.

- To select the default button — the button with the extra dark border around it — press Enter on your keyboard. (Return usually works, too.)
- To select the Cancel or Close button, press Esc or ⌘. on your keyboard.
- To select any button, hold down ⌘ and press the key corresponding to the first letter in the button name. For example, to choose Default in the Font dialog box, press ⌘D.

Edit Boxes

An edit or text box is a box where you can enter values. Click in the box to select its contents or position the insertion point within it, and then enter the appropriate text or value. Use Delete to make corrections — standard Macintosh editing techniques, which I'll discuss in Chapter 2, apply.

TIP/TRICK

Press Tab to move quickly from one edit box to another within a dialog box. If the edit box is empty, the insertion point will appear in it when you tab to it. If the edit box contains a value, that value will become selected when you tab to it.

FYI: Entering Measurements in Dialog Boxes

When an edit box requires a measurement, you can use either the default unit that appears in the edit box or choose points, inches, centimeters, lines, or picas. When using the default unit, it isn't necessary to enter the unit abbreviation. For example, in an edit box that shows a measurement of 8 pt (8 points), you can enter just 10 to change it to 10 points.

If you want to enter the new value in a different unit, you must type in the value followed by the correct abbreviation. Here's a table of the units, their abbreviations, and an example of each.

Unit	Abbreviation	Example
point	pt	8 pt
inch	in or "	.5 in or .5"
centimeter	cm	2 cm

Continued

Unit	Abbreviation	Example
line	li	2 li
pica	pi	2.5 pi

The space between the measurement number and unit abbreviation is optional. Word automatically converts whatever you type to the default unit for that edit box. You can change the default unit of measurement in the Options dialog box, which I'll discuss in Chapter 23.

Pop-up Menus

Some dialog boxes include pop-up menus with lists of options. These menus usually have arrows to the right of them. Click the arrow to display the menu, then choose an option from it.

Button/Menus

In Word version 6, Microsoft added a brand new interface item that I'll refer to throughout this book as a button/menu. Why? Because it looks like a button but it acts like a menu. Here's an example of one:

NEW IN WORD 6

Notice the tiny arrow on the button? That tells you that this button is more than just a push button. Click the button/menu to display the menu and choose an option from it.

Scrolling Lists

Many dialog boxes feature scrolling lists of options, like the ones for Font, Font Style, and Size in the Font dialog box. Use the scroll bar to view the items in the list. Click once on an item to select it. Sometimes these lists have an edit box where you can type in a value. For example, you can type a font size into the Size box to enter a value, including a value that does not appear on the Size pop-up menu.

Check Boxes

Check boxes are used to turn options on or off. Click the check box or label beside it to turn it on. An X appears in the box. Click it again to turn it off.

The X disappears. In most cases, any combination of check boxes within a group may be turned on or off.

Radio Buttons

Radio buttons, like check boxes, let you turn options on or off. Unlike check boxes, however, you can only turn on one radio button in each group. In fact, one radio button in each group *must* be turned on. Click the radio button or label beside it to turn it on. Any previously selected radio button in the group is turned off automatically. In some instances, turning on a radio button may activate or deactivate other options in a dialog box, like other radio buttons, check boxes, or edit boxes. You may be required to make a selection before you can continue.

Tabs

NEW IN WORD 6

In Word 6, some dialog boxes now include *tabs.* A tab lets you display different options in the same dialog box. The Font dialog box, for example, has two tabs: Font and Character Spacing. Click on a tab to display its options. It's like turning a page.

TIP/TRICK

You can move from tab to tab in a dialog box by pressing Control Tab on your keyboard.

Other Parts

Some dialog boxes include standard window elements like title bars, close boxes, and scroll bars. These were covered earlier in this chapter, in the discussion on Word's windows. These parts work the same way in dialog boxes as they do in windows — no surprises here.

Toolbars

NEW IN WORD 6

Word's toolbar, which was introduced in Word version 5.1, put a wide variety of menu commands where your mouse pointer can easily reach them. The toolbar feature was improved in version 6 by adding more toolbars. Word 5.1 users will notice many ribbon and ruler buttons on the Standard and Formatting toolbars which appear by default when you first launch Word.

Word version 6 has many toolbars. Various toolbars automatically appear, depending on the Word feature you're working with. You'll learn more about all of Word's toolbars and their buttons throughout this book.

Showing/Hiding Toolbars

You can display or hide any of Word's toolbars by choosing Toolbars. . . from the View menu. This command also lets you customize toolbars and make your own, something I'll tell you about in Chapter 24.

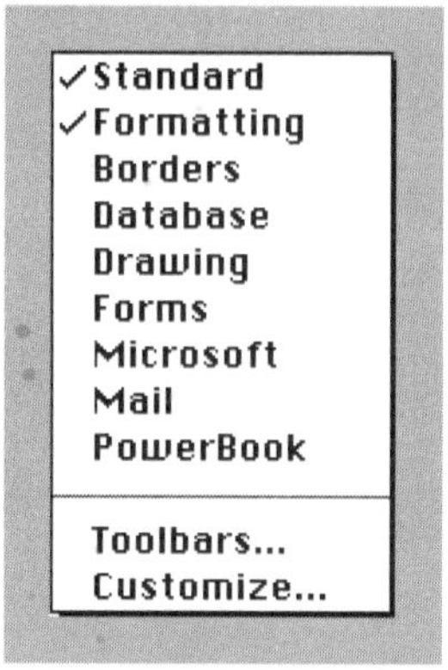

TIP/TRICK

If at least one toolbar is showing, you can use the toolbars shortcut menu to show or hide toolbars. Just hold down [Control] while clicking on a toolbar to display the shortcut menu. Each toolbar that is currently displayed has a check mark beside its name. Choose the toolbar you want to show or hide.

ToolTips

ToolTips is a great new Word 6 feature that works with its toolbars. When you use the mouse pointer to point to a toolbar button, Word displays the name of the button in a small box called a ToolTip. This takes all the guesswork out of the somewhat cryptic pictures on each button.

The Status Bar

NEW IN WORD 6

The status bar, which is new to Word 6, displays a variety of things, depending on what you're doing.

If you're just viewing your document or entering text, the status bar displays information about the text on the screen, like the page and section number, number of pages in the document, position of the insertion point on the page, current time, and various mode indicators. I'll tell you more about modes throughout this book.

If you're selecting a command or toolbar button, the status bar displays a description of that command or button. If Word is working on a task that may take a while and require that you wait for it to finish before continuing to work, the status bar displays a message telling you just that. Think of it as Word's way of communicating with you.

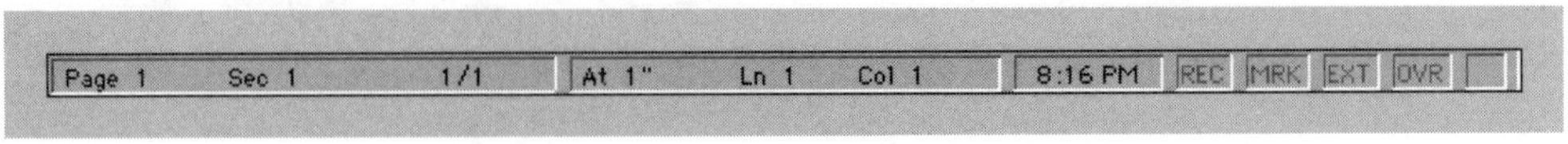

Getting Help

NEW IN WORD 6

Word's Help feature is greatly improved in version 6. The Help menu, which I mentioned earlier in this chapter, includes commands that make it easy to find the information you need. But, as you'll see in this section, the Help menu isn't the only way to get help.

Using the Help Menu

The Help menu offers commands that let you find Word information in a variety of ways. Use these commands to browse through Help topics or go right to a topic you're interested in.

Using Word Help Contents

The Help menu's Microsoft Word Help command (or the Contents button within the Help window) brings up a dialog box with a scrolling list of main Help topics, each with a corresponding icon:

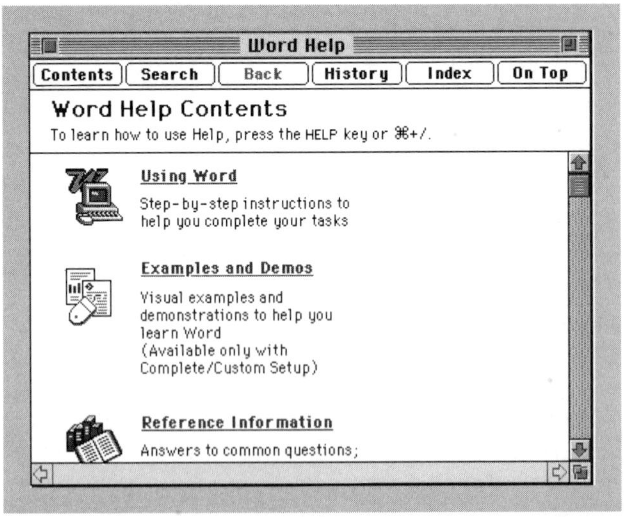

Use this list to begin browsing through Help. Simply click the underlined name of the topic you're interested in or the icon beside it. A

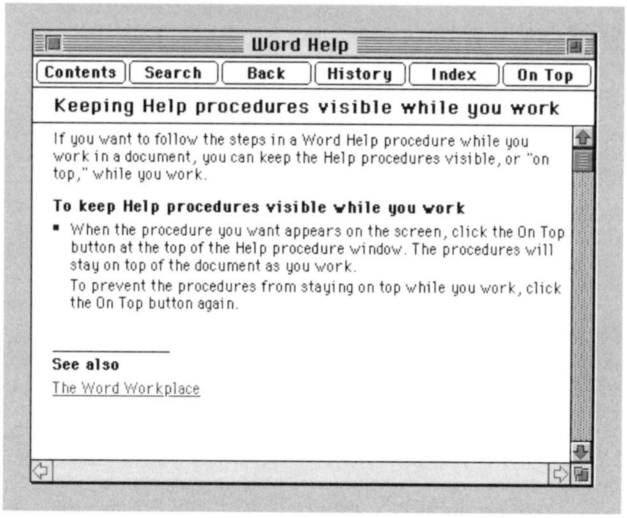

scrolling list of subtopics appears. Click the name of the subtopic in each list that appears to zero in on the exact information you need. Eventually, the subtopic's complete Help procedure, including information and step-by-step instructions, will appear in the window.

Searching

The Help menu's Search for Help On command (or the Search button within the Help window) lets you search for information about a specific topic. When you choose this command, the Search dialog box appears. In the edit box, type in a word for the topic you're looking for help on or choose a keyword from the list immediately below the edit box by clicking it. When you click the Show Topics button, a scrolling list of topics appears in the bottom of the dialog box. Choose the topic you want by clicking on it, then click the Go To button. Word displays the Help procedure for the topic you choose.

TIP/TRICK

If you're not fond of clicking an item in a scrolling list and then clicking a button to do something with it, skip the button clicking step by simply double-clicking on the list item. This not only selects the item but it "clicks" the button you'd have to click anyway. This technique works in many dialog boxes in many Macintosh applications.

Try It! Searching for Help

Try using Word's Search for Help On command to get information on creating a new document. Follow these steps:

1. Choose Search for Help On from the Help menu or, if the Help window is already displayed, click the Search button. The Search dialog box appears.

Continued

2. In the edit box at the top of the dialog box, type **new.** The scrolling list of key words immediately below the edit box automatically advances to the first item beginning with the characters *new*: "new columns, starting."

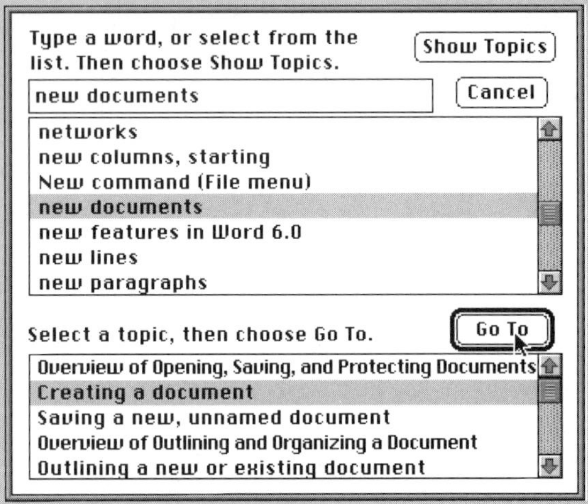

3. Click new documents to select it from the list and click the Show Topics button. (Or just double-click new documents in the list.) A list of topics appears in the bottom of the dialog box.
4. Click Creating a Document to select it from the list and click the Go To button. (Or just double-click Creating a Document in the list.) The Help procedure for creating a new document appears in the Help window.

Using the Index

The Help menu's Index command (or the Index button within the Help window) provides an alphabetical list of all topics. Simply click on the first letter of a topic to display a list of topics starting with that letter. Scroll through the list to find the topic you want

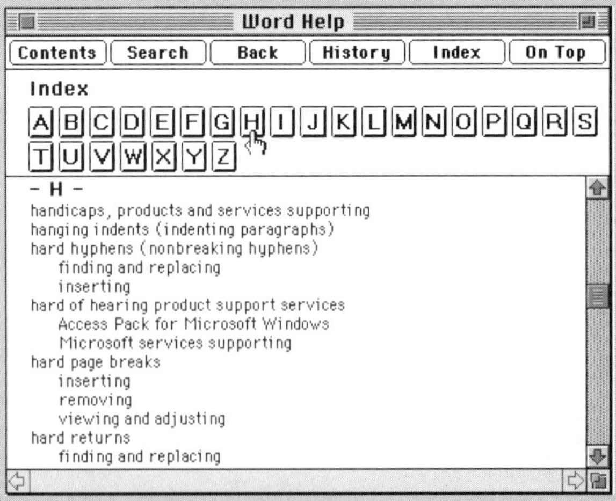

and click it to display it. Word's online index is huge, so don't be surprised if you need to do a lot of scrolling to get to the topic you want.

Other Help Menu Commands

The Help menu also offers these commands that provide more information:

- **About Balloon Help** — explains what System 7's Balloon Help feature is all about.
- **Show Balloons** — turns on System 7's Balloon Help feature. Use this command to display cartoon balloons containing brief information about screen objects you point to with the mouse. Choose Hide Balloon Help to turn this off when it starts to annoy you.

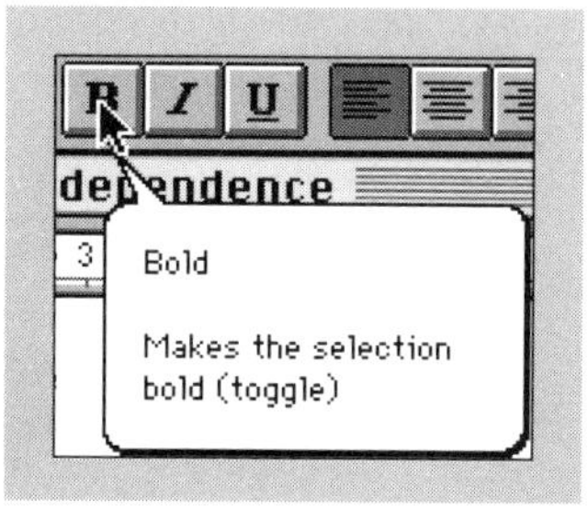

- **Tip of the Day** — displays a Word productivity tip. I discussed this feature earlier in this chapter.
- **Technical Support** — provides information on how you can get product support from Microsoft.

Help Window Buttons

Word's Help window has a total of six buttons for navigating from one Help topic to another. I already told you about the Contents, Search, and Index buttons. Here are the others.

- **Back** — displays the previous Help window, taking you back through topics you've already viewed since activating Help.
- **History** — displays a list of all the Help windows you opened since activating Help. To go to a topic you've already viewed, simply double-click it in the Help History window.

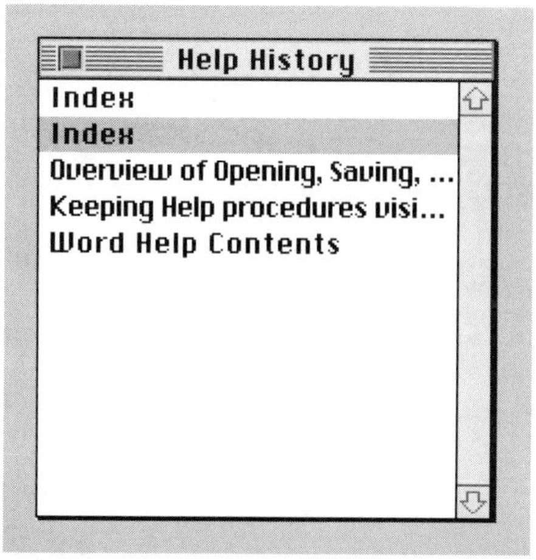

- **On Top —** keeps the Help window on top of your document window, even when you're working with your document. This keeps Help procedures visible so you can consult them while you work.

Tips for Using Help

TIP/TRICK

Here are a few more brief tips for working with Word's Help feature:

- Click any word or phrase in a Help window with a solid underline to jump to that topic. On a color screen Macintosh, these terms appear in green.
- Click any word or phrase in a Help window with a dotted underline to get a definition of it. A definition window appears. Click the definition window to close it.

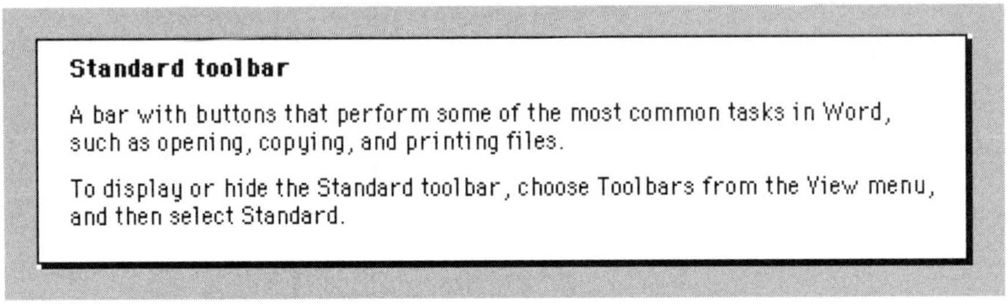

- Drag the title bar of a Help window to move that window anywhere on your screen.
- Drag the size box of a Help window to make it bigger or smaller. This makes it possible to view more than one window at a time.

Printing a Help Topic

NEW IN WORD 6

Word version 6 adds the ability to print any Help topic. Make sure the topic you want to print is in the active window (the one with the striped title bar) and choose Print Topic from Word's File menu.

Other Ways to Activate Help

There are several other ways to activate Word's Help feature.

Using the Keyboard

You can open a Help window and get context sensitive Help using keyboard keys. Press either [Help] (on an extended keyboard) or [⌘][/] (on any keyboard) and your mouse pointer turns into a question mark with a pointer, like this:

To get context sensitive Help, use your mouse to choose the menu command, Toolbar button, or window item for which you want help. A Help window with that topic displayed appears.

If you just want any Help at all, press [Help] or [⌘][/] again and the Search dialog box appears. Use that to get the information you need.

Using the Help Button on the Standard Toolbar

The Help button on the Standard Toolbar works the same way as the keyboard Help keys discussed above. Click it and your mouse pointer turns into a question mark with a pointer. Then select or click on the item for which you want help.

Using the Help Button in a Dialog Box

NEW IN WORD 6

Every single dialog box in Word version 6 now includes a Help button. Click this button to get context-sensitive help about options in the dialog box.

Closing Help

When you're finished using Help, click the close box of any open Help window or choose Close from the File menu.

TIP/TRICK

If you think you're going to use Help often during a Word session, don't close it each time you're finished with it. Instead, click on the Word document window to bring it to the front and make the Help window inactive. This speeds up the display of the Help window the next time you need it.

Closing Windows

When you're finished working with a document, it's a good idea to close it. This frees up memory within Word for use with other documents.

To Close a Window

There are two main ways to close a window.

- Click the close Box. You can close any window with a close box by clicking its close box.
- Use the Close Command. Choose Close from the File menu to close the active window. When you pull down the File menu, you might notice a shortcut key for the Close command: [⌘][W]. This is a standard keyboard shortcut that you'll find in many other Macintosh applications, including the Finder, so it's easy to remember.

If Changes Haven't Been Saved

When you try to close a document window without saving the changes you've made since the last time you saved it — or if you haven't saved it at all — a warning dialog box like this appears:

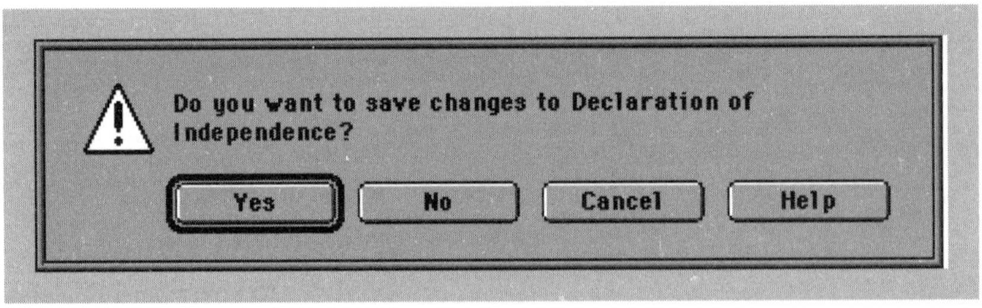

To save the changes, click Yes. To close the window without saving changes, click No. To change your mind and not close the window after all, click Cancel. To get more information about closing a document window, click Help.

As you can see, Word is watching out for you. It wants to make sure you don't forget to save your work before you put it away. I'll tell you more about saving documents in Chapter 3.

Quitting Word

When you're finished working with Word, it's a good idea to quit the program. Quitting frees up your computer's memory so that other applications can use it.

To quit Word, pull down the File menu and choose Quit. Or try the Shortcut Key, ⌘Q, which is the same in almost every Macintosh application.

When you quit Word, it does a number of things. First, if you have any open document windows, Word closes them. If you haven't saved changes in one or more documents, word displays the dialog box (shown in the previous section) for each document before closing them. Next, Word saves changes to any template files you may have changed while working with Word. I'll tell you more about templates in Chapter 9. If the Clipboard, something I'll discuss in Chapter 2, contains a large block of information, Word may ask if you want to save it. Finally, when everything is put away, Word quits.

FYI: Closing Windows vs. Quitting

I can't tell you how many people I've met who think that closing all the windows in an application is the same as quitting the application. It's not the same!

When you close a document window, you tell Word that you're done working with just that document. But Word is still active, waiting to do more work. It's still taking up your computer's random access memory (RAM). The RAM used by Word is RAM that isn't available to other programs. If you keep launching applications without properly quitting them, sooner or later, you're going to see a dialog box that looks something like this:

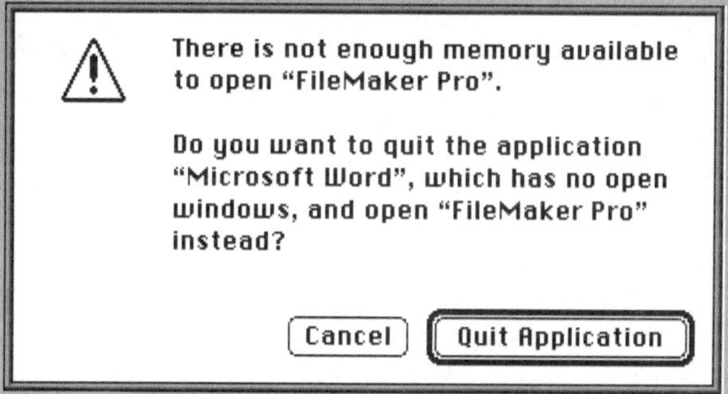

Continued

Although this dialog box offers the option of quitting Word, not all of them do. You may have to manually quit Word or some other program before you can launch another.

You can see what applications are open by pulling down the Application menu at the far right end of the menu bar. A list of open applications appears at the bottom of the menu. Choose the application you want to work with and its icon appears in the menu bar. To quit an application, choose it from the Application menu and then choose Quit from the File menu. Remember, you cannot quit Finder.

Chapter Summary

In this chapter, you took a good look at Word. You saw that there are a number of ways to launch Word and you learned the differences between them. You looked at Word's document window and learned about the parts you saw — both standard Macintosh window elements and elements specific to Word. I told you about Word's menus, including its new Shortcut Menus, and how to use them, even without a mouse. I also reviewed the parts of dialog boxes that appear when you choose certain menu commands. You saw Word's Standard and Formatting Toolbars and how the new ToolTips feature takes the guesswork out of using them. You learned how to use Word's improved Help feature. Finally, you saw how to close windows and quit word, and learned why closing and quitting are different.

In the next chapter, you'll create a Word document. I'll show you how to enter, edit, and select text, move the insertion point, and work with the Copy, Cut, and Paste commands. I'll also show you the command I call the "Oops!" command — it's one of my personal favorites and, in Word version 6, it's better than ever!

2

Chapter 2: Working with Text

IN THIS CHAPTER, YOU'LL CREATE A NEW DOCUMENT AND enter text into it. I'll tell you about Word's New dialog box and the options you'll find in it. I'll explain how to use Word's insertion point, as well as its new Overtype mode, to enter and change text. I'll show you 21 ways to move the insertion point and 17 ways to select text — don't worry, you don't have to remember them all! I'll tell you about two keyboard keys that delete text and how they differ. I'll show you how to move and copy text using Word's drag and drop text editing feature and the Cut, Copy, and Paste commands. Finally, I'll tell you about how you can undo your mistakes and repeat tasks you'd like to do more than once.

As you go through this chapter, you'll see that Word's text entering and editing techniques are very similar to those in other applications. As a result, if you can enter and edit text in another application, you can easily learn to do it in Word. And once you've learned to do it in Word, you can do it in most other applications.

Now flex your fingers and get ready to type. Here you go!

Creating a New Document

As you learned in Chapter 1, when you launch Word by double-clicking its application icon or an alias of its application icon, it displays a blank, untitled document. This is one surefire way to create a new document. But it isn't always convenient to quit Word and then relaunch it just to get a new document. Fortunately, Word offers the New command to create a new document any time, even when other documents are open. Version 6 of Word adds two new features called templates and wizards that are available when you create a new document. I'll show you these things in this section.

Using the New Command

Word offers several ways to activate the New command:

- Click the New button on the Standard Toolbar
- Choose New from the File menu *or*
- Press ⌘N

If you use the New button or shortcut key, Word creates a new document with the Normal template. I'll tell you more about the Normal template in a moment. If you use the New menu command, Word opens the New dialog box.

Using the New Dialog Box

NEW IN WORD 6

The New dialog box is brand new in Word 6. It lets you choose a template or wizard to use for the new document.

By default, the New dialog box offers to create a document with the

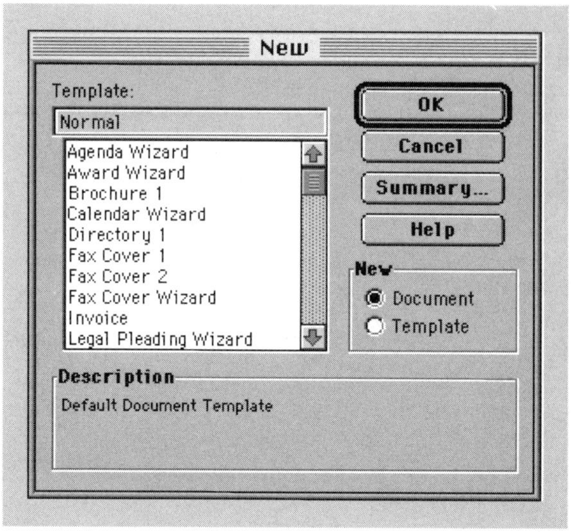

Normal template. You can choose a different template or a wizard from the list by clicking on it. Make sure the Document radio button is turned on. Then click the OK button or press Return or Enter to create the document.

TIP/TRICK

If you prefer, you can simply double-click a template or wizard name in the New dialog box to create a new document without clicking the OK button.

Templates

When you select a template from Word's New dialog box, a new document with that template's settings appears.

A *template* is a special Word document that can contain a collection of predefined text, formatting, styles, toolbar buttons, command settings, AutoText entries, and customized macros. (I'll cover all these things throughout this book.) You can use templates to make it quicker and easier to create a specific type of document, like a memo, fax transmittal form, or letter. For example, a memo template might include standard memo headings with special formatting and graphics, like a corporate logo, as well as AutoText entries to automatically enter commonly-used information. When you choose this template in the New dialog box, all of its settings become part of the new document.

The Normal template is a special template that contains all the default settings of Word and makes them global settings for all documents. Because it's an all-purpose template, it has standard settings that are useful in most documents. When you click the New button, Word creates a new document with this template.

Word comes with a number of other templates you can use to create documents. Each template is based on a template document stored in the default Document Templates folder. The Normal template, for example, is based on the Normal document template file. In Chapter 9, I'll tell you how you can modify the templates that come with Word or create your own.

FYI: All Documents Are Based on Templates

I think it's interesting to note that in Word 6, *every* document is based on a template. If you use the New button or shortcut key to create a new document, that document is based on the Normal template. If you use the New command and choose a template, that document is based on the template you chose. The template is *attached* to the document. It remains attached until you attach a different template. I'll tell you more about that in Chapter 9, too.

Wizards

A *wizard* is a special kind of file that takes you through the process of creating a specific kind of document, like a memo, letter, or fax transmittal. When you choose a wizard in the New dialog box and click OK, Word displays a series of dialog boxes that guide you, step by step, through the creation of that kind of document. Just follow the instructions that appear in the dialog boxes to choose among options or accept or reject proposed text. A Finish button closes the wizard when you're done and displays the document with the options and text you specified. You can then complete the document by typing in the remainder of the text.

As you can imagine, wizards are powerful tools for automating the creation of many routine documents. I'll tell you more about them in Chapter 26.

Entering Text

Entering text into a Word document is easy. Just type.

Typing Text

The text you type appears at the insertion point, that blinking vertical bar you first saw in Chapter 1. As you type, the insertion point moves so that it always appears after the last thing you typed. In addition, the insertion point location indicated in the status bar at the bottom of the screen changes.

When text you're typing reaches the end of a line, Word automatically begins a new line. This is called *word wrap,* and it's a standard feature of word processors. I discussed it in the chapter titled "Before You Start: Word Processing Basics."

FYI: Those Gray Dots and Characters

If Word is set to display nonprinting characters, you will see gray dots and characters like the ones shown in the following illustration. The paragraph mark, which I discussed in Chapter 1, is one of these marks. Spaces, which look like dots, and tabs, which look like right pointing arrows, are others.

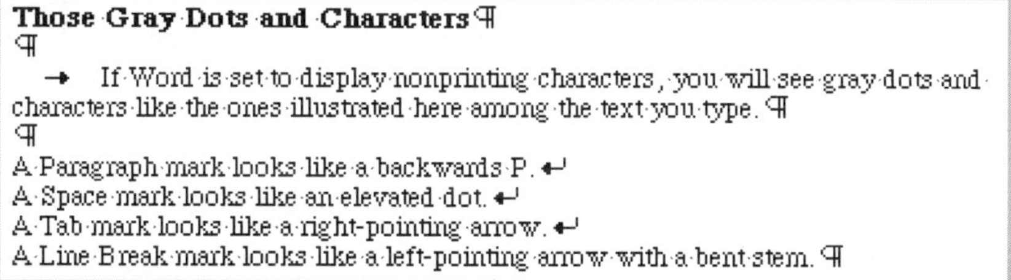

Those·Gray·Dots·and·Characters¶
¶
→ If·Word·is·set·to·display·nonprinting·characters,·you·will·see·gray·dots·and·characters·like·the·ones·illustrated·here·among·the·text·you·type.¶
¶
A·Paragraph·mark·looks·like·a·backwards·P.↵
A·Space·mark·looks·like·an·elevated·dot.↵
A·Tab·mark·looks·like·a·right-pointing·arrow.↵
A·Line·Break·mark·looks·like·a·left-pointing·arrow·with·a·bent·stem.¶

Don't worry, these characters will not appear on paper when you print. You can specify which nonprinting characters Word displays by changing settings in the Options dialog box, which I'll tell you about in Chapter 23. To turn the display of nonprinting characters on or off, click the Show/Hide ¶ button on the Standard Toolbar or press [⌘] [8].

Starting a New Paragraph

When you're finished typing a paragraph and want to begin a new one, press [Return]. This inserts a paragraph mark and moves the insertion point to the beginning of the next line. If you want a blank line between paragraphs, just press Return twice after each paragraph. Each time you press Return, Word inserts a paragraph mark and moves to the next line. When you press Return twice in a row, you get a paragraph mark sitting on a line all by itself. That creates a blank line. You can see an example in the previous illustration.

FYI: What is a Paragraph?

Word defines a paragraph as any line or group of lines ending with a paragraph mark. Since much of Word's formatting is paragraph-based, it's a good idea to display paragraph marks so you can see where each paragraph ends. I'll tell you more about paragraph formatting and styles in Chapters 6 and 7.

IMPORTANT NOTE

Do *not* press Return at the end of each line. Doing so defeats the word wrap feature and makes it impossible for Word to automatically adjust the way text flows from line to line when you insert or delete text.

Starting a New Line in the Same Paragraph

If you want to begin a new line in the same paragraph, hold down s and press Return. Word inserts a line break character, which looks like an arrow pointing to the left, and moves the insertion point to the beginning of the next line.

For Example: Why a New Line Rather Than a New Paragraph?

On the surface, there doesn't seem to be any difference between pressing Return and pressing Shift Return. In both cases, the current line ends and the insertion point moves to the beginning of the next line. But by pressing Shift Return to begin a new line in the same paragraph, you ensure that the new line always has the same paragraph formatting as the rest of the paragraph.

Continued

What do I use this for? A few things:

- Typing lists of names.
- Typing addresses in letters or on envelopes.
- Typing information in tab tables.

You'll get a better idea of how this can be useful when we discuss paragraph formatting and styles in Chapters 6 and 7. For now, just be aware that it isn't always necessary to begin a new paragraph just to begin a new line.

Moving the Insertion Point

As you can imagine, the insertion point is a VIP (very important point) in the Word window. Text is inserted wherever it appears. So unless you always want to type at the very end of your documents, it's a good idea to know how to move it.

There are several basic ways to move the insertion point. In this section, I'll tell you about them and then let you try specific techniques for yourself.

Using the Mouse

As you type, the mouse pointer disappears. (I bet you didn't even notice.) To get it back, just move your mouse. If the mouse pointer is within the window, it appears as an I-beam pointer.

To move the insertion point using the mouse, position the mouse I-beam pointer where you want the insertion point to be. Then click the mouse button once. The insertion point appears at that position.

It isn't enough to just move the mouse pointer to the new position. You *must* click the mouse button to move the insertion point. Otherwise, the insertion point remains right where it was before you reached for the mouse.

If you move the mouse while clicking, you may *select* or highlight some text. In that case, the insertion point disappears! I'll cover selecting text a little later in this chapter. If you select text by mistake while trying to move the insertion point, just try again. Be careful to keep the mouse still while you click.

Using the Keyboard

You can also use the keyboard to move the insertion point. My favorite keys for this are the arrow keys: ↑, ↓, ←, and →. Each time you press an arrow key, the insertion point moves one character or line, depending on which key you press. This is handy for moving short distances in your document. Extended keyboards offer more keys for moving the insertion point. The Pg Up and Pg Dn keys move the insertion point one windowful up or down. The Home and End keys move the insertion point to the beginning or end of a line. Holding down ⌘ while pressing any of these cursor movement keys moves the insertion point even farther.

If You Don't Have an Extended Keyboard

TIP/TRICK

Don't feel left out if you don't have an extended keyboard. I'll tell you a secret. If Num Lock is turned off, the number keys on your keyboard's numeric keypad can be used to move the insertion point as well. The following illustration shows which keys do the job.

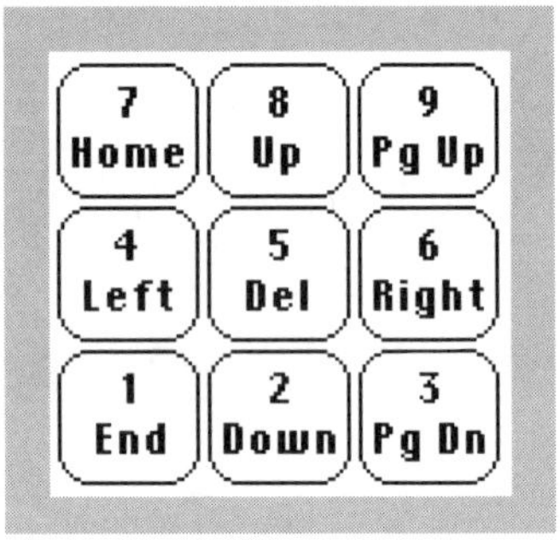

If You Don't have a Numeric Keypad

NEW IN WORD 6

What? Your PowerBook doesn't have a numeric keypad? Microsoft didn't leave you out in the cold. Word 6 offers a special PowerBook Toolbar. To display it, choose Toolbars from the View menu, turn on the check box to the left of PowerBook in the Toolbars scrolling list, and click OK. The PowerBook toolbar appears. It offers these buttons:

- **Start of Document —** moves the insertion point to the beginning of the document. (This is the same as pressing ⌘ Home.)

- **End of Document —** moves the insertion point to the end of the document. (This is the same as pressing ⌘ End.)

- **Start of Line** — moves the insertion point to the beginning of the current line. (This is the same as pressing [Home].)

- **End of Line** — moves the insertion point to the end of the current line. (This is the same as pressing [End].)

- **Page Up** — moves the insertion point up one screenful at a time. (This is the same as pressing — you guessed it — [Pg Up].)

- **Page Down** — moves the insertion point down one screenful at a time. (This is the same as pressing [Pg Dn].)

Using the Go To Command

NEW IN WORD 6

The Go To command, which was improved in Word version 6, lets you move the insertion point to a specific place in your document. There are three ways to activate it:

- Double-click on the page number in the status bar
- Choose Go To from the Edit menu *or*
- Press [F5] (extended keyboard) or [⌘][G] (any keyboard).

In each instance, the Go To dialog box appears

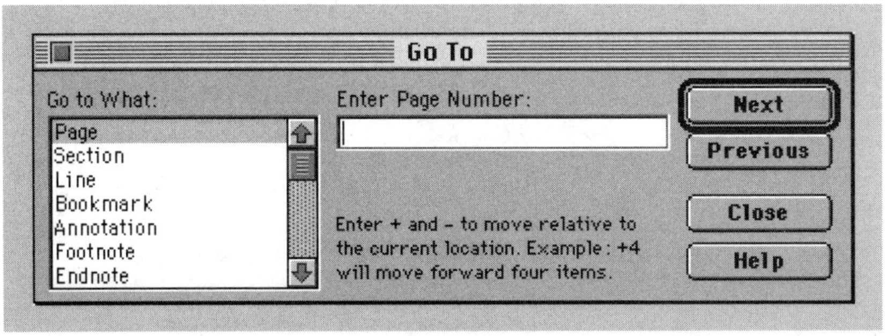

Choose the Go To What option from the scrolling list on the left side of the dialog box by clicking on it. Then enter the name or number of the item you want to go to in the Enter edit box. The exact label on this edit box depends on what you chose in the scrolling list. For example, if you chose Footnote in the left scrolling list, the label over the edit box will read Enter Footnote Number. Click Go To or press [Return] or [Enter] to move the insertion point to the place you specified. The Go To window does not disappear — if it's in your way, you can drag it by its title bar to a new position on your screen.

If you want to go to the next or previous occurrence of the option you chose in the Go To What list, leave the Enter edit box empty and click Next or Previous. When you're finished using the Go To dialog box, click the Close button or its close box or press Esc to dismiss it.

Using the Go Back Command

NEW IN WORD 6

Word 6 now remembers the last three places you used the insertion point. To revisit these locations, press Shift F5 or ⌘ Option Z. Word cycles through the last three locations, one at a time, and then brings you back to where you started.

Try This! 21 Ways to Move the Insertion Point

Here's a table of 21 ways to move the insertion point using the mouse, keyboard, and commands. Give each of them a try. If your Macintosh beeps at you when you're trying any of these keyboard techniques, that's probably because you're trying to move beyond the beginning or end of your document. That's a no-no and your Macintosh scolds you for it by playing the System alert sound.

To Move the Insertion Point Here:	Do This:
Anywhere in your document	Use the scroll bars to display the location you want to move the insertion point to, then position the mouse I-beam pointer at that location and click once *or* Activate the Go To command by double-clicking the page number in the Status bar, choosing Go To from the Edit menu, or pressing ⌘ G or F5, then specify the location and click the Go To, Previous, or Next buttons.
One character to the right	Press →
One character to the left	Press ←

Continued

To Move the Insertion Point Here:	Do This:
One line up	Press [↑]
One line down	Press [↓]
One window up	Press [Pg Up]
One window down	Press [Pg Dn]
The beginning of the current line	Press [Home]
The end of the current line	Press [End]
One word to the right	Press [⌘][→]
One word to the left	Press [⌘][←]
The beginning of the current paragraph	Press [⌘][↑]
The beginning of the next paragraph	Press [⌘][↓]
The beginning of the document	Press [⌘][Home]
The end of the document	Press [⌘][End]
The top of the window	Press [⌘][Pg Up]
The bottom of the window	Press [⌘][Pg Dn]
The top of the previous page	Press [⌘][Option][Pg Up]
The top of the next page	Press [⌘][Option][Pg Dn]
Back to one of the last three insertion point locations	Press [Shift][F5] or [⌘][Option][Z] one, two, or three times as required

FYI: Moving the Insertion Point vs. Scrolling

In Chapter 1, I discussed scrolling. In this chapter, I discussed moving the insertion point. What's the difference?

Continued

When you use the scroll bars to scroll around within your document, the insertion point does not move. When you use the mouse, keyboard, or commands to move the insertion point, the insertion point does move. Although in many cases you might not care whether the insertion point moves as long as you can view another part of your document, there may be times when you do care. That's when it's important to remember the difference between these two techniques.

Editing Text — The Basics

Entering text usually isn't enough for creating a document. You also have to know how to change it. In this section, I'll cover basic text editing, including inserting text, using Word's new Overstrike mode feature, and using the two deletion keys.

Inserting Text

Remember the insertion point? Remember why they call it that? Because text is inserted at its position.

To insert text in your document, move the insertion point to the position you want the new text to appear. Then type. The text you type is inserted at that point. All the text to the right of it shifts to the right. If you type a lot, you'll see the paragraph's word wrap change as Word shifts text to make room for incoming characters. You can use this method to insert as much text as you like — even whole paragraphs and pages of it.

Printing characters aren't the only things you can insert. You can also insert spaces, tabs, and paragraph marks. Just position the insertion point where you want the character to go and press the appropriate key: Spacebar, Tab, or Return. If you have Word set to display nonprinting characters (with the Show/Hide ¶ button on the Standard Toolbar), you'll see these characters appear where you insert them.

Try This! Dating Your Documents

NEW IN WORD 6

Word version 6 offers a new menu command that makes it easy to insert the current date or time in your document. Position the insertion point where you want the date or time to appear and choose Date and Time from the Insert menu. The Date and Time dialog box appears.

Choose the format you want to use from the scrolling list of Available Formats. If you turn on the check box for Insert as Field, Word inserts the date or time as a field that changes each time the document is printed. I'll tell you more about fields later in this book. Click OK to insert the date or time with the format you chose.

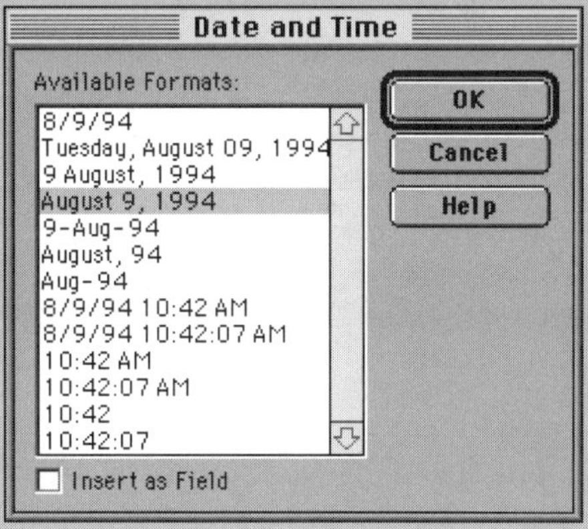

Using Overtype Mode

NEW IN WORD 6

In Word 6, Microsoft added an Overtype feature. When in Overtype mode, text you type is not inserted at the insertion point. Instead, it replaces the text already there, character for character.

To turn on Overtype mode, double-click the OVR mode indicator in the Status bar. The OVR characters in the indicator turn black when Overtype mode is turned on. To turn it off, double-click OVR again. The characters turn gray.

IMPORTANT NOTE

Be careful when using Overtype mode because it will replace existing text with whatever you type. If Overtype mode is turned on and you don't know it, you could lose text from your document without even realizing it!

Using the Deletion Keys

Sometimes you type in something and later realize you don't want it anymore. That's when deleting comes in handy. Word offers one or two deletion keys, depending on the kind of keyboard you have. They work similarly, but not exactly the same way.

The Delete Key

The Delete key, which is labeled [Delete], deletes characters immediately *before* the insertion point. Each time you press [Delete], one character to the left of the insertion point disappears and the insertion point moves one character to the left. You can use this method to delete characters, words, sentences, paragraphs — you get the idea — one character at a time.

The Del Key

The Del key appears on extended keyboards only. It's labeled [Del] and can be found beneath the [Help] key. [Del] deletes characters immediately *after* the insertion point. Each time you press [Del], one character to the right of the insertion point disappears. Characters to the right of the insertion point move one character to the left.

NEW IN WORD 6

You may notice that the Edit menu flashes briefly when you press [Del]. That's because [Del] is the shortcut key for the Clear command on the Edit menu. I'll tell you about the Clear command in a moment.

FYI: Which Deletion Key to Use

The only reason I make a point of mentioning both deletion keys in my Word classes and in this book is because so many people seem interested in being able to delete *forward* ([Del]) rather than *backward* ([Delete]). I think it's because many of my students have experience with other word processors that delete forward instead of backward.

But this is a Macintosh, not some weird, antiquated word processing machine. [Delete] is the standard deletion key that works — and works the same way — in every Macintosh application. Not so with [Del]. Although Microsoft products like Word and Excel take advantage of [Del], few other applications do. Perhaps it's because the key doesn't appear on all keyboards. Perhaps it's a conspiracy to get Macintosh users to delete backwards all the time. (A conspiracy that Microsoft isn't part of.) Who knows?

My recommendation to my students — and to you — is to use [Delete]. It will never fail you. And then you don't have to worry about remembering which to use.

The Deletion Keys and Selected Text

If text is selected, pressing either deletion key — Delete or Del — will remove it. This is a quick way to get rid of large blocks of text. After all, do you really want to press Delete 267 times to get rid of a paragraph that's 267 characters long?

If you want to know how to select text, read on. That's next on the agenda.

Selecting Text

To get beyond the basics of text editing and to be able to format text that's already been typed, you need to know how to select it. *Selecting* text — or *highlighting* it, as some people say — tells Word that you're going to do something with it, like delete, copy, move, format, or print it. You'll be working with selected text often when you work with Word, so text selection is a good skill to master.

As usual, there are several basic ways to select text. I'll give you an overview, then provide a list of specifics that you can try for yourself. If you're interested in special selection techniques for tables and graphics, consult Chapters 11 and 12.

Dragging the I-Beam Pointer

The most basic way to select text is to drag the mouse I-beam pointer over the text you want to select. Position the mouse pointer at the beginning of the text you want to select, press the mouse button down, and drag the pointer to the end of the text you want to select. As you drag, the text becomes highlighted — it turns black or some other color. (In case you're wondering, the color it turns depends on the setting in the Color control panel of your Macintosh.) When all the desired text is highlighted, let go of the mouse button. This is the most basic text selection technique and it works in every situation.

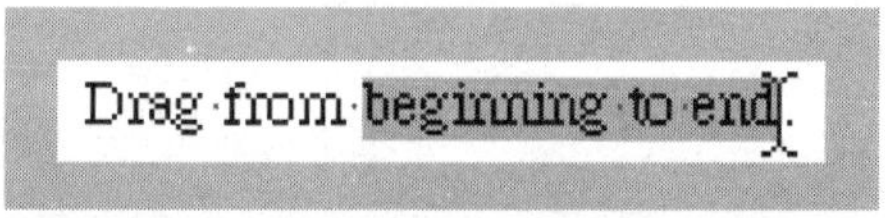

There are things to keep in mind when using this method. If the text you're trying to select is on more than one line, don't try to select it a line at a time. Just drag from the beginning to the end. Everything in the middle gets selected. Trust me. This works.

Do you have to select from the beginning to the end? No. You can select from the end to the beginning if you like. But you can't begin in the middle, drag backward to grab what you missed, and then drag forward to get the rest. You can only drag in one direction — forward or backward. So if you miss the first character(s) of what you want to select, you'll simply have to start over. Click elsewhere in the document window to cancel the selection (I'll talk more about that in a little while) and begin again.

One more thing. To select in increments less than a full line, your mouse pointer *must* look like an I-beam when you begin selecting. When your mouse pointer gets close to the first character on a line, it might turn into an arrow pointing in and up. If you click when your mouse pointer looks like this, that entire line becomes selected. If that isn't what you want, click elsewhere in the document window to cancel the selection and try again.

IMPORTANT NOTE

By default, Word is configured to select complete words when you drag over more than one word of text. If you want to select more or less than full words, you should turn this feature off. To do this, choose Options from the Tools menu to display the Options dialog box. Click the Edit tab to display its options. Click on the check box beside Automatic Word Selection to turn it off. I'll tell you more about the Options dialog box in Chapter 23.

TIP/TRICK

You might notice that dragging over text selects all the text. But sometimes you might need to select a vertical block of text, like a list or a column of a tab table. This is indeed possible with Word. Just hold down [Option] while dragging. You'll get something like this:

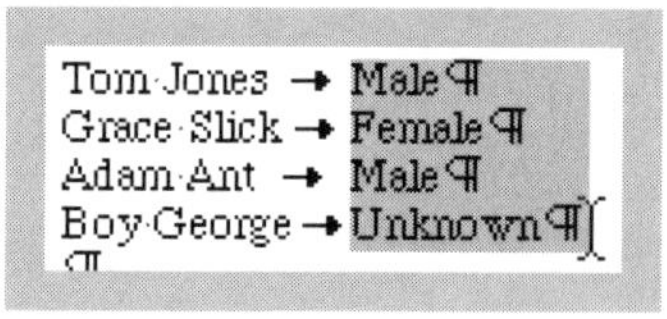

Clicking with the I-Beam Pointer

Now comes my favorite text selection technique: double-clicking a word. When you double-click a word, Word selects the entire word. If the word is followed by one or more spaces, Word selects them, too — just in case you want to delete the word and the space after it. And if a word isn't enough, triple-clicking anywhere in a paragraph selects the entire paragraph.

You want more? How about this: hold down ⌘ while clicking anywhere in a sentence to select the entire sentence, including any spaces after punctuation. This is another one of my favorite techniques. Just be forewarned: Word thinks the period after an abbreviation is the same as the period at the end of a sentence, so it might not get the whole sentence if there's a punctuated abbreviation (like Mr., Dr., or eg.) in it.

And here's one more, just for the heck of it. Click at the beginning of what you want to select. Now hold down Shift and click at the end of what you want to select. (Note that I said *click* and not *drag*.) Everything between the first click and the second click should become selected. This method has a name. It's called Shift-Click. It's great for selecting big or odd-shaped blocks of text.

Clicking or Dragging in the Selection Bar

The Selection bar is a mysterious place at the far left side of the Word document window. I say it's mysterious because it isn't labeled in any way. Lots of experienced Word users don't even know it exists. If they do know about it, most of them don't know what it's called. But now *you* know.

To find the Selection bar, slowly move your mouse pointer to the left within the document window. It looks like an I-beam pointer until it gets to the Selection bar, which normally begins to the left of the first character on the line. When your mouse pointer reaches the Selection bar, it turns into an arrow pointing to the right and up, like the one shown in the following illustration.

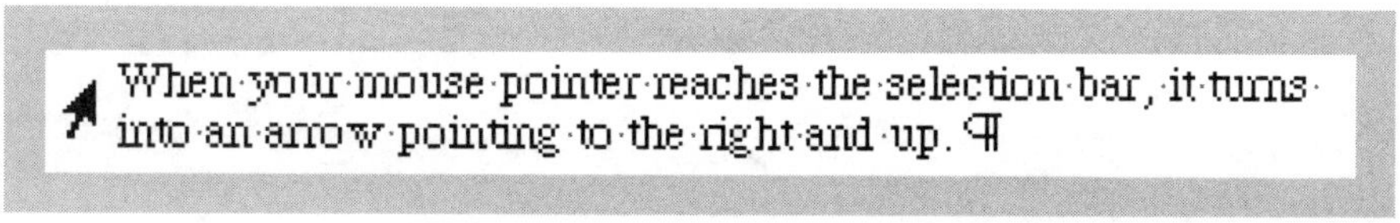

When your mouse pointer is in the Selection bar, clicking selects the entire line beside it. Double-clicking the Selection bar selects the entire paragraph beside it. Triple-clicking it selects the entire document. (So does holding down ⌘ while clicking once in the Selection bar.) Pressing the mouse button and dragging down the Selection bar selects multiple lines.

Using the Keyboard

You can also use the keyboard to select text. Although there are a lot of options, they aren't terribly easy to use or remember, but they are worth discussing, especially if you're a mouse-hater.

For example, you can simulate dragging by holding down Shift and using any of the cursor movement keys: ↑, ↓, ←, →, Pg Up, Pg Dn, End, or Home. Holding Shift, in effect, "locks" the starting point while pressing these other keys moves the insertion point. The result: a simulated drag that selects text along the way. Use Shift in combination with any of the techniques I covered earlier for moving the insertion point to select text.

TIP/TRICK

You can use Shift and cursor movement keys together to extend a selection. For example, say you selected a line and then decided you wanted to select multiple lines. Instead of starting from scratch, hold down Shift and press ↑ or ↓ to extend the selection to include additional lines. This works for any selection.

Using the Select All Command

If you need to select the entire document, use the Select All command:

- Choose Select All from the Edit menu *or*
- Press ⌘A

The entire document becomes selected.

Try This! 17 Ways to Select Text with a Mouse

Now for a complete list of text selection techniques. Try these for yourself to get the hang of them. The ones you find most useful will be the ones you remember best.

Continued

To Select This:	Do This:
Any amount of text	Drag the I-beam pointer over it *or*
	Click at the beginning of the text, hold down [Shift], and click at the end of the text *or*
	Position the insertion point at the beginning of the text, hold down [Shift], and use the cursor movement keys to select to the end of the text
A word	Double-click the word *or*
	Position the insertion point at the beginning of the word, hold down [Shift] and [⌘], and press [→]
A sentence	Hold down [⌘] while clicking on the sentence
A line of text	Click in the Selection bar beside the line
Multiple lines of text	Drag down the Selection bar beside the lines
A paragraph	Triple-click the paragraph *or*
	Double-click in the Selection bar beside the paragraph *or*
	Drag down the Selection bar beside the entire paragraph *or*
	Position the insertion point at the beginning of the paragraph, hold down [Shift] and [⌘], and press [↓]
Multiple paragraphs	Double-click in the Selection bar beside the first paragraph and drag down beside the remaining paragraphs
The entire document	Triple-click in the Selection bar *or*
	Choose Select All from the Edit menu *or*
	Press [⌘][A]
One or more columns of text	Hold down [Option] while dragging over the text

Canceling a Selection

Selecting text requires some skill. Canceling a selection doesn't. Simply click anywhere in the window other than on the selected text. Or, if you prefer, press one of the cursor movement keys. The selection disappears and the insertion point reappears.

IMPORTANT NOTE

It's a good idea to cancel a selection before making another selection, especially if your new selection includes text that's already selected. You may wind up dragging selected text to a new position with the drag and drop text editing feature, which I'll discuss in a moment.

Editing Text — Beyond the Basics

Now that I've discussed text selection, you can move on to some other text editing techniques.

Using the Clear Command

After you select text, there are a few ways to get rid of it. I already told you about using one of the deletion keys. You can also use the Clear command, which is under the Edit menu. Choose that command or press Del, its shortcut key, and whatever is selected is removed from the document.

Replacing Specific Text

Word's Overstrike mode, which I told you about earlier in this chapter, replaces text, character for character, as you type. But what if you only want to replace certain text? And what if the text you want to replace is a different length than what you want to replace it with?

No problem. Simply select the text you want to replace and then type in the new text. When you type while text is selected, the selection is automatically deleted and the insertion point placed where it was.

Moving and Copying Text with Drag and Drop

In Word version 5, Microsoft added a great feature for moving and copying text: drag and drop text editing. This feature lets you drag selected text to a new location. If you hold down Option while dragging, the text is copied. This works with any amount of text, from one character to pages and pages of it.

For this to work, the Drag and Drop Text Editing feature must be turned on in Word's Options dialog box. This feature is turned on by default when you install Word so you shouldn't have to change it. If this technique doesn't work, check the setting in the Options dialog box. Chapter 23 tells you how.

IMPORTANT NOTE

Try This! Using Drag and Drop Text Editing

Give drag and drop text editing a try. Follow these steps to move text:

1. Select some text using any of the text selection techniques discussed previously.
2. Position your mouse pointer inside the text. It looks like an arrow when inside the selection, as shown here:

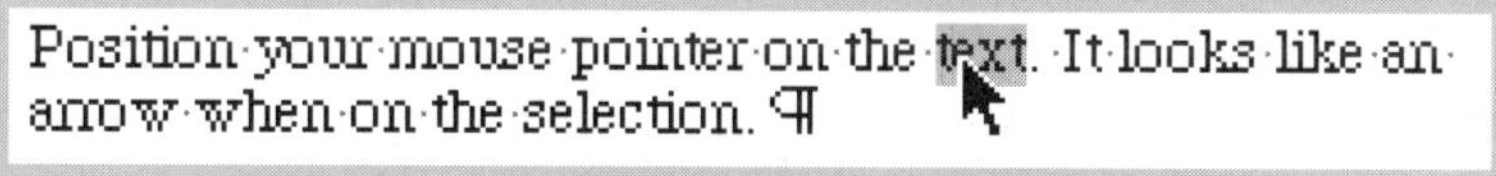

3. Press your mouse button down and drag the pointer to the place you want to move the selected text. As you move the mouse pointer, it changes to display a tiny document icon at its base. A dotted insertion point moves along with it, indicating exactly where the text will go when you release the mouse button. Like this:

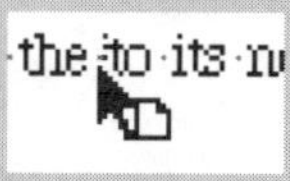

4. When you've positioned the pointer and dotted insertion point where you want them, release the mouse button. The text, which remains selected, moves.

Continued

Copying text with drag and drop text editing works almost the same way. The only difference is that you must hold down the Option key while dragging the selected text. Follow these steps:

1. Select some text.
2. Position your mouse pointer inside the selected text.
3. Holding down Option, press your mouse button down and drag the mouse pointer and dotted insertion point to the place you want to move the selected text. You may notice that a plus sign appears over the tiny document icon at the base of the pointer.
4. When you've positioned the pointer and dotted insertion point where you want them, release the mouse button. The selected text is copied to the new position. The copy remains selected.

Using the Cut, Copy, and Paste Commands

Drag and drop text editing is a great feature, but it isn't for everyone. There is another way. Like all other Macintosh programs, Word offers Cut, Copy, and Paste commands to move and copy text.

To move text using cut and paste, select the text to move, activate the Cut command, position the insertion point where you want the text to go, and activate the Paste command. To copy text using copy and paste, select the text to copy, activate the Copy command, position the insertion point where you want the text to go, and activate the Paste command.

Word offers several ways to activate the Cut, Copy, and Paste commands:

Method	Cut	Copy	Paste
Standard Toolbar button			
Menu and Command	Edit menu, Cut command	Edit menu, Copy command	Edit menu, Paste command
Shortcut Key (any keyboard)	⌘X	⌘C	⌘V
Shortcut Key (extended keyboard)	F2	F3	F4

NEW IN WORD 6

Word 6 features Smart-Cut-and-Paste. If this feature is turned on, Word automatically adjusts the spacing in a sentence when you cut or paste text there. For example, if you paste a word between another word and a punctuation mark like a period, Word automatically inserts a space between the two words. You can turn this feature on or off in the Options dialog box, which I'll discuss in Chapter 23.

IMPORTANT NOTE

If you use the Paste command while text is selected, the selection will be replaced with what you paste. This is something you might or might not want to do, so pay attention to the insertion point or selection when you use the Paste command.

Try This! Using Cut, Copy, and Paste

Give cut, copy, and paste a try. Follow these steps to move text:

1. Select some text using any of the text selection techniques discussed previously.
2. Activate the Cut command by clicking the Cut button on the Standard Toolbar, choosing Cut from the Edit menu, pressing ⌘X, or pressing F2. The selection disappears.

3. Position the insertion point where you want the text to go using any of the techniques previously discussed.

Continued

4. Activate the Paste command by clicking the Paste button on the Standard Toolbar, choosing Paste from the Edit menu, pressing [⌘][V], or pressing [F4]. The selection appears where you pasted it.

Copying text with copy and paste works almost the same way. Instead of using the Cut command, use the Copy command. The original selection doesn't disappear. Follow these steps:

1. Select some text.

2. Activate the Copy command by clicking the Copy button on the Standard Toolbar, choosing Copy from the Edit menu, pressing [⌘][C], or pressing [F3]. Nothing on your screen changes.
3. Position the insertion point where you want a copy of the text to go.

4. Activate the Paste command by clicking the Paste button on the Standard Toolbar, choosing Paste from the Edit menu, pressing [⌘][V], or pressing [F4]. A copy of the selection appears where you pasted it.

FYI: The Clipboard

When you use the Cut or Copy command, a copy of the selection is put on the Clipboard, a place in your Macintosh's random access memory (RAM). The Cut command also removes the original selection from the document.

Items on the Clipboard remain there until one of two things happens:

- You use the Cut or Copy command again. Then the new selection replaces the old one.
- Your Macintosh shuts down (or restarts). Then the Clipboard is wiped clean, just like the rest of RAM.

Continued

Now let's see how well you were reading. After using the Paste command, what's on the Clipboard?

If you said "nothing," go back and reread this sidebar. You weren't paying attention. The Paste command does *not* remove the contents of the Clipboard — it pastes a copy of the Clipboard contents where you indicate with the insertion point. After using the Paste command, the Clipboard remains the same. That means you can use the Paste command over and over to paste the contents of the Clipboard again and again.

You can see the contents of the Clipboard at any time by choosing Show Clipboard from Word's Window menu. A Clipboard window appears.

Although you can view the contents of the Clipboard, you can't change it. To close the Clipboard window, click in its close box, choose Close from the File menu, or press ⌘W.

Moving and Copying Between Word Documents

Drag and drop text editing and the Cut, Copy, and Paste commands also make it possible to exchange information between documents. This prevents a lot of time consuming retyping when information already in one document can be used in another.

To use drag and drop text editing to move or copy between documents, both document windows must be open and positioned so you can see their contents. Then simply drag a selection from one document window into the other. Use the dotted insertion point at the end of your mouse pointer to position the selection where you want it to go before releasing the mouse button.

To use Cut or Copy and Paste to move or copy between documents, simply cut or copy something in one document, make the other document active, position the insertion point where you want the selection to appear, and paste it in. I'll tell you more about working with multiple document windows in Chapter 3.

Changing Your Mind

Ever do something and immediately regret it? You know what I mean. The kind of thing you do and then say, "Oops!" In Word, the Undo and Redo commands can help you out of these situations.

Undoing the Last Thing You Did

Use the Undo command to undo or reverse the last thing you did. There are several ways to activate it:

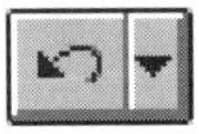

- Click the Undo button on the Standard Toolbar *or*
- Choose Undo from the Edit menu *or*
- Press [⌘][Z] or [F1]

The exact wording of the Undo command varies depending on the last thing you did. For example, if the last thing you did was to type in text, the command will be Undo Typing. If the last thing you did was format text, it'll be Undo Formatting. No matter what it says, it's always the first command on the Edit menu.

Undoing Multiple Things

NEW IN WORD 6

Word 6 has a better memory than previous versions. It now keeps track of the last 100 things you did. This makes it possible to undo more than just the very last thing. For example, using the Undo command again reverses the action before the one you just reversed. You can keep using the Undo command to reverse actions one at a time.

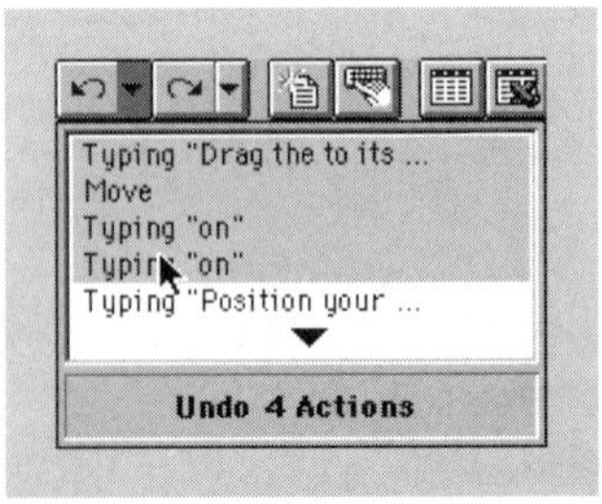

If you want to undo several actions at once, click on the arrow on the right side of the Undo button to pull down a list of the things you can undo. Drag down to select things to undo — the list scrolls and keeps count of the number of things you've selected.

Release the mouse button to reverse all the actions you've selected. As you can see, you can't skip actions — you must undo them in order.

FYI: Things That Can't Be Undone

There are a few things that the Undo command can't undo. Saving a file, which I'll cover in Chapter 3, is one of them. Switching from one document View to a different one is another. If you pull down the Edit menu and see that the first command, Can't Undo, appears in gray, that means you can't undo the last thing you did.

Don't worry, though. Word can undo most of the things you do.

Redoing the Last Thing You Undid

When you use the Undo command, Word offers a way to redo what you just undid: the Redo command. For example, say you deleted a word and then used Undo to get it back. The Redo command will Redo the deletion. Sound confusing? It isn't really. Just remember that if you use the Undo command, you can always use Redo to restore things to the way they were before you used it.

You can activate the Redo command by one of these methods:

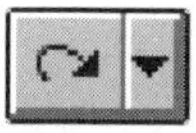

- Click the Redo button on the Standard Toolbar *or*
- Choose Redo from the Edit menu *or*
- Press ⌘Y

The exact wording of the Redo command varies depending on the last thing you undid. If you didn't just use the Undo command, the second command may be the Repeat command — I'll discuss that in a moment. The Redo button also has an arrow you can use to pull down a list of actions to redo. This works just like the Undo button's list of actions to undo.

Doing It Again

Since Word is paying close attention to the things you do, just in case it needs to undo them, it can also repeat them. For example, say you enter some text and want to enter the same text elsewhere in your document. Enter the text once, then move the insertion point and activate the Repeat command by one of these methods:

- Click the Repeat button on the Standard Toolbar *or*
- Choose Repeat from the Edit menu *or*
- Press ⌘ Y

The exact wording of the Repeat command varies depending on the last thing you did. If this command reads Redo command rather than Repeat or is gray, you cannot use it. When activated, the Repeat command retypes the text you typed again at the insertion point. You can use the Repeat command again and again. It will always repeat the last thing you did.

Chapter Summary

In this chapter, you started doing some serious work with Word. You created a document and took a look at Word's New dialog box. You took a first look at templates and wizards. You learned how to enter and edit text using the insertion point, Overtype mode, the Deletion key, drag and drop text editing, and the Cut, Copy, and Paste commands. You learned lots of ways to move the insertion point and select text. Finally, you became acquainted with the Undo, Redo, and Repeat commands.

In the next chapter, you'll learn about files. I'll show you how to save your work and explain the difference between the Save and Save As commands. You'll see the Summary Information Form and learn how it can help you keep track of files. I'll also show you how to open existing files for editing or printing and how to use Word's built in Find File feature to search for and work with files.

3

Chapter 3: Working with Files

WHEN YOU WORK WITH WORD DOCUMENTS, YOU'RE working with files — document files. Each document, when saved on disk, becomes a separate file on that disk. Once a document file has been saved, it can be opened at a later date, copied to another disk, or transferred to someone via network or modem connection.

In this chapter I tell you how to save and open Word document files. I'll show you the Summary Info dialog box and tell you how you can use it. The difference between the Save and Save As commands is explained, and you'll learn about some additional saving options that are covered in more detail later in this book. The Open command is also covered. This is where you'll find out how to open files already saved on disk. The secrets of using Word's Find File command are also revealed, and finally, you'll learn how to work with multiple document windows, something I touched on briefly in Chapter 2.

Give your typing fingers a rest — there's not much for them to do in this chapter. Instead, you'll give your disk a real workout.

FYI: Document vs. Application Files

A document file is very different from an application file. Since I've noticed that some of my Word students don't understand the difference between these two kinds of files, I thought it would be a good idea to talk about it here.

There are many different kinds of files on a Macintosh. The ones you work with most often are *application* and *document* files. Like other files, both appear as icons in Finder windows.

An application is a program. It lets you perform a specific task. Microsoft Word is a good example. It lets you create documents like letters, memos, reports, and even books like this one.

A document is a file created by an application. Think of it as the application's offspring. You must have an application to open a document. When you double-click the icon for a document, your Macintosh looks for the application that created it, launches the application, and opens the document within it. That's why you can double-click on a Word document icon to launch the Word application. When you do this, two files are actually open: the Word application and the Word document.

If you double-click on a document icon and your Macintosh can't find the application that created it, it tells you by displaying a dialog box like this:

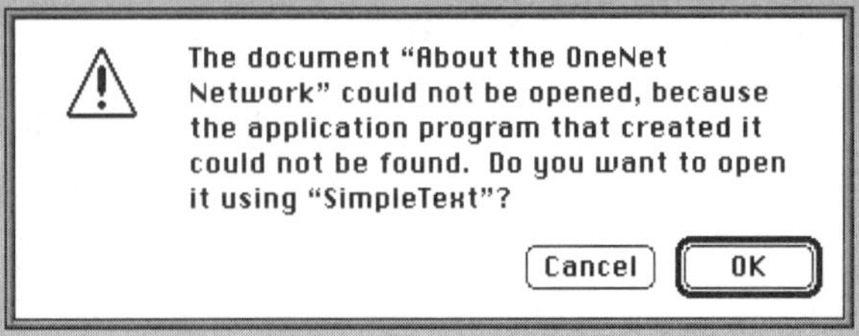

Continued

Sometimes it offers to open it with another application, like TeachText or SimpleText — two basic word processors provided by Apple Computer. But if these programs can't open the document, you have to find some other application that can. Some applications, like Microsoft Word, can open many kinds of documents, including documents created by other applications. We'll see that later in this chapter and again in Chapter 25.

One thing you need to understand: When you save a word document, you are not saving it as part of the Microsoft Word application. It is a separate file and it stays that way.

Saving a Document

A great thing about word processors is their ability to save documents on disk. Why bother to save a document? Here are some good reasons:

- You can save a document you created one day to edit or complete it another day. (Good thing for me. Do you think I could write this whole book in one day?)
- Saved documents often make good starting points for similar documents. For example, open a saved memo to someone, change a few things in it, and it becomes a memo to someone else. All without having to re-create the document from scratch.
- You can share saved documents electronically via network or modem connection. This means that your Macintosh can send a file to someone else's computer through special wires, either as a separate file or as an attachment to an electronic mail message. I'll tell you more about this in Chapter 25.
- When you save a document, you create an archival copy you can open at any time. Let's face it — a hard disk full of files takes up a lot less space than a file cabinet.

- You can copy saved documents to other disks to make backup copies in case your computer or main disk fails. You can also share these other disks with people who need copies of your documents.
- By saving a document as you work with it, you protect yourself against data loss in the event of a power failure or system crash.

Occasionally, you might create a document that you don't need to save, like a quick note to a friend or a fax transmittal form. In most cases, however, you'll want to save the documents you create. In this section, I'll tell you how.

Activating the Save Command

The Save command tells Word that you want to save the current document. The current document is the document you are viewing, the one with the striped title bar. I'll tell you more about working with multiple documents later in this chapter.

As usual, Word offers several ways to activate the Save command:

- Click the Save button on the Standard Toolbar *or*
- Choose Save from the File menu *or*
- Press ⌘S

If your document has not yet been saved, the Save As dialog box appears.

Using the Save As Dialog Box

The Save As dialog box, which is shown in the following illustration, lets you specify information about the file you are saving, like the file name, disk location, and file format. This dialog box contains components of the standard Macintosh Directory dialog box along with some additional buttons and a pop-up menu to access features specific to Word. Default settings for the file location and type automatically appear. You must provide at least a file name before you can save the file.

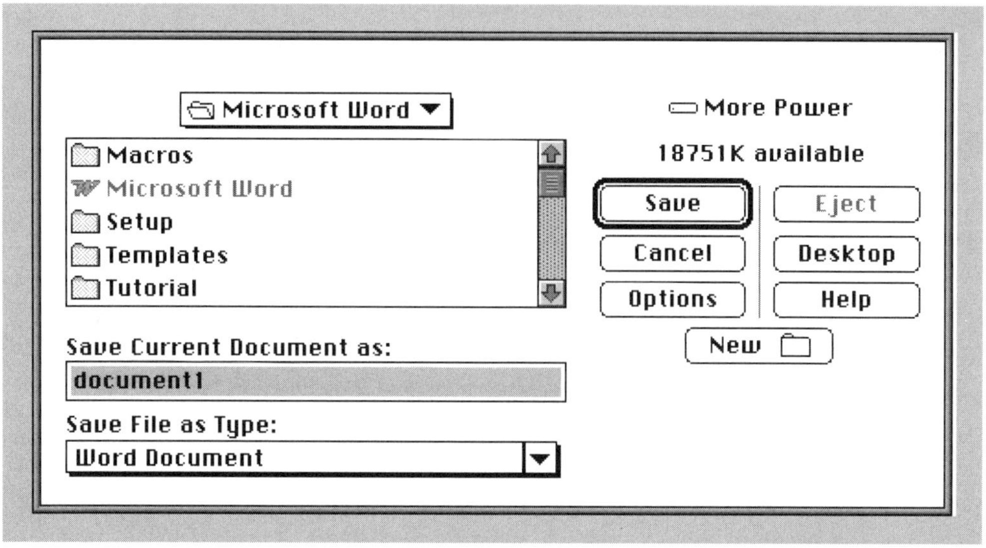

Naming Files. To give the file a name, simply type a name into the Save Current Document As edit box. The name you give the file must follow these rules:

- File names cannot be more than 31 characters in length.
- File names can include any character except a colon (:).
- You cannot give a file the same exact name as a file already existing in a folder unless you want the new file to overwrite the existing file.

TIP/TRICK

If you're saving a file that may be opened by a Word for Windows user, you might want to follow DOS file naming conventions. In that case, the file name must be no more than eight characters long followed by a period and then a three-character extension of DOC. For more information about naming files that may be opened on non-Macintosh computers, check Appendix B where cross-platform considerations are discussed in detail.

For Example: Tips for Naming Files

You've got a lot of flexibility with up to 31 characters in a file name. Take advantage of it. Give your files names that make them easy to identify. For example, say you've got a document that's a thank you note to your friend

Continued

Joe Smith. Why name it "Note" when you can name it "Joe Smith 6/30/94" or "Joe Thank You Note"?

Here are some tricks I use:

- When saving a letter, I name it with the name of the person, along with the date I sent it, like the first Joe Smith example above.
- When saving a fax transmittal, report, outline, proposal, or other specific type of document, I always include the type of document in the file name. The proposal for this book, for example, is named "Mac Bible Word Proposal".
- When saving a file I always want to appear at the top of a file list by name, I begin the file name with one or more spaces. If I want the file to appear at the bottom of a list, I begin its name with a bullet (•).
- When saving chapters of a book, I name them with the chapter numbers. For chapters 1 through 9, I name them 01 through 09 — this guarantees that when viewed in name order, Chapter 2 comes before Chapter 10.

Giving your files descriptive names helps take the guesswork out of identifying them. Take advantage of those 31 characters!

Changing the Disk Location. When you launch Word, the folder containing the Word application icon becomes the default folder. That means it appears in the directory portion of the Save As and Open dialog boxes. If you click the Save button without changing the directory location, the file is saved into the same folder as Microsoft Word.

While this isn't an earth shattering problem, it really isn't a good practice. If you do it all the time, the Word folder will soon be cluttered up with document files. It's like throwing all your paper files into the same drawer of a file cabinet — without bothering with file folders. It makes more sense to create folders for your documents and file them where they belong.

That's where the directory portion of the Save As and Open dialog boxes comes in. It lets you tell Word that you want to open a different folder — or even a different disk. Once the name of the folder you want appears in the pop-up menu above the scrolling list, you can click Save to Save the file within it.

Here's how you can use this dialog box to specify a different disk or folder.

- To change disks, click the Desktop button. Once at the desktop level, you can see all the disks on your Macintosh desktop. Double-click a disk name or click it once and then click Open to open it. The disk name appears in the pop-up menu at the top of the scrolling list as well as in the upper right corner of the dialog box. A list of the folders and files within the disk appears in the scrolling list.
- To eject a disk, click the Eject button. You can click this button only if the current disk can be ejected. Your internal hard disk, for example, cannot be ejected. If the current disk cannot be ejected, the Eject button will be gray. To eject a floppy disk, you must switch to the disk first.
- To go into a folder, double-click the folder name in the scrolling list or click it once and then click Open. The name of the folder you opened appears in the pop-up menu at the top of the scrolling list and the contents of the folder appear within the scrolling list. Repeat this procedure as necessary to open the folder you want.
- To come out of a folder, pull down the pop-up menu at the top of the scrolling list. A list of the different folder levels appears. Choose the level you want to switch to that disk or folder.
- To make a new folder inside the current folder, click the New Folder button. Enter a name in the edit box and click OK.

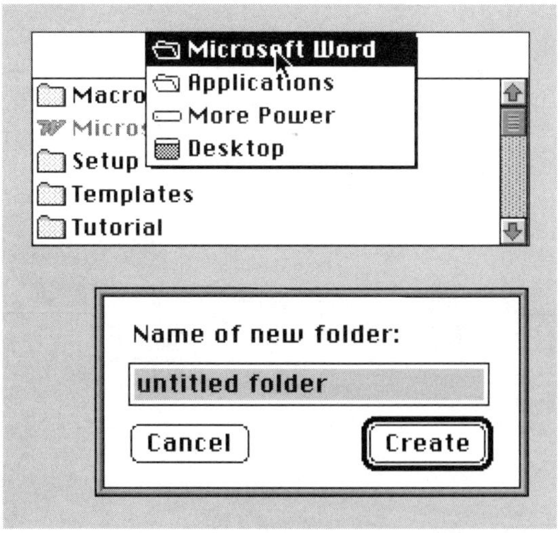

Remember, the location name that appears in the pop-up menu at the top of the scrolling list is the one you will save the file into when you click the Save button. You can change the default document folder — the one that automatically appears the first time you open the Save As or Open dialog box — by choosing a different one in the Options dialog box, which I'll discuss in Chapter 23.

The Save As and Open directory dialog boxes work much the same way. The difference is what you do with them. The Save As dialog box lets you save files. The Open dialog box lets you open files. I'll tell you more about opening files later in this chapter.

FYI: The File Hierarchy

The Macintosh has what's called a *hierarchical file system.* Although that might sound scary, it isn't. Most file cabinets use the same kind of system — files are organized based on labeled drawers and file folders. To find things on a Macintosh disk — or in a file cabinet — it's useful to understand how the filing system is organized. Since I'm getting a bit tired of the same old file cabinet and organization chart analogies — and I bet you are, too — I'll use one that my friend Mark suggested recently: the tree analogy.

Think of a tree. There is a main bough or trunk that goes up and branches off. Some of the branches split off into other branches. And all the branches have leaves.

Now think of a Macintosh disk as a tree. The main bough is called the *root level* or *root directory.* It's what you see in the Finder when you open the disk icon. Folders on the root level are branches that can contain more folders (branches) or files (leaves) or both.

If you wanted to find a specific leaf on the tree (or file on a disk), you'd have to know what path to take among its branches (folders) to find it. That's what navigating in Save As and Open directory dialog boxes is all about: finding a specific file (leaf) in a specific folder (branch) on a tree (disk).

This is a complex topic, one that many people don't fully understand right away. If you don't get it now, don't worry, you will soon. One day it will just click inside your head and everything will make sense.

Saving Files in Other File Formats. By default, Word saves new files in Word Document format. The Save File As Type pop-up menu in the Save As dialog box lets you save files in a variety of other formats. This is useful when exchanging files with someone who uses a different word processor or computer system. I'll cover this in Chapter 25. I'll talk about special kinds of file, templates and Stationery Pads, in Chapter 9.

Completing the Save

Once you've made necessary changes in the Save As dialog box, click the Save button or press Return or Enter to complete the save. Word saves your document with the file name you gave it on the disk location you specified. You can watch the save progress by checking the message Word displays in the status bar as it saves the document. You'll know that the document has been saved because the title bar of the document window will display the name you gave the file.

FYI: About Fast Saves

If you use the Save command to save a document that's already on disk, Word uses its Fast Save feature to save only the changes to the file since the last save. This speeds up the saving process, but can increase the overall size of the file. You can turn off the Fast Save feature in the Options dialog box, which I'll discuss in Chapter 23. This forces Word to save the entire file rather than just the changes to it. Either way, Word saves the latest version of the file.

Using the Summary Info Dialog Box

In Word version 5, Microsoft added a Summary Info feature that enables you to store information about a document with the document itself. This feature makes it easier to search for documents using the Find File command, which I'll discuss later in this chapter.

If the Prompt for Summary Info check box is turned on in the Options dialog box (something I'll discuss in Chapter 23), Word displays the Summary Info dialog box when you save a file for the first time. You can open the Summary Info dialog box for the active document by choosing Summary Info from the File menu. It looks like this:

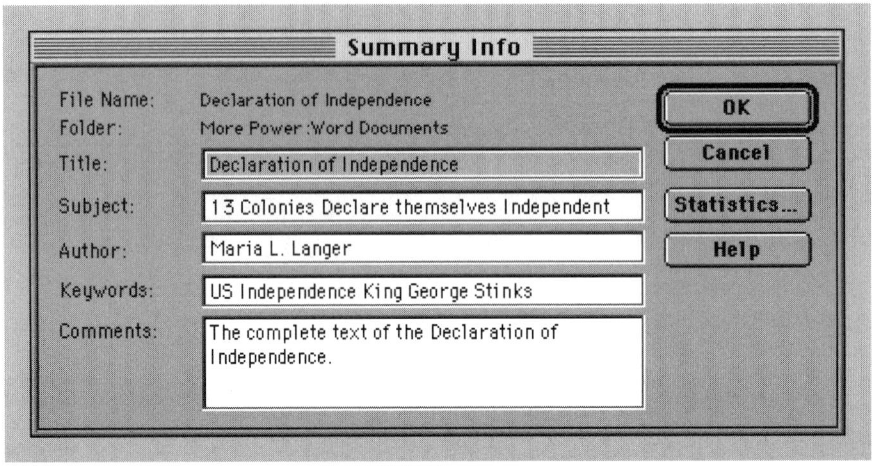

The dialog box already contains the name and location of the file. You can't change them within this box. But you can specify other information about the file, including:

- **Title —** Think of the file's title as an alternative name. It can be even more descriptive than the real file name.
- **Subject —** Every document is about something. Use this edit box to describe what the document is about.
- **Author —** Use this edit box to enter the name of the person who wrote or typed the document. Word automatically gets the author name from the settings in the Options dialog box, which I'll cover in Chapter 23.
- **Keywords —** Use this edit box to enter one or more keywords you might use when searching for this document.
- **Comments —** Use this edit box to enter more information about the file, including things like notes or file descriptions. Although this edit box does not have a scroll bar, if you type more than what can be displayed in the box, the contents scroll to accept it.

To enter information into this dialog box, move from one edit box to the next by clicking in the edit box or pressing [Tab]. Then type the information you want saved with the document. Click the OK button or press [Return] or [Enter] to accept your entries.

You can also use this dialog box to view document statistics. With the Summary Info dialog box open, click the Statistics button. A dialog box like the one below appears, showing you everything you always wanted to know about the document — and more.

NEW IN WORD 6

When you're finished viewing the statistics, click Close or press Return or Enter to dismiss the dialog box.

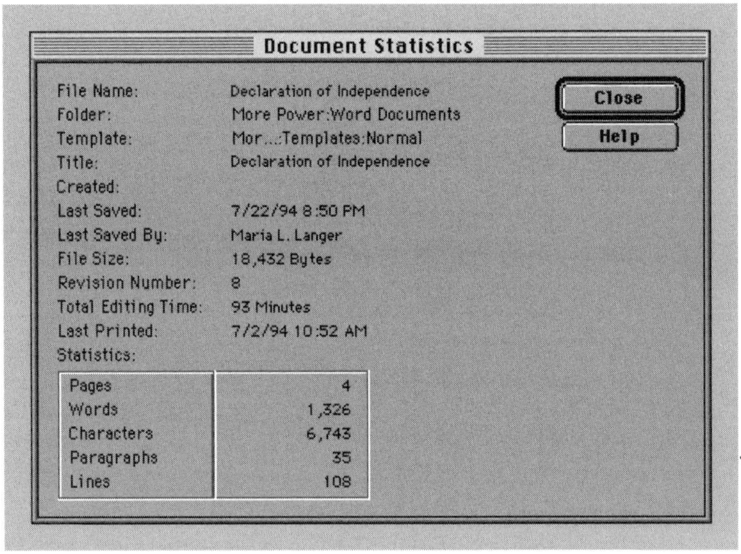

Saving Changes to a Document

You don't need to wait until a document is finished before you save it. In fact, it's good practice to save your documents as you work with them. This protects you from data loss in the event of a power failure or computer bomb. By saving every ten or fifteen minutes, you can never lose more than ten or fifteen minutes worth of work.

FYI: RAM and Document Files

When you first create a document, it exists only in your Macintosh's random access memory (RAM). RAM is a special kind of memory that requires electricity to hold information. While your Macintosh is running, the information in RAM remains right where your computer's central

Continued

processing unit (CPU) can use it. But if there's a power outage or your Macintosh crashes, RAM is wiped clean and the information that was in it is lost.

When you save a file, you copy the file in RAM onto your disk. At that point, two exact copies of the file exist — one in RAM and one on your disk. If there's a problem and RAM gets erased, you can always open the copy of the file that's on your disk — the saved file. When you open a file, you copy the file on your disk into RAM. Again, two exact copies of the file exist.

If you're wondering why we bother with RAM when it relies so heavily on power and can easily be wiped clean, it's because RAM is many times faster than any disk. If your Macintosh's CPU had to work directly with a disk rather than RAM, it would probably be faster to have a team of medieval monks create your documents by hand.

Once a document has been saved, activating the Save command does not display the Save As dialog box. Word already knows what the document is named and where you want it saved. It saves the document for you without bothering you for details. The original document is overwritten with the new version that incorporates all the changes since the last save.

Using the Save As Command

Sometimes you may want to save an existing document with a different name, disk location, or file type. That's when you use the Save As command, which can also be found under the File menu.

The Save As command displays the Save As dialog box. (Makes sense, right?) It contains all the current settings for the file, including its name, disk location, and file type. Make changes as desired and click Save or press Return or Enter to complete the save. If you don't change the file name or location, you'll see a dialog box like this, asking you to confirm whether you want to replace the existing file:

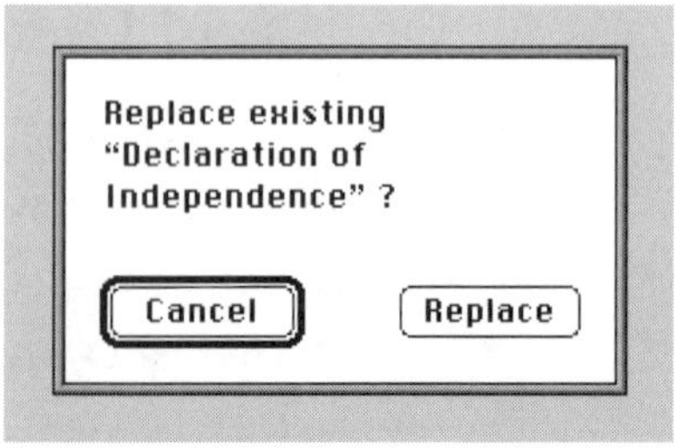

If you do want to replace the existing file, click Replace. If you don't want to replace the existing file, click Cancel or press [Return], [Enter], or [Esc] to go back to the Save As dialog box.

FYI: Save vs. Save As

There often seems to be some confusion over the difference between the Save and Save As commands. Here's a review:

- When a document has not yet been saved, there is absolutely no difference between the Save and Save As commands. Both display the Save As dialog box since the file does not yet have a name.
- Once a document has been saved, the Save command saves changes to the file since the last save without displaying a dialog box. The Save As command, on the other hand, always displays the Save As dialog box.

I always advise students to use the Save command unless they want to change the name, disk location, or file format of a file. That's what I do.

Other Save Options

In version 6, Word's Save As dialog box offers an Options button that you can use to specify Save options for the current file. These options offer additional features, such as the ability to password protect and automatically back up files. I'll cover all of these options in Chapter 23.

NEW IN WORD 6

FYI: Word's AutoSave Feature

Word version 6 adds a new feature called AutoSave, which is turned on by default. This feature works in conjunction with a built-in document recovery feature to help you recover unsaved documents in the event of a computer crash while working with Word.

NEW IN WORD 6

Continued

I'm not very happy with this feature and the way it works. First of all, the feature is called AutoSave, but it does *not* automatically invoke the Save command to save your document. Instead, it saves your document as a special temporary file with a weird name. If you quit Word, the temporary file is deleted. If Word crashes, it's moved to the Trash but is not deleted.

If your Macintosh crashes while you're working with Word, when you relaunch Word, it may automatically attempt to open the AutoSaved versions of the files that were opened when it crashed. If you launch Word by double-clicking on the icon for a document that was open when Word crashed, it might open two versions of the file — the version you last saved and the version Word had stored in its AutoSaved file. You have to figure out which is the version you want to keep and save it with the correct name.

Although the AutoSave and recovery features are powerful additions to Word that should help protect users from data loss in the event of a crash, I think they will confuse a lot of new Word users. I know that they've confused me enough times while I was writing this book! There's no real substitution for saving your work on a regular basis. Remember to use the Save command often as you work on any documents!

Opening an Existing Document

Once you've saved a file, it's a good idea to know how to open it again if you need to read, edit, or print it. That's what this section is all about.

Opening Recently-Opened Files

Word's File menu includes a list of up to nine recently-opened files that Word keeps track of automatically. To open one of these files, simply choose its name from the File menu. The file opens. It's as easy as that.

You can specify exactly how many files Word keeps track of in the Options dialog box, which I'll discuss in Chapter 23.

Using the Open Dialog Box

If the file you want to open is not listed on the File menu, you can use the Open command to open it. To activate the Open command, do one of the following:

- Click the Open button on the Standard toolbar *or*
- Choose Open from the File menu *or*
- Press ⌘O

The Open dialog box that appears looks like this:

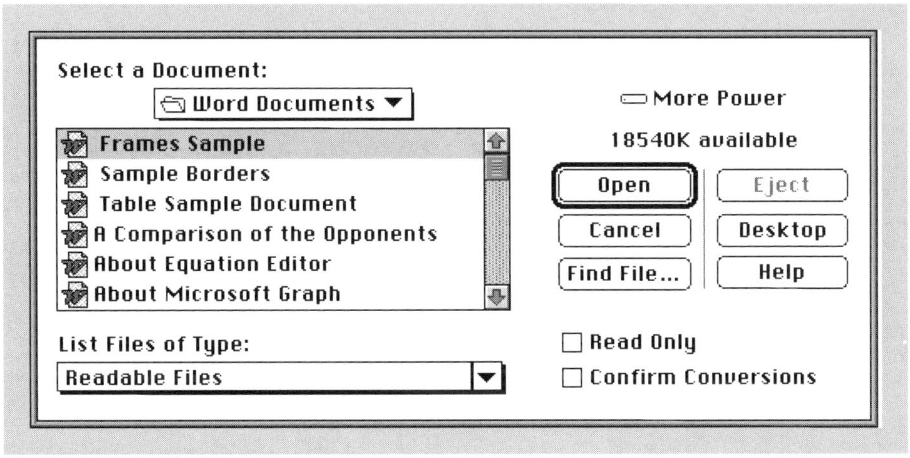

As you can see, it looks a lot like the Save As dialog box I showed you earlier in this chapter. All the Directory dialog box components I discussed earlier work the same way, so I won't bother explaining again how you use them to navigate through the Macintosh's hierarchical file system. (If you skipped that part of this chapter and don't know what I'm talking about, read the section entitled: "Changing the Disk Location".)

The scrolling list displays all the files and folders that you can open within the current directory. Double-click a folder or file or click it once and then click Open to open it. If you don't know where a file is on disk, you can click the Find File button to open Word's Find File dialog box, which I'll discuss a little later in this chapter.

Opening Specific Types of Files

If the file you want to open is not displayed in the scrolling list for a folder you know the file is in, look at the List Files of Type pop-up menu at the bottom of the dialog box. By default, Word looks for Readable Files — all the files it can read with its converters. If the file isn't displayed choose All Files to display every file in the folder. Keep in mind, however, that opening a non-Word file may yield unexpected results. I'll tell you more about opening files created with other applications in Chapter 25.

The List Files of Type pop-up menu can also limit the display of files. If you choose Text Files, for example, only plain text files are displayed. I'll talk more about this in Chapter 25, too.

Opening a Document as Read-Only

If you want to prevent a file from being accidentally changed and then saved with the changes, click the Read Only check box in the Open dialog box before clicking open. This opens the document but makes it impossible to save the document with the same name, thus overwriting the previous version. If you try to save it with the same name, you get a dialog box like this:

TIP/TRICK

The Read Only check box is also handy for network users. If you want to open a file over a network and leave the file available for other network users, turn this check box on before opening the file.

Using the Find File Command

When Microsoft added the Summary Info feature to Word version 5, it also added the Find File feature. Although these two features can operate independently, they complement each other perfectly, making it easy to locate and get information about files on your disks and work with more than one file at a time.

There are two ways to activate the Find File command:

- Choose Find File from the File menu *or*
- Click the Find File button in the Open dialog box

Searching for Files

The first time you use the Find File command, the Search dialog box appears.

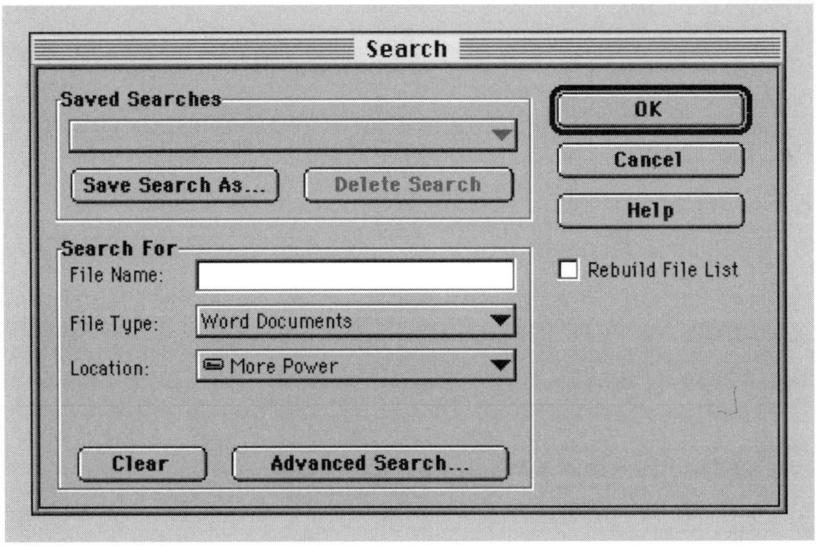

The Search dialog box lets you specify criteria that Word uses to look for files. In the Search For area of this dialog box, specify a File Name, File Type, and Location. The Rebuild File List check box instructs Word to disregard matches to previous criteria (if any) and build a new list from scratch. The Clear button clears out the current criteria so you can start fresh. When you click OK or press Return or Enter, Word searches the location disk based on your search criteria and displays a list of the files in the Find File dialog box.

TIP/TRICK

You don't have to enter an entire file name for Word to find a file. For example, entering *let* in the File Name edit box finds files with those characters anywhere in the file name.

Before I tell you about the Find File dialog box and what you can do with the files Word finds, let's get fancy with some advanced searching techniques.

Using Advanced Search Criteria

Sometimes you might find it necessary to search for files other than by name or location. Perhaps you don't know the name of the file or where it is. Or maybe you just want to search by other criteria. That's where advanced search criteria comes in.

Click the Advanced Search button in the Search dialog box to open the Advanced Search dialog box, which is illustrated in the following figure. It lets you search by Location, Summary, and Timestamp. Click on the tabs to view each of these categories and enter search criteria. You can enter criteria into all three categories if you like. Then click OK to go back to the Search dialog box. You'll have to click OK again in that dialog box to begin the search.

The more search criteria you specify, the longer the search takes and the fewer files Word finds. Word displays the results of the search in the Find File dialog box, which I'll discuss in a little while.

Searching by Location. To search by location, click the Location tab in the Advanced Search dialog box.

Enter a file name or type in the File Name edit box. Choose a file type from the File Type pop-up menu. Choose the folders Word should look into by clicking the Add button and using the directory dialog box that appears to open and select folders. Each folder you add appears in the Search In scrolling list. Do this for as many folders as you like. You can use the Remove button to remove a selected folder or the Remove All button to remove all folders from the list. Use the Include Subfolders check box to tell Word to look in folders inside the folders you chose.

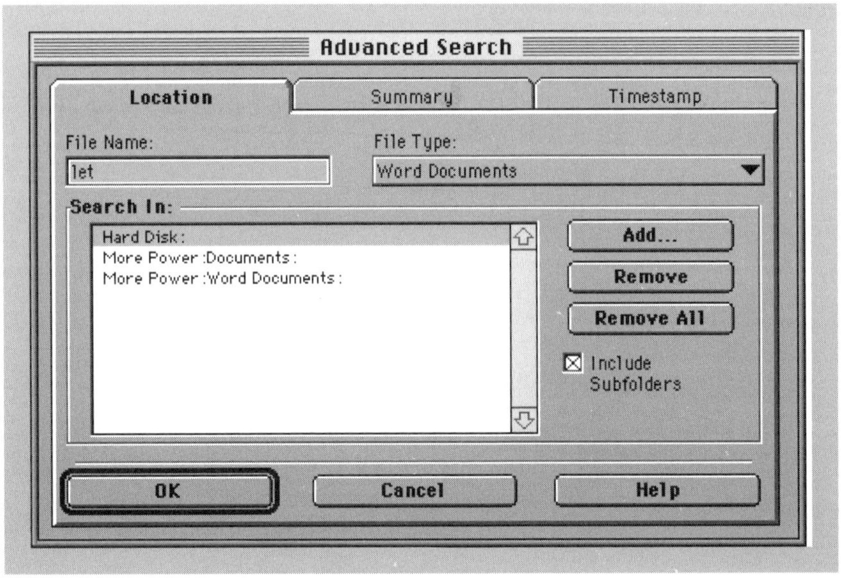

Searching by Summary Information. To search by summary information, click the Summary tab in the Advanced search dialog box.

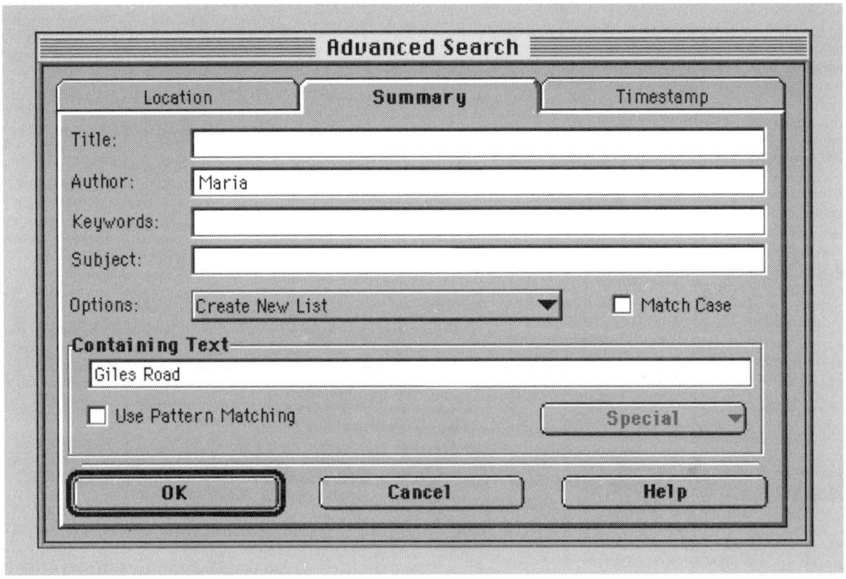

Press Tab or click in each of the edit boxes you want to use to type in search criteria. Click the Match Case check box to turn it on if you want to match upper-and lowercase characters of your search criteria. You can also use wildcard and search operator characters in your criteria. This increases the flexibility of the Find File feature by making it possible to search without exact criteria. Here's a list of special characters, along with examples of how to use them:

Character	Use	Example
?	Matches any single character	*wo?d* matches *wood* and *word*
*	Matches any number of characters	*wo** matches *wood, word, would, world, wonderland,* etc.
& (or space)	AND	*Microsoft & Word* matches only instances of both *Microsoft* and *Word*
,	OR	*Microsoft, Word* matches instances of either *Microsoft* or *Word*
~	NOT	~*word* excludes matches with instances of *word*
" "	Treats the special character within the quotes as a regular character	matches instances of * (rather than any character)

To search based on the contents of a document, enter the text you want to search for in the Containing Text edit box. You can use a variety of wildcard characters and advanced search operators in this edit box if you turn on the Pattern Matching check box. The Special button/menu offers these operators:

Character	Use	Example
?	Matches any single charcter	*wo?d* matches *wood* and *word*
[ ]	Matches one of the specified characters	*wor[de]* matches *word* and *wore*
[-]	Matches any single character in the range	*wor[a-l]* matches *word, wore,* and *work* but not *worm* or *worn*
[!]	Matches any character except the one in the brackets	*wor[!d]* matches *wore, work, worm,* and *worn* but not *word*

Continued

Character	Use	Example
[! -]	Matches any single character except one within the range inside the brackets	*wor[!a-l]* matches *worm* and *worn* but not *word*, *wore*, or *work*
( )	Matches the characters inside the parentheses	*(let)* matches *let* but not *letter*
{n}	Matches exactly n occurrences of the previous character	*10{2}1* matches *1001* but not *101*
{n,}	Matches exactly n occurrences of the previous character	*10{1,}1* matches *101* and *1001*
{n,m}	Matches from n to m occurrences of the previous character	*10{1,3}1* matches *101*, *1001*, and *10001* but not *100001*
@	Matches one or more occurrences of the previous character	*we@d* matches *wed* and *weed*
<( )	Matches at the beginning of a word	*<(to)* finds *to* and *total* but not *into*
>( )	Matches at the end of a word	*>(to)* finds *into* and *to* but not *total*
*	Matches any number of characters	*wo** matches *wood, word, would world, wonderland,* etc.

TIP/TRICK

To search for an operator character, put a backslash (\) before it in the Containing Text edit box.

Finally, you can use the Options pop-up menu to tell Word to either create a new list of matching files, add matching files to the existing list, or search for matches only in the existing list.

Searching by Date. To search by the date a file was created or last saved, or by the person who created or last saved the file, click the Timestamp tab in the Advanced search dialog box.

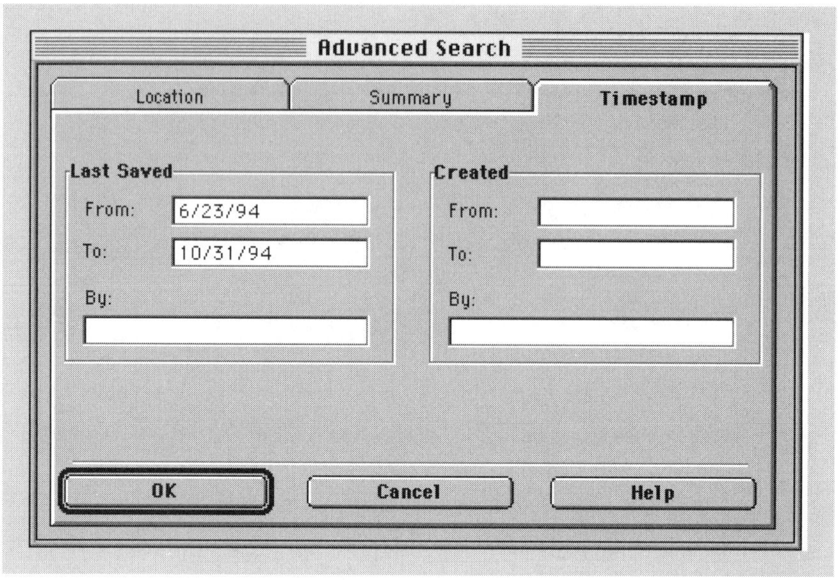

Enter the search criteria — date or name — in the appropriate edit box(es) for Last Saved or Created. To search for files last saved or created within a range of dates, be sure to enter a To and From date. To search by the person who last saved or created the file, you can enter any part of his or her name.

Reusing Search Criteria

Specifying advanced search criteria can be time consuming. Fortunately, Word lets you save and reuse search criteria. This is very useful if you often have to find files based on the same collection of complex criteria.

Here's how you can save, reuse, change, and delete search criteria.

Saving Search Criteria. Once you've specified search criteria (but before you begin the search), click the Save Search As button in the Search dialog box. The Save Search As dialog box appears:

Enter a name in the Search Name edit box and click OK. The name you specified appears in the Saved Searches pop-up menu in the Search dialog box:

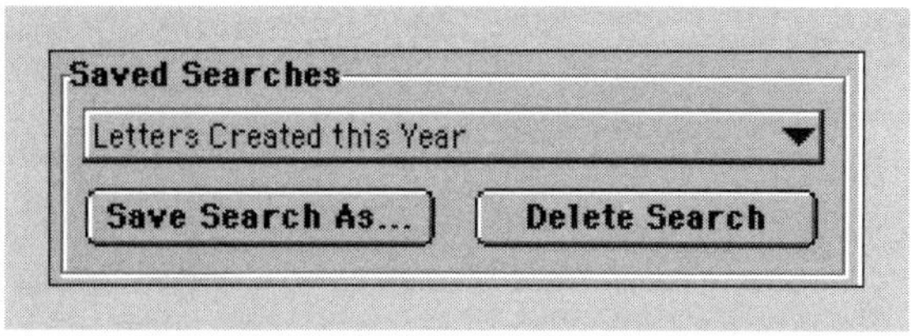

You can then perform the search by clicking the OK button in the Search dialog box.

Using Saved Search Criteria. To use saved search criteria, choose the name of the search from the Saved Searches pop-up menu in the Search dialog box. Then click OK to begin the search.

Changing Saved Criteria. Word also lets you change saved criteria. This is useful in two situations:

- You discover that a saved search isn't exactly what you need.
- You want to create a new search very similar to an existing search.

To change saved criteria, choose the name of the search from the Saved Searches pop-up menu in the Search dialog box. Then click the Advanced Search button to open the Advanced Search dialog box. The search criteria for the saved search you chose appears in the dialog box. Make desired changes to it in any of the three tabs and click OK to go back to the Search dialog box. Next, click the Save Search As button.

- To replace the search you originally chose with the new criteria, enter the same name in the Save Search as dialog box. Click OK and then click Yes to confirm that you want to replace the existing saved search.
- To create a brand new search based on the changed search criteria, enter a new name in the Save Search As dialog box. Click OK to complete the save.

Deleting Saved Criteria

You can also delete a saved search if you decide you don't need it anymore. Choose the name of the search you want to delete and click the Delete Search button. Click Yes in the confirmation dialog box that appears to complete the deletion.

Working with Found Files

NEW IN WORD 6

Once you perform a search, Word displays the results in the Find File dialog box, which is shown in the following illustration. While this dialog box is not brand new to Word 6, it has been greatly improved, both cosmetically and functionally, and has lots of new features.

A hierarchical list of disks, folders, subfolders, and found files appears in the Listed Files scrolling window on the left side of the dialog box. Click on a file name to display information about it in the right side of the dialog box.

The Find File dialog box also offers buttons and a pop-up menu to access other commands. Click the Search button to return to the Search dialog box. Click Open to open the currently chosen file. To close the Find File window when you're finished with it, click its Close button. I'll tell you about the View pop-up menu and Commands button/menu next.

Viewing File Contents and Information

The way the Find File dialog box appears depends on the current view. There are three views: Preview, File Info, and Summary. To switch from one view to another, choose the one you want from the View pop-up menu on the bottom of the dialog box.

Preview. Preview view, which is shown in the previous illustration, displays the contents of the file in the Preview Of window on the right side of the Find File dialog box. Use the scroll bars on the side of the window to preview the entire document.

If the file is not a Word file, Word uses its built-in converters to convert and display it. If the file is protected with a password (something I'll discuss in Chapter 23), you must type in the password before Word displays the file.

File Info. File Info view, shown in the following illustration, changes the dialog box to display one large scrolling window full of information about the files Word found. Information includes the Title, Size (in kilobytes), Author, and Last Saved date. The order this information is presented depends on how it was sorted — more on that in a moment. You can change column widths by dragging the border of a column to the right or left.

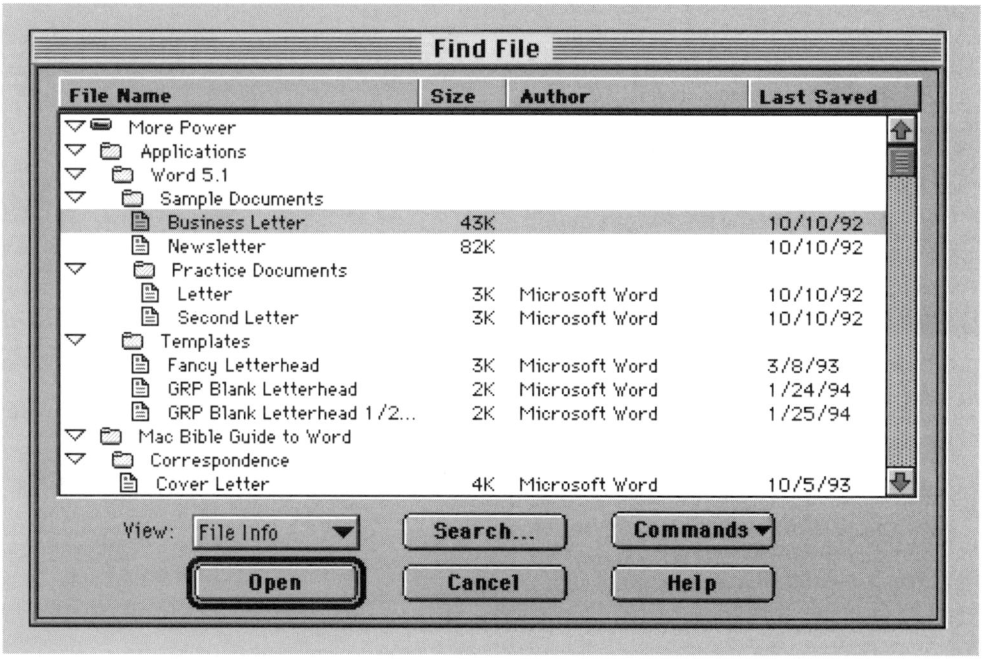

Summary. Summary view, which is shown in the following illustration, displays summary information and statistics for the chosen file on the right side of the Find File dialog box. The summary information that shows comes from the Summary Info dialog box I discussed earlier in this chapter. If you did not enter Summary Info for the file, the Title, Subject, Keywords, and Comments fields may be blank. Statistics like the creation, modification, and print dates, revision numbers, and document size are provided by Word.

Using Find File Commands

The Commands button/menu gives you additional options for working with found files. Most of the commands work on whatever file is selected in the list of files. You can select more than one file by holding down [⌘] while clicking on each file you want to select.

- **Open Read Only** — opens the selected document(s) as read-only documents. I discussed read-only documents earlier in this chapter.
- **Print** — prints the selected document(s). The Print dialog box displays only once, no matter how many documents are selected. I'll discuss printing in detail in Chapter 4.
- **Summary** — displays the Summary Info dialog box for the selected document.

- **Delete** — deletes the selected document(s). A confirmation dialog box lets you confirm that you really do want to delete them before Word removes them from disk.
- **Copy** — displays a standard directory dialog box you can use to copy the selected documents to another location on disk.
- **Sorting** — displays the Options dialog box shown below. Choose a radio button to sort files by Author, Creation Date, Last Saved By, Last Saved Date, Name, or Size. You can also tell Word whether it should list files by File Name or Title. A Show Folders check box lets you turn the display of folders on or off. With this check box turned off, more files fit in the file list window. Click OK to sort the files.

Working with Multiple Document Windows

As you saw briefly in Chapter 2, you can have more than one Word document window open at a time. Simply use the New or Open commands to create new documents or open documents on disk. As you open documents, their windows are stacked, one on top of the other, on your screen. You may not be able to see how many windows are open by looking at your screen since some windows may completely hide others. The topmost window is the active document — you can tell it from any others that might be displayed because it has a striped title bar.

In this section, I'll explain how you can switch from one window to another and resize windows so you can see more than one at a time.

Switching Between Open Documents

There are two main ways to switch from one open document window to another:

- Choose the name of the document you want from the Window menu *or*
- Click on any visible portion of the document window.

In either case, that document comes to the top and becomes the active window.

Resizing Document Windows

Unless you have a very large monitor, you probably won't be able to see more than one full-size document window on your screen at a time. Resizing windows to make them smaller makes it possible to see more than one document at a time. There are three ways to do this:

NEW IN WORD 6

- Choose Arrange All from the Window menu. This new command resizes and repositions all open windows so all are displayed.
- Position your mouse pointer in the window's size box and drag the corner of the window to make a custom window size. An outline of the window's right and bottom edges moves as you drag. When you let go of the mouse button, the window resizes.
- Click on the window's zoom box. This toggles the window between full size and a custom size.

Moving Document Windows

Sometimes making a window smaller isn't enough to see into other windows. Sometimes you also need to move a document window. To do this, position your mouse pointer on the window's title bar, anywhere except on the close box or zoom box. Then drag the title bar to a new position on the screen. An outline of the window moves as you drag. When you let go of the mouse button, the window moves.

Making Another Application's Window Active

Just as you can have more than one document open, you can also have more than one application open. The current application's windows are stacked atop any other applications' windows. There are two basic ways to switch from one application's windows to another's:

- Pull down the Application menu at the far right end of the menu bar and choose the application you want.
- Click on any visible portion of a document window for the application you want.

Chapter Summary

In this chapter, you worked with document files. You learned how to save, open, and search for Word documents, and how to use the Save As, Summary Info, and Open dialog boxes. Word's improved Find File command and its Search, Advanced Search, and Find File dialog boxes, plus some handy techniques for working with multiple document files were also covered.

In Chapter 4, you'll get it all on paper. You'll learn how to use Apple's Chooser to tell Word where to print documents, and how to use the commands and dialog boxes for Print Preview and Print.

4

Chapter 4: Printing Documents

ENTERING, EDITING, AND FORMATTING TEXT IS 95 PERCENT of the work you need to do to create a document. To finish the job, you just need to print. That's where Word, your Macintosh, and your printer work together to put your words on paper so you can share them with others.

In this chapter I'll tell you what you need to do to print your Word documents. I'll show you how to use Apple's Chooser to select a printer. I'll discuss commands and dialog boxes for Print Preview and Print. Finally, I'll offer some additional information for folks using System 7.5 with QuickDraw GX since they'll find that printing works a bit differently for them.

So fire up your printer, fill it with paper, and let's get to work.

Using Apple's Chooser

Apple provides a standard interface called the Chooser for selecting printers. It is automatically installed as part of your Macintosh's System software. To open the Chooser, pull down the Apple menu at the far left side of the Menu bar and choose Chooser. The Chooser window appears:

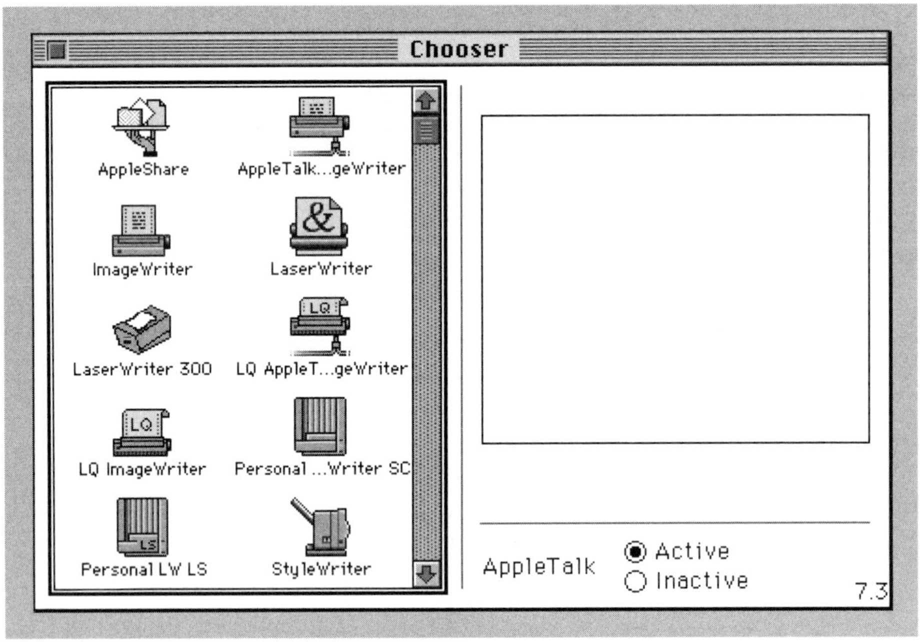

Choosing a Printer

Choosing a printer is a two- or three-step process, depending on whether you're using a Macintosh directly connected to a printer or one connected to a number of printers through a network. Either way, the first step is the same: choosing the icon for the kind of printer you want to use.

On the left side of the Chooser window is a scrolling window full of icons for printer drivers. Find the icon for the printer you want to use and click once on its icon to select it. If you do not see an icon for your printer, its printer driver has probably not been installed. Consult the manual that came with your Macintosh or printer for printer driver installation instructions.

FYI: Printer Drivers

A *printer driver* is a special kind of file your Macintosh uses to communicate with a specific kind of printer. It gives you access, through the Page Setup dialog box to options available on that printer. I'll tell you more about Page Setup in Chapter 8. If you don't choose the correct printer driver, not only will you be offered an incorrect set of options, but your Macintosh won't be able to print.

Printer drivers for Apple printers are normally installed when the rest of the System software is installed. Some common Apple printers include the LaserWriter, StyleWriter, and ImageWriter. Printer drivers for printers manufactured by companies other than Apple Computer — like Hewlett Packard, Sharp, or Canon — usually come on a disk with the printer. The proper printer driver must be installed before you can print.

In the Macintosh world, every program uses the same set of printer drivers. This means that if you can successfully print from one program, you'll probably be able to print from all others. Of course it also means that if you *can't* print from one program, you probably won't be able to print from *any* of them, but that's a rather pessimistic way of looking at things, isn't it?

Direct Connections

If your Macintosh is directly connected to a printer and you're not connected to a network, you're already half way done choosing your printer. All you need to do is locate and click on the name of your printer on the right side of the Chooser window.

Network Connections

If your Macintosh is connected to one or more printers through a network with zones, the Chooser window will have an additional scrolling window on the left, full of AppleTalk Zones, something like this:

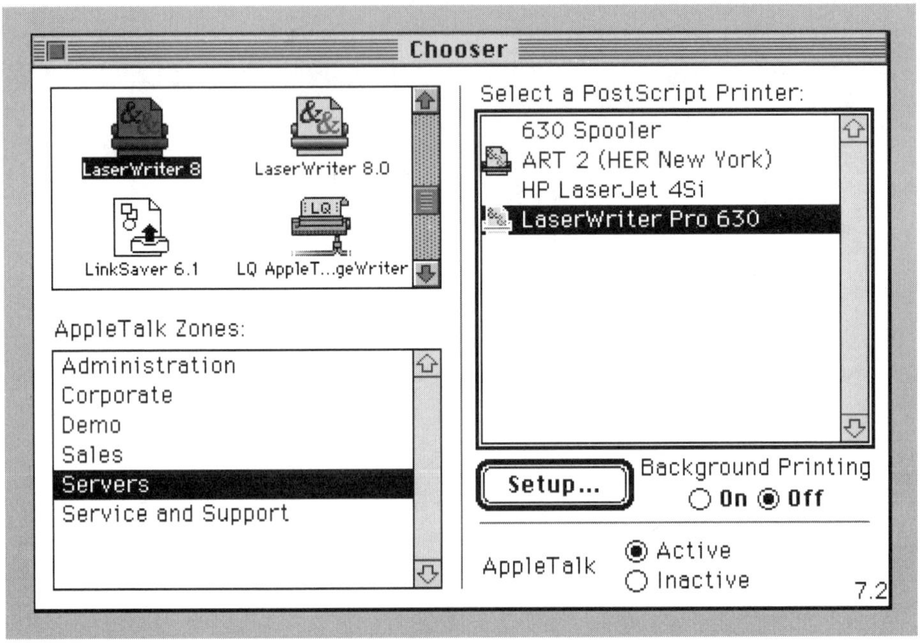

You've got two steps left to choose your printer. First, click once on the name of the AppleTalk Zone that contains the printer you want to use. A list of available printers in that zone appears on the right side of the dialog box. Click on the name of the printer you want to print on to select it. If you are unsure about the AppleTalk Zone or printer name, ask your Network Administrator or someone you work with.

Setting Other Options

The Chooser offers additional options you should be familiar with.

Background Printing

Background Printing should be available for most printers. By turning this on, your document is automatically sent to a special program called

PrintMonitor to print, thus freeing up Microsoft Word so you can continue working while the document prints. I'll tell you more about PrintMonitor later in this chapter. If you turn Background Printing off, you'll have to wait until the document finishes printing before you can perform other tasks with your Macintosh.

AppleTalk

In order to access any devices — including printers — on an AppleTalk network, AppleTalk must be set to Active. In addition, some printers require that AppleTalk be set to Active.

Setup

If you've chosen a PostScript printer, a Setup button may appear. Click this button to access printer setup options. Consult the manual that came with your printer for more information about these options.

Closing the Chooser Window

To tell your Macintosh to accept your choice of printer, close the Chooser window by using any of these methods:

- Click on its Close box *or*
- Choose Close from the File menu *or*
- Press [⌘][W]

A warning dialog box like this may appear:

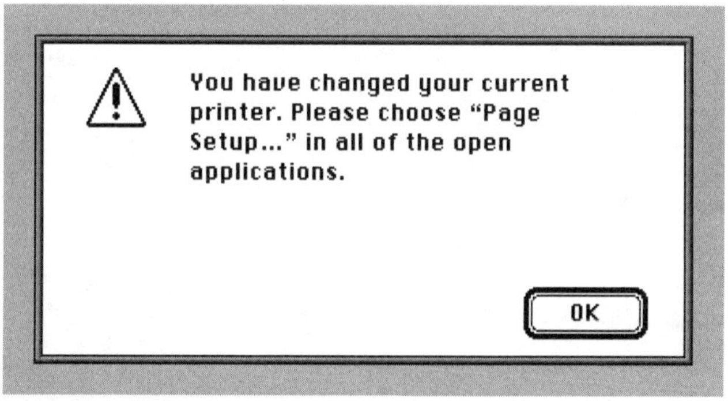

This dialog box reminds you that when you change the printer, you may have to make changes in the Page Setup dialog box. Click OK to dismiss it. I'll tell you about the Page Setup dialog box in Chapter 8.

IMPORTANT NOTE

When you choose a printer in Apple's Chooser, that printer remains your active printer until you change it. If you only have one printer, you can choose it once and never have to worry about it again.

Previewing a Document

As I mentioned in Chapter 1, Normal view, which is the fastest for entering and editing text, does not offer true WYSIWYG (What You See Is What You Get) page display. Instead, the entire document looks like one long, continuous page. Although most character and paragraph formatting is properly displayed, you can't get an overall idea of how your document will look, page for page, when printed.

That's where Print Preview comes in. Print Preview offers a bird's eye view of your document's pages. This gives you an idea of how text, graphics, and white space will appear on the printed page. You can also use Print Preview tools to examine each page more closely, edit the document, or adjust margins. All your changes are immediately displayed for your inspection. If you're satisfied with the way your document looks, use a Print button to print it.

For Example: Save a Tree!

It's the 1990s and the environment is a serious issue we should all be aware of. As joint owners and caretakers of the world, we should work hard to protect its resources. And, believe it or not, Word's Print Preview feature can help you do just that.

I use Print Preview before I print *any* Word document. Since Print Preview offers true WYSIWYG display, there aren't any surprises when I print. That means I only have to print a document once. That saves paper. Saving paper saves trees.

Here are some other ways I save paper. Why not try some of them yourself?

Continued

- If a document takes less than $1\frac{1}{4}$ pages, try adjusting its margins to squeeze it all on one page. Print Preview makes this easy to do, as you'll see later in this chapter.
- If you print something and it doesn't come out just right, don't throw the used paper away. After all, the unprinted side of it is still good. I use the back side of printed paper for draft documents or for taking notes. Sometimes I use a papercutter to cut batches of paper in half for telephone doodle sheets.
- If you receive a document electronically via network or modem, don't print it unless you really need to. As electronic communication becomes more popular in the business world, paper consumption should decrease. After all, you can read a document on your screen just as easily as you can read it on paper.
- Recycle all the paper you can. Businesses and communities are making recycling easier all the time. There's no excuse not to recycle!

And, in case you were wondering, this book was printed on recycled paper.

To open the Print Preview window, do one of the following:

- Click the Print Preview button on the Standard toolbar *or*
- Choose Print Preview from the File menu *or*
- Press ⌘ Option I

The Print Preview window is shown in the following illustration.

Displaying Pages in Print Preview

Print Preview can display from 1 to 36 pages of a document within its window. The more pages it displays, the smaller each page is on screen. For this reason, you may want to limit the number of pages you display at once.

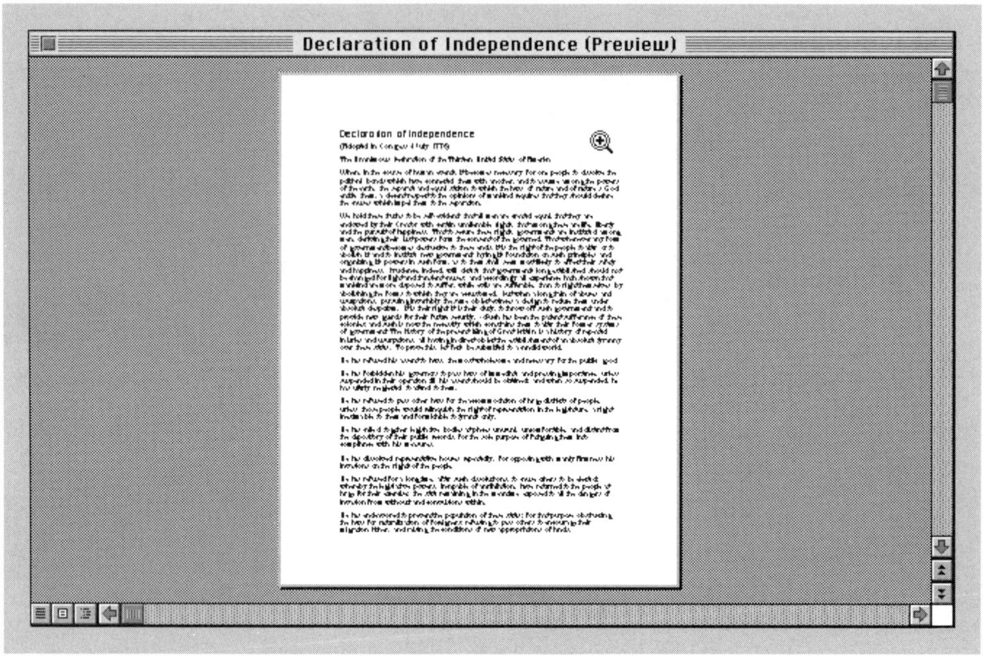

If your document is long and you're only displaying a few pages at a time, you'll need to scroll within Print Preview to see each page. There are several ways to do this:

- **Vertical Scroll bar:** Click the up or down arrow at either end of the Scroll bar to scroll through the document. Click in the gray area of the Scroll bar to move one screenful at a time. Drag the Scroll box to scroll more quickly — the page indicator in the Status bar tells you what page will appear when you release the scroll box.
- **Previous Page and Next Page:** These buttons, at the bottom of the Scroll bar, display the document one page at a time.
- **Pg Up and Pg Dn:** These keys move backward and forward through the document one screenful at a time.

Using the Print Preview Toolbar

NEW IN WORD 6

Word's Print Preview feature is not new, but, as experienced Word users can see, it is greatly changed for version 6. The Toolbar is a new addition. It replaces buttons that appeared along the left side of the window in previous versions of Word and adds a number of brand new features.

- **Print** — opens the Print dialog box so you can print the document. I'll discuss the Print command and dialog box later in this chapter.

- **Magnifier** — turns your mouse pointer into a magnifiying glass with a plus (+) or minus (-) sign in it when it is positioned over a document page. (You can see this in the previous illustration.) Click to magnify or reduce the view. You can also use the Zoom Control, which I'll discuss in a moment.

- **One Page** — displays the document one page at a time. (This is also shown in the previous illustration.)

- **Multiple Pages** — lets you tell Word how many pages to show. It works as a pop-up menu with a grid that lets you specify the number of pages and display configuration. Drag the mouse to expand the grid and choose the option you want. When you release the mouse button, the number of pages displayed changes.

- **Zoom Control** — displays the current magnification of a page. To change it, click on the arrow to the right of the box to pull down a menu of magnifications and choose the one you want. If you want a custom magnification, click on the Zoom Control box, type in a percentage, and press Return or Enter.

- **View Ruler** — shows or hides the Print Preview Rulers. The white portion of the ruler represents the part within the margins. I'll discuss Rulers and the markers you might find within them in greater detail in Chapter 6. In Print Preview, the Rulers let you

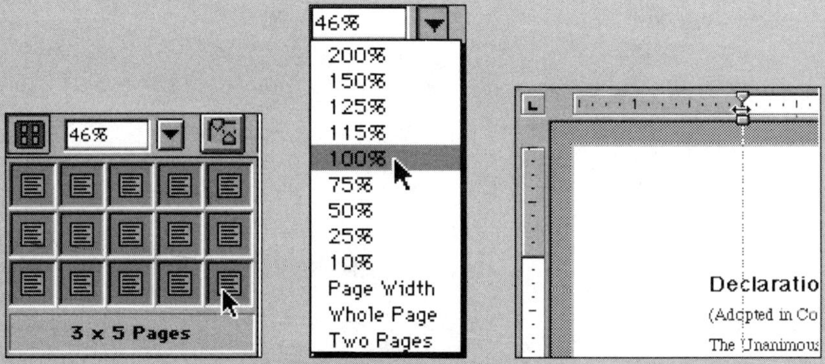

Multiple Pages pop-up **Zoom Control menu** **Print Preview Rulers**

adjust margins for a page. Display the page you want to change, then drag the end of a Ruler to change a margin. The Horizontal Ruler changes the right and left margins. The Vertical Ruler changes the top and bottom margins. I'll discuss margins in greater detail in Chapter 8 when I talk about Page Setup.

- **Shrink to Fit** — can be used to reduce the number of pages in a document if the last page has only a few lines of text on it. This helps you save trees and keeps your documents from looking silly — at least *I* think one or two lines on the last page looks silly. Click the Shrink to Fit button and wait while Word attempts to squeeze everything on one less page. If it can't do the job, it displays a dialog box telling you that it tried and failed.

- **Full Screen** — hides all the non-essential screen elements — like Scroll bars, Rulers, and the Status bar — so that only the displayed page(s) and the Print Preview Toolbar show. This can make the page display larger to provide more detail without zooming in. To bring the hidden screen elements back, click the Full Screen button again or press Esc.

- **Close** — closes the Print Preview window. (So does the Close box and the ⌘W shortcut key.) It does not close the document.

- **Help** — gives you access to Word's online Help feature, which I discussed in Chapter 1.

Try This! Adjusting Margins in Print Preview

As I mentioned a moment ago, you can use the Rulers in Print Preview to adjust margins. Give it a try.

1. If you haven't already done so, open a document and switch to Print Preview by clicking the Print Preview button, choosing Print Preview from the File menu, or pressing ⌘ Option I.

2. If the Rulers are not displayed, click the View Ruler button to display them.

Continued

3. Position your mouse pointer at the end of the white area of the Ruler. The mouse pointer changes to a double-headed arrow.
4. Press the mouse button down and drag the end of the Ruler. You'll see a dotted line follow your mouse as you drag. This indicates the new margin for the page.
5. When you've got the margin positioned where you want it, release the mouse button. The page reformats.

You can do this for the top, bottom, left, or right margin on a page. The benefit of doing it in Print Preview is that you can immediately see the results of your changes.

Printing a Document

You've chosen a printer. You've previewed your document. Now you're ready to print. Time for the Print command.

You can activate the Print command by using any of these methods:

- Click the Print button on either the Standard or Print Preview Toolbar *or*
- Choose Print from the File menu *or*
- Press ⌘P

When you click a Print button, Word prints one copy of the document without offering any options. A small Status box like the one shown here appears briefly to let you know what Word is up to. You can click Cancel or press ⌘. to prevent the document from printing. When the Status box disappears, you can go back to work.

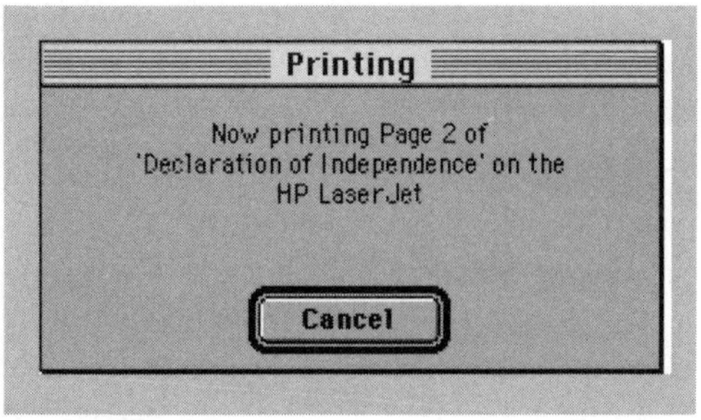

When you choose Print from the File menu or use the Print command shortcut key, Word displays the Print dialog box. Let's take a good look at that.

Using the Print Dialog Box

The Print dialog box lets you select printing options before you print. How this dialog box appears and what options it offers depends on your printer. Here's an illustration of the Print dialog box for an Apple LaserWriter printer:

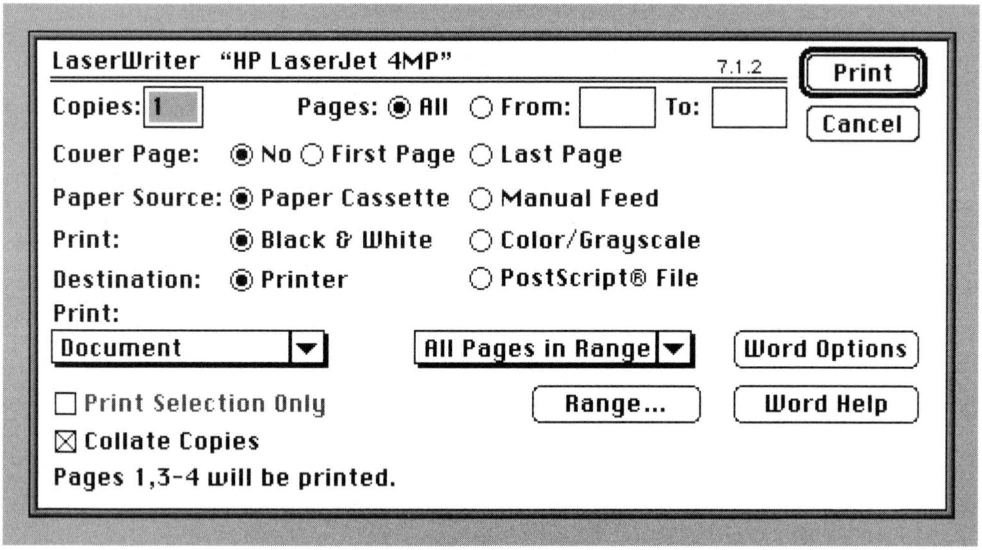

Think of this dialog box as having two parts: a printer-specific part and a Word-specific part. The printer-specific part at the top of the dialog box will always look the same for that printer in every application. You can learn more about its options in your Macintosh or printer manual. The Word-specific part at the bottom of the dialog box includes options that can only be found in Word. I'll tell you about them in this section.

Telling Word What to Print

NEW IN WORD 6

Two pop-up menus let you tell Word what to print. The first, which has a default value of Document, lets you choose among these options:

- **Document** — prints the active document.

- **Summary Info** — prints the contents of the Summary Info dialog box for the active document. I told you about Summary Info in Chapter 3.
- **Annotations** — prints any annotations that may be included in the active document. I'll tell you about annotations in Chapter 18.
- **Styles** — prints the descriptions of any styles in the active document. I'll tell you about styles in Chapter 7.
- **AutoText Entries** — prints the AutoText entries for the active document, inlcuding entries assigned to all templates. I'll tell you about AutoText in Chapter 16.
- **Key Assignments** — prints the names, shortcut keys, and descriptions for macros in the active document. It also prints any shortcut keys you created specifically for the active document. I'll tell you about macros and creating shortcut keys in Chapters 26 and 24.

If you chose Document from the first pop-up menu, you can also make a choice in the pop-up menu beside it. This menu is set to All Pages in Range by default. The options it offers are:

- **All Pages in Range** — prints all pages you specify with the Range button (which I'll tell you about in a moment) or with the standard Pages radio buttons and edit boxes at the top of the dialog box.
- **Odd Pages** — prints only the odd numbered pages in the range.
- **Even Pages** — prints only the even numbered pages in the range.

Specifying an Exact Page Range

NEW IN WORD 6

The Range button, which is only available if you chose Document from the pop-up menu above it, lets you specify exactly which pages of the document to print. Click the button to display the Range dialog box, which looks like this:

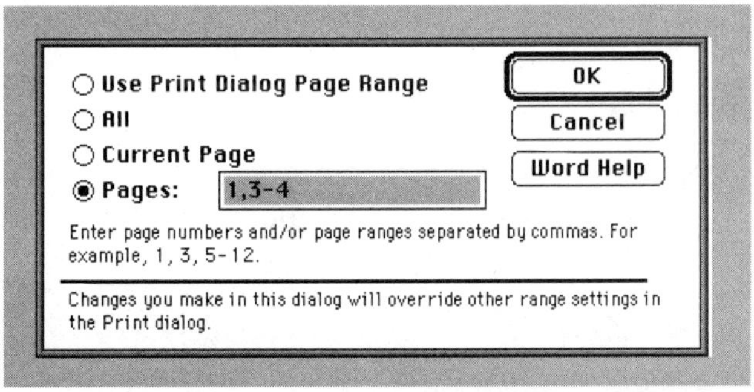

Use radio buttons to choose from among these options:

- **Use Print Dialog Page Range —** tells Word to use the page range specified in the Print dialog box.
- **All —** prints the entire document. No surprise there.
- **Current Page —** prints the page the insertion point was in when you opened the Print dialog box.
- **Pages —** lets you enter a range of pages to print. You can specify multiple, non-contiguous ranges. Use a hyphen to separate the beginning and end of a range. Use a comma to separate individual ranges. Use the letter *s* before a section number. (I'll discuss multiple-section documents in Chapter 8.) Here are some examples of valid ranges:

To print these pages:	Enter this in the Pages edit box:
Page 1 only	1
Pages 1 through 5	1-5
Pages 1 and 6 through 10	1,6-10
Pages 2 through 4, 6 through 10, and 12	2-4,6-10,12
Pages 1 through 5 and section 3	1-5,s3

Once you've made appropriate changes in the Range dialog box, click OK to accept your settings.

Using Other Options

The Print dialog box offers a few other options you should be aware of:

- **Print Selection Only —** tells Word to print only the text that was selected when you opened the Print dialog box. This option is only available if text is selected when you use the Print command; otherwise, it will be gray.
- **Collate Copies —** ensures that multiple copies of a document are printed in sets. With this check box turned off, Word prints multiple copies of each page before printing the next.
- **Word Options —** gives you access to Word's Print Options, which I'll discuss in Chapter 23.

Printing. Once you specify the options you want in the Print dialog box, click the Print button to print. A printing status box like the one I showed you earlier in this chapter appears to let you know Word is printing the document. To cancel printing, press ⌘. or Esc while the printing status box is showing on your screen. If you want to cancel a print job after the printing status box has disappeared, you need to open PrintMonitor, which I'll tell you about now.

Using PrintMonitor

When you turn on Background Printing in the Chooser, a special application called PrintMonitor intercepts all documents on their way to the printer. PrintMonitor is part of the Macintosh System software. It is automatically installed with the System software and works with all programs that print.

PrintMonitor's main job is to hold documents until the printer, which can only print a page at a time, can print them. This makes it possible for you to continue using your Macintosh even when printing long documents. Without PrintMonitor and Background Printing, you'd have to wait until a document finished printing before you could print another or do other work on your Macintosh. PrintMonitor is an example of a *print spooler* program. Others, like SuperLaserSpool, do the same basic thing.

As you saw in the previous section, a printing status box appears when you print a document. Once that message disappears, the document is out of Word's control and in the hands of PrintMonitor. You can view a list of the documents waiting to be printed by accessing the PrintMonitor application. Do this by choosing PrintMonitor from the System 7 Application menu. PrintMonitor's main window looks like this:

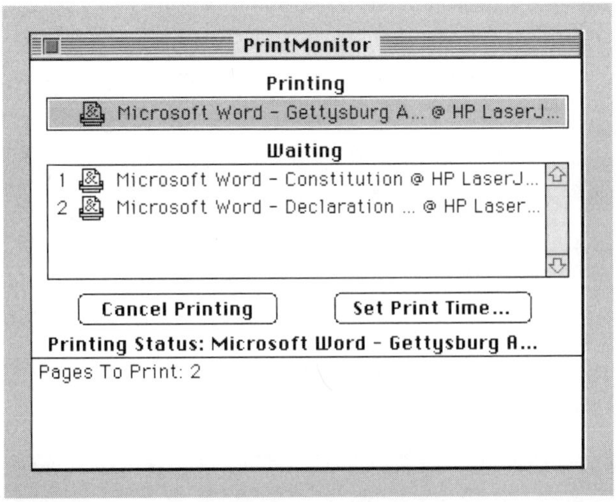

The Printing box shows the name and printer destination of the document currently being printed. The Waiting box lists all the names and destinations for other documents waiting to be printed. Click on the name of any document to view information about it in the Printing Status area at the bottom of the window. To cancel a print job, click once on its name to select it and then click the Cancel or Remove from List button. It usually takes a few seconds for PrintMonitor to cancel it, so be patient.

TIP/TRICK

To set a print date and time for a print job, click once on its name to select it and then click the Set Print Time button. Enter the desired date and time in the dialog box that appears and click OK to accept it.

PrintMonitor tells you when there are printing problems, too. It displays an informational dialog box that tells you when it can't find the printer, when the printer is out of paper, when you need to manually feed paper into the printer, or when the printer is jammed. By following instructions in these dialog boxes, you can solve most common printer problems.

Printing Multiple Documents

Sometimes, you may want to print more than one document at a time. There are several ways to do this.

- Group the documents you want to print together into a master document. I'll discuss that in Chapter 15.
- From the Finder, select the documents you want to print by holding down the Shift key and clicking once on each document icon. The icons must be within the same window to do this. Then choose Print from the Finder's File menu. The Finder opens each document in Word, displays the Print dialog box, and prints them.

Printing under System 7.5 with QuickDraw GX

Apple's System 7.5 introduced QuickDraw GX, which changes the way printing works on a Macintosh. You use the Chooser, which I discussed near the beginning of this chapter, to create a *desktop printer* for each printer attached to your Macintosh or available over a network. You can then select the printer you want to use right from within the Print dialog box, without ever using the Chooser again. If you're like me and have the luxury of multiple printers, you'll find this a lot more convenient than using the Chooser each time you need to change printers.

System 7.5 and QuickDraw GX also replaced PrintMonitor. Now, when you want to check printing status or change print time or date, you double-click on the desktop printer the document is scheduled to print to and make changes as necessary. Desktop printers make it possible to print to multiple printers at once — PrintMonitor could only handle one print job at a time.

In this section, I'll explain briefly how you use the Chooser, the Print dialog box, and desktop printers on a System 7.5 Macintosh. If you're not using System 7.5 yet, you can skip the rest of this chapter — unless, of course, you're curious about what you're missing!

IMPORTANT NOTE

This section was not written to cover every aspect of printing with QuickDraw GX. Instead, it provides enough information to get you started using QuickDraw GX with Microsoft Word. For more information about printing and using desktop printers, consult the manual that came with System 7.5. You'll find lots more information there.

Creating a Desktop Printer

In order to print on a System 7.5 Macintosh with QuickDraw GX, you must create at least one desktop printer. You do this with the Chooser. If you don't know how to use the Chooser and skipped over the "Using Apple's Chooser" section near the beginning of the chapter, go back and read it now since much of what I discussed applies in System 7.5, too. You may notice, however, that the Chooser looks a little different:

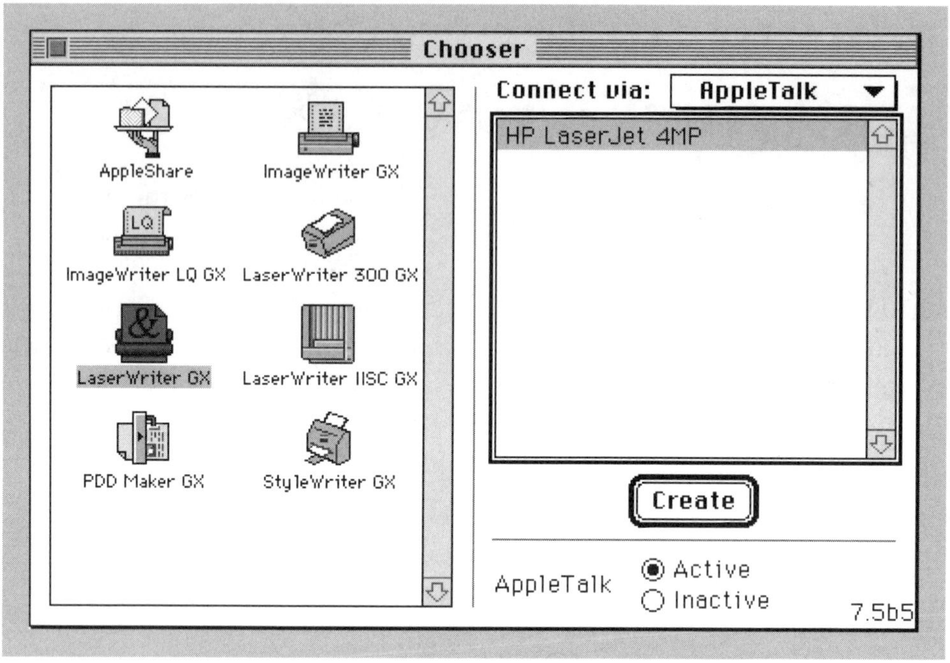

Instead of just selecting a printer driver on the left side of the window and choosing a printer in the upper right side of the window, you need to go a step further to create a desktop printer for any printer you plan to print to. To do this, click the Create button while the printer you want to use is selected. After a moment, a desktop printer icon appears on the desktop.

If you've got only one printer connected to your Macintosh, that's all you need to do. If several printers are available to your Macintosh through direction connections or a network, you can create a desktop printer for each one. When you're finished, click the Chooser's close box to dismiss it.

Using the Print Dialog Box

Choosing Print from the File menu on a Macintosh running System 7.5 displays a radically different print dialog box than the one I showed you earlier in this chapter:

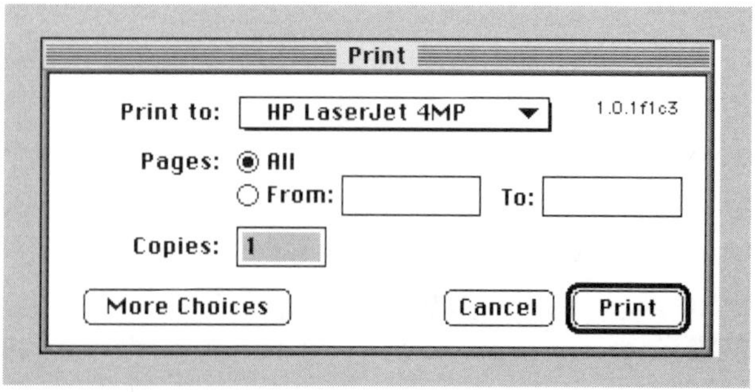

Basic Choices

The Print dialog box offers a number of basic options for printing:

- **Print To** — this pop-up menu displays the names of all the desktop printers you created. Choose the one on which you want to print the current document. The one you select remains selected each time you print a document until you change it to another.
- **Pages** — lets you tell your Macintosh whether it should print the entire document (All) or a range of pages. If you want to print less than the whole document, enter a value in the From and To edit boxes.
- **Copies** — is where you tell your Macintosh how many copies of the document it should print. Enter a value in the edit box.

More Choices

If you click the More Choices button, the Print dialog box expands so you can set additional options:

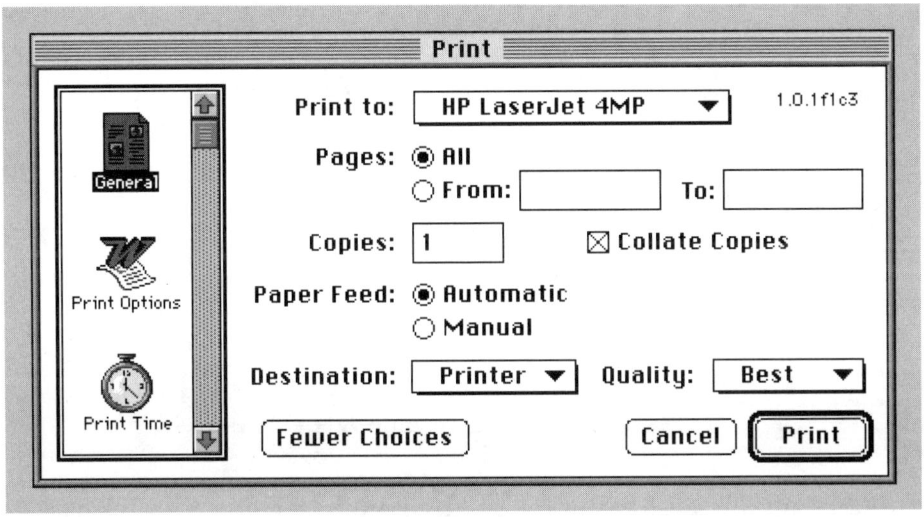

Click the icon for the type of options in the left side scrolling window. The options that appear in the main part of the window change accordingly. Here's a brief rundown of the available options.

General. The General Options include those I already covered as well as these:

- **Collate Copies** — when this check box is turned on and you are printing more than one copy of a document, the copies are collated automatically.
- **Paper Feed** — click the Automatic or Manual radio button to tell your printer how paper will be fed into it.
- **Destination** — on PostScript printers, you can print to the Printer or a PostScript file. Use this pop-up menu to choose. I discussed PostScript files earlier in this chapter.
- **Quality** — some printers offer more than one print quality. If yours does, use this pop-up menu to choose the quality for the current print job.

Print Options. When you click the Print Options icon on the left side of the window (the one that looks like a Word icon), the contents of the Print dialog box change:

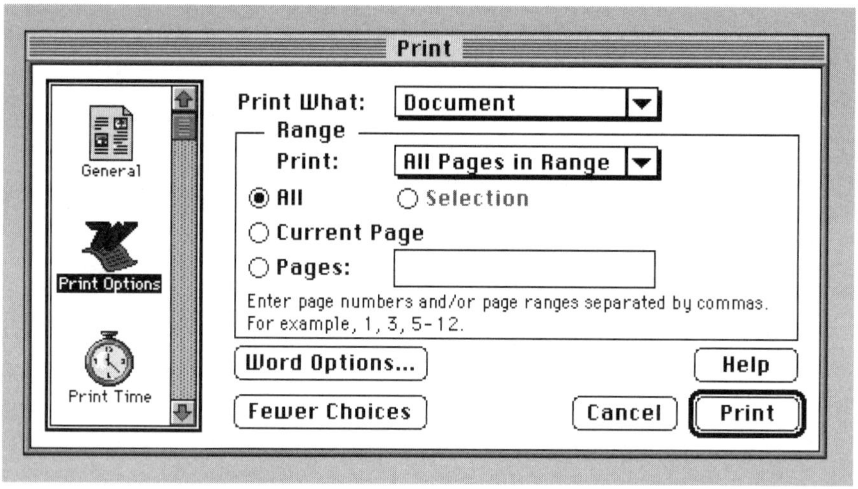

These options are the same as those I discussed in the "Telling Word What to Print" section of this chapter, so you can read up about them there. One thing that's important to remember is that any Range information you specify here will override the Pages options set under General options.

Print Time. When you click the Print Time icon, you get to tell your Macintosh when to print the document. This is a brand new feature of System 7.5 — one you'd normally have to use PrintMonitor for.

- **Priority** — four radio buttons let you determine how important it is to print the document. You can use the Print At option to set a time and date for printing.
- **Show Alert** — use two check boxes to tell your Macintosh to alert you Before Printing Starts, After Printing Finishes, or both.

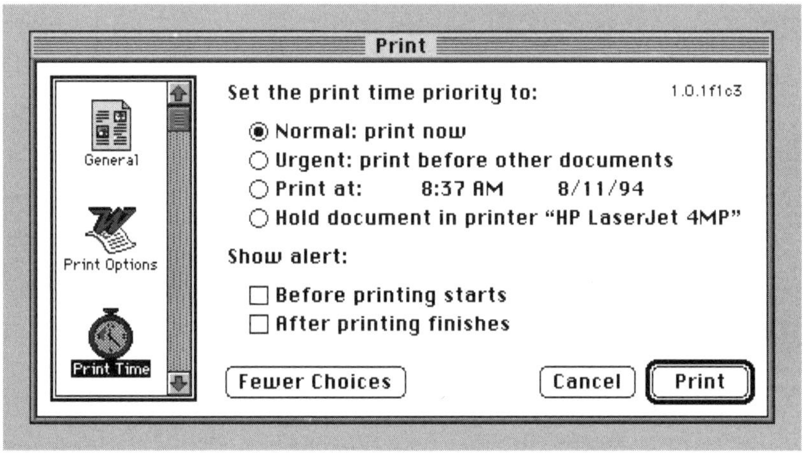

Paper Match. The last icon in the scrolling list is the Paper Match icon. Used this option if you have a fancy printer with multiple paper trays. You can tell your printer to match the paper to the tray or force it to use a specific paper tray and crop or scale the image accordingly.

Monitoring Printing Activity with Desktop Printers

On a System 7.5 Macintosh with Quick-Draw GX, there is no PrintMonitor. Instead, you can monitor printing by opening the desktop printer icon for the printer a document will be printed to. It might look something like this:

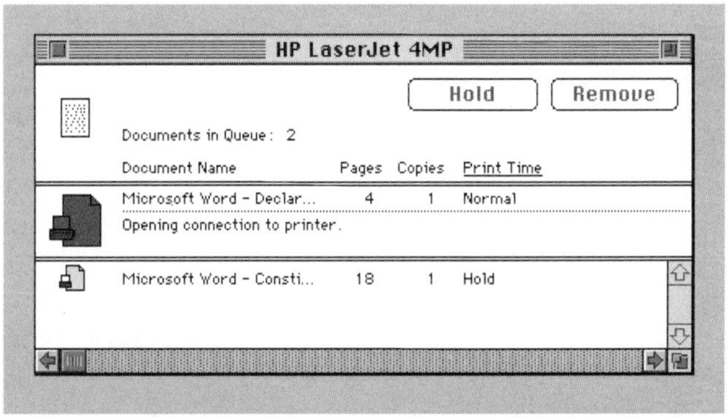

The desktop printer window displays the name, pages, copies, and print time of each document in the print queue. You can change a document's print time, remove it from the print queue, put it on hold, or even transfer it to another printer. Just click on the document to select it and use one of the commands under the Printing menu that appears whenever you select or open a desktop printer. Or drag the document's icon from one desktop printer window to another.

Chapter Summary

In this chapter, you learned how to get your Word documents on paper, how to use Apple's Chooser, and how to take advantage of Word's improved Print Preview feature to examine and make changes in your document. You also learned about the Word-specific buttons and pop-up menus in the Print dialog box. System 7.5 users also learned enough about printing with QuickDraw GX to get them started.

The next chapter starts Part 2 of this book, which covers formatting. In Chapter 5, I'll tell you all about font formatting — getting the individual characters of your document to look just the way you want.

PART

2

Using Standard Formats and Styles

THIS PART OF THE BOOK EXPLAINS FONT, PARAGRAPH, SECTION, and document formatting options. In these five chapters, readers learn how to use Word's menu commands, toolbars, rulers, and styles feature to format their documents.

Chapter 5: Font Formatting

Chapter 6: Paragraph Formatting

Chapter 7: Paragraph and Character Styles

Chapter 8: Section and Document Formatting

Chapter 9: Templates and Automatic Formatting

5

Chapter 5: Font Formatting

ONE OF THE GREAT THINGS ABOUT WORD PROCESSORS IS THAT they make it possible to spice up documents with formatting not available on typewriters. With a few mouse clicks or keystrokes, you can change the appearance of your document to add emphasis and personality.

Word lets you do all kinds of formatting, as you'll see in the next few chapters. This chapter concentrates on *font formatting* — making text characters look different. You'll learn how to use Word's Formatting Toolbar and Font dialog box to change characters. You'll also learn how to insert special characters like symbols and bullets. This is where you start having some real fun with Word.

Overview of Font Formatting

Font formatting helps make your documents better communication tools. You can draw the reader's attention to important points by making them bold, italic, or underline; make a document easier to read by formatting section headings with larger or different typestyles, and use special characters like bullets and check marks to set off items in lists. The combinations and possibilities are endless.

FYI: Don't Get Carried Away!

It's important not to get carried away with character formatting. I remember the first time I wrote a letter on my Macintosh after years of working on an Apple //c and an IBM-compatible PC. Suddenly, I had easy access to different fonts, sizes, and styles. I wrote a letter to a friend that must have used ten different fonts, a dozen different sizes, and each of the different styles. When I printed it, I thought it looked really cool. (Remember what computers I'd been using up until then!) But was it an effective communication tool? No! It was a jumbled, confused mess.

Although font formatting can help communication, there's a limit to how much you can do before it becomes distracting. When every third word is bold, italic, underlined, or (heaven forbid) shadowed, the reader can't tell what's really important. A two-page document written with ten different fonts would probably tire out the reader before it got its message across. And a serious business letter written in a funky display font probably won't get you too much business.

How much is enough? How much is too much? It depends on the document, its purpose, and its reader. If you've got a good eye for design, you'll know what's right. If you're like me and don't have a good eye for design, stay on the safe side and try to keep your documents simple.

There's an important distinction that needs to be made here. Font formatting can be applied either *directly* or through the use of a *character style*. This chapter will discuss methods for directly applying font formatting — making changes to the default font. In Chapter 7, I'll discuss character styles, which work a bit differently.

IMPORTANT NOTE

Changing Font Formatting

When you begin a new document, the appearance of the characters you type depends on the default font settings stored as part of the Normal style in the template the document is based on. The Normal style defines the characteristics of plain text, including its font, size, style, character and line spacing, and a variety of other options. I'll discuss styles in Chapter 7.

There are two main ways to change font formatting. Let's take a look at each one.

Type First, Then Format

The first method — the one I like to use — is to select the text you want to change, and then use the appropriate toolbar button, menu command, or shortcut key to change it. This requires that you type the text first, then go back and change it. I prefer this method for two reasons: First, I'm a reasonably fast typist and don't like to stop to make formatting changes. Second, I like to do all my formatting at once, usually right before I preview and print my documents.

Here's an example. Say you want to type the text "I love Microsoft Word" with the word "love" in italics for emphasis. First, type the entire phrase in plain text. Then use your mouse to select the word "love." Finally, use the appropriate toolbar button, menu command, or shortcut key to italicize the selected word. (If you're not sure what to use right now, just click the Italics button on the Formatting toolbar. It's illustrated in the margin. I'll tell you more about the available formatting buttons and commands in a moment.)

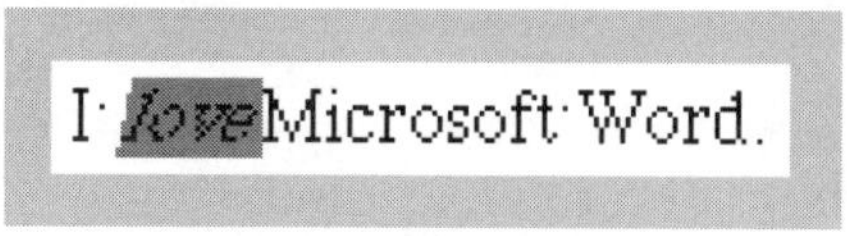

Format as You Type

The other method is to change font formatting as you type. To do this, you must choose the toolbar button, menu command, or shortcut key for the formatting you want *before* you type the text. This, in effect, turns the formatting on or off. Then, when you type, the text appears in the formatting you chose.

Let's reexamine our previous example using this method. First type the word "I" followed by a space in plain text. Then use the toolbar button, menu command, or shortcut key to turn italics on. Next, type the word "love" — it appears in italics. Then use the toolbar button, menu command, or shortcut key to turn italics off. Finally, finish typing the phrase — it appears in plain text.

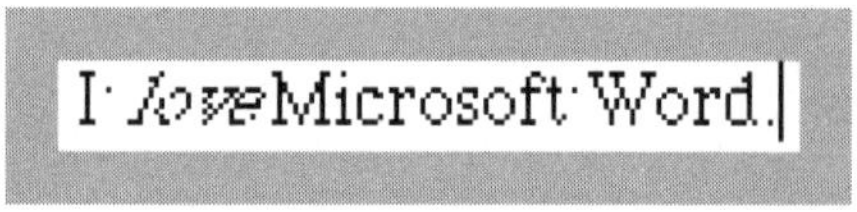

How Font Formatting Works

As the examples in the previous section show, font formatting is applied to characters. It's like wearing makeup to change their appearance. Even nonprinting characters like spaces have formatting.

Now here's where it gets a little tricky. If you position the insertion point in a block of text and then start typing, the text you type will have the same formatting as the text at the insertion point. So, in the above examples, if I put the insertion point right after the word "love" and typed the words " to use " those words would appear in italics because they carry forward the formatting of the word at the insertion point, which is italic.

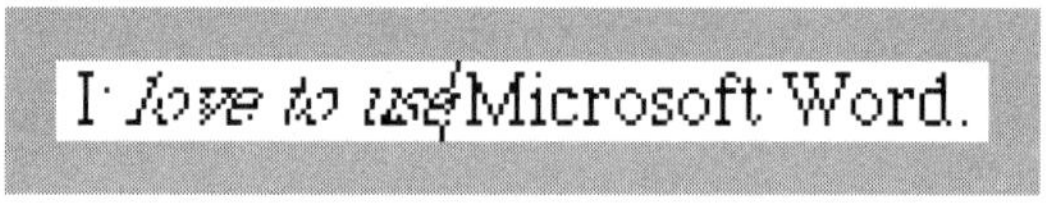

Sometimes you might want the font formatting to be carried forward. In that case, great! But sometimes you'll want the formatting to be different. If that's the case, there's no problem. Just select the text you typed and change it. Simple as that.

Seeing Font Formatting

Word displays characters on screen the way they appear when printed. This is WYSIWYG (What You See Is What You Get). Sometimes, however, it isn't clear what formatting is applied to text. Word offers two ways for you to find out.

Revealing Formats

NEW IN WORD 6

Microsoft added a new feature to Word version 6 that makes it easy to find out exactly what formatting is applied to text. It's called Reveal Formats and it does just that.

Click the Help button on the Standard Toolbar or press Shift Help or ⌘ Shift /. The mouse pointer turns into a pointer with a question mark. Now click the text you want to see the formatting of. A Reveal Formats window appears, like the one in the following illustration. It provides information about the paragraph and font formatting, including styles and directly applied format changes. A box surrounds the character you're checking.

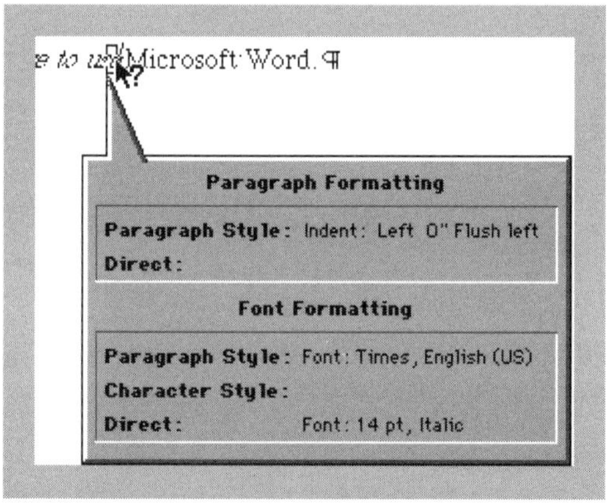

Each time you click on text, a new Reveal Formats window appears. When you're finished checking text, press Esc or ⌘ . to turn off the Reveal Formats feature.

Looking at Buttons, Boxes, and Other Settings

Toolbar buttons and boxes, as well as the settings inside dialog boxes, can also tell you what formatting is applied to text. For example, the Font box on the Formatting toolbar displays the name of the font for the selected text or text at the insertion point. The Bold button, also on the Formatting toolbar, looks dark and kind of "pushed in" when selected text or text at the insertion point is bold. In the following illustration, I can tell that the selected text is New York, 10 points, and italic. The Font dialog box similarly displays current settings with its boxes, menus, check boxes, and radio buttons.

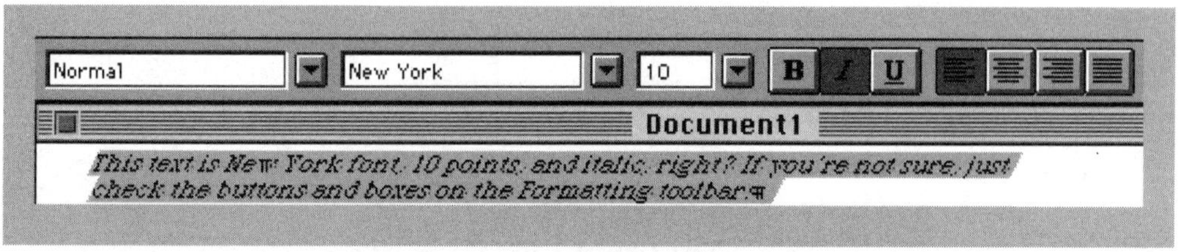

When a toolbar or dialog box setting appears blank, gray, or unselected, your selection may contain more than one setting. Word can only display one setting at a time. When it needs to display more than one, it simply doesn't display anything. That doesn't mean you can't change a selection. Buttons, boxes, and other settings work the same way, no matter what they indicate. In the following illustration, the selected text is New York font, with multiple sizes. Some text is italic and some isn't, but none is bold or underlined. Note how the Formatting toolbar displays this.

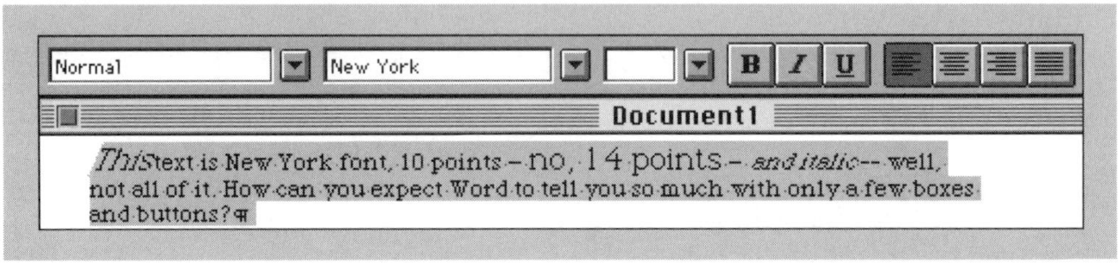

I'll discuss the Formatting toolbar and Font dialog box in detail later in this chapter.

FYI: About Fonts

NEW IN WORD 6

One of the changes you can make to text is to change its font. A *font* is a character set or typeface. Some common examples in the Macintosh world include Times, Helvetica, Courier, New York, Monaco, Geneva, and Chicago. There are thousands of fonts available to Macintosh users. Some, like the ones listed above, come as part of the Macintosh operating system and are installed when the System files are installed. Others are sold by font vendors like Adobe Systems, Letraset, and Image Club Graphics. Word version 6 comes with a number of fonts, including several that help keep your Word for Macintosh documents compatible with Word for Windows. (Appendix B provides more information about cross-platform considerations.) To use any font, you must first install it in your System file (System 7.0.x) or the Fonts folder inside your System Folder (System 7.1.x and 7.5).

IMPORTANT NOTE

It's important to remember that because fonts are installed in your System, the fonts available in Microsoft Word are the same ones available in all other programs you use on your Macintosh. This includes any fonts

Continued

that come with Word that you install in your System. The fonts are *not* part of Microsoft Word.

Macintosh computers use three main kinds of fonts: TrueType, PostScript, and bitmapped fonts.

- **TrueType:** These fonts are scalable outline fonts — that means they can be viewed and printed at virtually any size. TrueType versions of the fonts I mentioned above come with System 7. They work both on-screen and in printers to provide correctly sized, clear characters.
- **PostScript:** These fonts work with PostScript printers. That's why they're sometimes called *printer fonts.* They're either installed in the printer or are automatically downloaded from your Macintosh to the printer when needed. To display a PostScript font on a Macintosh screen, you need the bitmapped version of the same font. A program called Adobe Type Manager by Adobe Systems Incorporated can also scale PostScript fonts for on-screen display.
- **Bitmapped:** These fonts, which are sometimes called *screen fonts* are used primarily to display fonts on screen. Each PostScript font comes with a bitmapped version of the same font. Many TrueType fonts also come with bitmapped versions of the same font for on screen display. Since bitmapped fonts are not scalable, more than one size is normally provided. Your Macintosh can scale bitmapped fonts, but the results are usually less than perfect. If a font appears jagged on the screen, you're looking at a bitmapped font that your Macintosh has scaled to the desired size. If you've got a PostScript version of the same font and you're printing on a PostScript compatible printer, the printed output should be fine.

One more thing: font size. Fonts size is expressed in terms of points. A *point* is a typographical measurement approximately equal to $^1/_{72}$ of an inch. The larger the size number, the larger the character appears.

Using the Formatting Toolbar

NEW IN WORD 6

The Formatting toolbar is a new addition to Word in version 6. The tools it includes to format text, however, have been available since Word version 5, on the Word Ribbon. The ribbon is gone now, but the tools remain. Let's take a look at them.

IMPORTANT NOTE

Remember, the changes you make with the Formatting toolbar will only affect text that is selected or text that is typed at the insertion point. If you want to try any of these toolbar buttons, be sure to select text in your document first.

Font Box

The Font box lets you choose a font. You can use it one of two ways:

- Click the arrow to the right of the Font box. A pop-up menu of available fonts appears. The one with the check mark is the current font. (Remember, if none of the fonts in the menu have a check mark, that means your selection contains multiple fonts.) The fonts listed above the double line are those most recently selected. This makes it quicker to access the fonts you use most often. All fonts available are listed below the double line, in alphabetical order by name. Choose the font you want from the menu to apply it to selected text or begin using it at the insertion point.

- Click in the Font box to select it. Then type in all or part of the font name. Press [Enter], [Return], or [Tab], or click in the document window to complete the choice.

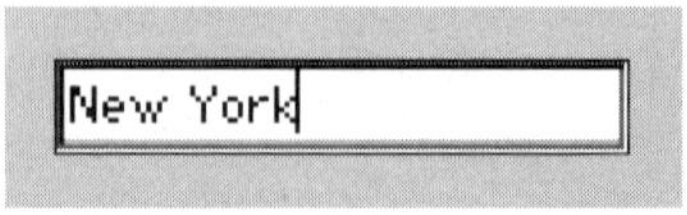

Font Size Box

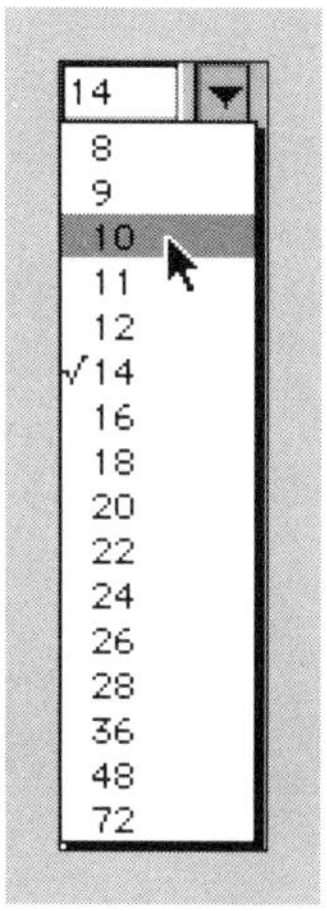

The font size box lets you choose a font size. You can use it one of two ways:

- Click the arrow to the right of the Font Size box. A pop-up menu of sizes appears. Not every possible size is displayed — the menu would get too long — but all standard sizes should be available. Again, the one with the check mark (if there is a check mark) is the current size. Choose the size you want to apply.
- Click in the Font Size box to select it. Then type in the size you want. You can enter just about any number as a size. Press Return, Enter, or Tab or click in the document window to complete the choice.

In Word version 6, you can enter numbers in increments of .5 — so 15.5 would be a valid measurement.

NEW IN WORD 6

Bold Button

The Bold button makes text bold. Click it to turn bold formatting on or off.

Italic Button

The Italic button makes text italic. Click it to turn italics on or off.

Underline Button

The Underline button puts a single, continuous underline under text. Click it to turn single underline formatting on or off.

Try This! Font Formatting with Toolbar Buttons

If you haven't given any of these buttons a try, what are you waiting for? Here's a quick exercise that gives the font formatting buttons on the Formatting Toolbar a 30-second workout.

Continued

1. In a Word document, type the following text: **I'm reading a great book about Microsoft Word version 6.**
2. Select all the text. (If you're not sure how to select text, go back to Chapter 2 where I discussed it in detail.)
3. Choose Courier from the Font box menu on the Formatting Toolbar. The text changes to Courier font. (It should look like it came out of a typewriter!)
4. Click in the Font box on the word Courier. Type **Helvetica** and press [Enter]. The text changes to Helvetica.
5. Choose 18 points from the Size box. The text gets larger.
6. Click in the Size box on number 18. Type **14.5** and press [Enter]. The text gets smaller.
7. Select the word "great" in the sentence.
8. Click the Bold button on the Formatting Toolbar. The word becomes bold. Notice how the Bold button gets dark.
9. Click the Bold button on the Formatting Toolbar again. The word returns to plain text.
10. Click the Bold button on the Formatting Toolbar yet again. The word becomes bold again. Now click on the Underline button on the Formatting Toolbar. The word is now bold and underlined.
11. Select the words "Microsoft Word" in the sentence.
12. Click the Italic button. The words become italic.

Don't be afraid to experiment with these buttons. They will not delete text. And if you ever make a formatting change you really don't like, you can always undo it. I discussed the Undo command in Chapter 2.

Using the Font Dialog Box

NEW IN WORD 6

The Formatting Toolbar may put often-used font formatting options in a convenient place, but it doesn't give you access to all the options Word offers. There are far more. You can find them in the Font dialog box, which replaces the old Character Format dialog box found in previous versions of Word. Not only does this dialog box offer more formatting options, but it lets you apply several changes at once — and view a sample of changed text before accepting it.

To open the Font dialog box, do one of the following:

- Choose Font from the Format menu *or*
- Press [⌘] [D]

The Font dialog box is shown in the following illustration. As you can see, it has two tabs: Font and Character Spacing. We'll take a good look at the options under each.

Under the Font Tab

The Font tab offers a wide variety of font formatting options. Use scrolling lists, pop-up menus, edit boxes, and check boxes to make selections. A new preview area shows you a sample of what the formatted characters will look like when you accept your changes by clicking OK or pressing [Return] or [Enter].

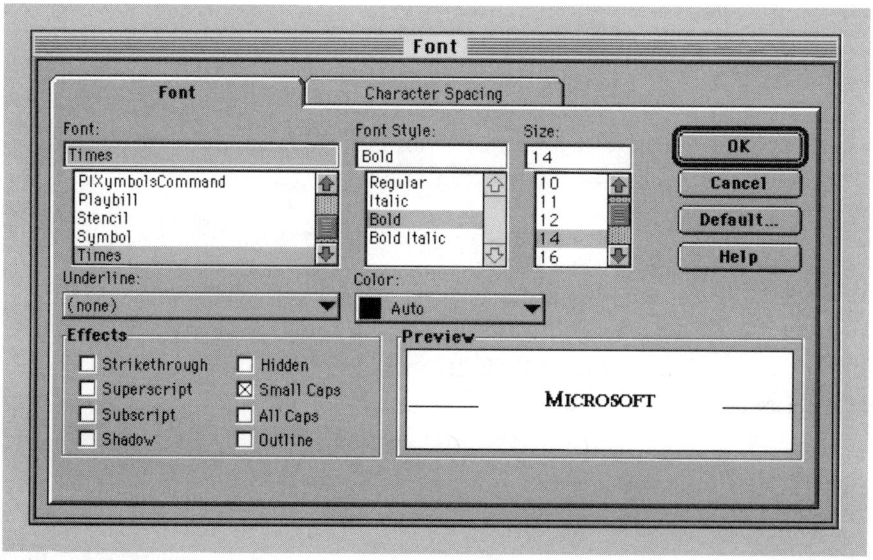

Font

The Font box lets you change the font. Click on the name of a font in the scrolling list. If you prefer, you can click in the edit box at the top of the scrolling list and type in a font name.

Font Style

NEW IN WORD 6

The Font Style box lets you apply italic and bold formatting to characters. Click on the name of a font style in the scrolling list to choose it. You can normally choose from among four options, although other options may be available depending on the font.

Regular does not apply bold or italic formatting

This is an example.

Italic applies italic formatting

This is an example.

Bold applies bold formatting

This is an example.

Bold Italic applies both bold and italic formatting

This is an example.

This scrolling list replaces the Bold and Italic check boxes in the Character dialog box of previous versions of Word.

Size

The Size box lets you change the size of characters. There are two ways to use it:

- Click on the number for a size in the Size scrolling list to choose it. Not all possible sizes are shown, but most standard sizes are.
- Click in the Size edit box and type in a size. This method makes it possible to use any number. As I mentioned earlier, font sizes must be in increments of .5.

Underline

The Underline pop-up menu lets you underline characters. Word offers five underline options:

None does not underline text at all

This is an example.

Single puts a single line under text, including any spaces and punctuation between words. It's the same as using the Underline button on the Formatting toolbar.

This is an example.

Words Only puts a single line under the text of words but not spaces or punctuation

This is an example

Double puts a double line under text, including any spaces

This is an example

Dotted puts a dotted line under text, including any spaces and punctuation between words

This is an example

Color

The Color pop up menu lets you apply color to text. There are 16 choices, including Auto, which normally displays text as black. The text appears in the color you choose on a color monitor. If you have a color printer, you can print in color as well. Otherwise, you'll print in black and white or shades of gray, whichever your printer supports.

Effects

The Effects area of the dialog box offers a number of additional formatting effects. Click on a check box to turn the effect on or off. There are eight options:

Strikethrough puts a line through text. This is useful for indicating changes in a document. As you'll see in Chapter 18, however, Word's new Revision feature offers a better way to manage changing documents.

~~This is an example.~~

Superscript raises characters 3 points above the invisible baseline. You can set a custom measurement under the Character Spacing tab of the Font dialog box.

This is an example.

Subscript lowers characters 3 below the invisible baseline. You can set a custom measurement under the Character Spacing tab of the Font dialog box.

This is an example.

Shadow adds a shadow effect beneath characters

This is an example.

Hidden formats characters so they do not display or print unless you indicate that they should. To display hidden characters, use the Show/Hide ¶ button on the Standard Toolbar. When displayed, hidden text has a dotted underline under it. To print hidden characters, use the Options command under the Tools menu or the Options button in the Print dialog box. I'll discuss Options in Chapter 23. Hidden text is useful for entering information you want to include in your document but you don't always want to display or print.

Small Caps converts all lowercase characters to uppercase characters in a smaller font size. I like this format for document headings.

THIS IS AN EXAMPLE.

All Caps converts all lowercase characters to uppercase characters

THIS IS AN EXAMPLE.

Outline puts an outline around characters

This is an example.

You can turn these check boxes on or off in any combination with the following two exceptions:

- Text cannot be superscript and subscript at the same time
- Text cannot be small caps and all caps at the same time

TIP/TRICK

If you're interested in using superscripts and subscripts to create mathematical formulas, you might be better off taking advantage of Word's Equation Editor. I'll tell you about that in Chapter 12.

Under the Character Spacing Tab

The Character Spacing tab offers additional formatting options for character spacing. Use the pop-up menus, edit boxes, and check box to make changes. Again, the preview area shows the affects of your changes as you make them.

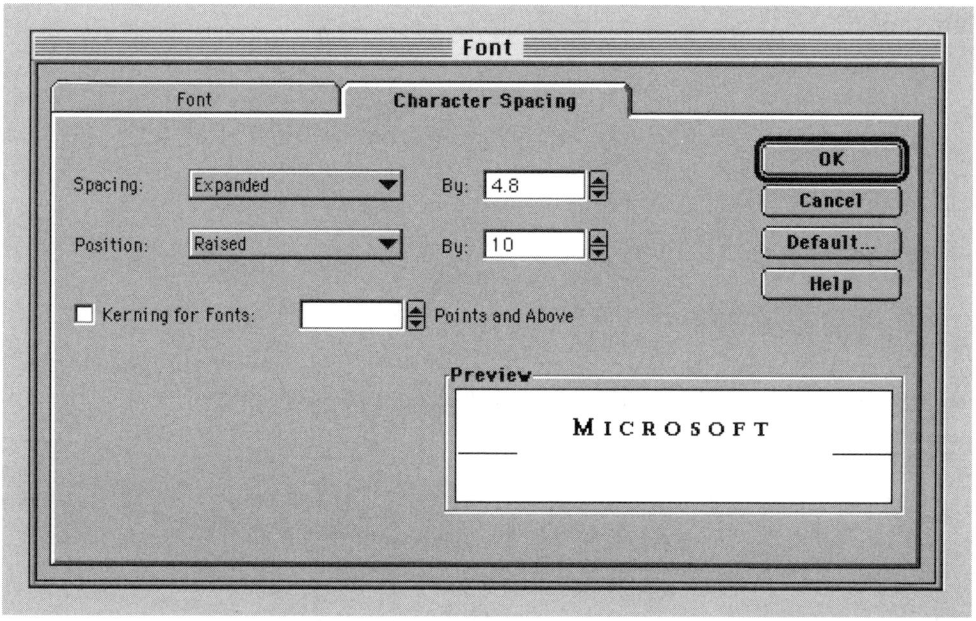

Spacing

The Spacing pop-up menu and edit box let you set the spacing between characters. Your options are:

Normal uses regular spacing between characters

This is an example.

Expanded adds 1 point of space between characters

This is an example.

Condensed removes 1 point of space between characters

This is an example.

If you choose either expanded or condensed, you can enter a value in the By edit box to specify the exact spacing. If you prefer, use the tiny up and down arrows beside the edit box to have Word enter values for you.

Position

The Position pop-up menu and edit box let you enter exact measurements for superscripts and subscripts — characters raised or lowered on the baseline.

Normal places text right on the baseline

This is an example

Superscript raises characters 3 points above the invisible baseline

This is an example.

Subscript lowers characters 3 below the invisible baseline

This is an example.

If you choose either Raised or Lowered, you can enter an exact measurement in the By edit box. Or use the tiny up and down arrows beside the edit box to have Word enter values for you.

Kerning

NEW IN WORD 6

Automatic Kerning is a new feature of Word version 6. Kerning refers to the spacing between certain pairs of characters, like the combination "To". When kerned, the lowercase letter o should move in under the horizontal stroke of the uppercase letter T. This is more visually pleasing since it removes large gaps between certain pairs of characters. Most of the professionally prepared documents you read these days have kerned pairs.

The Kerning check box lets you turn kerning on or off so you can give your documents a more polished, "typeset" look. Once turned on, specify the minimum font size to kern by entering a value in the Points and Above edit box. Again, Word offers tiny arrows you can click to have Word enter a value for you. The minimum value is 8 points.

Accepting Your Changes

None of the changes you make in the Font dialog box are applied to selected text in your document until you click OK or press Return or Enter. This applies the changes and dismisses the dialog box. If you decide you don't want to make the changes after all, click Cancel or press Esc. If you've already accepted the changes and want to reverse them, use the Undo command, which I discussed in Chapter 2.

TIP/TRICK

If you want to apply the same changes to text here and there throughout your document, you can use the Repeat command, which I also discussed in Chapter 2. Immediately after accepting changes in the Font dialog box, select other text to apply the same changes to and choose Repeat from the Edit menu or press ⌘Y. I'll tell you another way to apply the same font formats a little later in this chapter.

Try This! Font Formatting with the Font Dialog Box

It's your turn to give it a try.

1. In a Word document, type the following text: **The Font dialog box offers so many more font formatting options!**
2. Select all the text. (If you're not sure how to select text, check Chapter 2.)
3. Open the Font dialog box by choosing Font from the Format menu or pressing ⌘D.
4. Now have some fun with Font formatting. Choose different fonts, sizes, and styles from the Font, Font Size, and Font Style scrolling lists. Use the Underline and Color pop-up menus to change underlining and text color. Turn the different Effects check boxes on and off. Every change you make in this dialog box is reflected in the sample text within the dialog box.

Continued

5. Click the Character Spacing tab to view and change Character spacing options. Use the Spacing and Position pop-up menus and edit boxes to change spacing between characters and vertical position. Try turning on the Kerning check box. All changes, with the possible exception of kerning changes, are reflected in the sample text.

6. If desired, click the Font tab to go back to Font formatting options. You can switch from tab to tab at any time.

7. To accept your changes, click OK or press Return or Enter. The text selected in your document changes.

Changing the Default Font

NEW IN WORD 6

The default font for a document is based on the font settings for the Normal style in the template the document is based on. You can use the Font dialog box to change the default font for the Normal style. This will automatically change all Normal style text in the current document and any new documents based on the current template.

To change the default font, choose the settings you want in the Font dialog box and click the Default button. A dialog box like the one shown here appears, asking if you want to change the default font for the current template. Click Yes. Word immediately changes any text based on the Normal style. In addition, since it also changed the default font for the current template, any new document you create with that template will use the default style you specified.

I'll talk about styles in Chapter 7. I discussed templates briefly in Chapter 2 and will discuss them in more detail in Chapter 9.

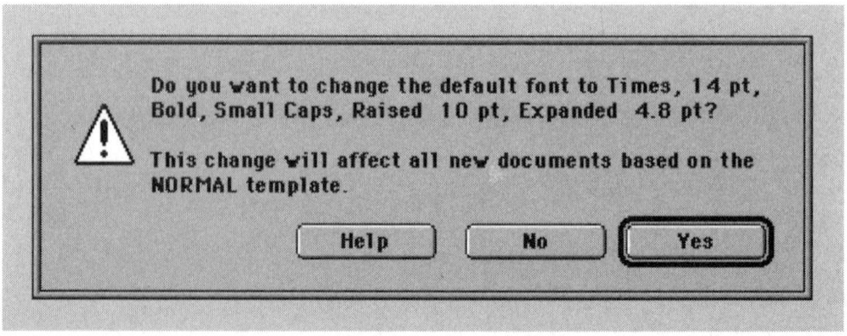

If you need to change the formatting of certain text throughout your document — for example, change all underlined text to italicized text — you can use the Replace command. I'll tell you about that in Chapter 16.

TIP/TRICK

Using Shortcut Keys

You can make many font formatting changes with shortcut keys. To format text that has already been typed, select the text first, then use one of these key combinations to change it. To begin different font formatting at the insertion point, use one of these key combinations to change the formatting, then type.

Formatting	Shortcut Key
Font	[⌘][Shift][F], then type in all or part of the font name and press [Return] or [Enter]
Symbol Font	[⌘][Shift][Q]
Next Larger Font Size	[⌘][Shift][.]
Next Smaller Font Size	[⌘][Shift][,]
One Point Size Larger	[⌘][]]
One Point Size Smaller	[⌘][[]
Bold	[⌘][B]
Italic	[⌘][I]
Single Underline	[⌘][U]
Word Underline	[⌘][Shift][W]
Double Underline	[⌘][Shift][D]
Hidden	[⌘][Shift][H]
Small Caps	[⌘][Shift][K]
All Caps	[⌘][Shift][A]
Change Case (cycles through Upper, Lower, and Title Case)	[Shift][F3] or [⌘][Option][C]
Superscript	[⌘][=]
Subscript	[⌘][Shift][=]

Try This! Font Formatting with Shortcut Keys

Your turn. Let's type and format some text without touching the mouse even once!

1. Press [⌘N] to create a brand new Word document based on the Normal template. Don't type anything in it yet.
2. Press [⌘Shift F] to activate the Font box in the Formatting toolbar. Type **Helvetica** and press [Enter]. This sets the text at the insertion point to Helvetica font.
3. Press [⌘Shift .] two times. This increases the font size at the insertion point twice. You should see the Font Size box on the Formatting Toolbar change accordingly.
4. Type **Who says I.** The text appears in Helvetica font in the size specified in the Font Size box on the Formatting Toolbar.
5. Press [⌘I]. This turns on italics at the insertion point.
6. Press [⌘B]. This turns on bold formatting at the insertion point.
7. Type **can't.** The new word is bold and italic.
8. Press [⌘I]. This turns off italics at the insertion point.
9. Press [⌘B]. This turns off bold formatting at the insertion point.
10. Type **type and format text.** The new words are in the same format as the first few words.
11. Press [⌘Shift D]. This turns on double underlining at the insertion point.
12. Type **without.** The new word is double underlined.
13. Press [⌘Shift D]. This turns off double underlining at the insertion point.
14. Type **using my mouse?**

Of course, you can also use these shortcut keys with text that has already been typed. Just make sure you select the text to be formatted before you use the shortcut key.

Changing Case

Have you ever typed a whole sentence or paragraph before you noticed that the Caps Lock key was down and all characters had been typed in uppercase? I have. In the old days, when Word 4 was the current version, you'd have to type the whole darn thing over. In version 5, Microsoft added the Change Case command, which makes changing the capitalization of characters fast and easy. Word 6 also offers this great feature.

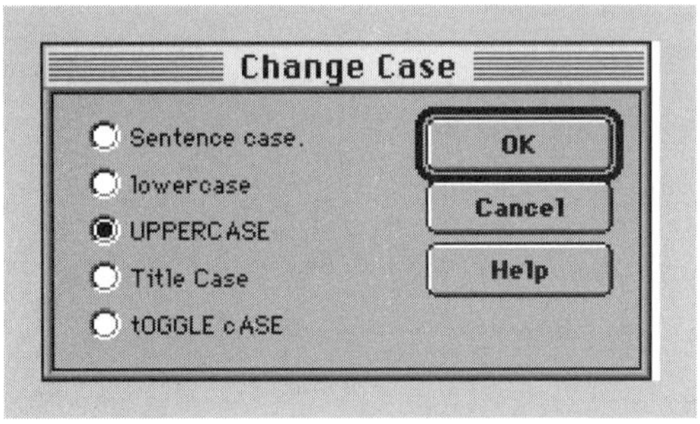

To change the capitalization of selected text, choose Change Case from the Format menu. The Change Case dialog box, which offers five options, appears:

Sentence Case makes the first character of each sentence an uppercase character

This is an example.

Lowercase makes all characters lowercase characters

this is an example.

Uppercase makes all characters uppercase characters

THIS IS AN EXAMPLE.

Title Case makes the first character of each word an uppercase character

This Is An Example.

Toggle Case turns uppercase characters into lowercase characters and turns lowercase characters into uppercase characters

tHIS IS AN EXAMPLE.

IMPORTANT NOTE

The Change Case command does not apply character formatting like the Small Caps and All Caps formats I mentioned earlier. Change case actually changes the *characters*. Small Caps and All Caps just change the *appearance* of lowercase characters. As far as Word is concerned, the characters it changes are still lowercase characters, no matter how they look on screen or paper.

FYI: A Theory about the Caps Lock Key

I've been teaching Word for about four years now and must have worked with close to a thousand students. One thing I noticed is that some students insist on typing in class with the Caps Lock key down. Everything they type comes out in uppercase characters and looks pretty bad. But since I teach them how to use Word and not how to type, I let them do as they like with the Caps Lock key.

I've got a theory about these people, though. I think they have a subconscious fear of the Shift key. By keeping Caps Lock down, they don't have to worry about using the Shift key at the beginning of sentences and proper names. It takes a big load off their minds.

Funny thing is, every single student I've seen with the Caps Lock key affliction has been male. It must be genetic and carried on the Y chromosome.

Copying Font Formats

In many instances, you'll apply formatting to a block of characters and then want to apply the same formatting to other characters in your document. Word offers you the ability to copy and paste font formatting. You can do this two different ways.

Using the Format Painter Button & Pointer

NEW IN WORD 6

The Format Painter button is a new tool on Word's Standard Toolbar. To copy font formats with the Format Painter button, select some text with the formatting you want to copy. Click on the Format Painter button. The mouse pointer changes to the Format Painter pointer, which looks like an I-beam pointer that has a plus (+) sign on its left side. Use this pointer to select the text you want to format. When you release the mouse button, the text you selected changes and the mouse pointer returns to normal.

To copy one format to multiple places, double-click the Format Painter button after selecting text with the formats you want to copy. The mouse pointer changes to the Format Painter pointer and stays that way. You can make multiple selections to change formats throughout your document. When you're finished, press Escape to return the mouse pointer to normal.

TIP/TRICK

Using Shortcut Keys

Previous versions of Word offered shortcut keys to copy and paste formatting, but these have changed in Word 6. Copying formats is now easier to do.

NEW IN WORD 6

To copy formats with shortcut keys, select some text with the formatting you want to copy and press ⌘ Shift C. To paste the font formatting, select the text you want to format and press ⌘ Shift V. To paste formatting in multiple places, just select the text to format and press ⌘ Shift V again. You can paste the selected format until something new is copied to the Clipboard.

These Shortcut Keys should be easy to remember because they're so similar to the ones for Copying and Pasting text, ⌘ C and ⌘ V. I discussed the Copy and Paste commands in Chapter 3.

Removing Font Formats

You can remove any directly applied font formatting quickly and easily with a shortcut key. Simply select the characters you want to remove formatting from and press ⌘ Shift Z. This removes all character formatting you applied with the Formatting toolbar, Font dialog box, or shortcut keys. It does not remove character formats that are part of a character style. I'll discuss character styles in Chapter 7.

Inserting Bullets and Other Special Symbols

If you think the characters you see on your keyboard are the only ones you can include in a document, you're missing out on the dozens of symbols and other special characters Macintosh computers put at your fingertips. While available characters vary slightly from one font to another, symbols like bullets (•), copyright (©), trademark (™), registered trademark (®), and cents (¢) are available in just about any font. Also available are the accents (´), umlauts (¨), and tildes (~) widely used in foreign languages. You can put them in your documents by either typing them in with the keyboard or using Word's Symbol command. Word's Symbol command also offers easy access to special characters in the Symbol font that comes with your Macintosh.

In this section, I'll show you a few ways you can get special characters into your Word documents.

Using the Symbol Command

NEW IN WORD 6

Word's Symbol command first appeared in version 5. For version 6, Microsoft made some functional improvements to the Symbol dialog box.

To use the Symbols command to insert symbols or special characters into your document, begin by positioning the insertion point where you want the character to go. Then choose Symbol from the Insert menu. The Symbol dialog box appears.

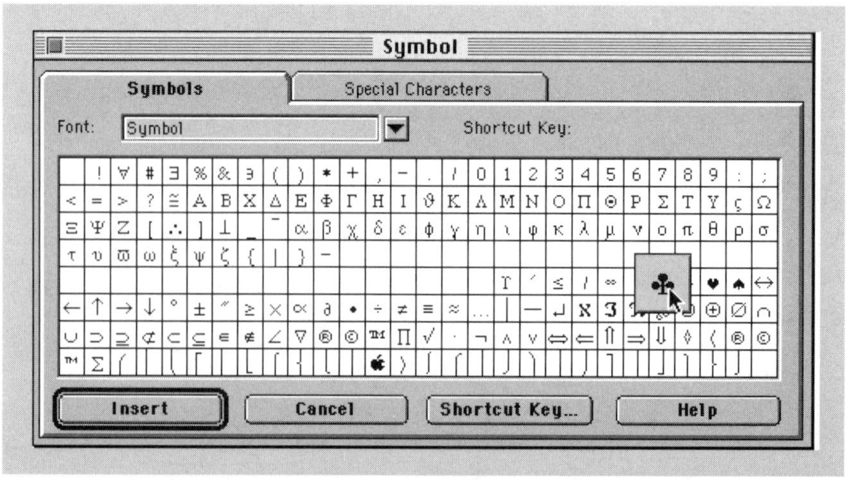

Choose the tab for either Symbols or Special Characters. The Symbols tab shows all the characters available in the Symbols font. These are mostly letters in the Greek alphabet and special symbols commonly used in science and mathematics. You can change the Symbol font to another font by pulling down the Font menu within the dialog box.

To see an enlarged view of a character, click it. Any shortcut keys for a character are indicated to the right of the font pop-up menu. You can use the Shortcut Key button to specify a new shortcut key for the selected character. I'll tell you how to do that in Chapter 24.

The Special Characters tab, which is illustrated here, shows special characters available in the current font, along with the name of the character and its shortcut key.

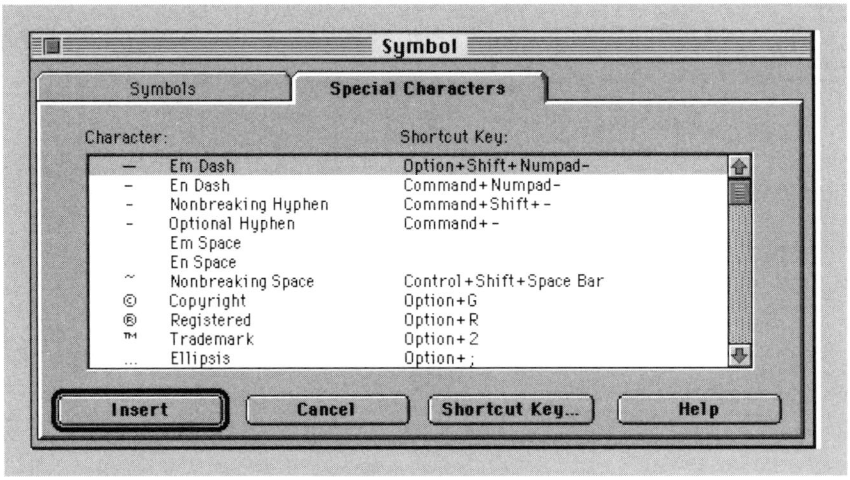

To insert a character into your document, click a character on either tab to select it and then click the Insert button. The dialog box remains open until you click its close box or the Cancel button or press Esc. This way, you can insert multiple characters if you need to.

IMPORTANT NOTE

When you use the Symbols command to insert symbols and special characters, those characters are *protected*. This prevents characters from changing if you change a character's font. To change a protected character, you have to delete it first and then replace it, either with the Symbol command or by typing it in manually.

Typing Special Characters

You can type special characters directly from the keyboard if you prefer. This is often a little quicker than using the Symbol command. The trick is knowing what to type in. Here's a table of some of the more popular special characters, along with their keystrokes. As you can see, the Option key is used to type all special characters.

Character Name	Example	Keystroke
Bullet	•	Option 8
Copyright	©	Option G
Trademark	™	Option 2
Registered Trademark	®	Option R
Cents	¢	Option 4
Pound (British currency)	£	Option 3
Paragraph	¶	Option 7
Check	√	Option V
Not Equal	≠	Option =
Plus or Minus	±	Shift Option 8
Apple		Shift Option K
Upside Down Question Mark	¿	Shift Option ?
Delta	Δ	Option J
Omega	Ω	Option Z
Sigma	Σ	Option W
Beta	ß	Option S

Don't feel that you have to memorize all these. They're just examples. There are many more. Remember the ones you use. If you forget them, you can always use Word's Symbol command to insert them into Word documents.

FYI: Key Caps

Key Caps is a desk accessory that comes with your Macintosh. It is installed with the System software. You can use it to display the characters in a font.

To open Key Caps, choose Key Caps from the Apple menu. The Key Caps window, which is shown here, appears. Use the Key Caps menu on the menu bar to choose a font. The tops of the keys in the Key Caps window change to look like that font. To see uppercase characters, hold down [Shift]. To see special characters, hold down [Option] or [Shift] and [Option] together.

The position of special characters on the Key Caps keyboard indicates that position on your keyboard. For example, if you display Helvetica font in Key Caps and hold down [Option] as shown above, you'll see that there's a check mark where the letter V should be. This means that holding down [Option] and pressing [V] gives you a check mark in Helvetica font.

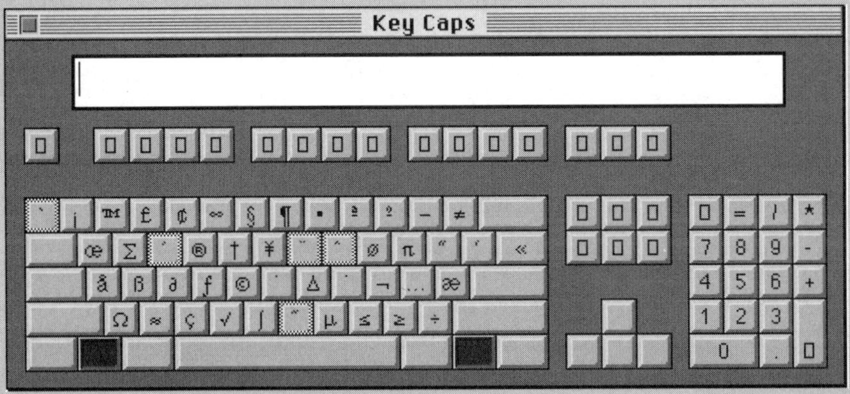

FYI: Smart Quotes

Smart quotes are special typesetter's quotation marks and apostrophes that curve in toward what they enclose. They improve the overall appearance of your documents without calling attention to themselves. For example, which looks better to you?

This has “smart quotes.”

This doesn't have "smart quotes."

Word's new AutoCorrect feature, which I'll tell you about in Chapter 16, can automatically insert smart quotes as you type (and previous Word versions could do it with the Smart Quotes command). Smart quotes are also among the special characters offered in most fonts. In fact, you can type them in manually if you like. Their keystrokes are as follows:

Character	**Keystroke**
‘	Option]
’	Shift Option]
“	Option [
”	Shift Option [

Using the Bullet Button

Bullets are a great way to set off items in a list. You've already seen two ways to insert bullets into your documents: with Word's Symbol command or by typing Option 8. But Word offers another way: the Bullet button.

The Bullet button on the Formatting toolbar inserts bullets and tab characters before each new line in a list. To use it, type a list and select it. Then click the Bullet button. Word changes the paragraph style of the text, and inserts a bullet, followed immediately by a tab character, at the beginning of each line. The result is a bulleted list with hanging indents, as shown in the following figure.

I'll discuss paragraph formatting in more detail in Chapter 6. In Chapter 15, I'll tell you about some other ways to format lists.

Chapter Summary

In this chapter, you learned how you can directly apply font formats to text within your documents. I showed you three ways to change the way characters look: with the Formatting toolbar, the Font dialog box, and shortcut keys. You learned how to use the Change Case command to change the case of typed characters without retyping them. You learned two ways to copy font formats from one place to another within your document and how to remove applied formats. You also learned how to insert bullets and special symbols into your documents with the Symbols command, shortcut keys, and the Bullet button.

In the next chapter, you'll find out about paragraph formatting, which you can use to change the format of entire paragraphs. You'll see how to change text alignment, line spacing, spacing between paragraphs, tabs, and indentation, using the Ruler, dialog boxes, and, of course, shortcut keys. All these formatting changes can help make your documents more effective communication tools.

6

Chapter 6: Paragraph Formatting

CENTERING TEXT, DOUBLE-SPACING LINES, CREATING HANGING indents, and using tabs to create tables of information are things that can make documents easier to read and more effective as communication tools. These things can also be done with a typewriter and a bit of manual effort, but word processors take it a step further with automatic formatting and the ability to change things at any time.

In this chapter, you'll learn about *paragraph formatting* — changing the appearance of entire paragraphs. You'll see how to use Word's Formatting toolbar, ruler, Paragraph dialog box, and shortcut keys. You'll learn how to set paragraph formatting options like alignment, line spacing, indentations, and tabs.

Overview of Paragraph Formatting

Paragraph formatting lets you change the appearance of entire paragraphs. You can change the alignment of text in a paragraph, change the line spacing or spacing between paragraphs, indent text to set it off from other text in the document, use tabs to create simple tables — all these things are examples of paragraph formatting in Microsoft Word.

IMPORTANT NOTE

The most important thing to keep in mind when dealing with paragraph formatting is that **paragraph formatting affects entire paragraphs.** For example, if you want to center text, the entire paragraph that the text is part of must be centered. You can't have one line in a paragraph centered and the others left justified. To do that, you'd have to split the paragraph into two separate paragraphs and center just the first one.

FYI: Why Paragraph Marks Are Important

Back in Chapter 2, I gave you Word's definition of a paragraph: *any line or group of lines ending with a paragraph mark.* This is a very important concept to remember when dealing with paragraph formatting. It explains how Word processes your formatting changes. If you position the insertion point anywhere within a paragraph and make a paragraph formatting change, the entire paragraph changes.

Word stores paragraph formatting information in the paragraph mark at the end of each paragraph. You can use the Show/Hide ¶ button on the Standard toolbar or press ⌘ 8 to show or hide paragraph marks. I highly recommend that you show paragraph marks as you work with Word, especially when you need to make changes to paragraph formatting. Seeing these important nonprinting characters will help you understand and correctly format your documents.

Paragraph Formatting Options

Before I tell you how to make paragraph formatting changes, let's take a closer look at each of the kinds of changes you can make.

Alignment

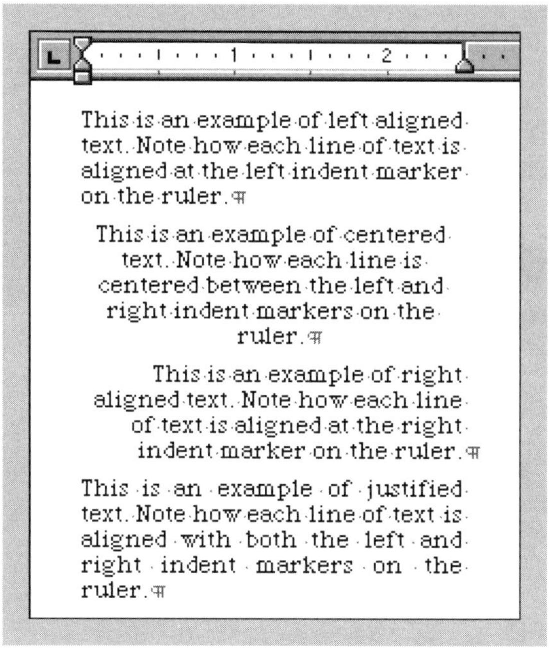

Alignment or *justification* refers to the way text is positioned across the page. Word offers four kinds of alignment: left justified, centered, right justified (or flush right), and justified (or full justified).

Word offers three ways to change the alignment of paragraphs: the Formatting toolbar, the Paragraph dialog box, and shortcut keys. I'll show you each of these methods later in this chapter.

IMPORTANT NOTE

Alignment works with indent settings, which I'll discuss in a moment. To have paragraphs aligned with margins, indents must be set to the margins. This is especially important for centering paragraphs on a page.

Line Spacing and Spacing Before and After Paragraphs

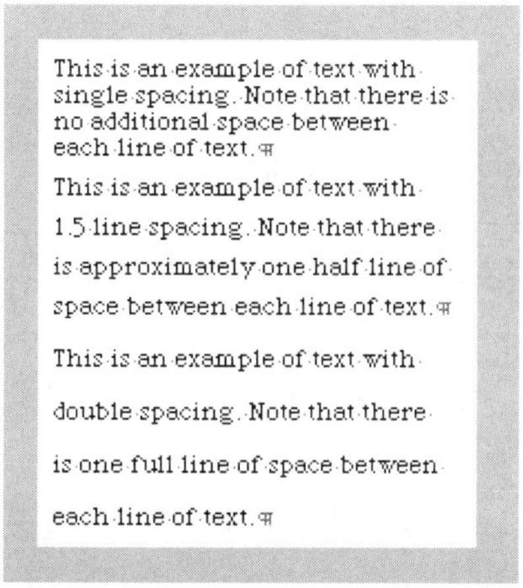

Line spacing refers to the amount of space between lines of text within the paragraph. Word offers three standard line spacing options: single, 1.5 line, and double. Word also lets you specify exact or minimum line spacing if you need to.

In addition to spacing between the lines of a paragraph, Word gives you the ability to set spacing before and after paragraphs.

This makes it possible to have additional space between paragraphs without pressing [Return] to create empty paragraphs.

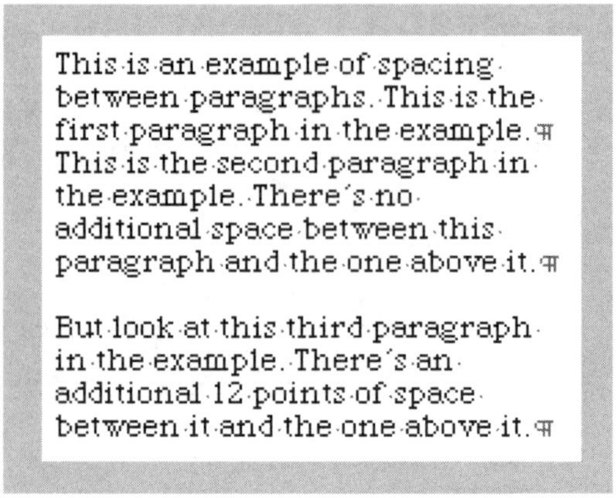
This is an example of spacing between paragraphs. This is the first paragraph in the example.¶
This is the second paragraph in the example. There's no additional space between this paragraph and the one above it.¶

But look at this third paragraph in the example. There's an additional 12 points of space between it and the one above it.¶

Set line spacing and spacing before and after paragraphs with the Paragraph dialog box or shortcut keys. We'll look at these methods and spacing options in greater detail later in this chapter.

FYI: Leading

Line spacing is also sometimes referred to as *leading*, an old typesetters' term. Back in the days when metal type was set by hand, leading was additional strips of lead inserted between lines of type. This increased the amount of space between lines. Many desktop publishing applications, like QuarkXPress and PageMaker, use this term.

Indentation

Indentation refers to the amount of space between the margin and printed text. Indents are often used to make paragraphs stand out from other text in the document. Word offers three kinds of indents:

- **Left Indent —** By adjusting the left indent, you change the position of all lines in the paragraph in relation to the left margin.
- **Right Indent —** By adjusting the right indent, you change the position of all lines in the paragraph in relation to the right margin.
- **Special Indent —** Word offers two special indentation options: First Line and Hanging. Both change the left indent of just the first line in the paragraph.

By setting indents, you can create effects like indented first lines, hanging indents, indented paragraphs, and text running outside the margins. I'll show you examples later in this chapter.

Word gives you four ways to change indents: with the Formatting toolbar, the ruler, the Paragraph dialog box, and shortcut keys. Of these methods, the ruler and Paragraph dialog box offer the most flexibility. I'll show you how to use all these methods later in this chapter.

FYI: Indents vs. Margins

IMPORTANT NOTE

It is very important not to confuse margins with indents. They are different.

Indents determine the amount of space between the left and right margins and text. They are measured in relation to the margins. For example, a one-inch left indent means text will begin one inch to the left of the left margin. Indents can be different in every paragraph of your document.

Margins, on the other hand, determine the amount of space between the edge of the paper and the main text area. For example, a one-inch left margin means the main text area begins one inch from the left edge of the paper. Margins must be the same for every paragraph within a section of your document. I briefly discussed margins in Chapter 4 and will discuss them again in more detail in Chapter 8.

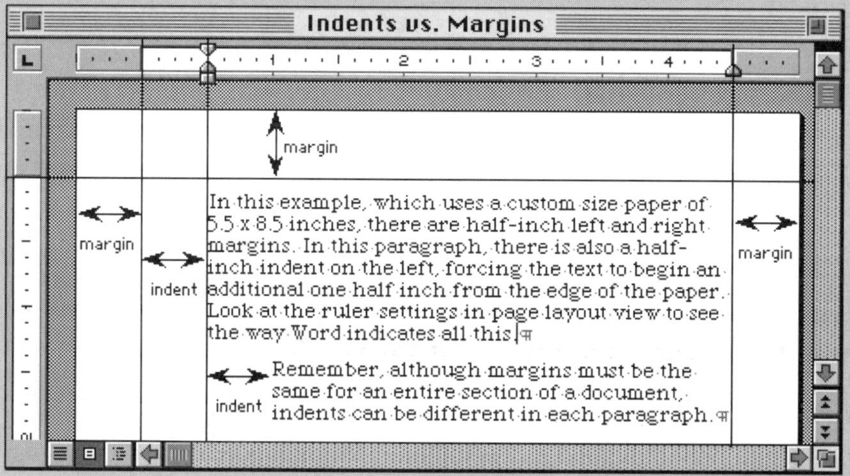

Tab Stops

Tab stops work in conjunction with the Tab key to position text horizontally on the page. When you press Tab, Word inserts a tab character and moves the insertion point to the next tab stop. Whatever you type lines up with that tab stop on the ruler. Press Tab again to insert another tab character and type at the next tab stop. Most often, tabs are used to manually indent the first line of text in a paragraph or create simple tables of information.

By default, Word has tab stops every half inch. You can override them by setting your own custom tab stops in the Tabs dialog box. (I'll show you how later in this chapter.) Word offers four types: left-aligned, centered, right-aligned, and decimal. It also offers a "Bar" tab (no, this isn't the thing you run up when you go out with your drinking buddies) to put a vertical line between columns in a tab table. Use the ruler or Tabs dialog box to set tab stops. Here's an example of a simple table created with all five kinds of tabs:

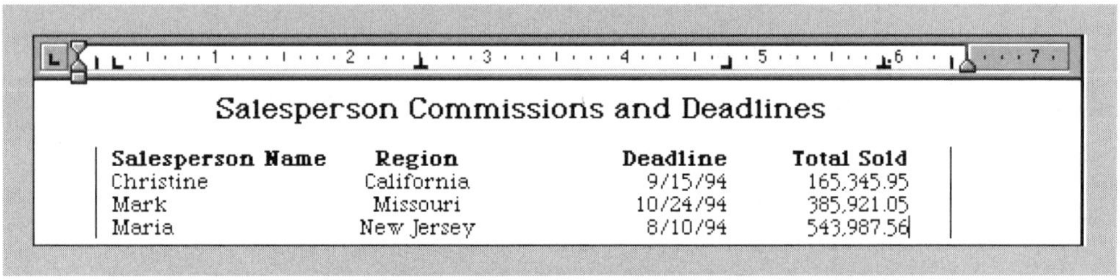
Salesperson Commissions and Deadlines

Salesperson Name	Region	Deadline	Total Sold
Christine	California	9/15/94	165,345.95
Mark	Missouri	10/24/94	385,921.05
Maria	New Jersey	8/10/94	543,987.56

IMPORTANT NOTE

To effectively use tabs within your document, it's best to set your own tab stops rather than pressing Tab repeatedly and depending on Word's default tab stops. Custom tabs are far more flexible for formatting, as you can see in the previous illustration. In addition, pressing Tab multiple times inserts multiple tab characters. If you later decide to set custom tab stops, you'll have to remove all these unnecessary tab characters.

Borders, Shading, Frames, and Drop Caps

Borders, shading, frames, and drop caps are also paragraph formatting options. Borders let you put lines on any or all sides of a paragraph. Shading lets you color in the background of paragraphs. Frames let you position text or graphic objects anywhere on a page and have text flow around it. Drop Caps uses a frame to position one or more enlarged text characters within the first few lines of a paragraph. I'll discuss these four special formatting options in Chapter 13.

Changing Paragraph Formatting

When you begin a brand new document, its paragraph formatting depends on settings stored as part of the Normal style for the template the document is based on. The Normal style defines the characteristics of plain text, including its font formatting, alignment, line spacing, indents, and a variety of other options. I discussed font formatting in Chapter 5 and will discuss styles in Chapter 7.

There are two main ways to change paragraph formatting. Let's take a look at each one.

Type First, Then Format

One method is to select the paragraphs you want to change and then use the appropriate toolbar button, ruler setting, menu command, or shortcut key to change it. This requires that you type the text first, then go back and change it.

Here's an example. Say you're typing a double-spaced report. The report contains a long quote that you want indented and single-spaced. Type the whole report first. Then select the paragraphs you want double-spaced and use the Paragraph dialog box or shortcut key to make them double-spaced. Finally, select the paragraph containing the quote and use the ruler, paragraph dialog box, or shortcut Key to change the indentation.

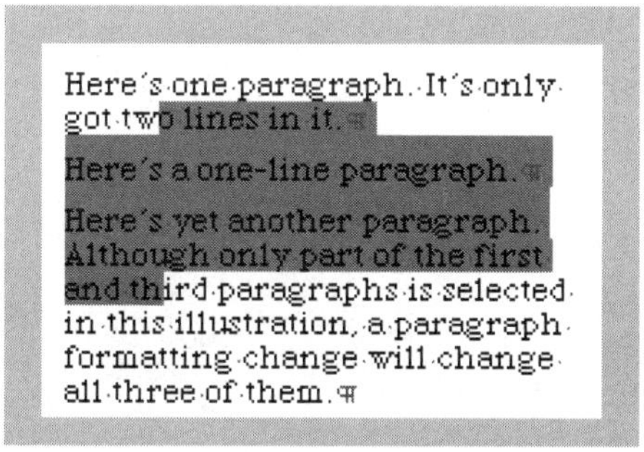

TIP/TRICK

You don't have to select an entire paragraph to change its formatting. If you only need to change the paragraph formatting of one paragraph, click to position the insertion point anywhere inside it. Then make the change. The entire paragraph changes. If you need to change several paragraphs at once, select any part of those paragraphs and make the change. As long as some part of a paragraph is selected, when you make a paragraph formatting change, the entire paragraph changes.

Format As You Type

The other method is to change paragraph formatting as you type. To do this, you must choose the toolbar button, menu command, or shortcut key for the formatting you want *before* you begin typing a new paragraph. Then, when you type, the paragraph has the formatting you chose. Paragraph formatting is carried forward each time you press [Return].

Let's look at our previous example. First use the Paragraph dialog box or shortcut key to set paragraph formatting for double-spaced text. Then type the report up to the paragraph that will contain the quote. Each time you press [Return] to begin a new paragraph of the report, the double-spaced paragraph formatting is carried forward to the next paragraph. Be sure to press [Return] to end the last paragraph before the quote. Then use the ruler, Paragraph dialog box, or shortcut key to change the indentation and line spacing. Now type the paragraph containing the quote. It appears with the indentation and line spacing you specified. Press [Return] at the end of it. Finally use the ruler, Paragraph dialog box, or shortcut key to change the indentation and line spacing back to what it was set for at the beginning of the document. Finish typing.

Inserting and Deleting Paragraph Marks

As I mentioned earlier, a paragraph's formatting is stored in the ending paragraph marker. If you position the insertion point in the middle of a paragraph and press [Return], Word inserts a paragraph mark with the same format settings as the one at the end of that paragraph. Likewise, as you type, each time you press [Return], you are inserting a paragraph mark with the same formatting as the current paragraph. This is why paragraph formatting is automatically carried forward to the next paragraph.

When you delete a paragraph mark, you delete the formatting information for that paragraph. As a result, that paragraph takes on the formatting of the paragraph immediately after it.

Seeing Paragraph Formatting

Word displays most paragraph formatting on screen the way it appears when printed. This is WYSIWYG (What You See Is What You Get). Sometimes it isn't clear what formatting is applied to paragraphs. Word offers two ways to find out.

Revealing Formats

Microsoft added a new feature to Word version 6 called Reveal Formats that makes it easy to find out exactly what formatting is applied to paragraphs. I discussed how this feature applies to font formatting in Chapter 5; now I'll tell you about how it applies to paragraph formatting.

Click the Help button on the Standard toolbar or press Shift Help or ⌘ Shift /. The mouse pointer turns to a pointer with a question mark. Click the paragraph and a window like the one in the following illustration appears. It provides information about the paragraph and font formatting, including styles and directly applied format changes.

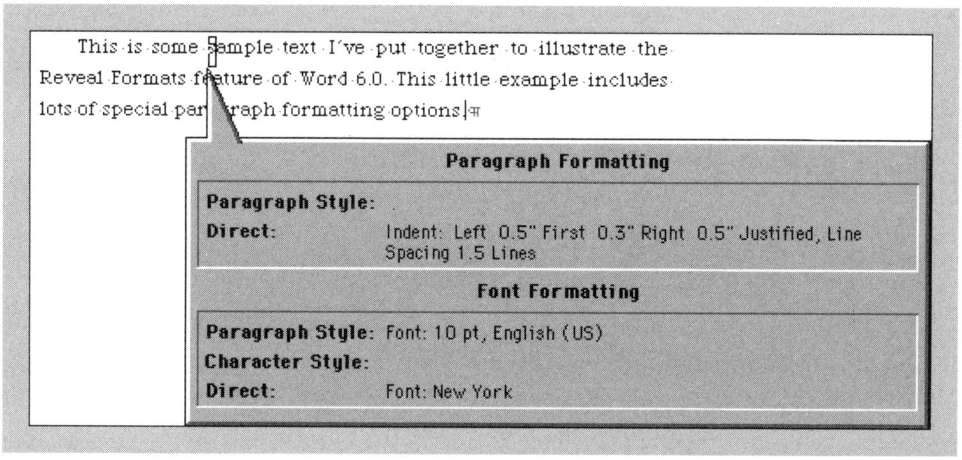

When you're finished checking formats, press Esc to turn off the Reveal Formats feature.

Looking at Buttons, Boxes, and Other Settings

Toolbar buttons and ruler and dialog box settings can also tell you what formatting is applied to paragraphs. For example, the justify button on the Formatting toolbar looks darker when the paragraph at the insertion point or selected paragraph is justified. The ruler, Paragraph dialog box, and Tabs dialog box similarly display current settings with their tab and indent markers, boxes, menus, check boxes, and radio buttons.

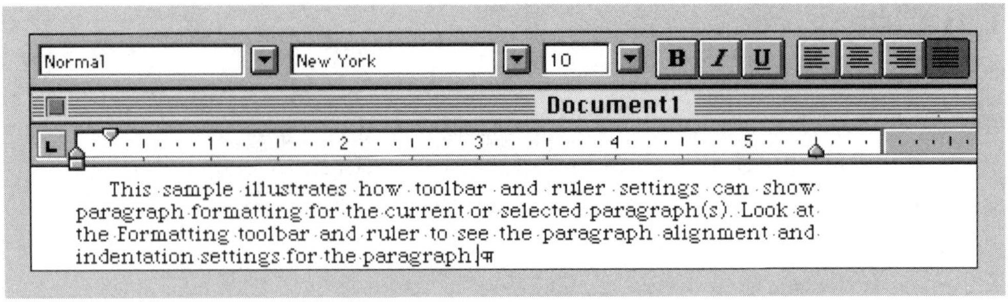

When a setting on the ruler appears blank, gray, or unselected, your selection contains more than one setting. Word can only display one setting at a time. When it needs to display more than one, it simply doesn't display anything. That doesn't mean you can't change a selection. Buttons, boxes, and other settings work the same way, no matter what they indicate.

Using the Formatting Toolbar

NEW IN WORD 6

The Formatting toolbar offers alignment buttons that could be found on the ruler in previous versions of Word as well as two new buttons for changing indentation.

Changing Alignment

Four alignment buttons on the Formatting toolbar let you change the alignment of text between the indents. Click the appropriate button to change the alignment for the current or selected paragraphs.

Align Left — aligns text with the left indent.

Center — centers text between the left and right indents.

Align Right — aligns text with the right indent.

Justify — aligns text with both the left and right indents.

Changing Indentation

Two indentation buttons on the Formatting toolbar let you change the indentation of the current paragraph or selected paragraphs with a click. Each time you click one of these buttons, you increase or decrease the indentation by one tab stop. Word uses default or custom tab stops to change the indentation with these buttons.

Decrease Indent — decreases left indentation by one tab stop. You cannot use this button to set indentation to the left of the left margin.

Increase Indent — increases left indentation by one tab stop.

Using the Horizontal Ruler

NEW IN WORD 6

Word's ruler has undergone a major facelift for Word version 6. All the buttons it carried in previous versions of Word have been removed. It's now used for setting only two paragraph formatting options: indentation and tab stops. To display the ruler if it is not already showing, choose Ruler from the View menu.

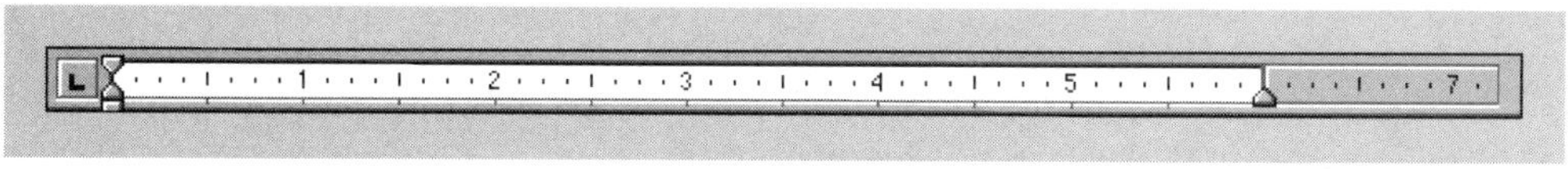

Reading the Ruler

To get the most out of the ruler, it's a good idea to learn how to read it. Here's some basic information:

- On a color or grayscale monitor, the ruler uses gray and white areas to indicate the parts of the document that are outside (gray) and inside (white) the margins. Where the gray and white meet on either end of the ruler are the margins. The left margin is always the zero mark on the ruler, even though a 0 never appears there. In Chapter 4, I showed you how you can use the ruler to change margins in Print Preview. I'll show you how to do the same thing in Page Layout view in Chapter 8.

- The tick marks and numbers on the ruler show actual measurements. By default, the US version of Word displays the ruler in inches with one-eighth inch increments. You can change the default measurement unit in the Options dialog box. I'll tell you how in Chapter 23.
- Indent and tab markers are used to set indents and tabs (that makes sense, right?). I'll tell you more about them next.

FYI: The Mystery of the Changing Ruler

Unlike some other word processing applications, Word has only one horizontal ruler. Rather than display a separate ruler on screen each time there's a formatting change, Word changes the settings on the ruler. The ruler always shows the settings for the current or selected paragraphs.

I've found that the ruler is a source of confusion for many new Word users. Many of my Word students complain that the ruler changes all by itself. Contrary to what they may believe, the ruler is not possessed by some demonic presence intent on making Word users insane. It appears to change simply because the student moves the insertion point into a paragraph with different settings.

For example, one student wanted to indent some text in her document. She used the scroll bar to see the place she wanted to indent the text. Then she used the indent markers on the ruler to make the changes. She didn't see any change so she selected the paragraph containing the text she wanted to indent and looked at the ruler again. The changes she'd made to the indent markers were gone. She complained that the ruler had changed.

What really happened was this: When she used the scroll bar to change her view of the document, the insertion point did not move. It remained in another paragraph in her document, one that didn't appear on the screen. When she adjusted the ruler settings, she adjusted the current paragraph, the one she couldn't see. The ruler reflected settings for that paragraph, but nothing on her screen changed. Then, when she selected

Continued

the paragraph she wanted to change, the ruler reflected the settings for that paragraph. The ruler changed because the selected paragraph hadn't been changed yet.

If I had a dollar for every time I saw this happen in a Word class, I'd be writing this book from poolside in Maui.

The moral to this story is this: Word's ruler always reflects the settings in the current or selected paragraphs. To change the settings for a paragraph, you *must* select it first.

Changing Indentation

The Ruler gives you complete control over indentation. Drag any of the four markers to set left, right, and first line left indents for the current or selected paragraphs.

The left indent marker has three parts:

- Drag the top, inverted triangle to set only the first line left indent. It moves independently of the other two parts.
- Drag the bottom triangle to set the left indent. It moves with the rectangle below it but independently of the top triangle.
- Drag the bottom rectangle to set all left indents, including the first line indent. When you drag the rectangle, all three markers move.

The right indent marker has only one part. Drag it to set the right indent.

For Example: Some Common Indent Settings

Perhaps the best way to explain how indent settings work is to provide some illustrated examples for commonly used indent settings. In each of these illustrations, note the position of the indent markers on the Ruler and the way text in each line of the paragraph lines up with them.

Continued

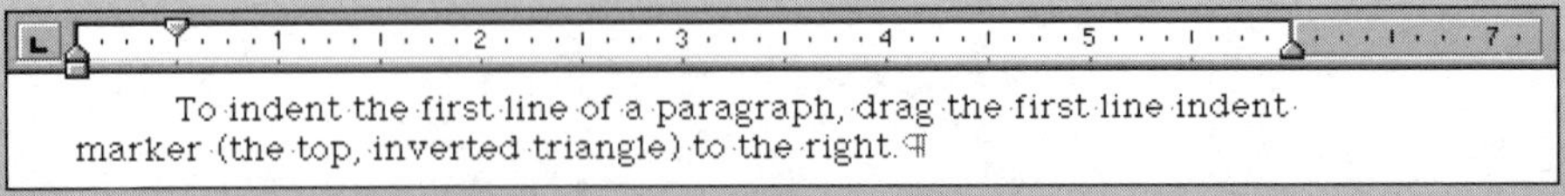

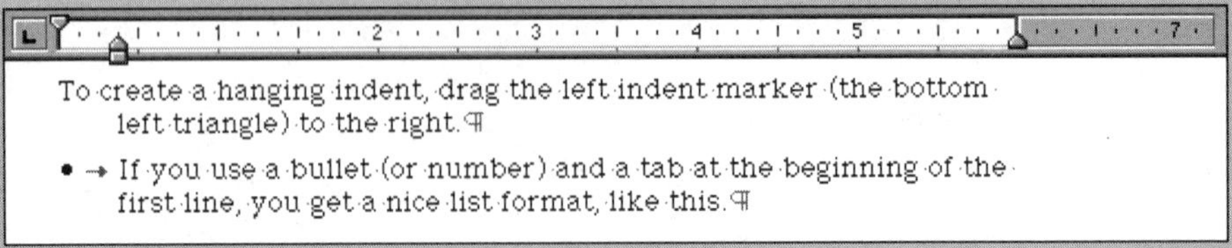

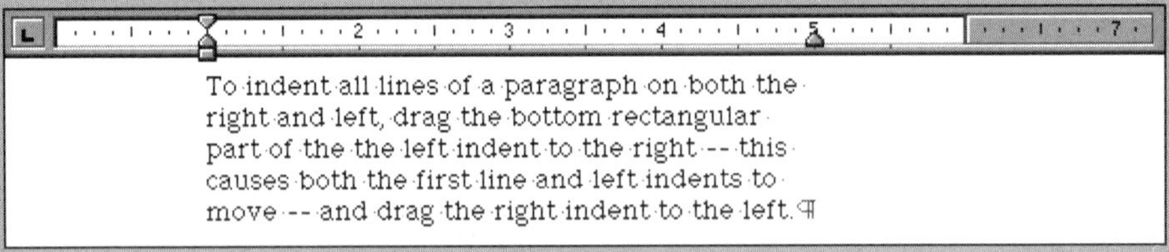

TIP/TRICK

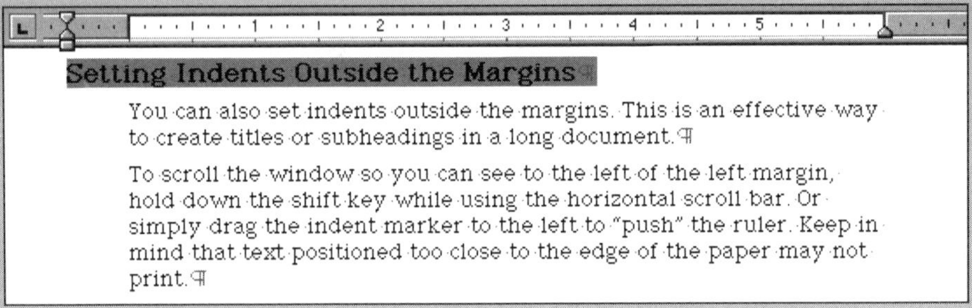

Setting Tabs

If you look closely at the ruler, you may be able to see tiny marks along the bottom indicating Word's default tab stops. (If you don't see them, it might be time for reading glasses.) The ruler lets you set custom tab stops that override these defaults. When you set a custom tab stop, all the default tab stops to the left of it disappear.

Word lets you set four kinds of tab stops with the ruler: left-aligned, centered, right-aligned, and decimal. When placed on the ruler, they look like this:

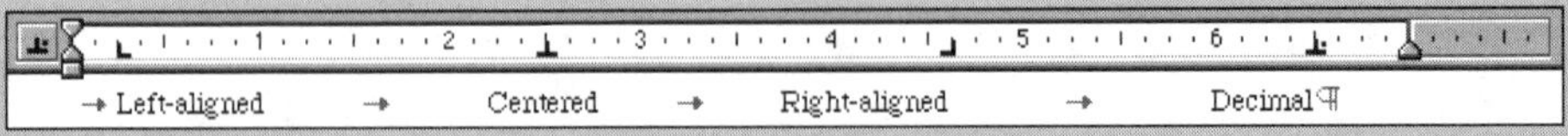

To set tab stops with the ruler, choose the kind of tab you want and then click on the ruler to set it. You can choose a tab by clicking the Tab Alignment button at the far left end of the ruler to cycle through the different tab markers until the one you want appears. They look like this:

 Left-aligned tab

 Centered tab

 Right-aligned tab

 Decimal tab

Once you've selected a tab type, click on the ruler to set the tab. A tab stop mark appears where you click. If necessary, drag the mark to the right or left to change its location. To remove a tab stop mark, drag it off the ruler and let go.

IMPORTANT NOTE

Remember, changes to the ruler — including changes to tab stops — only affect selected paragraphs. To set or change tab stops, you *must* select the paragraph(s) first, then make the change.

Using the Tabs Dialog Box

The Tabs dialog box, which was slightly changed for Word version 6, gives you precise control over custom tab stop locations, offers access to tab leaders, and makes it easy to clear one or all custom tab stops. It also lets you specify the distance between default tab stops. When you are finished making changes in the Tabs dialog box, click the OK button or press [Return] or [Enter] to accept your settings.

There are several ways to open the Tabs dialog box:

- Double-click on a tab stop on the Ruler *or*
- Choose Tabs from the Format menu *or*
- Choose Paragraph from the Format menu and then click the Tabs button in the Paragraph dialog box that appears. I'll tell you about the Paragraph dialog box later in this chapter.

Here's what the Tabs dialog box looks like with the tabs set in the previous illustration:

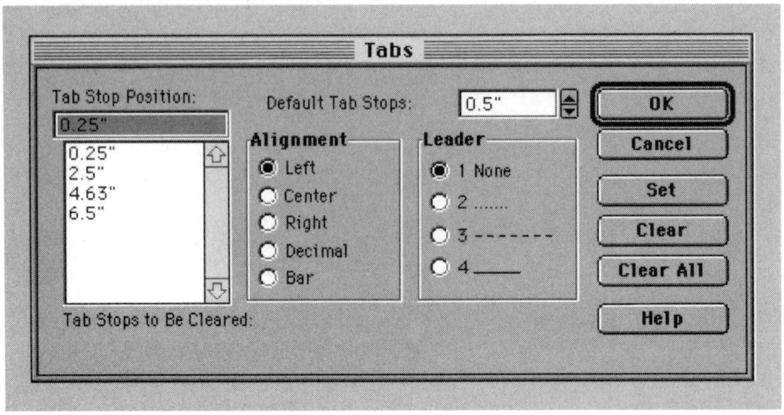

Setting a New Tab Stop

To create a new tab stop, enter a measurement in the Tab Stop Position edit box. Change the Alignment and Leader radio buttons as necessary and click Set.

Setting a Tab Leader

A tab leader is a character that appears between the insertion point where you press t and the character typed at the tab marker. It's called a tab leader because it's a character that leads up to the tab stop. Word offers four options: None, dots, dashes, and lines.

Tab leaders are commonly used in tables of contents. I often use them to create signature lines, like those you might find at the bottom of a legal document.

Try This! Using Tab Leaders to Create a Signature Line

In my Word classes, I'm often asked how to create signature lines. Many people try to do it with the underscore character. Although you can do it this way, using tab stops and the line tab leader may be more effective. Give this a try and see what you think.

Continued

1. In the paragraph you want the line to appear, set two tab stops on the ruler, one where you want the line to begin and one where you want it to end. It doesn't matter which kind of tab stop you use.
2. Double-click on the tab stop for the second tab. In the Tabs dialog box that appears, make sure the second tab in the Tab Stop Position scrolling list is selected. Then choose the line tab leader (the last one under Leader). Click Set to change the Tab stop so it includes the leader. Click OK to close the Tabs dialog box.
3. Press Tab once. The insertion point moves to the first tab stop, where you want the line to begin. Now press Tab again. The insertion point moves to the second tab stop and a line appears between them.

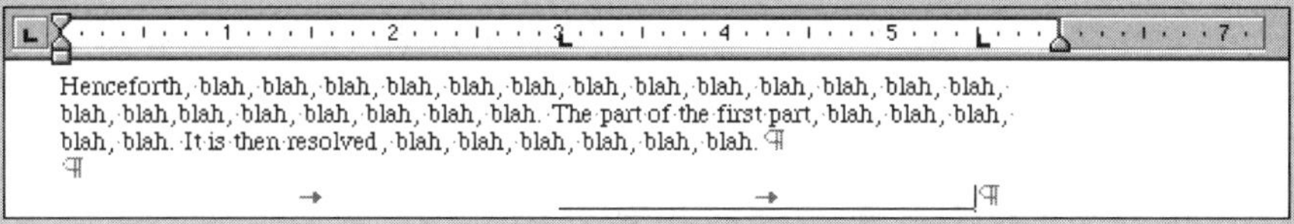

4. To type in the name or title of the person who will sign on the line, press Return to create a new paragraph. The tab stops you set for the previous paragraph are carried forward.
5. Remove the tabs for that paragraph by dragging them off the ruler or using the Tabs dialog box's Clear All command.
6. Click the Tab Alignment button at the far left end of the ruler until the Centered tab marker shows. Then click on the ruler to position the tab stop so it lines up with the middle of the line.
7. Press Tab once to move the insertion point to the tab stop. Type whatever you want to appear under the signature line. Because you used a centered tab stop, whatever you type is centered at the tab marker.

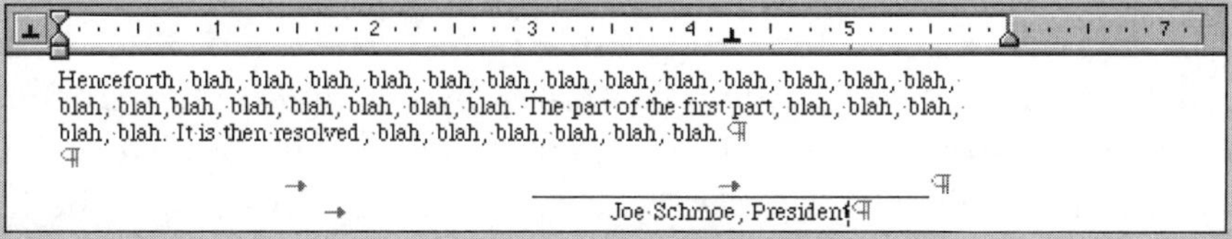

Continued

You can do this for as many signature lines as you need. To have multiple lines on one line of your document, remember to use two tab stops per line and only include a leader in the second tab stop of each pair.

Changing and Clearing Tab Stops

To change a tab stop, choose the one you want to change in the Tabs dialog box scrolling list of tab stop positions. Type a new value in the Tab Stop Position edit box. Click Set to make the change.

To clear a tab stop, choose the one you want to clear in the scrolling list of tab stops, and then click the Clear button. The tab disappears from the list and is added to the Tab Stops to Be Cleared list below it. To clear all tab stops, click the Clear All button. When you click OK, all tabs listed at Tab Stops to Be Cleared are removed.

Changing Default Tab Stops

The Default Tab Stops box lets you set the distance between each of Word's default tab stops in your document. Type a new value into the Default Tab Stops edit box or use the arrows beside it to increase or decrease the value. Then click OK. You can see the new default tab stops as tiny marks on the ruler.

Using the Paragraph Dialog Box

The Paragraph dialog box gives you control over most aspects of paragraph formatting. To open the Paragraph dialog box, choose Paragraph from the Format menu.

The dialog box has two parts you can access by clicking on tabs: Indents and Spacing and Text Flow. Select the appropriate tab and make changes. If you like, you can make changes under both tabs. The Preview area at the bottom of the dialog box shows you how the current or selected paragraphs will look with your settings. The Tabs button lets you open the Tabs dialog box, which I discussed a moment ago, to set paragraph tab stops. When you are finished making changes in the Paragraph dialog box, click the OK button or press Return or Enter to accept your settings.

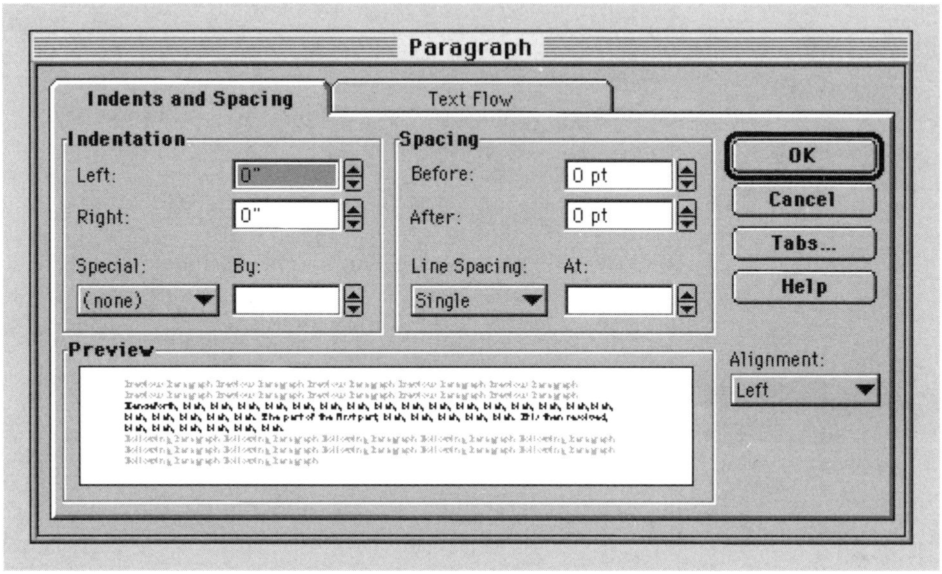

Let's take a closer look at what's available under the two tabs.

Under the Indents and Spacing Tab

The Indents and Spacing tab, shown here, gives you access to edit boxes and menus for Indentation, Spacing, and Alignment.

Indentation

The Indentation area of the Paragraph dialog box lets you set indentation for the left and right sides of a paragraph or selected paragraphs, as well as set special indentation. Values for each of the Indentation edit boxes is normally expressed in the default measurement unit — inches in US versions of Word. To change a value, enter a new value in the appropriate edit box or click the tiny arrows beside the edit box to change the value already there.

Left. The Left edit box lets you set the amount of space between the left margin and the left indent.

TIP/TRICK

To extend text to the left of the left margin, enter a negative value in the Left edit box. For example, -.5 causes the text to extend one half inch to the left of the margin. Remember, however, text that's set to print too close to the edge of the paper may be cut off by your printer.

Right. The Right edit box lets you set the amount of space between the right margin and the right indent.

Special. The Special pop-up menu offers three special indentation options you can use in conjunction with the By edit box beside it:

- **None —** keeps the first line left indent set the same as the left indent.
- **First Line —** shifts the first line left indent to the right of the left indent. This enables you to indent the first line of a paragraph without pressing Tab.
- **Hanging —** shifts the left indent to the right of the first line left indent. This results in all lines other than the first being further indented than the first line. The first line "hangs" over the other lines.

Spacing

The Spacing area of the Paragraph dialog box lets you set spacing before and after a paragraph or selected paragraphs, as well as the line spacing for each line within a paragraph or selected paragraphs. Values for each of the Spacing edit boxes is normally expressed in points, the same measurement used for font size. To change a value, enter a new value in the appropriate edit box or click the tiny arrows beside the edit box to change the value already there.

Spacing Before. The Before edit box lets you change the amount of space before the current or selected paragraphs. Word ignores additional spacing for paragraphs that begin at the top of a page unless that paragraph is also the first paragraph in the document, in a section of the document, or immediately after a manual page break. I'll discuss sections and manual page breaks in Chapter 8.

After. The After edit box lets you change the amount of space after the current or selected paragraphs.

By setting line spacing before or after a paragraph, you can add space between paragraphs without pressing [Return] to insert empty paragraphs. This helps you keep control over spacing since you can specify an exact measurement which is more or less than a full line of text.

TIP/TRICK

Line Spacing. Line spacing is determined by the size of the largest character in a line of text and the line spacing option for the paragraph. For example, the line spacing for 12-point text would be slightly more than 12 points. If a line included an 18-point character, the line spacing for that line would be slightly more than 18 points. You can use the Line Spacing pop-up menu to choose from six line spacing options:

- **Single** — does not add any additional space between lines of text.
- **1.5 Lines** — adds half a line height to the spacing. For example, for 12-point text, line spacing would increase to approximately 18 points: 12 points plus 6 points.
- **Double** — adds a whole line height to the spacing. For example, for 12-point text, line spacing would increase to approximately 24 points.
- **At Least** — lets you specify a minimum line spacing measurement in the At edit box to the right of the Line Spacing pop-up menu.
- **Exactly** — lets you specify an exact line spacing measurement in the At edit box to the right of the Line Spacing pop-up menu. This is particularly useful if the lines of a paragraph contain a variety of font sizes.
- **Multiple** — lets you specify line spacing in terms of lines. When you choose it, enter the number of lines of spacing in the At edit box to the right of the Line Spacing pop-up menu.

Alignment

The Alignment pop-up menu lets you choose from Word's four alignment options: Left, Center, Right, and Justified.

Remember, text is always aligned with the indents, not the margins!

IMPORTANT NOTE

Under the Text Flow Tab

The Text Flow tab in the Paragraph dialog box, which is shown here, gives you access to options that can change the way text flows from line to line and from page to page.

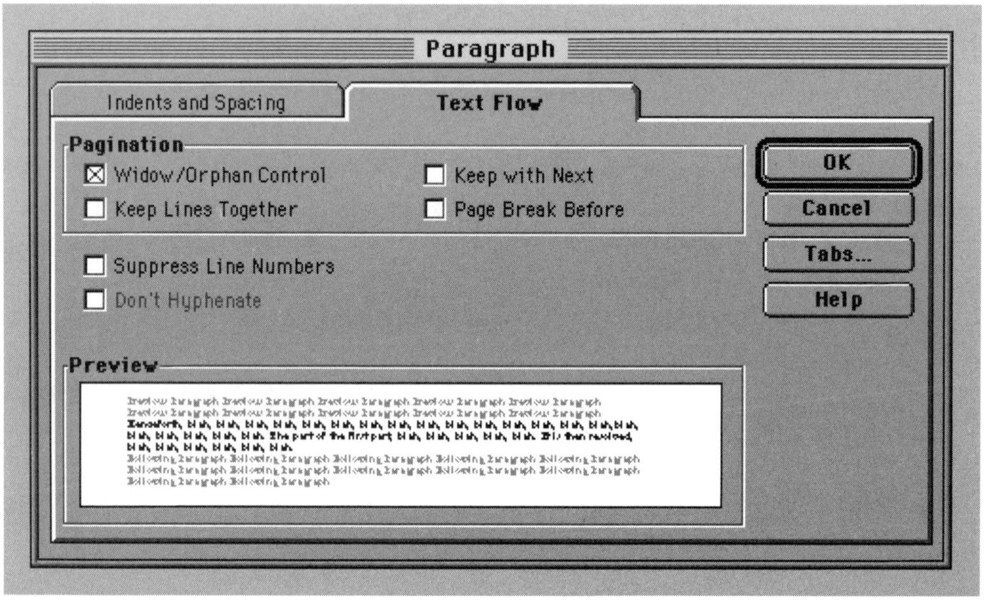

Pagination

The Pagination check boxes tell Word how it should handle automatic page breaks that fall within or immediately after the current or selected paragraphs. There are four options.

- **Widow/Orphan Control —** may sound like part of the plot of a Dickens novel but it isn't. It refers to the number of lines Word allows at the top or bottom of a page when a page break falls within a paragraph. Widow and orphan lines are single lines of text from a multiple line paragraph. A widow appears alone at the bottom of a page and an orphan appears alone at the top of a page. With Widow/Orphan Control turned on, Word will not allow an automatic page break to create a widow or orphan line. There will always be at least two lines of a paragraph at the bottom or top of a page unless the paragraph is only one line long.

- **Keep Lines Together —** prevents an automatic page break from falling in the middle of a paragraph. With this option turned on, if the entire paragraph does not fit together on a page, it is carried forward to the top of the next page.
- **Keep with Next —** prevents a page break from falling between the end of the paragraph and the beginning of the next one. If a page break would normally fall between the paragraphs, the end of the first paragraph is carried forward to the top of the next page. With Widow/Orphan Control also turned on, at least two lines of the first paragraph will be carried forward to the next page. With Keep Lines Together also turned on, the entire first paragraph will be carried forward to the next page.

TIP/TRICK

The Keep with Next option is especially useful when applied to headings in a document. It ensures that the heading isn't at the bottom of a page with the information it relates to on the top of the next page. By including Keep with Next in heading styles, you're ensured this is set for all headings without having to manually set it each time. I'll discuss styles in Chapter 7.

- **Page Break Before —** forces a page break before a paragraph. This ensures that the paragraph always begins at the top of a page.

IMPORTANT NOTE

Although the Page Break Before option may seem to be the same as setting a manual page break, it isn't. When you insert a page break, you're inserting a character into your document. The Page Break Before option doesn't insert any additional characters. I'll discuss page breaks in more detail in Chapter 8.

Line Numbering

Word can automatically number lines in a list, as you'll see in Chapter 15. The Suppress Line Numbers option prevents a paragraph from being included when Word's automatic line numbering feature is used.

Hyphenation

Word can automatically hyphenate words in a document. I'll tell you about that in Chapter 17. The Don't Hyphenate option prevents the paragraph from being hyphenated when Word's hyphenation feature is used.

Using Shortcut Keys

You can also make many paragraph formatting changes with shortcut keys. To format one or more paragraphs that have already been typed, select the paragraphs first, then use one of these key combinations to change it. To begin different paragraph formatting in the paragraph containing the insertion point, use one of these key combinations to change the formatting, then type.

Show/Hide Nonprinting Characters	⌘ 8
Left-align	⌘ L
Center	⌘ E
Right-align	⌘ R
Justify	⌘ J
Single Line Spacing	⌘ 1
1.5 Line Spacing	⌘ 5
Double Line Spacing	⌘ 2
Add/Remove 12 points Before Paragraph	⌘ 0
Create/Increase Indent from Left Margin	⌘ M
Remove/Decrease Indent from Left Margin	⌘ Shift M
Create/Increase Hanging Indent	⌘ T
Remove/Decrease Hanging Indent	⌘ Shift T
Remove Paragraph Formats	⌘ Option Q

Copying Paragraph Formats

In many instances, you'll apply formatting to one or more paragraphs and then want to apply the same formatting to other paragraphs in your document. Word lets you copy and paste paragraph formatting two different ways.

Using the Format Painter Button & Pointer

The Format Painter button is a new tool on Word's Standard toolbar. I discussed it in Chapter 5, where I showed you how to use it to copy font formats. You can also use it to copy the formats of selected paragraphs.

NEW IN WORD 6

To copy paragraph formats with the Format Painter feature, select part or all of a paragraph with the formatting you want to copy. You *must* include the paragraph mark at the end of the paragraph since that's where Word stores paragraph formatting information. Click the Format Painter button. The mouse pointer changes to the Format Painter pointer, an I-beam pointer with a plus sign on its left side. Use this pointer to select the paragraph(s) you want to copy the format to. When you release the mouse button, the paragraphs you selected change and the mouse pointer returns to normal.

To copy one format to multiple places, double-click the Format Painter button after selecting a paragraph with the formats you want to copy. The mouse pointer changes to the Format Painter pointer and stays that way. You can make multiple selections to change formats throughout your document. When you're finished, press – to return the mouse pointer to normal.

Using Shortcut Keys

You can also use shortcut keys to copy paragraph formats. I discussed this in Chapter 5, too.

TIP/TRICK

Select a paragraph with the formatting you want to copy. Again, it's important to include the paragraph mark at the end of the paragraph in your selection. Then press [⌘][Shift][C] to copy the formatting. To paste the paragraph formatting, select the paragraphs you want to format and press [⌘][Shift][V]. To paste formatting in multiple places, just select paragraphs to format and press [⌘][Shift][V] again. This will work until something new is copied to the Clipboard.

FYI: How Word Copies Formats

The Format Painter tool and shortcut keys can copy directly applied font and paragraph formatting, character styles, and paragraph styles. I discussed font formatting in Chapter 5 and will discuss styles in Chapter 7. What Word copies depends on what you select.

- To copy just character styles and directly applied font formatting, select text only and no paragraph marks. Word copies the character style and any formatting applied directly to the first character of the selection.
- To copy just paragraph styles and directly applied paragraph formatting, select only the paragraph mark at the end of the paragraph. Remember, that's where Word stores paragraph formatting.
- To copy all styles and formatting, select both text and a paragraph mark. Word copies the paragraph style and any additional directly applied paragraph formatting as well as the character style and any additional font formatting applied directly to the first character of the selection.

Removing Paragraph Formats

You can remove any directly applied paragraph formatting quickly and easily with a shortcut key. Simply select the paragraphs you want to remove formatting from and press [⌘] [Option] [Q]. This removes all paragraph formatting you applied with the Formatting toolbar, ruler, Tabs or Paragraph dialog boxes, or shortcut keys. It does not remove paragraph formats that are part of a paragraph style. I'll discuss paragraph styles in Chapter 7.

Chapter Summary

In this chapter, you learned all about paragraph formatting — starting with an overview of the kinds of formatting available in Word, including text alignment, indentation, line spacing, and tabs, and then moving on to specific methods of changing formatting: using the Formatting toolbar, ruler, Tabs dialog box, Paragraph dialog box, and shortcut keys. Finally, you learned how to copy and remove paragraph formatting.

In the next chapter, you'll learn about character and paragraph styles. The Styles feature of Word makes it quick and easy to apply the same formatting over and over within a document. Not only is it a real time-saver, but it helps keep formatting consistent throughout a document, eliminating the possibility of distracting formatting errors.

7

Chapter 7: Formatting with Styles

In Chapters 5 and 6, you learned all about Word's font and paragraph formats which enable you to change the way text characters and entire paragraphs appear. In this chapter, I'll tell you about Word's styles feature. You'll learn what paragraph and character styles are and how you can create and apply them to format your documents quickly and consistently.

If you skipped over Chapters 5 and 6 and aren't familiar with font and paragraph formatting, go back and read them before getting started with this chapter. You'll need the information there to get the most out of this chapter.

Overview of Styles

A style is a collection of formats — font, font size, font style, effects, line spacing, alignment, indentation, etc. — with a name. When you apply a style to text, all the formats that are part of the style are applied to the text. This makes it quick and easy to apply the same formatting over and over to text throughout your document.

It gets better, though. If you use styles in your document and then change the definition of a style, the formatting of all the text that uses that style changes automatically. You don't have to go through your document and make manual formatting changes. How's that for a real time saver?

Kinds of Styles

Word now offers two kinds of styles: paragraph and character styles.

- **Paragraph** — These styles can include any kind of paragraph or font format, including formats you can apply with a toolbar button, the ruler, or the Font, Paragraph, or Tabs dialog boxes. A paragraph style determines the appearance of the entire paragraph. The Paragraph Style feature is not new to Word version 6 — it has been around for years.

NEW IN WORD 6

- **Character** — These styles are new to Word version 6. A character style includes only the kind of formatting you can apply with the Font Formatting toolbar buttons or the Font dialog box.

For Example: Using Styles

I use styles in almost all of my Word documents. I find it easier to simply apply a predefined style to text in my document than to manually format each block of text I want to change.

Continued

This book is a good example of a document that uses styles. Look at the pages before you. See the headings, subheadings, blocks of plain text, and lists with bullets or numbers? Although I did not prepare final book pages in Microsoft Word, I did use it to prepare my manuscript. I used paragraph styles to identify different heading levels and different paragraph formatting. As I spent more time working with Word 6, I began using character styles to format words that needed to stand out. This formatting helped organize and indentify different parts of my manuscript, making it easier for my editors to work with.

Using styles to format text benefits me in three main ways:

- Using styles takes most of the work out of formatting text. I save time and can concentrate on the words rather than the way they look.
- Using styles ensures almost effortless consistency throughout my document. I use the same styles over and over throughout my manuscript documents.
- Using Word's built-in Heading styles makes it easy for me to automatically generate a detailed table of contents. I'll tell you how in Chapter 15.

If you find yourself applying the same formatting changes over and over to different parts of your documents, it's time to consider using styles. I'm sure you'll find them as useful as I do.

Displaying Styles

Word offers several easy ways to see what styles are applied to text. Two of these methods are new to Word version 6.

Reveal Formats

NEW IN WORD 6

As I showed you in Chapters 5 and 6, you can always see what styles are applied to text by using Word's new Reveal Formats feature. Click the Help button on the Standard Toolbar or press [Shift][Help] or [⌘][Shift][/]. The mouse pointer changes to an arrow with a question mark. Click on the text you want to check. A Reveal Formats window appears. In the following illustration, you can see that the text being checked has both paragraph and character styles applied to it but no directly applied formats.

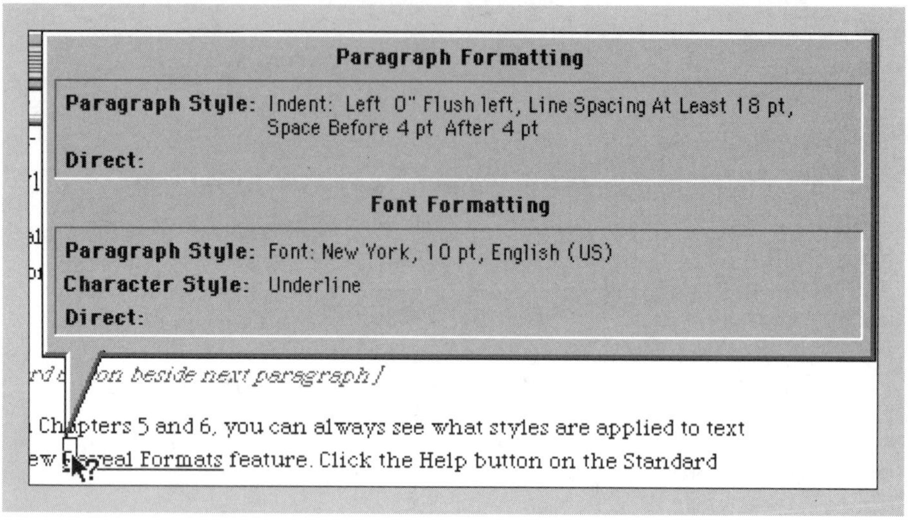

Style Box

The Style box on the Formatting toolbar displays the name of the style applied to selected text or text at the insertion point.

- If the text has a character style applied to it, that style name appears in the Style box.
- If the text does not have a character style applied to it, the paragraph style name appears in the Style box.
- If a selection includes some text with a character style and some text without it, the paragraph style name appears in the Style box.
- If the selection includes text with multiple paragraph styles, the Style box remains empty.

The Style Dialog Box

The Style dialog box, which I'll tell you about later in this chapter, also displays the name of the style applied to selected text or text at the insertion point. But unlike the Style box, which can only display one style at a time, the Style dialog box can display both the paragraph and character formatting for selected text or text at the insertion point. This is true only if the selection contains just one paragraph style and one character style; if the selection contains multiple paragraph or character styles, even the Style dialog box cannot display all the styles applied to the selection.

Style Area

NEW IN WORD 6

Word version 6 includes a style area along the left side of the window that can be used to display paragraph styles applied in your document. When turned on, it looks like this:

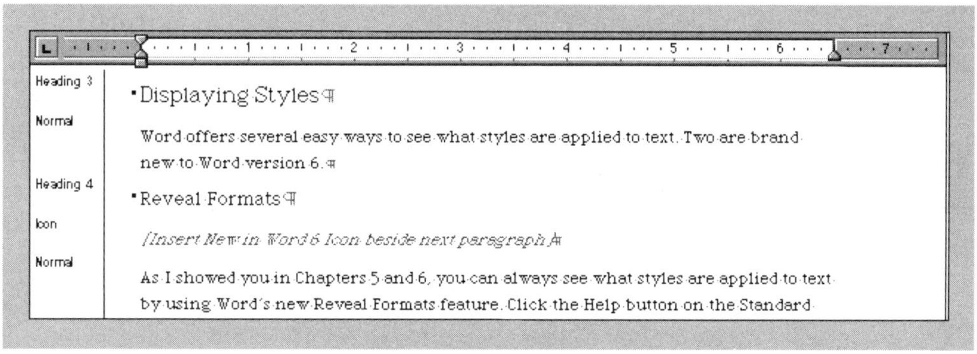

To turn on this feature, choose Options from the Tools menu. If necessary, click the View tab. In the Window area, enter a value greater than 0 in the Style Area Width edit box. (Unless your styles have long names, 0.8 should be enough.) Click OK to close the Options dialog box. The style area appears.

You can change the width of the style area at any time by dragging the vertical style area boundary line to the right or left. When you position your mouse pointer over the line, your mouse pointer changes to a double line with arrows coming out of it. Press your mouse button down and drag. When you let go, the width of the style area changes.

To hide the style area, either set the style area Width to 0 in the View tab of the Options dialog box or drag the style area boundary to the far left side of the window and let go.

I'll discuss the Options dialog box in detail in Chapter 23.

Printing Style Definitions

NEW IN WORD 6

Word version 6 gives you the ability to print a document *style sheet* — a list of the styles in use and their definitions. The printout includes the name of the style (printed in bold) and the formats it includes. You might find this helpful if you need to keep track of the styles used in a document.

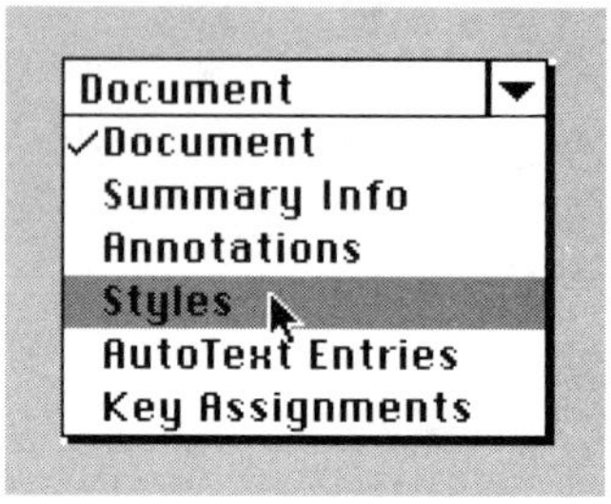

To print style definitions, choose Print from the File menu. In the Print dialog box that appears, choose Styles from the pull down menu. Then click the Print button or press [Return] or [Enter] to begin printing. I discussed printing in Chapter 4.

Word's Built-In Styles

Each Word template includes several built-in styles. Since every Word version 6 document is based on a template, many styles are available in all documents. Other styles are available only in specific templates. I'll discuss templates in Chapter 9. In this section, I'll tell you about the styles you'll find in many Word template files.

TIP/TRICK

Just because a style is built into a Word template, it doesn't mean you're stuck with using it exactly the way it is defined. You can change any style's definition. Or, if you prefer, you can create and use your own custom styles. I'll tell you how later in this chapter.

The Normal Style

The Normal style is the default style for documents based on the Normal template. It's the style that is automatically used when you begin typing in a new document. By default, Normal is set at single-spaced, left-aligned, 12-point Times font. If you prefer another font or size, you can always change it by using the Default button in the Font dialog box. I told you how back in Chapter 5.

IMPORTANT NOTE

One of the most important things to remember about the Normal style is that many other styles within a template are based on it. That means changing the definition of the Normal style may change the definition of other styles within the document. This is both good and bad — good if you want those other styles to change for consistency but bad if you don't want those other styles to change. I'll tell you how to change style definitions later in this chapter.

Automatically Applied Styles

Some of Word's built-in styles are applied automatically when you use certain features, like the header and footer, footnote, index, and table of contents features. For example, if you use the Caption command (Insert menu), the text you enter as a caption will have the Caption style automatically applied to it. (I'll tell you about the Caption feature in Chapter 14.) This automates part of the task of formatting your documents and helps ensure consistency.

Here's a list of built-in styles that are automatically applied, along with the name of the commands or features that apply them.

Annotation Text	Annotation (Insert menu)
Annotation Reference	Annotation (Insert menu)
Caption	Caption (Insert menu)
Footer, Footer Even, Footer Odd, Footer First	Header and Footer (View menu)
Endnote Text	Footnote (Insert menu)
Footnote Text	Footnote (Insert menu)
Endnote Reference	Footnote (Insert menu)
Footnote Reference	Footnote (Insert menu)
Header, Header Even, Header Odd, Header First	Header and Footer (View menu)
Heading 1 through Heading 9	Outline feature
Index 1 through Index 9	Index and Tables (View menu)
Line Number	Document Layout (File menu)
Macro Text	Macro (Tools menu)
Page Number	Page Numbers (Insert menu)
Table of Authorities	Index and Tables (Insert)
Table of Figures	Index and Tables (Insert)
TOC 1 through TOC 9	Index and Tables (Insert)

You'll get a better idea of how these styles look and work when you read about the commands and features that apply them throughout this book.

Other Template Styles

Other Word version 6 templates offer other styles. For example, the template called Letter 1 uses paragraph styles called Return Address, Date, Inside Address, Salutation, Body Text, Closing, Signature Name, Signature Job, Reference Initials, Enclosure, and CC. Each of these styles can be used to format a specific part of a general purpose business letter. Many additional paragraph and character styles are included in the template for your use.

Defining Styles

If Word's built-in styles aren't enough for you, you can create your own from scratch. This makes it possible to have and use styles that meet your exact needs.

Word offers two ways to create paragraph styles and one way to create character styles. Let's check them out.

Defining with the Style Dialog Box

NEW IN WORD 6

The Style dialog box lets you define both paragraph and character styles. While it isn't exactly new in Word version 6, it certainly has changed from previous versions. It's bigger now and offers access to a lot more features.

To open the Style dialog box, use one of the following methods:

- Choose Style from the Format menu *or*
- Double-click on a style name in the style area of the document window (if it is displayed)

The Style dialog box, shown here, appears.

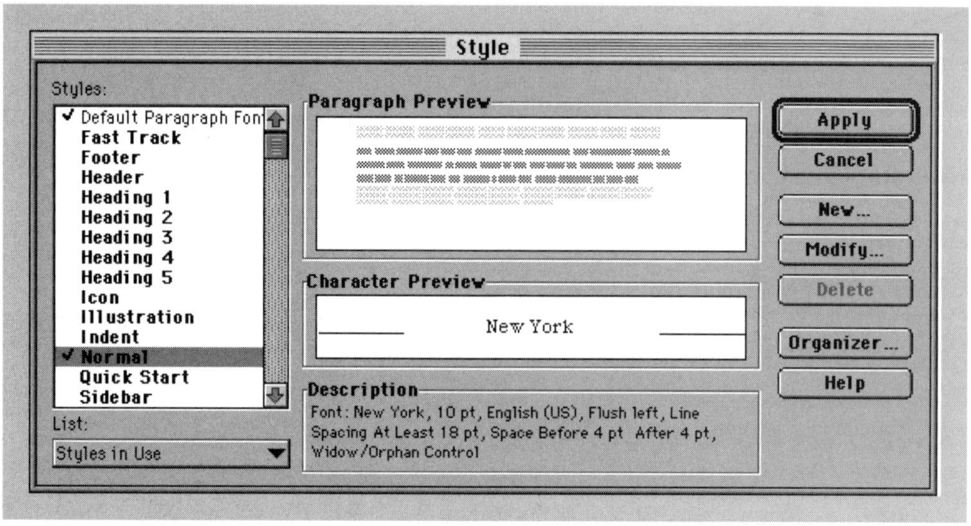

Overview of the Style Dialog Box

Let me take a minute to explain what you're seeing inside this busy dialog box.

Styles. The Styles scrolling list displays styles within the document. Paragraph styles are displayed in bold text while character styles are displayed in plain text. Check marks beside style names indicate the style applied to selected text or text at the insertion point. I discussed how this works earlier in this chapter. You can click on a style name to select it.

List. The List pop-up menu lets you tell Word which styles it should display in the Styles scrolling list above it. The options are:

- **Styles in Use** — displays only the styles used within the document.
- **All Styles** — displays all the styles available in the template the document is based on. This includes Word's built-in styles.
- **User-Defined Styles** — displays only the styles you created in the document.

Paragraph Preview. The Paragraph Preview window displays a sample of what the paragraph would look like with the selected style applied. Unless the font for the paragraph is very large, you won't be able to read what's in the preview window. It will, however, let you see paragraph spacing, alignment, indentation, and tab settings.

Character Preview. The Character Preview window displays a sample of the font formatting with the selected style applied. The text within the Character Preview window is always the name of the font for the selected style. The two horizontal lines represent the invisible baseline, just like you'll find in the Font dialog box, which I discussed in Chapter 5.

Description. The Description window displays a complete description of the selected style. If the style is based on another style, like Normal, the description will begin with the name of the style followed by a plus sign (+) and the changes that define the style. Here's an example:

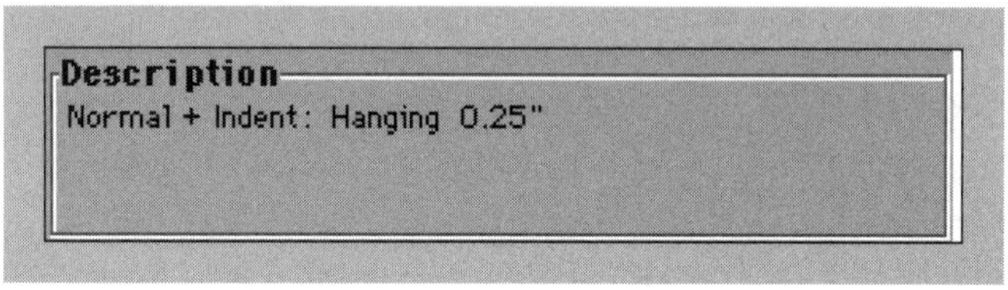

Buttons. The Style dialog box has a bunch of buttons. I'll discuss them throughout the rest of this chapter.

Defining a New Style

NEW IN WORD 6

To create a new style with the Styles dialog box, begin by clicking the New button. The New Style dialog box, which is new in Word version 6 and illustrated below, appears.

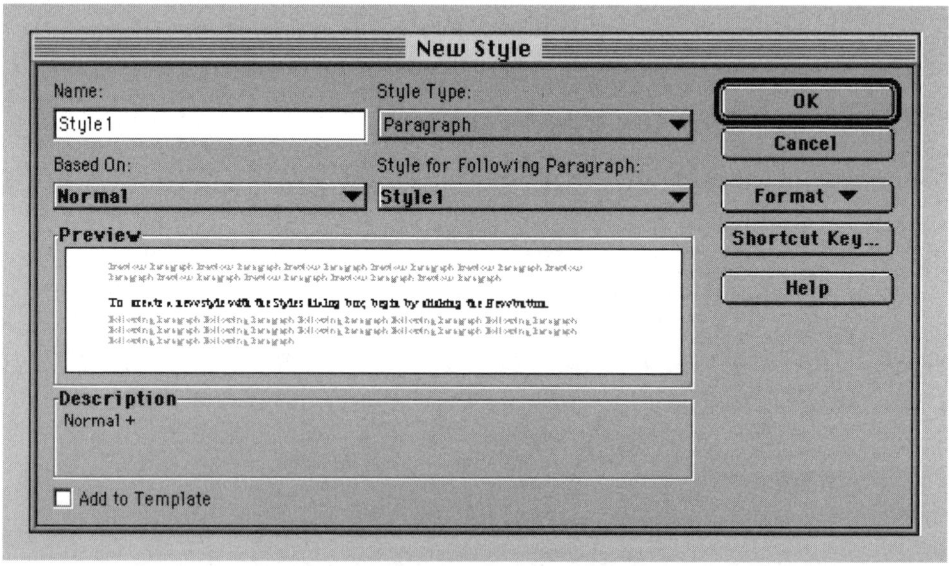

Name. Enter a name for the style in the Name edit box. The name must be unique. In Word version 6, style names are no longer case sensitive. That means you can't create a new style named "Heading" if a style named "heading" already exists. Style names can include up to 253 characters and cannot include the colon (:) or semicolon (;) characters.

NEW IN WORD 6

Style Type. Select a type of style from the Style Type pop-up menu. Your choices are Paragraph or Character. Choosing a type of style here will determine what formatting options are available from the Format button/menu in this dialog box, as you'll see in a moment.

Based On. A style can be based on another style. For example, if you base a style on Normal, the new style begins with all the formatting of the Normal style. Any changes you make with the Format button/menu determine how that style differs from Normal. If the definition of the Normal style changes, any characteristics the new style shares with the Normal style will also change.

Basing a style on another style can save you time if you need to make global formatting changes in your document. For example, if all your styles are based on Normal, which uses the Times font, you can change all styles to Helvetica font simply by changing the Normal style so it uses Helvetica font.

TIP/TRICK

The Based On pop-up menu displays a complete list of all styles in the current document. The list, which is in alphabetical order, may be very long. If you do not want to base the new style on an existing style, choose (no style), which you'll find at the top of the list.

Style for Following Paragraph. The Style for Following Paragraph pop-up menu determines which style will be automatically applied to the next paragraph when you press Return in a paragraph your new style is applied to. For example, say you're creating a new style you plan to use as a section heading in a document. When you apply this style and press Return, do you want the next paragraph's style to also be formatted as a heading? Probably not. You may want the Normal, Body Text, or another plain text style applied. Use the Style for Following Paragraph pop-up menu to choose the next paragraph's style.

If you chose Character in the Style Type pop-up menu, the Style for Following Paragraph pop-up is gray and cannot be used.

Format. The Format menu/button offers access to dialog boxes you can use to make character and paragraph formatting selections. The type of style you selected from the Style Type pop-up menu determines what options are available. If you chose Character, you can access the Font and Language dialog boxes. If you chose Paragraph, you can access both of these dialog boxes as well as the Paragraph, Tabs, Border, Frame, and Numbering dialog boxes. I discussed the Font dialog box in Chapter 5 and the Paragraph and Tabs dialog boxes in Chapter 6. I'll discuss the Language dialog box in Chapter 17, the Border and Frame dialog boxes in Chapter 13, and the Numbering dialog box in Chapter 15.

Once you've used the Format button/menu to access a dialog box and make changes in it, you can click OK in that dialog box to return to the New Style dialog box. You can then use the Format button/menu again to change other formatting until you've got the new style completely defined.

Preview. The Preview window displays a preview of what the new style will look like. It works like the Paragraph Preview window in the Style dialog box.

Description. The Description window lists the entire description for the new style. If the style is based on another style as previously discussed, the description begins with that style name. This works exactly like the Description window in the Style dialog box.

Add to Template. The Add to Template check box tells Word to add the new style to the template the document is based on. I'll discuss templates in Chapter 9.

Other Buttons. The New Style dialog box offers three buttons other than the Format button/menu I discussed above and the Help button you'll find in every dialog box:

- **OK** — accepts the style definition, adds it to the list of user-defined styles, and returns you to the Style dialog box. This is the button you click when you're done defining your new style.
- **Cancel** — tells Word to forget all about the new style you're defining and returns you to the Style dialog box.
- **Shortcut Key** — displays the Customize dialog box. I'll discuss this dialog box in Chapter 24.

Finishing the Style Definition

When you've finished defining a style and find yourself back in the Styles dialog box, you've got two choices to continue working with your document.

- Click Apply to close the Style dialog box and apply the new style *or*
- Click Close to close the Style dialog box without applying the new style. If you haven't just created a new style, this button will be labeled Cancel. The Cancel button also closes the dialog box without applying a style.

Choose carefully! The button you click will determine whether the selected text or text at the insertion point changes. I'll discuss applying styles a little later in this chapter.

IMPORTANT NOTE

Try This! Creating a New Style with the Style Dialog Box

Here's your chance to try creating a new style. In this example, you'll create a paragraph style called Main Heading that is based on Normal and will automatically apply the Normal style to the following paragraph.

1. In a Word document, choose Style from the Format menu. The Style dialog box appears.
2. Click the New button. The New Style dialog box appears.
3. In the Name edit box, type the name: **Main Heading.**
4. Choose Paragraph from the Style Type pop-up menu.
5. Choose Normal from the Based On pop-up menu.
6. Choose Normal from the Style for Following Paragraph pop-up menu.
7. Use the Format button/menu to choose Font. The Font dialog box appears.
8. Use the Font dialog box to make the font larger and more distinctive. Remember, this is for a main heading! If you need a suggestion, try Helvetica, 18 points, bold, single underline.

Continued

9. When you've finished making changes, click OK. The Font dialog box disappears and you'll find yourself looking at the New Style dialog box again.
10. Use the Format button/menu to choose Paragraph. The Paragraph dialog box appears.
11. Use this dialog box to change the paragraph spacing. By adding additional space before and after a heading, you help make it stand out from the rest of the text. If you need a suggestion, try 12 points of spacing before and 4 points of spacing after. Make sure the Line Spacing option is set to at least the same size as the font you used in Step 8 above.
12. When you've finished making changes, click OK. The Paragraph dialog box disappears, leaving you in the New Style dialog box again.
13. Click OK to dismiss the New Style dialog box. The Style dialog box, which has been waiting underneath it all this time, is displayed again. The Main Heading style appears in the Styles scrolling list.
14. Click Close to close the Style dialog box without applying the new style. You'll see how this works a little later when you learn how to apply styles.

Defining by Example

Word offers a quicker way to define paragraph styles. Rather than use the Style dialog box, begin by formatting existing text to create an example of the style you want. Then, with the insertion point anywhere within the example paragraph, click on the Style box or press [⌘][Shift][S] and type in a new style name. Remember, the name must be unique, have less than 253 characters, and not use the colon or semicolon characters. When you press [Return] or [Enter] to accept the name, the new style is defined and applied all at once.

NEW IN WORD 6

Although this method is not new to Word version 6, the dialog box that appeared in previous versions no longer appears. This makes it even faster to create paragraph styles this way.

IMPORTANT NOTE

When using this method to define new paragraph styles, if the text in the example paragraph has multiple font formats, the new style will have whatever font formats are applied to the first character in the paragraph. Also keep in mind that you can only use this method to define paragraph styles. To define a character style, you must use the Style dialog box.

Try This! Defining a Style by Example

Now try defining a style by example. Following these steps, you'll create a new style called Quoted Text that can be used for long quoted passages of text in a document.

1. In a Word document, select some typed text. If the document doesn't have any text yet, type some and then select it.
2. Use the ruler to indent the left and right sides of the paragraph by one inch.
3. Click the Justify icon on the Formatting Toolbar.

4. With the text still selected, use the Font and Font Size boxes on the Formatting toolbar to choose Helvetica 10 point font.

5. Click on the Style box on the Formatting Toolbar or press (⌘)(Shift)(S) to make the Style box active. The name of the style that appears in the box becomes selected.

6. Type in the new style name: **Quoted Text.** Press (Return) or (Enter) to accept the name. The name in the Style box changes as the new style is created and applied to the selected text.

Applying Styles

It wouldn't be very practical to create styles if you couldn't apply them to text in your document. In this section, I'll discuss applying styles.

Before you apply a style, however, you must tell Word what you want to apply the style to.

- To apply a character style to existing text, select the text.
- To apply a character style to text before you type it, position the insertion point where you plan to type. Immediately after applying the style, anything you type at that point has the character style you applied.
- To apply a paragraph style to one paragraph, either position the insertion point inside the paragraph or select all or part of the paragraph.
- To apply a paragraph style to multiple contiguous paragraphs, select all or part of the paragraphs.
- To apply a paragraph style to multiple non-contiguous paragraphs, select the first paragraph(s) and apply the style. Then repeat these two steps for each group of paragraphs you want to apply the style to. Unfortunately, you cannot make multiple, noncontiguous selections.

You can apply a style to an empty paragraph — a paragraph marker on a line all by itself. If you later type information in that paragraph, whatever you type will have the style you specified.

FYI: How Word Applies Styles

Word applies styles differently, based on whether a character or paragraph style is being applied. When Word applies a character style, it adds the style's formats to whatever formats the text already has. For example, when a character style consisting of bold and italic formatting is applied to text that is already 12 point, plain, Times font, the result is text that is 12 points, Times, bold, and italic.

In this example, a character style with ***bold and italic*** formatting was applied only to the words "bold and italic" in the first line.

Continued

When Word applies a paragraph style, it applies all the formatting options included in the style to all the text in the paragraph. This can change the appearance of the entire paragraph, even if the entire paragraph was not selected when the style was applied.

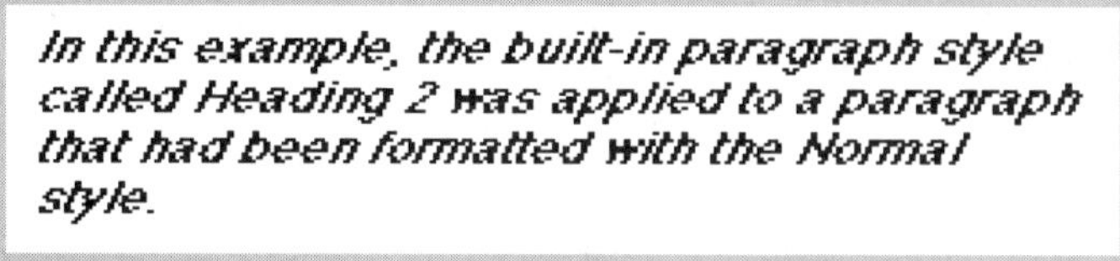
In this example, the built-in paragraph style called Heading 2 was applied to a paragraph that had been formatted with the Normal style.

Some kinds of font formatting work like on/off toggle switches. Bold and italic are perfect examples. If a character style utilitizing one of these font formats is applied to text that already includes the same font format, the format is, in effect, "turned off" for the text the character style is applied to. The same thing goes for paragraph styles applied to text already including the same directly applied font formatting. It's almost as if having the format turned on twice cancels it out.

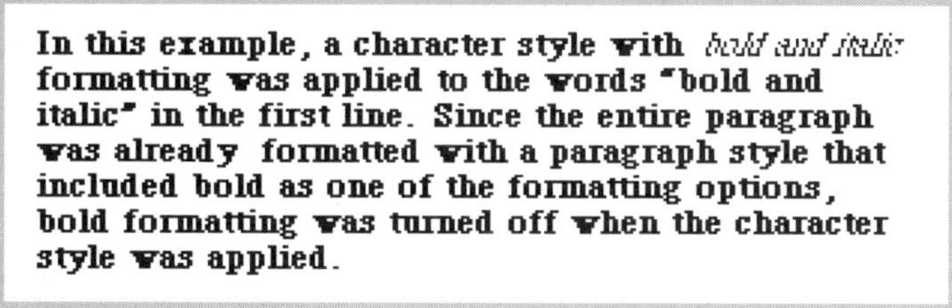
In this example, a character style with *bold and italic* **formatting was applied to the words "bold and italic" in the first line. Since the entire paragraph was already formatted with a paragraph style that included bold as one of the formatting options, bold formatting was turned off when the character style was applied.**

Applying with the Formatting Toolbar

The Formatting toolbar offers two quick and easy ways to apply a style. Both utilize the Style box.

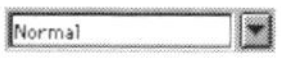

- Click on the arrow beside the Style box to display a menu of all the styles you defined or modified as well as commonly used built-in styles. Remember, paragraph styles appear in bold text while character styles appear in plain text. Choose a style from the menu to apply it to selected text.
- Click on the Style box or press [⌘] [Shift] [S] to activate it. Then type in the name of the style you want to apply and press [Return] or [Enter].

IMPORTANT NOTE

Be careful when entering the name of the style you want to apply. If you enter a name that does not exist, you'll wind up defining a brand new style exactly like the style currently applied to the text! I'll tell you how to delete styles a little later in this chapter.

Applying with the Style Dialog Box

You can also use the Style dialog box to apply a style. Choose Style from the Format menu. Find the style you want to apply in the Styles list. If the style is not displayed, use the List pop-up menu to change the display. Click on the name of the style in the list to select it and click Apply or press [Return] or [Enter] to apply it.

TIP/TRICK

Although this may take a bit longer than using the Style box on the Formatting Toolbar, there is the added benefit of seeing a preview of the style in the two Preview windows before actually applying it.

Applying with Shortcut Keys

As usual, Word offers a number of shortcut keys you can use to get the job done. Here's a list to get you started:

Activate Toolbar Style box (or Open Style dialog box)	[⌘] [Shift] [S]
Apply Normal style	[⌘] [Shift] [N]
Apply Heading 1 style	[⌘] [Option] [1]
Apply Heading 2 style	[⌘] [Option] [2]
Apply Heading 3 style	[⌘] [Option] [3]
Apply List Bullet style	[⌘] [Shift] [L]

In Chapter 24, I'll tell you how to create shortcut keys to apply any style you like.

Try This! Applying Styles Four Ways

Here's your chance to apply the styles you created earlier in this chapter using all the methods previously discussed.

1. In a Word document, press [Return] to start a new paragraph.
2. Choose Main Heading from the Style menu on the Formatting Toolbar. Now type a few words of text and notice how they are formatted.
3. Press [Return] again and type some more text. If you carefully followed the instructions I provided when you created the Main Heading style, this second line should appear in the Normal style since that was specified under Style for Following Paragraph.
4. While the insertion point is in the same paragraph, click on the Style box or press [⌘][Shift][S] to make it active. Then type the name of one of Word's built-in styles: **<u>Heading 1.</u>** Press [Return] or [Enter] to accept the name. The text changes to the Heading 1 style, which is bold, 14 point Helvetica.
5. Press [⌘][Shift][N] to use a shortcut key to reapply the Normal style to the paragraph the insertion point is in. Try some of the other shortcut keys if you like.

Other Ways to Apply Styles

Here are a few other ways to apply styles:

TIP/TRICK

- To apply a style more than once, use the Repeat command or its shortcut key, [⌘][Y]. I discussed this in Chapter 2.
- To apply a style used elsewhere in your document, use the Format Painter button or the Copy and Paste formats feature. I discussed this in Chapters 5 and 6.

- To apply heading styles, use Outline view and buttons on the Outline Toolbar. I'll discuss this in Chapter 15.
- To change one style to another throughout your document, use the Replace command. I'll discuss this in Chapter 16.

Removing Applied Styles

When you remove an applied style, you tell Word to return the text to the default style.

- To remove an applied character style, begin by selecting the text that has the character style applied to it. Then apply the Default Paragraph Font style using one of the methods discussed previously or by pressing [⌘][Shift]Z.
- To remove an applied paragraph style, begin by positioning the insertion point in the paragraph that has the style applied to it or by selecting all or part of multiple paragraphs that have the style applied to it. Then apply the Normal style, using one of the methods previously discussed or by pressing [⌘][Shift][N].

Modifying, Renaming, and Deleting Styles

Once a style has been defined, it's not engraved in stone. You can change it any time. You can add or remove formatting, change the style name, or delete it entirely. You can do any of this with the styles you create or the styles that are built into Word. I'll tell you how in this section.

Modifying with the Formatting Toolbar

Just as you can define a style with the Style box on the Formatting Toolbar, you can also modify an existing style. To do this, first modify an example of the style and then tell Word that the modified example has the style's definition.

Begin by selecting text that has the style you want to change. It can be a character style or a paragraph style. Make sure the style name appears in the Style box on the Formatting Toolbar. Then make whatever formatting changes you want to the selected text using Toolbar buttons or formatting dialog boxes. When you've finished making changes, click the name of the style in the Style box on the Formatting Toolbar and press [Return] or [Enter].

The Reapply Style dialog box, which is illustrated below, appears.

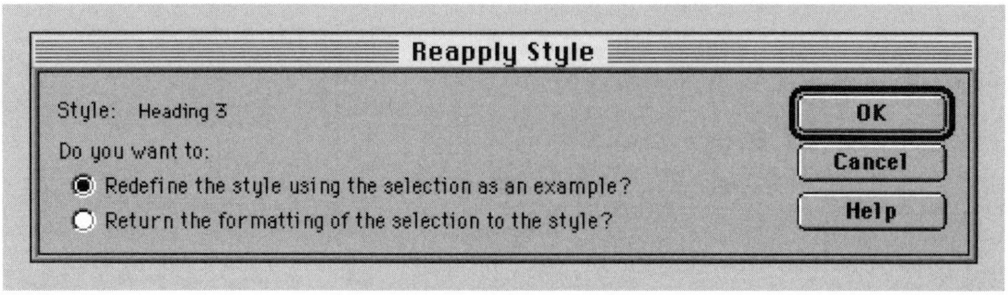

Make sure the radio button: *Redefine the style using the selection as an example?* is chosen and then click OK or press Return or Enter to change the style definition. If you change your mind and want to reapply the style as it already exists to the selection, click the radio button: *Return the formatting of the selection to the style?* and click OK.

Modifying with the Style Dialog Box

The Style dialog box includes a Modify button you can use to modify an existing style. Find the name of the style you want to modify in the Styles scrolling list. If the style you want to modify does not appear in the list, use the List pop-up menu beneath it to change what the list includes. Click the name of the style to select it, and then click Modify. The Modify Style dialog box that appears looks and works exactly like the New Style dialog box I discussed earlier in this chapter. Use its pop-up menus and buttons to change the format of the style you selected. When you've finished making changes, click OK to return to the Styles dialog box.

IMPORTANT NOTE

You cannot use the Modify button to change the definition of the Default Paragraph Font character style. You must use the Default button in the Font dialog box, which I discussed back in Chapter 5.

Renaming with the Style Dialog Box

You can also use the Modify button in the Style dialog box to rename a style. Click the style you want to rename in the Styles Scrolling list. Then click the Modify button. Type a new name into the Name edit box of the Modify Style dialog box. Click OK to accept the name change and return to the Style dialog box.

You cannot rename any of Word's built-in styles, although you can give them aliases, as discussed below.

Creating an Alias with the Style Dialog Box

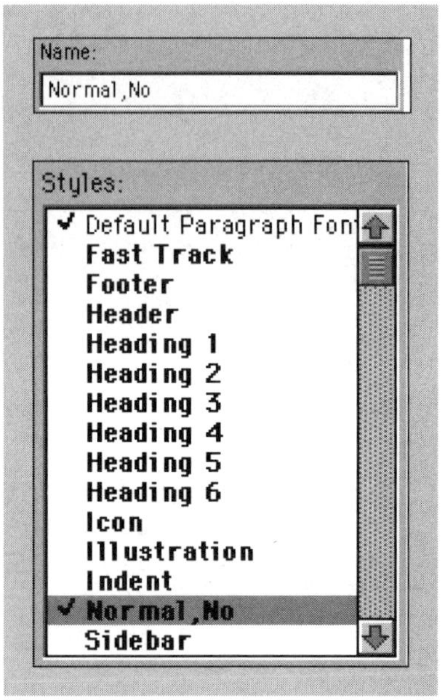

TIP/TRICK

You can also use the Modify button to create an *alias* of a style name. An alias is usually a shorter name that's quick to type into the Style box on the Formatting toolbar when you want to apply a style. In the Modify Style dialog box, enter a comma and a new name after the style name in the Name edit box.

Click OK to accept the alias and return to the Style dialog box. The style name appears in the Styles scrolling list, followed by its alias.

Deleting with the Style Dialog Box

You can also delete a style if you decide you don't need or want it. When you delete a paragraph style, any text that has that style applied to it reverts to Normal style. When you delete a character style, any text that has that style applied to it loses the font formatting of that style.

To delete a style, use the Delete button in the Styles dialog box. (Makes sense, doesn't it?) Click on the name of the style you want to delete in the Styles scrolling list to select it. Then click Delete. A confirmation dialog box appears. Click Yes to delete the style.

IMPORTANT NOTE

Some, but not all, of Word's built-in styles may be deleted this way. If you click a style name in the Styles scrolling list and the Delete button is gray, that style cannot be deleted.

Chapter Summary

In this chapter, you learned about formatting text with paragraph and character styles. You learned to define, apply, modify, rename, and delete styles using a variety of methods: the Style dialog box, the Style box on the Formatting toolbar, and shortcut keys. In Chapter 9, you'll continue this discussion of styles by learning about Word's new AutoFormat feature.

In the next chapter, you'll explore formatting on a larger scale: document sections and entire documents. Among other things, you'll learn how to divide your document into multiple sections, insert page breaks, adjust margins, and work with newsletter-like columns. You'll also get a chance to work with another handy view of your document: Page Layout view.

8

Chapter 8: Section and Document Formatting

SO FAR, YOU'VE LEARNED TO FORMAT THE INDIVIDUAL characters, words, and paragraphs that form the building blocks of your documents. In this chapter, you'll step back and look at the big picture: the individual pages of your document. You'll start by learning about sections and how you can use them to have multiple paper sizes, orientation, and margins (among other things) throughout your documents. Then you'll learn how to set up document pages. You'll see the options available in Word's new Document Layout dialog box, as well as the standard Page Setup dialog box. You'll learn to insert page, column, and section breaks and exactly what each of these things can do for you. Finally, you'll create and format newspaper-style columns within your documents.

If you'd like to follow along and try all these things on your Macintosh, prepare yourself by opening a Word document that's at least two pages long. You'll give that document a real workout by the time you finish this chapter.

About Sections — Read This First!

NEW IN WORD 6

Each Word document can be divided into multiple *sections*. While this isn't new in Word version 6, the ability to apply certain document formatting to less than the whole document is a new feature. You can now have different paper sizes, orientations, and margins for different pages within the same document. This is something my Word students have been asking about for years.

Multiple Orientations in One Document

Here's how it works. Say you've got a report that includes a very wide table. To best fit the table on a page, you decide to print it sideways on the page using Landscape orientation. But you don't want your entire document to be printed that way — just the one page containing the table.

With Word version 6, this is easy to do. Begin by typing the report up to the point where you want to create the table. Position the insertion point where you want the table to begin. Then use the Page Setup dialog box to change the orientation to landscape. I'll show you the Page Setup dialog box and explain orientation later in this chapter. What's important right now is that you notice the Apply Size and Orientation To pop-up menu, which is illustrated here.

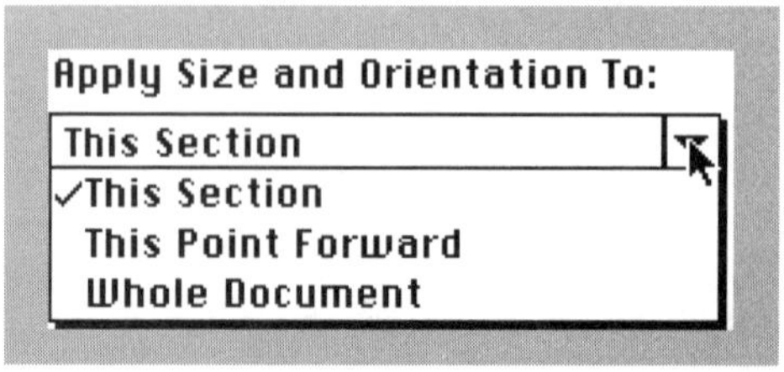

This pop-up menu lets you tell Word whether to apply the changes in the dialog box to the Whole Document, This Point Forward, or This Section. (If text is selected when you open the dialog box, you'll get the option

Selected Text rather than This Point Forward.) In the wide table example, you'd choose This Point Forward and click OK or press Return or Enter to accept the settings. Word inserts a section break at the insertion point like the one in the following illustration. In Normal view, it stretches right across the page; in Page Layout view, it appears at the end of the previous line.

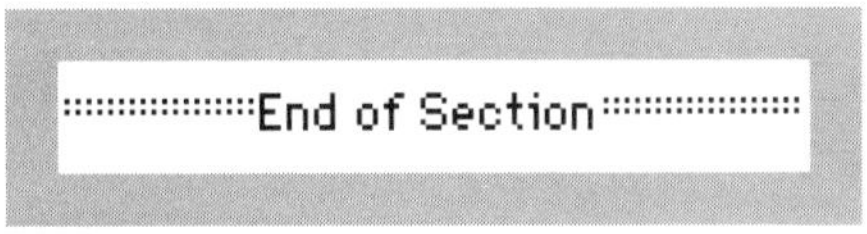

What does this mean? It means your document now has two sections. The first section contains the pages of the report up to the section break Word inserted. The second section contains a single blank page in Landscape orientation. You can confirm this by looking at the document in Print Preview, which I discussed in Chapter 4. Simply choose Print Preview from the File menu and then use the Multiple Pages button to view several pages of your document at once. You might see something like this:

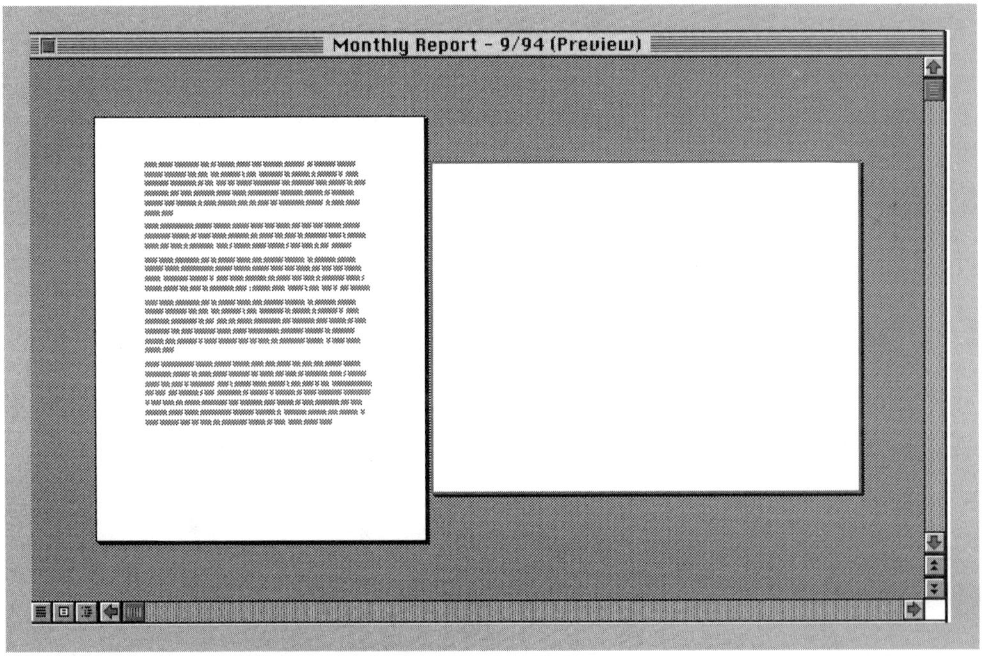

At this point, you'd go back to Normal or Page Layout view and create and format the wide table. When you're finished and want to complete the remaining pages of the document, just use the Page Setup dialog box again to begin a new section with portrait orientation.

This technique works for the Paper size and Orientation options in the Page Setup dialog box and all options in the Document Layout dialog box. (You'll find that the Document Layout dialog box, which I'll show you later in this chapter, includes an Apply To pop-up menu that works exactly like the Apply Size and Orientation To pop-up menu in the Page Setup dialog box.) This gives you complete control over these options for every single page of your document!

Determining What Part of the Document is Formatted

The key to working with the options in the Page Setup and Document Layout dialog boxes is selecting the correct part of your document before you open the dialog box to make a change. Here are the rules. **Read them carefully** to understand how this works, since they'll come into play whenever you use the Page Setup or Document Layout dialog box.

Formatting the Entire Document

TIP/TRICK

To format the entire document, it doesn't matter where your insertion point is or what's selected when you open the Page Setup or Document Layout dialog box. What's vital is that you select Whole Document from the Apply To pop-up menu before you click OK to accept the changes. Then, no matter how many sections your document has, all will receive the formatting changes you make.

If you're planning to create a multi-section document and most sections will have Page Setup or Document Layout options that differ from Word's defaults, format the entire document first and then make adjustments to the individual sections as you create them. This can prevent a lot of repetitive formatting.

Formatting from the Insertion Point to the End of the Document

To format from the insertion point to the end of the document, position the insertion point where you want the new formatting to begin. Then use the Page Setup or Document Layout dialog box to make the change. Be sure to select This Point Forward from the Apply To pop-up menu before clicking OK to accept the changes. Word inserts a section break to create a new section. This is just like the wide table example I used above.

Formatting One or More Paragraphs

To add document formatting to one or more paragraphs of a document, first select the paragraph(s) you want to change. Then use the Page Setup or Document Layout dialog box to make the change. Be sure to select This Selection from the Apply To pop-up menu before clicking OK to accept the changes. Word inserts a section break before and after the selection to create two new sections: the section containing the selection and the section after it.

Formatting One Section

To format one section of your document, position the insertion point anywhere within that section — that means *after* the section break that begins the section but *before* the section break that ends the section. Then use the Page Setup or Document Layout dialog box to make the change. Be sure to select This Section from the Apply To pop-up menu before clicking OK to accept the changes.

Formatting Multiple Sections

To format multiple sections of your document, begin by positioning the insertion point anywhere within the first section you want to change. Use the Page Setup or Document Layout dialog box to make the change. Be sure to select This Section from the Apply To pop-up menu before clicking OK to accept the changes. Then position the insertion point anywhere within the next section you want to change. Choose Repeat (the second command) from the Edit menu or press [⌘][Y]. Do this for each of the sections you want to change.

Creating Sections with Section Breaks

As mentioned earlier, Word creates section breaks automatically when you choose This Point On or This Selection in the Apply To pop-up menu of the Page Setup or Document Layout dialog boxes. You can create sections yourself by inserting section breaks. Here's how.

Using the Break Dialog Box

To insert a section break, begin by positioning the insertion point where you want the break to occur. Then choose Break from the Insert menu. The Break dialog box, shown here, appears. It offers four section break options.

(I'll tell you about the other options later in this chapter.) Click the appropriate radio button to select the one you want and then click OK to insert the section break.

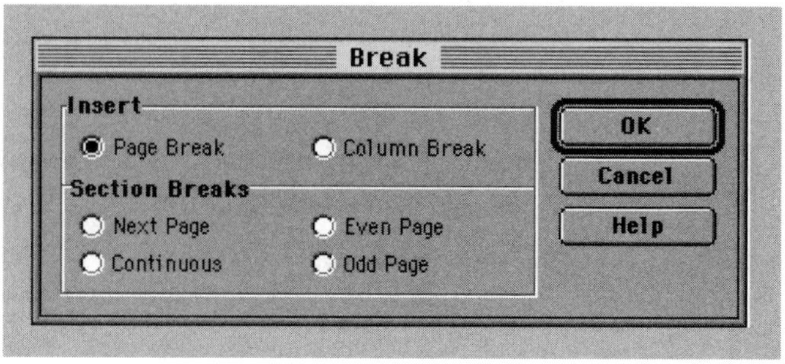

- **Next Page** — inserts a section break and starts the new section on a new page.
- **Continuous** — inserts a section break and continues the new section right after the previous one, without starting a new page.
- **Even Page** — inserts a section break and forces the new section to begin on an even numbered page.
- **Odd Page** — inserts a section break and forces the new section to begin on an odd numbered page.

IMPORTANT NOTE

Even Page and Odd Page may cause pages to be skipped. For example, if you insert an Even Page section break on an even page of a document, Word leaves the odd numbered page that would have come next blank to give you the even numbered page you want.

Using a Shortcut Key

To insert a section break without dealing with the Break dialog box, try ⌘ Enter. (Make sure you use the Enter key on the numeric keypad, not the Return key!) When you use this shortcut key, Word inserts a section break with the same formatting as the section the insertion point was in when you used it.

Deleting a Section Break

A section break is a character. To delete it, simply double-click it to select it and press Delete. It disappears.

IMPORTANT NOTE

When you delete a section break, two sections become one because there is no longer a break between them. Both sections wind up with the section formatting of the section after the break you deleted. This includes paper size, orientation, margins, line numbering — any change you made to the section with the Page Setup or Document Layout dialog boxes.

Setting Up Document Pages

Margins and page size are possibly the two most important page-related pieces of information a word processor needs in order to format a document. Header and footer positions, gutter widths, line numbering options, and vertical alignment are others. Word lets you specify values for each of these options, either before you begin entering text into a new document or later, when the document is halfway or even completely done. That's what the Document Layout and Page Setup dialog boxes are for. In this section, I'll show you how to set up your document pages using these two dialog boxes and Page Layout view.

FYI: Word's Document Layout Defaults

Word includes default settings for document layout options. That means when you create a new document, certain values are always used unless you change them. You may find that these default values meet your needs for most documents. If that's the case, you might not need to change your document layout or page setup for most of the documents you create.

Here's a list of the more common default values:

Top and Bottom Margins	At least 1 inch
Left and Right Margins	1.25 inch
Header and Footer Position	0.5 inch from edge of paper
Gutter	0 inch
Mirror Margins	Off
Vertical Alignment	Top
Line Numbers	Off
Suppress Endnotes	Off
Orientation	Portrait
Paper Size	US Letter

Continued

You can change these defaults using the Document Layout or Page Setup dialog boxes. I'll tell you more about these default settings and how you can change them later in this chapter.

Setting Paper Size and Orientation with the Page Setup Dialog Box

The Page Setup dialog box lets you set options that affect the way your document prints. The way it appears and the options it offers depends on the printer that's selected in Apple's Chooser and whether you're using System 7.5's QuickDraw GX. I discussed the Chooser and QuickDraw GX in Chapter 4.

IMPORTANT NOTE

If you're using System 7.5 with QuickDraw GX, the Document Layout and Page Setup dialog boxes look and work a bit differently. Read this section for general information about Page Setup options. Then be sure to read "Setting Paper Size and Orientation with QuickDraw GX" near the end of this section for information specific to your system.

The Page Setup dialog box for an Apple LaserWriter is shown here. To access this dialog box, choose Page Setup from the File menu.

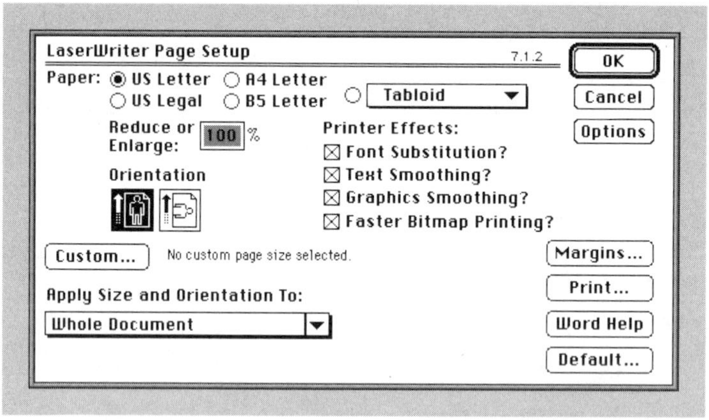

Two options will always be offered: Paper and Orientation. I'll discuss them here. For other printer-specific options like Reduce or Enlarge, Printer Effects, and Options, consult the manual that came with your printer or your Macintosh Owner's Guide.

Setting the Paper Size

The paper size is part of what determines how much text can fit on a page. The default paper size is US Letter, which measures 8.5 by 11 inches. Many printers can accept other paper sizes as well.

No matter how the dialog box looks for your printer, chances are, the Paper option will be at the very top. Use radio buttons to select from among the paper sizes your printer supports. Some common options include US Legal (8.5 by 14 inches) and Tabloid (11 by 17 inches). A4 and B5 are two European paper sizes. The pop-up menu under Tabloid in the illustration above offers even more options, including envelopes. I'll tell you how to print envelopes in Chapter 19.

Specifying a Custom Page Size

NEW IN WORD 6

Although Word has supported custom paper sizes for some time now, Word version 6 added a Custom button to the Page Setup dialog box to make it easy to specify a custom paper size. Click this button to display the Custom Paper Size dialog box.

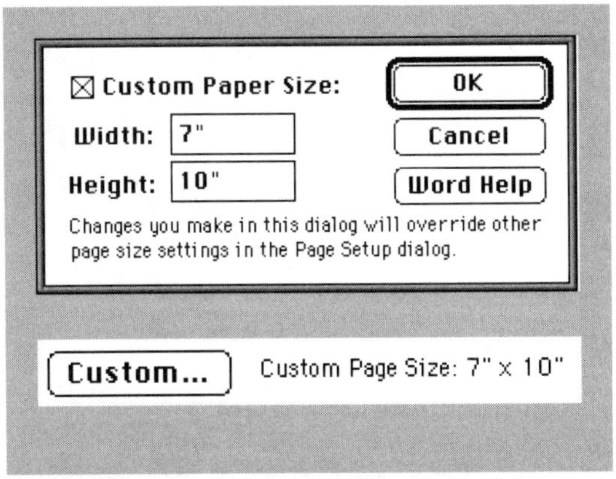

Turn on the check box beside Custom Paper Size to tell Word to override any other page size setting in the Page Setup dialog box. Then enter the Width and Height of the custom paper you want to use. Click OK to accept your settings. You'll see the custom page size indicated in the Page Setup dialog box beside the Custom button.

To go back to a standard paper size, click the Custom button in the Page Setup dialog box and turn off the check box beside Custom Paper Size. Then click OK.

Setting the Orientation

Orientation refers to the direction the page will print. The options are Portrait and Landscape. In Portrait orientation the paper is held lengthwise while in Landscape orientation, the paper is held sideways. The Macintosh System software illustrates these options with standard icons. I like to think of them as "the standing man" (Portrait) and "the sleeping man" (Landscape).

Setting Paper Size and Orientation with QuickDraw GX

If you're using System 7.5 with QuickDraw GX, you can set orientation and paper size in the Paper Size tab of the Document Layout dialog box. Choose Document Layout from the File menu. If necessary, click the Paper Size tab to display its options. This tab is not available unless you're using System 7.5 with QuickDraw GX.

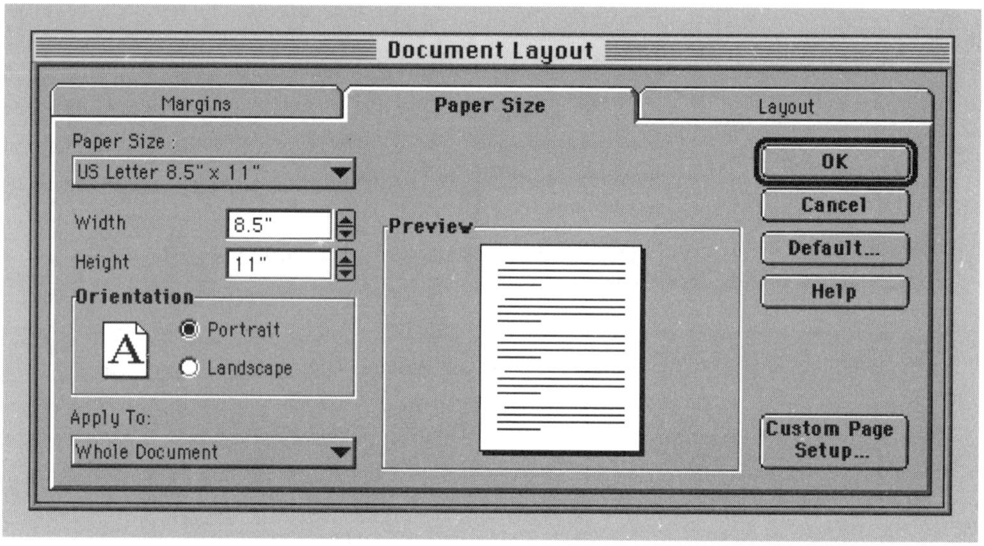

- **Paper Size** — use this pop-up menu to select a paper size from among standard options. If you choose Custom, you can enter the paper's Width and Height in the edit boxes below the pop-up menu.
- **Orientation** — click the appropriate radio button for Portrait or Landscape.

- **Apply To —** use this pop-up menu to tell Word what it should apply the paper size and orientation to. This works just like the Apply Size and Orientation To pop-up menu in the Page Setup dialog box, which I discussed earlier.

As you make changes, the Preview area of the dialog box changes accordingly. Click OK to accept your changes.

FYI: How Page Size and Orientation Affects Page Width and Margins

The paper size and orientation options you specify in the Page Setup dialog box will change the page width and margins. For example, you'll be able to fit less across a page if it is set for Portrait orientation than if it is set for Landscape orientation. That's because the page is wider when in Landscape orientation. If you doubt my words, hold a piece of paper sideways and see for yourself.

What you might not realize, however, is that Word's default right and left margins of 1.25 inches become the top and bottom margins when the page is set for Landscape. Why is that? Beats me. But you can always adjust them — I'll tell you how next.

Setting Margins with the Document Layout Dialog Box

A margin is the distance from the edge of the paper to the main printing area in the document. I showed you how to change margins in Print Preview back in Chapter 4, and I'll show you how to change them in Page Layout view a little later in this chapter. For now, let's look at how you can change Margins with the Document Layout dialog box.

NEW IN WORD 6

The Document Layout dialog box in Word version 6 replaces the Document and Section dialog boxes in previous versions of Word. Not only does this dialog box combine old features of Word in one place, but it adds brand new features. You'll learn about them throughout this chapter. To open the

Document Layout dialog box, choose Document Layout from the File menu or double-click on the ruler anywhere except on a tab marker.

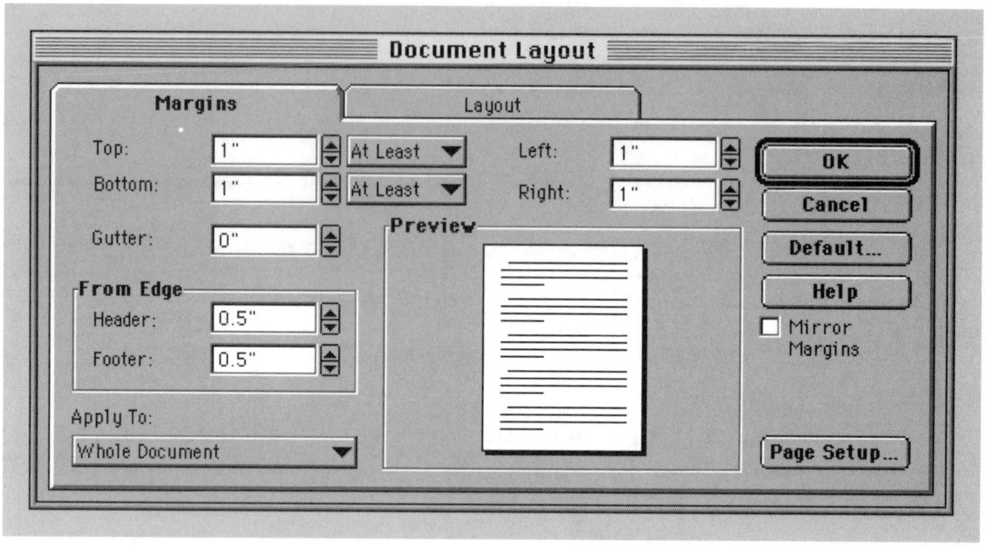

The Document Layout dialog box has two tabs (unless you're running System 7.5 with QuickDraw GX, discussed earlier): Margins and Layout. Make sure Margins is selected so the dialog box looks like the one illustrated here. If you've worked with previous versions of Word, you may recognize many of these options from the old Document dialog box.

Setting Margin Measurements

Use the four margin measurement edit boxes to enter measurements for the top, bottom, left, and right margins. Inches is the normal measurement unit for these boxes. If you don't want to enter an amount, you can use the tiny arrows beside each box to change the value already in there.

NEW IN WORD 6

The two pop-up menus beside the Top and Bottom edit boxes give you two options for those measurements:

- **At Least —** sets the margin so that it can change if it has to. For example, if your document includes a multiple-line header, the header may end below the measurement you set for the top margin. By using the At Least setting, you prevent the header and text at the top of the document page from printing in the same area, thus overwriting each other. I'll tell you more about headers and footers later in this chapter and in Chapter 10.

- **Exactly** — sets the margin at exactly the measurement you specify. This ensures that the margin never changes.

IMPORTANT NOTE

When entering measurements for the margins in a document, remember that the minimum margin size may be determined by your printer. As I discussed in Chapter 4, many laser printers cannot print very close to the edge of the paper. If you set your margins for less than the allowable amount, a dialog box may appear, telling you that one or more of your margins is too small. Click Fix to have Word automatically adjust the margin. Click Ignore to keep the margin as you set it. Keep in mind, however, that if you click Ignore, part of your document may get cut off.

Mirror Margins

Mirror Margins refers to the margins on facing pages, like the ones in a book. Rather than set a right and left margin, you can set an inside and outside margin. The result is that the pages seem to "mirror" each other — hence the name.

When you turn on the Mirror Margins check box, the first thing you may notice is that the Preview window, which normally shows only one page, displays two pages. At the same time, the Right and Left edit boxes change their names to Inside and Outside. If you enter different values in each box, the Preview window will give you a better idea of what Mirror Margins are all about, as illustrated here:

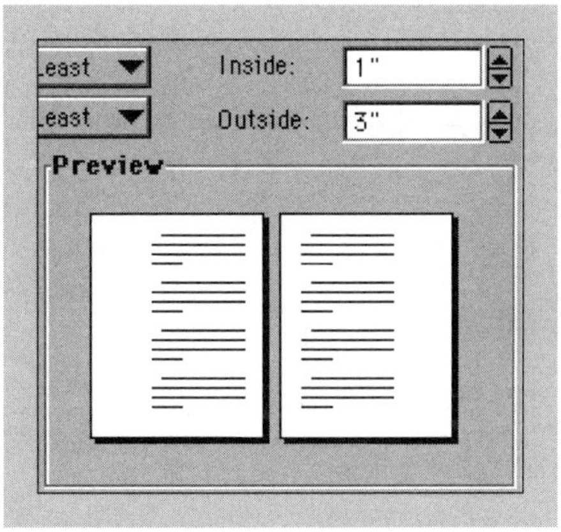

Gutter

When a book is bound, part of each page is lost. If information is printed too close to the binding, it simply cannot be read. A *gutter* is an area set aside for the binding

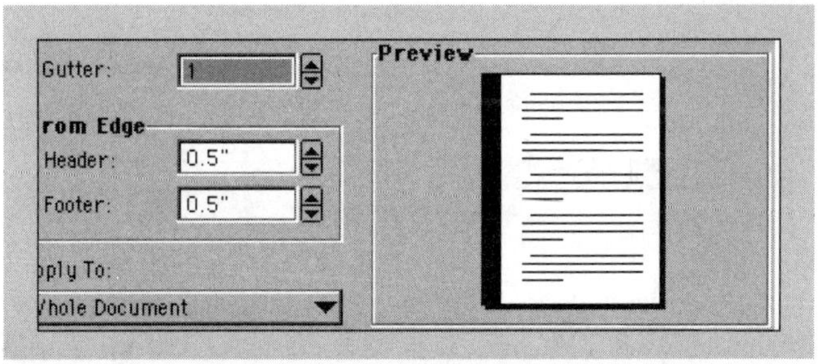

process. When you enter a measurement in the Gutter edit box, the Preview window displays a black bar corresponding to the gutter, as shown here.

If Mirror Margins is also turned on, the gutter is displayed in the Preview window in addition to the inside margin for both pages.

Setting Margins in Page Layout View

NEW IN WORD 6

If you prefer, you can set margins in Page Layout view. This is a new feature of Word version 6.

To switch to Page Layout view, either choose Page Layout from the View menu or click the Page Layout View button in the bottom left corner of the document window. Your view of the document changes to display it the way it will print. You see everything that will appear on the page, including headers and footers, which I'll discuss in detail in Chapter 10. Page numbers also appear. You'll learn about these later in this chapter. As you scroll, you can see the nonprinting area between the edge of the paper and the margin. You can also see a gray background that represents the area beyond the edge of the paper. The following illustration provides a good sample.

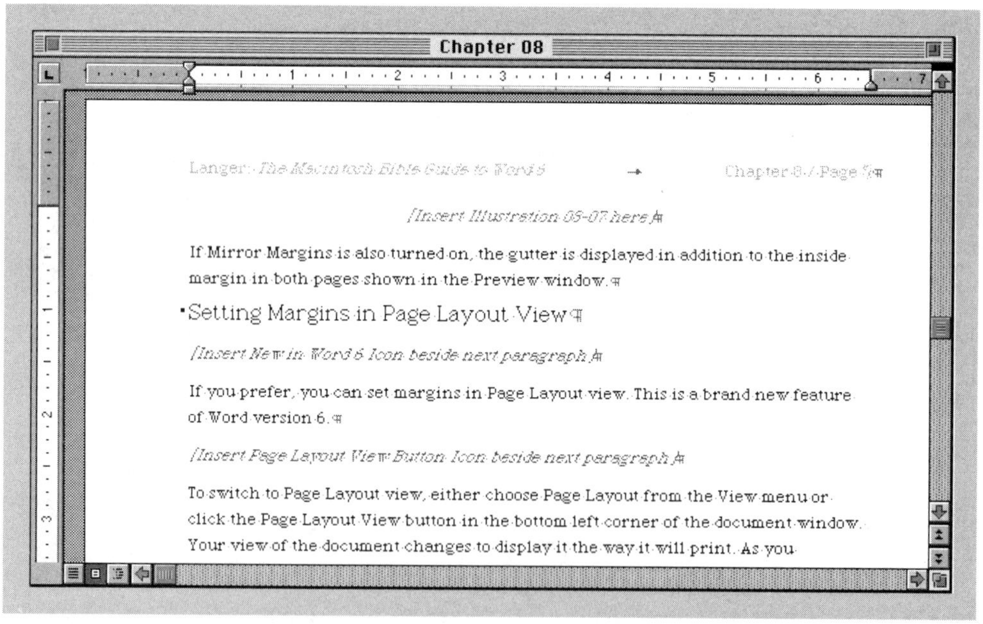

You can enter and edit text in Page Layout view. What you might notice, however, is that Word takes longer to scroll and change documents in Page

Layout view than it does in Normal view. Why? Because in order to display your document exactly the way it will print, page for page, Word needs to perform many more calculations than if it just displayed your document as one scrolling sheet. The more complex your document, the longer it takes. That's why Normal view is the best view for most of your work with Word.

Let's get back to changing margins. In Page Layout view, Word displays two rulers, a horizontal ruler and a vertical ruler. (If the rulers are not showing, choose Ruler from the View menu to display them.) The vertical ruler, which I mentioned briefly in Chapter 1, is new to Word version 6. You can use these rulers to change the margins for a page, just like you can in Print Preview, which I discussed in Chapter 4.

To change a margin in Page Layout view, drag the margin boundary — the line on the ruler between the gray nonprinting area and the white printing area — up or down (vertical ruler) or right or left (horizontal ruler). When you position your mouse pointer over the margin boundary, it turns into a two-headed arrow, as shown in the following illustration. As you drag, a dashed line moves along with your mouse and the ruler shifts. The zero mark, which never appears, is always the location of the top and left margins on the ruler. When you let go, Word repaginates the document and displays your pages with the new margins.

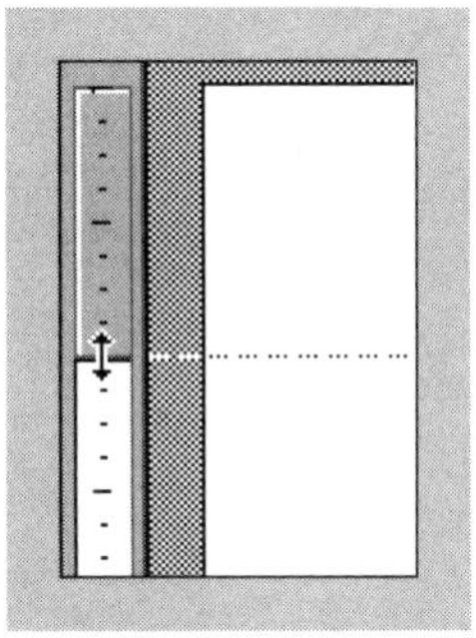

Setting Some Header and Footer Options

A header is text that appears at the top of each page. A footer is text that appears at the bottom of each page. I'll tell you more about headers and footers in Chapter 10. For now, I'll tell you about some header and footer options available in the Document Layout dialog box.

Header and Footer Locations

The Margins tab in the Document Layout dialog box has a From Edge section that lets you specify the position of the header and footer from the edge of the page. Enter values in the Header and Footer edit boxes or use the tiny arrows to change the values already there. Click OK to accept the changes.

Remember, not all printers can print right up to the edge of the page. Experiment to see what the minimum measurement is for your printer.

Different Headers or Footers

The Layout tab in the Document Layout dialog box, which is shown here, has a Headers and Footers section that offers two options you can use to set different headers and footers.

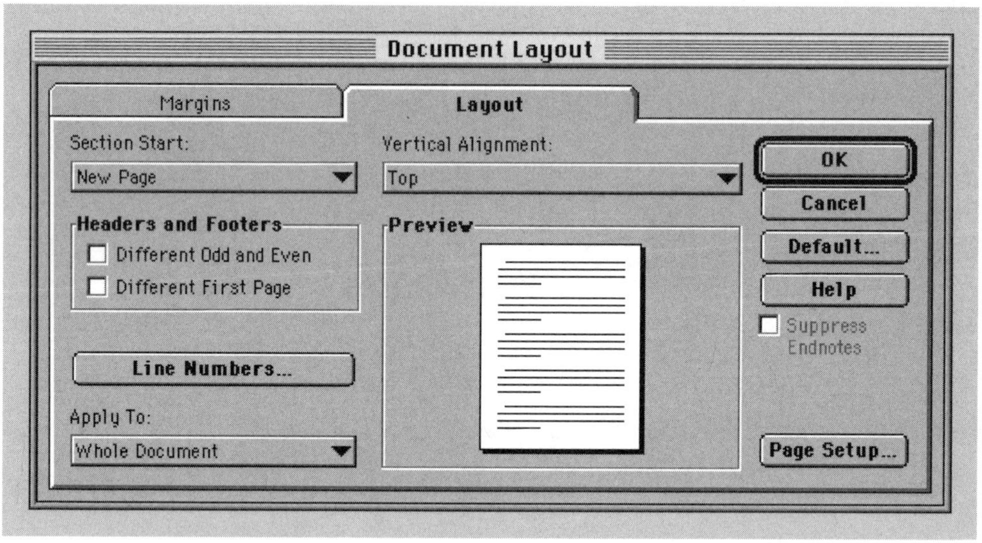

Odd and Even Headers and Footers

The Different Odd and Even check box makes it possible to create different headers and footers for odd and even pages. This is commonly used in bound documents, like books.

First Page Headers and Footers

The Different First Page check box tells Word that the first page of the document (or section) should have a different Header and Footer. When you turn this on, you can create a different header and footer for the first page — or leave the first page headers and footers blank.

Numbering Lines

One of Word's document formatting options is the ability to number lines in a document. Line numbers appear in the left margin of text or between columns in a multi-column section. I've personally never had a use for this feature, but folks who work with legal documents and the like might use it daily. I'll take a moment to discuss it here.

Adding Line Numbers

To number lines in your document or a section of your document, choose Document Layout from the File to open the Document Layout dialog box. Click the Layout tab to display its options. Then click the Line Numbers button. The Line Numbers dialog box, which is illustrated here, appears.

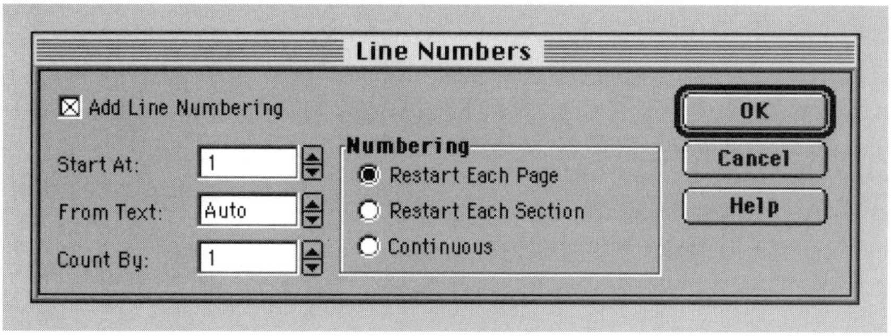

To turn on line numbering for the document or section, turn on the Add Line Numbering check box. All options become active. You can then enter values and make selections.

- **Start At** — This edit box lets you enter a starting number for the lines of your document.
- **From Text** — This edit box lets you specify the distance between the line numbers and the text. If you leave it set to Auto, Word uses 0.25 inch for single-column text and 0.13 inch for multi-column text.

IMPORTANT NOTE

Be sure the value you enter in the From Text edit box does not exceed the width of the margins or cause numbers to be printed in the area your printer cannot print in. If you want to increase the distance between the text and the line numbers, you should consider increasing the left margin of your document.

- **Count By** — This edit box lets you specify which lines should be numbered. For example, if you want every tenth line numbered, enter a 10 in this edit box.
- **Numbering** — These radio buttons let you tell Word how to number the document. They're pretty self-explanatory.

When you're finished setting options in the Line Numbers dialog box, click OK to accept your settings. You'll be returned to the Document Layout dialog box, where you can use the Apply To pop-up menu to specify what part of the document should include line numbers. When you click OK in that dialog box, the line numbers will appear. They may look something like this:

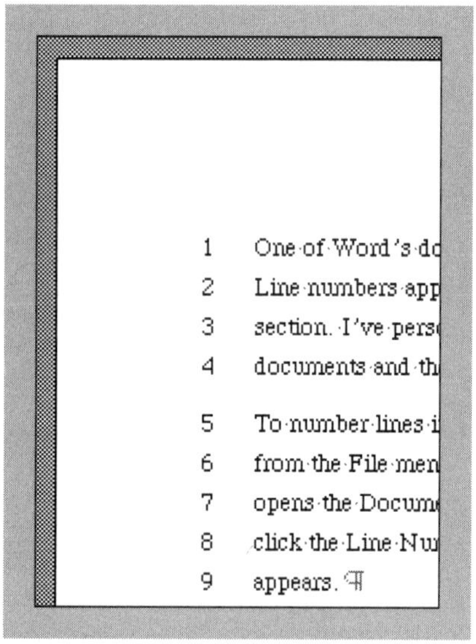

Line numbers appear only in Page Layout view or Print Preview — they do not appear in Normal view. To see line numbers, choose Page Layout view from the View menu or click the Page Layout View button in the bottom left corner of the document window.

TIP/TRICK

If you don't like the way the line numbers look, you can change their appearance by modifying the Line Number style, one of Word's built-in styles. I discussed modifying styles in Chapter 7.

Excluding Paragraphs from Line Numbering

You can use the Paragraph dialog box to exclude paragraphs from automatic line numbering. I mentioned this back in Chapter 6. First select the paragraph(s) you don't want to number. Choose Paragraph from the Format menu. Click the Text Flow tab to display its options. Then turn on the check box beside Suppress Line Numbers. Click OK to accept the change.

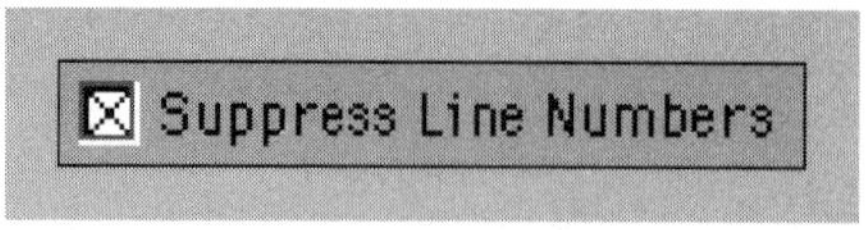

Word skips the entire paragraph(s) when it numbers the lines. If you've got nonprinting characters displayed, you'll see a little black box beside the beginning of the paragraph to indicate that it has special formatting.

Removing Line Numbers

To remove line numbers from your document or a section of it, choose Document Layout from the File menu. Click the Layout tab to display its options and click the Line Numbers button. Turn off the check box beside Add Line Numbers. Click OK to accept the change. When you click OK in the Document Layout dialog box, the line numbers disappear.

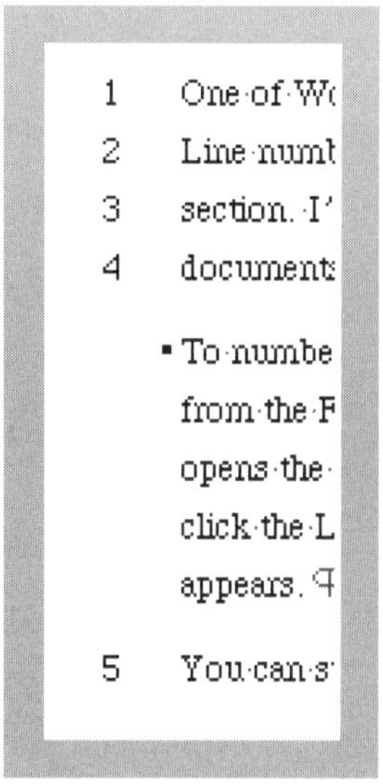

Numbering Pages

Word offers two ways to number pages. One, which I personally prefer, uses headers or footers, which I'll discuss in Chapter 10. The other uses the Page Numbers command. I'll tell you about that now. To number pages, choose Page Numbers from the Insert menu.

FYI: About Page Numbers

Although Word offers two ways to put page numbers in your documents, both methods put the page number in the header or footer of your document. This means you cannot see the page number unless you are in Page Layout view or Print Preview or have used the Header and Footer command.

There's also a difference in the way the page number is inserted with each method. When you use the Page Numbers command, the page number is enclosed in a *frame.* A frame is an object that can be resized, formatted, and positioned anywhere on the page by dragging it or using the Frame command. I'll tell you about frames in Chapter 13. When you use the Header and Footer command to insert a page number, the page number is entered without a frame. Although this may limit where you can position the page number on the page, it also makes it easier to reformat or delete the page number. Regular font formatting buttons and commands apply. I'll tell you more about page numbers in headers and footers in Chapter 10.

NEW IN WORD 6

Continued

One more thing. When Word inserts a page number, it really inserts a PAGE field. Fields are new to Word version 6 — I'll discuss them more throughout the book. All you need to know right now is that Word substitutes the current page number for the PAGE field when it displays and prints the document. (It will not display the page number if you have Field Codes turned on in the View tab of the Options dialog box. I'll discuss the Options dialog box in Chapter 23.)

Setting Position and Alignment

The Page Numbers dialog box lets you set the position and alignment of the page numbers. A Preview window shows you where the page number will appear on the page, based on your selections from two pop-up menus. You can also tell Word whether a page number should appear on the first page of the document or section.

Position

The Position pop-up menu offers only two options: Top of Page (Header) or Bottom of Page (Footer). They're pretty straightforward.

Alignment

The Alignment pop-up menu offers five options:

- **Left, Center, Right —** place the page number in the left side, center, or right side of the header or footer. Makes sense to me.
- **Inside, Outside —** create facing pages with the page numbers in the inside or outside of the pages. When you choose one of these options, the Preview window displays two pages with the page number positioned just where you'd expect.

Show Number on First Page

The Show Number on First Page check box tells Word whether it should include the page number on the first page of the document or section. Turn this off if you don't want a page number on the first page.

Formatting Page Numbers

The Format button in the Page Numbers dialog box lets you set certain page number formatting options. Click it to display the Page Number Format dialog box, which is shown here:

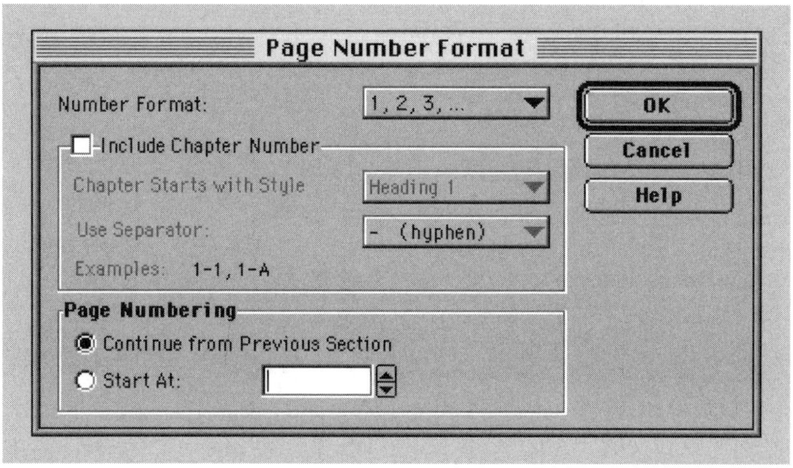

TIP/TRICK

To change the appearance of the page number, modify the Page Number style. I discussed modifying styles in Chapter 7.

Number Formats

The Number Format pop-up menu lets you select from among several common number formats, including alphabetical and Roman numerals. The pop-up menu displays examples of each one, making it easy to find just the one you want.

Including a Chapter Number

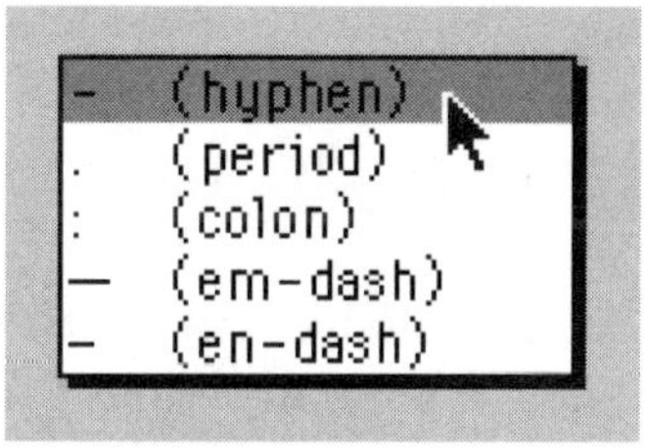

If you turn on the Include Chapter Number check box, the options immediately below it become active. Use this feature to have Word search one of the nine heading styles for a chapter number and include it as part of the page number. The Use Separator pop-up menu lets you choose a separator character to place between the Chapter number and page number. The menu displays the name of the separator, as well as the character itself, as shown above:

Specifying a Starting Page Number

Use the Page Numbering area of the dialog box to tell Word whether it should continue the page numbers from the previous section or start page numbering at a specific number. You can enter a page number by typing it in. If Continue from Previous Section is selected, and there is no previous section, Word begins numbering with page 1.

Removing Page Numbers

To remove a page number, you must open the header or footer it is in. In Page Layout view, simply double-click on the header or footer to make it active. Or, if you prefer, select Header and Footer from the View menu and, if necessary, click the Switch Between Header and Footer button to view page number. Then click on the page number to select it and press Delete to get rid of it. Once again, you'll learn lots more about headers and footers in Chapter 10.

IMPORTANT NOTE

The previously described technique will delete the page numbers in an entire section of your document (or the entire document, if there's only one section). Be sure to position the insertion point in or select the section(s) you want to remove page numbers from first. If you have set one or more sections to have a different first page header and footer (something I discussed earlier in this chapter), you must be sure to delete the page number from that page as well.

Reformatting a Section Start

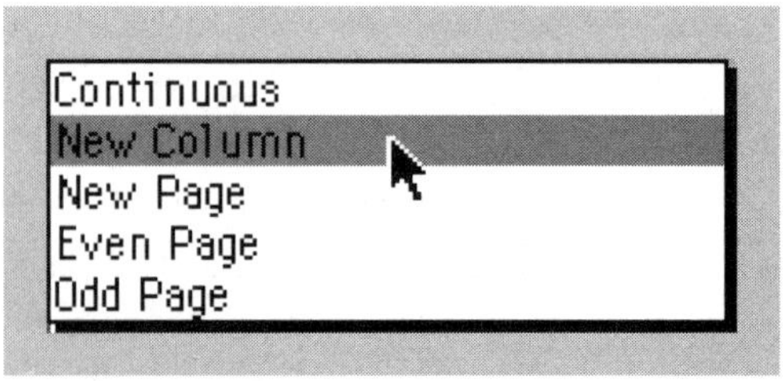

If you've already got a section break and you want to change it, position the insertion point in the section you want to change and choose Document Layout from the File menu. Click the Layout tab to display its options. Then choose one of the five options from the Section Start pop-up menu.

As you can see from the illustration, the options are just about the same as those offered in the Break dialog box. You'll learn about New Column later in this chapter.

Aligning Text Vertically

NEW IN WORD 6

Word version 6 added the ability to align text vertically on a page. This is especially handy if you have a short page of text and want to center or justify it on the page.

Choose Document Layout from the File menu. Click the Layout tab to display its options. Choose the kind of alignment you want from the Vertical Alignment pop-up menu:

- **Top —** the default vertical alignment, begins the text at the top of the page.
- **Center —** centers the page's text on the page.
- **Justified —** spreads the text vertically on the page, adding additional space between lines and paragraphs so the text fills the page. The first line on the page begins at the top margin and the last line on the page ends at the bottom margin.

The Preview window displays an illustration of the option you choose.

Changing Default Document Options

Both the Page Setup and Document Layout dialog boxes include Default buttons. If you find yourself changing options in either of these dialog boxes on a regular basis, you can use this button to make a permanent change to Word's default settings.

For example, say you don't like right and left margins set at 1.25 inches, Word's default value. (I don't know about you, but I prefer equal margins all around.) Open the Document Layout dialog box, click the Margins tab to display its options, and change the contents of the Right and Left edit boxes to the value you prefer. Then click the Default button. Word displays a confirmation dialog box that looks like this:

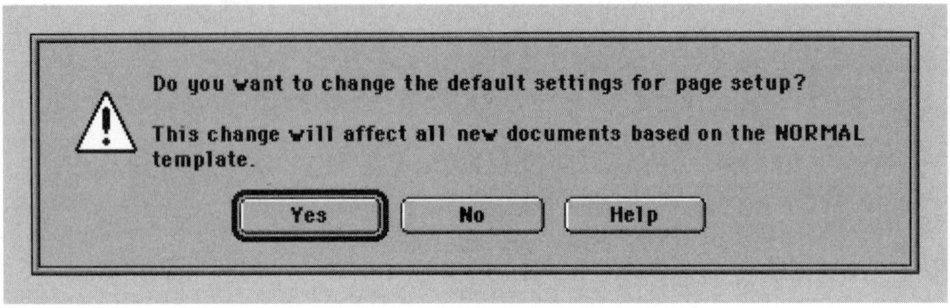

If you click Yes, the changes you made in the dialog box will become the defaults for all new documents based on the current template. If you click No, Word retains the default settings it has.

Inserting and Removing Manual Page Breaks

As you create a long document, at some point, a dotted line will appear across the screen in Normal view. In case you haven't guessed yet, that dotted line is an automatic or *soft* page break.

Often, Word will indicate an automatic page break in a place you don't want one. That isn't a problem. You can always insert a manual or *hard* page break which will override the automatic page break. Word will use your page break and repaginate the document from that point forward.

FYI: Where Automatic Page Breaks Come From

You may not realize it, but as you work with Word, typing and formatting text, Word is busy doing all kinds of calculations in the background. One of those calculations concerns determining where pages begin and end.

Continued

The amount of text that can fit on a page is determined by many factors. How large is the paper? How wide are the margins? What size is the text? What kind of spacing is there between lines and paragraphs? Are there graphics that take up additional space? If so, how much? Word is constantly evaluating these things as you work. The dotted line that represents an automatic page break in Normal view is the result of Word's evaluations and calculations. If you're working in Page Layout view, not only does Word have to indicate where one page ends and the next begins, but it must show you graphically by drawing the edge of the pages with the text in the right place — not to mention any headers or footers you may have set up. No wonder Page Layout view is a bit sluggish when compared to Normal view!

You may be able to speed up Word's operation by turning off background repagination in Normal, Outline, and Master Document views. You do this with the Options dialog box, which is discussed in Chapter 23.

TIP/TRICK

Inserting a Page Break with the Break Dialog Box

To insert a manual page break in your document, begin by positioning the insertion point where you want the break to occur. Then choose Break from the Insert menu. The Break dialog box, which I showed you much earlier in this chapter, appears. Make sure the Page Break radio button is selected and click OK to insert the break. A page break indicator like the one illustrated here stretches across the entire document window. If you are in Page Layout view, Word displays nothing on the page (except possibly your footer) after the page break.

Inserting a Page Break with a Shortcut Key

If you don't want to bother with the Break dialog box, use a shortcut key to insert a page break: Shift Enter. (Make sure you use the Enter key on the numeric keypad, not the Return key; it makes a difference here!)

Removing Page Breaks

A manual page break is a character. To delete the page break, simply double-click on the page break to select it and press Delete to get rid of it. It's as simple as that.

Tips for Working with Page Breaks

TIP/TRICK

Here are a few brief tips for working with manual page breaks:

- If you want to override an automatic page break, you must insert the manual page break somewhere *above* it. Otherwise, you'll just insert another page break after the automatic one.
- Don't try to force an automatic page break to occur where you want it by adding blank paragraphs above it. This messes up your document formatting and makes it look silly if you insert or delete text before it in the document.
- To prevent an automatic page break from occurring between a heading and its following text or between lines of a paragraph, use the Pagination options in the Text Flow tab of the Paragraph dialog box. I told you about them in Chapter 6.
- If you plan to use manual page breaks in your documents, insert them last, after you've already written and edited the text. If you add or remove large blocks of text after inserting manual page breaks, you may need to adjust the page breaks again before you print.
- Always use Print Preview to review your pages before printing. This can save time and paper by making sure your document is set up correctly before you print. I discussed Print Preview and printing in Chapter 4.

Working with Multiple Columns

NEW IN WORD 6

Word gives you the ability to set up newspaper-style columns within your document. Although this feature is not new to Word version 6, it has been improved to provide more flexibility over column widths and formatting.

FYI: Columns and Sections

Column formatting works on a section by section basis, just like the Page Setup and Document Layout options I've been telling you about throughout this chapter. In order to have three columns in part of your document, one column in another part of your document, and two columns in a third part of your document, each part must be a separate section.

I explained how to create multiple sections in your document near the beginning of this chapter. Go back and read up on it if you find yourself having trouble getting columns to work properly for you.

Viewing Columns

In Normal view, multiple column text looks like one long, narrow column of text along the left side of the document window. That's because Normal view does not display document pages as they print. Instead, it displays a document's column as a continuous stream of text. This makes Normal view somewhat awkward for working with multiple column text.

To see and work with multiple columns, switch to Page Layout view by clicking the Page Layout View button on the bottom left side of the document window or by choosing Page Layout from the View menu. The columns of text appear as they will print and you can still edit and format them.

Setting Columns with the Columns Dialog Box

NEW IN WORD 6

The Columns dialog box, which is new in Word version 6, lets you set the number of columns in a section, as well as much of the formatting for the columns. To open it, choose Columns from the Format menu. Make appropriate changes in the dialog box and then click OK to accept them.

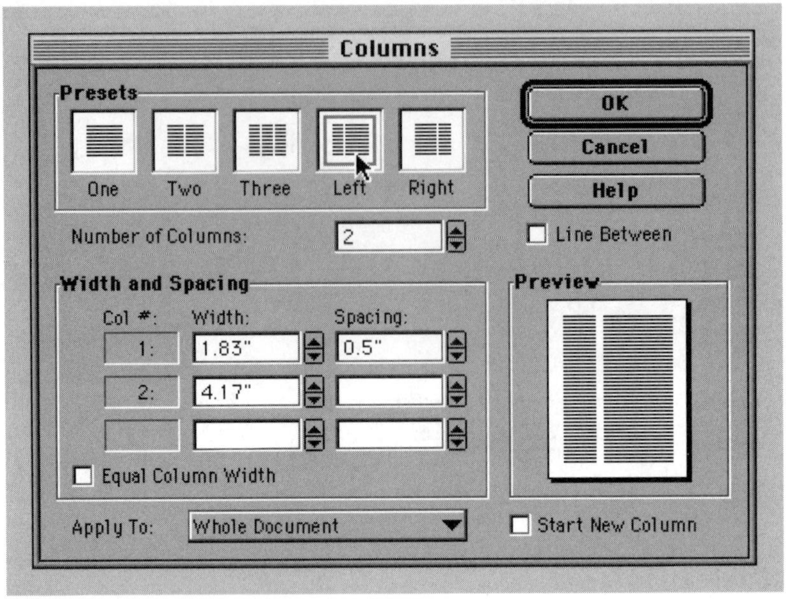

Using the Presets

The Presets section of the dialog box offers five common preset options. The first three — One, Two, and Three — create columns of equal width. The last two — Left and Right — create columns of unequal width. You can select any of these options by clicking on them. The Preview window changes to reflect your choice.

Creating Custom Columns

Of course, you don't have to use the presets if you don't want to. That's what the Number of Columns and the Width and Spacing options in the dialog box are for.

- **Number of Columns —** lets you specify — you guessed it — the number of columns. You can have up to 45 columns. (Why you'd want that many is beyond me.) Just remember that the more columns you have, the narrower the columns will be.
- **Width and Spacing —** lets you set the column width and spacing for up to the first three columns. Type values in the edit boxes or use the tiny arrows to change the values already there. If you turn the Equal Column Width check box on, all columns will be the same width.

Setting Columns with the Columns Button

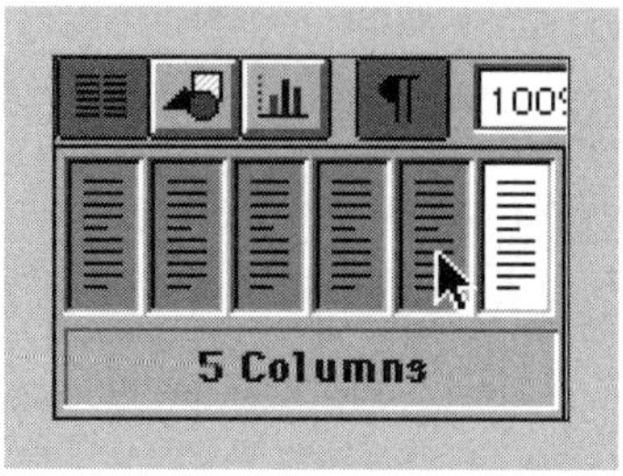

The Columns button on the Standard Toolbar gives you a quick way to set up to six columns of equal width. Press your mouse button down on it and a menu like the one in the following illustration pops out of it. Drag your mouse down and to the right to specify the number of columns. When you let go, the number of columns changes to what you specified.

Adjusting Column Width

NEW IN WORD 6

Once you've set multiple columns, you can change a column's width at any time. This is a new feature in Word version 6. Previous versions of Word could only vary column width by changing the spacing between columns, indent settings, and margin widths. Now Word offers two ways to adjust column width.

Using the Columns Dialog Box

As I showed you a moment ago, the Columns dialog box can be used to set the column widths for all columns of equal width or for up to three columns of unequal width. Choose Columns from the Format menu to change the settings for columns. Use the Width and Spacing area of the dialog box to specify exact measurements for column widths. When you click OK to accept your changes, the column widths change.

Dragging a Column's Boundary

A better way to change a column's widths is to simply drag the column marker on the Horizontal Ruler. The column marker is a gray bar between columns. To move one, put your mouse pointer on it. When your mouse pointer changes to a double-headed arrow, press your mouse button down and drag to the right or left. A vertical line appears, indicating the new column boundary, as shown in the following illustration. When you let go, the column width changes and the section reformats.

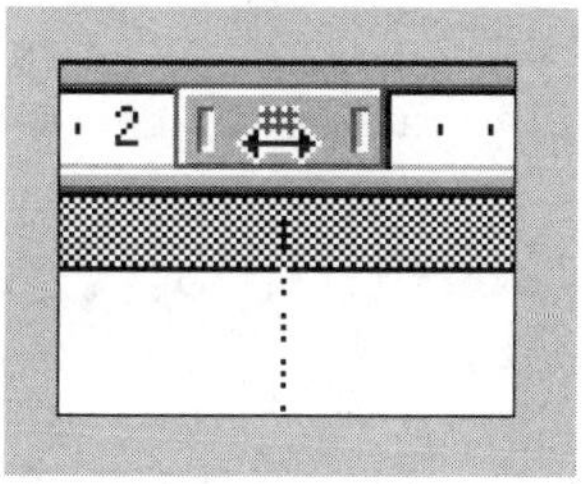

If columns are set to equal width, changing the width of one column this method changes all of them. If columns are set to be unequal width, you can set each column's width separately.

TIP/TRICK

You can use almost the same method to adjust the amount of space between each column. Use your mouse pointer to drag one end of the column marker to the right or left to make the marker wider or narrower. This increases or decreases the space between columns.

Creating Headlines

Newspapers rarely have the same number of columns throughout every page. Often, a headline spans two or more columns so it stands out on the page. Word version 6 makes this easy to do.

Start by selecting the headline, including the paragraph marker immediately after it. Position your mouse pointer over the columns button, press your mouse button down, drag down so 1 Column is selected, and then release the mouse button. Word inserts a section break before (if the headline is not at the beginning of the document) and after the headline, and formats the section containing the headline so that it spans the width of the page.

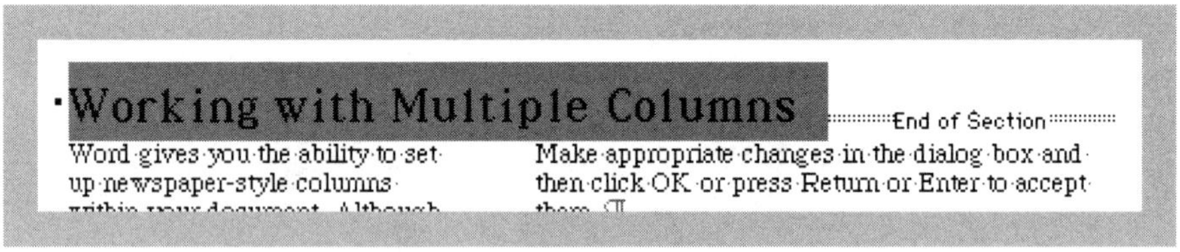

Adding a Line Between Columns

To have Word automatically place a vertical line between columns, use the Columns dialog box. Choose Columns from the Format menu and turn the Line Between Columns check box on. When you click OK to accept the settings, a line appears between columns. This can help make text in multiple columns a little easier to read.

Starting a New Column

Just as Word automatically calculates page breaks, it also automatically calculates column breaks. When a column is full, Word begins a new column.

NEW IN WORD 6

You can force text to start a new column by inserting a column break. Although column breaks are new to Word version 6, they have the same functionality as a section break formatted to start a new column — something that was available in previous versions of Word.

Position the insertion point where you want the new column to begin. Then choose Break from the Insert menu. The Break dialog box, which I showed you earlier in this chapter, appears. Click the radio button beside Column Break and click OK to insert the break. A column break, shown here, appears. Any text after the break will start in a new column.

TIP/TRICK

Here are a few tricks for starting new columns:

- If you don't want to use the Break dialog box, you can use a shortcut key to insert a new column: ⌘ Shift Return. (Make sure you use the Return key rather than the Enter key on the keypad. It makes a difference here.)
- Another way to force text to start a new column is to format a section break to start a new column. I discussed how to reformat section breaks earlier in this chapter. Use the Section Start pop-up menu on the Layout tab of the Document Layout dialog box.
- A column break can be deleted just like a section break or a page break. Simply double-click on it to select it and press Delete.

Balancing Columns

In a perfect world, when you create a multiple-column document, all columns of the document would be exactly the same length. As you've probably realized by now, we don't live in a perfect world. Columns will seldom balance out.

Fortunately, Word can handle the problem of unbalanced columns. To balance them out, put a section break at the bottom of the last column.

Position the insertion point at the very end of the last column and choose Break from the Insert menu. In the Break dialog box that appears, click the radio button beside Continuous. Then click OK to insert the break. The columns should balance.

Formatting Text and Paragraphs in Columns

Text displayed in multiple columns is no different than text displayed in a single column. You can use the same font and paragraph formatting techniques I showed you in Chapters 5 and 6. You can even use styles, which I discussed in Chapter 7.

TIP/TRICK

To prevent automatic column breaks from occurring between a heading and the text following it or between the lines of a paragraph, use the Pagination options available under the Text Flow tab in the Paragraph dialog box. I mentioned this earlier in this chapter and discussed it in detail in Chapter 6.

Chapter Summary

Whew! This chapter was certainly a long one. But it covered a lot of ground. You learned all about document and section formatting, including the options available in the Page Setup, Document Layout, and Columns dialog boxes. You learned how to separate your document into sections and how to format each section differently for incredible document formatting flexibility. You also learned how to insert page breaks and about one of the ways you can number pages. Finally you saw how to add and format newspaper-style columns using Word's new Columns dialog box and a bunch of related commands.

In the next chapter, you'll learn more about document templates, which I've been mentioning throughout the book. You'll learn what a template is, what it can do for you, and how you can create your own. You'll also see just how easy it is to format your documents with Word's new AutoFormat feature.

9

Chapter 9: Templates and Automatic Formatting

NEW IN WORD 6

AS MENTIONED BACK IN CHAPTER 2, EVERY WORD VERSION 6 document is based on a template file. When you choose New from the File menu, Word displays the New dialog box, which lets you create a document based on any template in the default templates folder. When you create a document with the New button on the Standard toolbar or the ⌘N shortcut key, Word creates a new document based on the Normal template.

In this chapter, you'll learn all about template files: what they are, what they can do for you, how you can use them, how you can modify them, and how you can create your own. Then I'll continue the discussion of styles, which began in Chapter 7, in which you'll learn all about Word's AutoFormat and Style Gallery features. By the end of this chapter, you'll have plenty of ideas for putting these features to work.

Working with Templates

NEW IN WORD 6

The template feature — and everything related to it in this chapter — is brand new to Word version 6. Templates take the idea of System 7 Stationery Pads a step further by enabling you to incorporate specific Word features into a file. Like stationery, however, when you open a Word template file, you're presented with an untitled document that contains all the text and formatting found in the template file. You can use this as a starting point for creating your own documents.

In this section of the Chapter, I'll tell you all about template files so you can understand their power and use them effectively in your day to day work.

What Is a Template?

A template is a special kind of Word document that can include the following components:

- **Document Layout —** settings for margins, line numbering, header and footer locations, and vertical alignment. I discussed the options in the Document Layout dialog box in Chapter 8.
- **Page Setup —** options for paper size and orientation. I discussed the options in the Page Setup dialog box in Chapter 8.
- **Character and Paragraph Styles —** including any font or paragraph formatting. I discussed font formatting in Chapter 5, paragraph formatting in Chapter 6, and styles in Chapter 7.
- **Text and Graphics —** commonly used in documents created with templates. Some examples include boilerplate text in reports, signature lines in letters, and company logos on letterheads.

- **AutoText** — entries that make it quick to insert predefined, preformatted text and graphics. I'll discuss Word's AutoText feature (which was known as the Glossary feature in previous versions of Word) in Chapter 16.
- **Custom Toolbars and Menus** — to create the kind of document the template will be used for. I'll discuss custom toolbars and menus in Chapter 24.
- **Macros** — to automate repetitive tasks. I'll discuss Word's new Macro feature in Chapter 26.

FYI: Templates vs. Stationery Pads

I mentioned stationery Pads back in Chapter 3 and again in this chapter. If you don't know what a stationery Pad is, you probably feel as if you're missing out on something. You are.

A stationery Pad is a special type of System 7 file that can be used as a template for creating other documents. Think of it as a pad or package of printed stationery you might buy in an office supply store or have custom made. It contains standard text and formatting that you can use to create a specific type of document. You fill in the blanks and you're done.

Of course, any file can be used like this. But the benefit of using stationery is that when you open a stationery file, Word opens it as an untitled document. That means you're prompted to give the file a new name when you save it. This prevents you from accidentally overwriting the original file with your changes.

To create a stationery file, create a document with the text and formatting that will be the same for every document of that type. Then activate the Save command. In the Save As dialog box, give the file a name, specify a disk location, and choose stationery from the Save File As Type pop-up menu. Click Save or press Return or Enter to complete the save. The name you gave the file does not appear at the top of the document window. Instead, it remains an untitled document.

You can also convert an existing document into a stationery Pad by using the Finder's Get Info window. Click the document icon to select it and choose Get Info from the File menu. Turn on the check box beside stationery Pad to convert the document. The icon changes immediately.

Continued

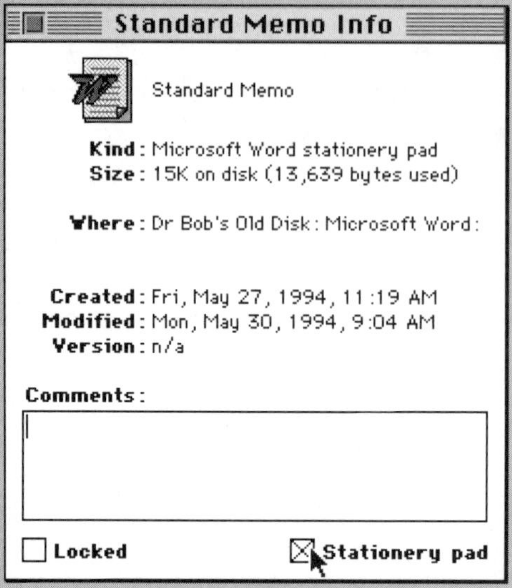

At this point, you're probably wondering what the difference is between stationery and template files. There's a big difference as far as Word is concerned. A stationery file can include any of the features previously listed for template files except AutoText entries, custom toolbars and menus, and macros. Those are features that can only be included in a Word template file. Word templates offer you more options than stationery files. Rather than spending a lot of pages telling you about stationery files, I'll concentrate on Word template files. I think you'll get more out of them.

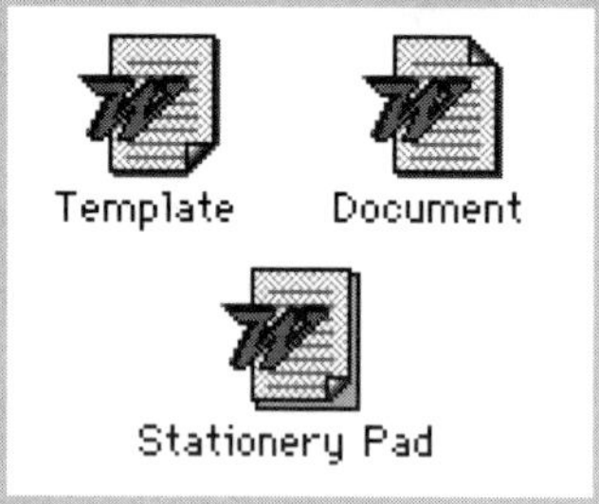

One more thing: if you've got sharp eyes, you can identify the different kinds of Word files by their icons. Here's an illustration of the icons for a template, a document, and a stationery pad. Note the subtle differences.

TIP/TRICK

FYI: About the Normal Template

The Normal template is the template Word automatically chooses when you use the New button or ⌘N shortcut key to create a new document. It's the default template that appears in the New dialog box when you choose New from the File menu. It's also the template that is used when you launch Word and Word displays a blank document window. Because of this, it's probably the template you'll use most. I know I do.

Continued

The Normal template is based on a Word template file called Normal. Although it does not include any text or graphics, it does include all the other features I listed above for template files. Features stored in the Normal template are available to all documents. That's what makes the Normal template special. Any change you make to its features affects not only the documents you create with the Normal template but the ones you create with all templates. If you make a change to the AutoText entries, toolbars or menus, or macros for the Normal template, your change is applied throughout the Word environment to all documents you create or modify.

TIP/TRICK

To quickly restore Word's default global settings, simply delete the Normal template file in the Templates folder. When you launch Word and it can't find this file, it creates a new one based on values stored within the Word program by Microsoft.

Using a Template

Word comes with dozens of template files. You'll find them in the Templates folder that the Word installer places inside the main Microsoft Word folder. Use them to prepare specialized documents like letters, memos, fax cover sheets, brochures, reports, manuscripts, and resumés.

There are four *families* of templates: 1. Classic, 2. Contemporary, 3. Typewriter, and 4. Elegant. The family a template belongs to defines its overall styling. The number in the template name identifies the family. For example, Fax Cover 2 is a template for a fax cover sheet in the Contemporary family. Not all templates are available in all families.

To create a document based on a template, choose New from the file menu. The New dialog box appears. By default, Normal appears as the selected template. To create a document based on the Normal template, click OK. To create a document based on another template, click on the template name in the scrolling list. A description of the template appears in the Description area at the bottom of the dialog box, as shown here. Click OK, and the new document appears as an untitled document window.

IMPORTANT NOTE

If the Templates scrolling list in the New edit box is empty, Word may not know where to look for template files. Use the File Locations tab in the Options dialog box to tell Word where user and workgroup templates are located. I'll tell you how to do this in Chapter 23.

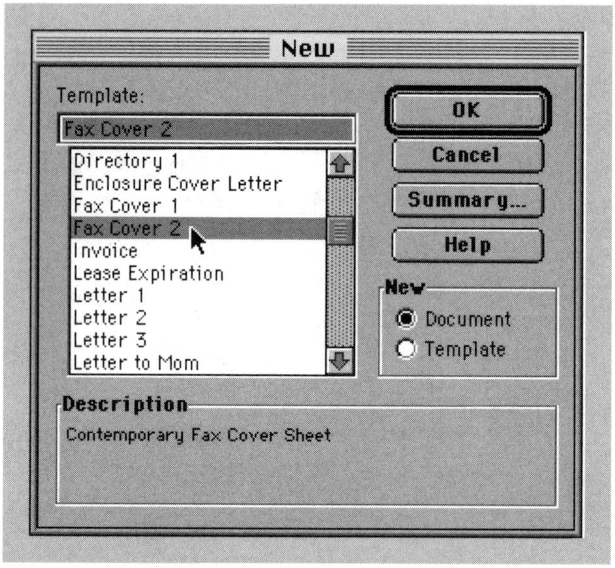

Most templates include some kind of text, which is used as a placeholder for your own information. Fax Cover 2, which is illustrated here, includes placeholders for all the usual fax cover sheet information.

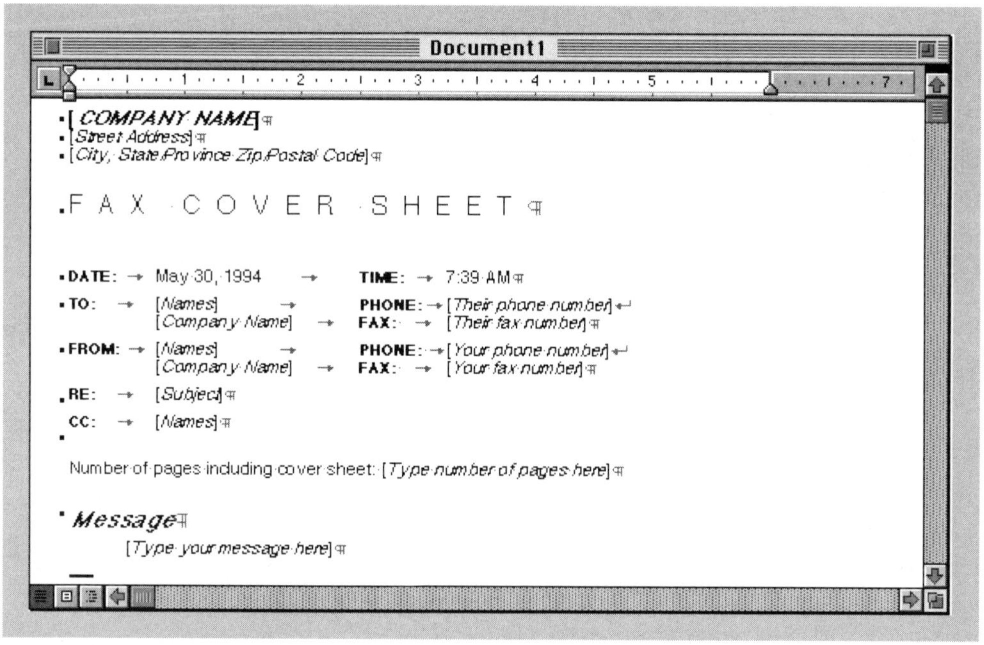

IMPORTANT NOTE

Some of Word's template files utilize fonts that come with Word. These fonts are automatically installed on your hard disk when you do a complete installation of Word. Appendix A discusses installing Word; check it for instructions.

To use a template, delete the text you don't want and replace it with the text you do want. For example, you probably wouldn't want your fax cover sheet to begin with the word "Company" in brackets. So you select that text (including the brackets) and type in your own company name to replace it. Or, if you don't have a company name, just delete the whole line.

Here are a few extra tips for using the template files that come with Word:

TIP/TRICK

- Word's templates make extensive use of styles. You can use the styles that come with a template or modify them for your own needs and tastes. I told you about styles in Chapter 7.
- You don't have to include all the information in the template in your finished document. Add or delete any information using standard editing techniques.
- To get the most out of Word's templates, modify them to meet your own needs. This way, you won't find yourself replacing the same information over and over each time you create a new document based on an often-used template. I'll tell you how to modify templates next.

Modifying a Template

Although Word's templates are generic in nature and should meet the needs of many Word users, you may find them a lot more useful once you customize them. For example, why replace the [Company] placeholder in the Fax Cover 2 template every single time you use it? Why not simply replace it once in the template file?

To change a template, begin by using the Open command under the File menu to open it. Then make whatever changes you like to the template file. Replace placeholders with the information that won't change, like your company name and address and your name and title. Change styles and formatting. Make adjustments to Document Layout and Page Setup options. You can even add AutoText Entries, customize the toolbar and menus, and add macros — I'll tell you how to do those things in Chapters 16, 24, and 26. You can see examples of some of the changes you might want to make in the following illustration.

When you're all finished making changes, choose Save from the File menu to save the changes to the template. Then close the template's window. Now, when you choose New from the file menu, the template you changed appears among the list of available templates.

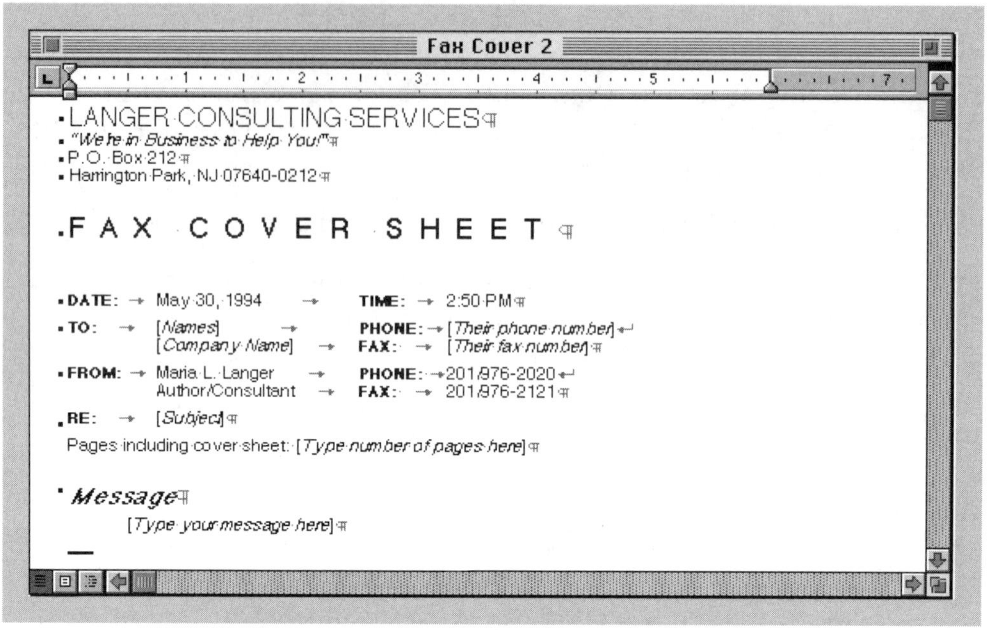

TIP/TRICK

Another way to modify a template is to use the Default button in the Font, Document Layout, Page Setup, and Language dialog boxes while a document based on the template is open. This establishes the settings in the dialog box as the default settings for the template. I discussed the Font dialog box in Chapter 5 and the Document Layout and Page Setup dialog boxes in Chapter 8. I'll discuss the Language dialog box in Chapter 17.

Try This! Modifying a Template

You saw what I did to the Fax Cover 2 file in the previous illustration. Now it's your turn. Open one of the templates that come with Word and customize it for your own use.

1. Choose Open from the File menu or press [⌘][O]. The Open dialog box appears.
2. Use the directory portion of the dialog box to locate the default templates folder. It should be called Templates and be located within the Microsoft Word folder.
3. Choose a template you'd like to modify and double-click it to open it.

Continued

4. Go through the template and make changes as you see fit. Replace placeholders for any information that won't change with the actual information. Delete placeholders and other text you don't need. Add text you do need. Change the font or paragraph formatting or redefine the styles used throughout the template file. Change margins, paper size, orientation, and vertical alignment. I told you how to do all these things throughout the first eight chapters of this book.
5. Choose Save from the File menu or press [⌘][S] to save the template with your changes.
6. Close the template file.
7. To check your handiwork, choose New from the File menu. Locate the template you just changed in the Templates scrolling list. Click it once to select it and click OK to open it. The modified template should appear in a new untitled window.

Creating a New Template

If your template needs go beyond those that come with Word (and they probably will), you can create your own custom templates. Word offers two ways to create a new template.

Creating a Template with the New Dialog Box

The New dialog box, which appears when you choose New from the File menu, has a pair of radio buttons that let you tell Word what new thing you want to create: document or template. Choose Template. If desired, select a template from the scrolling list of templates. When you click OK, a window titled with the word "template" followed by a number appears. Its contents are based on either the Normal template or another template you chose.

Make changes within the window or appropriate dialog boxes to create the custom template you want. Consult the list above for ideas about the kinds of things you can include in a template file. Finally choose Save or Save As from the File menu to save the template file. Use the directory portion of the

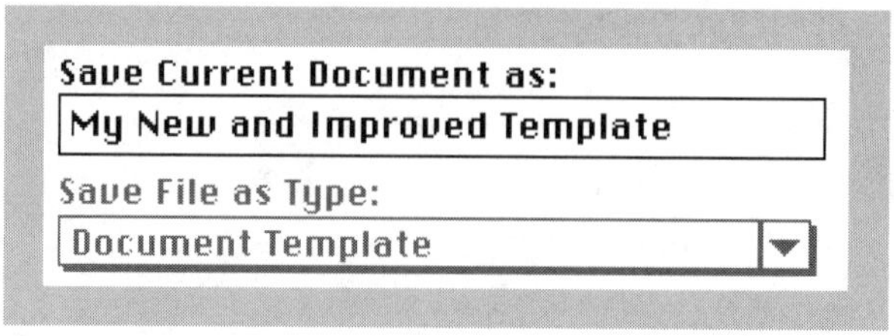

dialog box to locate the folder that contains Word's template files and give the file a name. The Save File As Type pop-up menu in the Save As dialog box will be gray, so when you click Save, the file is automatically saved as a document template.

Creating a New Template from a Document

You can also create a new template from a new or existing document. Create or open a document that includes all the text and other features a template file allows. Use placeholders if desired to remind yourself where certain information should go.

When you're all finished making changes, choose Save As from the File menu to save the changes to the template. In the Save As dialog box that appears, use the directory area to locate the folder containing Word's templates. Enter a name for the template file. Then choose Document Template from the Save File As Type pop-up menu. Finally, click Save to save the template file.

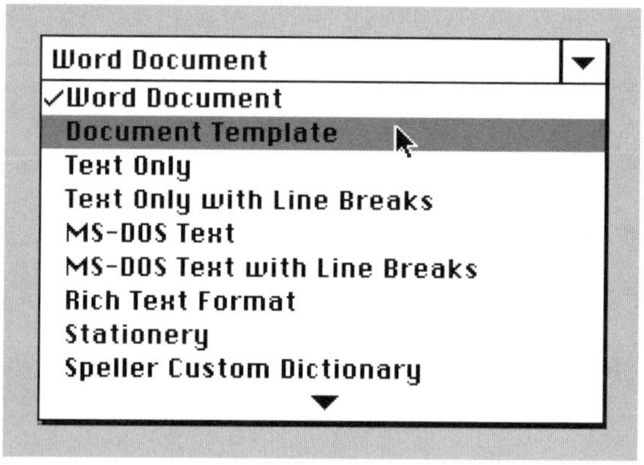

Changing a Document's Template

When you create a new document, the template that document is based on is said to be *attached* to the document. That means all its features are available for your use while you work with the document. The template remains attached until you attach a different template.

Why would you want to attach a different template? Perhaps the template you originally selected does not have the features — especially AutoText entries, customized toolbars and menus, or macros — you need for the document. Perhaps you or someone else has created a better template for that kind of document since the document was originally created. To attach a different template to a document, choose Templates from the File menu. The Templates and Add-ins dialog box appears.

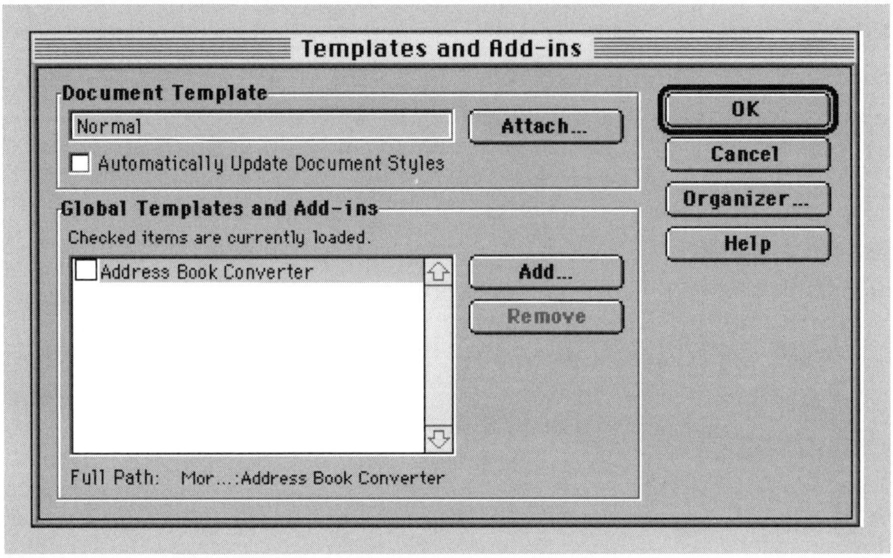

This dialog box lets you do two main things: attach a different template to the current document and identify global templates and add-ins.

Attaching a Different Template

To attach a different template to the current document, click the Attach button. A standard Open dialog box appears. Use the dialog box to locate and Open a template file.

TIP/TRICK

If you know the exact name of the template file and it is located with the other templates in the templates folder, you can simply type the template name into the Document Template edit box.

When you change the template attached to a document, any AutoText entries, custom toolbars and menus, and macros in the newly attached template are automatically available to you in the current document. The text, graphics, margin settings, paper size and orientation, and other document settings are not changed. Style definitions will change only if you turn on the check box labeled Automatically Update Document Styles. Not only can this change the styles when you first attach the new template, but it can change them in the future if you modify the style definitions for the template.

Identifying Global Templates and Add-ins

A global template is a template file that makes its features available to all files when you work with Word. An Add-in is a separate program that adds features to Word.

There are two ways to identify a global template: with the Templates and Add-ins dialog box and with the Word Startup Folder (6) folder.

Adding Templates. To identify one or more templates as global templates, click the Add button in the Templates and Add-ins dialog box. A standard Open dialog box appears. Use it to locate and open a template you want to add. It appears in the scrolling list under Global Templates and Add-ins. Do this for as many templates as you like — or as many as available memory allows. The check box before each template in the list indicates whether it's loaded and its features are available in the current work session.

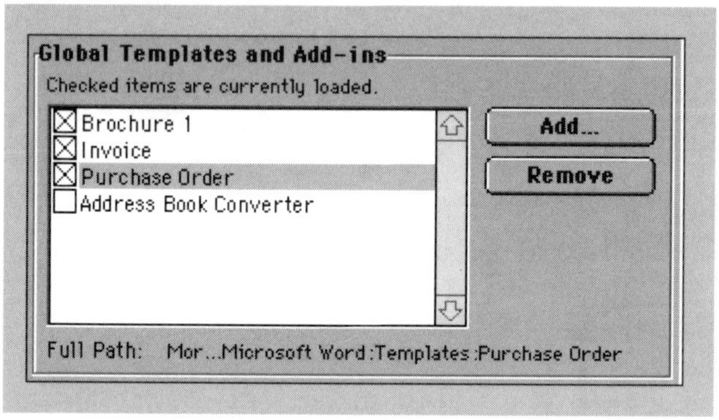

Word remembers what templates are in this list from one Word session to another, although it does not automatically turn on the check boxes for any of them. To load a template in this list, simply open the Templates and Add-ins dialog box and click the check box before the item you want to load.

You can also use the Templates and Add-ins dialog box to remove global templates. To remove a template for the current work session only, turn off the check box before the template's name in the scrolling list. To remove it permanently, click on it to select it and click the Remove button.

Ensuring That a Template's Features Are Always Available. To make a template's features available every single time you work with Word, use the Finder to make an alias of the template file and store it in the Word Startup Folder (6) folder. You'll find this folder inside the Preferences folder inside your System Folder.

The next time you launch Word, the AutoText entries, custom toolbars and menus, and macros included in the template will be immediately available for use. You'll also see the template listed in the Templates and Add-ins dialog box, although you won't be able to use the Remove button to delete it from the list. (You'll have to drag it out of the Word Startup Folder (6) folder to remove it permanently.)

TIP/TRICK

To launch Word without loading any global templates or add-ins, hold down Shift while double-clicking the Word application icon and keep it held down until the Word document window appears. This sets Word to its original "out-of-the-box" default values for the current work session only.

Copying Template Components

Word makes it easy to use components of one template in another. The Organizer lets you copy styles, AutoText entries, toolbars, and macros from one template to another. You can open the Organizer by clicking the Organizer button in the Templates and Add-ins dialog box. (Choose Templates from the File menu to display the Templates and Add-ins dialog box.) Click the Styles tab and it should look something like this:

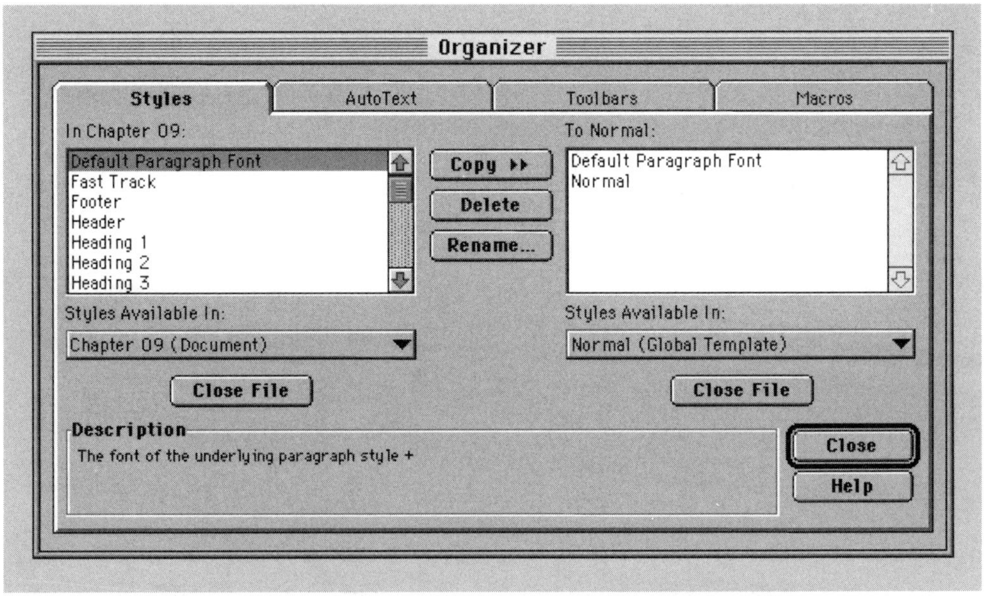

FYI: Look Familiar?

If you've been using a Macintosh since the days of System 6, you might see some similarities between the Organizer dialog box and the one that is displayed by the old Apple utility, Font/DA Mover. It also looks a lot like Apple File Exchange, another Apple utility that lets you work with IBM-formatted disks on your Macintosh. Here's a secret: they don't just look similiar. They work similiarly, too.

The dialog box is separated into two sides, one for each document or template you can work with. By default, the contents (in this case, styles) of the current document or template appears on the left side. You can use the pop-up window beneath the left scrolling list to switch from document to template. By default, the Normal template appears on the right side. To copy a style from one template (or a document) to the other, click on the name of the style in one scrolling window and click the Copy button to copy it to the other scrolling window. You can hold down [⌘] while clicking to select multiple items to copy. As you can probably guess, the Delete and Rename buttons let you delete and rename items you select. Keep in mind that not all of Word's built-in styles can be deleted from a document or template and none of them can be renamed.

If you want to work with another document, no problem. Click the Close File button under the scrolling window for the file you're finished with. The window's contents disappear and the button turns into an Open File button. Click that to open another template or document file. Once it's contents are displayed in the scrolling window, you can copy, delete, or rename to your heart's content.

The Organizer also has tabs for AutoText, Toolbars, and Macros. We'll discuss those features of Word in Chapters 16, 24, and 26 respectively. For now, don't be afraid to peek at the tabs in this dialog box. You'll find that they look surprisingly similiar to the Styles tab and they work the same way.

When you're all finished making changes in the Organizer, click Close. Your changes take effect immediately.

Automatically Formatting Documents

If you're looking for a quick way to format your documents, try Word's AutoFormat feature. This feature, which is new in Word version 6, makes it possible to automatically apply styles to an entire document.

NEW IN WORD 6

Word's AutoFormat feature examines each paragraph of the document in an effort to determine how it's used. It then applies built-in styles to the document and lets you review and approve the changes it made.

FYI: What AutoFormat Can — and Can't — Do

Word's AutoFormat feature is very powerful. Not only can it apply styles to make your document look more polished, but it can actually fix typing and formatting blunders. Here are a few examples:

- Replaces incorrectly used tabs and multiple spaces with proper paragraph indentation.
- Replaces abbreviated symbols like (C) and (TM) with correct symbols like © and ™.
- Replaces asterisks (*) and dashes (-) used in lists with the more professional-looking bullet (•) character.
- Replaces empty paragraphs with additional spacing between paragraphs.
- Removes Return characters incorrectly used at the end of each line of text.

You can specify exactly what the AutoFormat command does by setting options on the AutoFormat tab of the Options dialog box. You'll learn more about this in Chapter 23.

AutoFormat is a cool feature of Word — no doubt about that. But it can't perform miracles. In the sample document I created, it missed several

Continued

formatting changes I think it should have caught. And it ignores tables — that's what the Table AutoFormat command is for. I'll tell you about tables in Chapter 11.

What it all comes down to is something you knew all along: AutoFormat can't take the place of someone like you who really knows what each part of the document is used for. Your job is secure, at least until Word version 7.

Using the AutoFormat Feature

You've just written a letter to a new business associate with Word version 6. You had no trouble typing in what you had to say, but when you look at the letter on your Macintosh screen you feel that it lacks the pizzazz it needs to get her attention.

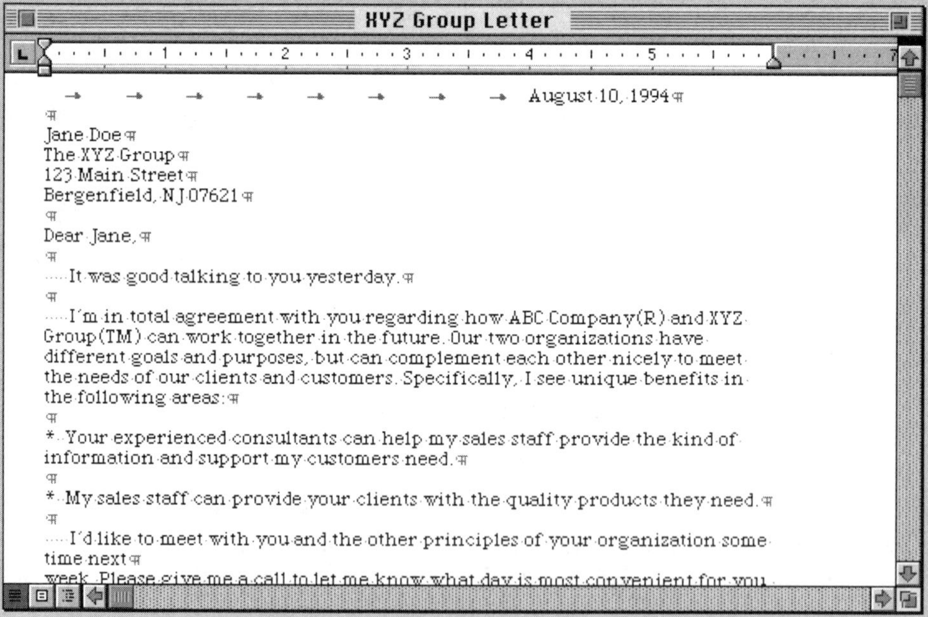

Unfortunately, you don't have the time to play around with the different font and paragraph formatting options you read about in Chapters 5 and 6. What do you do?

Use the AutoFormat feature, of course. To use the AutoFormat feature on the entire document, position the insertion point anywhere within the document. Then choose AutoFormat from the Format menu or click the AutoFormat button on the Standard Toolbar. The AutoFormat dialog box appears.

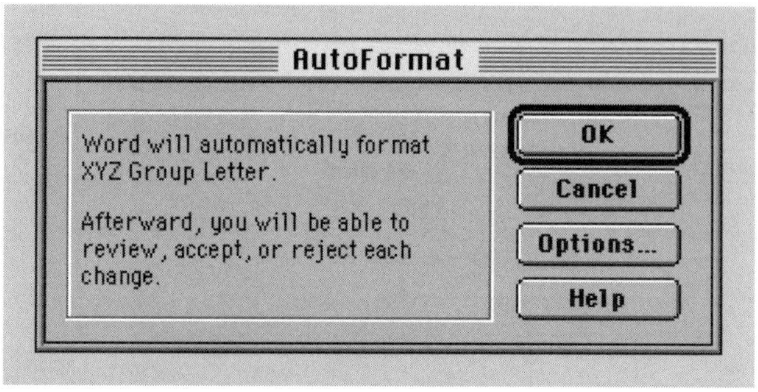

TIP/TRICK

You can use the AutoFormat feature on less than the entire document by selecting the part of the document you want to format first.

The AutoFormat dialog box begins by kindly telling you exactly what Word plans to do (automatically format the document) and what you can do when it's done (review, accept, or reject each change). At this point, you can click OK to put Word to work or click Options to view the AutoFormat options. For now, click OK. I'll discuss Options in Chapter 23.

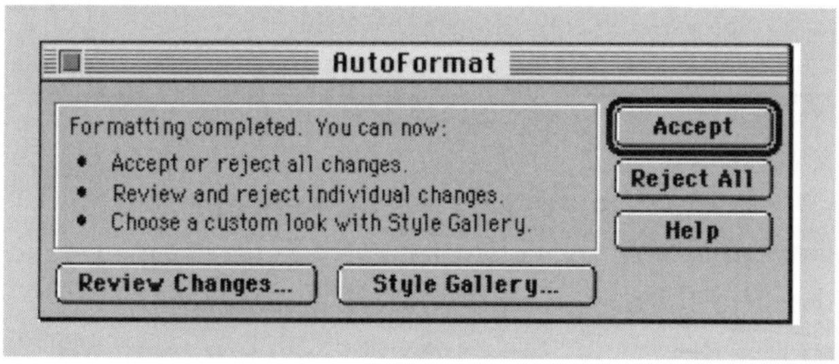

Word begins formatting. You know what it's up to because the status bar at the bottom of the screen tells you. When it's finished, it displays an expanded version of the AutoFormat dialog box.

Reviewing Changes

You can see the changes Word made in the background, behind the AutoFormat dialog box. If you're in a hurry, just move the dialog box by dragging its title bar with your mouse pointer so you can see the contents of the window. If you like them, click Accept or press Return or Enter to accept the changes. If you hate them, click Reject All to go back to the way the document originally looked.

If you've got a few minutes and would like to give your document the attention it deserves, click the Review Changes button. This displays the Review AutoFormat Changes dialog box, with your revised document in the background. The document includes revision marks that indicate all the changes made. (I'll tell you about Word's new Revision feature in Chapter 18.) The first revision is selected in the document and the Description area of the Review AutoFormat Changes dialog box tells you what the change was.

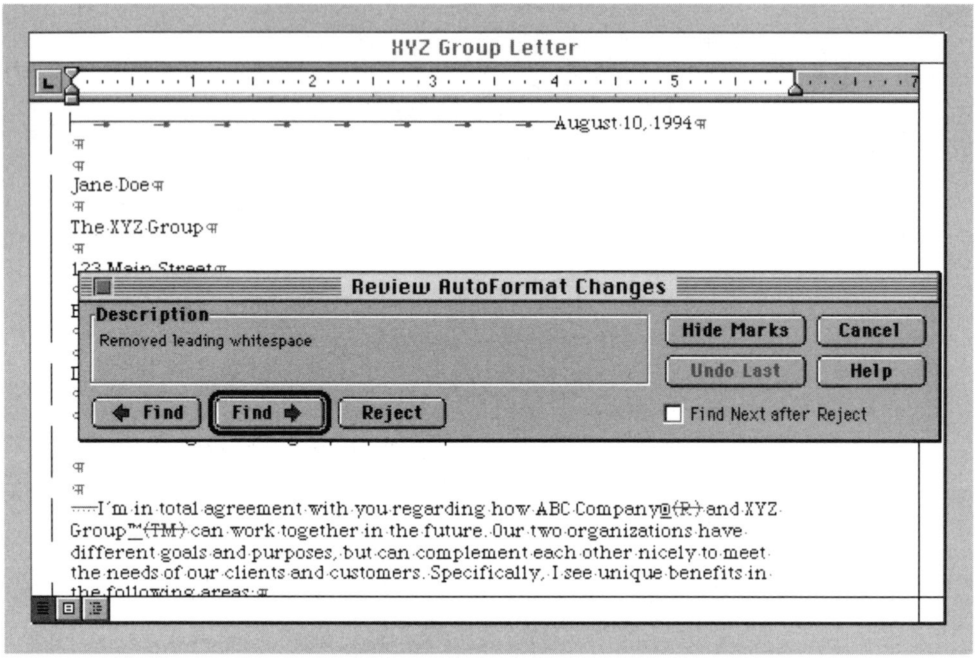

To review the changes one by one, click the Find button. The next revision appears. You can click Find to accept it and move on (in either direction) or Reject to reject it. If you turn on the Find Next After Reject dialog box, Word automatically advances to the next revision when you click Reject. You can click the Hide Marks button to view the document without the revision marks. You can also choose Undo Last to reverse your last change.

When you get to the end of the document, a dialog box appears, giving you the opportunity to continue reviewing from the beginning of the document (if the insertion point wasn't already there when you began the AutoFormat process) or telling you that you're done.

Completing the AutoFormat Process

When you're done reviewing changes, the expanded AutoFormat dialog box I showed you earlier reappears. Now that you know what the changes are, you can make an informed decision. Accept accepts the changes except the ones you rejected in the review process. Reject All rejects all the changes. You'll learn about the Style Gallery next.

Using the Style Gallery

The Style Gallery is yet another new feature of Word verison 6. It lets you change the formatting of a document by automatically copying styles from a template you choose.

NEW IN WORD 6

In order to really benefit from the Style Gallery, you need to either have styles already applied in your document or you need to be willing to apply them. That's why the Style Gallery works so well with the AutoFormat feature. AutoFormat applies the styles and the Style Gallery makes it easy to pick the styles that look best in your document.

TIP/TRICK

You can open the Style Gallery two ways:

- Click the Style Gallery button in the AutoFormat dialog box *or*
- Choose Style Gallery from the Format menu

The Style Gallery dialog box, a big monster of a thing, appears. It includes a scrolling window that lets you choose from among the templates in Word's default template folder. The Name of the currently selected template appears in an edit box at the top of the list. *(Current)* refers to the template of the current document. Most of the dialog box's real estate is taken up with a preview window that can show one of three things you choose with the preview radio buttons:

- **Document** — displays your document with the styles of the currently selected template. Remember, if your document doesn't already have applied styles, you won't see anything special here.

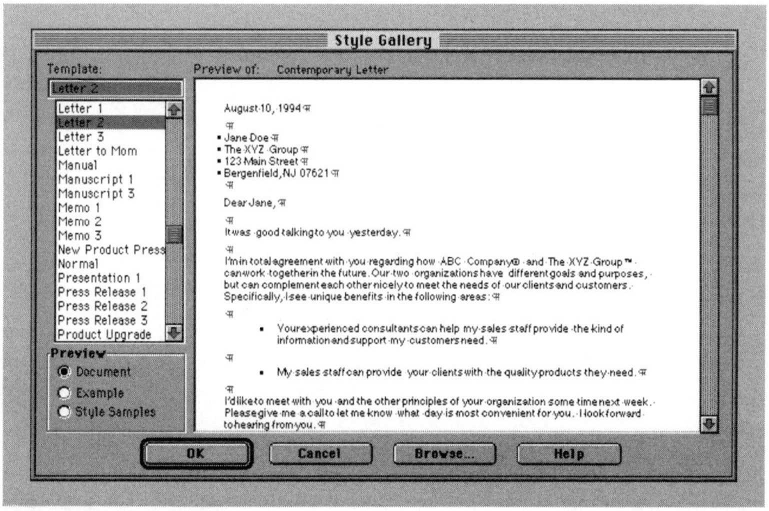

- **Example —** displays a sample document that is formatted with the styles of the currently selected template.

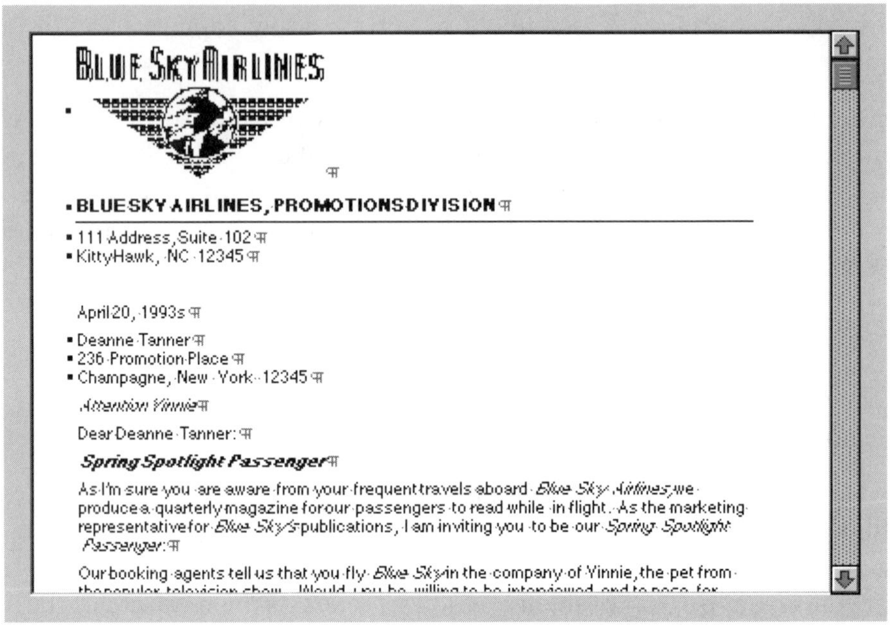
BLUE SKY AIRLINES

BLUE SKY AIRLINES, PROMOTIONS DIVISION

111 Address, Suite 102
Kitty Hawk, NC 12345

April 20, 1993s

Deanne Tanner
236 Promotion Place
Champagne, New York 12345

Attention Yinnie

Dear Deanne Tanner:

Spring Spotlight Passenger

As I'm sure you are aware from your frequent travels aboard *Blue Sky Airlines*, we produce a quarterly magazine for our passengers to read while in flight. As the marketing representative for *Blue Sky's* publications, I am inviting you to be our *Spring Spotlight Passenger*.

Our booking agents tell us that you fly *Blue Sky* in the company of Yinnie, the pet from

- **Style Samples —** displays a list of all the styles in the currently selected template, in alphabetical order, formatted with the styles they represent.

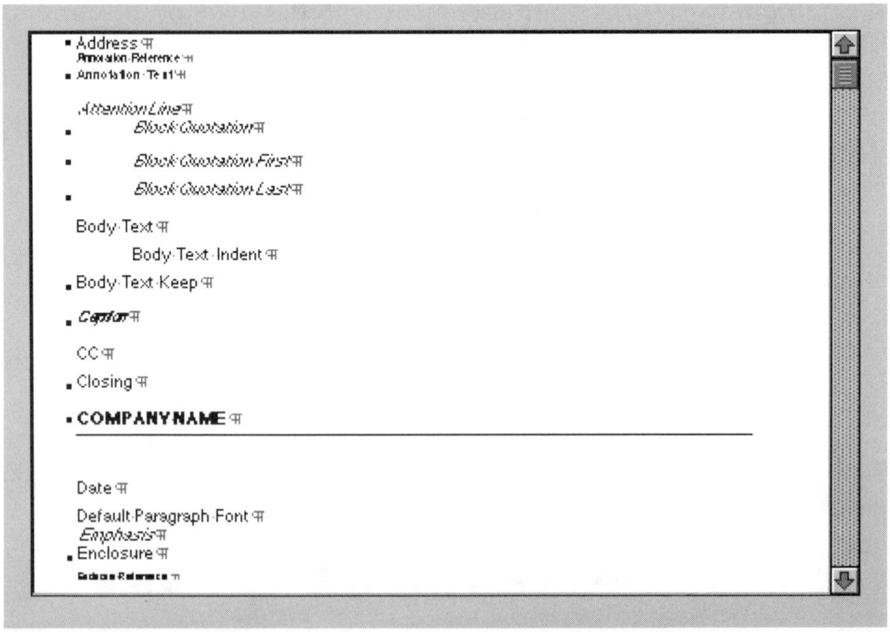
Address
Annotation Reference
Annotation Text
Attention Line
Block Quotation
Block Quotation First
Block Quotation Last
Body Text
Body Text Indent
Body Text Keep
Caption
CC
Closing
COMPANY NAME
Date
Default Paragraph Font
Emphasis
Enclosure
Enclosure Reference

Previewing Styles

To see what your document will look like with the styles from another template, choose a template from the scrolling list by clicking on it and make sure the Document radio button is selected. It may take a moment for the preview to appear. Try different templates to get a better idea of what Word offers.

Browsing Other Templates

If you have other templates on disk but they're not in Word's default templates folder, they won't appear in the scrolling list. You can use the Browse button to open templates located in other folders or on other disk drives, including drives available over a network.

Accepting a Template's Styles

Once you've found a template you like, click OK to accept it. The template's styles are automatically applied to your document. If you prefer not to use any of the styles you've seen in the Style Gallery, click Cancel to close it without accepting anything.

IMPORTANT NOTE

Using the Style Gallery to apply a template's style to your document is not the same as attaching that template to your document. The originally attached template is not changed. It's just the styles that are changed. I discussed attaching different templates earlier in this chapter.

Chapter Summary

In this chapter, you learned about three new features of Word 6: templates, AutoFormatting, and the Style Gallery. You learned what templates are, how you use them, and how you can modify them and create your own. You saw how the AutoFormat feature can help you format your documents by applying a template's styles. And, if you don't like the styles in the template your document is based on, you can always use the Style Gallery to change them to another template's styles.

This ends Part II of the book. In the next part, you'll learn about some special text and graphics formats, such as tables, borders, shading, frames, outlines and lists, and footnotes. You'll also explore some special programs that come with Word: the Equation Editor and Microsoft Graph. Chapter 10 begins with a thorough discussion of headers, footers, footnotes, and endnotes.

PART

3

Working with Graphics and Special Formats

THIS PART OF THE BOOK EXPLAINS SPECIAL TEXT AND GRAPHICS formatting options. In these six chapters, readers learn how to use a variety of Word features — including Add-in applications — to format text and graphics in their documents.

10

Chapter 10: Headers, Footers, Footnotes, and Endnotes

HEADERS, FOOTERS, FOOTNOTES, AND ENDNOTES ARE FOUR kinds of special text you may want to include in your documents. I call them special because they're not part of the body of the document. Instead, they appear at the top or bottom of the page, beneath text, or at the end of a section or document. They're not "required reading," if you know what I mean.

You were introduced to headers and footers briefly back in Chapter 8 when the subject was page numbering. In this chapter, you'll learn how to create, format, and position headers and footers. You'll see how you can specify different headers and footers throughout your document, another thing mentioned back in Chapter 8. You'll also learn about footnotes and endnotes — how to insert them, edit them, and position them in your document. I'm sure you'll agree that using Word for footnotes is almost enough to make you want to go back to school and write term papers again.

Headers and Footers

A header is text or graphics or a combination of the two that appears on the top of each printed page of a document. A footer is basically the same, but it appears on the bottom of each printed page. Both print within a document's margins, outside the area normally occupied by the document itself.

Headers and footers are commonly used in long documents to identify different parts of the document, number pages, or provide additional information about the document, its author, or release date. Most books include headers, footers, or both. This book is a good example.

Creating a Header or Footer

NEW IN WORD 6

Microsoft made a few changes to the way headers and footers work in Word version 6. The separate Header and Footer commands under the View menu are gone, replaced by a single Header and Footer command. In this section I'll show you how this new command works.

> **FYI: Seeing Headers and Footers**
>
> You can only see a document's headers and footers in Page Layout view or Print Preview. Headers and footers cannot be viewed in either Normal, Outline, or Master Document view.

Opening the Header or Footer

To create a header or footer, begin by choosing Header and Footer from the View menu. No matter what view your document is in when you choose this command — Normal, Page Layout, Outline, or Master Document — Word displays the top of the current page in Page Layout view. The header area, which has a dotted line around it, becomes active. The rest of the page turns gray and can't be edited. Finally, the Header and Footer toolbar appears for your use.

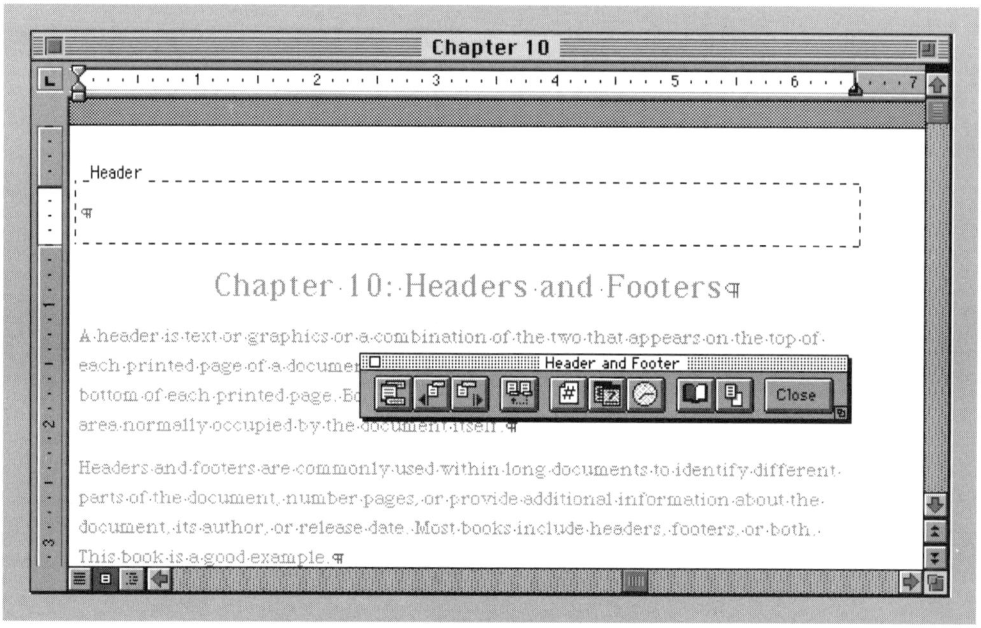

Switching Between Header and Footer

To switch from the header to the footer, click the Switch Between Header and Footer button. The bottom of the page and the footer are displayed.

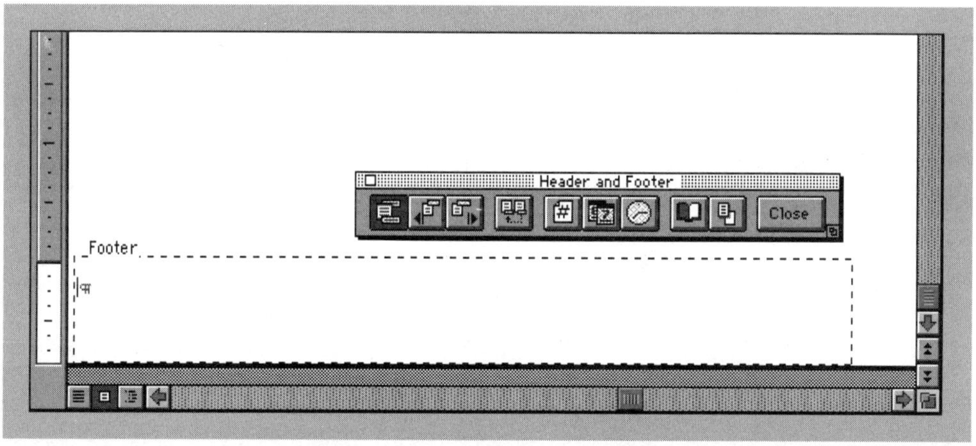

Entering Text in the Header or Footer

To enter text or graphics into either the header or footer, simply type at the insertion point. Think of the header or footer area as a tiny word processing document. You can enter and edit text just as you can anywhere else in a Word document. You can even use Copy and Paste to paste in text or graphics. I'll tell you more about graphics in Chapter 12.

Including Page Numbers, Dates, and Times in a Header or Footer

Word's Header and Footer toolbar provides buttons that make it easy to include page numbers, dates, and times in a header or footer. Begin by positioning the insertion point where you want the page number, date, or time to go. Then click the appropriate button:

- **Page Numbers —** inserts the PAGE field, which is used by Word to insert the correct page number on each page.

TIP/TRICK

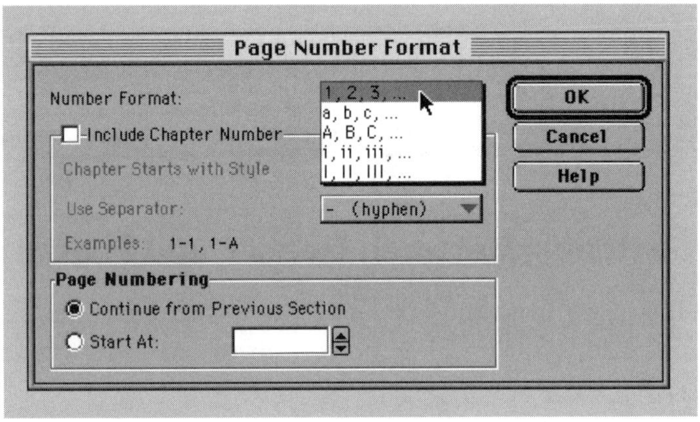

The format and starting number for page numbers are set in the Page Number Format dialog box, which I discussed in Chapter 8. Choose Page Number from the Insert menu to display the Page Number dialog box. Then click the Format button to display the Page Number Format dialog box. Set the page number format and starting page number. Click OK to close the Page Number Format dialog box and click Close (*not* OK) to close the Page Number dialog box. This formats the page number without inserting it in a frame as discussed in Chapter 8.

- **Date —** inserts the DATE field, which displays the current date in the format month/day/year (for example, 10/15/94).
- **Time —** inserts the TIME field, which displays the current time in the format hour:minutes AM/PM (for example, 11:58 AM).

FYI: A Brief Word about Fields

A field is a special code that tells Word what information to insert. By using fields, the information entered is dynamic — it can change if it needs to. For example, the PAGE field changes on each page, the DATE field changes each day, and the TIME field changes each minute (although you won't actually see it change on your screen).

These are just examples of fields available through buttons on the Header and Footer toolbar. They are not the only fields Word offers. You can use the Field command on the Insert menu to insert fields rather than current information in your header or footer. I'll tell you more about fields throughout this book.

TIP/TRICK

For Example: Why I Use the Page Numbers Button in a Header or Footer

Back in Chapter 8, I mentioned that Word offers two ways to include a page number in Word documents: with the Page Number command and with the Header and Footer command. Both commands put the page number in the header or footer, but the Page Number command also encloses the page number in a frame. Frames, which I'll discuss in Chapter 13, add flexibility in positioning the page number — you can place the framed page number anywhere you like on the entire page.

At first glance, it may seem as if the Page Number command is the way to go for numbering pages. But I prefer using the Header and Footer command and its Page Numbers Toolbar button. Why? When you use the Page Numbers button, it inserts the PAGE field at your insertion point. The page number becomes part of the paragraph of text you're typing. That means it will flow with the rest of the text and can be formatted like any other text: with standard font, paragraph, and document formatting. This just isn't the case with a page number (or any other text, for that matter) in a frame. You'll see what I mean when you get to Chapter 13.

Formatting Header or Footer Text

The text you enter into a header or footer can be formatted like any other text. Use toolbar buttons, menu commands, and dialog boxes to change the formatting of characters or paragraphs, either before or after you type them. Chapters 5 and 6 tell you all about font and paragraph formatting. Here's an example of the standard header I used for the manuscript of this book:

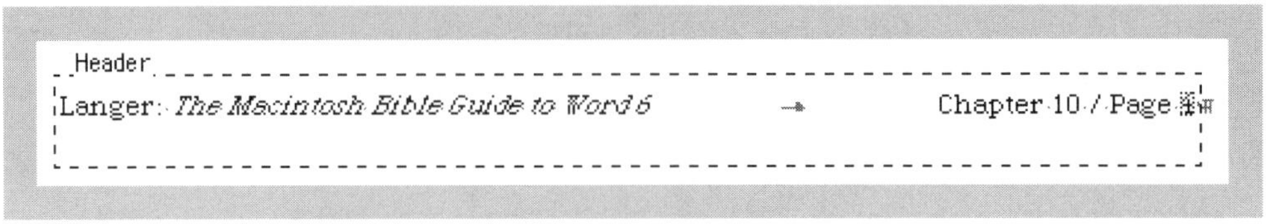

Header and Footer Styles

When you create a header or footer, Word automatically applies the Header or Footer style to it. The Header and Footer styles are built-in styles based on the Normal style for the document. A peek at the style definition in the Styles dialog box (choose Styles from the Format menu) reveals the following definition for each style:

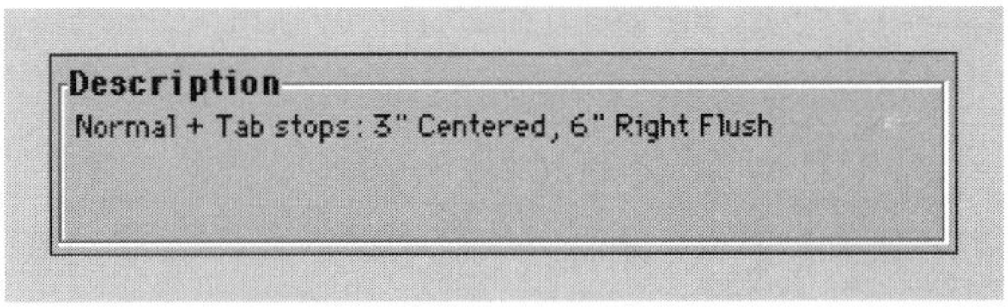

By including tab settings in the Header and Footer, Word makes it easy to have three-part headers and footers: left aligned text, centered text, and right aligned text. In addition, by basing the Header and Footer styles on the Normal style, if you change the definition of the Normal style, the header and footer will change accordingly, helping you maintain consistent formatting throughout your document. This is another good reason to take advantage of Word's Styles feature. I discussed styles in detail in Chapter 7.

Try This! Creating and Formatting Headers and Footers.

Enough talk! Now it's your turn to give it a try. Follow the steps provided here to create a header and footer in a Word document.

Continued

1. With a Word document open, choose Headers and Footers from the View menu to open the document Header. The document appears in Page Layout view with the Header displayed. If the footer is displayed, click the Switch Between Header and Footer button.

2. Type **December 1994.** Press Tab. Type **Monthly Report.** Press Tab. Type **Page** (be sure to include a space after the word "Page"). Click the Page Numbers button.

3. Select the Words "Monthly Report" and use buttons on the Formatting toolbar to make it 14 points and bold. At this point, the header should look like this:

4. Click the Switch Between Header and Footer button to switch to the footer.

5. Type **Prepared by:** followed by your name. Press Tab. Click the Date button. Type **at** (include spaces around the word). Click the Time button.

6. Press Return twice. Type **This document has been prepared for the internal use of XYZ Company and may not be distributed outside the organization.** The text should wrap to the next line and the footer should move up to make room for all the text.

7. With the insertion point in the last line of the footer, click the Center button on the Formatting toolbar to center the last paragraph of the footer. The footer should look something like this:

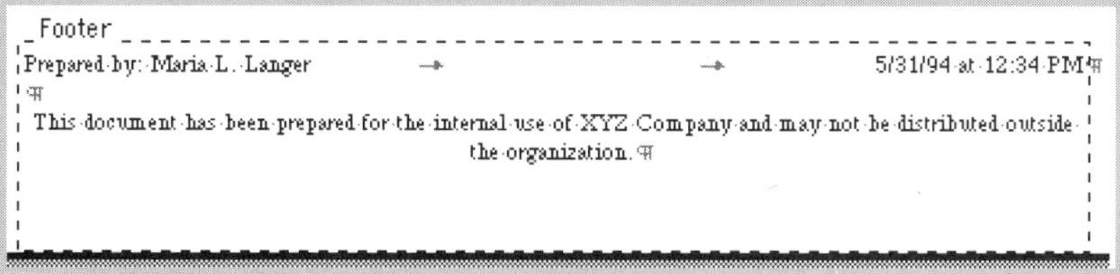

If you like, experiment further with formatting to get a good idea of the kinds of things you can do.

Returning to Your Document

To return to your document after creating and formatting a header or footer, click the Close button on the Header and Footer toolbar or double-click in the main document area. This makes your document active again, returning you to the view you were in when you chose Header and Footer from the View menu. The Header and Footer Toolbar disappears.

Editing a Header or Footer

Once you've created a header or footer, you can edit it at any time. Simply choose Header and Footer from the View menu. The header and footer become active. Use the techniques you just learned to enter, edit, and format the contents of the header or footer.

TIP/TRICK

If you're in Page Layout view, you can double-click on the header or footer of any page to make it active for editing.

IMPORTANT NOTE

If your document has the same header and footer throughout, it doesn't matter which page the insertion point is in when you choose Header and Footer from the View menu. When you change the header and footer, it changes for every page of the document. If your document has multiple headers and footers, however, you must position the insertion point on the page containing the header or footer you want to edit before choosing Headers and Footers from the View menu. I'll discuss this in more detail later in this chapter.

Positioning Headers or Footers on the Page

Headers and footers are positioned on the page relative to the top or bottom edge of the paper. In Chapter 8, I showed you how to adjust the position of headers and footers with the Document Layout dialog box. Let's take a closer look at that.

Choose Document Layout from the File menu or click the Document Layout button on the Header and Footer toolbar. The Document Layout dialog box appears. If necessary, click the Margins tab to display its options.

Setting the Distance from the Edge of the Paper

The From Edge area lets you set the distance from the edge of the paper to the top or bottom of the header or footer. Enter a value or click the tiny arrows to change the value already there.

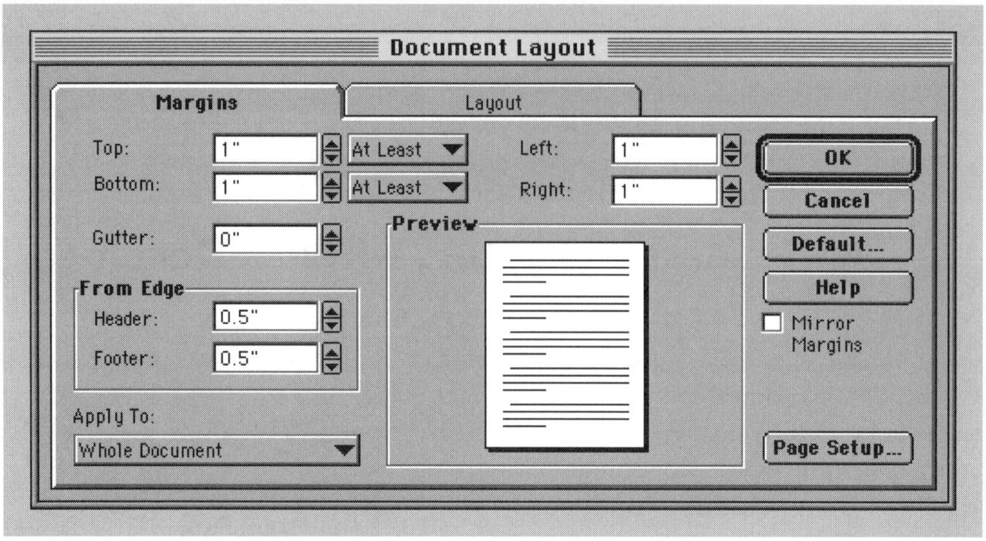

As I mentioned back in Chapters 4 and 8, not all printers can print right up to the edge of the page. Check your printer manual or experiment to see what results you can get.

FYI: Setting the Distance from the Rest of the Text

The amount of space taken up by the header or footer is determined by the amount of text or graphics you put into it. Once you type more than a few lines, the header or footer may become too large to fit within the margins. In that case, Word shifts the margins down (for a header) or up (for a footer) to prevent header or footer text from printing in the same space as your document.

This is where the Margin area of the Document Layout dialog box comes into play. If you find that the header or footer print too close to the first or last lines of text on the page, increase the size of the Top or Bottom margin. If you prefer, you can adjust the top or bottom margin in Page Layout view or Print Preview. I discussed how to do this in Chapters 4 and 8.

If the Top and Bottom margins are set for Exactly a certain measurement, the top and bottom margins won't move to allow space for a large header

Continued

or footer. As a result, the header or footer text may print in the same space as the first or last lines of the document page. To prevent this from happening, avoid using the Exactly setting.

Varying Headers or Footers within a Document

You don't have to have the same headers and footers throughout your document. You can have a different header or footer on the first page, different headers or footers on odd or even pages, or different headers or footers in each section of the document. To do either of these things, you'll need to use options under the Layout tab of the Document Layout dialog box.

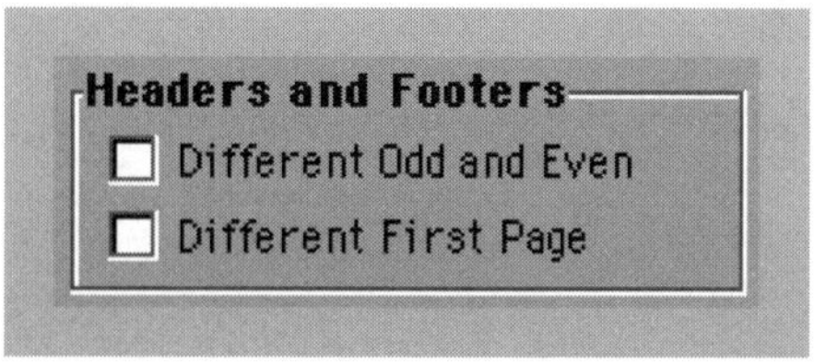

Setting a Different First Page Header or Footer

You're working on a long document and have included the document title and page number in the header. When you preview the document, however, you realize that the first page looks silly with the document title in the header and again, in big, bold type, an inch below it on the page. You want to remove the header from just the first page.

If your document has multiple sections, make sure the insertion point is in the first section. If your document has only one section, it doesn't matter where the insertion point is. Choose Document Layout from the File menu. The Document Layout dialog box appears. Click the Layout tab to display its options. Turn on the check box beside Different First Page. Then click OK to accept your changes.

If you view your document in Page Layout view or Print Preview, you'll see that the first page now has no header or footer. By telling Word you want a different first page header and footer but not specifying either one, you've removed them from the first page.

To specify a different header or footer for the first page, choose Headers and Footers from the View menu. Use the Show Previous button on the Headers and Footers Toolbar to move through the headers and footers in your document until the first page header or footer is displayed. Enter and edit information in them just like any other header or footer.

Setting Different Headers or Footers on Odd and Even Pages

You can set different headers and footers for odd and even numbered pages within your document. This makes it possible to have mirror headers and footers — left justified on the left (even) page and right justified on the right (odd) page. Or provide one piece of information on the left page (like the document name) and a different piece of information on the right page (like the document author's name).

Begin by positioning the insertion point anywhere in the section whose headers or footers you want to change. If your document has only one section, it doesn't matter where the insertion point is. Then choose Document Layout from the File menu. The Document Layout dialog box appears. If necessary, click the Layout tab to display its options. Turn on the check box for Different Odd and Even. If you have multiple sections in your document and only want the change to apply to the current section, be sure to select This Section from the Apply To pop-up menu. Then click OK to accept the settings.

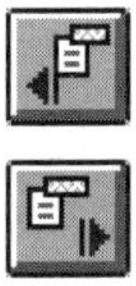

Now, when you choose Header and Footer from the View menu and use the Show Previous and Show Next buttons to look at headers, you'll see that your headers are labeled Odd Header and Even Header. You'll find the same for the footers, of course. The Odd Header and Odd Footer automatically acquires the contents of the original header and footer. You can change any of the headers or footers by displaying and editing them.

Setting Different Headers or Footers for Each Document Section

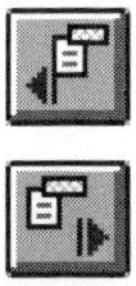

If your document has multiple sections you can set different headers and footers for each section. First insert section breaks to separate your document into sections. I told you how to do this back in Chapter 8. Then choose Header and Footer from the View menu to open the headers and footers. Use the Show Previous and Show Next buttons to view and edit the different headers and footers in your document. As you'll see, each header and footer is clearly labeled so you know which one you're working with.

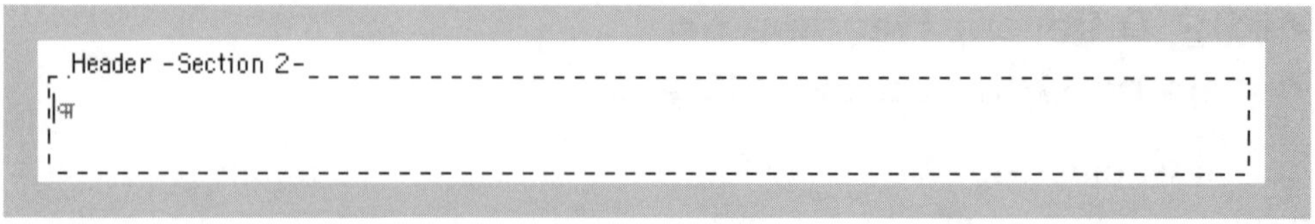

Disconnecting Headers or Footers. When you've got a document that already includes headers or footers and you separate that document into sections, each section inherits the same header and footer as the previous section. The headers and footers for the sections are said to be *connected.* You can tell when a header or footer is connected to the previous section's header or footer because the words Same as Previous appear:

In order to make the current section's header or footer different from the previous section, you must disconnect them. Otherwise, changing the current header or footer will also change all the headers or footers connected to it. Disconnect a header or footer from the previous one by clicking the Same as Previous button on the Header and Footer Toolbar to turn it off. The link is severed and the current section's header or footer can be changed without affecting previous sections. The current section's header or footer will still be connected to any headers or footers in the sections following it. Use the Show Next button to view, disconnect, or change any subsequent headers or footers.

Connecting Headers or Footers. If you later decide that you want a section's header or footer to be the same as the previous section, you can connect it. Click the Same as Previous button to turn it on. If the header or footer has information in it, you may see a dialog box like this one asking if you want to delete the current header or footer to reconnect it to the previous one:

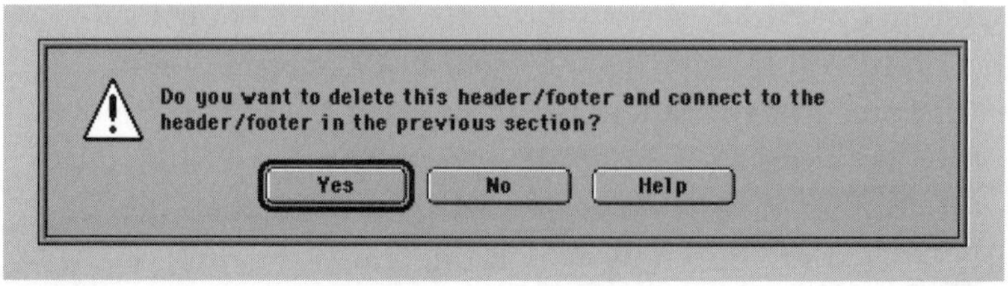

Click Yes to reconnect it. Click No to keep it separate (and different).

Deleting a Header or Footer

To delete a header or footer, use one of the previously discussed techniques to view it. Then select the header or footer text and press Delete.

IMPORTANT NOTE

When you delete a header or footer, you are deleting it for the entire section of the document — not just one page. To delete a header or footer from just one page, you must either set that page as a separate section or use the Different First Page option I discussed above.

Footnotes and Endnotes

Ah, footnotes. If you read the "Before You Start" chapter of this book, you'll know how I feel about typing footnotes with a typewriter. Thank heaven I don't have to do *that* anymore!

A footnote is a note that provides additional information about text in your document. It's commonly used to provide complete reference information for sources of information or comments about the text. A footnote consists of a small reference mark immediately after the text plus the note text, which is usually placed right after the text or at the bottom of the page.

NEW IN WORD 6

An endnote is basically the same thing as a footnote, but it usually appears at the end of a section of your document or at the very end of the document. In previous versions of Word, there was no distinction between footnotes and endnotes. Word version 6, however, not only distinguishes between the two types of notes, but can automatically keep track of both types if you use both in a document. As you'll see, working with footnotes is the same as working with endnotes.

FYI: Parts of a Footnote or Endnote

Each footnote or endnote consists of two parts: the reference mark and the note text. The reference mark is the mark that appears in the body of the text to indicate that the text has a note. The note text is the note itself, which you can position in a variety of different places.

Continued

The important thing to remember here is that the two parts of a footnote or endnote are linked. If you delete the reference mark, you automatically delete the note text. If you move the reference mark to another page, the note text may move, too — this depends on where it's set to print. I'll tell you more about moving, copying, and deleting footnotes and endnotes later in this chapter.

Inserting a Footnote or Endnote

To insert a footnote or endnote, begin by positioning the insertion point immediately after the text you want to comment on. Choose Footnote from the Insert menu. The Footnote and Endnote dialog box appears:

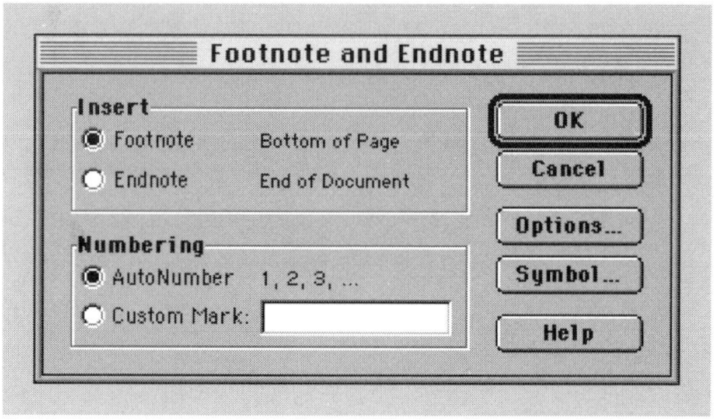

This dialog box lets you tell Word whether you want to insert a footnote or an endnote. It also tells you what the default positioning and numbering options are:

- Footnotes appear at the bottom of the page and are automatically numbered with arabic numerals.
- Endnotes appear at the end of the document and are automatically numbered with lowercase roman numerals.

One of the really great things about Word's footnote and endnote feature is that you can insert or delete notes in any order you want and Word will automatically update the numbers so they're in sequential order. You don't have to worry about the numbers at all.

You can accept Word's defaults by choosing the kind of note you want and clicking OK. If you prefer, you can use the other components of the dialog box to customize your note reference marks. I'll tell you how next.

Specifying Reference Mark Characters

If you don't want numbered footnotes or endnotes, you can click the radio button beside Custom Mark and enter the character(s) of your choice in the edit box beside it. If you don't know the keystroke for a specific symbol you want to use, click the Symbols button. An abbreviated version of the Symbols dialog box, which I discussed back in Chapter 2, appears.

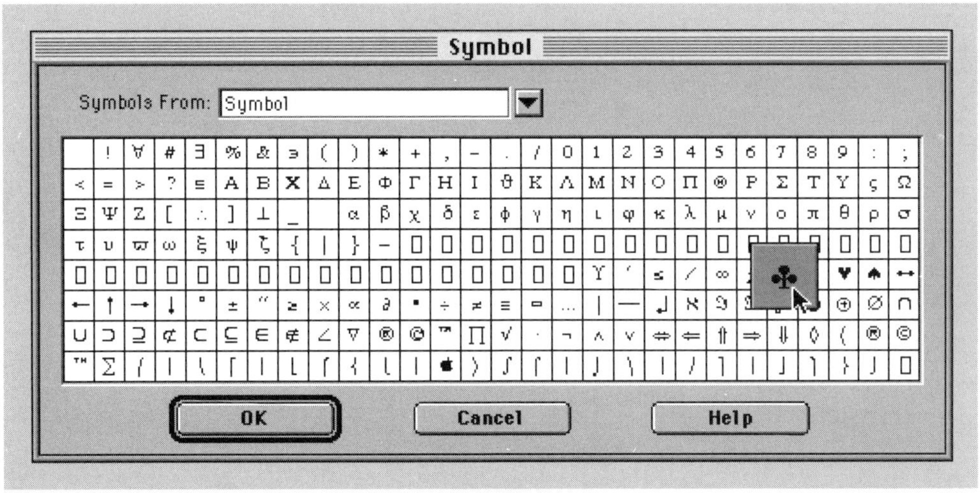

Locate the character you want. If you click on a character, a larger version appears, making it a bit easier to see. If desired, use the Symbols From pop-up menu to choose another font. When you've found the symbol you want to use, click on it to select it, and then click OK to enter it into the Custom Mark edit box.

Footnote and Endnote Options

If you don't like the default settings for footnotes or endnotes, you can change them. Click the Options button in the Footnote and Endnote dialog box. The Note Options dialog box appears. It has two tabs: All Footnotes and All Endnotes. The two tabs are virtually identical and let you change several of the default values for footnotes and endnotes.

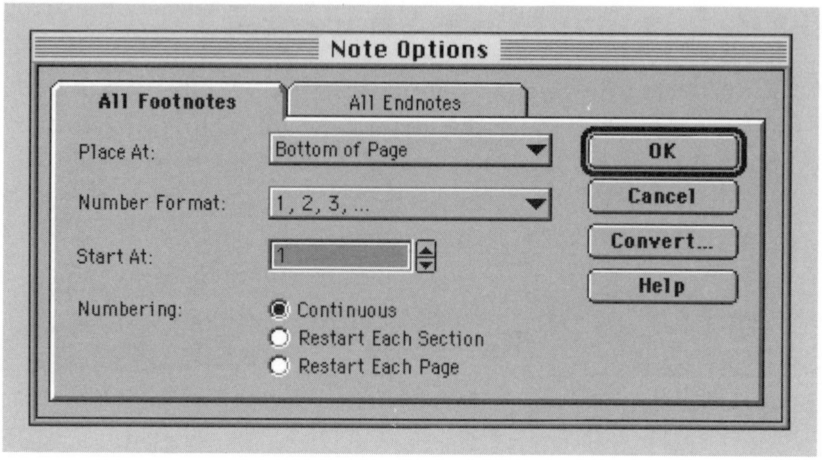

Changing the Reference Mark Number Format

To change the number format, choose a new format from the Number Format pop-up menu. Word offers several common options, including arabic numerals, letters, roman numerals, and symbols.

Changing the Note Text Position

You can also change where the notes will print in your document. Use the Place At pop-up menu. The choices under the All Footnotes tab are Bottom of Page and Beneath Text. The choices under the All Endnotes tab are End of Section and End of Document. These are pretty straightforward and easy to understand.

Specifying a Starting Number

Don't want to start numbering with 1? No problem. Enter a new value in the Start At edit box.

Setting Number Restarts

By default, Word numbers footnotes and endnotes continuously throughout the document. If you prefer, you can have Word restart the numbering of notes more frequently. Radio buttons on each tab offer these options:

- The All Footnotes tab offers Continuous (the default), Restart Each Section, and Restart Each Page.

- The All Endnotes tab offers Continuous (the default) and Restart Each Section.

Inserting Notes with a Shortcut Key

If you're looking for a quicker way to insert a footnote or endnote into your document, try ⌘Option F to insert a footnote or ⌘Option E to insert an endnote. Both of these shortcut keys insert notes with the same settings as the previously inserted note — without displaying the Footnote and Endnote dialog box.

Entering Note Text

Once you click OK to accept the settings in the Footnote and Endnote dialog box, Word displays the note text area. In Normal, Outline, and Master Document views, this is the Note Pane, the bottom half of a special split window.

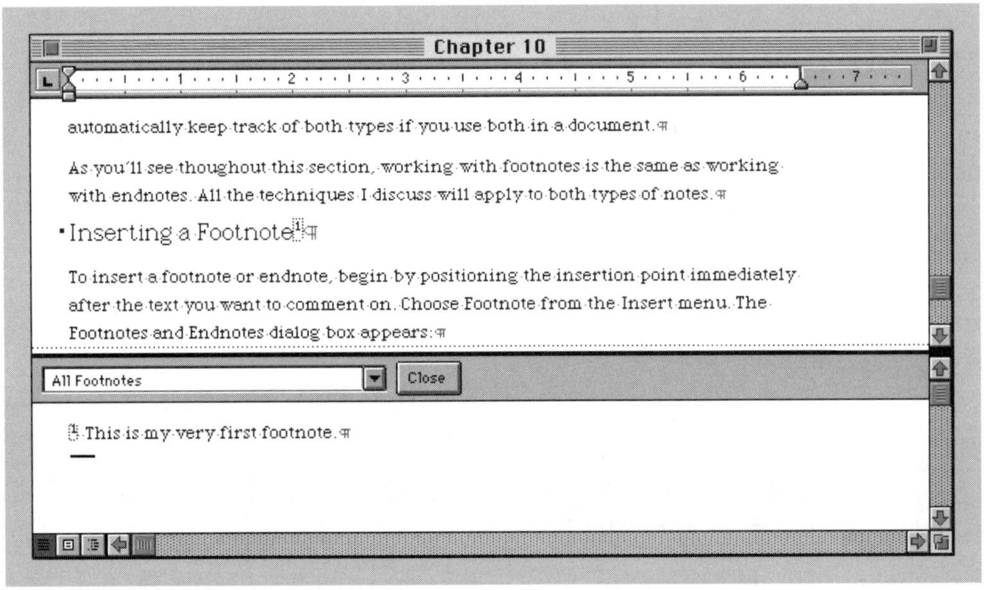

In Page Layout view, when you click OK to insert the note, Word displays the note where it will print.

To enter the footnote or endnote text, simply type it in beside the note reference in the Note Pane or note area.

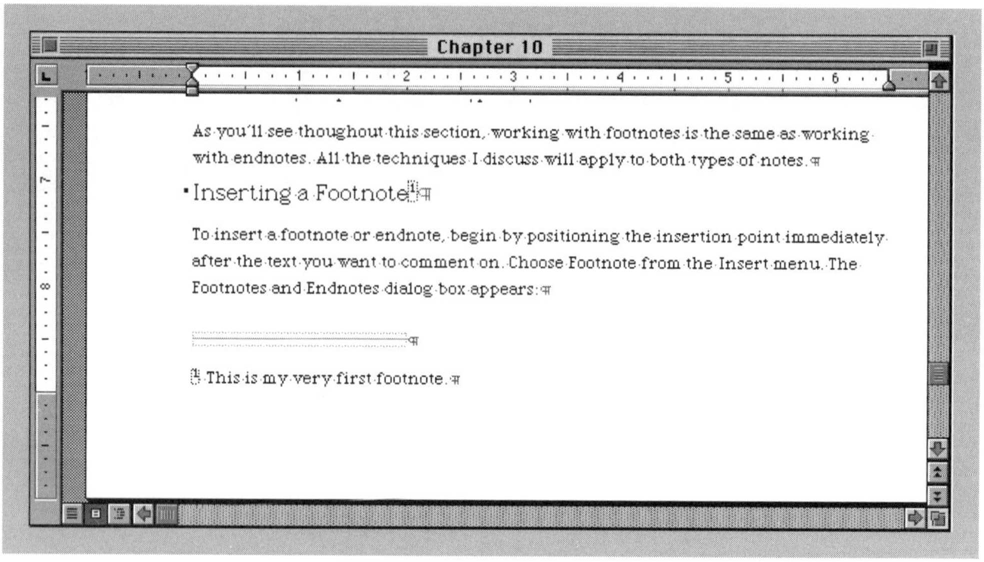

Hiding and Viewing Notes

In Normal, Outline, and Master Document view, you can only view footnotes and endnotes in the Note Pane, which automatically appears when you create a footnote or endnote in one of these views. Here are a few tips for hiding and viewing notes in the Note Pane:

- Resize the Note Pane by dragging the split box in the scroll bar or the black border between the two window panes.
- Close the Note Pane by double-clicking the split box or clicking the close button at the top of the Note Pane.
- Reopen the Note Pane by either double-clicking a reference mark in your document or choosing Footnotes from the View menu.
- Switch the notes view from footnotes to endnotes or from endnotes to footnotes by choosing All Endnotes or All Footnotes from the Note Pane's pop-up menu.

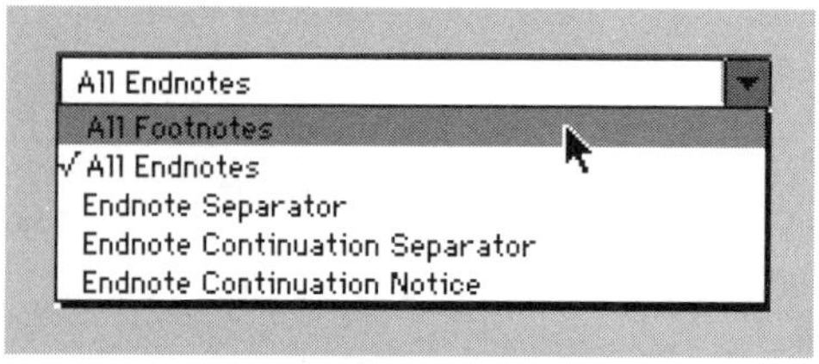

- View a note's reference mark by selecting the note in the Note Pane. The top half of the split window changes to display the reference mark for the note you selected.
- Move from note text to its reference mark in the document by double-clicking the reference mark before the note text in the Note Pane. This also closes the Note Pane.

In Page Layout view, notes appear where they print. Here are a few tips for viewing notes in Page Layout view:

- Move quickly to a specific footnote or endnote by double-clicking its reference mark in the document.
- View notes, by choosing Footnotes from the View menu. If your document has both footnotes and endnotes, a dialog box like the one in the following illustration appears, letting you pick which area you want to view. If your document contains just footnotes or just endnotes, the window shifts to show the first footnote or first endnote.
- Move from note text to its reference mark in the document by double-clicking the reference mark before the note text in the note area.

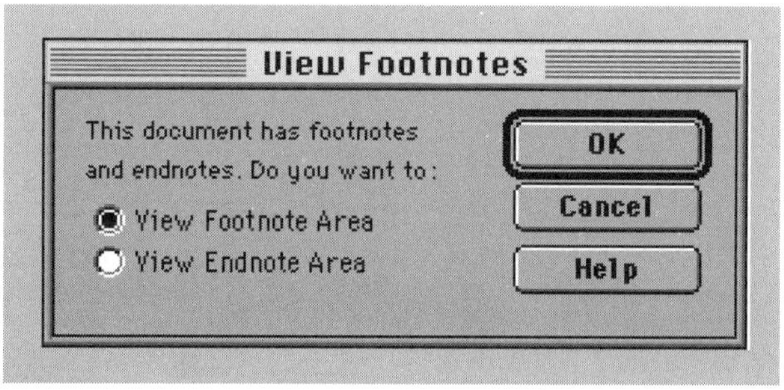

You can use the Go To command, which I discussed in Chapter 2, to view footnotes or endnotes. Choose Go To from the Edit menu or press ⌘G or F5. The Go To dialog box appears. Choose Footnote or Endnote (whichever applies) from the Go To What scrol-ling list. Then enter a footnote or endnote number in the Enter Footnote (or EndNote) Number edit box. Click Go To to view that reference mark and click Close to dismiss the Go To dialog box. Double-click on the reference mark to view the note.

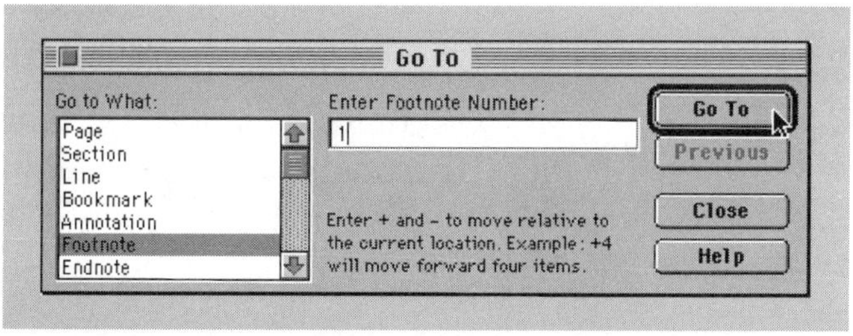

Changing Notes

Footnote and endnotes can be changed at any time. You can edit the text of the note, convert footnotes to endnotes or endnotes to footnotes, format reference marks and note text, move and copy notes, and delete notes.

Editing Notes

To edit note text, use one of the previously discussed techniques to view it. Then edit the note text as you would any other text.

Converting Notes

The Note Options dialog box lets you convert footnotes to endnotes or endnotes to footnotes. You can convert some or all of the notes.

To convert all footnotes or endnotes, begin by choosing Footnote from the Insert menu. The Footnote and Endnote dialog box appears. Click Options. The Note Options dialog box appears. Click Convert. The Convert Notes dialog box, which is illustrated here, appears:

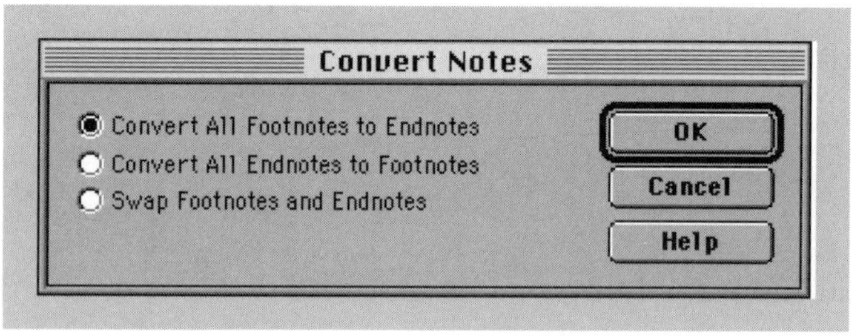

The options this dialog box offers depend on the kinds of notes you have. In this example, the document has both footnotes and endnotes. As you can see, you can convert all footnotes to endnotes, all endnotes to footnotes, or swap footnotes and endnotes. Click the appropriate radio button and Click OK to make the conversion and close the dialog box. Then click OK in the Note Options dialog box. Finally, click Close (*not* OK) in the Footnote and Endnote dialog box. (Clicking OK in the Footnote and Endnote dialog box will insert another footnote or endnote in your document.)

TIP/TRICK

To convert only some footnotes or endnotes, use one of the techniques you've learned to view the notes you want to convert. Select the notes, hold down [Control], point to the selection, and press the mouse button down. Word displays the Note shortcut menu.

Choose Convert to Endnote or Convert to Footnote (whichever appears) from this menu. Word makes the conversion instantly.

Formatting Notes and Reference Marks

You can change the font and paragraph formatting of footnote and endnote text. Use the techniques covered in Chapters 5 and 6 to select text and make the changes.

If you want to make global changes to the formatting of note text or reference marks, modify the definitions of their styles. Word automatically applies the following built-in styles to notes and reference marks: Footnote Reference, Footnote Text, Endnote Reference, and Endnote text. The two reference styles are character styles while the two text styles are paragraph styles. I covered modifying styles in Chapter 7.

Copying and Moving Notes

You can also move or copy notes within your document. To do this, begin by selecting the note's reference mark (not the note itself) in the document. Then use the Edit menu's Copy or Cut command to copy or cut the note from the document. Position the insertion point where you want the note to go and use the Edit menu's Paste command to paste it there. The note is copied or moved. If necessary, the reference number and note position changes.

TIP/TRICK

Of course, you can also use shortcut keys or toolbar buttons to invoke the Copy, Cut, or Paste commands. Or use drag and drop text editing. I discussed all this back in Chapter 2.

Deleting Notes

To delete a note from your document, delete its reference mark. Select the reference mark and press [Delete]. Both reference mark and note text are deleted. If necessary, other notes after it are renumbered.

TIP/TRICK

You can also use the Replace command to delete all automatically numbered footnotes or endnotes in your document. I'll tell you how in Chapter 16.

Working with Separators and Continuation Notices

Footnotes and endnotes are kept separate from the body of your document with a line called a separator. A *note separator* is a 2-inch line that separates note text from the rest of the text on the page. If a note is too long to fit on a page, it is continued on the next page, after a *continuation separator,* which is a line that stretches from margin to margin. You can also include a continuation notice to tell readers that a long note is continued on the next page.

You can edit all three of these things, for footnotes, endnotes, or both, in the Note Pane. To open the Note Pane, switch to Normal view and choose Footnotes from the View menu, or double-click on any footnote or endnote reference mark in your document. Use the Note Pane's pop-up menu to display either All Footnotes or All Endnotes. Then use the pop-up menu to choose the separator or notice you want to edit. The following illustration shows the note separator all ready for editing.

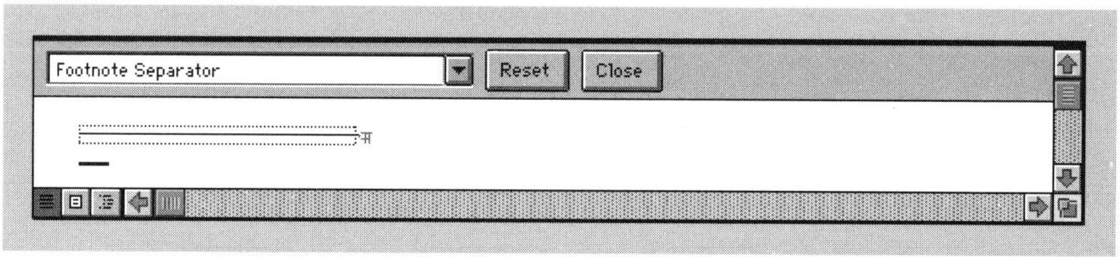

The separator is a graphic object. You cannot edit it within the Note Pane. You can add text before, after, over, or under it using the insertion point and standard editing techniques. You can delete it entirely by selecting it and pressing [Delete]. You can restore it to its default by clicking the Reset button. The continuation separator works the same way. The continuation notice does not include a line. Instead, it's just text you can use to tell the reader that the notes are continued on the next page. Enter any text you like. You can apply font and paragraph formatting to any of the changes you make to the separators or continuation notices.

You can see the results of your changes when viewing footnotes or endnotes in Page Layout view or Print Preview.

Cross-Referencing Notes

NEW IN WORD 6

Ever need to reference the same source more than once in your document? For example, say you've quoted this book five times in a report discussing new features of Word version 6. Do you want to type in the same reference five times? Of course not. That's what cross-referencing is for. Coincidentally, it's a brand new feature of Word version 6.

Begin by inserting a footnote or endnote the first time the source is referenced, and then position the insertion point where the next reference should occur. Choose Cross-reference from the Insert menu. The Cross-reference dialog box appears.

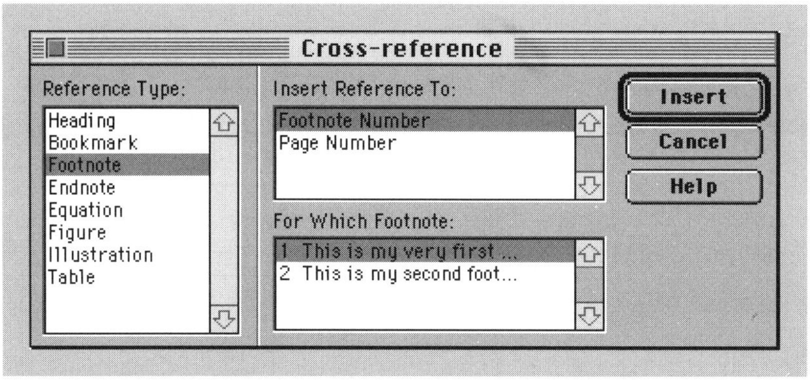

Choose Footnote or Endnote (whichever applies) from the Reference Type scrolling list. Choose Footnote (or Endnote) Number from the Insert Reference To scrolling list. Finally, choose the footnote (or endnote) number from the For Which Footnote (or Endnote) scrolling list. Click Insert and then click Close.

The cross-reference is added to your document in the current font. To format it so that it looks like a footnote or endnote, simply select it and apply the Footnote Reference or Endnote Reference character style to it using the Style menu on the Formatting Toolbar or Style dialog box. I discussed applying styles in Chapter 7.

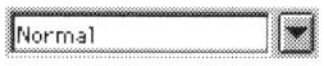

You can use this same method to insert a reference to one footnote or endnote in the note text of another. Simply position the insertion point within the note text when inserting the cross-reference.

TIP/TRICK

IMPORTANT NOTE

When you insert or delete footnotes or endnotes, cross-references are automatically updated in Page Layout view, Print Preview, and when your document prints. They are not updated automatically in Normal view. To force Word to update a cross-reference in Normal view, select the reference number in the document (or select the whole document) and press ⌘ Option Shift U. (Hey, I don't make them up, I just tell you about them). If you delete a note referred to by a cross-reference, you may see an error message rather than a reference mark. To delete the error message, simply select it and press Delete. I'll discuss cross-references in greater detail in Chapter 14.

Suppressing Endnotes

The Layout tab of the Document Layout dialog box, which I discussed in detail in Chapter 8, includes a Suppress Endnotes check box.

If you set up your document to place endnotes at the end of each section, you can use the Suppress Endnotes check box to prevent the endnotes from printing in a specific section. Position the insertion point in the section for which you want to suppress the endnotes. Then choose Document Layout from the File Menu. The Document Layout dialog box appears. If necessary, click the Layout tab to display its options. Turn on the Suppress Endnotes check box. Make sure This Section is selected in the Apply To pop-up menu and click OK to accept the new setting. The endnotes will not be printed at the end of that section. Instead, they'll be printed at the end of the following section.

Chapter Summary

In this chapter, you learned about headers, footers, footnotes, and endnotes — how to create, edit, and format them. You also learned how to set up multiple headers or footers in your document and how to use and customize the lines that separate footnotes and endnotes from the rest of the document text.

In the next chapter, you'll learn about cell tables and all about the commands and features under Word's new Table menu. You'll see why cell tables can be a lot easier to work with than tables created with tabs.

11

Chapter 11: Tables

Back in Chapter 6, you learned to use Word's tab feature to create simple tables. My definition of a "simple table" is a table that contains small bits of information laid out in columns and rows. But what if you need to create a more complex table — a table where text doesn't always fit in its column, a table containing graphics, or a table you'd like to embellish with borders and shading? Well, this is when you should forget about tabs and move on to Word's Table feature.

Word's Table feature creates tables made up of cells. A cell is a box that can contain any amount of text or graphics. Each cell is like a tiny word processing document that expands vertically as you fill it. You can format text within each cell using the standard font and paragraph formatting techniques discussed in Chapters 5 and 6. A collection of cells arranged in columns and rows makes up a table. You can format a table either manually or with Word's new Table AutoFormat feature.

NEW IN WORD 6

In this chapter, you'll learn all about tables — how to create them from scratch or from existing text, how to move the insertion point, and how to select cells, columns, rows, or the whole darn thing. You'll also learn how to enter and edit text and how to format the table so it looks just the way you need it to. You'll explore all the commands on the new Table menu. Throughout this chapter, you'll learn how flexible tables can be. Before long, you'll be coming up with all kinds of uses.

FYI: What I Use Tables For

First of all, I have to confess that I never use tab tables. I always take advantage of Word's Table feature, no matter how simple or complex the table I need to create is. Think of a résumé. You know how some people like to put dates in the left margin area and education or job experience in the main body of the document? A table is a perfect way to do this.

Think of a menu in a fancy Italian (or French or whatever) restaurant. You know the kind. The names of the dishes are in a foreign language with an English translation or description below them and prices going down the right column. I've created menus like this with tables.

Think of a glossary at the end of a book or software manual. The first column has words, the second column has definitions. I've done this with a table. There's also the added benefit of being able to easily sort the whole thing when I'm done.

These are just examples. Think carefully about what you need to type before typing it. If a table can do the job, don't be afraid to use it. You won't regret it.

Creating a Table

Word offers two ways to create a table. You can create an empty table from scratch or you can take text that's already typed into your document and convert it into a table. I'll discuss both methods in this section and tell you how you can get around in the tables you create.

Creating a Table from Scratch

When you create a table from scratch, you're inserting a table grid into your document. Although you can add columns or rows to your table at any time, it's a good idea to know, at a minimum, how many columns your table will need. Word automatically sizes your table to fit from margin to margin across your document. If you tell Word you want three columns and later realize you need four, you'll have to change the column widths of the existing columns to fit the fourth column in. While this is neither impossible nor difficult, it is an additional step that you might be able to avoid by planning ahead.

To create the table, position your insertion point where you want your table to begin and use either the Insert Table button on the Standard Toolbar or the Insert Table command on the new Table menu. I'll discuss both methods next.

Using the Insert Table Button

The Insert Table button is actually a menu. Position your mouse pointer on it and press your mouse button down. A grid comes out of the button, as shown in the figure.

Drag your mouse down and to the right to select the number of rows and columns you want. The number of rows and columns appears at the bottom of the grid. When you get the size you want, let go of the mouse button. The table appears in your document.

Using the Insert Table Command

The Insert Table command under the Table menu displays the Insert Table dialog box, which looks like this:

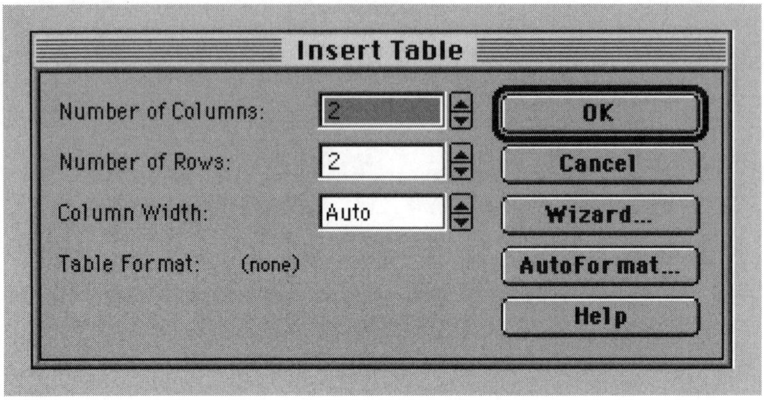

Use this dialog box to enter the number of columns, the number of rows, and the column width. You can type in the numbers or use the tiny arrows beside the edit boxes to change the values already in there.

If you leave Column Width set to Auto, Word automatically divides the total table width (the distance between margins) into equal-width columns. You can always change this later if you like. If you enter a value that's too wide to fit within the margins of the document, part of your table might not print, so be careful when using the Column Width edit box.

TIP/TRICK

If you want Word to help you create the table, click the Wizard button. A series of dialog boxes appears, one after the other, asking questions about the table you want to create. Answer the questions to create a formatted table. I'll tell you more about wizards in Chapter 26.

TIP/TRICK

You can click the AutoFormat button to select a predefined format for your table. When you create the table, it's automatically formatted for you, too. I'll discuss this feature later in this chapter.

When you click OK or press Return or Enter, the table you specified is inserted in your document.

Converting Text to a Table

If you find yourself struggling with a tab table that just isn't doing the job for you, you can easily convert the existing text into a cell table. Begin by selecting the text you want to convert into a table. Then choose Convert Text to Table from the Table menu. Word "looks" at the selected text, guesses how many columns and rows it has, and displays the Convert Text to Table dialog box.

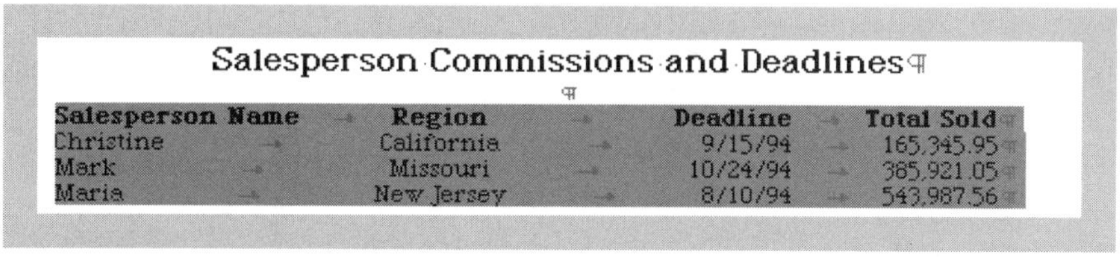

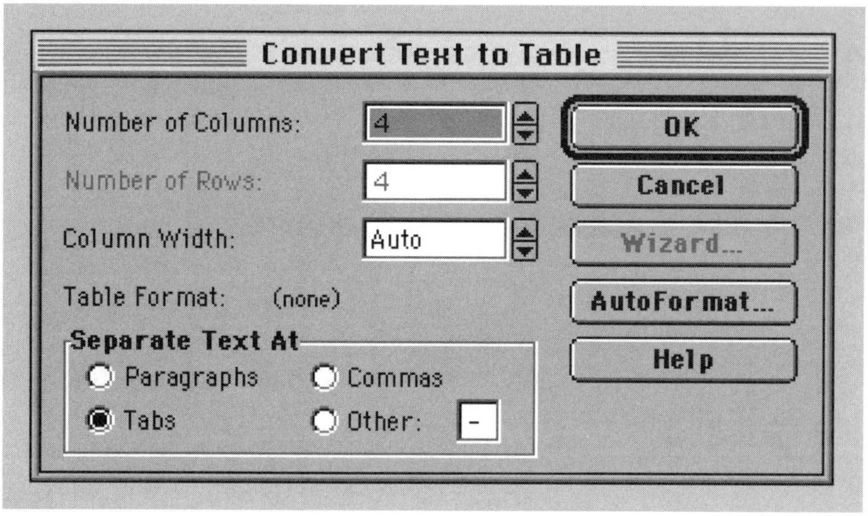

Word looks for standard separators in the text to help determine how many columns a table has. In the example shown here, Word "sees" that the selected text includes tabs between columns. Since a tab is a standard separator, it selects the Tabs radio button in the Separate Text At area of the dialog box. You can override whatever Word selects by entering a different number of columns, clicking another separator option, or entering a custom separator in the box beside Other, but in most cases you'll find that Word gets it right. When the settings are correct, click OK to make the conversion. You may need to adjust column widths when the new table appears — I'll tell you how to do that later in this chapter.

Rather than using the Convert Text to Table command, you may want to try the Insert Table button. It can convert text to a table without the Convert Text to Table dialog box and may be quicker to use. If Word messes up the conversion, you can always undo it and try again with the dialog box.

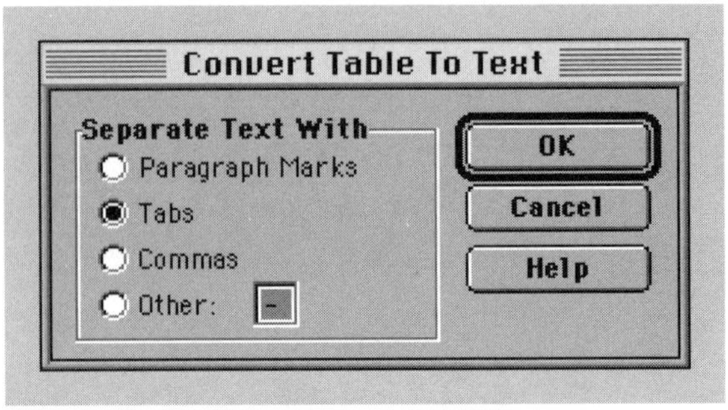

You can also convert a table back to text. Select the table and choose Convert Table to Text from the Table menu. The Convert Table to Text dialog box, which is shown here, appears. Specify the character you want to use to separate each column of the table's information once it is converted and click OK to convert it.

Parts of a Table

When you create a table, Word displays its gridlines, end-of-cell marks, and end-of-row marks. It might look something like this:

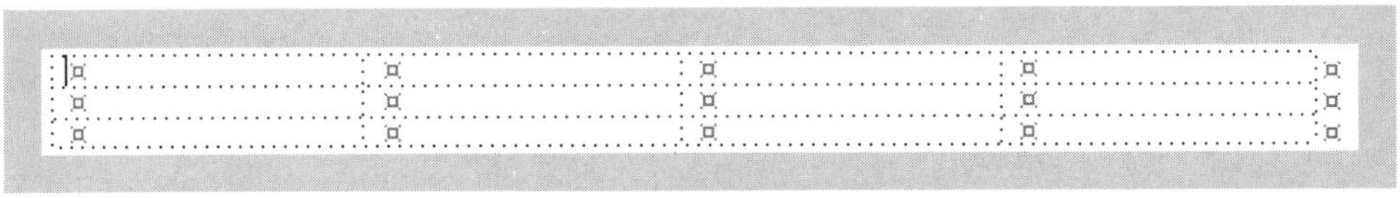

The dotted lines are the table's gridlines. They mark the boundaries of each cell. In the example shown here, there are 12 cells organized in 4 columns and 3 rows. Each cell contains an end-of-cell mark which indicates the end of the cell's contents. Since each of the cells in the illustration are empty, the end-of-cell mark is at the beginning of each cell. At the end of each row, just outside the table, is an end-of-row mark. These marks indicate the end of a table row. None of these marks — gridlines, end-of-cell marks, or end-of-row marks — will print.

If you don't see the end-of-cell or end-of-row marks in your table, you've got Word set to hide non-printing characters. Click the Show/Hide ¶ button to display these marks. If you don't see the gridlines of your table, choose Gridlines from the Table menu to turn them on. Although you can work with a table with both nonprinting characters and gridlines turned off, it's very difficult to do. Trust me — I've tried it.

Moving the Insertion Point

To enter information into the table, you'll need to position the insertion point where you want the text to go — that shouldn't be a surprise to you. You can always move the insertion point by clicking with the mouse. Here are a few more techniques you can use when moving around inside a table:

These Key(s):	Do This:
Tab	Moves to the next cell *or*
	when in the last cell, adds another row
Shift Tab	Moves to previous cell
→	Moves one character to the right *or*
	when at the end of a cell's contents, moves to the next cell
←	Moves one character to the left *or*
	when at the beginning of a cell's contents, moves to the previous cell
↓	Moves down a row
↑	Moves up a row
Option Home	Moves to the first cell in the current row
Option End	Moves to the last cell in the current row
Option Pg Up	Moves to the first cell in the current column
Option Pg Dn	Moves to the last cell in the current column

Selecting Parts of a Table

To move, insert, delete, and format cells, columns, and rows, you'll need to know how to select them. Here are a few selection techniques that work in tables.

To Select This:	Do This:
A Cell	Drag over the contents of the cell *or* click in the cell's Selection bar (the far left side of the cell, where the mouse pointer turns to an arrow pointing up and to the right) *or* triple-click in the cell
A Row	Drag over the contents of the row *or* click in the row's selection bar (just outside the left boundary of the first cell in the row) *or* click in any cell of the row and choose Select Row from the Table menu
A Column	Drag over the contents of the column *or* hold down [Option] and click anywhere in the column *or* click in any cell of the column and choose Select Column from the Table menu
Contiguous Cells	Drag over the contents of the cells *or* click in the first cell, then hold down [Shift] and click in the last cell
The Entire Table	Drag over the contents of all the cells in the table *or* hold down [Option] and double-click anywhere in the table

Entering and Editing Text and Graphics

You can enter text or paste graphics into the cells of a table. You can also sort columns or rows, number cells, and perform calculations.

Entering Information

To enter text or graphics into a table, begin by positioning the insertion point where you want the text or graphics to go. Then type or paste it in. I'll tell you more about working with graphics in Chapter 12.

If you enter more text than will fit across a cell, the text automatically wraps within the cell. At the same time, the cell stretches vertically to accommodate additional lines. If you want to, you can press Return within a cell to begin a new paragraph. Think of a cell as a tiny word processing document.

TIP/TRICK

To insert a tab character within a cell, hold down the Control or Option key while pressing Tab. Pressing Tab by itself will move the insertion point to the next cell, select the next cell's contents, or add a row at the bottom of the table as previously discussed.

Editing Information

Editing information in a table is just like editing in any other part of Word. All the standard editing techniques work. So do the Cut, Copy, and Paste commands and their Shortcut Keys.

Sorting by Column

NEW IN WORD 6

If you want to put information into alphabetical or numerical order, Word's sort feature can do the job. Although this feature is not new to Word version 6, it has been greatly improved and now has its own dialog box.

To sort the contents of a table, begin by selecting the rows you want sorted. Then choose Sort from the Table menu. The Sort dialog box appears.

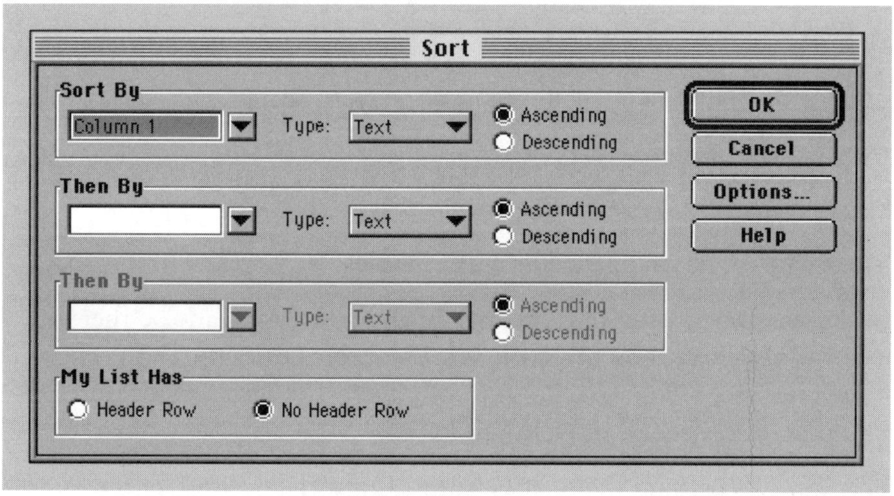

Enter the column you want to sort by in the Sort By edit box. If you're not sure what column it is, pull down the Sort By menu to display the first entry in each column and choose the one you want. Choose the type of sort — Text, Number, or Date — from the Type pop-up menu. If you want to sort in reverse order, be sure to click the Descending radio button.

These steps tell Word what you want as your "primary sort" but Word lets you sort by up to three columns. Why three? Well, say you have a table with columns for First Name, Last Name, Job Title, and Hire Date. You want to sort by Last Name, but there are five people named Jones and you want to be able to specify which comes first. You can use the Then By area to choose First Name as the secondary sort column. And, if there are two people named John Jones, you can use a second Then By area to choose another column, like the one for Hire Date, as a tertiary sort column. Think of the Then By areas as tie-breakers.

If the first row of your table contains headings for each column, be sure to turn on the radio button beside Header Row under My List Has. This tells Word not to sort in the headings. Otherwise, your headings might end up in the middle of the table!

The Sort dialog box has an Options button that offers additional options. If you click it, the Sort Options dialog box appears.

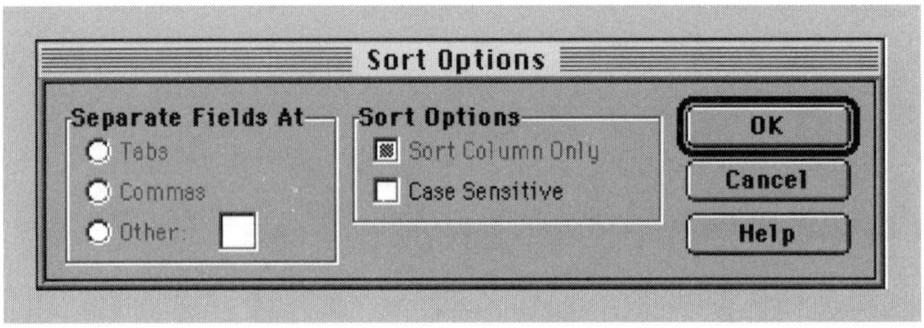

Two options can apply when sorting within tables:

- If you have selected only one column of the table, you can use the Sort Column Only check box to sort just the contents of that column. If you have selected more than one column of a table, the Sort Column Only check box will be gray as it is shown here.

Be very careful when using the Sort Column Only check box! If you sort just one column of a table, the information in the rest of that row will no longer correspond with the cell from the sorted column. This could mess up your data!

- The Case Sensitive check box lets you specify a case sensitive sort. That means uppercase letters come before lowercase letters when sorting.

When you're all finished making changes in the Sort Options and Sort dialog boxes, click OK to accept the settings and perform the sort.

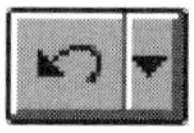

If you perform a sort and get undesirable results, choose Undo Sort from the Edit menu, press [⌘ Z], or click the Undo button to reverse it. You can then try again.

Numbering Cells

You can also number all or some of the cells within a table. Begin by selecting the cells you want to number. Then click the Numbering button on the Formatting Toolbar. The Table Numbering dialog box appears.

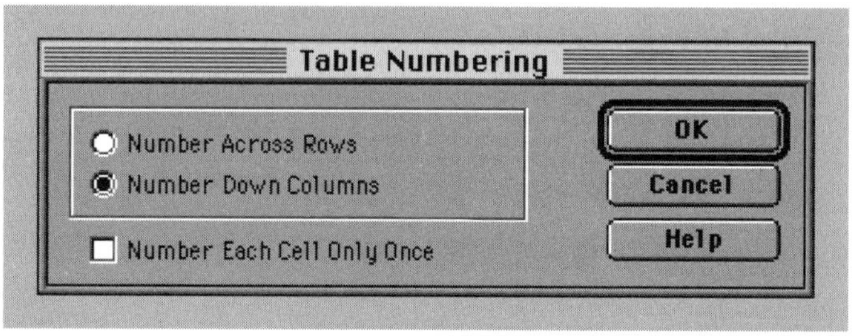

Choose the appropriate radio button for numbering across rows or down columns. If you turn on the check box for Number Each Cell Only Once, if a cell contains multiple paragraphs, only one number will be added to the cell. Otherwise, with the check box turned off, each separate paragraph within the cell will be numbered. When you click OK to accept your settings, the cells you selected are numbered. An example is shown in the following illustration. Note the ruler settings for the numbered cells. Word has automatically set indents for the numbered cells. I told you about indent settings back in Chapter 6.

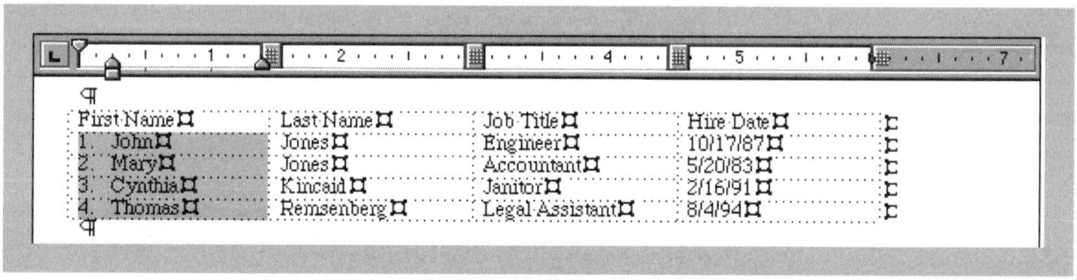

To remove numbers from cells, select the numbered cells and click the Numbering button again. The numbers are removed and the ruler settings return to normal.

If you want special number formatting, choose Bullets and Numbering from the Format menu to display the Bullets and Numbering dialog box. Click the Numbering tab if necessary to display its options and choose the format you want. I'll tell you more about the Bullets and Numbering command in Chapter 15.

Performing Calculations

NEW IN WORD 6

In Word version 6, Microsoft has greatly improved the Calculation feature, making it much more powerful and flexible. It now utilizes formulas to calculate values. The Table menu offers a Formulas command to make formulas easy to write and insert.

TIP/TRICK

If you work with Microsoft Excel, you may find it convenient to copy worksheets from Excel and paste them into your Word documents. You may be surprised to see them inserted as Word tables with all the formatting you applied in Excel. I'll tell you more about exchanging information between applications in Chapter 25.

To insert a formula in a cell, position your insertion point where you want the results of the calculation to appear. Then choose Formula from the Table menu. The Formula dialog box, which is shown here, appears.

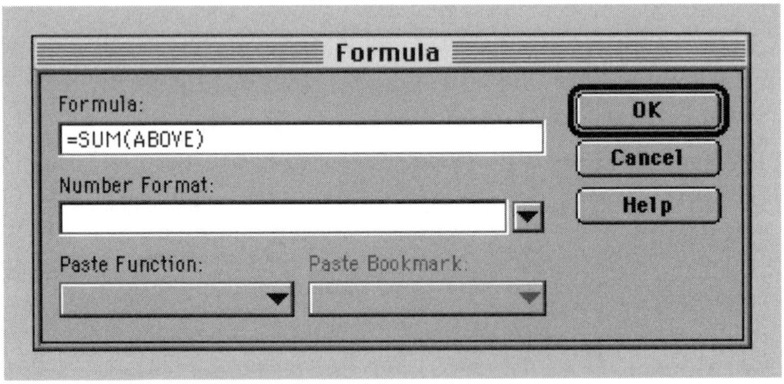

Using Word's Formula Command

When you use the Formula command, Word examines the current document and insertion point position and makes a guess at the formula you need. The =SUM(ABOVE) formula tells Word to add up (or *sum*) the contents of all the cells above the current cell. Since the insertion point was in an empty cell below a column of numbers when Formula was chosen, this makes sense. Clicking OK in this dialog box will total the column of numbers.

Writing Simple Formulas

You can also write your own formulas, using references to rows, columns, or cells in the table. References in Word work like they do in most spreadsheet programs: the column is referred to by a letter (A, B, C, etc.) and the row is referred to by a number (1, 2, 3, etc.). For example, in the previously illustrated table, the column for Last Name information would be column B (referenced as B:B), the row for Cynthia Kincaid's information would be row 4 (referenced as 4:4), and the cell containing the word "Accounting" would be C3. Column and cell address letters are not case sensitive — you can type them in capital or lowercase letters. Use standard mathematical symbols like +, -, *, and / to add, subtract, multiply, or divide one cell and another. Just remember that each formula must begin with an equal (=) sign.

Here are some examples of simple formulas:

Formula	**Purpose**
=A1+B1	Adds the contents of cell A1 and B1
=A1-B1	Subtracts the contents of cell B1 from the contents of cell A1
=A1*B1	Multiplies the contents of cell A1 by the contents of cell B1
=A1/B1	Divides the contents of cell A1 by the contents of cell B1
=A1*(B1+C1)	Adds the contents of cell B1 to the contents of cell C1, then multiplies the results by the contents of cell A1 (the parentheses tell Word what to do first)

Using Functions

Word supports a number of common functions, like those you'd find in a spreadsheet program. The Paste Function pop-up menu lets you paste them into the Formula edit box. The function name tells Word what kind of calculation to perform. The list or range of columns, rows, or cells in the parentheses after the function name tells Word which cells to perform the calculation on. Use a comma to separate references in a list and use a colon to separate the beginning and ending references in a range.

Here's a list of the most commonly used functions Word supports, along with an example of each:

Function	Purpose	Example
AVERAGE( )	Calculates the average of a list or range of numbers	=AVERAGE(A1:A6)
COUNT( )	Counts the number of entries in a list or range of cells	=COUNT(1:1)
IF(x,y,z)	Evaluates the expression x; if x is true, returns the value in y; otherwise returns the value in z	=IF(A1>B1,A5,A6)
MAX( )	Returns the value of the highest number in a list or range	=MAX(A1:D1)
MIN( )	Returns the value of the lowest number in a list or range	=MIN(A1:D1)
PRODUCT( )	Multiplies the numbers in a list or range	=PRODUCT(A1,D1)
SUM( )	Adds the numbers in a list or range	=SUM(A1:A5)

Choosing a Number Format

The Number Format pop-up menu lets you specify a specific format for the results of the calculation. Choose from among the following options for the following effects:

Format	Example
#,##0	12,345
#,##0.00	12,345.67
$#,##0.00;($#,##0.00)	$12,345.67 if positive ($12,345.67) if negative

Continued

Format	Example
0	12345
0%	67%
0.00	12345.00
0.00%	67.89%

Pasting a Bookmark

The Paste Bookmark pop-up menu only works if your Word document contains Bookmarks. Bookmarks let you reference cells anywhere in your document. I'll tell you more about Word's new Bookmark feature in Chapter 14.

Try This! Writing Formulas

If you'd like some practice writing your own formulas, create the table illustrated here and try each of the example formulas. Remember to select the contents of cell B7 (the one to the right of the word "Results") and press Del to delete its contents before you use the Formula command to write a new formula. Check your results with those provided to see how you did. You'll have to use the Number Format pop-up menu in the Formula dialog box to format some of the numbers so they look just like the results shown here:

245	236	145	258
125	456	978	354
167	256	874	236
956	483	975	453
236	987	249	995
236	254	263	684
Results			

Continued

Formula	Result	Number Format
=A1+B1	481	none
=A1-B1	9	none
=A1*B1	57820	none
=A1/B1	1.04%	0.00%
=A1*(B1+C1)	93,345	#,##0
=AVERAGE(A1:A6)	327.50	#,##.00
=COUNT(1:1)	4	none
=IF(A1>B1,A5,A6)	236	none
=MAX(A1:D1)	258	none
=MIN(A1:D1)	145	none
=PRODUCT(A1,D1)	$63,210	$#,##0.00;($#,##0.00)
=SUM(A1:A5)	1727	none

Modifying a Table's Layout

Once you've created a table, you might discover that your table doesn't look exactly as you need it to. No problem. You can modify the table's layout to add or remove cells, columns, or rows, change column width and row height, merge or split cells, and create headings. This section covers all of these tasks and more.

NEW IN WORD 6

If you've used previous versions of Word, you'll be pleased to learn that Microsoft changed the way many of its table-related tasks are accomplished. The Table Cells and Table Layout dialog boxes are gone, replaced with easy to access menu commands. If you're like me and could never remember which table dialog box did what, this will be a welcome change.

Inserting Columns, Rows, or Cells

When you insert a column, row, or cell, it is inserted to the left or above the currently selected column, row, or cell. In a way, the new column, row, or cell steps in front of the selected one, pushing it down or to the right. For this reason, it's important to begin with a selection. What you select determines what insertion option is offered on the Table menu as well as the ToolTip name that appears when you point to the Insert Table button on the Standard Toolbar. Your selection also determines how many columns, rows, or cells are inserted — for example, if you select three rows, you'll insert three rows.

Inserting a Column

To insert a column, select the column you want to appear on the right of the inserted column and choose Insert Columns from the Table menu or click the Insert Columns button. The column is instantly inserted.

To insert a column at the far right side of the table, select the end-of-row markers there. They can be selected just like any other column. Then choose Insert Column from the Table menu or click the Insert Columns button.

TIP/TRICK

Inserting a Row

To insert a row, select the row you want beneath it and choose Insert Rows from the Table menu or click the Insert Rows button. The row is instantly inserted.

You can also insert a single row anywhere in the table by positioning the insertion point at the end-of-row marker and pressing Return. To insert a row at the bottom of a table, position the insertion point in the last cell of the table or at the last end-of-row marker and press Tab.

TIP/TRICK

Inserting a Cell

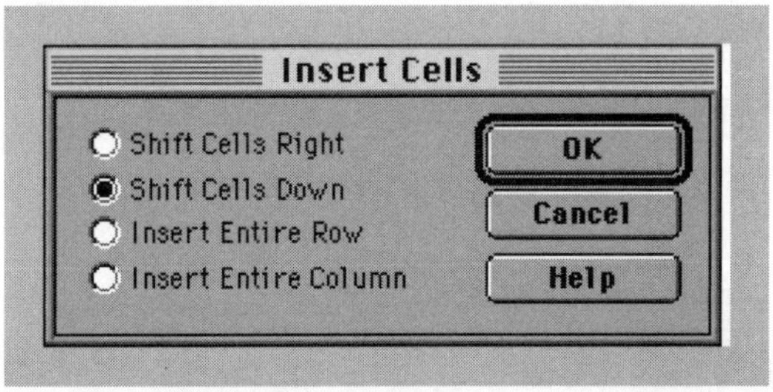

To insert a cell, select the cell and choose Insert Cells from the Table menu or click the Insert Table button. The Insert Cells dialog box appears. Use radio buttons to tell Word

where to shift the cells that begin with the selected cell. The first two options insert only one cell, shifting the others to the right or down. The last two options insert an entire row or column. When you click OK, the cell (or column or row) is inserted.

TIP/TRICK

By inserting (or deleting) cells, you can create interesting effects. The tables often used to indicate mileage on maps is a good example. Here's one I threw together to put Harrington Park in perspective:

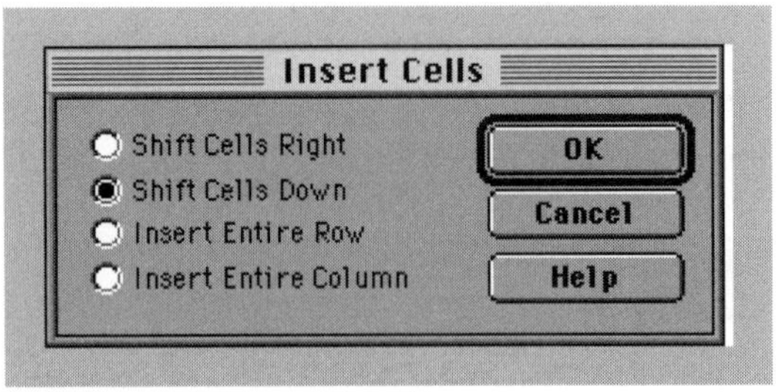

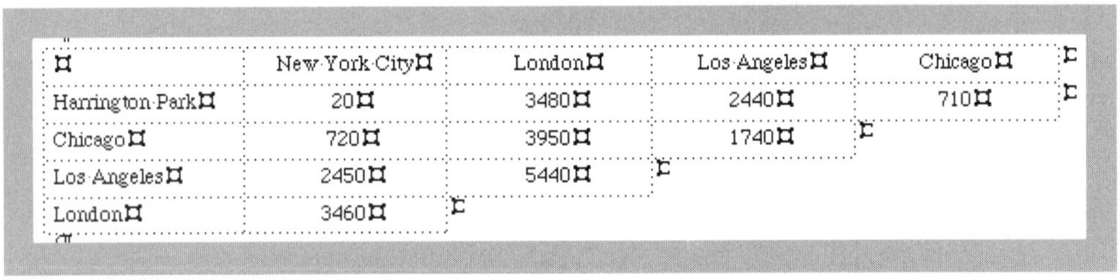

	New York City	London	Los Angeles	Chicago
Harrington Park	20	3480	2440	710
Chicago	720	3950	1740	
Los Angeles	2450	5440		
London	3460			

Deleting Columns, Rows, or Cells

When you delete columns, rows, or cells, you begin by selecting what you want to delete. Then choose the appropriate command from the Table menu: Delete Columns, Delete Rows, or Delete Cells. Columns and rows are instantly deleted. When deleting cells, however, the Delete Cells dialog box appears. Use it to specify whether Word should shift the cells to the right of the selection to the left, shift the cells below the selection up, or delete whole columns or rows. When you click OK, the cells are deleted.

TIP/TRICK

You can also delete an entire column or row by selecting it (including the end-of-row marker if you are selecting a row) and choosing Cut from the Edit menu or clicking the Cut button on the Standard Toolbar.

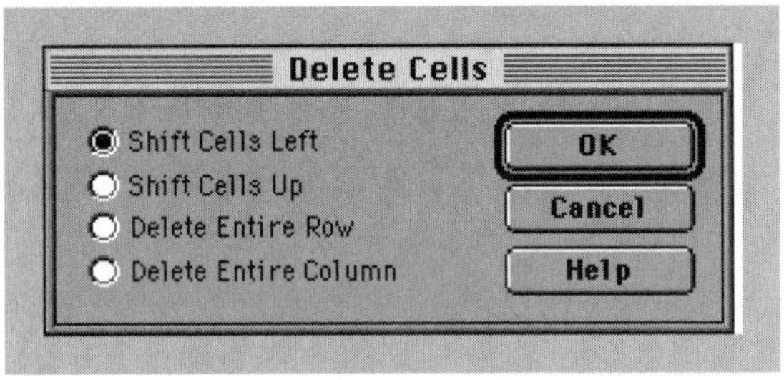

Copying or Moving Columns, Rows, or Cells

You can use Word's Copy, Cut, and Paste commands from the Edit menu, the Copy, Cut, and Paste buttons on the Standard toolbar, or drag and drop text editing to copy or move columns, rows, or cells. If you copy or move part of a table immediately before or after the table, it becomes part of the same table. If you copy or move part of the table elsewhere in your document or in another document, it becomes a separate table.

Begin by selecting what you want to copy or move and then use one of these procedures:

- To copy the selection, choose Copy from the Edit menu, click the Copy button, or press ⌘C. Position the insertion point where you want the copy to go and choose Paste from the Edit menu, click the Paste button or press ⌘V. Or, if you prefer, hold down Option while dragging the selection to a new position.

- To move the selection, choose Cut from the Edit menu, click the Cut button, or press ⌘X. Then position the insertion point where you want the selection to go and choose Paste from the Edit menu, click the Paste button, or press ⌘V. Or, if you prefer, simply drag the selection to a new position.

TIP/TRICK

If you select text within a single cell and omit the end-of-cell marker from the selection, you can copy or move the text without otherwise copying or changing the table layout.

Changing Width, Height, and Spacing

How often do you think you'll create a table that has perfect column widths? Not very often, I'll bet. Well, changing column width couldn't be easier in Word version 6. Word now gives you three ways to get the job done. The new Cell Height and Width Dialog box lets you make other adjustments to cell dimensions, too.

Dragging the Column Boundaries

Simply position the mouse pointer along the cell boundary at the end of the column you want to change. The mouse pointer turns into a double line with arrows coming out of it, like this:

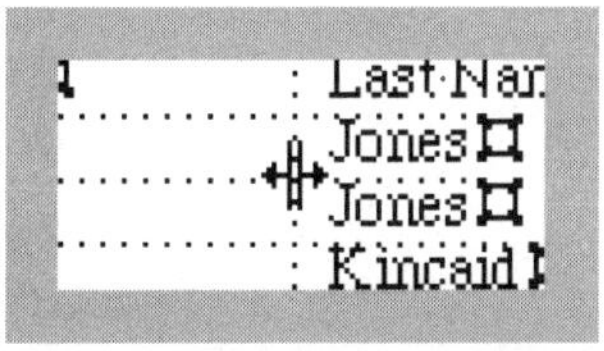

NEW IN WORD 6

Press the mouse button down and drag to the right or left to change the column width. You'll see a vertical line move along with the mouse as you drag. When you let go of the mouse button, the column width changes. All columns to the right of the column boundary you dragged are also resized in proportion to their original size. This makes it possible to change the width of a column without changing the total width of the table. Users of previous versions of Word may recognize this as a change in the way Word handles column width changes.

Dragging the Table Column Markers

If you prefer, you can also change column width by dragging the table column markers on the ruler. When you position the mouse pointer over one of these markers, it turns into a two-headed arrow. Press the mouse button and drag. When you release the mouse button, the column width changes.

TIP/TRICK

Here are some additional tips for dragging column boundaries and table column markers:

- Hold down [Shift] while dragging to change the width of only the current column and the column immediately to its right.
- Hold down [⌘] while dragging to make all columns to the right of the current column the same width.
- Hold down [⌘] and [Shift] together while dragging to change only the width of the current column. This will also change the total width of the table.
- Double-click on a column boundary to automatically adjust the column width to the widest it needs to be to accommodate information within its cells.
- To show the column widths in the Ruler, hold down [Option] while clicking on or dragging a table column marker.
- In Page Layout view, you can drag the table row markers to change the height of rows. They look like double gray lines on the vertical ruler:

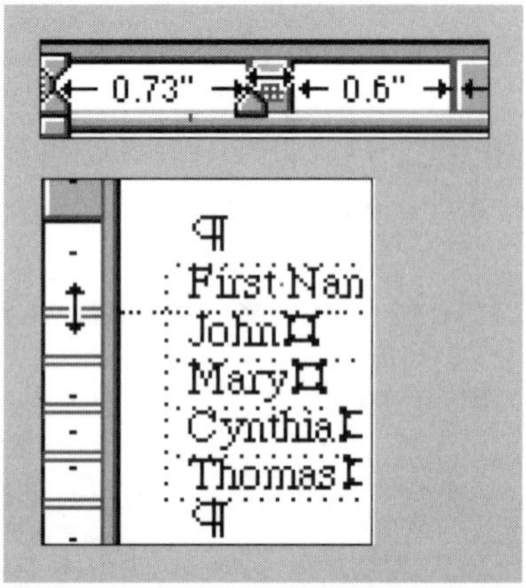

Using the Cell Height and Width Dialog Box

The Cell Height and Width dialog box lets you adjust the height of rows, the width of columns, and the spacing between columns. Begin by selecting the row or column you want to change. If you want to change the entire table, select the entire table, and then open the dialog box by choosing Cell Height and Width from the Table menu or double-clicking on a Table Column Marker on the Ruler. As you can see from the following illustration, the dialog box offers two tabs. I'll tell you about the Column tab's options first.

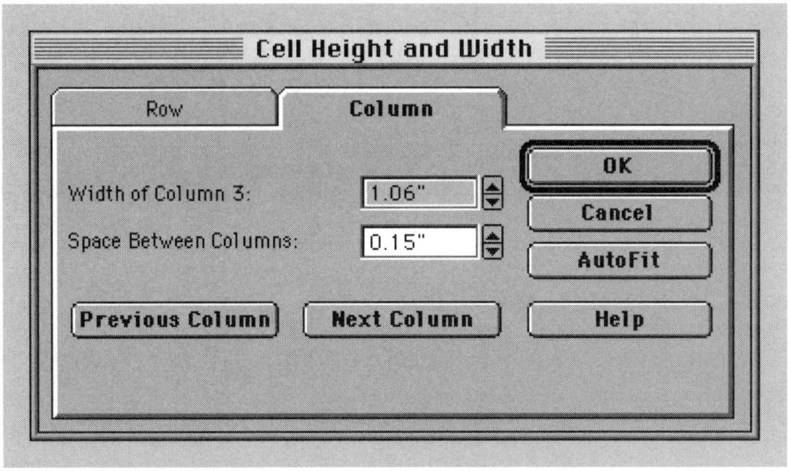

Changing Column Widths. The Column tab lets you change the width of selected columns, or, by using the Previous Column and Next Column buttons, any column in your table. Enter a new value in the Width edit box. If you click the AutoFit button, Word calculates the width of the widest cell in the column, adds a little padding, and adjusts the column width automatically.

Changing Spacing between Columns. The Space Between Columns edit box lets you specify the amount of space between each column in the table. Enter a value between 0 and 0.35. Word changes the space between columns without changing the total width of the table.

Changing Row Height. The Row tab in the Cell Height and Width dialog box lets you change the height of the selected rows, or, by using the Previous Row and Next Row buttons, any row in your table.

Use the Height Of pop-up menu to choose among the row height options:

- **Auto** — automatically adjusts the row height to accommodate all lines of text or the total height of graphics in the cell. This is the default setting.
- **At Least** — lets you specify a minimum row height for the row. Enter the value in the At box or use the tiny arrows to change the value that appears there when you choose this option.
- **Exactly** — lets you specify an exact measurement for the row height. Enter the value in the At box.

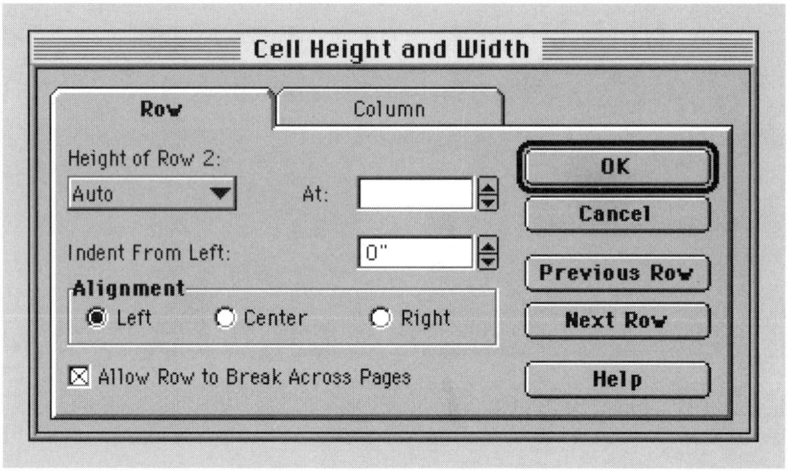

IMPORTANT NOTE

If you set an exact row height, any text or graphics that do not fit in the cells of that row will be cut off.

Merging or Splitting Cells

Word offers the ability to merge and split cells. When you merge cells, you remove the column boundary between them, turning two or more cells into one. When you split a cell, you insert a column boundary in the middle of it, turning one cell into two.

Merging Cells

To merge two or more cells, begin by selecting the cells you want to merge. They must be next to each other in the same row. Then choose Merge Cells from the Table menu. Word turns the cells into one cell and places a paragraph mark after the text or graphics that was in each individual cell before the merge.

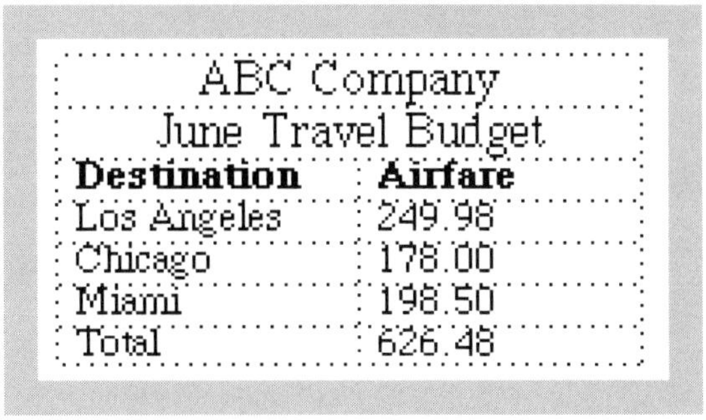

ABC Company	
June Travel Budget	
Destination	**Airfare**
Los Angeles	249.98
Chicago	178.00
Miami	198.50
Total	626.48

By merging all the cells in the first row or two of a table, you can create table headings like the one shown here.

TIP/TRICK

Splitting Cells

To split a cell, select the cell and choose Split Cells from the table menu. The Split Cells dialog box appears. Enter the number of columns you want to split the cell into. Then click OK to accept your settings. The cell splits to your specifications.

TIP/TRICK

If the cell you're splitting is not empty, you can have Word automatically distribute its contents among the new cells it creates when you split it. Position your insertion point after the contents you want placed in each new cell and press [Return]. Then make sure the number of columns you specify in the Split Cells dialog box corresponds to the number of paragraphs in the cell you're splitting.

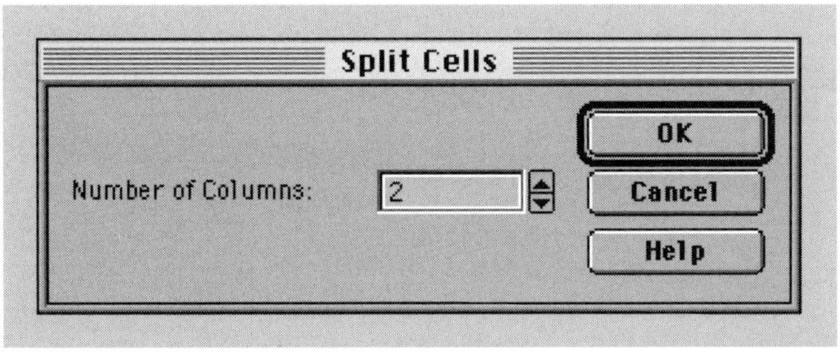

Splitting a Table

NEW IN WORD 6

Word version 6 now lets you split a table. This makes it possible to insert non-table text in the middle of a table.

Position the insertion point anywhere in the row that will be the first row in the new table. Then choose Split Table from the Table menu. Word breaks the table in two and inserts an empty paragraph between the parts.

To put a split table back together, select the paragraph mark between the two parts and choose Cut or Clear from the Edit menu, press [⌘][X] or [Del], or click the Cut button on the Standard toolbar. With the paragraph mark removed, the two tables become one.

Handling Page Breaks within a Table

If your table is long, it may not all fit on a page. You can let Word paginate your table for you, along with the rest of the document, or insert your own page breaks.

Preventing a Page Break from Occurring within a Row

NEW IN WORD 6

Word version 6 automatically inserts a page break within a row if the entire row can't fit at the bottom of a page. To prevent a page break from occurring within a row, position the insertion point anywhere within the row and choose Cell Width and Height from the Table menu. If necessary, click the Row tab to display its options. Then turn off the check box beside Allow Row to Break Across Pages. When you click OK to accept your settings, Word repaginates so that the page break falls before the selected column.

To set this for all rows in your table, select the entire table first, then use the Cell Width and Height dialog box to turn off the Allow Row to Break Across Pages check box.

Inserting a Manual Page Break

You can insert your own page breaks if you don't like the ones Word automatically calculates. I discussed page breaks in detail in Chapter 8.

To insert a page break within a table, position the insertion point in the row where you want the new page to begin. Then choose Break from the Insert menu. Make sure the Page Break radio button is selected in the Break dialog box and click OK. Word splits the table and inserts a page break and a paragraph marker.

Creating Headings

NEW IN WORD 6

If an automatic page break occurs within a table, Word version 6 is smart enough to carry table and column headings over to the next page. First, however, you must tell it that the table has headings and specify which row(s) contain them.

Select the row(s) of text containing the headings, including the first row of the table. Then choose Headings from the Table menu. If a page break occurs within the table, Word copies the row(s) you selected to the next page for the rest of the table. In fact, it'll copy the headings to every page of the table no matter how many pages your table takes up.

To remove the headings setting from the row(s), make sure they're selected and pull down the Table menu. You should see a check mark beside the Headings command. Choose that command to turn off the setting for the row(s).

IMPORTANT NOTE

In Normal view, you can't see that headings are carried forward. To check that headings are carried forward properly, view the document in Page Layout view or Print Preview. Also note that the headings setting does not work if you insert a manual page break since doing so splits the table into two separate tables.

Formatting a Table

So far, all the tables I've shown you are pretty dull. Formatting is one way to spice them up by changing the way text characters look, changing alignment and indentation within cells, changing line and paragraph spacing and adding borders and shading. You can do all this manually or have Word's Table AutoFormat feature do it for you.

Formatting Table Contents

I won't spend a lot of time telling you how to format the contents of a table's cells. Why? Because I already told you all about formatting in Chapters 5, 6, and 7. That's right. All the techniques I discussed there can be applied to tables. Begin by selecting the cells or cell contents you want to format. Then use the Formatting Toolbar buttons; ruler; Font, Paragraph, or Tabs dialog box; or Styles feature to format the selection. Chapters 5, 6, and 7 have the details.

Adding Borders and Shading

You can add borders and shading to tables, as well as paragraphs and framed objects. The command you need to use is the Borders and Shading command under the Format menu. But rather than discuss borders and shading three times, I'll discuss it all at once in Chapter 13. Don't worry, Chapter 13 pays special attention to tables.

Automatically Formatting a Table

NEW IN WORD 6

Back in Chapter 9, I told you about Word's new AutoFormat feature. It uses styles to automatically format documents based on the way text is used. The Table AutoFormat feature, which is also new to Word version 6, is specifically designed to format tables. It includes predefined formats that combine font, border, shading, color, and column width adjustments to give your table a special look — with very little effort on your part.

To use the Table AutoFormat feature, begin by selecting the table you want to format and choosing Table AutoFormat from the Table menu. The Table AutoFormat dialog box appears.

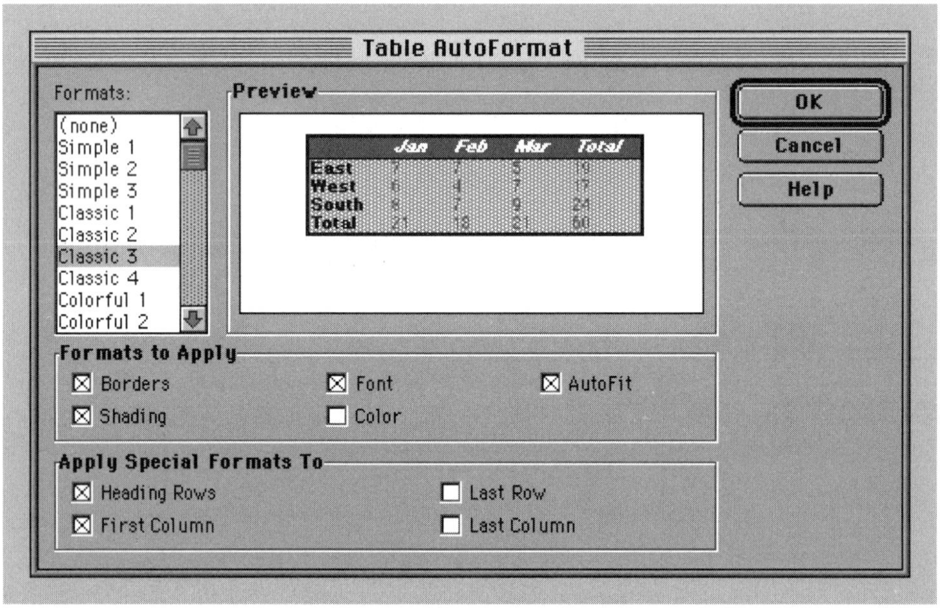

The dialog box has several parts. The Formats scrolling list provides a list of predefined formats. Click on one to see a sample of it in the Preview window. As you try the different formats, you'll get an idea of the way Table AutoFormat combines different formatting options for different looks.

The Formats to Apply check boxes let you tell Word which of the Table AutoFormat attributes you want to use. For example, say you like everything about the Classic 3 format except the shading. Simply turn off the Shading check box. You can use these check boxes in any combination.

IMPORTANT NOTE

If your table contains rows with varying numbers of columns, be sure to turn off the AutoFit check box. If you leave it on, Word may adjust the outer boundaries of your table, resulting in a table that is not rectangular.

The Apply Special Formats To check boxes let you tell Word that parts of your table should get special formatting. For example, the Classic 3 style has special formatting for the first row and columns, which include headings. If your table includes headings you've set with the Headings command, be sure to turn on the check boxes for Heading Rows and First Column.

Each time you make a change in the Table AutoFormat dialog box, the Preview window changes to reflect your change. This gives you a better idea of how your table will look when formatted. When you're all done making changes, click OK or press [Return] or [Enter] to apply the formatting.

Not bad, considering the amount of effort that went into it: one Menu command, one check box, one OK button. Done!

TIP/TRICK

If you ever use the Table AutoFormat command and find your table a mess when you're done, remember the Undo command, which I discussed in Chapter 2.

Positioning a Table on the Page

If you've got a small or narrow table like the previously shown airfares table, you can tell Word where to place it horizontally on the page. There are two ways to do this: with the Cell Height and Width dialog box or with Word's Frame feature. I'll save the Frame feature for Chapter 13. Right now, let's take a closer look at the Rows tab of the Cell Height and Width dialog box.

IMPORTANT NOTE

Before you choose Cell Height and Width from the Table menu, be sure you're selecting the part of the table you want to position. In most cases, this will be the entire table, not just a column, row, or cell. If you choose just a single table row and use the Cell Height and Width dialog box to change its position, only that row will shift. This may not be what you intended.

Indenting a Table

To indent a table, select the table and then choose Cell Height and Width from the Table menu. If necessary, click the Row tab to display its options. Enter a value in the Indent from Left edit box or use the tiny arrows to change the value already there. When you click OK to accept the settings, the table is indented from the left margin.

IMPORTANT NOTE

Indenting a table (or a table's rows) is not the same as indenting the cells in the table. To indent the cells in a table, use the ruler or the Paragraph dialog box. I discussed both of these in Chapter 6.

Aligning a Table

To align a table, select the table and then choose Cell Height and Width from the Table menu. Click the Row tab, if necessary, to display its options. Then choose one of the three alignment options: Left (the default), Center, or Right. When you click OK, the table shifts.

IMPORTANT NOTE

Changing the alignment of a table (or its rows) is not the same as changing the alignment of the contents of table cells. To change the alignment of the contents of cells, use the Formatting Toolbar. I discussed this in Chapter 6.

Chapter Summary

In this chapter, you learned all about working with tables — creating them from scratch, converting existing text into a table, the parts and nonprinting characters inside tables, and how you can move the insertion point and select cells, columns, and rows. You also learned how to enter and edit information in a table, sort table contents, number and calculate cells, modify a table's layout by inserting and deleting, and how to change column width, row height, and the spacing between columns. Finally, you learned to format your tables and how Word's Table AutoFormat feature can help you create sharp looking tables in a snap.

In the next chapter, you'll learn about graphics. You'll see how you can paste graphics into a Word document and how you can create your own graphics from scratch with Word's built-in drawing tools. You'll also learn a little bit about Microsoft Graph and the Equation Editor — two useful programs that come with Word.

12

Chapter 12: Graphics and Objects

IT ISN'T UNCOMMON THESE DAYS FOR DOCUMENTS TO CONTAIN non-text objects like graphics and charts. While Macintosh users have always had the ability to paste graphic objects into word processing documents, Word takes this a step further by including commands and tools specifically for working with graphics, stylized text, mathematical and scientific equations, and charts.

In this chapter, you'll learn how you can include non-text objects in your documents. You can either paste or import objects created with another application — like your favorite drawing program — or create and edit graphics using Word's built-in drawing tools. You can also use WordArt, a new feature in Word version 6, to create special text effects. You'll also learn how to use the Equation Editor to create complex equations, and Microsoft Graph to add custom charts to your documents. It's time to get graphic!

FYI: "Object" Defined

I've been throwing around the word "object" and I'll continue to throw it around for the rest of this chapter. It might be a good idea to explain what an object is before I continue.

An *object* is a graphic, equation, chart, table, or other collection of information that you can insert in a Word document. Objects are often created and edited with applications other than Word. An object differs from text primarily in the way it is selected and edited. Once an object has been inserted into a Word document, it can be edited, positioned, resized, or cropped. It can even be linked to its source document so if the source changes, the version inside the Word document changes. I'll tell you about linking in Chapter 25.

Inserting Pictures and Other Objects

If you've got a graphic in another file, it's easy to get it into a Word document. In this section, I'll tell you how you can paste in all or part of a graphic or import an entire graphic file. I'll also tell you how you can make a graphic fit where you want it to go.

Using Copy and Paste

Pasting pictures created with other applications into a Word document — or any other word processing document, for that matter — isn't anything new. It's been available since the early days of Macintosh, when MacWrite and MacPaint were among the few available applications. It should come as no surprise that the steps to copy and paste a graphic are very similar to the steps to copy and paste text, which I covered in Chapter 2.

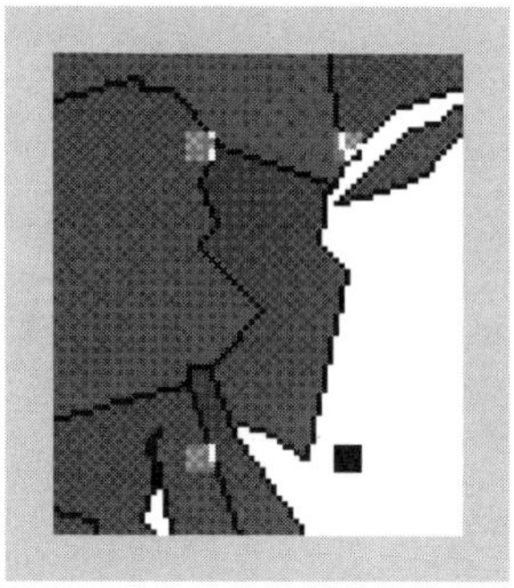

To copy a graphic from a non-Word document into a Word document, begin by opening the document that contains the graphic. Then use the selection tools offered by that application to select the part of the graphic you want in your Word document. In the following illustration, I've selected the state of New Jersey from a US Map that I opened with MacDraw Pro — you can see the selection handles in the four corners of the object boundary. Keep in mind that the selection method and tool you use to select a graphic will vary depending on the application the graphic is in. Once the graphic has been selected, choose Copy from the Edit menu or press ⌘C to copy it to the Clipboard.

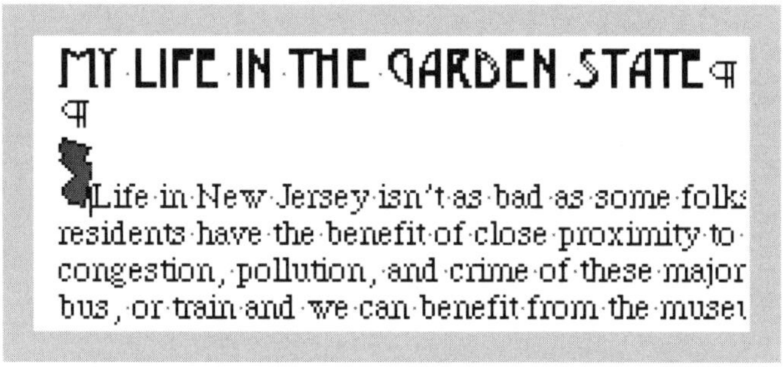

With the graphic on the Clipboard, half the job is done. Open the Word document you want to paste the graphic into, position the insertion point where you want the graphic to appear, and choose Paste from the Edit menu, press ⌘V, or click the Paste button on the Standard Toolbar. The graphic is pasted at the insertion point, as shown here.

FYI: Special Steps for EPS Graphics

EPS, which stands for Encapsulated PostScript, is a special file format created by certain graphics applications. EPS files contain PostScript codes that a PostScript printer uses to print images. But that isn't enough to display the image in a Word document. Word needs an additional screen version. To copy both versions of a selected EPS graphic to the Clipboard,

Continued

hold down Option while choosing Copy in the graphics application. The graphic is copied to the clipboard in PICT with Embedded PostScript format.

While all EPS images include PostScript printing code, not all of them include additional screen display information. If you paste one of these graphics into Word, a placeholder appears to mark the graphic's location. The actual image appears when printed.

Using the Insert Menu's Picture Command

Although Copy and Paste is an effective way to get a graphic into a Word document, it isn't always practical. Say, for example, that you've got a graphics file but don't have an application that can open it. Or that your Macintosh doesn't have enough RAM to open both the graphics application and Word at the same time and you're already working with Word. In either case, you can use the Picture command to insert an entire graphic file into a Word document.

Begin by positioning the insertion point in a Word document where you want the graphic to appear. Then choose Picture from the Insert menu. The Insert Picture dialog box appears.

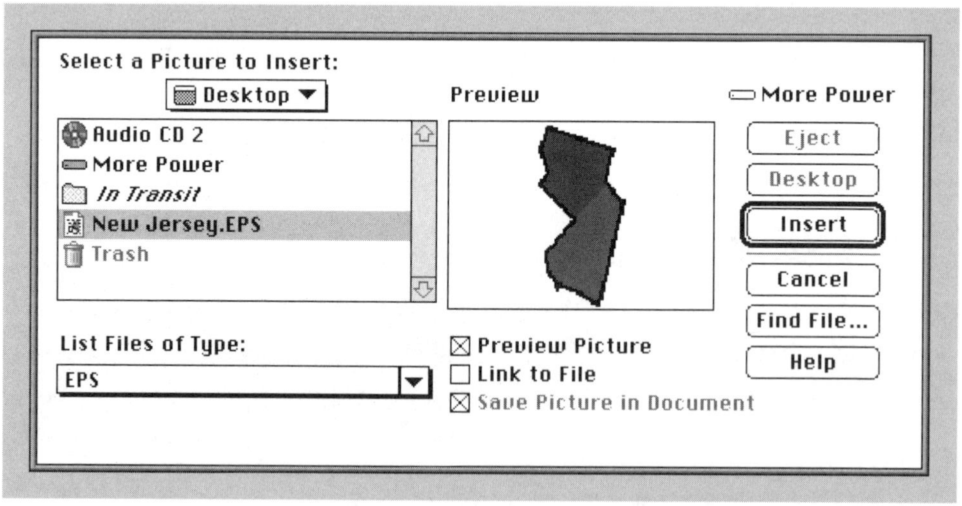

The left side of the dialog box contains a standard directory window you can use to locate and select a graphic file. You can widen or narrow the search by choosing a type of file from the List Files of Type pop-up menu beneath the window. (The options that appear there are discussed in the Graphics Filters sidebar.) If you can't find the file you want, use the Find File button to look for it with Word's search feature, which I discussed back in Chapter 3.

Once you find the picture you want to insert, click once on it to select it and then click the Insert button to paste it in (or just double-click the graphic file name). You'll see a Progress bar appear in the status area at the bottom of the screen as Word converts the graphic to a format it can use in the document. This may take a while, depending on the speed of your Macintosh and the size of the file. When the conversion is done, the graphic appears at the insertion point.

If you'd like to see a preview of the graphic before pasting it in, click the Preview Picture button in the Insert Picture dialog box before clicking Insert. Word searches the selected file for a preview (if one is available) and displays it in the Preview window — this helps ensure you've got the right picture. Since Word needs to translate the file first, it may take a few moments for the preview to appear.

TIP/TRICK

FYI: Clip Art

Word version 6.0 includes clip art — graphics files you can use in your documents. If you did a complete installation of Word, you should find a Clip Art folder inside the Microsoft Word program folder. You can preview or open a clip art file inside this folder from the Insert Picture dialog box. For more information about installing Word features, see Appendix A.

Clip art is widely available through other sources too. You can put clip art graphics into your Word documents using the Copy and Paste commands or the Picture command under the Insert menu. I think you'll find clip art a lot quicker and easier to use than creating your own drawings from scratch.

FYI: Graphics Filters

Word depends on translators and graphics filters to read graphics files. Certain translators, like those for paint and PICT files, are built into Word. Graphics filters, which are programs that tell Word how to read certain kinds of files, give Word the ability to read files in formats like TIFF (tag image file format), EPS (encapsulated PostScript), WMF (Windows metafiles), and WPG (WordPerfect graphics files). Graphics filters are stored in the Word Extensions folder and can be added or removed at any time to increase or decrease the number of file formats Word can read.

If a filter does not exist for a file format, Word will not be able to read the graphics it contains. In that case, you'll get a message telling you that Word couldn't convert the file.

One more thing. Word's translators and graphics filters are only used when you use the Picture command on the Insert menu. If you copy and paste a graphic into Word, Word doesn't need to do any conversion to insert the graphic. I guess you can consider that a benefit of copy and paste over inserting a picture.

Editing Imported Graphics

Once you've got the graphic in your document, you can crop it, or add additional graphic objects to it. I'll tell you how to do some of these things in this section and others later in this chapter.

Resizing and Cropping Graphics by Dragging

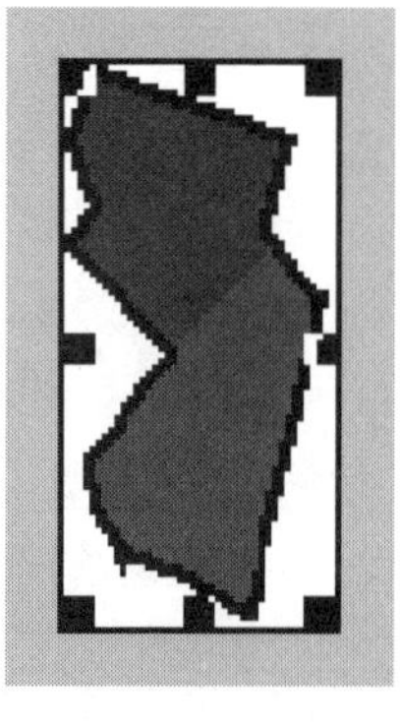

You can resize or crop a graphic object by dragging one of its sizing handles. To display the sizing handles, click once on the graphic. A box appears around the graphic. Each corner and side of the box has a sizing handle. There should be eight in all.

When you position the mouse pointer over a sizing handle, the pointer changes to either a double-headed

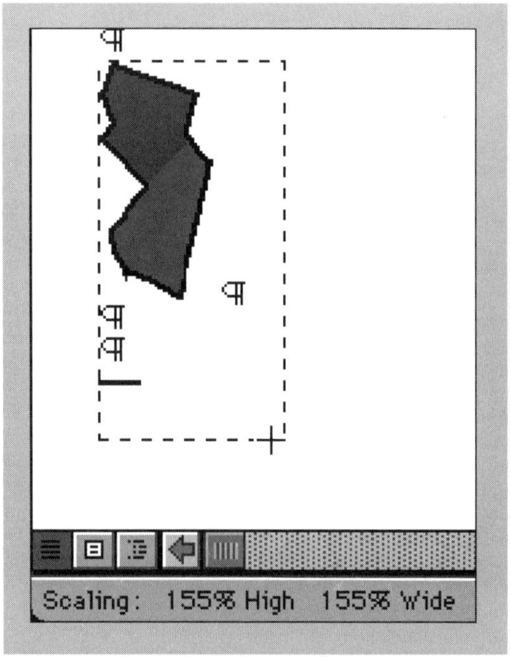

arrow (for resizing) or a cropping tool (for cropping). As you drag, a dotted-line box shows you how large or small the graphic will be while the Status bar indicates the exact change in size. When you let go, the graphic changes.

Here's how to resize or crop a graphic. If you've used previous versions of Word, read carefully since the procedures have changed a bit in Word version 6.

- To resize a graphic while retaining its original proportions, drag a corner handle.
- To stretch a graphic widthwise, drag a side handle.
- To stretch a graphic lengthwise, drag a top or bottom handle.
- To crop (or cut) out a portion of a graphic, hold down Shift while dragging the appropriate handle toward the graphic.
- To add additional white space around a graphic, hold down Shift while dragging the appropriate handle away from the graphic.

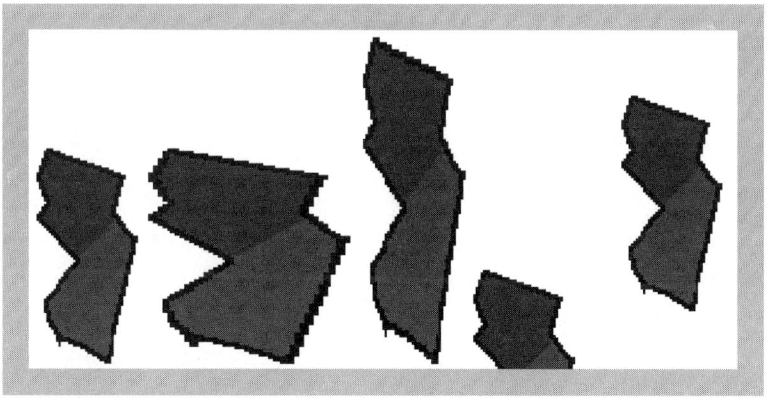

Resizing and Cropping Graphics with the Picture Dialog Box

NEW IN WORD 6

While it isn't difficult to resize or crop a graphic by dragging, if you're interested in exact measurements, you might want to use Word's new Picture dialog box. Click once on the graphic to select it and choose Picture from the Format menu. The Picture dialog box appears.

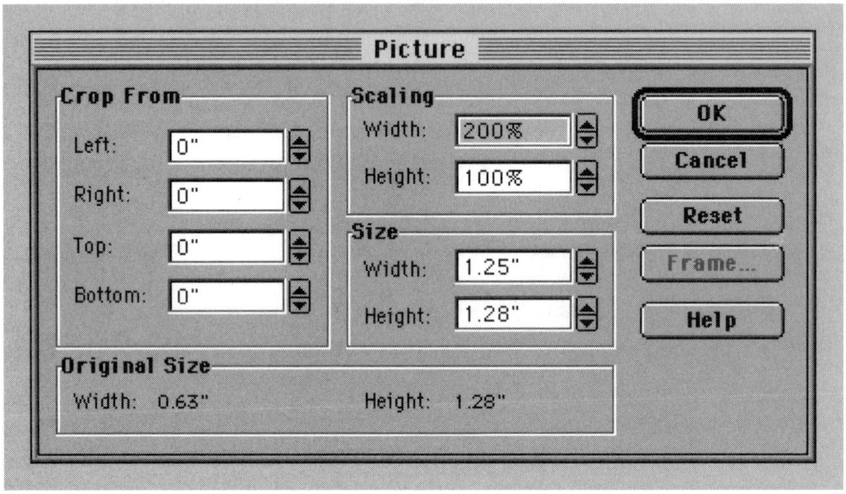

- **Crop From:** These edit boxes let you enter measurements to crop from the Left, Right, Top, or Bottom of the graphic. Positive amounts crop the graphic while negative amounts add white space.
- **Scaling:** These edit boxes let you enter scaling percentages. The percentage you enter will be applied to the original graphic size. Numbers greater than 100 make the object larger than the original while numbers smaller than 100 make the object smaller than the original. To keep the same proportions while resizing, make sure the percentages you enter in the Width and Height edit boxes are the same.
- **Size:** These edit boxes let you enter an exact Width and Height for the graphic. As you may notice, making changes in the Crop From or Scaling edit boxes changes the values in these boxes. If you enter a value in either of these boxes, it affects the scaling percentages, not cropping.
- **Original Size:** This section of the dialog box displays the Width and Height of the object as it originally appeared in the Word document.

When you're finished making changes in the Picture dialog box, click OK to accept them. The graphic changes immediately to reflect your changes.

Restoring Resized or Cropped Graphics

If you get carried away while dragging graphic handles, you can always restore a resized or cropped graphic to its original appearance. Word offers two ways to do this:

- Hold down [⌘] and double-click on one of the graphic's sizing handles *or*
- Click once on the graphic to select it and choose Picture from the Format menu, then click Reset and OK

Adding Borders and Shading to Graphics

If you're interested in adding borders or shading to a graphic object, check out Chapter 13 which discusses borders and shading in detail, and how to position a graphic object anywhere you like on a page with the use of frames.

Creating and Editing Drawing Objects

NEW IN WORD 6

Word version 6 has a brand new Drawing Toolbar filled with tools you can use to add graphics to your Word documents. Use this feature to create simple graphics composed of shapes, lines, and arrows. The new Callout and Text Box features make it easy to add and position text anywhere on your document page.

In this section, I'll tell you how to display the Drawing Toolbar and use its tools to create and edit drawing objects. I'll also tell you how you can add drawing objects to an imported graphic.

Using the Drawing Toolbar

To display the Drawing Toolbar, click the Drawing button on the Standard Toolbar. Word switches to Page Layout view, resizes the document window if necessary, and displays the Drawing Toolbar.

IMPORTANT NOTE

In order to use the Drawing Toolbar, you must be in Page Layout view or Print Preview. Drawing objects are not displayed in any other view. This is why Word automatically switches to Page Layout view when you display the Drawing Toolbar. If you switch to another view and attempt to use a Drawing Toolbar button, Word offers to switch to Page Layout view so you can use it.

Drawing Lines and Shapes

The first five buttons on the Drawing Toolbar let you draw lines and shapes. They work much like drawing tools you'd find in drawing or painting applications. To use a tool, click on it to select it and then drag in the document window to draw. After drawing a line or shape, the tool you used becomes deselected. If you want to draw more than one object with the same tool, double-click it to select it and lock it in until you choose another tool, press Esc, or click in the document window.

- **Line** — draws straight lines. If you hold down Shift as you drag, you can force the line to be horizontal, vertical, or at an angle of 30°, 45°, or 60°.

- **Rectangle** — draws a rectangle. If you hold down Shift as you drag, you can draw a square.

- **Ellipse** — draws an oval or ellipse. If you hold down Shift as you drag, you can draw a circle.

- **Arc** — draws an arc, which is a line representing one quarter of an ellipse. If you hold down Shift as you drag, you can draw the arc of a circle.

- **Freeform** — combines a freeform drawing tool with a straight line tool. Click to anchor starting and ending points with straight lines between them. Drag to draw freeform lines. To create a closed freeform shape, click the first point to close the shape. To create an open freeform shape, double-click the last point or press Esc. To delete the last segment of a freeform shape as you are creating it, press Delete.

FYI: About those Anchors

When you select a drawing object, an anchor icon appears in the left margin. Did you notice? If not, draw something, make sure it's selected, and see for yourself. You may have to click the Show/Hide ¶ button to see it.

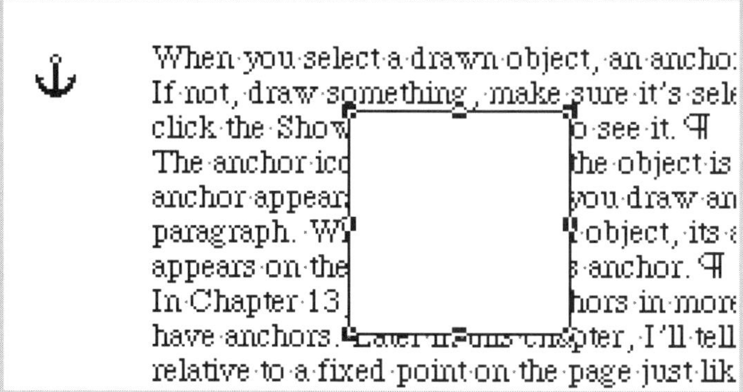

The anchor icon indicates that the object is anchored to a specific paragraph — the one the anchor appears beside. When you draw an object, it is automatically anchored to the nearest paragraph. When you move an object, its anchor moves, too. A drawing object always appears on the same page as its anchor.

In Chapter 13, I'll discuss anchors in more detail when I talk about frames, which also have anchors. Later in this chapter, I'll tell you how you can position a drawing object relative to a fixed point on the page just like you can do with frames.

Creating Text Boxes

A text box is a graphic object you can fill with text and position anywhere on the page. While frames, which I'll discuss in Chapter 13, also let you position text anywhere on the page, text boxes can be placed on top of another object or document text. This may make them a bit more flexible than frames for certain purposes.

To create a text box, click the Text Box tool to select it and drag a box anywhere on the document page. The text box appears, complete with an insertion point and paragraph mark inside it. (If you don't see the paragraph mark, click the Show/Hide ¶ button on the Standard Toolbar to display it.) A gray border around the text box indicates that it is selected. The text box also has a thin line around it; I'll tell you how to remove that a little later in this chapter.

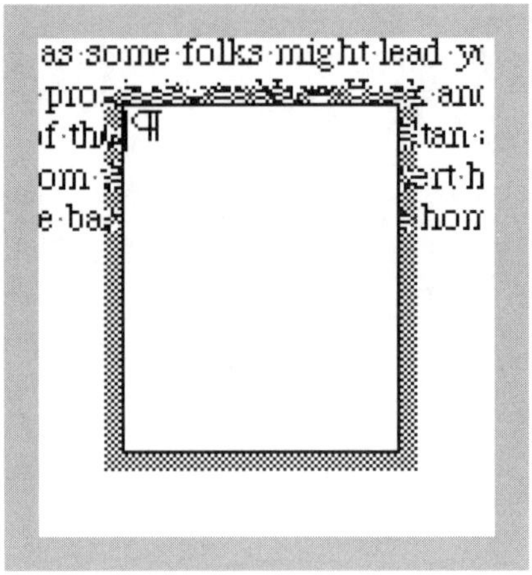

To enter text in the text box, simply type at the insertion point inside it. Treat the text box like a little word processing document. You can enter, edit, and format text just as you can in a Word document. You can even change paragraph justification and spacing and add tabs. These are all things I covered in Chapters 5 and 6. If the text box isn't big enough for the text you want to put into it or if it's too big, you can resize it. I'll tell you how to do that in a while.

Creating and Formatting Callouts

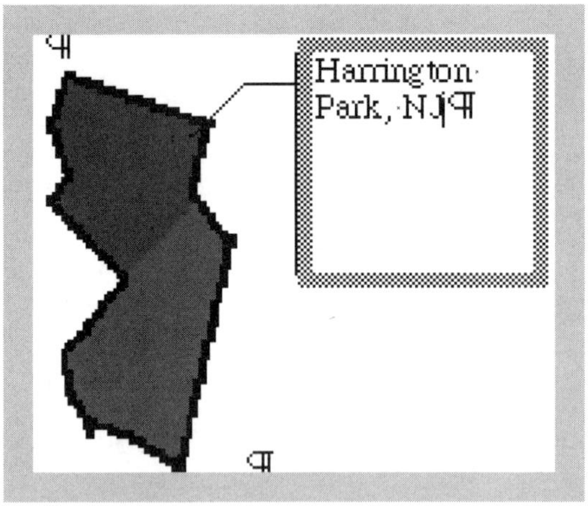

A callout is a text box with a line attached to it. When you draw a callout, you can enter text into its text box and position the line so that it points to something in your document. The result can be impressive.

To create a callout, click the Callout button to select it and draw a line beginning at the item you want to point to and ending where you want the callout text to appear. Word automatically formats the callout line and text box — I'll tell you how to change them in a moment. Type the callout text into the text box. You can format it just like any other text box or a Word document.

The Format Callout button lets you change the appearance of the callout. Click the callout to select it and then click the Format Callout button. The Format Callout dialog box appears.

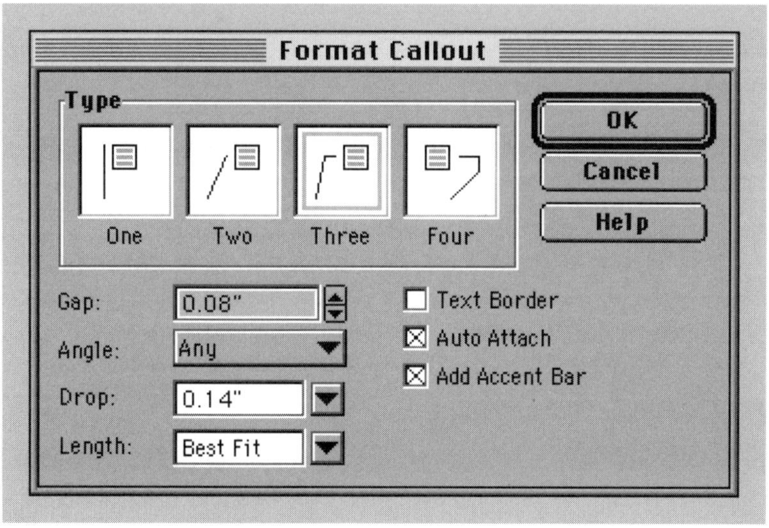

- **Type** — lets you select from among the different types of callout lines. The numbers beneath each illustrated type represent the number of points in the callout line. Although One and Two each have two points, One must be either horizontal or vertical but Two can also be diagonal at any angle. The default selection is three, which gives you a two-segment line like the one in the previous figure.
- **Gap** — lets you enter a value for the distance between the callout text and the callout line.
- **Angle** — lets you choose from among standard angles — 30 degrees, 45 degrees, 60 degrees, or 90 degrees — for the angle of the callout line. You can choose Any to have Word automatically adjust the angle for you based on how you drag the callout text box. The Angle option is gray if you choose One from Type.
- **Drop** — lets you select a position — Top, Center, or Bottom — for the placement of the callout line in relation to the callout text. If you prefer, you can type a value into the edit box representing the distance from the top of the callout text to the callout line.

- **Length** — lets you enter a measurement to change the length of the first segment of the callout line. To have Word automatically adjust the length of the line as you drag callout text, choose Best Fit. The Length option is gray if you choose One or Two from Type.
- **Text Border** — when turned on, places a border around the callout text box.
- **Auto Attach** — when turned on, moves the callout line to the bottom of the callout text box if the box is moved to the left of the object the line points to.
- **Add Accent Bar** — when turned on, adds a vertical line beside the callout text box.

When you're finished making changes in this dialog box, click OK to accept them. You'll see your changes immediately.

To change the default callout settings, click the Format Callout button when no callout is selected. Make changes in the dialog box and click OK. From then on, all callouts you create will have the settings you specified.

TIP/TRICK

Working with Graphic Objects

Once you've drawn a graphic object, you can select it, edit it, copy it, move it, change its stacking order in relation to other objects, or group it with other objects. I'll tell you how to do all these things in this section.

Selecting Objects

To select a graphic object, click on it. As the mouse pointer moves over a drawing object, it turns into a smaller pointer with a four-headed arrow. When you click, the object is selected and sizing handles appear around it. Some objects, such as text boxes and callout text boxes, get gray borders around them when selected. To select multiple objects, hold down Shift while clicking on each one. To deselect an object that is part of a multiple-object selection, hold down Shift and click on it.

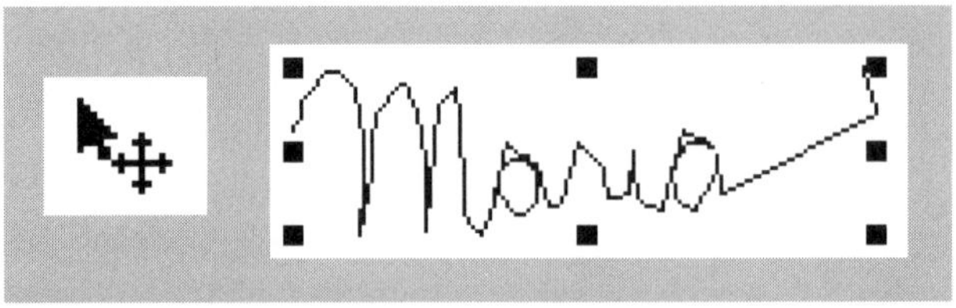

If you need to select a drawing object that is beneath text, use the Select Drawing Objects tool. Click on the tool to select it and then click on the object. It becomes selected. You can also use the Select Drawing Objects tool to select multiple objects. Drag a selection marquee around the objects you want to select. When you release the mouse pointer, any drawing object that was entirely inside the marquee is selected.

To deselect any selected objects, click anywhere in the document window, other than on a selected object, or press [Esc].

Deleting Drawing Objects

To delete a drawing object, select it and press [Delete] or [Del], or choose Clear from the Edit menu.

Resizing and Reshaping Drawing Objects

As you may have already guessed, the resizing handles that appear around a drawing object can be used to resize or reshape the object. Position the mouse pointer over one of the handles and it turns into a two-headed arrow. Press the mouse button down and drag to resize or reshape the object. This works with any drawing object, including text boxes, callout boxes, and freeform lines or shapes.

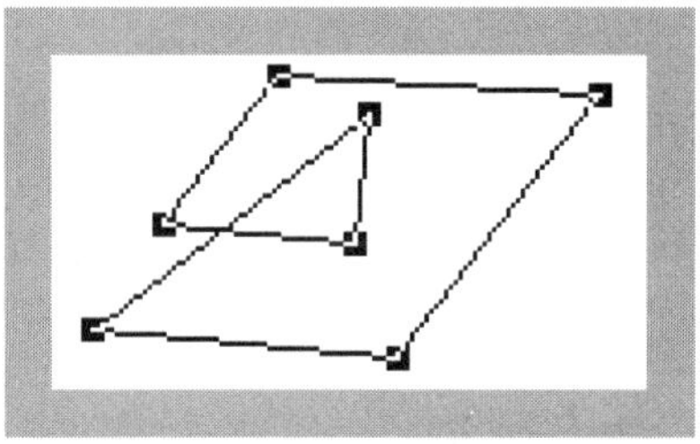

TIP/TRICK

To break a freeform shape into its component lines, click the Reshape button. An example is shown here. You can then drag any of the selection handles to a new position to reshape the freeform shape. When you're finished, click the Reshape tool again to accept the change.

Moving Drawing Objects

You can also move a drawing object. Position your mouse pointer on the object anywhere except on a sizing handle. (If the object is not filled, you may have to position the mouse pointer on a border of the object.) Then press the mouse button down and drag. You'll see the outline of the object move as you drag. When you let go, the object moves to its new position.

TIP/TRICK

To move a drawing object without using the mouse, use the arrow keys. Each time you press an arrow key on your keyboard, the selected object moves one grid space in the direction of the arrow. (I'll tell you about the grid in a little while.) To move an object a tiny bit at a time, hold down Option while pressing an arrow key. Each time you press the arrow key, the object moves one pixel. This is referred to as *nudging*. This is a precise way to position drawing objects when your mouse hand can't seem to get it right.

Copying Objects

One way to copy an object is with the ever-popular, Copy and Paste commands. Select the object you want to copy and choose Copy from the Edit menu or click the Copy button. Then choose Paste from the Edit menu or click the Paste button. The pasted copy may wind up right on top of the original, so you may have to drag it from there to see it.

The other way to copy a drawing object is to hold down Option while moving an object. When you let go of the mouse button, a copy of the object appears.

Grouping Objects

You can group two or more drawing objects together. Doing this turns them into a single object that you may find easier to select and position in your document. Grouped objects are also much faster for Word to display.

To group multiple objects into one object, begin by selecting all the objects you want to include in the group. I told you how earlier in this section. Then click the Group button. The separate sizing handles around each object disappear, replaced by a set of sizing handles that surround all the objects in the group, like this:

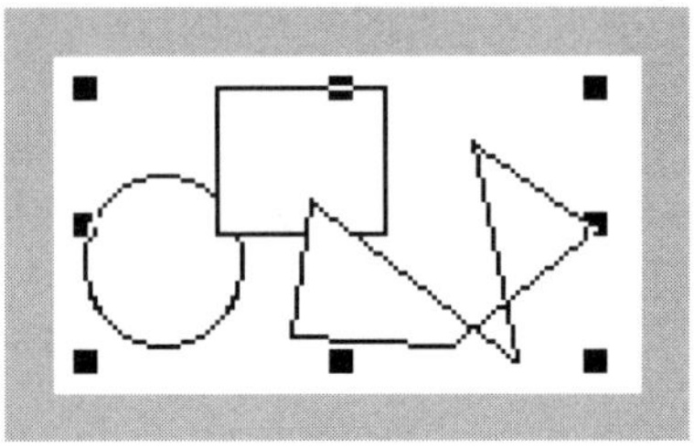

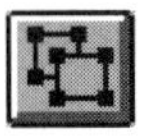

To ungroup objects in a group, select the group and click the Ungroup button. If a group consists of multiple groups, you may have to click the Ungroup button more than once to separate all components.

Aligning Objects

The Align Drawing Objects button makes it easy to align drawing objects. Select the objects you want to align and click the Align Drawing Objects button. The Align dialog box appears.

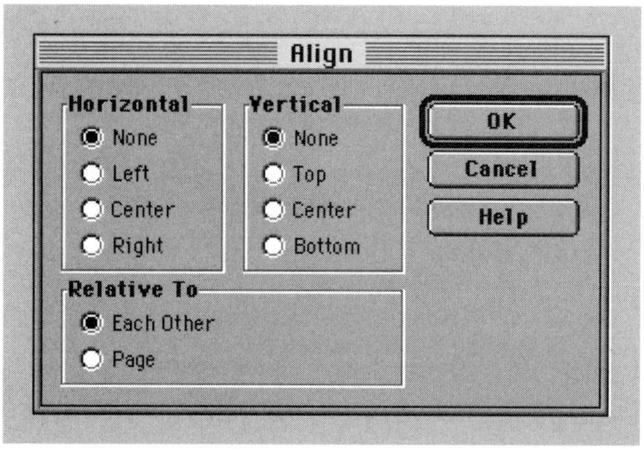

- **Horizontal** — offers four radio buttons to set horizontal alignment: None, Left, Center, or Right.
- **Vertical** — offers four radio buttons to set vertical alignment: None, Top, Center, and Bottom.
- **Relative To** — lets you tell Word whether you want to align objects relative to each other or the page. If you choose Each Other, the objects remain in the same area on the page. If you choose Page, the objects are moved to the edges or center of the page, depending on your other choices in the dialog box.

When you're done setting options, click OK to accept them. The objects align.

TIP/TRICK

Remember the Oops! command: Undo. If the settings you make in the Align dialog box yield unexpected results, it's a lot easier to undo the change and try again than to try to fix whatever mess you made.

Changing Object Stacking Order

As you may have noticed while drawing, the lines, shapes, text boxes, and callouts you create are drawn in different layers of the document. Each time you draw an object, imagine that it is drawn on a fresh transparency placed over the document page. There's a new transparency or layer for each object. If you draw an object on top of an existing object or text, the object or text beneath it is hidden from view. This is referred to as layering or stacking order.

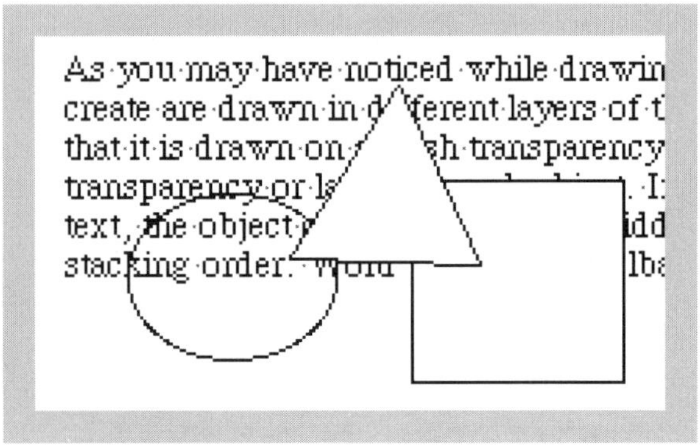

Although a Word document has three main layers — the text layer, the layer in front of the text, and the layer behind the text — the two non-text layers can have as many "sublayers" as objects placed in them. You can get a rough idea of this by looking at the following illustration. In it, the circle is in a layer behind the text and the triangle and rectangle are in layers in front of the text. The triangle is in a layer in front of the rectangle. See?

Word's Drawing Toolbar gives you four tools to change layering. This makes it possible to, in effect, "shuffle" the transparencies.

- **Bring to Front —** moves the selected object to the front or topmost layer.

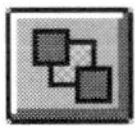

- **Send to Back —** moves the selected object to the back or bottom layer. The bottom layer, however, is still above the text layer, so using this button will not send an object behind the text.

- **Bring in Front of Text —** moves the selected object to the layer in front or on top of the text layer. If the object is already in front of the text, this button won't do anything except make your Macintosh beep at you.

- **Send Behind Text —** moves the selected object behind the text layer. If the object is already behind the text, this button won't work.

FYI: Drawing Objects vs. Pictures and Imported Graphics

The time has come to make an important distinction: the difference between a drawing object and a picture or imported graphic.

A drawing object is something you draw on the page with the drawing tools. You must draw it and view it in either Page Layout view or Print Preview. Once drawn, the object is in its own layer either in front of or behind the text layer. A drawing object is never in the text layer.

Continued

A picture or imported graphic, however, is always in the text layer. You can view it and work with it in any view, including Normal, Outline, and Master Document view.

TIP/TRICK

Here are a few tips you might find helpful when you need an object or graphic in a different layer.

- To move a pasted or imported graphic out of the text layer, draw a text box large enough to contain it, cut it out of the document, and paste it into the text box. If desired, you can move it behind the text layer by selecting it and clicking the Send Behind Text button.

- To move a drawing object to the text layer, select it and click the Insert Frame button. This creates a frame the same size as the object and places the object in it. Since frames are in the text layer, the object moves to the text layer. I'll tell you more about frames in Chapter 13.

Flipping and Rotating Drawing Objects. Word offers three tools to let you flip or rotate a drawing object.

- **Flip Horizontal** — flips the selected object horizontally. That means it flips from right to left.

- **Flip Vertical** — flips the selected object vertically. That means it turns it upside down.

- **Rotate Right** — rotates the selected object 90° to the right or clockwise.

Using the Grid. Each document page includes an invisible grid. Although you can't see it, you can modify it and use it. You may find it helpful when drawing and manually aligning objects. To use the grid, click the Snap to Grid button. The Snap to Grid dialog box appears.

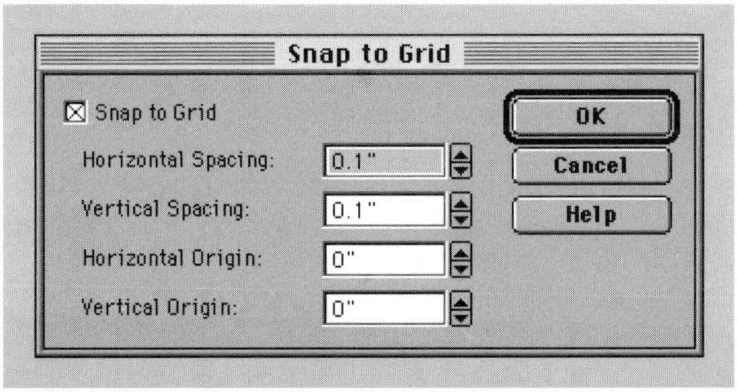

By default, the grid has spacing of $^{1}/_{10}$ of an inch horizontally and vertically and begins at the very top left corner of the document page. The Snap to Grid dialog box lets you change all that as well as turn the Snap to Grid feature on or off.

- **Snap to Grid** — when turned on, forces all objects you draw or move to align with the invisible grid.
- **Horizontal Spacing** — lets you enter a measurement for the amount of space horizontally between grid lines.
- **Vertical Spacing** — lets you enter a measurement for the amount of space vertically between gridlines.
- **Horizontal Origin** — lets you enter a measurement from the left edge of the paper to begin the grid.
- **Vertical Origin** — lets you enter a measurement from the top edge of the paper to begin the grid.

TIP/TRICK

I like to work with Snap to Grid turned on. I find that it helps me draw consistently-sized and positioned objects. In addition, holding down the [⌘] key while drawing or moving an object temporarily reverses the Snap to Grid setting. So I can disable it at any time without opening the Snap to Grid dialog box.

Changing the Appearance and Position of Drawing Objects

So far, all I've told you is how to draw objects and juggle them around a bit. I haven't told you how you can add color, change line thicknesses, and position them precisely where you want them on the page. That's what this section's all about.

IMPORTANT NOTE

While Word enables you to add color to drawing objects, remember that if you do not have a color printer, the objects will not print in color. Instead, they will print in varying shades of gray or black and white, depending on your printer and the Print dialog box options you choose. For more information about printing, check Chapter 4.

Using the Fill and Line Buttons

Word's Drawing Toolbar offers three buttons to change the appearance of a selected object.

The Fill Color button is like a menu. When you position your mouse pointer on it and press your mouse button down, a menu of colors and shades of gray appear. The default selection is white, but you can change it to any color by choosing a color from the menu and releasing the mouse button. The inside color of the object changes.

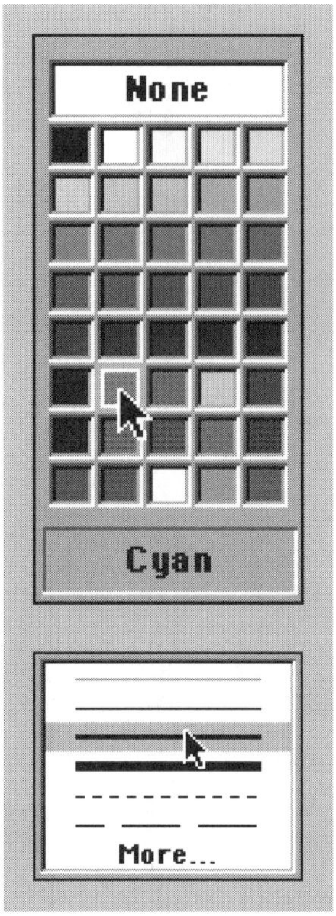

If you choose None, the object becomes transparent. In order to select that object from then on, you'll have to click on the border of the object.

The Line Color button looks and works the same way as the Fill Color button. Choose a color from it to change the color of the line.

The Line Style button is also a menu. Position the mouse pointer on it and press the mouse button down to display several line styles. If you choose the More option, Word opens the Drawing Object dialog box, which I'll discuss next.

TIP/TRICK

The choices you make with the Fill Color, Line Color, and Line Style dialog box affect selected objects. If no object is selected, the choices you make affect all objects you draw. This is how you can change the default settings for these three options.

Using the Drawing Object Dialog Box

The Drawing Object dialog box offers more options for drawing objects. To display it, use one of these methods:

- Select the object you want to change and choose Drawing Object from the Format menu *or*
- Double-click on the object you want to change

The Drawing Objects dialog box has three tabs: Fill, Line, and Size and Position. Let's look at them one at a time.

Changing Object Fill Color and Pattern

The Fill tab lets you change the color and pattern of an object's fill.

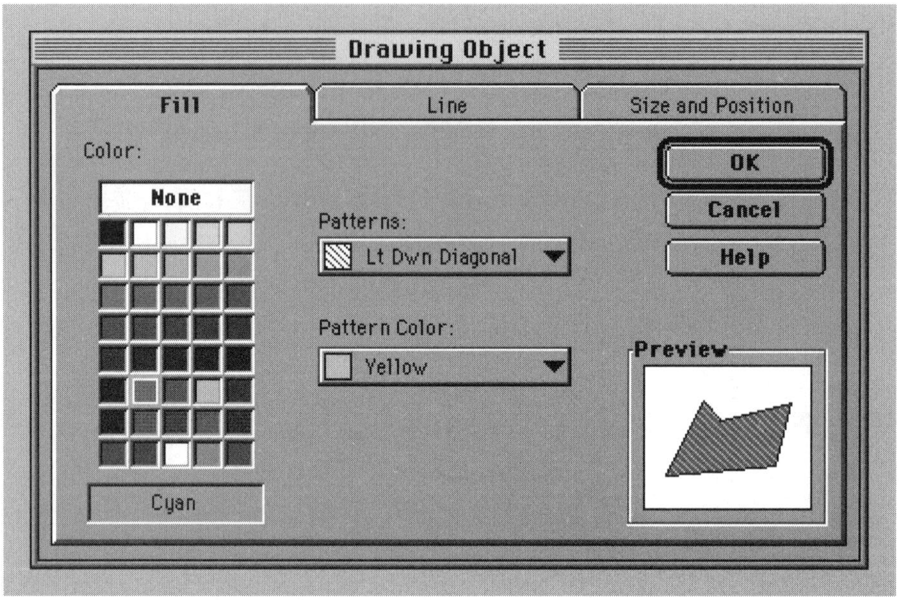

- **Color —** offers the same color options as the Fill Color button. These are background colors. Click on a color to select it. The name of the color appears at the bottom of the palette of choices.
- **Patterns —** has a pop-up menu of patterns. The percentages represent shading percentages or tints of color. Actual patterns appear further down on the menu. A sample of each pattern appears beside it.
- **Pattern Color —** has a pop-up menu of colors and shades of gray for the foreground of a pattern.

As you make changes in the dialog box, the Preview area shows you how the fill will look when you click OK.

Changing Line Thickness, Style, Color, and Arrowhead

The Line tab lets you change the appearance of an object's line. This works for lines drawn with the Line or Arc tool or the line around any other object you draw.

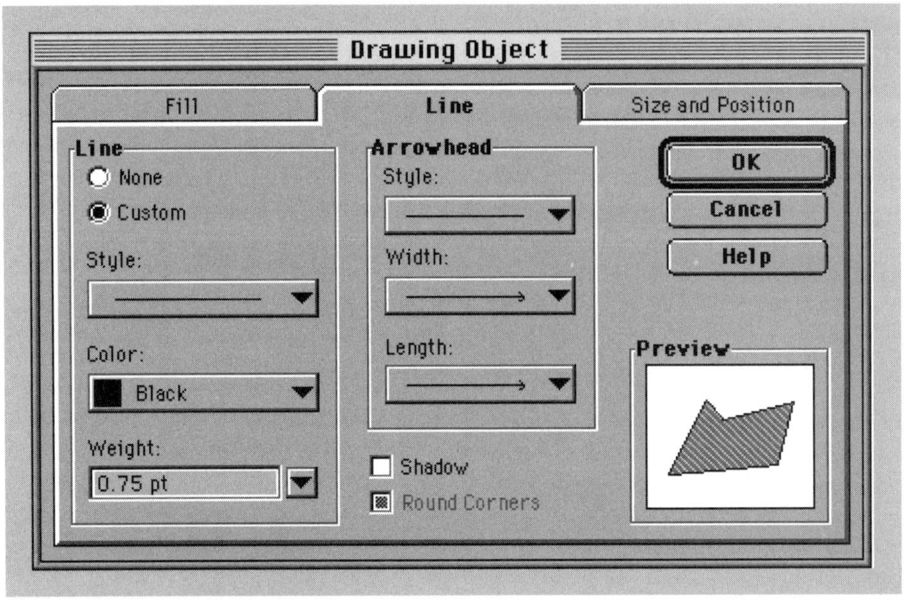

- **Line** — lets you change the appearance, style, color, and weight of a line. Click the None or Custom radio button to tell Word whether it should include a line at all. If you choose None, the line is removed from the object. Use the Style pop-up menu to choose from among a variety of line styles, including non-breaking, dashed, and dotted lines. Use the Color pop-up menu, which offers the same options as the Line Color button, to select a line color. Use the Weight edit box and pop-up menu to enter or select a line thickness. Weights are measured in points — a typographical measurement roughly equal to $^1/_{72}$ inch.
- **Arrowhead** — lets you add or customize arrowheads on straight lines. These options will be gray if a closed shape or arc is selected. Use the Style pop-up menu to choose an arrowhead style and determine which side of the line the arrowhead appears on. Choose the top option without the arrowheads if you want a plain line without arrowheads. Use the Width pop-up menu to choose an arrowhead (not line) width. Use the Length pop-up menu to choose an arrowhead (not line) length.
- **Shadow** — when turned on, places a shadow to the lower right of the object. This gives the object a three dimensional effect.
- **Round Corners** — when turned on, rounds the corners of rectangles, squares, text boxes, and callout boxes.

The Preview area shows an example of the object with the changes applied.

Positioning and Sizing Objects

The Size and Position tab lets you position the drawing object on the page and specify an exact size for it. It works a lot like some of the options in the Frame dialog box, which I'll talk about in the next chapter.

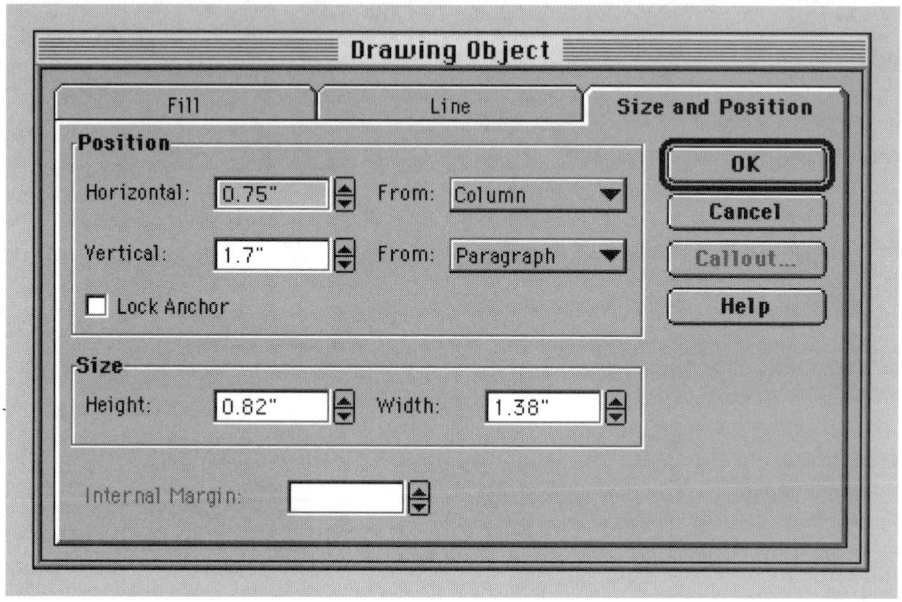

- **Position —** lets you specify the horizontal and vertical measurements that determine the drawing object's position on the page. Enter horizontal and vertical measurements in relation to locations you choose from the From pop-up menus beside them. You can position an object horizontally in relation to the left side of the margin, page, or column. You can position an object vertically in relation to the top of the margin, page, or paragraph containing the object's anchor.
- **Lock Anchor —** when turned on, locks the object's anchor to its current position so that it doesn't move, even when the object is moved.
- **Size —** lets you enter measurements for the exact Height and Width of the selected object.
- **Internal Margin —** which only appears if a text box or callout box is selected, lets you specify the distance between the edge of the box and the text within it.

If a callout is selected, you can click the Callout button to open the Format Callout dialog box, which I discussed earlier in this chapter.

Working with Pictures

So far, I've told you about pasted or imported graphics and drawing objects. But that isn't the only kind of graphic you can work with in Word. Word also lets you draw pictures.

A picture is similar to a pasted or imported graphic since it resides on the text level. That means you can view pictures in any Word view: Normal, Outline, Master Document, Page Layout, or Print Preview. Drawing objects, if you recall, reside either in front of or behind the text level and must be viewed in either Page Layout view or Print Preview.

Creating a Picture

To add a picture to a Word document, position the insertion point where you want the picture to appear and click the Create Picture button on the Drawing Toolbar. (If the Drawing Toolbar is not already showing, click the Drawing button on the Standard Toolbar to display it.) Word opens a new window in Page Layout view and displays the tiny Picture Toolbar. A dotted line box inside the document window indicates the boundaries of the picture you're about to create. A blinking insertion point and paragraph marker are inside the box. (Why? Because pictures are created on the text level.)

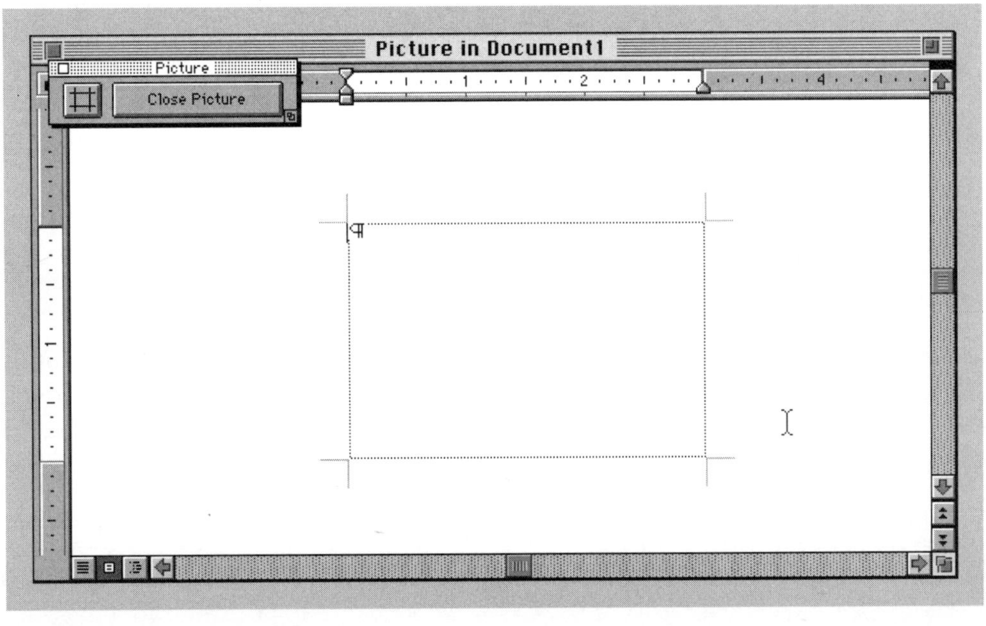

To create the picture, use the drawing tools I've been telling you about throughout this chapter. Start drawing inside the box. If your picture doesn't fit, don't worry about it for now. Just make the picture look exactly the way you want it to, using whatever Drawing tools and Menu commands you need to get the job done.

When your picture is finished, click the Reset Picture Boundary button on the Picture Toolbar. This automatically adjusts the boundaries of the picture so that the box enclosing the picture is exactly the size it needs to be to display the picture. Then click the Close Picture button. Word closes the window it opened and inserts the picture in your document, right at the insertion point.

Adding Drawing Objects to an Imported Graphic

Sometimes, you might find yourself with a pasted or imported graphic that you'd like to embellish with additional graphics or text. Word lets you edit graphics in a picture window. To edit a picture, simply double-click on it. Word opens a picture window with the graphic inside it. You can then add drawing objects to the graphic using the drawing tools. When you're finished, click the Reset Picture Boundary button to adjust the size of the picture and the Close Picture button to close the picture window.

IMPORTANT NOTE

If you double-click on an EPS graphic, Word displays a dialog box warning you that the picture contains embedded PostScript information and that converting it will discard PostScript data. Click OK only if you don't mind losing the PostScript information.

Positioning Pictures

To position a picture precisely on the page, you must put it inside a frame or inside a drawing object text box.

- To put a picture inside a frame, click on the picture to select it and click the Insert Frame button. I'll tell you more about frames, including how to position them, in Chapter 13.

- To put a picture inside a text box, use the Text Box tool to draw a text box, then cut the graphic out of the document and paste it into the text box. I told you how to position drawing objects earlier in this chapter.

WordArt, Equation Editor, and Microsoft Graph

When you do a complete installation of Microsoft Word, several additional applications are installed. Among these are WordArt, Equation Editor, and Microsoft Graph. These programs have two things in common: they utilize OLE (object linking and embedding) and they insert graphic objects into Word documents.

In this section I'll tell you how you can use WordArt, Equation Editor, and Microsoft Graph to spice up your documents. I'll tell you more about OLE in Chapter 24 and about installing Word features in Appendix A.

WordArt

NEW IN WORD 6

WordArt is a brand new Word application you can use to create special text effects like arched text, text flowed into a shape, or three dimensional text. With a little imagination, you can even use WordArt to create company logos.

Not only is WordArt cool, but it's incredibly easy to use. Begin by positioning the insertion point where you want the WordArt object to appear. Then choose Object from the Insert menu. The Object dialog box appears.

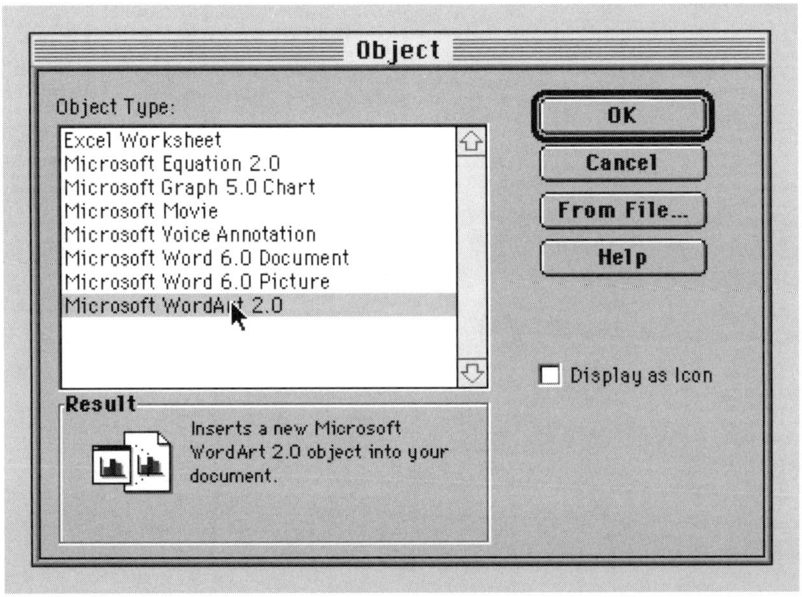

Choose Microsoft WordArt 2.0 from the Object Type scrolling list and click OK. Word launches Word Art and displays the WordArt window.

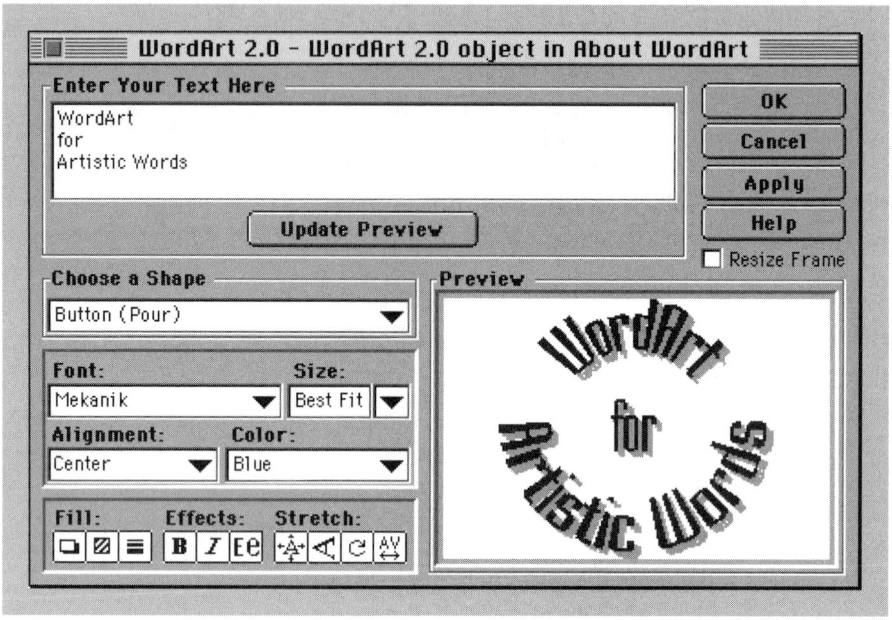

Begin by entering the text you want to stylize in the Enter Your Text Here edit box. Press Return each time you want to start a new line. Click the Update Preview button to display the text in the Preview area of the WordArt window. Once the text is entered, the fun begins. Watch the Preview area to see the results of each change.

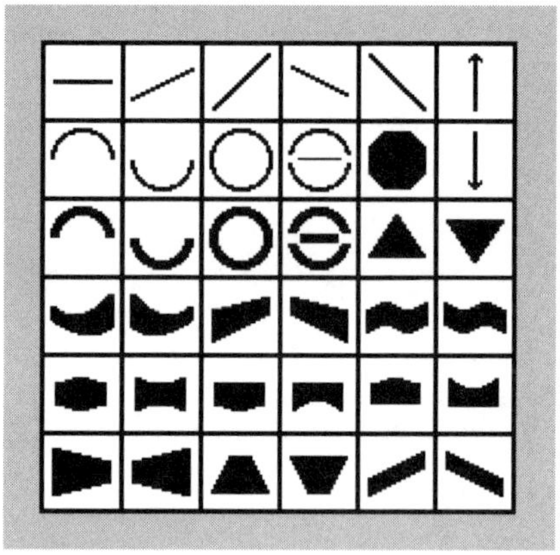

- **Choose a Shape** — offers a pop-up menu of shapes, as shown here.
- **Font** — gives you access to all the fonts available to your system, including any fonts installed by Word.
- **Size** — lets you specify the size of font characters. If you choose Best Fit, the characters are sized according to the size of the WordArt object in the document.
- **Alignment** — lets you choose an alignment for the text in the WordArt object. By default, the text is centered.

- **Color** — lets you choose a color for the text in the WordArt object. White/Black reverses the image, placing white text on a black background.
- **Fill** — offers three buttons to change the line and fill of the object. The first button displays the Shadow dialog box, which you can use to choose a shadow style and color. The second button displays the Shading dialog box which you can use to choose a shading style and colors. The third button displays the Border dialog box, which you can use to choose an object border, thickness, and color.
- **Effects** — offers three buttons to change the style of text. The first button makes the text bold. The second button makes the text italic. The third button makes all letters the same height.
- **Stretch** — offers four buttons to change the overall appearance of the text. The first button stretches the text horizontally and vertically to fill the object. The second button flips the text to its side without rotating the object. The third button opens the Special Effects dialog box where you can change the rotation and slider values to rotate or change the shape of the object. The fourth button opens the Spacing Between Characters dialog box to change the tracking and kerning of text characters.
- **Resize Frame** — if turned on, automatically resizes the WordArt object boundaries in your document to fit the WordArt object. This option is not available if you've already adjusted the size of the boundaries.

You can create an infinite number of combinations by playing around with the menus, buttons, and dialog boxes available in WordArt. It's a lot of fun and probably pretty addictive. Once you've got the effect you want, click Apply to see it in your Word document without closing the dialog box or OK to close the dialog box and return to your document.

Equation Editor

Equation Editor is an application you can use to create properly formatted, complex mathematical and scientific equations. Equation Editor automatically applies formatting such as superscripts and subscripts and sizes special symbols so the equation looks just the way it should. I wouldn't say that it's particularly easy to use, but then again, if you're writing these complex equations, you shouldn't have much trouble with it.

Begin by positioning the insertion point where you want the equation to appear, then choose Object from the Insert menu. Select Microsoft Equation 2.0 from the Object Type scrolling list and click OK. Word launches Equation Editor. The Equation Toolbar appears, an empty equation object is inserted in your document, and the Menu bar changes to reflect Equation Editor menu options.

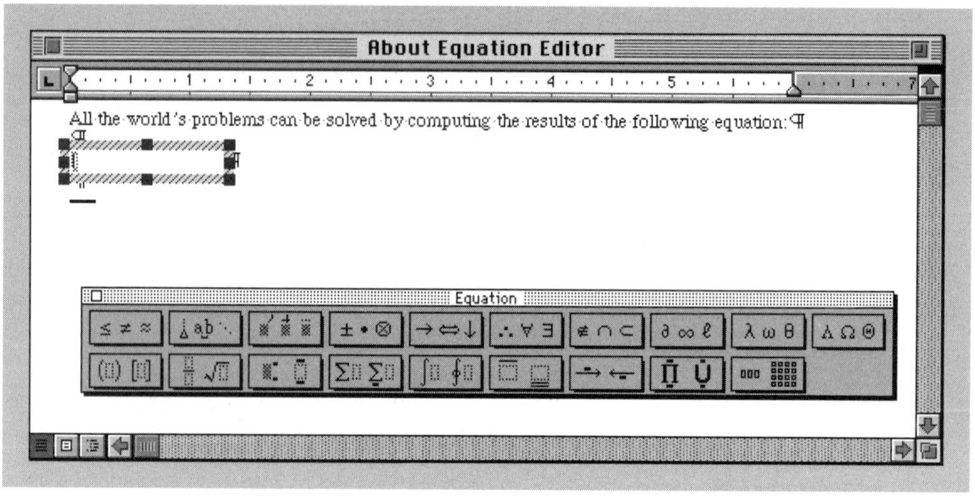

To create an equation, use the buttons on the Equation Toolbar to insert special symbols. Each button is really a menu full of the kinds of symbols and formatting templates used in equations. When you position your mouse pointer over a button and press the mouse button down, a menu pops up. Choose the symbol or template you want and it is inserted in the equation at the insertion point. You can then click in template "slots" — they have gray boxes around them — and type in letters, numbers, or other symbols.

You can move the insertion point within the equation object at any time by clicking where you want it to go or by using the arrow keys. You can edit equations by highlighting parts you don't want and deleting them or by moving them around within the equation object. The Menu bar gives you access to additional commands for formatting, changing the style, and changing the size of the equation.

When you're finished, click anywhere in the Word document outside the equation object. The object is inserted in your document and you're returned to Word.

Microsoft Graph

NEW IN WORD 6

Microsoft Graph is an application you can use to incorporate charts in your Word documents. Graph is relatively flexible, offering many of the same charting options you'd find in Microsoft Excel, which has powerful charting capabilities. Although it is not new to Microsoft Word, it has been modified considerably since previous versions. It now has its own toolbar and builds the chart right in the Word document window.

To create a chart in a Word document, begin by positioning the insertion point where you want the chart to appear. Then do one of the following:

- Click the Insert Chart button on the Standard Toolbar *or*
- Choose Object from the Insert menu, select Microsoft Graph 5.0 Chart from the Object Type scrolling list, and click OK

Word launches Microsoft Graph. It places a chart in the document window and displays a Datasheet window that contains all the information that makes up the chart. It also displays its own version of the Standard Toolbar, which contains buttons and commands you can use to use to create and format charts.

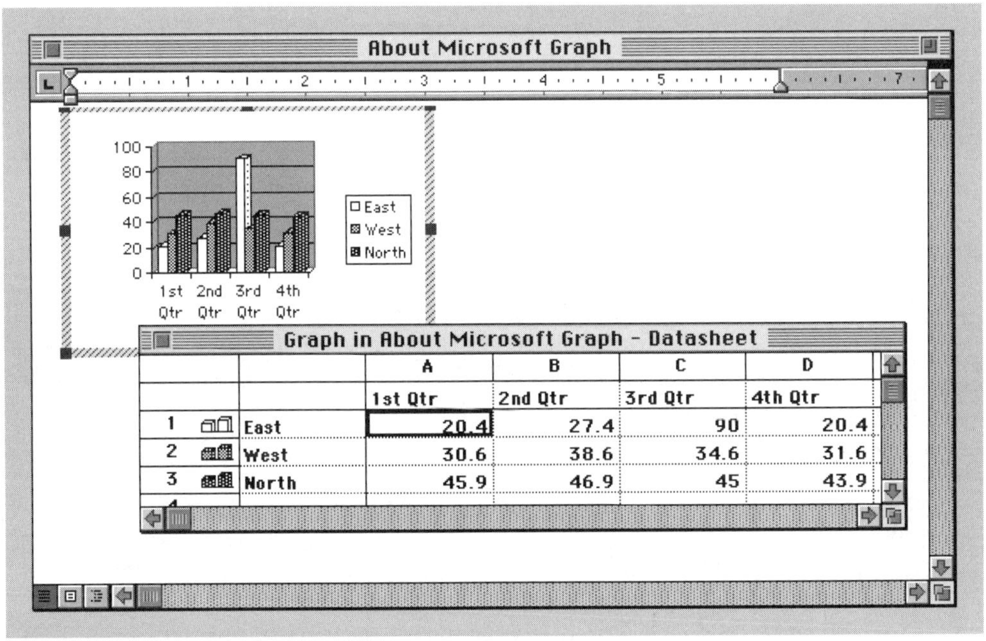

The Datasheet contains lettered columns and numbered rows, just like a spreadsheet. To change the chart to reflect your data, edit the information in the datasheet window. Use the arrow keys or click with the mouse pointer to position the cell pointer (the dark box) around the cell you want to change. Type new information to replace what's already there and press Return or Enter to accept it. Your changes take effect immediately. You can use this method to change values and row or column headings.

To change the type of chart, click on the arrow on the right side of the Chart Type button in the Standard Toolbar. An icon menu of chart types appears. Choose the one you want and the chart changes. The Insert, Format, and Tools menus offer several other Graph options you might find useful. I could spend a whole chapter telling you about them, but I won't. You can explore them for yourself. Microsoft Graph has a good help feature that'll guide you if you need help.

Once you've finished creating and modifying your chart, click in the Word document window outside the chart to return to Word.

TIP/TRICK

If you want to create a chart based on the contents of a Microsoft Word table, select the table or portion of the table you want to chart and click the Insert Chart button on the Standard Toolbar. The sample chart and Datasheet that appear when Microsoft Graph launches will contain the table information. I told you about cell tables in Chapter 11.

TIP/TRICK

If you already have a chart you created in Microsoft Excel, you can use the Copy and Paste commands or buttons to paste a copy of it right into a Word document. I'll tell you more about that in Chapter 25.

Editing WordArt, Equation Editor, and Microsoft Graph Objects

Once you've created and inserted a WordArt, Equation Editor, or Microsoft Graph object in your document, you can edit it a number of ways. Here are some examples:

- To edit the object in the application that created it, double-click on it. The appropriate application is launched and you can edit to your heart's content.
- To resize the object, click it to select it and drag its sizing handles. WordArt, Equation Editor, and Microsoft Graph objects are treated just like imported graphics for resizing and cropping.

- To position or add borders around the object, click it to select it and click the Insert Frame button on the Drawing Toolbar to enclose it in a frame. (You may have to click the Drawing button on the Standard Toolbar to display the Drawing Toolbar first.) I'll tell you about borders and frames in Chapter 13.
- To remove the object from the document, click on it to select it and press the Delete or Del key, or choose Clear from the Edit menu.

Chapter Summary

In this chapter, you learned about the graphics capabilities of Microsoft Word — how to paste in and import graphics created with other programs, about the clip art that comes with Word, and how to draw objects right on the word document page, format them, and position them. You also learned to create and edit pictures, and how to use the three graphics applications that come with Word: WordArt, Equation Editor, and Microsoft Graph. All these features help you add color and life to your documents by giving them visual appeal.

In the next chapter, you'll learn about other special formatting options — borders, shading, and frames — how to apply borders and shading to paragraphs and tables, how to use frames to position text, tables, and graphics anywhere on a page, and how all these formatting options can give your plain documents professional polish.

13

Chapter 13: Frames, Borders, and Shading

BACK IN CHAPTER 6, WHEN YOU FIRST LEARNED ABOUT PARAgraph formatting, I mentioned that frames, borders, and shading could also be used to format paragraphs. In this chapter, you'll find out what each of these Word features do and how you can use them to change the appearance and position of text, tables, and graphics in your document.

Frames

Word's Frame feature lets you position text, graphics, tables — virtually any Word object except a footnote, endnote, or annotation — anywhere you want on a page. The frame holds the object. Once an object is inside a frame, you can drag it anywhere you like on the page and have text flow around it. For best results, it's a good idea to work with frames in Page Layout view. In fact, as you'll see in a moment, Word offers to switch to Page Layout view when you create a frame in your document. If you need to switch to Page Layout view, click the Page Layout view button at the bottom left side of the document window or choose Page Layout from the View menu.

A frame is a paragraph formatting feature. That means anything you frame must be separated from the rest of the document by a paragraph mark. You can, however, have multiple paragraphs inside a frame. Information about the position of a frame is stored in the paragraph mark at the end of the framed object. If you delete the last paragraph mark, you delete the frame. To show paragraph marks, click the Show/Hide ¶ button on the Standard Toolbar.

For Example: Using Frames

At this point, you might be wondering why you'd use frames in your document. The main reason is to enable you to exactly position objects on the page. What you'll find, however, is that frames give you the ability to create what I call "special effects" in a document , effects that are normally available only in page layout programs like PageMaker and QuarkXPress. Here are some examples:

- Use a frame to create multiple-line headings in the margin or sidebars.
- Use a frame to position a table of information and the text that refers to it side by side in a document. Or position a chart based on a table beside the table.

Continued

- Use a frame to create a block of text with a quote from the document or interesting tidbit of information. Position it in the middle of the page or outside the margin. Make the text larger so it stands out. Put a border around the frame so it isn't confused with the rest of the text. This technique, which is used often in magazines, gets a reader's attention and draws him into the document.
- Use a frame to position a graphic, like your company logo, beside information about your company. By doing this, you can create an impressive letterhead that'll print on any paper.

For more ideas, browse through newspapers, magazines, and catalogs. Once you get comfortable working with frames, I'm sure you'll think of lots of applications for them.

Creating a Frame

A frame can be inserted around existing text, graphics, or another object within your document. A frame can also be empty so you can fill it later on.

Inserting a Frame around an Existing Object

To place a frame around an existing object, begin by selecting the object, including any paragraph marks within or immediately after the object. Then choose Frame from the Insert menu. If you're in Normal view, a dialog box, like the one shown here, warns you that you can only view, resize, or reposition frames in Page Layout view. Click Yes and Word switches the view for you and inserts the frame.

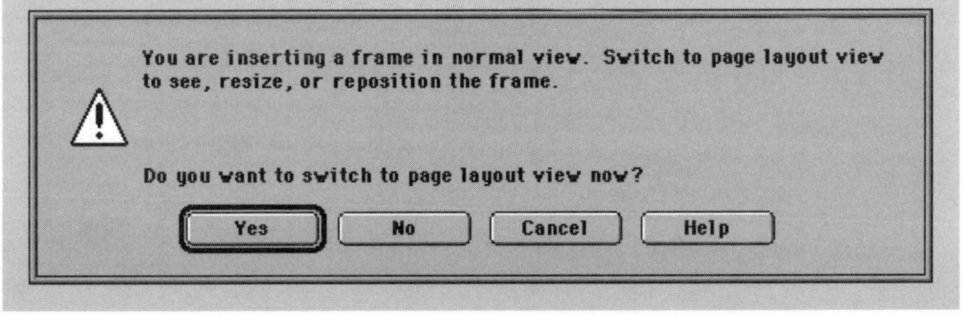

If you're already in Page Layout view, Word simply inserts the frame. If you've framed a graphic, it might look something like this:

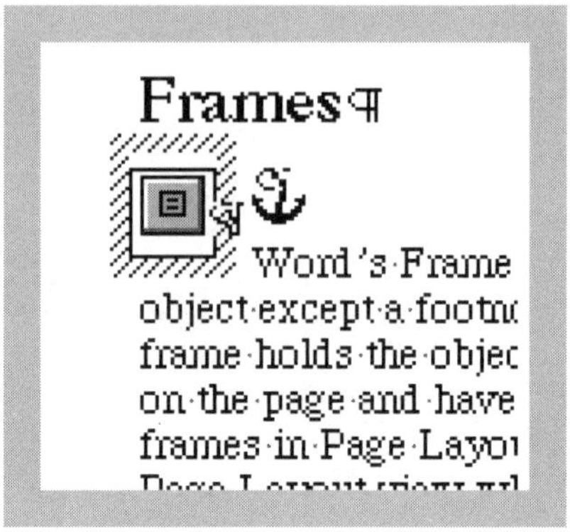

Inserting an Empty Frame

You can also insert an empty frame in a document. An empty frame can be used as a placeholder for text or graphics you plan to position in your document in the future.

To create an empty frame, choose Frame from the Insert menu. If you're in Normal view, the dialog box, previously illustrated, appears. Click Yes to switch to Page Layout view. Once in Page Layout view, the mouse pointer turns to a cross hair pointer and a message appears in the Status bar: "Click and drag to insert a frame." Use the mouse pointer to drag a box to the desired size and position right on the document window.

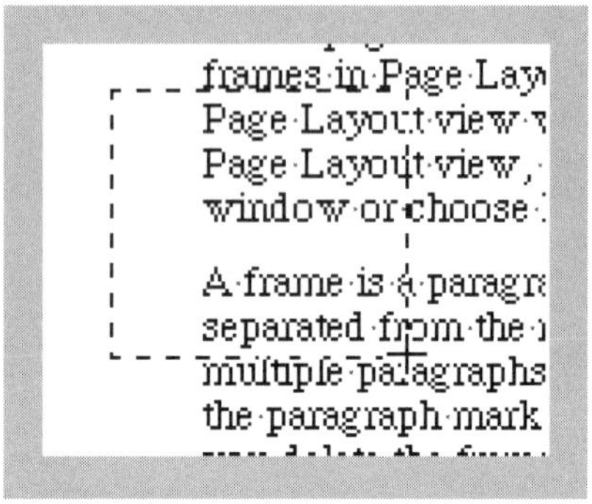

When you let go of the mouse button, Word inserts the frame. It might look something like this:

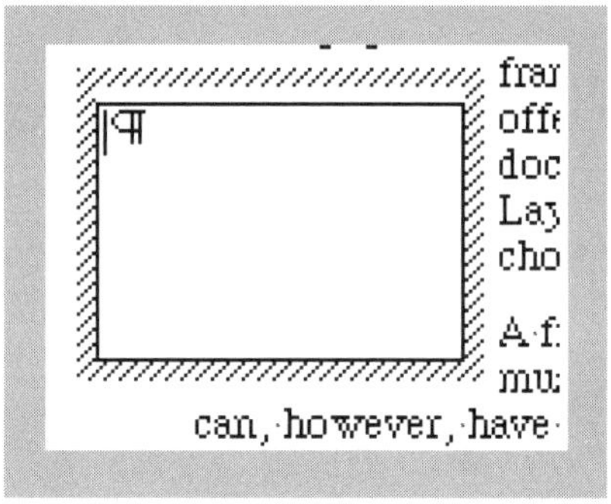

Notice that there is an insertion point inside the frame. This means you can enter text or paste graphics right into the frame. Try it and see. In the following example, I copied some text from the body of the document and pasted it into the frame.

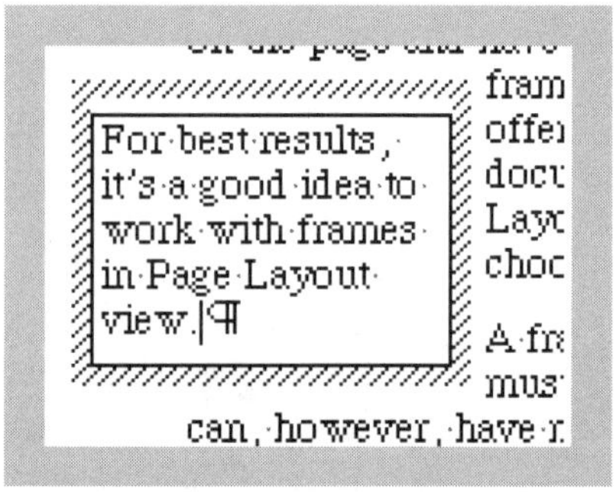

Anatomy of a Frame

Let's take a closer look at the frames you've learned about so far. Each frame includes a printable border (which you can remove — I'll tell you how later in this chapter). There's a paragraph mark within the frame, although depending on the size of the frame, it may appear as if it's outside the frame. When the frame is selected — you can click on it to select it — a thick border of diagonal dashed lines appears around it and an anchor symbol appears nearby. If you don't see the paragraph mark or anchor symbol click the Show/Hide ¶ button to turn on invisible characters. Finally, Word pushed aside all the text near the frame, so that it does not overlap. The surrounding text flows around the frame. As you'll see later, you have some control over the way text wraps around a frame.

When Word frames a graphic that's already in a document, it automatically makes the frame roughly the same size as the selected object. It'll do that if you select a graphic, an equation created with the Equation Editor, a table, a chart created with Microsoft Graph, or a chart or worksheet pasted in from a spreadsheet program like Excel. In each case, Word knows how big the object is and makes the frame just the right size. If you select text, however, Word makes the frame as wide as the area between the indent markers for that paragraph. You'll learn how to resize or reposition a frame next.

Editing a Frame by Dragging

Once you've got a frame within your document, you can move or resize it. Perhaps the easiest way to change the location or size of a frame is to simply drag it.

Positioning a Frame

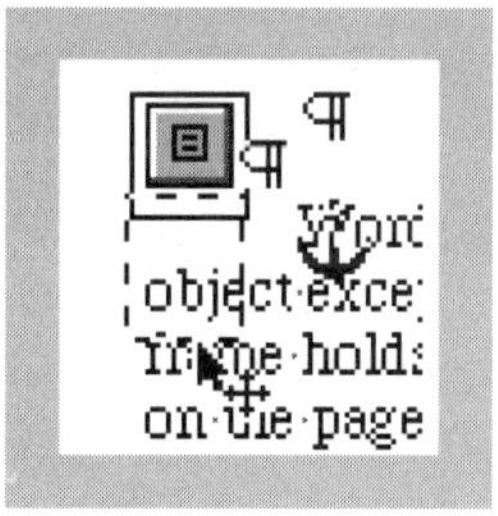

When you position the mouse pointer on a frame border, it turns into an arrow with a tiny four-headed arrow beside it. This is called a *positioning pointer.* Press the mouse button down and drag the object to a new position. As you drag, a dashed outline of the object moves. The anchor may move, too, as shown here. When you let go of the mouse button, the frame appears in its new position.

FYI: About the Anchor

Every frame is *anchored* to a paragraph. When you first insert a frame, it is anchored to the closest paragraph. The anchor symbol appears beside it. This indicates that Word will place the frame on the same page as the paragraph marked with the frame's anchor.

I'll tell you how you can move an anchor without moving a frame and do other anchor-related tasks later in this chapter.

Resizing a Frame

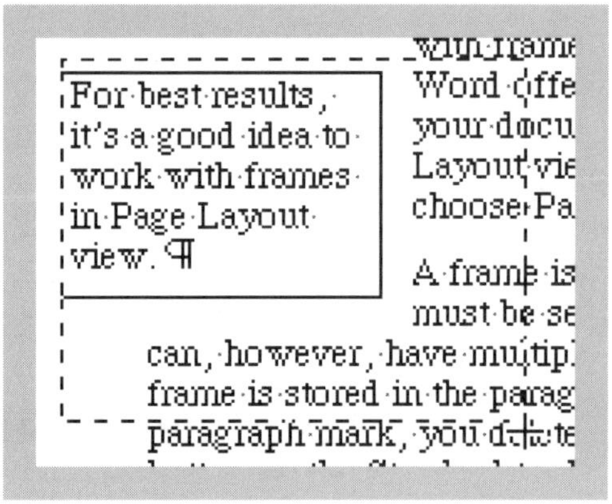

If you click on the border of a frame that has not been automatically sized by Word, eight selection handles appear: one in each corner and one on each side. To resize a frame, simply position the mouse pointer on one of these handles, press the mouse button down, and drag. When you release the mouse button, the frame is resized.

IMPORTANT NOTE

Word will not display handles for frames that have been automatically sized. To resize a frame that does not display handles, you must use the Frame dialog box.

Editing a Frame with the Frame Dialog Box

The Frame dialog box lets you reposition and resize a frame. It also lets you change text wrapping, position a frame relative to specific parts of the page, and lock an anchor to specific text. I'll cover all of these things in this section.

To open the Frame dialog box, click on the border of the frame you want to edit and choose Frame from the Format menu or simply double-click on the frame border.

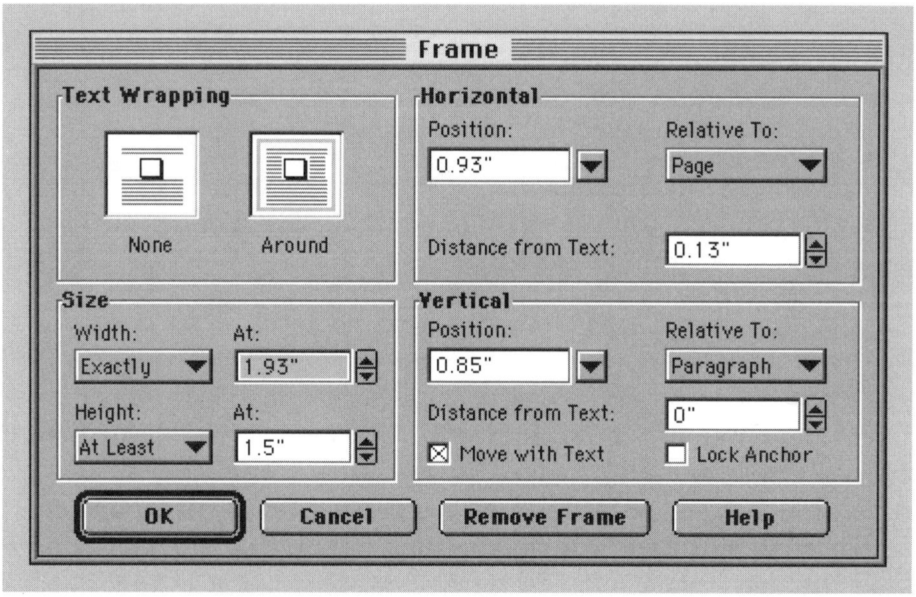

Setting Text Wrapping

The first part of the Frame dialog box is the Text Wrapping area. Two sample illustrations show how text will wrap around the frame. By default, text wraps all the way around a frame, but if you'd prefer the text to break at the frame and continue after it, click the None illustration to select it.

Resizing a Frame

The Size area of the Frame dialog box lets you specify exact measurements for the width and height of the frame. The Width pop-up menu offers two options:

- **Auto** — tells Word to automatically adjust the width of the frame.
- **Exactly** — lets you specify the width of the frame. If you choose Exactly, enter a value in the At edit box beside the pop-up menu to set the width.

The Height pop-up menu offers both of these options. As you can imagine, they work the same way, but for the height of the frame. There's one additional option:

- **At Least** — lets you specify a minimum height for the frame. If you choose At Least, enter a value in the At edit box beside the pop-up menu to set the minimum height. Word uses that height unless the frame contains too much information to fit inside it. Then Word makes the frame larger to accommodate the information. This setting is useful for frames containing text since changes to the text formatting can affect the amount of space it takes up.

TIP/TRICK

If you want to change the size of a frame that was automatically sized by Word, make sure Auto is not selected in either of the Size pop-up menus. Enter your measurements in the At edit boxes.

Repositioning a Frame

The Horizontal and Vertical areas of the Frame dialog box give you complete control over the position of a frame. By using the options in this dialog box, you can set the position of the frame with a reference point. For example, you can set a frame so that it is always placed beside a certain paragraph or a certain distance from the left margin. This can prevent a lot of frame positioning adjustments if the contents, margins, or overall layout of your document changes.

Relative To Settings. The Relative To pop-up menus are very important components of this dialog box; they tell Word what reference point to use. The Horizontal options are:

- **Margin** — tells Word to position the frame horizontally relative to the left and right margins of the page.
- **Page** — tells Word to position the frame horizontally relative to the left and right edges of the paper.
- **Column —** tells Word to position the frame horizontally relative to the left and right edges of the column.

The Vertical options are:

- **Margin —** tells Word to position the frame vertically relative to the top and bottom margins of the page.
- **Page —** tells Word to position the frame vertically relative to the top and bottom edges of the paper.
- **Paragraph** — tells Word to position the frame vertically relative to the paragraph containing the frame's anchor. When you choose the paragraph option, the Move with Text check box below it is automatically turned on. If the paragraph moves, the frame moves along with it, even from one page to the next.

IMPORTANT NOTE

Remember, not all printers can print to the very edge of a page. Use caution when specifying the Page option. Check your document in Print Preview before printing it to make sure the entire frame will print if positioned outside the margin. I told you about printing and Print Preview back in Chapter 4.

Position Settings. Once you've decided what reference point to use to position the frame, use the Position edit box and pop-up menu to either enter a position measurement or choose an alignment option. If you enter a measurement, Word measures from the left or top (for horizontal or vertical, respectively).

If you decide not to enter a measurement, click the arrow beside the edit box to display a menu of alignment options. Remember, these options are relative to whatever you select in the Relative To pop-up menu. The Horizontal options are:

- **Left** — tells Word to position the frame horizontally against the left margin, edge of the page, or edge of the column.
- **Right** — tells Word to position the frame horizontally against the right margin, edge of the page, or edge of the column.
- **Center** — tells Word to center the frame horizontally between the left and right margins, edges of the page, or edges of the column.
- **Inside** — tells Word to position the frame horizontally at the inside edge of the margin, page, or column. The inside edge is the left side on odd-numbered pages and the right side on even-numbered pages.
- **Outside** — tells Word to position the frame horizontally at the outside edge of the margin, page, or column. The inside edge is the right side on odd-numbered pages and the left side on even-numbered pages.

The Vertical options are:

- **Top** — tells Word to position the frame vertically against the top margin, edge of the page, or paragraph.
- **Bottom** — tells Word to position the frame vertically against the bottom margin, edge of the page, or paragraph.
- **Center** — tells Word to center the frame vertically between the top and bottom margins, edges of the page, or paragraph.

Try This! Positioning a Frame

The best way to learn about positioning with the Frame dialog box is to experiment with the different settings and see exactly what they do. Create a one-page document filled with text and put a 2.5 x 2.5 inch frame (either empty or filled) anywhere in it. Then try these examples. You should get the results shown here:

Horizontal Settings		**Vertical Settings**		
Position	**Relative To**	**Position**	**Relative To**	**Expected Results**
1.5	Page	2.5	Page	
Center	Page	Top	Margin	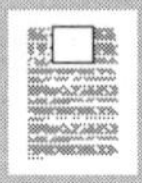
Right	Margin	Center	Margin	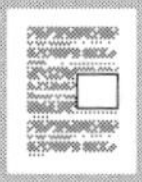
2	Margin	Center	Page	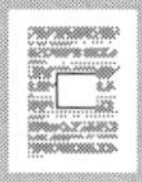
Inside	Column	Bottom	Margin	

Setting the Distance from Text

The Horizontal and Vertical areas of the Frame dialog box also let you specify the distance from the edge of the frame to the text around it. Enter a value in either or both Distance from Text edit boxes. The text shifts accordingly when you accept the settings.

Controlling Frame Movement

You can control how a frame moves with the Move with Text and Lock Anchor check boxes in the Frame dialog box.

- To assure that a frame moves to whatever page a paragraph appears on, drag the frame's anchor to the paragraph and turn on the Lock Anchor check box for the frame. If the Move With Text check box is turned on, the frame will also move up or down on the page depending on whether text is inserted or deleted before the paragraph containing its anchor. If the Move With Text check box is turned off, the frame will remain positioned as specified by the other Vertical positioning options.
- To prevent a frame from moving to another page when the paragraph containing its anchor moves, turn off both the Lock Anchor and Move With Text check boxes for the frame. This keeps the frame on its current page and enables the anchor to move.

Removing a Frame

You can use the Frame dialog box to remove the selected frame. Click the Remove Frame button. Word removes the frame, no questions asked. If the frame was not empty, Word places the contents of the frame above the paragraph that had the frame's anchor.

TIP/TRICK

You can also remove a frame by simply deleting the frame's last paragraph mark. Or, to remove the frame and its contents, select the frame and press Delete. The whole frame, contents and all, disappears.

Formatting Text within a Frame

You can change the appearance of text within a frame the same way you do anywhere else in a Word document. Select the characters or paragraphs you want to format and use the appropriate toolbar buttons, ruler markers, menu commands, or dialog boxes to make the change. I discussed font and paragraph formatting in Chapters 5 and 6, and styles in Chapter 7. Use any of the techniques discussed in those chapters to format text within a frame.

TIP/TRICK

When you insert a frame around text already in your document, the text retains any font or paragraph formatting applied to it. So don't think you have to wait until after you frame text to format it.

Creating a Dropped Cap

A *dropped cap* is a character or word at the beginning of a paragraph that has been enlarged and shifted down. Text can flow around the enlarged character(s) or the character(s) can be positioned in the margin. Dropped caps are commonly used in desktop publishing and can add a nice touch to reports and other documents. Here are two examples of dropped caps:

FYI: What Kind of Formatting Is a Dropped Cap, Anyway?

I think of dropped caps as a sort of formatting hybrid. First of all, you're enlarging characters, so it has an element of font formatting. Second, you're working with the first characters in a paragraph, so it has an element of paragraph formatting. Finally, the enlarged character is enclosed in a frame, so it has an element of frame formatting. A formatting hybrid, don't you agree?

To create a dropped cap, select the characters you want to enlarge. You can select as many characters as you like from the beginning of the paragraph. If you just want to enlarge the first character, position the insertion point anywhere in the paragraph. Then choose Drop Cap from the Format menu. The Drop Cap dialog box appears.

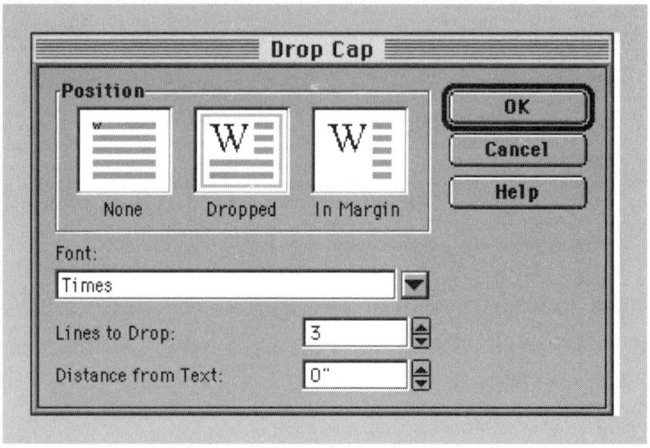

The Position area offers the following options:

- **None** — the default.
- **Dropped** — places the enlarged letter within the margins of the document and wraps text around the dropped cap character(s).
- **In Margin** — places the enlarged letter outside the margin.

Use the Font pop-up menu to choose the font for the dropped cap character(s) — it doesn't have to be the same as the font used for the rest of the paragraph. Enter a number between 1 and 10 in the Lines to Drop edit box to specify the height, in lines, for the dropped cap character. Finally, if you want the character spaced away from the rest of the text in the paragraph, enter a measurement in the Distance from Text edit box.

When you've finished setting up the dropped cap, click OK or press Return or Enter to accept the settings. Word creates the dropped cap to your specifications. If you click on it, you'll find that it is indeed a framed character. It even has an anchor linking it to the paragraph.

Borders and Shading

Borders and shading are yet another form of special formatting. Borders let you place lines around or between paragraphs and table cells, as well as around graphic or framed objects. Shading lets you highlight paragraphs, table cells, or framed text with shades of gray or color. If you read the Table AutoFormat section of Chapter 11, you should have an idea of the places where borders and shading would be useful in your documents. In this chapter you'll learn how to apply borders and shading manually.

IMPORTANT NOTE

Word applies borders or shading (or both) to whatever is selected when you use the Border toolbar buttons or Borders and Shading dialog box. If you click in a paragraph, select part of a paragraph, or select an entire paragraph, Word applies borders or shading to the entire paragraph. If you select multiple paragraphs, Word applies it to the selected paragraphs. If you select a part of a table, Word applies it to whatever part of the table is selected. If you select a picture or a paragraph within a frame, Word applies it to the entire frame. Select carefully before applying borders and shading. If you wind up with something unexpected, remember your trusty friend, the Undo command.

Using the Borders Toolbar

NEW IN WORD 6

Word version 6 adds a new toolbar button and a whole new toolbar just for borders and shading. Click the Borders button on the Formatting toolbar and the Borders toolbar appears. It offers a bunch of buttons you can use to apply borders and shading to a selection, no matter what that selection is.

TIP/TRICK

Another way to display the Borders toolbar is to click the Show Toolbar button in the Borders and Shading dialog box. You'll see that a little later in this chapter. You can always hide the Borders toolbar by clicking the Borders button on the Formatting toolbar again when it is selected.

The Line Style pop-up menu lets you select among a variety of line styles and thicknesses. Use your mouse to click on the arrow and open the menu. The point sizes indicate the thickness of the lines. The illustration beside each one shows how the line will look. Choose the line style you want before clicking one of the other buttons to place a line.

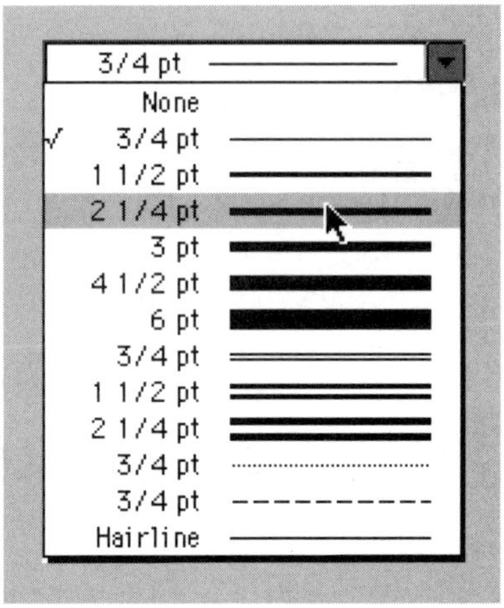

The Top Border button places a border at the top of the selection. Click it to turn it on or off.

The Bottom Border button places a border at the bottom of the selection. Click it to turn it on or off.

The Left Border button places a border along the left edge of the selection. If the selection is a paragraph, it places the border along the left indent. Click it to turn it on or off.

The Right Border button places a border along the right edge of the selection. If the selection is a paragraph, it places the border along the right indent. Click it to turn it on or off.

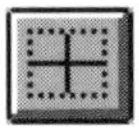

The Inside Border button places a border between parts of the selection. For example, if you have multiple paragraphs selected, the Inside Border button places a border between the paragraphs. If you have table cells selected, the Inside Border button places a border between the cells. Click it to turn it on or off.

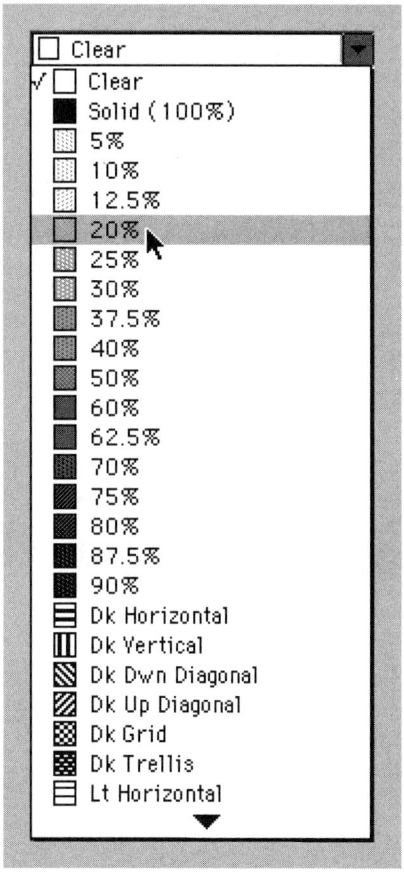

The Outside Border button places a border around the entire selection. Click it to turn it on or off.

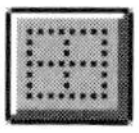

The No Border button removes all borders from the selection.

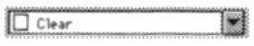

The Shading pop-up menu lets you select from among various shading options. Click on the arrow to open the menu. Shading is listed by its percentage of darkness. No shading is Clear. When fully extended, the menu also offers a number of patterns that can be used as shading.

Using the Borders and Shading Dialog Box

The Borders and Shading dialog box offers another way to add borders or shading (or both) to a selection. Its main benefit over the buttons on the Border toolbar is that it gives you access to colors. To open the Borders and Shading dialog box, choose Borders and Shading from the Format menu. There are three versions of the dialog box. The one that appears depends on what you've got selected when you open it. In the following illustration, since a paragraph was selected, the Paragraph Borders and Shading dialog box appears. There's also a Table version and a Picture version.

The Borders and Shading dialog box has two tabs: Borders and Shading. (Makes sense, doesn't it?) I'll show you the main components of each of these, then discuss specifics about placing borders around paragraphs, tables, and pictures.

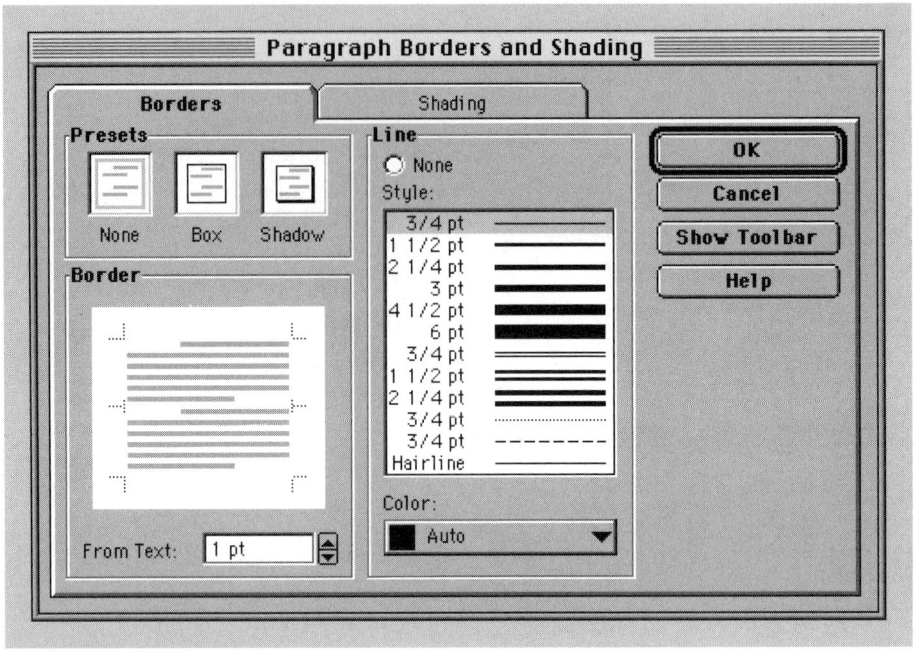

Using Preset Borders

The Presets area of the Borders and Shading dialog box offers the following options:

- **None** — removes all borders from the selection.
- **Box** — puts a simple box around the selection.
- **Shadow** — puts a drop shadow border around the entire selection, adding a sort of three dimensional effect.

The Presets area looks a little different when cell tables are selected, as shown here. The None and Box options are still there, but rather than the Shadow option, Word offers Grid. Grid puts a heavy border around the entire selection with thinner border lines between each cell.

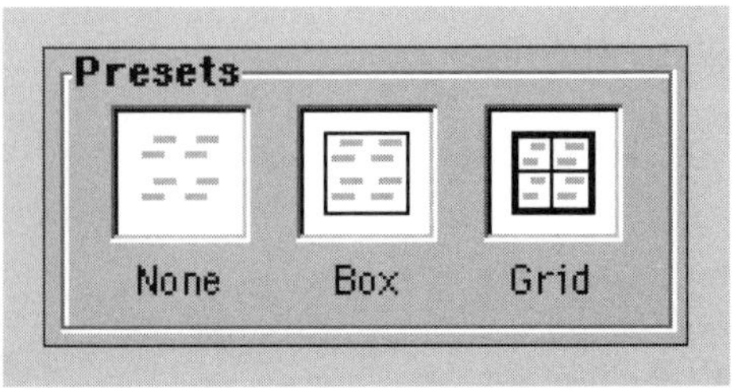

TIP/TRICK

When adding borders to a selection, you can start with one of Word's preset borders and then modify it to look exactly the way you want by changing the model in the Border section of the dialog box. I'll tell you how to change the model later in this chapter.

Choosing a Border Line and Color

The Line area of the Borders and Shading dialog box offers a selection of line styles and thicknesses. The number in front of each sample line in the Style list indicates the thickness of the line in points. Choose a line by clicking on it. It is automatically applied to any selected line in the Border area model. If no line is selected in the model, the line is used when you select a line in the model.

If you'd like to add color to your borders, use the Color pop-up menu to choose from among 16 colors. Auto, the topmost option that is selected by default, sets borders to black. When you change colors, the line styles change accordingly. The color is automatically applied to any selected line in the Border area model or used when you select a line in the model.

Using the Model to Apply Styles

Each version of the Borders and Shading dialog box includes a model of the type of selection. The model for paragraphs is shown in the previous Borders and Shading dialog box illustration. The models for tables and pictures are shown here. Note the subtle differences.

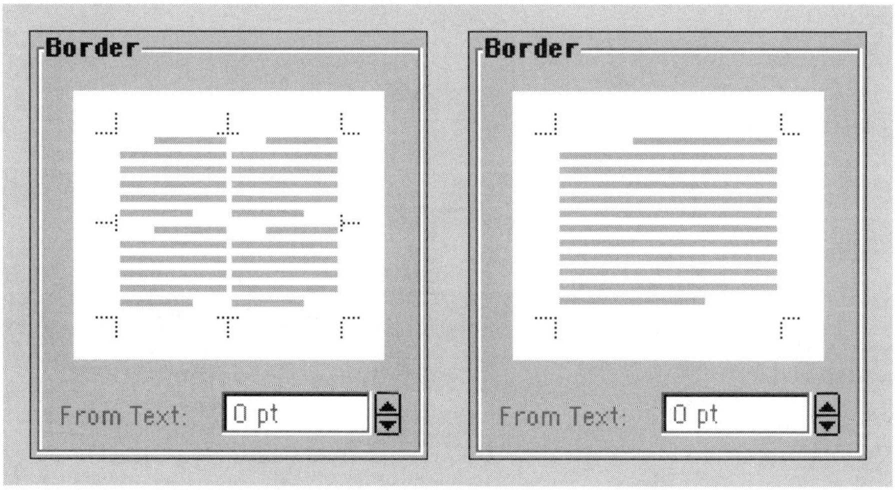

To use the model, imagine that it is a sample of your selection. If you look closely at it, it represents either paragraphs, table cells, or a block of text — whatever you've got selected. To apply a border, click on the model between the dotted line markers where you want the border to appear. The line becomes selected — two tiny triangles mark either end of it. It might look like this:

If a line style is already selected, that line is applied. If None is selected in the Line area, choose a line style to apply it. To remove an applied line, simply click it again with the same line style selected. It disappears.

IMPORTANT NOTE

The models are not exact representations of what you've got selected. They always look the same for the specific type of selection. The paragraph model always looks as if it contains two paragraphs. The table model always looks as if contains four cells (two across and two down). The picture model always looks as if it contains one paragraph of text. By placing lines on the model, you can place lines anywhere you like on your selection.

The Border area also includes an edit box you can use to specify the distance between the text within a paragraph border and the border itself. Enter a value in points to increase spacing. This option is only offered when adding borders to paragraphs. It's gray when you work with tables and pictures.

TIP/TRICK

Here are a few additional tricks for placing borders in paragraphs, tables, and around pictures:

- Right and left paragraph borders are applied at the paragraph's indents. To adjust the position of a paragraph's right and left borders, simply adjust the indents for that paragraph.
- When applying borders to a table, it might be necessary to do it in steps. For example, to create the effect shown here, begin by selecting the entire table and applying a thick, box border to it. Then select the third row and apply a thinner top and bottom border to it — do not change the borders that already appear in the model.

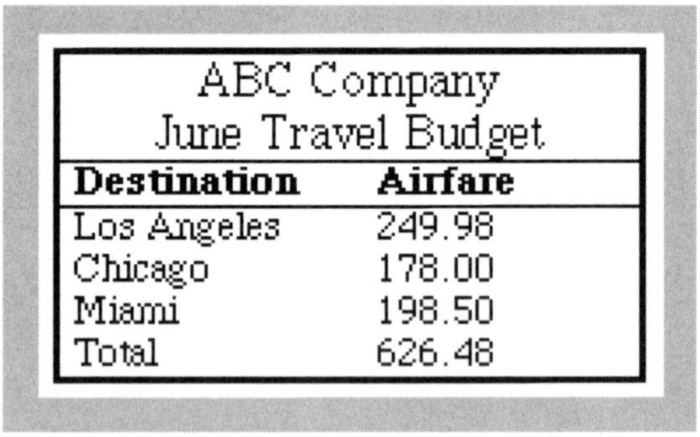

ABC Company June Travel Budget	
Destination	**Airfare**
Los Angeles	249.98
Chicago	178.00
Miami	198.50
Total	626.48

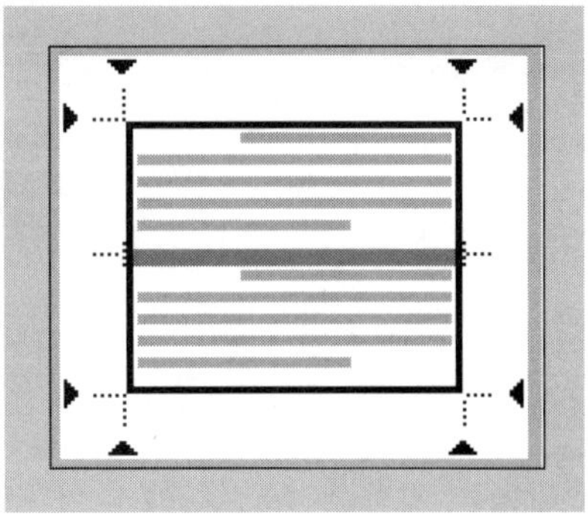

- When viewing the Borders and Shading dialog box for a selection that already contains some borders, gray lines may appear on the Border model. These gray lines indicate that some of the selection has lines in that position, but not all of them. Removing the gray line removes the borders from that position throughout the selection. Turning the gray line to a regular border line adds borders at that position throughout the selection.
- If you're trying to place a border around a group of paragraphs with different indentation settings and Word insists on putting borders between some of the paragraphs, put the entire selection into a one-cell table and put a border around that.
- If you're having difficulty using the Borders and Shading dialog box to place borders and each attempt only makes your selection look worse, select everything you've applied a border to, open the Borders and Shading dialog box, click the None preset, and click OK to remove all borders. Then take a deep breath (or, better yet, grab a cup of coffee or soda), and try again from scratch. Starting over is often easier than trying to repair damage done by errors. And believe me, the Border models can make you nuts if you're not sure how to use them.
- If you find yourself with some spare time, experiment with a few empty tables or meaningless paragraphs. You might pick up a few tricks you can use in the future.

Shading a Paragraph, Table, or Frame

The other part of the Borders and Shading dialog box is the Shading tab. Click the tab to display its options.

The Fill area has the following radio buttons:

- **None** — which is the default, turns off all shading in the selection.
- **Custom** — lets you select a shading percentage or pattern and colors for the foreground and background.

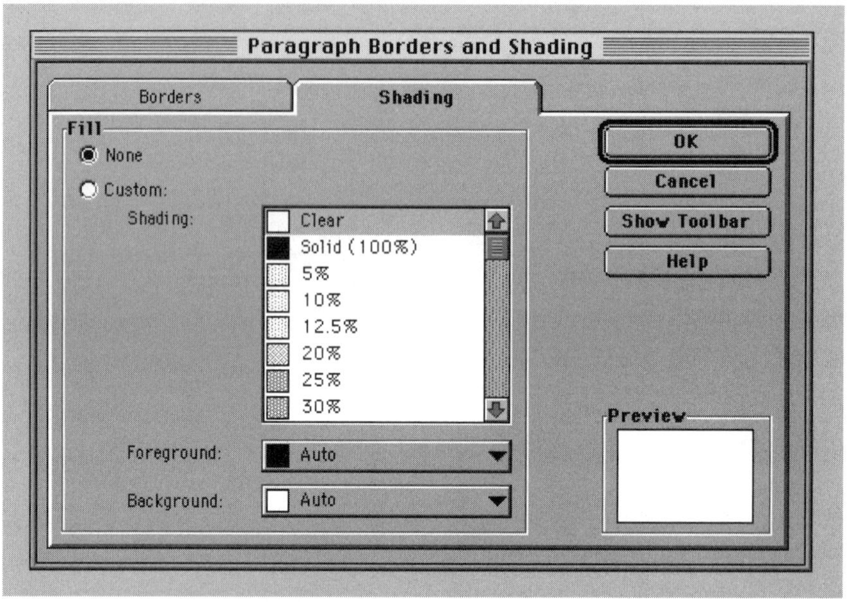

IMPORTANT NOTE

When choosing a shading percentage, remember that the higher the percentage number, the darker the shading will be. Text inside darkly shaded areas may be difficult to read so stick to the lower numbers when shading text areas. You can also apply bold formatting to text in shaded areas to help it stand out.

The foreground color specifies the color of the dots or lines that make up the shading or pattern. This is normally black, but you can make it any color you like. For example, if you want your document shaded with a pinkish color, try a foreground of red or magenta at 10% or 12.5%. The background color specifies the color of the area that forms the background for the dots or lines of the shading or pattern. This is normally white, but again, you can change it to anything you like. The preview window lets you see exactly how the shading will look when applied.

FYI: Printing Colors

Borders and shading is not limited to black, white, and shades of gray. You can make your Word documents as colorful as you like. But if you don't have a color printer, there's no way to make those colors appear on paper. Instead, your printer will either convert the colors to black and white or shades of gray — whatever option you chose in the Print dialog box. I told you about printing in Chapter 4.

Chapter Summary

In this chapter you learned what a frame is and how you can create, resize, and position one anywhere on a page; to create a dropped cap, which can give your documents a "desktop published" look; and how you can apply borders and shading to paragraphs, tables, and pictures or frames using the Borders toolbar and the Borders and Shading dialog box.

In the next chapter, you'll learn about captions, cross-references, and bookmarks, three brand new features of Word version 6 that help you identify specific information in your documents.

14

Chapter 14: Bookmarks, Captions, and Cross-References

NEW IN WORD 6

AS YOU LEARNED IN CHAPTERS 11 AND 12, WORD MAKES IT easy to include tables, graphics, charts, and figures in your documents. Keeping track of all these elements can be quite a chore, especially when working with a long document (like a book about Microsoft Word). Fortunately, Word version 6 offers three new features that can help: bookmarks, captions, and cross-references. In this chapter, you'll learn to use these new features.

For Example: How I Use Bookmarks, Captions, and Cross-References

For a writer, Word's new Bookmark, Caption, and Cross-Reference features are like gifts from heaven. Here are some ways I take advantage of these features:

- Using bookmarks to identify and keep track of manuscript sections I need to do further work on before submitting them to my editors.
- Using captions to identify and properly number figures and illustrations throughout my manuscripts. That might not seem like a big deal to you, but when you're inserting figures and your editors are pulling figures out, keeping track of figure numbers can be a real chore. By having Word automatically add captions each time I insert a screen shot, I don't have to worry about numbering them at all!
- Using cross-references to properly refer to figures in my manuscripts. While Peachpit didn't make me refer to every single screen shot in this book with a figure number in the text, other publishers often expect me to. The Cross-Reference feature certainly helps me keep my sanity.

Bookmarks

Bookmarks let you give names to text, graphics, tables — almost anything in your document. Once a bookmark is defined, the item you marked can be found simply by looking for its bookmark. You can also use bookmarks to create cross-references, mark a page range for an index, or perform calculations on numbers scattered throughout your document. I'll tell you more about indexes in Chapter 20. I told you about Word's calculation feature in Chapter 11 and will discuss it again in Chapter 22 when I tell you about forms.

Defining a Bookmark

To define a bookmark, select the item you want to mark. The item can be any amount of text, all or part of a table, or a graphic or drawing object. Then choose Bookmark from the Edit menu or press ⌘ Shift F5 (on an extended keyboard only). The Bookmark dialog box appears.

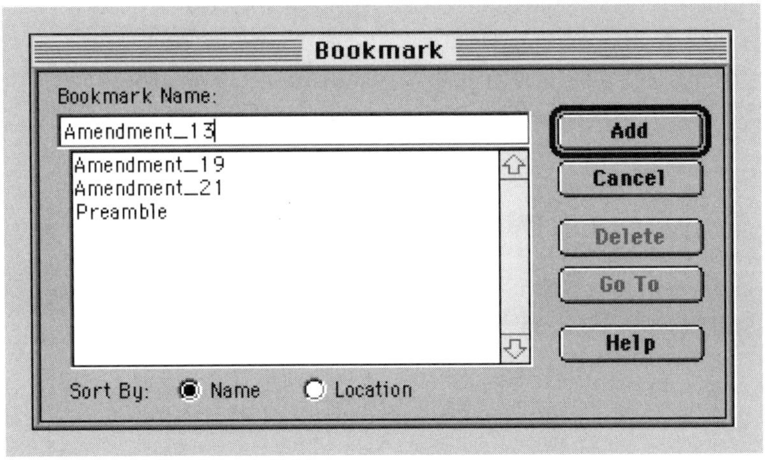

Enter a name in the Bookmark name edit box. The name is limited to 40 characters and can only include letters, numbers, and the underscore character (_) — no spaces! Click the Add button to add the bookmark to the list of bookmarks in the scrolling window beneath the Bookmark Name edit box. The Bookmark dialog box closes.

Seeing Bookmarks

Word uses gray brackets to display the beginning and end of text or other items marked with a bookmark. By default, however, these marks are not displayed on screen. To see them, choose Options from the Tools menu. Click the View tab and turn on the check box beside Bookmarks. Click OK to close the Options dialog box. The gray brackets should appear around any marked text. I'll tell you more about the Options dialog box in Chapter 23.

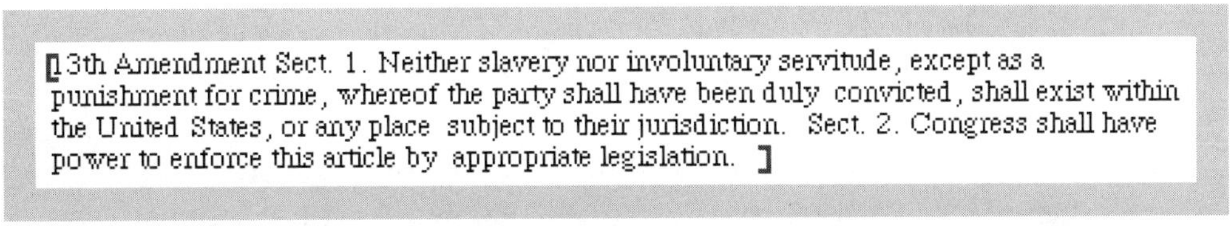

Revising a Marked Item

You can revise the contents of a marked item by simply typing or deleting text within the bookmark brackets. As long as new text is included within the brackets, it's included as part of the marked item. If you delete part of a marked item, what remains in the document retains the bookmark.

If you want to reassign the bookmark name to a new item, select the new item and choose Bookmark from the Edit menu or press ⌘ Shift F5. Select the name of the bookmark you want to use from the scrolling list and click Add. Word changes the definition of that bookmark to include the selected text.

Copying or Cutting a Marked Item

When you copy a marked item, what you copy and where you copy it to will determine whether the bookmark is copied, too.

- If you copy all or part of a marked item to another location in the same document, the bookmark is not copied and remains with the original item.
- If you copy all of a marked item to another document, both documents have the same bookmark. The only time this will not be true is if the other document already had a bookmark with the same name. In that case, the copied text does not carry its bookmark with it.
- If you copy part of a marked item to another document, the other document does not get a bookmark.

When you cut a marked item and paste it into the same document, the bookmark moves with it to the new location. This is true when you cut a marked item and paste it into another document, unless the other document already had a bookmark with the same name.

Deleting a Bookmark

There are two ways to delete a bookmark:

- To delete a bookmark without deleting the text it marks, choose Bookmark from the Edit menu or press ⌘ Shift F5 to open the Bookmark dialog box. Click the name of the bookmark in the scrolling list and click the Delete button. The bookmark is removed from the list. When you click Close to close the Bookmark dialog box, you'll see that the bookmark brackets are removed.

- To delete a bookmark and the text it marks, select *all* the marked text, including the bookmark brackets and press Delete or Del. If you select only part of the text or include only one of the bookmarks in the selection, the bookmark definition changes to include the text up to the point you deleted.

Using Bookmarks to Find Text

Once you've got a bookmark in your document, you can use it to find the item it marks. Choose Bookmark from the Edit menu or press ⌘Shift F5 to open the Bookmark dialog box. Click on the name of the bookmark you want to find and click the Go To button. The text marked by that bookmark becomes selected. The Bookmark dialog box remains open so you can go to other bookmarks if desired. To dismiss it, click Close.

TIP/TRICK

You can also use the Go To dialog box, which I discussed in Chapter 2, to find text marked with a bookmark. Open the Go To dialog box with one of these methods:

- Choose Go To from the Edit menu *or*
- Press F5 (extended keyboard only) *or*
- Double-click on the page number in the Status bar at the bottom of the screen

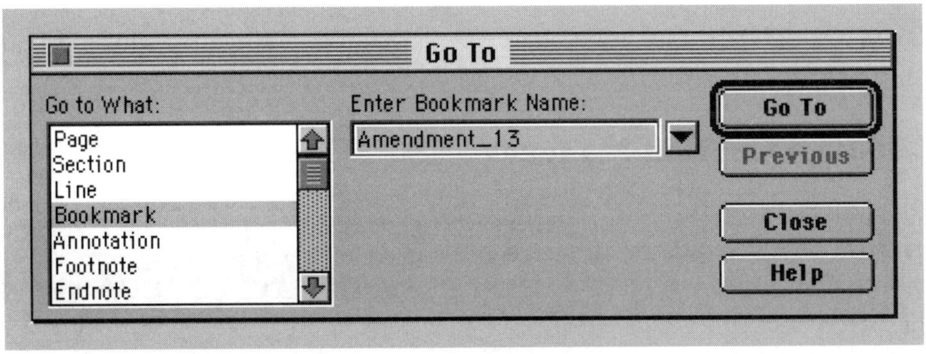

In the Go To dialog box, select Bookmark from the Go To What scrolling list. Then either enter the bookmark name in the Enter Bookmark Name edit box or use the arrow beside it to display and choose from a list of all the bookmarks in the document. When you click Go To, the item marked by that bookmark becomes selected.

Captions

Captions are labels you can attach to figures, tables, graphics, or other items in your Word document. Although you could always type text into your documents to identify these items, the caption feature goes a step further by making it easy to update caption numbers. The AutoCaption feature makes it possible to have Word do all the caption work for you. In this section, I'll tell you how you can include captions in your documents.

FYI: Captions, Cross-References, and Fields

When you insert a caption number or cross-reference into a document, Word inserts it as a field. As I mentioned back in Chapter 10, a field is a special code that tells Word what information to insert. This enables Word to keep track of and, if necessary, change caption numbers and cross-references. Word also uses fields to insert page numbers, dates, and times in headers and to perform calculations in tables. I discussed this in Chapters 10 and 11.

Adding a Caption

There are two ways to add a caption: manually and automatically. Let's take a look at each method.

Adding a Caption Manually

To add a caption to an item, select it and choose Caption from the Insert menu. The Caption dialog box appears.

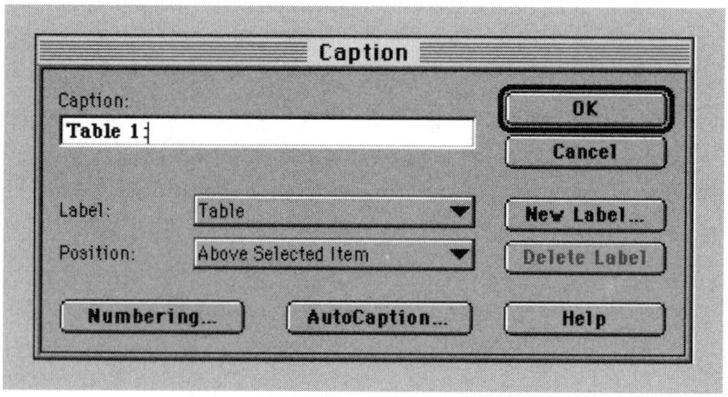

Word automatically includes a label and caption number in the

Caption edit box. If desired, enter additional text for the caption after the caption number. You can change the label by choosing a new option from the Label pop-up menu. Your options are Equation, Figure, or Table. If you don't like those options, you can click the New Label button to create your own; it is automatically added to the Label menu. Choose a position for the caption — Above Selected Item or Below Selected Item — from the Position pop-up menu. Then click OK. The caption is added to your document. In the following illustration, I added a caption to a table that was placed in a frame and positioned on the right side of the document window. Looks good, doesn't it?

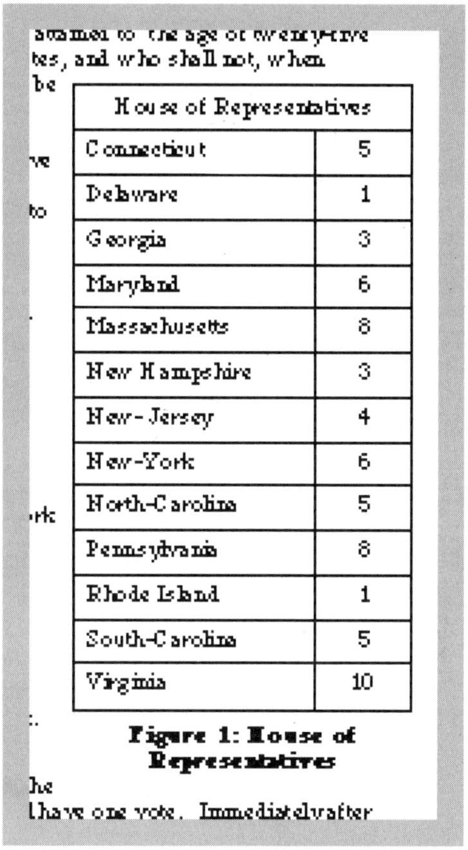

House of Representatives	
Connecticut	5
Delaware	1
Georgia	3
Maryland	6
Massachusetts	8
New Hampshire	3
New-Jersey	4
New-York	6
North-Carolina	5
Pennsylvania	8
Rhode Island	1
South-Carolina	5
Virginia	10

Figure 1: House of Representatives

Using the AutoCaption Feature

The AutoCaption feature adds captions automatically to your document whenever you create or insert a particular type of item. To use this feature, choose Caption from the Insert menu and click the AutoCaption button in the Caption dialog box. The AutoCaption dialog box appears.

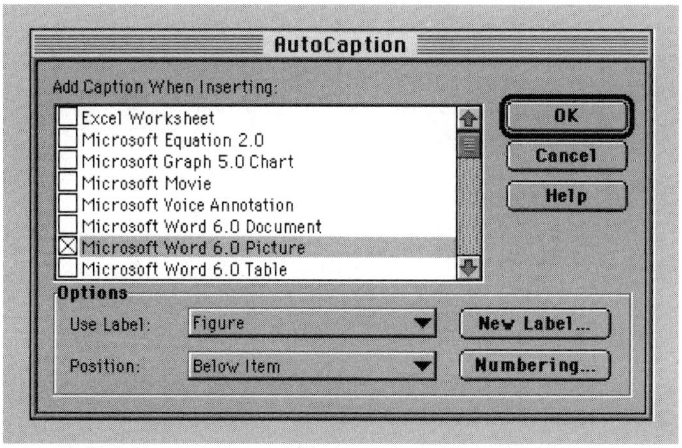

This dialog box displays a scrolling list of items that can be inserted into a Word document.

If you were paying attention back in Chapter 12, you'll recognize this as the same list that appears when you use the Object command under the Insert menu. To have Word automatically add a caption to a specific kind of object, click the object to select it and turn on its check box. Then choose the appropriate label and position from the Use Label and Position pop-up menus. The Label button lets you create a new label if you don't like the ones Word offers. Click OK to accept the settings. From then on, any time you insert that kind of object, Word automatically creates a caption for it.

TIP/TRICK

You can turn on as many check boxes as you like in the AutoCaption dialog box. Just remember to choose the appropriate label and position while the item is selected.

Changing Caption Numbering Options

The Numbering button in the Caption dialog box lets you change the format of caption numbers. It also lets you tell Word to automatically include chapter numbers in the caption number.

To change caption numbering options, choose Caption from the Insert menu and click the Numbering button. The Caption Numbering dialog box appears.

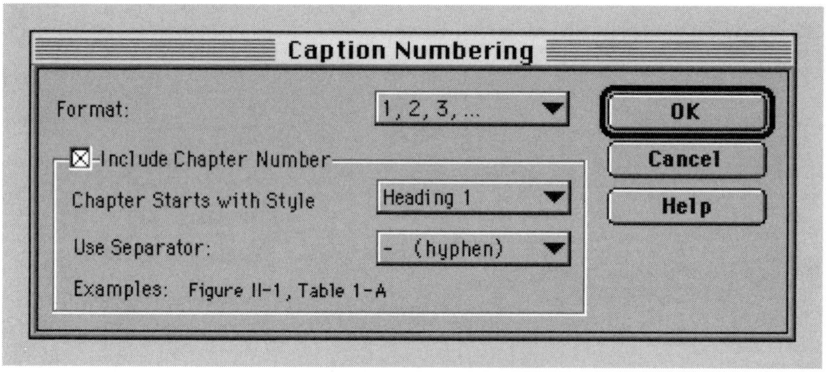

Choose a numbering format from the Format menu — the choices include Arabic numerals, letters, and roman numerals. To include the chapter number in the caption, turn on the Include Chapter Number check box and make sure the correct style is selected from the Chapter Starts with Style pop-up menu. I'll tell you more about including chapter numbers in headings in Chapter 15. When you're finished making changes in the dialog box, click OK. In the Caption dialog box, click OK to insert a new caption or click Close to accept the numbering change without inserting a caption.

The numbering format you select in the Caption Numbering dialog box applies to whatever label is selected in the Caption dialog box. If you like, you can assign a different numbering scheme to each label.

TIP/TRICK

Formatting a Caption

Captions are automatically formatted based on the Caption style. I told you about styles back in Chapter 7. To change the way captions appear, modify the Caption style. Or, if you want to make a quick change to a caption, select the text you want to change and use the appropriate Toolbar button, Menu command, Shortcut Key, or dialog box option to make the change. I told you about formatting text back in Chapters 5 and 6.

Revising a Caption

You can revise the text in a caption — either the label or the text you typed in — at any time. You can also delete a caption.

- To change the text you typed into a caption, select the text you want to change and enter new text to replace it.
- To change the label of a single caption, select the label and number of the caption and press [Delete] or [Del] to delete it. Then choose Caption from the Insert menu and choose the new label. Remember, you can use the New Label button to add a different label to the list. Click OK to complete the change.
- To change the labels of all captions to another label, select the label and number of the caption and choose Caption from the Insert menu. Select a new label for the caption and click OK. All captions using the old label will change to the new one.
- To delete a caption, select the entire caption, including the return character at the end of it, and press [Del] or choose Clear from the Edit menu. The caption disappears.

Updating Caption Numbers

When you insert captions, Word automatically renumbers the captions that come after it. But when you delete captions or move captions around in your document, Word doesn't update caption numbers until you print. You can force Word to update all caption numbers by choosing Select All from the Edit menu or pressing ⌘A and then pressing ⌘ Option Shift U. To update only one caption number, select it and press ⌘ Option Shift U.

Cross-References

Cross-references are commonly used to refer document readers to where they can find additional information. Back in Chapter 10, you took a brief look at cross-references when I told you about footnotes and endnotes. Now I'll tell you more about cross-references, including how you can create them and use them throughout your documents.

Creating a Cross-Reference

Each cross-reference has two parts: the text you type to introduce the reference and the reference itself. In the following illustration, I've created a cross-reference to a table. The text within the parentheses that isn't bold is the introductory text that I typed. The text that is bold is the cross reference Word inserted. I made it bold so I could talk about it here — it's not automatically bold.

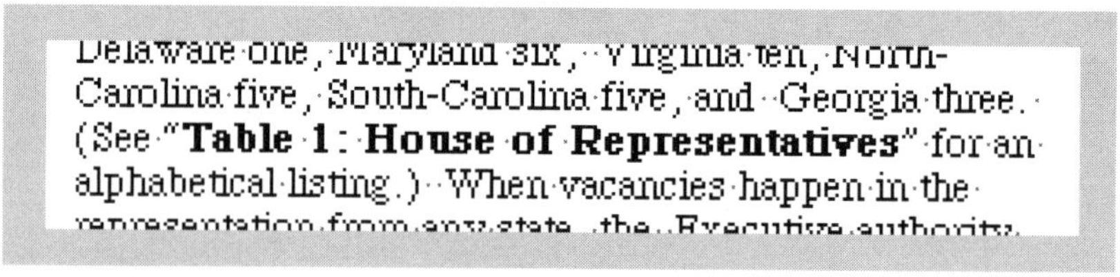
Delaware one, Maryland six, Virginia ten, North-Carolina five, South-Carolina five, and Georgia three. (See "**Table 1: House of Representatives**" for an alphabetical listing.) When vacancies happen in the representation from any state, the Executive authority

All that said, to create a cross-reference, begin by typing in the beginning of the introductory text. If you want the cross-reference to be enclosed in quotes, type a quotation mark too. Then, with the insertion point right after the quotation mark, choose Cross-reference from the Insert menu. The Cross-reference dialog box appears.

Under Reference Type, choose the kind of thing you want to refer to. As you can see, there are several options. I'll tell you about headings in Chapter 15. I told you about bookmarks earlier in this chapter. I told you about footnotes and endnotes in Chapter 11. Equation, figure, and table are three caption labels, which I told you about in the previous section of this chapter — if you added labels, they'd appear here, too.

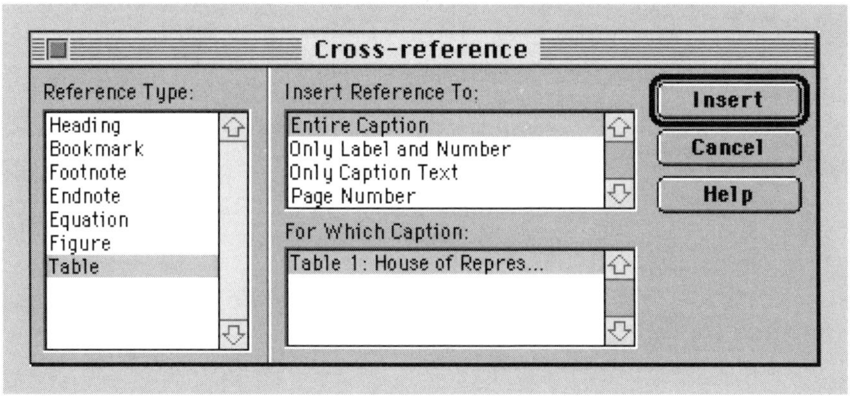

Once you've selected the type of reference, choose an option from the Insert Reference To scrolling list. The options that appear there depend on the reference type you selected. In the previous illustration, I'm referring to a Table which is a type of caption. I've selected Entire Caption as what I want to refer to. That'll include the caption label, number, and text.

The For Which Caption scrolling list displays all the available items of the reference type you selected. Choose the one you want to refer to. When you click Insert, the reference is inserted into your document. The Cancel button changes to a Close button and the dialog box remains open. You can reposition the insertion point in your document, type some more text, and then insert another reference. When you're finished inserting references, click Close.

As you can imagine, the cross-reference feature can be extremely handy when working with long documents. By referring to bookmarks, which can be placed anywhere in your document but don't print, you can create cross-references to any word, phrase, or page in your document.

If your document is part of a master document, which is something I'll discuss in Chapter 15, you can even have a cross-reference to another document within that master document.

TIP/TRICK

Revising a Cross-Reference

You can revise the introductory text or reference of a cross-reference at any time. You can also delete cross-references.

- To revise the introductory text of a cross-reference, select the text and type new text to replace it. Be careful not to delete part of the cross-reference Word inserted.
- To revise a cross-reference inserted by Word, select it and choose Cross-reference from the Insert menu. Select a different cross reference from among the dialog box options and click Insert. Then click Close to dismiss the Cross-reference dialog box.
- To delete a cross-reference, select it and press [Delete] or [Del], or choose Clear from the Edit menu. The cross-reference disappears.

Updating Cross-References

As your document grows, cross-references may need to change. Word updates all cross-references in a document when you print it. You can force Word to update all cross-references by choosing Select All from the Edit menu or pressing [⌘][A] and then pressing [⌘][Shift][Option][U]. To update only one cross-reference, select it and press [⌘][Shift][Option][U].

IMPORTANT NOTE

If you delete an item that is referred to by a cross-reference, Word displays an error message in its place when it updates the references: "Error! Reference source not found." This is a good reason to update and check cross-references before using the Print command. To remove the error message, either revise or delete the cross-reference that generates the error.

Chapter Summary

In this brief chapter, you learned about three new features in Word version 6: bookmarks, captions, and cross-references. As you probably noticed, these features work together to help you manage and refer to information in long documents.

In the next chapter, you'll learn about lists, outlines, and master documents, three more features you might find useful for organizing information and working with long documents.

15

Chapter 15: Lists, Outlines, and Master Documents

EVER USE A SHOPPING LIST? OR A TO-DO LIST? OF COURSE you have. How about when you needed to write a term paper for school — didn't you start out with an outline? You probably did, in one form or another. If you're like me, you discovered in school that lists and outlines are two great ways to organize information. If you haven't discovered it yet, perhaps this chapter will convince you.

In addition to covering lists and outlines in this chapter, you'll also learn about a new feature in Word version 6: master documents. If you normally split a long document into separate documents to make it easier to work with, you'll embrace the master document feature as I have. It makes it possible to work on the chapters or sections of a long document separately or together, making your work far easier to manage.

Working with Bulleted or Numbered Lists

Look at the following illustration and answer the two questions immediately after it.

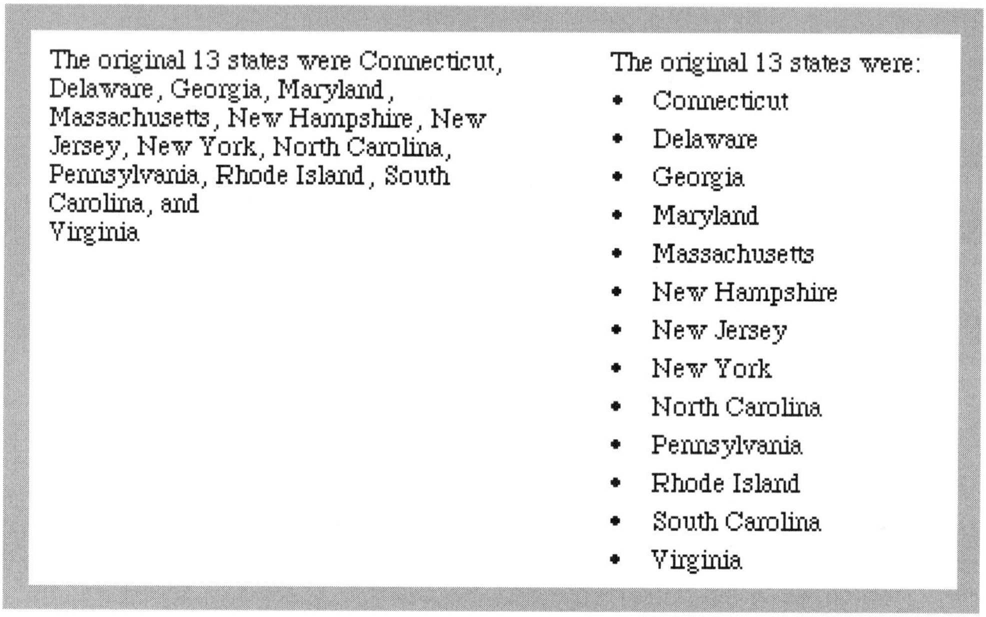

The original 13 states were Connecticut, Delaware, Georgia, Maryland, Massachusetts, New Hampshire, New Jersey, New York, North Carolina, Pennsylvania, Rhode Island, South Carolina, and
Virginia

The original 13 states were:

- Connecticut
- Delaware
- Georgia
- Maryland
- Massachusetts
- New Hampshire
- New Jersey
- New York
- North Carolina
- Pennsylvania
- Rhode Island
- South Carolina
- Virginia

- Which side of the illustration was easier to read?
- Which side of the illustration were your eyes drawn to first?

Both sides of the illustration contained exactly the same information: a list of the first thirteen states, presented in alphabetical order. Chances are, you found the right side, which presents the information as a bulleted list, easier to read. In fact, your eyes probably moved to the list first, even though it was on the right side of the illustration. Why? I haven't done any real research or study, but I suspect that our eyes know an easy job when they spot one and try to tackle the easy jobs first.

This example reinforces something I've been telling people for years: one of the best ways to organize and present information is in list form. When properly presented and formatted, readers are drawn to lists. They read lists before they read tightly packed text around them. That's why you find lists used so frequently in magazine articles, presentations, and, yes, even computer how-to books.

In this section, I'll tell you how you can create and format lists — bulleted lists like the one illustrated here, numbered lists, and even fancy, multilevel lists. As you'll see, Word can keep track of list item numbers for you, making it easy to insert, delete, or even rearrange list items. Word also handles list formatting for you, although you can modify the default formats it uses. Finally, I'll show you how to use the Sort command, which I first introduced back in Chapter 11, to change the order of items in a list.

Creating a List

To create a list, begin by typing in the list items. Be sure to press Return after each one to begin a new paragraph. Select the paragraphs containing the list items and do one of the following:

- For a bulleted list, click the Bullets button on the Formatting toolbar.

- For a numbered list, click the Numbering button on the Formatting toolbar.

In either case, Word inserts the appropriate character (a bullet or number) in front of the text and changes the ruler settings to set a hanging indent. I told you about the ruler and hanging indents in Chapter 6 when I covered paragraph formatting.

Using the Formatting toolbar buttons is actually one of two ways to create a list. The Bullets and Numbering dialog box is another. I'll discuss that a little later in this chapter when I tell you how to change a list's formatting.

TIP/TRICK

To convert a bulleted list to a numbered list or a numbered list to a bulleted list, simply select the list items and click the appropriate toolbar button to make the change.

Adding to a List

You can add items to the list and have them formatted the same way as the other items in the list. Word will even automatically renumber numbered items if necessary.

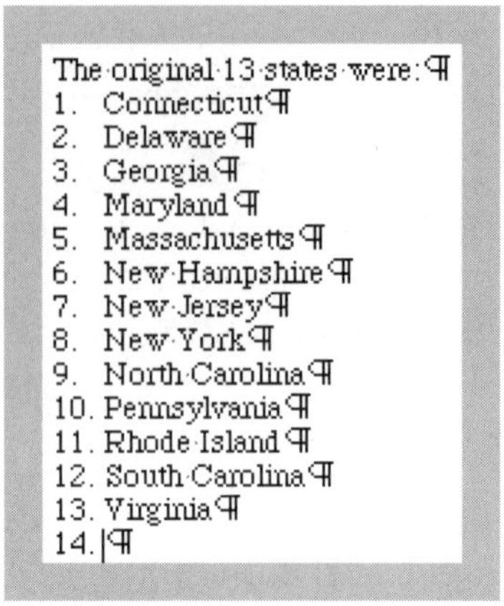

- To add an item to the end of a list, position the insertion point immediately after the last item in the list and press [Return]. Word carries forward the same formatting as the rest of the list. If you've got a numbered list, Word adds another number in the sequence.

- To add an item to the middle of a list, position the insertion point immediately after the item above where you want to insert. Press [Return] to insert a new line. Word renumbers all the items after the inserted item.

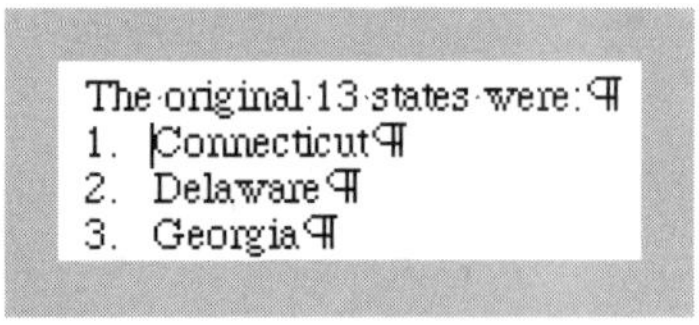

- To add an item to the beginning of the list, position the insertion point immediately before the first item in the list. You won't be able to position the insertion point before the bullet or number so don't bother trying. Type in the text for the new item and press [Return]. The item that was the first item becomes the second item. If the list is numbered, Word adjusts the numbers accordingly.

Deleting Items from a List

Deleting items from a list is easy. Simply select the item, including the paragraph mark at the end of it, and press [Delete] or [Del] to remove it. You won't be able to select the bullet or number before the list item, so don't worry about it. It disappears along with the list item. If the list is numbered, Word adjusts the numbers.

Rearranging the Items in a List

You can rearrange the order of items in a list by using the Cut and Paste commands or buttons, or drag and drop text editing. I discussed all these things back in Chapter 2. Be sure to include the paragraph mark at the end of a list item when you move it — that's where Word stores the list formatting information.

When you rearrange list items in a numbered list, Word automatically updates the numbers for you. When you copy list items from one list to another, Word carries the list formatting with the item. This makes it possible to move an item from one numbered list to another and have the numbers update properly all around.

Removing Bullets or Numbers

You can remove or "turn off" the bullets or numbering feature. There are several ways to do this, depending on why you want to turn them off. The Shortcut menu, which I first mentioned back in Chapter 1, offers commands to skip or stop numbering. To display the Shortcut menu for an item, hold down the [Control] key while pointing to the item and press your mouse button down. (Yes, this will require two hands.) Or try pressing [Shift][F10] (on an extended keyboard) while pointing to the list item. The menu appears and you can select one of its options.

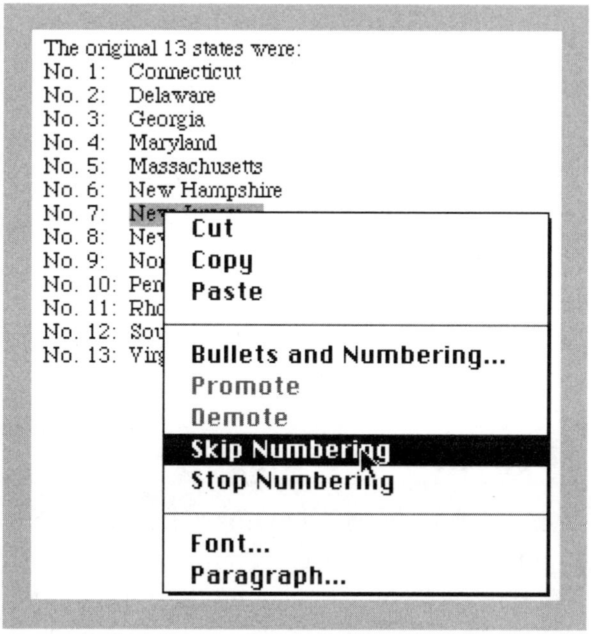

Here's what you want to look for:

- To skip the numbering of one or more list items, choose Skip Numbering from the Shortcut menu to turn the list formatting off for the item. Or, if you prefer, simply click the appropriate toolbar button — Bullets or Numbering — to turn it off. As you can see in the illustration, numbering continues after the item(s) you skipped.

The original 13 states were:
1. Connecticut
2. Delaware
3. Georgia
4. Maryland
5. Massachusetts
6. New Hampshire
New Jersey
7. New York
8. North Carolina
9. Pennsylvania
10. Rhode Island
11. South Carolina
12. Virginia

- To end one list so you can begin another, select the items you don't want numbered and choose Stop Numbering from the Shortcut menu. Or, if you prefer, choose Bullets and Numbering from the Format menu and click the Remove button. (I'll tell you more about the Bullets and Numbering dialog box in a moment.) This makes it possible to have two consecutive lists, each with different numbering, like this:

8 of the original 13 states were:
1. Connecticut
2. Delaware
3. Georgia
4. Maryland
5. Massachusetts
6. New Hampshire
7. New Jersey
8. New York
The other 5 were:
1. North Carolina
2. Pennsylvania
3. Rhode Island
4. South Carolina
5. Virginia

TIP/TRICK

If you're working with a bulleted list, it doesn't matter which command you pick since you don't have to worry about getting numbers right.

Formatting a List

You may have noticed by now that you can't select and edit the bullets or numbers in a list. That's because most list formatting is done internally by Word. While you can change the font and paragraph formatting with techniques I told you about in Chapters 5 and 6, and you can apply styles with techniques I told you about in Chapter 7, to change the look of the bullet or number, you'll have to use the Bullets and Numbering dialog box. As you'll see in this section, this dialog box lets you choose from among different preformatted list styles, as well as modify styles to meet your specific needs.

To modify the formatting of a list, select all the list items and choose Bullets and Numbering from the Format menu. The Bullets and Numbering dialog box, which has three tabs, lets you select, modify, or remove a specific type of list format.

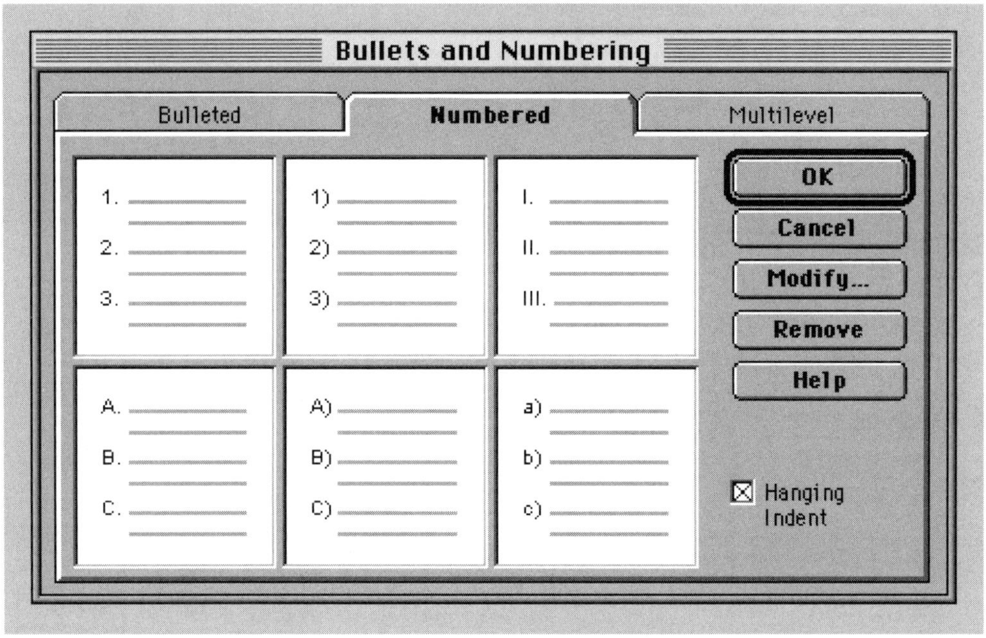

Each tab looks and works basically the same way. Most of the dialog box real estate is taken up with six big preview buttons that illustrate the different preformatted options. As you can see, the options vary primarily by the bullet or number format. To use one, just click on it. You can turn hanging indents on or off for the Bulleted and Numbered tabs by turning the Hanging Indent check box on or off. The preview buttons change accordingly.

Modifying a Bulleted List

If you want a bulleted list but the six preformatted options aren't exactly what you're looking for, make sure the Bulleted tab is displayed and then click the Modify button. The Modify Bulleted List dialog box appears. It lets you change a variety of the formatting options.

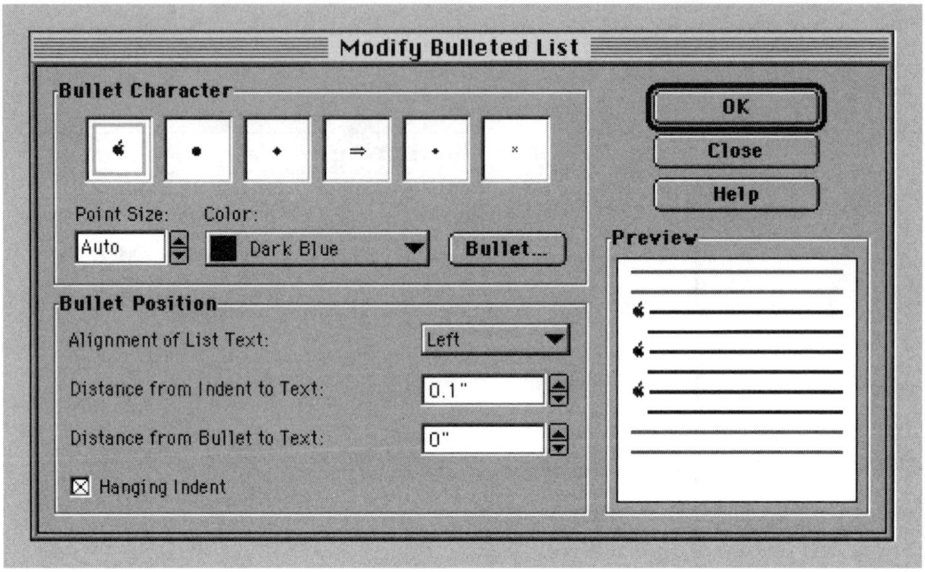

- **Bullet Character:** This area lets you select a character to use as a bullet. Click on one of the six standards or, if you don't like them, click the Bullet button to open the Symbol dialog box, which I told you about in detail back in Chapter 5. You can also specify a size for the bullet character by entering a value into the Point Size edit box. If you enter Auto, the bullet will be the same size as that specified by the paragraph formatting of each list item. You can even choose a color from the Color pop-up menu. Remember, you must have a color monitor to see colors and a color printer to print in color.
- **Bullet Position:** This area lets you specify the bullet position in relation to the margins and text. Choose Left, Centered, or Right from Alignment of List Text. Enter a value in the Distance from Indent to Text edit box to specify the distance between the left indent setting and the text of the list. Enter a value in the Distance from Bullet to Text to specify the distance between the bullet and the text. Again, a Hanging Indent check box lets you turn hanging indents on or off.

Modifying a Numbered List

You can also modify one of the preformatted options for numbered lists. Make sure the Numbered tab is displayed in the Bullets and Numbering dialog box and click the Modify button. The Modify Numbered List dialog box appears.

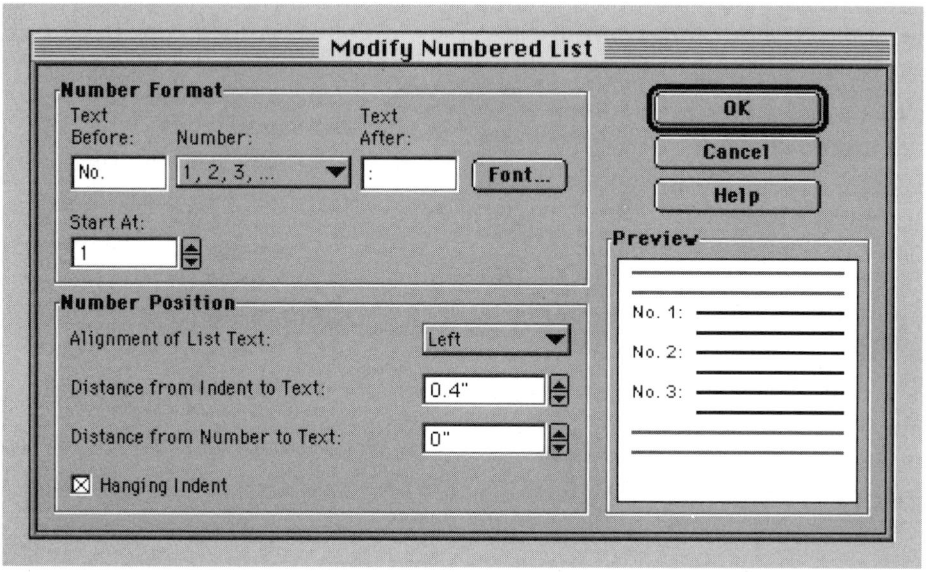

- **Number Format:.** This area lets you set the number format. Enter up to 32 characters (total) in the Text Before and Text After edit boxes to insert characters like parentheses, dashes, or periods before or after the number. If desired, use the Font button to display the Font dialog box. I told you about this back in Chapter 5; it lets you format text characters. By default, the list numbers will use the same font and size as determined by the paragraph formatting of the list item. You can also enter a value in the Start At box to specify a starting number for the list.
- **Number Position:** This area lets you specify number position in relation to the margin and text. It works just like the Bullet Position options in the Modify Bulleted List dialog box, which I discussed above.

The Preview area changes to reflect your settings. When you're satisfied with your changes, click OK to accept them and return to your document.

Working with Multilevel Lists

Word also lets you create multilevel lists with up to nine levels. For example, say you've got a list of things to do today and tomorrow. You want the days to be on one level and the items that need to be done each day on a sublevel. That's a perfect application for a multilevel list. When you're finished creating it, it might look something like this:

1) Things to Do Today
   - Meet the Group for a Ride
   - Finish Chapter 15
   - Make Dinner
2) Things to Do Tomorrow
   - Start Chapter 16
   - Go to the Post Office
   - Call Jeremy
   - Make Reservations for Dinner

IMPORTANT NOTE

Although multilevel lists are similar to outlines, they're created with the List feature of Word, not the Outline feature. This is an important distinction that affects paragraph styles and the generation of a table of contents. I'll tell you about outlines later in this chapter and about tables of contents in Chapter 20.

Creating a Multilevel List

You can format text as a multilevel list as you type it or take existing text and convert it into a multilevel list. In either case, you'll need to use the Multilevel tab in the Bullets and Numbering dialog box.

- To format text as a multilevel list as you type it, position the insertion point in an empty paragraph and choose Bullets and Numbering from the Format menu.
- To format existing text as a multilevel list, select the text and choose Bullets and Numbering from the Format menu.

Click the Multilevel tab in the Bullets and Numbering dialog box to display the predefined formats for multilevel lists.

As you can see, the formats combine numbers with letters, numbers with bullets, and numbers with numbers. Click on the one you like to select it and click OK to accept it and return to your document.

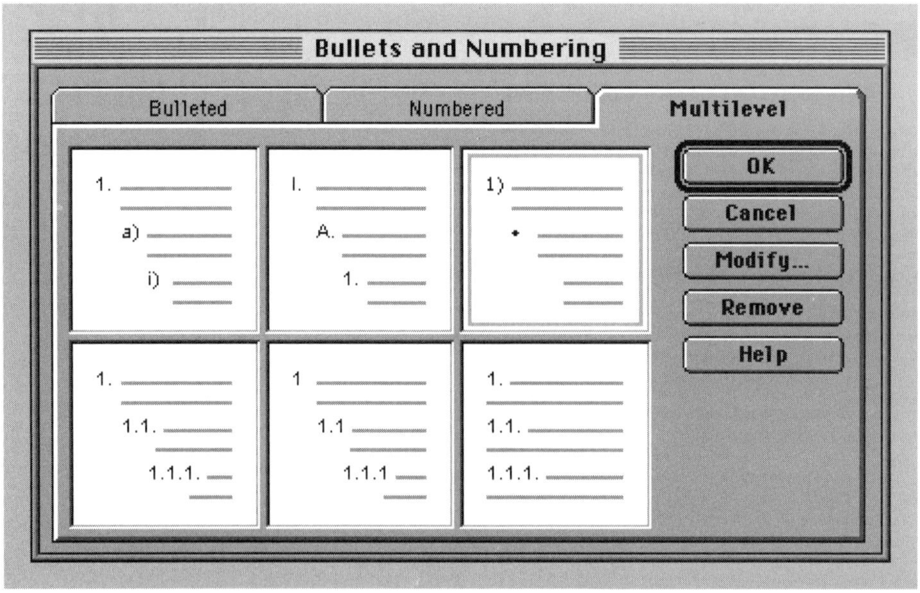

If your list doesn't exist yet, begin typing. You'll see that the list formatting for the first level of the format you selected is used for each paragraph. To move an item to the next lower level or *demote* that item, select it and click the Increase Indent button on the Formatting toolbar or press Option Shift →. To *promote* an item, select it and click the Decrease Indent button on the Formatting toolbar or press Option Shift ←. You'll see the selected item move accordingly. If you press Return after a second level item, you create a new second level item. You can demote or promote that item as necessary to get the formatting you want.

If you selected an existing list before using the Bullets and Numbering command, all the text in the list is formatted with first level formatting. Use the techniques discussed in the previous paragraph to demote or promote list items. Remember, you can select more than one list item at a time to save time while changing them.

Formatting a Multilevel List

The Multilevel tab of the Bullets and Numbering dialog box offers a Modify button, too. Click it to create a custom multilevel list format. The Modify Multilevel List dialog box that appears lets you change the formatting of each level of your list. This dialog box works very much like the Modify dialog boxes for bulleted and numbered lists, so you can consult my discussions of those for details. Here are a few exceptions worth noting:

- A Level area is included above the Preview area. Use the scrolling list to select the level you want to change before making changes on the left side of the dialog box.
- Bullet or Number is a pop-up menu with all kinds of bullet and number formats, including any special formats you may have created for other lists in the document. The New Bullet option displays the Symbol dialog box.
- When you've selected any level other than Level 1, an Include from Previous Level pop-up menu appears. This makes it possible to include the previous level's number or number and position in the level you're modifying.

As you might expect by now, all changes you make are reflected in the Preview area. When you're happy with what you've created, click OK to return to your document.

Sorting a List

I discussed sorting information in detail back in Chapter 11 when I talked about tables. Sorting a list works much the same way. Begin by selecting the list items you want to sort. It doesn't matter whether the items are numbered — Word ignores the numbers and you can't select them anyway. Choose Sort Text from the Table menu to display the Sort Text dialog box.

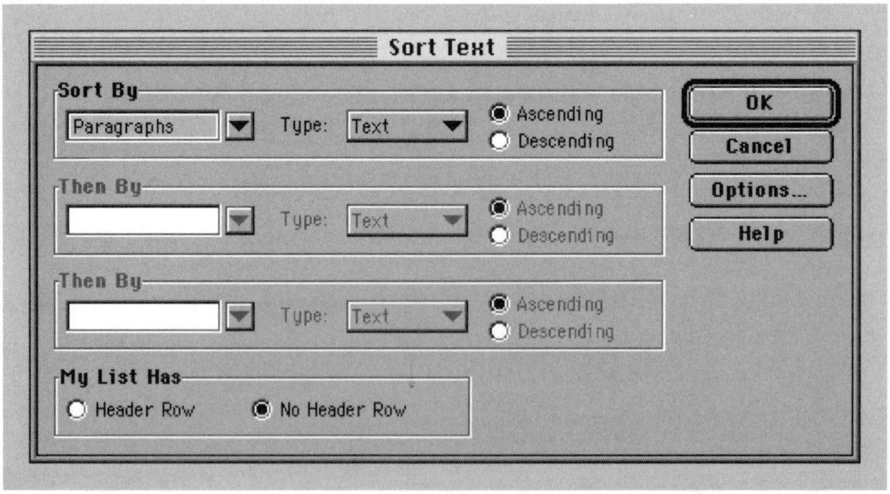

In most cases, you'll be sorting paragraphs so make sure Paragraphs is selected in the pop-up menu/edit box under Sort By. If the list is part of a tab table, you may want to sort by different fields or columns. In that case, choose the appropriate field from the pop-up list. From the Type pop-up menu, choose the type of thing you're sorting by: text, number, or date. If you want the items sorted in reverse order, be sure to click the Descending radio button. All this defines what the primary sort will be. For more information about sorting by multiple fields or columns, check Chapter 11.

The Sort Text dialog box has an Options button that displays the Sort Options dialog box. Two options in this dialog box apply to sorting lists:

- If each list item contains separate fields of information — like in a tab table — use the Separate Fields At radio button to tell Word what character separates one field from another.
- A Case Sensitive check box lets you tell Word whether it should sort uppercase letters before lowercase letters when sorting.

If you've specified sort options, click the OK button in the Sort Options dialog box to accept them and dismiss the dialog box. Then click OK in the Sort Text dialog box to perform the sort. Word sorts the list in the order you specified and, if necessary, renumbers any numbered items.

TIP/TRICK

You can sort any text in your document using the Sort Text command under the Table menu. Don't let the menu name fool you! Use the same procedures outlined here to sort paragraphs of text, cell table format information, words, numbers, or dates.

IMPORTANT NOTE

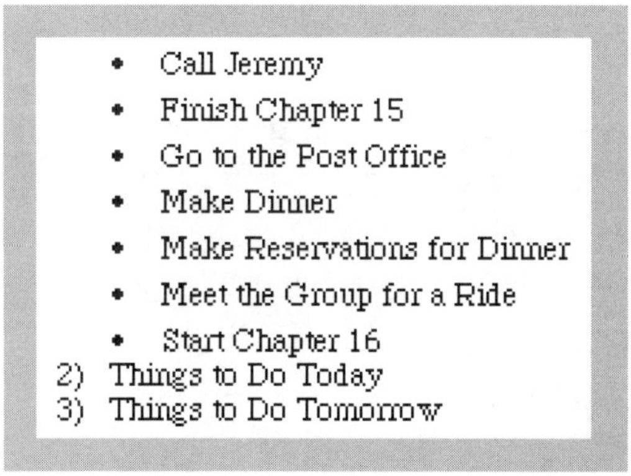

If you select and sort a multilevel list, you'll find that the entire list is sorted — not just the items under each level. That could make a mess, as shown here.

To prevent this from happening, select only list items in the same level when sorting. This may require a separate sort for each group of items in a particular level of the list.

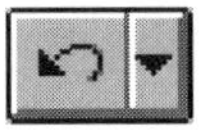

The Sort command is another one of those commands that can really mess up a document. If you sort a list and get unexpected results, click the Undo button or choose Undo Sort from the Edit menu.

Outlines

Like lists, outlines are a great way to organize information. By separating ideas into main topics and putting related subtopics beneath them, you can create a document or presentation "skeleton." Use the outline as is to present information to someone else, or add body text to build a document.

In this section, I'll tell you how you can create and use outlines to organize information and create finished documents. If you've been looking for a way to organize long, complex documents, outlines might just be the answer.

NEW IN WORD 6

Word's outline feature is not new to version 6.0, but like other Word features, it has undergone some minor changes. If you already use Word's outline feature, be sure to look for the New in Word 6 icon throughout this section. It'll mark the changes you should be aware of.

For Example: Why Use Outlines?

If outlines remind you so much of high school English class that you're ready to skip this section, stop and read this first.

Word's outline feature may look like just an organizational tool, but it goes far beyond that. Let me give you some examples.

- A Word outline can be collapsed or expanded to display different levels or sections of the document. When you collapse an outline, you can see more topics on screen at once. Outlines also make it a bit easier to select and move entire topics with drag and drop text editing.
- When you create an outline, you automatically apply Heading styles to the various heading levels in your document. This helps you consistently format the final document. I told you about styles back in Chapter 7.

Continued

- A table of contents is much easier to generate when the document has been created or formatted with Word's outlining feature. As you'll see in Chapter 20, a table of contents can be based on the Heading styles automatically applied by Word.
- If you use Microsoft PowerPoint to give presentations, Word's outlining feature is something you should learn and use. PowerPoint can read and write Word outline files. So the report you create in Word can easily be turned into a PowerPoint presentation. I'll tell you a little more about this in Chapter 24.

I use Word's outlining feature whenever I write a book. I start by creating a very basic outline that goes to my editor with the initial book proposal. When I get the book contract, I modify and expand the outline to help organize my thoughts and establish the book's complete contents. Then I add body text to build the final manuscript. About 50 percent of this book was written in Word's Outline view. In fact, I'm in Outline view as I write this now.

As you'll see in this chapter, Word's outline feature has hidden perks that'll make it useful anytime you need to create a long document.

Creating an Outline

There are two ways to create an outline. You can create it from scratch in an empty document window and add text or convert an existing document's text to an outline. I'll tell you about each method here.

IMPORTANT NOTE

An outline does not have to remain an outline. Word's outline feature adds special outlining capabilities and commands while you work with a document in Outline view. You can switch from one view to another and continue working with your document at any time. So don't think that once you create an outline you're "stuck" working with it forever. Another view is just a mouse click away.

Creating an Outline from Scratch

To create an outline from scratch, simply create a new document and click the Outline view button on the lower left side of the window or choose Outline from the View menu. Once in outline view, you can begin to enter text. I'll tell you how in a moment.

Converting Existing Text into an Outline

To convert an existing document into an outline, open the document and click the Outline view button on the lower left side of the window or choose Outline from the View menu. Once in outline view, you can promote and demote existing text to the heading levels you need. I'll tell you how in a little while.

Outline View Symbols

Before I tell you how to enter text and promote and demote headings, let me tell you about the Outline view symbols that you'll see in your documents. Here's an illustration of an outline in progress with the Style area displayed. I told you about the Style area back in Chapter 7.

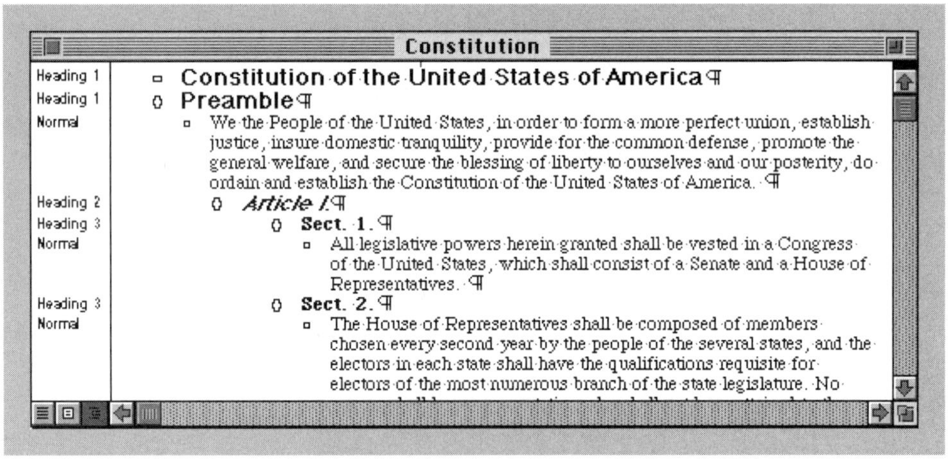

As you can see, this outline uses three different Heading styles: Heading 1, Heading 2, and Heading 3. Each heading has a different look and indentation in Outline view. The appearance of a heading is determined by the Heading style, which you can change if you like. The indentation is determined by its level in Outline view. Indentation may or may not be part of a Heading style in other views. I'll tell you more about that later.

Font formatting of Heading styles is only displayed when the Show Formatting button on the Outlining toolbar is turned on. If everything appears as plain text, click the Show Formatting button to turn it on.

Each heading is marked with a hollow plus or minus sign. The hollow plus sign indicates that the heading has subheadings or subtext. The hollow minus sign indicates that the heading does not have subheadings or subtext. In the previous illustration, all the heading levels displayed have subtext except the first one.

Body text, which is automatically formatted in the Normal style, is marked with a little hollow box. Its indentation depends on which heading level it falls below. As you already know, indentation is not part of the Normal style. As you'll see when I switch to Normal view in a little while, body text is not indented.

You might also notice that there's a new toolbar when you're in Outline view. This is the Outlining toolbar and it appears automatically when you switch to Outline view. I'll tell you about its buttons throughout the Outlines section of this chapter.

Entering Text

Let's go back to our new outline. You created a new document and clicked the Outline view button. Now you're ready to create your outline. Well, go ahead. Type.

The first text you type is automatically assigned Heading 1. You can tell by looking at the Formatting toolbar or the Style area, if you have them displayed. Think of headings now, not body text — the skeleton, not the flesh.

When you press Return, you get a new paragraph at the same heading level. If you want to create a heading at a different level, you'll need to *demote* that heading to a lower level. You can demote or *promote* (raise) a heading before or after you type it.

Promoting and Demoting Headings and Body Text

Promoting and demoting headings changes their level of importance in the outline. When you demote a heading, it becomes a subheading or subtopic of the heading at the next higher level before it. In our example, the headings Sect. 1. and Sect. 2. are subheadings under Article I. Article I. is a subheading under Preamble. (I know this isn't right, but I'll fix it in a while.) Word gives you nine heading levels in your documents.

Headings are fine for creating the document skeleton, but when it's time to add flesh to the bones, body text is what you want. Body text is the text beneath a heading level which is formatted with the Normal style. To create body text, you demote a heading level to body text. You can also, if desired, promote or demote body text to a heading.

There are three ways to promote or demote headings or body text: with toolbar buttons, shortcut keys, and the mouse.

With Toolbar Buttons

To promote or demote a heading or body text with the Outlining toolbar, begin by clicking anywhere in the heading or body text you want to change. Then use one of these buttons:

Click the Promote button to promote a heading to the next higher level. The heading and any body text beneath it shift to the left. You cannot promote a Heading 1 heading since there's no higher level. If you promote body text, it shifts to the same level as the heading above it.

Click the Demote button to demote a heading to the next lower level. The heading and any body text beneath it shifts to the right. You cannot demote a Heading 9 heading since there's no lower level. If you demote body text, it shifts to the heading level below the heading above it.

Click the Demote to Body Text button to demote a heading to body text. The heading becomes part of the body text beneath the heading above it.

With Shortcut Keys

NEW IN WORD 6

To promote or demote a heading or body text with shortcut keys, begin by clicking anywhere in the heading you want to change. Then use one of the key combinations listed below. These keys differ from those in previous versions of Word, so if you already use Word's outlining feature, take note of the changes!

To...	Shortcut Keys
Promote a Heading or Body Text	Option Shift ←
Demote a Heading or Body Text	Option Shift →
Demote a Heading to Body Text	⌘ Shift N (this applies the Normal style)

With the Mouse

To promote or demote a heading with the mouse, position the mouse pointer on the hollow plus or minus sign. It turns into a four-headed arrow and the heading (as well as any body text or subheadings beneath it) becomes selected. Press the mouse button down and drag to the left to demote or to the right to promote. As you drag, the mouse pointer turns into a two-headed arrow pointing to the right and left and a vertical line appears, indicating the new position of the heading. It might look something like this:

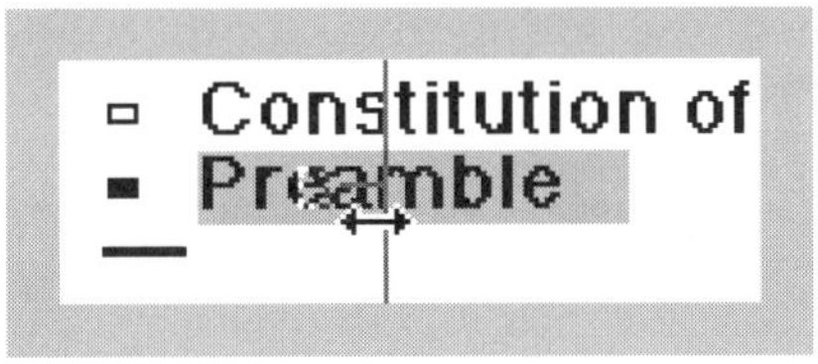

When the vertical line reaches the level you want, release the mouse button. The heading and any body text and subheadings beneath it shifts.

You can also use this method to promote or demote body text. Position the mouse pointer over the hollow box before the body text and drag as instructed above. The body text becomes a heading.

IMPORTANT NOTE

As you'll find by experimenting with this method of promoting and demoting heading levels, when you click on a hollow plus sign, the heading it marks, as well as any body text and subheadings beneath it, becomes selected. When you drag to promote or demote, you're promoting or demoting all of the subtext and subheadings. You can see this in the following illustration. If this is not what you intended, use the toolbar buttons or shortcut keys to promote or demote the heading.

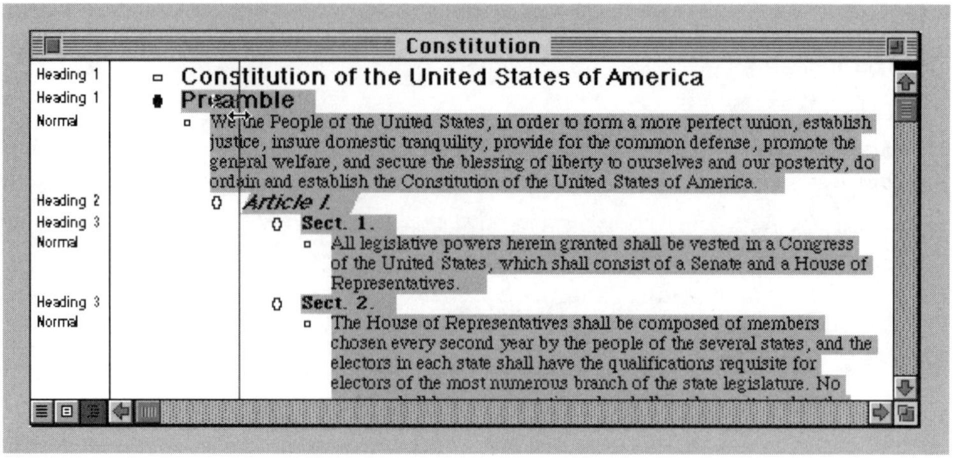

Selecting Headings and Text

As you may have noticed, selecting text in Outline view is a little different from selecting text in other Word views. Here are some selection techniques you might find useful.

- To select only a heading or only a paragraph of body text, click in the Selection bar (the area immediately to the left of the left indent) beside the heading or paragraph.
- To select multiple headings and paragraphs of body text, click in the Selection bar beside the first heading and drag down to select the text you want.
- To select an entire paragraph of body text, click on the hollow box to the left of the paragraph.
- To select a heading and all subtext and subheadings beneath it, click on the hollow plus sign to the left of the heading.

IMPORTANT NOTE

Be careful when you drag to select text! If you drag one of the outline symbols (hollow plus, minus, or box), you'll move the entire selection. I'll tell you about moving headings and text next.

Moving Headings and Text

You can move headings and text to rearrange or reorganize your outline or the information it contains. While the Cut and Paste commands, Cut and Paste toolbar buttons, and drag-and-drop text which I told you about in Chapter 2 can do the job, in Outline view you have additional options to move blocks of text.

With Toolbar Buttons

The Outlining toolbar offers two buttons to let you move selected parts of your outline up or down. With that said, I bet you can guess which buttons I'm talking about.

Click the Move Up button to move selected headings and body text up. Each time you click, the selection moves up one paragraph.

Click the Move Down button to move selected headings and body text down. Each time you click, the selection moves down one paragraph.

With the Mouse

You can also rearrange your outline or document with the mouse. This works similarly to drag and drop text editing, but you're limited to where you can drag selected headings and body text.

To move a heading and any subheadings or body text beneath it, position your mouse pointer on the hollow plus sign before the heading and press the mouse button down. The mouse pointer turns into a four-headed arrow and the heading and any subheadings and body text beneath it become selected. Drag up or down in the document window. As you drag, the mouse pointer turns into a two-headed arrow pointing up and down and a horizontal line appears, showing you where the selection will be inserted when you release the mouse button. The horizontal line will always appear between paragraphs — it will never appear in the middle of a paragraph.

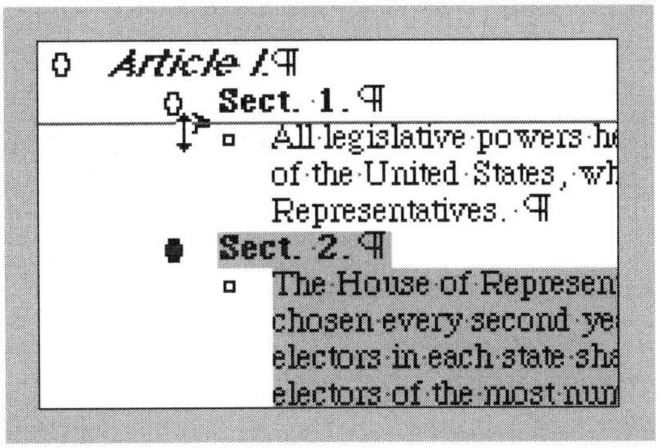

When the horizontal line appears where you want to move the selection, release the mouse button. The entire selection moves.

TIP/TRICK

This technique also works for body text. Drag the hollow box up or down to rearrange paragraphs.

With Shortcut Keys

NEW IN WORD 6

You want shortcut keys? You've got 'em. Here are the keys you can use to rearrange selected parts of your outline. These differ from keystrokes in previous versions of Word, so if you've already got keystrokes in your mind, check them against these.

To...	Shortcut Keys
Move a Heading or Body Text Up	Option Shift ↑
Move a Heading or Body Text Down	Option Shift ↓

Collapsing and Expanding Outline Levels

As I mentioned earlier, you can expand and collapse outline levels. By collapsing an outline so that only certain heading levels are displayed, you can get a better idea of the overall organization of your document. Collapsing an outline also makes it quicker and easier to rearrange your document — without body text and subheadings displayed, there's less to move.

In the following illustration, I've collapsed my outline so that only levels 1 and 2 are displayed. The gray line beneath the Level 2 headings indicate that there's subtext beneath that level.

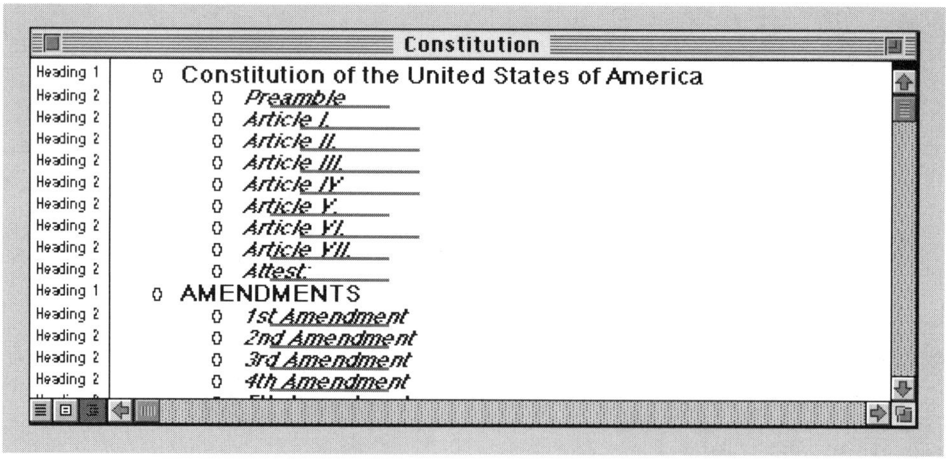

In the next illustration, I've expanded part of the outline — the part under Article III — to view and work with its contents. You can collapse or expand almost any combination of outline sections and levels to meet your needs.

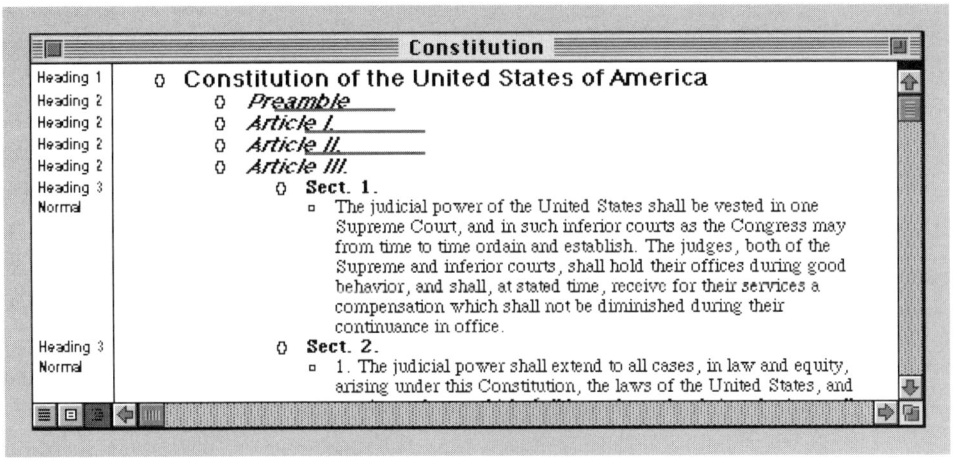

Word offers three ways to expand or collapse all or part of an outline: with toolbar buttons, the mouse, or shortcut keys.

With Toolbar Buttons

Word's Outlining toolbar features a bunch of buttons to change the outline levels displayed in selected sections or the entire document. Experiment with these to get a good feel for how they work.

To expand only part of an outline, select the part you want to expand or position the insertion point in the heading you want to expand and click the Expand button. The view changes to display the next level of the outline and the heading's body text.

To collapse only part of an outline, select the part you want to collapse or position the insertion point in the heading you want to collapse and click the Collapse button. The view changes to display one less level of the outline.

The Show Heading 1 button collapses the outline so only the first or top level of the outline is displayed.

The Show Heading 2 button collapses or expands the outline so only the first and second levels of the outline are displayed.

NEW IN WORD 6

As you can probably guess, the Show Heading 3 through Show Heading 8 buttons (numbered 3 through 8), show the levels they indicate. Each button shows only headings, however — not body text. This is an improvement over previous versions of Word, which only offered buttons to display levels 1 through 4.

The All button displays the entire outline, including body text.

The Show First Line Only button displays only the first line of each paragraph of body text under each heading. The body text is only displayed if you have selected the All button or expanded part of the outline another way. At the end of the line, Word displays an ellipsis to indicate that there's more text in the paragraph. It might look something like this:

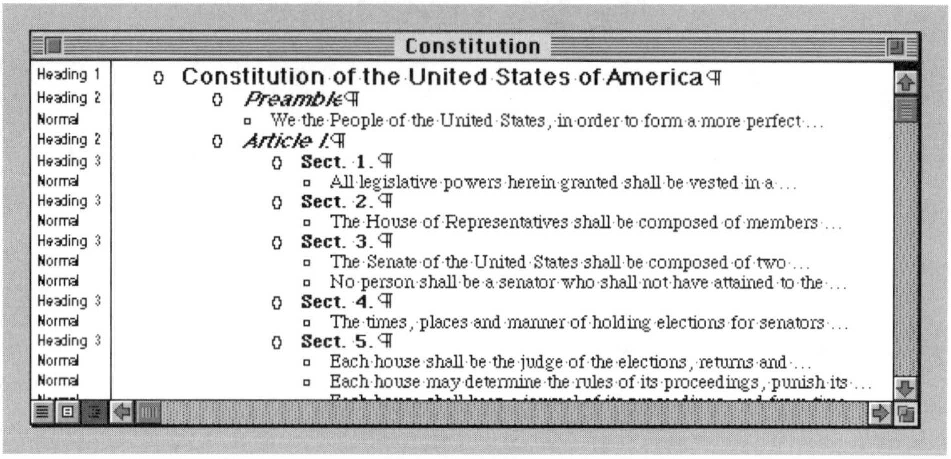

With the Mouse

You can also expand or collapse outlines with the mouse. Simply double-click on the hollow plus sign to the left of the heading you want to expand or collapse. Word either fully expands or completely collapses everything under that heading.

With Shortcut Keys

NEW IN WORD 6

If you prefer using shortcut keys over buttons and mouse movements, Word has got you covered again. Here are the Shortcut Keys you can use to expand or collapse outlines. Remember to select the heading level you want to expand or collapse first, before using these keystrokes. If you've used previous versions of Word, take note of these keystrokes since they're different from what you might be used to.

To...	Shortcut Keys
Expand Subheadings and Body Text under the Selected Heading	Control Shift =
Collapse Subheadings and Body Text under the Selected Heading	Control Shift -
Expand to Show Entire Outline or Collapse to Show Only Headings	Control Shift A (Same as clicking All button on Outlining toolbar.)
Expand or Collapse Entire Outline to a Specific Level	Control Shift *number* (1-8 on main keyboard) For example, Control Shift 2 collapses the entire outline to show only levels 1 or 2. (Same as clicking Show Heading 2 button on the Outlining toolbar.)
Show All Body Text or Show Only First Line of Body Text	Control Shift L (Same as clicking the Show First Line Only button on the Outlining toolbar.)

Modifying an Outline's Format

The appearance of headings and text in an outline is determined by the Heading and Normal style sheets applied. While the headings and text appear indented in Outline view, heading styles do not include indentation when viewed in Normal or Page Layout views or Print Preview.

You can modify the format of an outline by changing the style sheets as I discussed in Chapter 7 or by using the font and paragraph formatting techniques I discussed in Chapters 5 and 6. Formatting capabilities in Outline view are limited to formatting you can apply with toolbar buttons, Shortcut Keys, or Menu commands. You cannot apply paragraph formatting with the Ruler or Paragraph dialog box because the Ruler doesn't display and the Paragraph command is unavailable in Outline view. To make formatting changes you can't make in Outline view, switch to Normal or Page Layout view.

Word gives you the ability to turn character formatting on or off while in Outline view. To show or hide character formatting, click the Show Formatting button on the Outlining toolbar or press / on the numeric keypad. This button only affects text in Outline view. If you switch to another view (other than Master Document view), the formatting is displayed no matter what.

TIP/ TRICK

You can work on your document in two views at the same time by splitting the screen. To do this, drag the Split box at the top of the Vertical Scroll bar down to the middle of the document window and let go of the mouse button. Or simply double-click on the Split box. The window divides into two separate panes. You can then assign different views to each pane by clicking in the pane you want to change and clicking the appropriate View button at the bottom of the window.

In the following illustration, I've split the screen so that the top pane shows Outline view while the bottom pane shows Normal view. Any change I make in either pane will be reflected in the other pane. In addition, when I scroll one pane, the other pane scrolls to display the same part of the document. This is something you might find really useful, especially if you've got a large monitor and can make both panes a reasonably large size. (This isn't something you'd want to do regularly with a 9-inch monitor.)

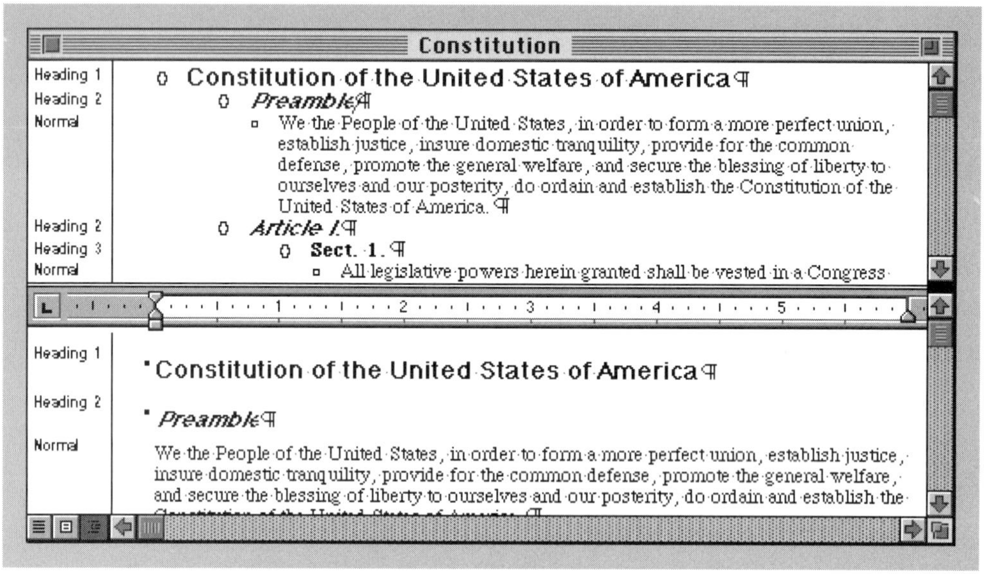

FYI: About Heading Styles

Heading styles are designed to look like document headings. They utilize standard fonts like Helvetica and Times in a variety of sizes and styles. They also include spacing before and after the heading paragraph to help make the heading stand out from the rest of the document text. Headings

Continued

1 through 4 utilize the Keep with Next option in the Paragraph dialog box to assure that the heading is never separated from the text that follows it.

You can use the Styles command under the Format menu to modify the definition of any style in your document, including Heading styles. You can use the Styles tab in the Organizer dialog box to copy modified Heading styles to the Normal template so all future outlines have the styles you want to use. I told you about that in Chapter 9.

Numbering Headings

A useful Word version 6 feature that works with Heading styles applied by the Outlining feature is the ability to automatically number headings. This is particularly handy when headings include chapter, section, or paragraph numbers and you find yourself shuffling them around as you refine the document.

NEW IN WORD 6

To have Word automatically assign and keep track of heading numbers in your document, choose Heading Numbering from the Format menu. The Heading Numbering dialog box, which looks and works a lot like the Bullets and Numbering dialog box I showed you earlier, appears.

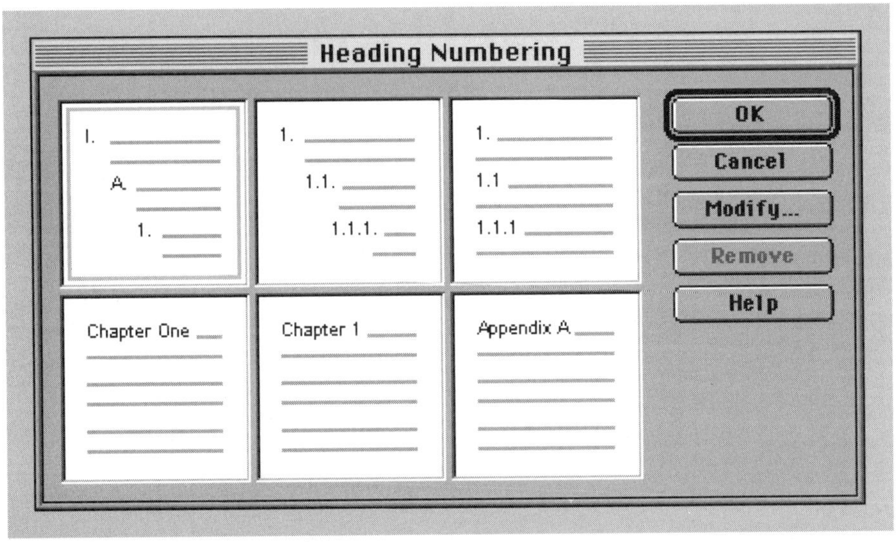

Choose one of the six predefined formats offered by preview buttons in the dialog box by clicking on it. If the predefined formats don't meet your needs, click the Modify button to create your own custom format. The Modify Heading Numbering dialog box that appears works just like the Modify Multilevel List dialog box I talked about earlier in this chapter, so I won't repeat myself here. An important thing to remember is that each level is applied to the corresponding Heading level in your outline. With a little imagination, you can have this dialog box automatically create all your headings for you.

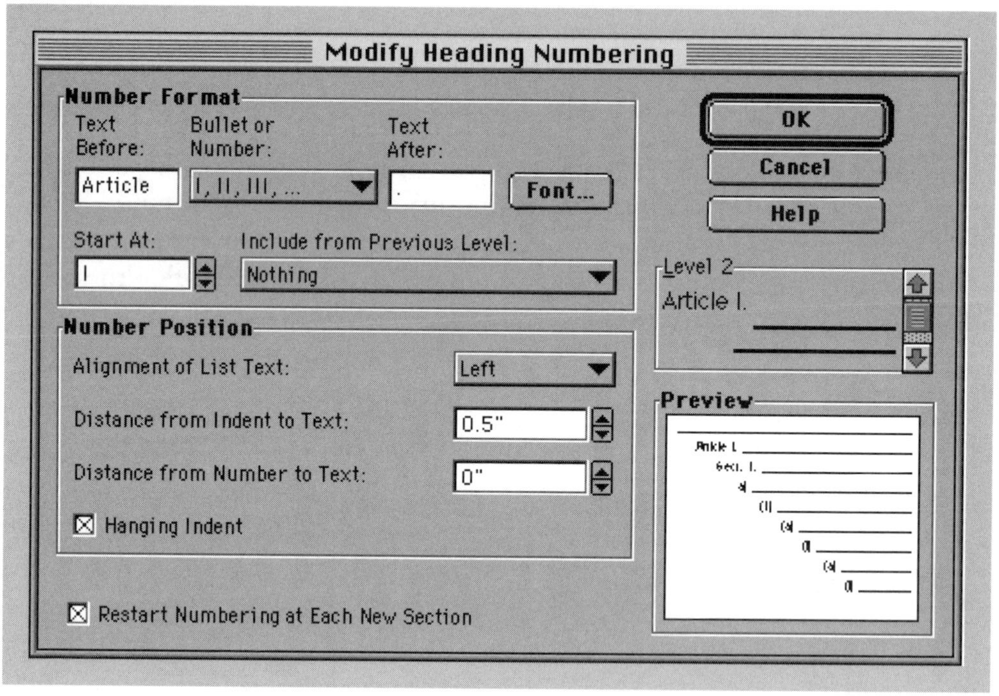

IMPORTANT NOTE

When you use the Heading Numbering command to number heading levels in your document, Word also makes changes to the heading style to add indentation. You can control this with the Distance from Indent to Text and Distance from Number to Text edit boxes in the Modify Heading Numbering dialog box or by changing the style of the heading with the Modify Style dialog box.

Printing an Outline

You can also print an outline, complete with Outline view indentation. Begin by expanding or collapsing the outline so it shows just the information you want to print. Then choose Print from the File menu, make necessary adjustments in the Print dialog box, and click the Print button. I covered printing back in Chapter 4.

TIP/TRICK

If desired, you can insert manual page breaks in an outline to control where one page ends and the next begins. These page breaks will remain when you switch to another view, however, so be prepared to remove them before you print in another view. I told you about page breaks in Chapter 8.

Master Documents

NEW IN WORD 6

Word's brand new Master Document feature takes outlining a step further. It enables you to create a single master document comprised of up to 80 documents. You can work on the entire master document as one document or work on any of the documents that are part of it.

In this section of the chapter, I'll tell you how you can create and work with a master document and its component documents. If you work with long documents, which you normally have to separate into smaller parts to work with and manage effectively, this section is for you.

NEW IN WORD 6

In case you're wondering, the File Series feature of previous versions of Word is no longer available in Word version 6. If you used and depended on that feature for chaining together the parts of a document, I think you'll find the Master Document feature a much better replacement.

Master Document view is, in a way, an extension of Outline view. If you skipped the Outline part of this chapter, you may want to go back and read it — or at least skim through it. As you'll see, outlining concepts are used extensively in the master document feature.

For Example: Why I'm Excited about Master Documents

One of the dilemmas I've always encountered when working on a long document like a book is how to store the document on disk. If I store the document as a single file, that file would be extremely large, tedious to scroll through, and slow to save. In addition, if there's a power outage or some other catastrophe while I'm saving the file, I run the risk of losing the entire document so I've got to be even more concerned about backups. On the other hand, if I store the document as separate files (usually one for each chapter), it's more time consuming to move text from document to document, generate a table of contents, and get page numbers just right.

The Master Document feature of Word version 6 is another gift from heaven for a writer. Using this feature, I can have the best of both worlds. Each chapter can remain a separate document but be included in the master document. I can write the bulk of the book by working on the separate chapter documents, but do major revisions, create a table of contents and index, cross-reference one document in another, and print the whole thing all at once. What more can I ask for?

Creating a Master Document

There are three ways to create a master document. You can create one from scratch when you're just beginning a long document, convert an existing document into a master document, or combine existing documents into a master document. I'll cover each method in this section.

Creating a Master Document from Scratch

To create a new master document, begin by creating a new Word document. When the empty document window appears, choose Master Document from the View menu. This switches you to Master Document view and displays the Outlining and Master Document toolbars. Use the techniques I discussed in the Outlining section of this chapter to create an outline for the master document. You can even include body text if you like.

To separate the document into subdocuments, select the headings and text you want to include in subdocuments. Make sure the first heading in the selection is the heading level you want to start each subdocument. For example, in the following illustration, each Heading 2 heading will begin a new document.

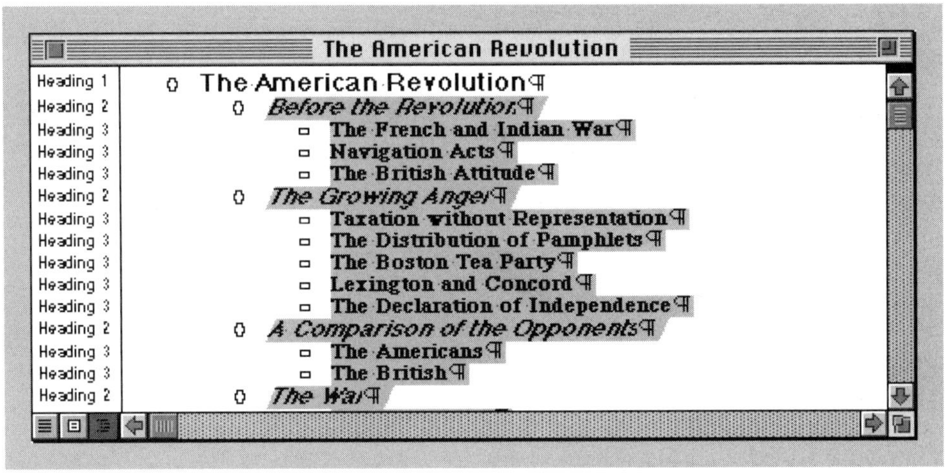

Click the Create Subdocument button on the Master Document toolbar. Word breaks the document into sections according to the heading level you specified with your selection. I'll tell you more about how it displays the master document in a little while.

Converting an Existing Long Document into a Master Document

Converting an existing long document into a master document is similar to creating a master document from scratch. The only difference is that the document text already exists so you don't have to type it. What you may have to do, however, is use Word's Outlining feature to add headings and rearrange the document. (Remember, Word uses the headings to determine how to split the document into subdocuments.) Then follow the previous steps to separate the document into subdocuments.

Combining Existing Documents into a Master Document

To combine a number of existing documents into a master document, begin by opening or creating a master document and choosing Master Document from the View menu. Position the insertion point where you want to add a document and click the Insert Subdocument button on the Master Document toolbar. A standard Open File dialog box appears. Use this dialog box to locate and open the document you want to insert. Repeat these two steps for each subdocument you want to add.

Saving a Master Document and its Subdocuments

When you save a master document, you save it and all of its subdocuments. To save a master document, choose Save from the File menu.

- If the master document hasn't been saved yet, use the Save As dialog box that appears to enter a name and specify a location for the master document. Word saves the master document with the name you specified. It uses the heading that starts each subdocument to name and save each one. For example, when I saved the master document I created in the previous illustration, I got new files with the names Before the Revolution, The Growing Anger, etc.
- If the master document has already been saved, Word automatically saves any changes to it and, if necessary, creates and saves new files for each subdocument, using the first heading in the subdocument as the document name.

Once you save a master document, you can open and work with each subdocument either from within the master document or by simply opening the subdocument file.

Master Document View Symbols

Like Outline view, Master Document view has its own collection of symbols. You should already know about the hollow plus, minus, and box. These symbols work exactly as they do in Outline view. In the following illustration, you can see some other symbols specific to Master Document view.

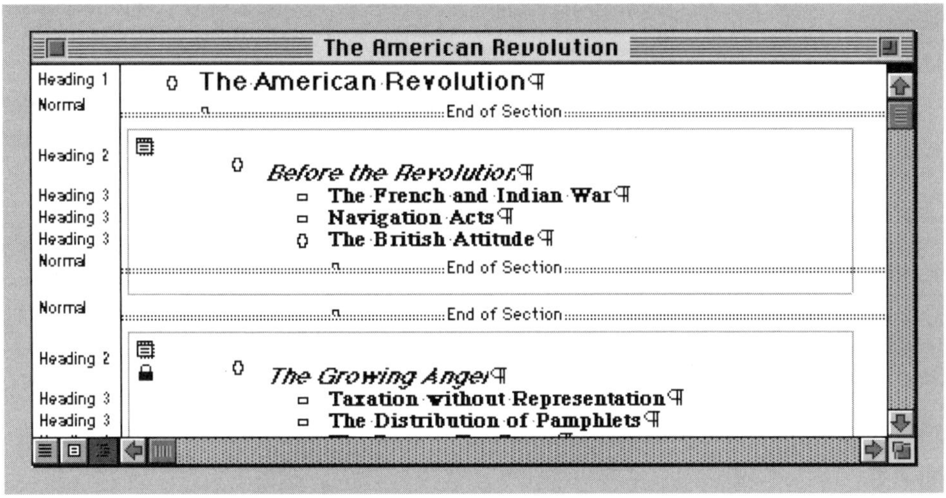

Word surrounds the text of each subdocument with a gray box to indicate what that document contains. It also places section breaks between subdocuments. I told you about section breaks and how you can use them to format parts of a document back in Chapter 8. You'll only be able to see them if paragraph marks are showing. If they're not, click the Show/Hide ¶ button to display them.

At the beginning of each subdocument, Word places a subdocument icon. By double-clicking this icon, you can quickly open the subdocument as a separate file. If a subdocument file is open, a lock appears beneath its subdocument icon. That indicates that the subdocument is locked and cannot be changed in Master Document view. Instead, you must switch to the open subdocument file to make the change or close the subdocument file to unlock it in the master document.

Working with Subdocuments

You can work with subdocuments two ways: by changing them in Master Document view or by opening them as separate files and changing them in their own document windows.

Opening Subdocuments

I already told you one way to open a subdocument in its own window — double-click on the subdocument icon in master document view. But you can also open a subdocument the same way you open any other Word document:

- Choose Open from the File menu and use the Open dialog box that appears to locate and open the subdocument *or*
- Double-click the subdocument icon (or an alias of it) in a Finder window *or*
- Drag the subdocument icon onto the Word application icon (or an alias of it)

I discussed all these techniques in detail way back in Chapters 1 and 3.

Rearranging Subdocument Information

A master document is just a big outline composed of a bunch of little outlines. You can use any of the techniques I covered in the outlining section of this chapter to rearrange headings, body text, or other contents. As you might expect, the Cut and Copy commands and buttons and drag and drop text editing also work fine. Just watch out for the lock symbol; as I mentioned above, if a subdocument is locked, you can't change it in Master Document view.

TIP/TRICK

You can move information from one subdocument to another or to the master document itself by dragging it. This makes it very quick and easy to change the contents of documents.

Renaming or Moving Subdocuments

A master document knows where to find its subdocuments by name and disk location. Because of this, it's vital that you use the correct technique to rename or move a subdocument. If you use the Finder to rename or move a subdocument, the master document simply won't be able to find it.

To rename or move a subdocument, open the master document and double-click on the subdocument icon to open the subdocument. Then choose Save As from the File menu. Use the Save As dialog box that appears to give the file a new name, a new disk location, or both. Click Save to complete the change.

You'll now have two versions of the file on disk. Delete the old one (the one with the original name or disk location) if you don't need it. Word might not get confused if you keep it hanging around, but *you* might.

You must open the subdocument from within the master document to change its name or give it a new disk location. In addition, you must keep the master document open until after you've changed the subdocument name or location. Otherwise, the master document will not receive the updated information.

Locking Subdocuments

IMPORTANT NOTE

Word automatically locks a subdocument in Master Document view when that document is open in another window. Although you cannot unlock a subdocument without first closing the subdocument window, you can lock a subdocument even when its document window is not open. To lock a subdocument, click anywhere in the subdocument's gray box in Master Document view and then click the Lock Document button. The lock symbol appears just below the subdocument icon and prevents the subdocument from being changed in Master Document view.

You can also lock a master document to protect it from being overwritten on disk. To do this, position the insertion point anywhere in the Master document but not in a subdocument. Then click the Lock Document button. If you have made changes to the document since the last time you saved it, Word asks if you want to save changes. Click Yes or No. Word then closes the master document and reopens it as a Read-Only document. You can change it to your heart's content, but you won't be able to save it with the same name or in the same disk location.

Splitting and Merging Subdocuments

If a subdocument gets too large, you can split it into two separate subdocuments. You can also merge subdocuments into one subdocument. Here's how.

- To split a subdocument, in Master Document view, position the insertion point at the beginning of the heading or other paragraph where you want to create the split. Click the Split Subdocument button on the Master Document toolbar to make the split. When you save changes to the master document, the new document is created and saved on disk.

- To merge two or more subdocuments, make sure those documents are positioned one after the other in Master Document view. Select the subdocuments you want to merge by holding down Shift while clicking once on each subdocument icon. Click the Merge Subdocuments icon on the Master Document toolbar to merge the subdocuments together. You may have to delete additional section breaks between the two merged documents. When you save changes to the master document, the merged documents are saved under the first document's name. You may want to delete any documents you no longer need.

Removing a Subdocument from the Master Document

You can remove a subdocument from a master document two ways: by making the subdocument part of the master document or by deleting the subdocument and its contents from the master document.

- To make a subdocument into part of the master document, click its subdocument icon and then click the Remove Subdocument button. The subdocument becomes part of the master document. You may want to remove any section breaks remaining between them.
- To delete a subdocument and its contents from the master document, click its subdocument icon and then press Del or choose Clear from the Edit menu. The subdocument is removed from the master document. You may want to remove any unnecessary section breaks that remain.

When you remove a subdocument from a master document, the subdocument file remains on disk. If you no longer need this file, be sure to delete it.

Formatting a Master Document

At the risk of sounding like a broken record, I'll make my formatting proclamation again: formatting a master document is just like formatting any other Word document. You can use the same font, paragraph, and style formatting techniques I discussed in chapters 5, 6, and 7. Here are a few additional considerations you should keep in mind.

- When you create a subdocument from scratch, the formatting of the document is based on the styles and template of the master document. All subdocuments inherit this formatting.
- When you create a subdocument by adding existing documents to a master document, Master Document view displays the styles and template of the master document. When you open a subdocument, however, it utilizes the styles and template it was based on, which might be different from the master document's styles and template. I discussed styles and templates in Chapters 7 and 9.

- To use the headers or footers of a master document in all subdocuments, make sure the subdocuments don't have headers or footers. I discussed headers and footers in Chapter 10.
- Remember how section breaks affect options in the Document Layout dialog box. I told you about section breaks and Document Layout options in Chapter 8.

Printing a Master Document

Print a master document just as you would any other document.

- If you want only an outline of the entire document, make sure you're in Master Document view and use the Outlining toolbar buttons to select exactly what you want to print before using the Print command.
- If you want the entire document or a range of pages printed, make sure you're in Normal or Page Layout view before using the print command.
- If you want only a single subdocument printed, open that subdocument, switch to the appropriate view (Normal, Page Layout, or Outline), and then choose the Print command.

I discussed printing in detail in Chapter 4.

Chapter Summary

I don't know about you, but I'm exhausted. We covered a lot more than I thought in this chapter. You learned to create and work with bulleted and numbered lists, saw how Outline view adds additional features to Word to help you organize your documents as you create them, and also learned how to create and use master documents to make managing long documents easier.

This wraps up Part III of the book. In the next chapter, you'll begin learning to put some of Word's productivity features to work — starting with Find and Replace and moving on to "power user" features like AutoText, AutoCorrect, Print Merge, and Forms.

PART

4

Putting Word's Features to Work

THIS PART OF THE BOOK SHOWS YOU HOW YOU CAN TAKE advantage of some of the productivity features and tools in Microsoft Word. These features make it easy to perform both basic and advanced word processing tasks.

16

Chapter 16: Find and Replace, AutoText, and AutoCorrect

IN CHAPTER 2, YOU LEARNED SOME BASIC TEXT EDITING techniques, like how to insert and delete text, how to copy and paste text, and how to move text around with drag and drop text editing. While those are important techniques that you'll use every day, Word offers more powerful text editing features that can automate much of the text editing job. I'm talking about Find and Replace, AutoText, and the new AutoCorrect feature.

In this chapter, you'll learn how to use Find and Replace to look for text and formatting in your document and replace it with what you specify. Then you'll also learn about Word's AutoText feature, which users of previous Word versions might know as the Glossary. Finally, you'll explore a cool new feature called AutoCorrect, which looks for and fixes your mistakes — as you make them!

Find and Replace

Find and replace are among the most basic features of a word processor. Almost every word processor I've ever seen includes a Find or Replace command. (TeachText and SimpleText are two notable exceptions, but what do you expect from a pair of freebies?) Word's Find and Replace commands, however, go far beyond those of most word processors. Not only do they let you search for and replace text, but you can also find and replace special characters and formatting within your document. In this section, I'll tell you how you can use the Find and Replace commands to make changes in your documents.

Finding Text

The Find command lets you search for text, including special characters and formatting in your document. You tell it what to find by entering text or making selections in the Find dialog box. To open the Find dialog box, choose Find from the Edit menu or press ⌘F.

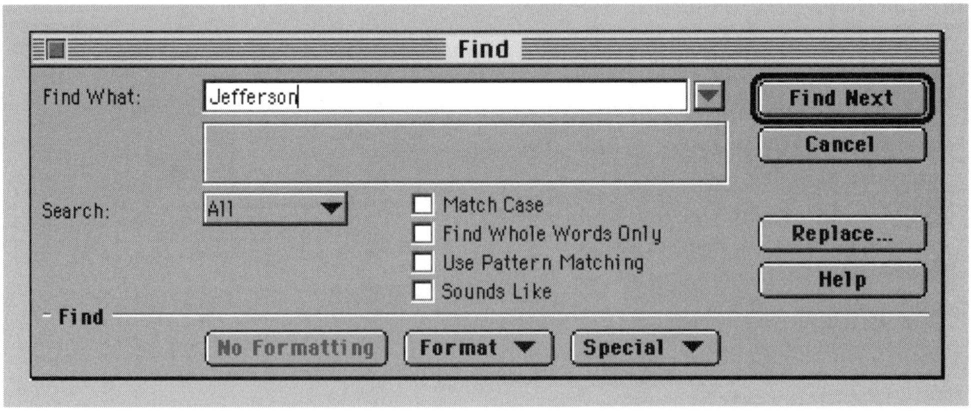

Entering Text to Find

You tell Word what you want to find by typing it into the Find What edit box. Word remembers the last four text searches you made during your work session, so if you want to repeat a search, you can click the arrow beside the Find What box to display a menu of the last few searches and choose the one you want.

You can paste the contents of the Clipboard into the Find What edit box. Make sure the Find What edit box is selected or has an insertion point blinking in it and choose Paste from the Edit menu, click the Paste button on the Standard Toolbar, or press ⌘V. This can be helpful if you need to search for a long or complex string of characters and you already know of one occurrence in your document.

TIP/TRICK

Finding Special Characters

Word also lets you find special characters. Use the Special menu/button to display a menu of the characters Word can look for. When you choose one of these options, Word puts the appropriate code in the Find What edit box. For example, say you want to find manual page breaks in your document. When you choose Manual Page Break from the Special menu/button, Word inserts ^m into the Find What edit box. The Find What edit box can contain any combination of text and codes necessary to find exactly what you want to find.

If you know the code for the characters listed under the Special menu/button, you can type it yourself. Here's a list of them, along with descriptions or examples and the Word code to find them.

TIP/TRICK

Character Name	Character or Description	Code
Paragraph Mark	The character that results when you press [Return].	^p
Tab Character	The character that results when you press [Tab].	^t
Annotation Mark	The mark that appears when you insert an annotation. I'll cover annotations in Chapter 18.	^a
Any Character	Any character you can type. For example, if you ask Word to find *wor^?*, it could find words like *word*, *wore*, *work*, or *worm* since it would exactly match the first three characters and look for any other character as the fourth.	^?
Any Digit	Any numerical character you can type. This works like the Any Character option, but specifically looks for a number.	^#
Any Letter	Any alphabetic character you can type. This works like the Any Character option, but specifically looks for a letter. (The Any Character option looks for any character at all.)	^$
Caret Character	^	^^
Column Break	The mark that appears when you insert a column break. I discussed column breaks in Chapter 8.	^n
Em Dash	—	^+
En Dash	–	^=
Endnote Mark	The mark that appears when you insert an endnote. I discussed endnotes in Chapter 10.	^e
Field	An item inserted with the Field command. I mentioned fields in Chapters 10 and 14 and will discuss them again in other chapters of this book.	^d
Footnote Mark	The mark that appears when you insert a footnote. I discussed footnotes in Chapter 10.	^f

Continued

Character Name	Character or Description	Code
Graphic	A graphic object. I discussed graphics in Chapter 12.	^g
Manual Line Break	The character that results when you press Shift Return.	^l
Manual Page Break	The character that appears when you insert a page break. I discussed page breaks in Chapter 8.	^m
Nonbreaking Hyphen	The character that results when you press ⌘ Shift -. I'll discuss nonbreaking hyphens in Chapter 17.	^~
Nonbreaking Space	The character that results when you press Control Shift Spacebar. I'll discuss nonbreaking spaces in Chapter 17.	^s
Optional Hyphen	The character that results when you press ⌘ -. I'll discuss optional hyphens in Chapter 17.	^-
Section Break	The character that appears when you insert a section break. I discussed section breaks in Chapter 8.	^b
White Space	Any number and combination of spaces, tab characters, and paragraph marks.	^w

The Special menu/button does not list any symbols or special characters like those you can insert with the Symbol command, which I discussed back in Chapter 5. The Symbol command isn't even available when the Find edit box is active, so you can't use it to insert symbols into the Find edit box. If you want to search for one of these symbols, you must know the keystroke and, if necessary, the character font. I'll tell you more about specifying fonts in the Find dialog box in a little while.

IMPORTANT NOTE

Telling Word Where to Look

The Search pop-up menu lets you tell Word where it should search for the characters you specified. The options are Down, Up, and All (the default). It works like this:

- To search the entire document, choose All. When Word has finished searching the document, it displays a dialog box telling you. Click OK.

- To search from the insertion point to the end of the document, choose Down. When Word reaches the end of the document, it displays a dialog box offering to continue searching from the beginning of the document. Click Yes or No.

- To search from the insertion point to the beginning of the document, choose Up. When Word reaches the beginning of the document, it displays a dialog box offering to continue searching at the end. Click Yes or No.

- To search only a part of the document, select the part of the document you want to search before opening the Find dialog box. It doesn't matter which search option you choose — when you perform the search, only the text you selected is searched. When Word finishes searching the selection, it displays a dialog box offering to search the remainder of the document. Click Yes or No.

Narrowing the Search

You can narrow down the search by turning on the Match Case and Find Whole Words only check boxes.

- When Match Case is turned on, Word finds only the occurrences of the character string that exactly match — case and all. For example, say you tell Word to look for occurrences of the word "report" and turn on the Match case check box. Word finds only occurrences where "report" is spelled in all lowercase characters. It would not find "Report." To have Word ignore the case of characters, make sure this check box is turned off.

IMPORTANT NOTE

All Caps and Small Caps are font formatting options that do not affect the true case of characters. Word matches case based on the way the characters were originally typed or changed with the Change Case command. I discussed these options in Chapter 5.

- When Find Whole Words Only is turned on, Word finds only the occurrences of the character string that match exact words. Using the "report" example again, with Find Whole Words Only turned on, Word would find "report" but would not find "reported," "reporting," or "reporter." If you're in the habit of searching for words or phrases by entering just part of what you're looking for, make sure this check box is turned off.

Advanced Searches

NEW IN WORD 6

In version 6.0 of Word, Microsoft added two new check boxes. One of them is Use Pattern Matching. When turned on, this check box tells Word that you want to use special search operators. You can then use operators and wildcard characters like the ones available in the Advanced Search dialog box that's part of Word's Find File feature. Advanced searches work the same in that feature as they do in this one. I discussed Find File back in Chapter 3.

IMPORTANT NOTE

When using the Any Character, Any Digit, or Any Letter option available from the Special menu in the Find What dialog box, you don't need to turn on the Pattern Matching check box. Use this check box only if you are performing advanced searches using the advanced search wildcard characters.

Using Sounds Like

NEW IN WORD 6

The Sounds Like check box is another new addition to the Find dialog box. It lets you find a word based on the way it sounds.

Remember homonyms from your school days? They're words that sound alike but are spelled differently. Some examples include their, they're, and there or would and wood. Word is smart enough to know that these words sound alike. When you turn on the Sounds Like check box and tell word to find *their*, it finds *their*, *they're*, or *there*.

Turning on the Sounds Like check box can slow down Word's find feature because Word has to search for more than just one word. Use this feature only if you really need it.

Starting the Search

Once you've set up your search criteria, click the Find Next button to begin the search. Word finds the first character string that matches the search criteria and selects it. The Find dialog box remains on screen. You have three options:

- To work with the text Word found but keep the Find dialog box on screen, click in the document window to make it active and work with the text. If the inactive Find dialog box is in your way, move it aside by dragging its Title bar.

- To find the next occurrence of the character string, click the Find Next button. Word selects the next occurrence. You can continue to click Find Next until Word displays a message telling you it's done searching.
- To dismiss the Find dialog box, press [Esc], click Cancel or Close, or click the close box.

You can cancel a search at any time by pressing [Esc] or clicking Cancel in the Find dialog box.

TIP/TRICK

To repeat a search you've just completed, press [⌘][Option][Y] or [Shift][F4] (on an extended keyboard). Word conducts the search without displaying the Find dialog box.

Replacing Text

Word's Replace command lets you tell word to find something and then replace it with something else. This information goes into the Replace dialog box. You can open the Replace dialog box one of three ways:

- Choose Replace from the Edit menu *or*
- Press [⌘][H] *or*
- With the Find dialog box open, click the Replace button

As you can see from the illustration, the Replace dialog box is an extension of the Find dialog box. The only thing it adds is a Replace With edit box and a Replace All button. In fact, if the Find dialog box is open and you click the Replace button, you'll see it grow from one to the other.

Using the Replace With Edit Box

Use the Replace With edit box to tell Word what you want to replace the found item with. Click in it with your mouse pointer or press Tab to make it active. An indicator at the bottom left side of the Replace dialog box shows whether you're working with Find or Replace options. (It says Replace in our example; see how the insertion point is in the Replace With edit box?) Enter the text you want to replace what's showing in the Find What edit box. Word remembers the last four items from the Replace With edit box, so you can use the arrow beside the dialog box to display a menu of them and choose one. You can also use the commands under the Special menu/button to add special characters. You'll have fewer options but two new ones: Contents of Clipboard and Find What Text. Don't change the check boxes — they're just for the contents of the Find What edit box.

Making the Changes

When you've got the Find What and Replace With edit boxes filled in and ready to go and have told Word where to look with the Search pop-up menu, you have two choices:

- To replace the Find What occurrences with the Replace With item one at a time, click Find Next. Word finds the first occurrence and displays it on your screen. To replace it, click the Replace button. Word replaces it and finds the next occurrence. To skip it, click Find Next. When Word's finished searching, it tells you.

- To replace the Find What occurrences with the Replace With item all at once, click Replace All. Word replaces all occurrences and displays a dialog box telling you how many replacements it made.

Don't use the Replace All button unless you're really sure that you want Word to replace. If you use this command by mistake and get unexpected results, remember the Undo command!

IMPORTANT NOTE

Try This! Find and Replace Tricks

Here are a few Find and Replace tricks you can use in your own documents.

- You can use Word's Space Before and Space After options in the Paragraph dialog box to add additional space between paragraphs. I told you about this in Chapter 6. This makes empty paragraphs between paragraphs of text unnecessary. To remove empty paragraphs from your documents, set the Replace dialog box like this and click Replace All:

- To add empty paragraphs to your document, set the Replace dialog box like this and click Replace All:

- To remove a word or phrase from your document, enter the word in the Find What edit box and leave the Replace With edit box completely empty. Then click Find Next and Replace until all the occurrences you want to delete are gone.

Continued

- To remove additional spaces from between sentences, enter two spaces in the Find What edit box and one space in the Replace With edit box. Then click Replace All. If your document has three and four spaces between sentences, you can repeat this process until Word finds no more occurrences.
- To replace straight quotes with smart quotes (which I told you about in Chapter 5) in a document that has already been typed, first choose AutoCorrect from the Tools menu and make sure the Change Straight Quotes to Smart Quotes check box is turned on. Then open the Replace dialog box and enter a single quote in the Find What and the Replace With edit boxes. Click Replace All to replace the single quotes. If your document also has double quotes, enter a double quote in the Find What and Replace With edit boxes and click Replace All again.
- If your replacement text is long and has already been typed in the document or another document, copy it to the Clipboard before opening the Replace dialog box. Then, in the Replace dialog box, use the Special menu/button's Clipboard Contents command to enter the appropriate code in the Replace With edit box. When you tell Word to make the replacement(s), the contents of the clipboard are inserted in your document in place of the found text.

Finding and Replacing Formatting

So far, I've only told you about the most basic find and replace function: finding and replacing text. Word's Find and Replace feature is very powerful. It also enables you to find specific types of formatting, like font and paragraph formatting. This makes it possible to change underlined text to italicized text or double-spaced paragraphs to single-spaced paragraphs throughout your document. These are just two examples. With a little imagination, you can get Word to reformat an entire document!

Telling Word What to Find

To Find or Replace text and formatting, begin by opening the Find or Replace dialog box. Then tell Word what to Find.

If you want to find specific text with specific formatting, start by entering the text you want to find in the Find What edit box. You can include whatever options from the Special menu/button that you like. You can even include advanced search criteria. I explained all this earlier in this chapter and in Chapter 3.

If you want to find only specific formatting and don't care what text it has been applied to, make sure the Find What edit box is empty. You can clear it out by selecting any contents and pressing Delete.

To specify the formatting you want to find, choose an option from the Format menu/button. The choices are Font, Paragraph, Tabs, Border, Language, Frame, and Style. Whichever option you choose, the corresponding dialog box appears. For example, in the following illustration I chose Font and the Find Font dialog box appeared.

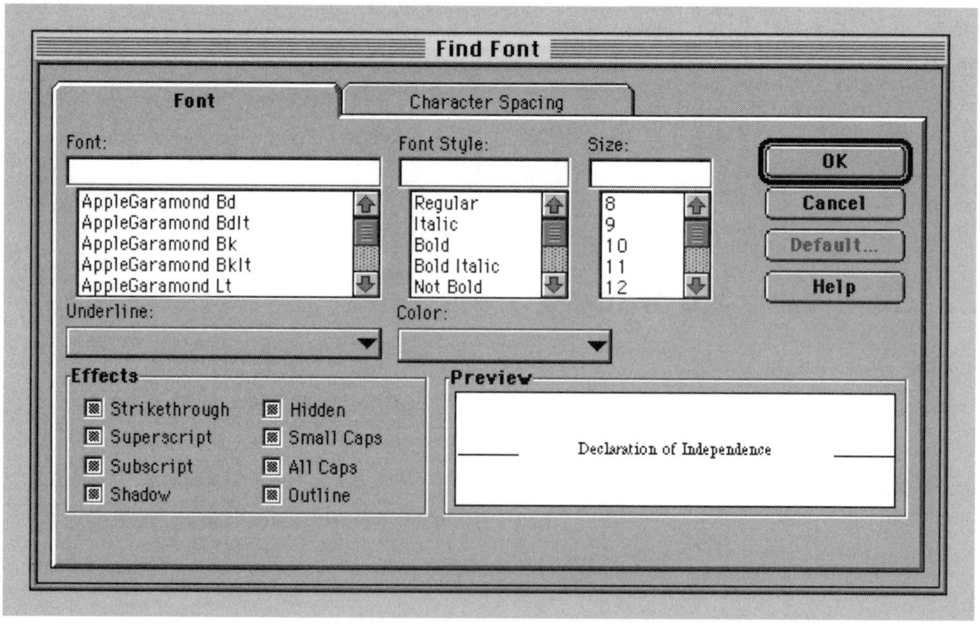

The dialog boxes look remarkably like the dialog boxes you use to apply the various kinds of formatting. I discussed the Font dialog box in Chapter 5, the Paragraph and Tabs dialog boxes in Chapter 6, and the Border and Frame dialog boxes in Chapter 13. I'll discuss the Language dialog box in Chapter 17. The Find Style dialog box is simpler than the Styles dialog box I discussed in Chapter 7, as shown here.

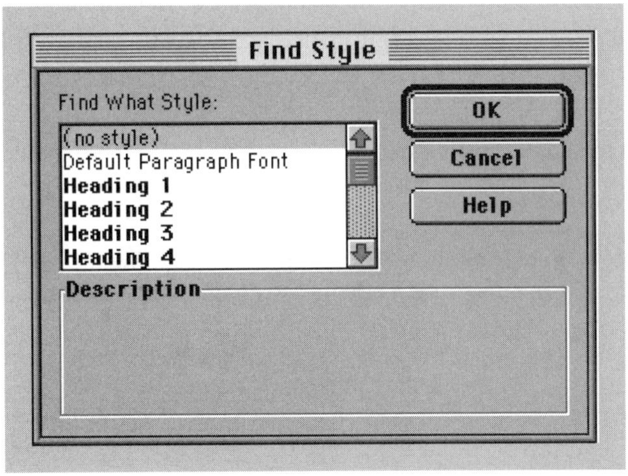

The most important thing to note about these dialog boxes is that when you first open them from the Find dialog box, nothing is selected. You can see that in the Find Font and Find Style dialog boxes. No font, no size, no underline, no color, no effects, no style — *nothing*. (Remember, if a check box is gray or an edit box or pop-up menu is blank, nothing is selected.) If you don't change a thing in the dialog box and click OK, Word won't search for any specific formatting within it. To search for specific formatting, you must set it in the dialog box and click OK.

TIP/TRICK

If you prefer, you can use toolbar buttons or shortcut keys to specify certain types of formatting. For example, if you want to specify bold formatting, click the Bold button on the Formatting toolbar or press ⌘-B. You'll see the Bold or Not Bold option get entered into the Format area beneath Find What.

Use the Format menu/button to choose each kind of formatting you need to specify. Each time you set options in a dialog box, Word adds it to the list of what you're searching for, right under the Find What dialog box. In the following example I told Word to find the phrase *Declaration of Independence* if it is Bold and Underlined (the Find Font dialog box) and in the Normal Style (the Find Style dialog box).

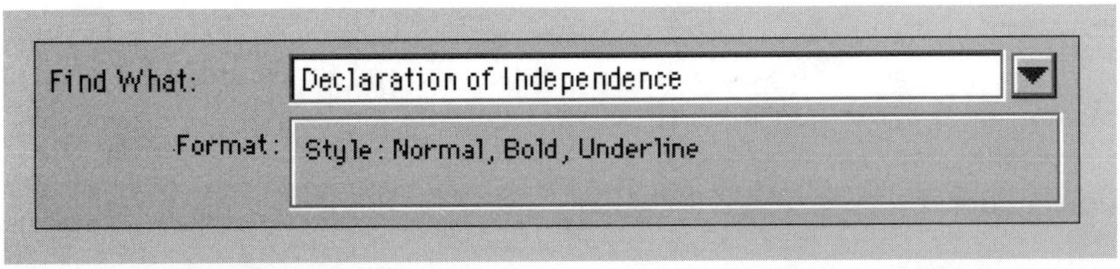

If you make a mistake while specifying what Word should find, you'll discover that you can't always remove an option from the specific formatting dialog box. Say, for example, that I change my mind and don't care whether *Declaration of Independence* is underlined when Word looks for it. If I go back to the Find Font dialog box and try to clear out the Single Underline option, I'll find that I can't completely clear the Underline option. As you can see in the following illustration, when I choose none (which seems at first to be the right choice), Word will search for the Find What text only if it's *not* underlined. That isn't what I want!

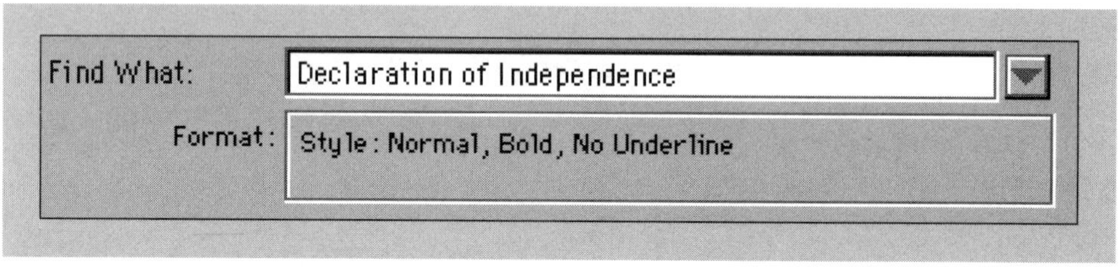

In order to clear out any formatting options, click the No Formatting button. Word clears out the formatting options you specified so you can start over.

If you're using the Find dialog box and just want to find text and/or formatting, set the Search option and click the Find Next button to start the search. The Find dialog box works just like a regular text-only search from this point on.

If you're using the Replace dialog box and want to replace what you find, however, read on. You'll need to fill in the Replace With part of the Replace dialog box.

Telling Word How to Replace What It Finds

As you can probably guess, the Replace With part of the dialog box works the same way as the Find What part. If necessary, click in the Replace With edit box or press Tab to make it active. Type in the replacement text or choose it from the pop-up menu of recent replacements. If you want the text to remain the same — in other words, you only want to change the formatting — type the text exactly as it appears in the Find What edit box or choose Find What Text from the Special menu/button. You can also use the Special menu/button to enter special codes if you need to. Then use options under the Format menu/button to specify the replacement formats.

Here comes the tricky part. You must use the various formatting dialog boxes to specify what kind of formatting you want to apply or remove. Don't set an option if you don't want it to change. Here's an example. I'm looking for *Declaration of Independence* in Normal style with Bold and Single underline formatting. I want the text and style to remain the same, but I want to change the font formatting to remove the underline and make the text Small Caps. Here's how I'd set the Replace Font dialog box. (Remember, check boxes are white when turned off and have X's in them when turned on.)

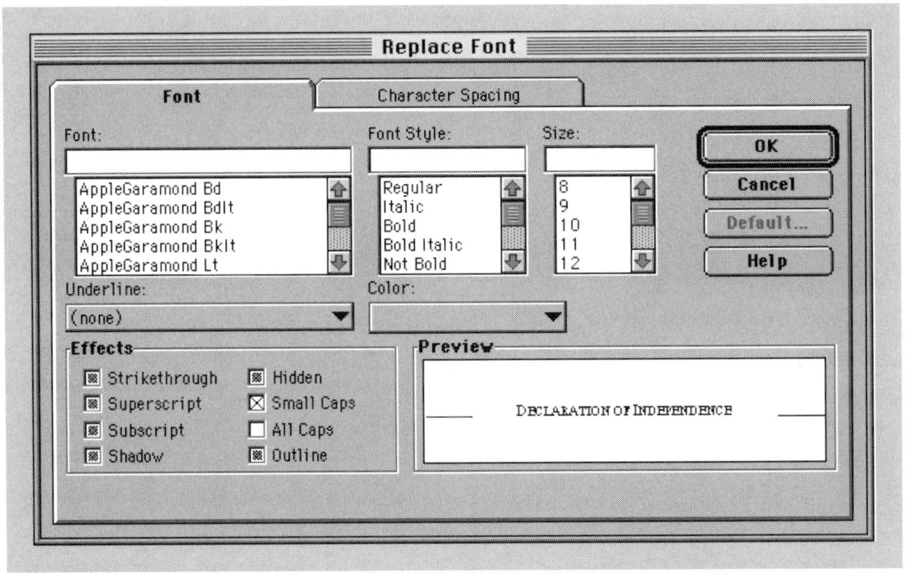

Would I change anything in the Replace Style dialog box? No. I don't want to change that. When I'm finished making settings in the Replace dialog box, it should look like this:

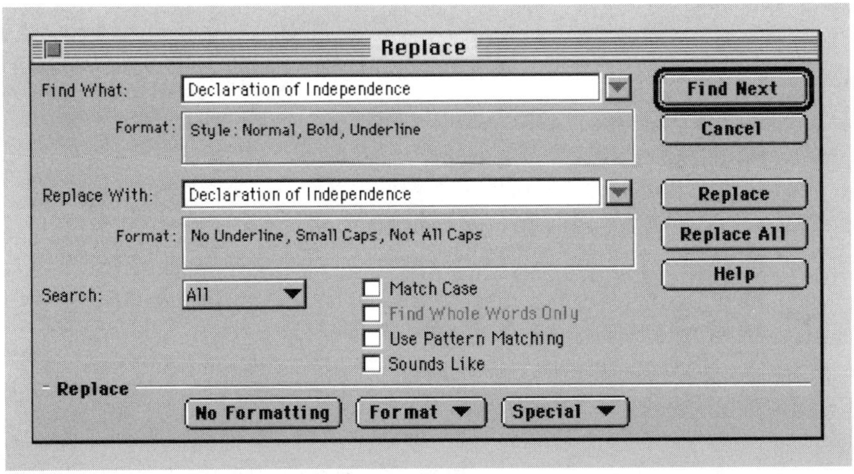

To continue the replacement, make sure you've got the right thing set in the Search pop-up menu and click either Find Next or Replace All. From here on, it works just like a regular plain text replacement.

TIP/TRICK

Replacing text and formatting sometimes take folks a while to fully comprehend, so if you don't get it right now, don't feel like a dummy. (Despite what some people may lead you to believe, *none* of us are really dummies.) The best advice I can offer you is to experiment. Think out what you want to do and give it a try. Pay attention to the results of specific settings. If the replacement isn't what you expected, remember your buddy, the ever-present Undo command. Undo the replacement and try again.

AutoText

Do you get tired of typing the same text passages over and over into your documents? Things like your name and address, the *Yours Truly* stuff at the end of a letter, and the boilerplate disclaimers or confidentiality notices that seem to go into every report you type? How about graphics? Sick of pulling out the Scrapbook to paste in your company logo or your boss's digitized signature a dozen times a day? If so, Word's AutoText feature is for you.

The AutoText feature lets you save passages of text and graphics as part of a template (usually the Normal template) file. Each item becomes an AutoText entry with its own unique name. When you need to insert the entry into your document, use a Menu command, toolbar button, or shortcut key to stick it in. As you can imagine, AutoText entries can save time and effort.

NEW IN WORD 6

If you've used previous versions of Word, all this might sound familiar. The AutoText feature is the new name for Word's old Glossary feature. It works similarly, but not exactly the same. Read on and you'll see what's new and improved.

Creating an AutoText Entry

To create an AutoText entry, begin by selecting what you want to include in the entry. The selection can include any amount of text or graphics — whole pages of it if you like. If you want to include paragraph formatting as part of the entry, be sure to include all paragraph marks within it, including the one at the very end. Then open the AutoText dialog box by clicking the Edit AutoText button on the Standard Toolbar or choosing AutoText from the Edit menu.

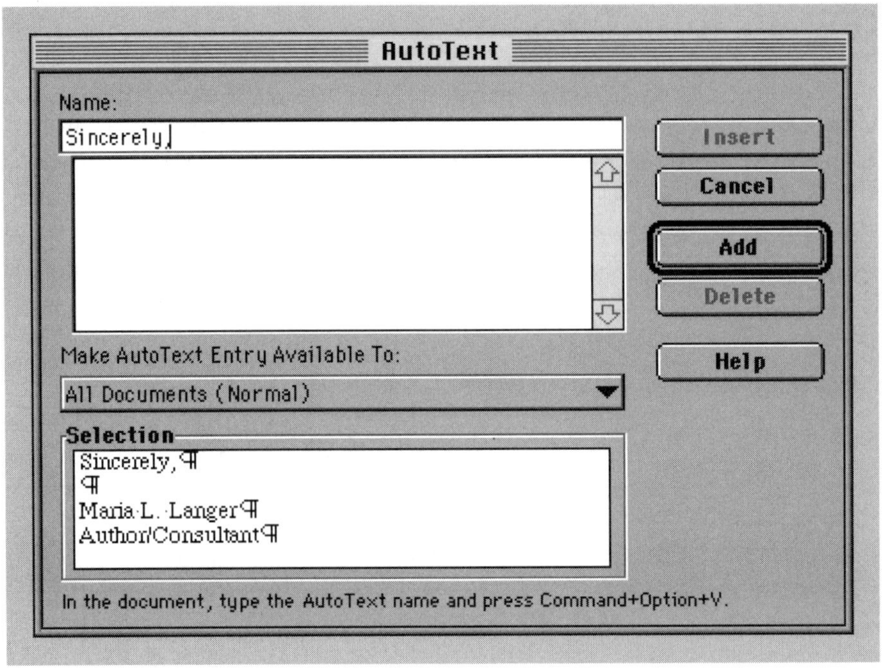

Word suggests a name for the AutoText entry in the Name edit box. Word doesn't have much of an imagination, so it usually uses the first bunch of characters in the selection. You can accept the name or change it by editing the contents of the Name edit box. An AutoText entry name can be up to 32 characters long, including spaces and symbols. I recommend keeping the name short and to the point. You'll see why a little later.

You can use the Make AutoText Entry Available To pop-up menu to select the template you want to save the AutoText entry in. Your options will always include All Documents (Normal). By saving an AutoText entry in the Normal template, it's available in all documents, no matter what template created it. Remember one important thing: if you delete a template, you will delete all the AutoText entries saved in it.

The Selection area of the AutoText dialog box displays the first few lines of the selection. This window neither scrolls nor allows editing. If you want to get a better look at what you've selected in your document to make sure it includes just what you want in the AutoText entry, you can move the AutoText dialog box to the side by dragging its Title bar.

To add the selection as an AutoText entry, click the Add button. It's added to the list of AutoText entries (if there are any) and the dialog box disappears.

Inserting an AutoText Entry

Word gives you three ways to insert an AutoText entry into a document: with a Menu command, toolbar button, or shortcut key. No matter how you do it, you must start the same way, by positioning the insertion point where you want the entry to appear. If text is selected when you insert an entry, that text will be replaced with the contents of the AutoText entry, so be careful! Once you've got the insertion point in place, try one of the following techniques.

With the AutoText Command

Choose AutoText from the Edit menu. The AutoText dialog box appears. A list of all AutoText entries available to the document appears in a scrolling list beneath the Name edit box. Click on the name of the entry you want to insert. As you can see in the following illustration, the dialog box gives you the option of inserting the entry as Formatted Text or Plain Text. An entry inserted as Formatted Text retains the original formatting of the entry. An entry inserted as Plain Text gets the formatting of the text immediately before the insertion point.

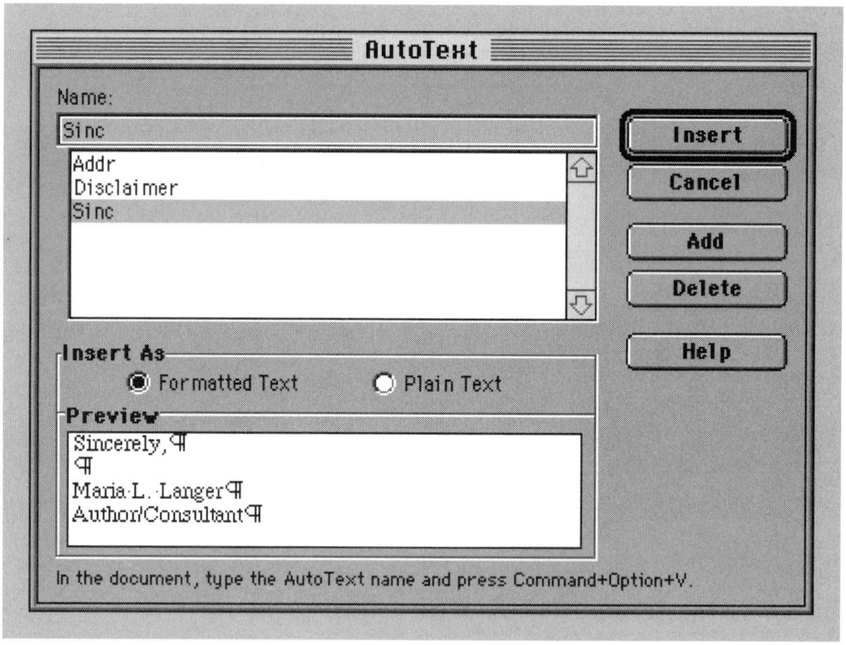

Choose the appropriate radio button and click Insert. The entry is inserted into your document and the AutoText dialog box disappears.

With the Insert AutoText Button

A quicker way to insert an AutoText entry is to type in the name of the entry at the insertion point and then click the Insert AutoText button (which is the same as the Edit AutoText button). AutoText names are not case sensitive — *Sinc* is the same as *sinc*.

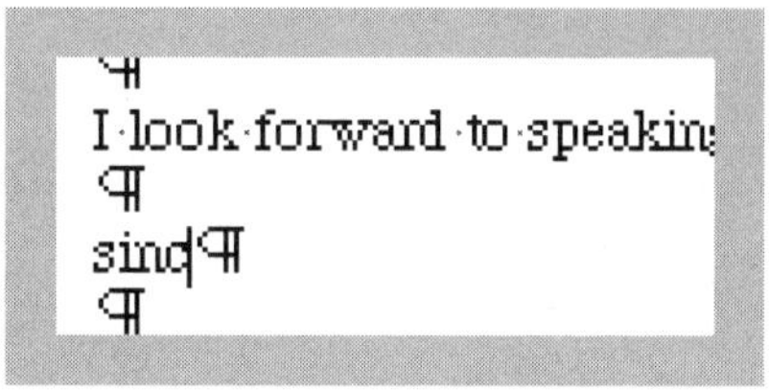

If you typed in a correct name, Word instantly replaces the entry name with the actual entry. (See why it's a good idea to have short names?) If you typed in an incorrect name, Word beeps at you and displays an error message in the Status bar, telling you that the specified text is not a valid AutoText entry name.

TIP/TRICK

You don't have to type in the entire AutoText entry name before clicking the Insert AutoText button. Just type in enough of the name to distinguish it from the other AutoText entry names. In the previous example, I could type in *si* rather than *sinc* to have Word insert the correct entry. But if I had another entry named *Since*, I'd have to type in the whole name.

With a Shortcut Key

Using a Shortcut Key is similar to using the Insert AutoText button. Type in the name of the AutoText entry and press [⌘][Option][V]. Word instantly inserts the AutoText entry in place of the entry name.

NEW IN WORD 6

If you are used to pressing [⌘][Delete] and typing the entry name to insert an entry in a previous version of Word, the change in shortcut key can drive you bonkers until you get used to it. In Word version 6, [⌘][Delete] deletes the word immediately in front of the insertion point. If you do this by mistake, count to ten and press [⌘][Z] to bring back any lost text.

Changing an AutoText Entry

You can change an AutoText entry two ways: by renaming it or by editing its contents.

- To change the name of an AutoText entry, begin by inserting it in your document. Then select it and choose AutoText from the Edit menu. In the scrolling list of entry names, click the old name of the entry to select it. Click delete. Now type in a new name for the item and click Add. The new name is added to the list and the dialog box disappears.

TIP/TRICK

You can also change the name of an AutoText entry in the AutoText tab of the organizer. I'll talk about the organizer a little later in this section.

- To change the contents of an AutoText entry, begin by inserting it in your document and editing it so it looks the way you want it. Then select it and choose AutoText from the Edit menu. In the scrolling list of entry names, click the name of the entry to select it. Then click Add. A confirmation dialog box appears, asking if you want to redefine the AutoText entry. Click Yes. The entry is redefined and both dialog boxes disappear.

Deleting an AutoText Entry

To delete an AutoText entry, choose AutoText from the Edit menu to display the AutoText dialog box. Click on the name of the entry you want to delete to select it. Then click Delete. The entry disappears, but the dialog box remains. You can delete other entries if you like. When you're finished with the AutoText dialog box, click Close to dismiss it.

Using the Spike

NEW IN WORD 6

The Spike is a new feature of Word. It enables you to cut multiple pieces of information out of a document and paste them as a group somewhere else. This can save a lot of document switching when you have to repeatedly cut items out of one document and paste them into another.

- To add items to the Spike, select the first item you want to cut from the document and press ⌘ F3. The item disappears and is added to the Spike. Repeat this procedure for each item you want to add to the Spike.

- To insert the contents of the Spike in a document, insert the AutoText entry named Spike which Word automatically created for you as you spiked items. You can do this by using the AutoText command, the Insert AutoText button, or the [⌘][Option][V] shortcut key as I discussed earlier in this section.

IMPORTANT NOTE

The Spike does not use the Clipboard. It uses the AutoText feature. The Paste command cannot restore the contents of the Spike to a document. In addition, if you use the Spike often, you may want to clear the Spike by pressing [⌘][Shift][F3] before adding items to it or the previously spiked items will become part of the collection of newly spiked items.

If you don't have an extended keyboard and want to use the Spike, check Chapter 24 for instructions on how you can change shortcut keys.

Printing AutoText Entries

TIP/TRICK

You can print the AutoText entries for the current and Normal templates. Choose Print from the File menu or press [⌘][P]. In the Print dialog box that appears, choose AutoText Entries from the Print pop-up menu.

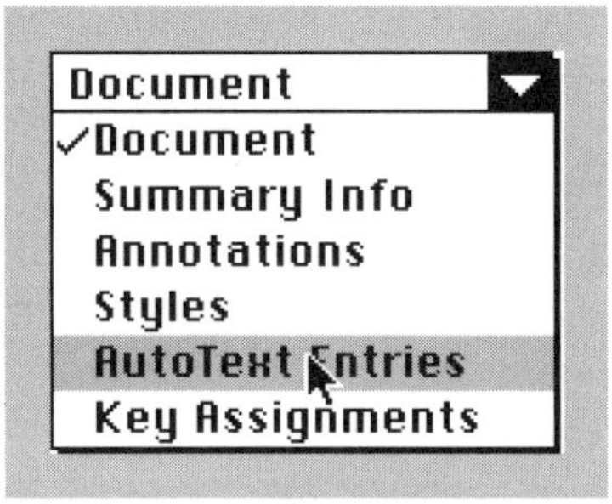

Click Print. Word prints a complete list of all the AutoText entries and their names in alphabetical order. The entries in the current template print first, followed by the entries in the Normal template. I discussed printing in detail in Chapter 4.

Using the Organizer to Work with AutoText Entries

NEW IN WORD 6

As I showed you back in Chapter 9, the Organizer dialog box can be used to copy styles from one template or document to another. It also includes an AutoText tab that can be used to copy, rename, or delete AutoText entries.

To open the Organizer, choose Templates from the File menu. In the Templates and Add-ins dialog box that appears, click the Organizer button. If necessary, click the tab for AutoText to display the AutoText options.

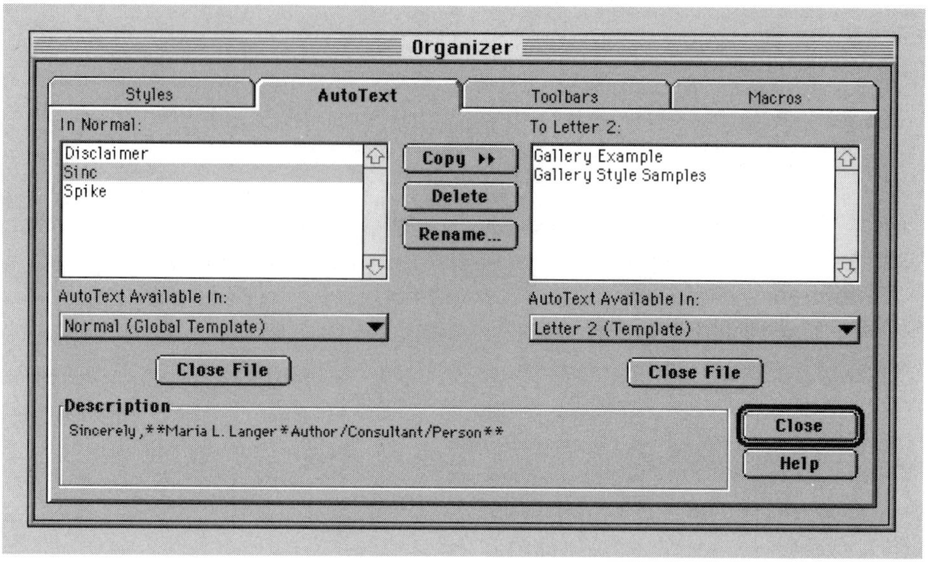

- To copy an AutoText entry from one template to another, make sure the name of each template appears at the top of each scrolling window. If necessary, use the Close button at the bottom of one window to close its template and then click the Open button to open another template. Then click the name of the AutoText entry you want to copy and click the Copy button. The entry is copied to the other template.
- To rename an AutoText entry with the Organizer, click the name of the entry you want to rename and click the Rename button. The Rename dialog box appears. Enter a new name for the entry and click OK.
- To delete an AutoText entry with the Organizer, click the name of the entry you want to delete and click the Delete button. A confirmation dialog box appears. Click Yes to complete the deletion.

TIP/TRICK

You can copy or delete more than one AutoText entry at a time. Hold down the Shift key while clicking AutoText entry names to select more than one. Then click the Copy or Delete button. If you're deleting multiple entries, be sure to click Yes to All in the confirmation dialog box. Otherwise, Word displays the confirmation dialog box for each entry.

AutoCorrect

NEW IN WORD 6

AutoCorrect is a new feature of Word version 6. It's kind of like having an editor reading over your shoulder and making changes to your document as you type. But this is an editor you have complete control over. You tell it what you want it to change and that's all it changes. If it annoys you, you can always turn it off.

In this section, I'll show you how to use AutoCorrect as your own personal editor.

TIP/TRICK

While at first glance, AutoCorrect appears to be a feature to help poor typists type, it goes well beyond that. Use AutoCorrect to automatically type in the same kind of information you'd use AutoText for. This skips a whole step — the AutoText command, button, or shortcut key.

Setting AutoCorrect Options

AutoCorrect options are set in the AutoCorrect dialog box. To open it, choose AutoCorrect from the Tools menu.

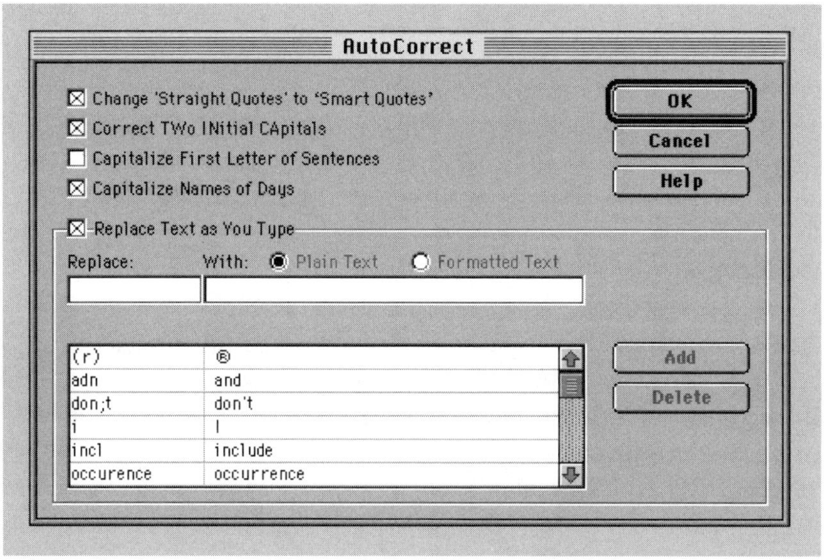

The dialog box offers four standard options and the ability to create custom entries. I'll talk about the check boxes here and tackle the Replace Text as You Type entries separately.

- Change 'Straight Quotes' to 'Smart Quotes' — tells Word to automatically convert straight quote characters like ' and " to curly quote characters like ‘ ’ and “ ” as you type them. These characters look better in your documents, as I discussed in Chapter 5.

IMPORTANT NOTE

Remember, by turning this check box on, Word will change the characters as you type them. If you want to convert quote characters already existing in the document, you'll need to use the Replace command, which I discussed earlier in this chapter.

- **Correct TWo INitial CApitals —** tells Word to watch out for instances when you type the first two letters of a word in uppercase. This is a problem that fast typists often have. (It's certainly a problem *I* have!) With this turned on, if you type two uppercase characters in a row at the beginning of a word, Word automatically converts the second one to lowercase.

- **Capitalize First Letter of Sentences —** tells Word to watch out for words that start with a lowercase letter at the beginning of a sentence. With this turned on, if you start a sentence with a lowercase letter, Word automatically converts it to uppercase. How does Word know what the beginning of a sentence is? If a word starts a paragraph or comes after a period, exclamation point, or question mark, Word considers it the beginning of a sentence.

- **Capitalize Names of Days —** tells Word to watch out for the names of days of the week that aren't capitalized. With this turned on, if you type the name of a day of the week in lowercase (for example, *wednesday*), Word automatically capitalizes the first letter. How does Word know? It's smart.

About AutoCorrect Entries

The Replace Text as You Type check box refers to the entries in the scrolling list below it. If you turn the check box on, Word examines every character you type. If you type any of the character combinations on the left side of the scrolling list followed immediately by a space, Word automatically steps in, removes the characters you typed, and replaces them with the corresponding text on the right side of the scrolling list. If you've got sharp eyes and are paying attention, you may even see Word do it.

TIP/TRICK

The Replace Text as You Type check box is like the master power switch for this feature. If you prefer that Word mind its own business and let you correct your own typos, turn this check box off.

Let's look at a few of the built-in AutoCorrect examples. My favorite is *teh*, which doesn't appear in the previous illustration. You can use the down arrow in the scrolling window to see it. I probably type the letters *teh* more than I type the correct letters: *the*. With AutoCorrect turned on, I don't have to worry about it. As soon as I type *teh* and press Spacebar, Word fixes my error. No more Delete Delete Delete to fix this particular boo-boo. The other built-in entries are similarly useful. If they're not enough for you, you can add your own.

Creating an AutoCorrect Entry

There are two ways to create an AutoCorrect entry. The first method is good for creating short entries of unformatted text. The second method is good for creating entries that are long, formatted, or include graphics. Let's take a look at both.

- To create a short entry, choose AutoCorrect from the Tools menu to display the AutoCorrect dialog box. Enter a name for the entry in the Replace edit box. The name can be up to 31 characters long and cannot contain any spaces. In the With dialog box, enter the text you want Word to automatically type when you type the entry name followed by a space. Click the Add button to add the entry to the list. It appears in alphabetical order among the other entries.
- To create an entry that is long, formatted, or contains graphics, begin by entering, formatting, and selecting the replacement information in a document window. Then choose AutoCorrect from the Tools menu. The information you selected automatically appears in the With edit box. If the entry contains formatted text or graphics, be sure to click the Formatted Text radio button over the With edit box. Then type a name for the entry in the Replace edit box and click Add. The entry appears with the others.

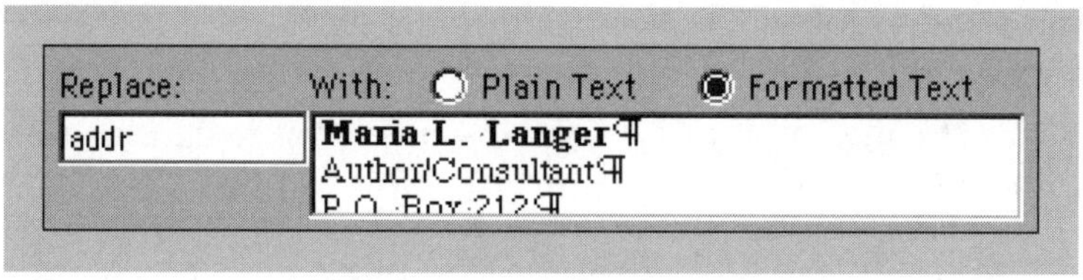

Changing an AutoCorrect Entry

There are two ways to change an AutoCorrect entry: rename it or edit the replacement text. Here are the details.

- To change the name of an AutoCorrect entry, begin by selecting it in the scrolling list of entries. Make sure the name is selected in the Replace edit box and click Delete. The entire entry is deleted, but the information remains in the Replace and With edit boxes. Type a new name in the Replace edit box and click Add. The entry reappears with its new name.
- To change the replacement text of a plain text AutoCorrect entry, begin by selecting it in the scrolling list of entries. Change the text in the With edit box and click Replace. A confirmation dialog box appears, asking if you want to redefine the AutoCorrect entry. Click Yes. The entry is redefined.
- To change the replacement text of a formatted text AutoCorrect entry, begin by inserting the entry in your document. Make any changes you need to and select it. Then choose AutoCorrect from the Tools menu. Type the name of the entry in the Replace edit box and click Replace. A confirmation dialog box appears, asking if you want to redefine the existing AutoCorrect entry. Click Yes. The entry is redefined.

Deleting an AutoCorrect Entry

Deleting an AutoCorrect entry is easy. Choose AutoCorrect from the Tools menu to open the AutoCorrect dialog box. Click on the name of the entry you want to delete to select it. Then click Delete. All gone.

Chapter Summary

In this chapter, you learned about some great features that take a lot of work out of repetitive editing. Find and Replace lets you find and replace text and formatting throughout your documents. AutoText lets you insert commonly used text and graphics in your documents with just a few key-strokes or mouse clicks. AutoCorrect, my favorite of the three, tells Word to automatically correct some of your typos and expand abbreviations to words, phrases, sentences, and even paragraphs of information.

In the next chapter, you'll find out about some real proofing tools, Word's spelling checker, grammar checker, thesaurus, and Hyphenation feature. I'll also tell you about the new Language feature, which let's you tell Word what language you're writing in. And, if you're getting paid by the word, you'll find the Word Count feature handy for writing invoices.

17

Chapter 17: Proofing Tools

ONE OF THE MOST POPULAR FEATURES OF ANY WORD PROCESSOR is its spelling checker. Many people depend on it as a "proofreader" to catch and correct errors. Nowadays, a spelling checker is only one of several proofing tools offered by word processors. Word includes not only a spelling checker, but a grammar checker, a thesaurus, a Hyphenation feature, and a Word Count feature.

In this chapter, you'll learn to use Word's proofing tools in your documents. Even if you flunked high school English, Word can help make sure your documents have correct spelling, grammar, and punctuation, and that you use just the right words to get your message across.

Specifying a Language

NEW IN WORD 6

Before I tell you about each of Word's proofing tools, let me take a minute to talk about Word's new Language command. The Language command lets you tell Word what language document text is written in.

Word's Language feature works hand in hand with its spelling checker and other proofing tools. Word uses the language settings of a document to determine which dictionary to use for a spelling check. Since different parts of the document can be set for different languages, this can be very handy for a document that contains text in more than one language.

Word assumes that your documents are written in English unless you tell it otherwise. To change the language of a document or a portion of a document, select the text you want to change and choose Language from the Tools menu. The Language dialog box appears.

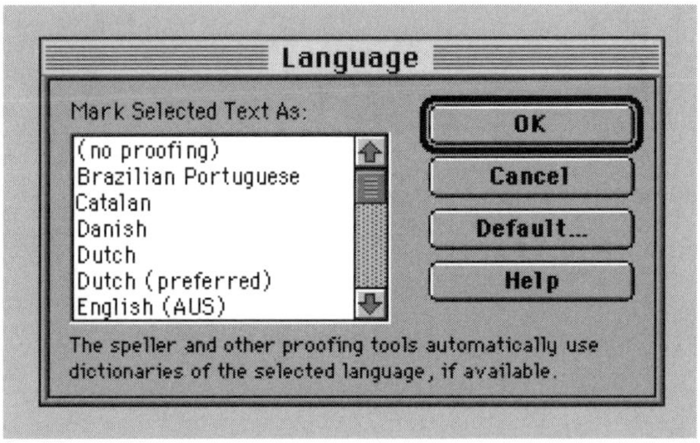

Choose a language from the scrolling list of languages. If you want to exclude selected text from proofing by Word's proofing tools, choose the first option, no proofing. If you want to specify which English your document is written in, choose from among Australian (AUS), British (UK), or American (US). This tells Word which spellings it should use in its English Dictionary when performing a spelling check.

To set the default language for all documents based on the current template, click Set Default. A confirmation dialog box appears, asking if you're sure you want to change the default language. Click Yes and the new language is saved as part of the current template.

When you're all finished with the Language dialog box, click OK to accept the settings and dismiss it.

IMPORTANT NOTE

Word does not come with a dictionary for every single language listed in the Language dialog box. Foreign language dictionaries, as well as dictionaries of technical terms, are available from third party sources. Contact Microsoft

Customer Service for information on where you can obtain additional dictionaries. If you specify a language and don't have the proper dictionary, when you do a spelling check, Word will first have you attempt to find the right dictionary and then give up and tell you it can't find it. It will then skip the spelling check for the portion of text set in that language.

TIP/TRICK

If you use the Language feature often in your documents, make it part of a style that you can apply to text in your documents. I told you about styles in Chapter 7.

The Spelling Checker

Word's spelling checker can check your documents for spelling errors based on a main dictionary file called English Dictionary. It examines each word in the document or selection and compares it to its own list of words. If it finds a match, it checks the next word. If it doesn't find a match, it displays the unknown word in the Spelling dialog box for you to act on. As you'll see, you can tell Word to ignore the unknown word, change it to one of the suggestions Word comes up with, change it to a word you type in, or add the word to a custom dictionary of words you commonly use.

NEW IN WORD 6

Word's spelling checker has undergone some minor changes since previous versions of Word. You can now undo the last change you made or add a change to Word's AutoCorrect feature, which I discussed in Chapter 16.

In this section, I'll cover the spelling checker in detail. If you'd like to follow along, create or open a document with spelling errors in it. You can then put Word to the test.

IMPORTANT NOTE

If you did not do a complete installation of Word, the spelling checker may not be available. If the Spelling command does not appear on the Tools menu, you will probably have to install it. Check Appendix A for Word installation information.

Starting the Spelling Checker

You can have Word check an entire document, part of a document, or even a single word within a document. What Word checks depends on where you position the insertion point or what you select.

- To check the whole document from beginning to end, position the insertion point at the very beginning of the document. When Word is finished checking the document, it tells you.
- To check the document from the insertion point to the end of the document, position the insertion point where you want to begin checking. When Word reaches the end of the document, it offers to continue checking from the beginning.
- To check only a portion of the document, select what you want to check. When Word is finished checking the selection, it offers to check the rest of the document.

Once you've positioned the insertion point or selected text, start the spelling checker using one of these methods:

- Click the Spelling button on the Standard Toolbar *or*
- Choose Spelling from the Tools menu *or*
- Press [⌘] [Option] [L] *or*
- Press [F7] (on an extended keyboard only)

Word doesn't waste any time. It immediately gets to work checking the document. If you look in the Status bar at the bottom of the screen, a message there tells you exactly what Word is up to. It isn't until Word finds a problem word that it stops and tells you about it. It does this by selecting the problem word in the text and displaying the Spelling dialog box.

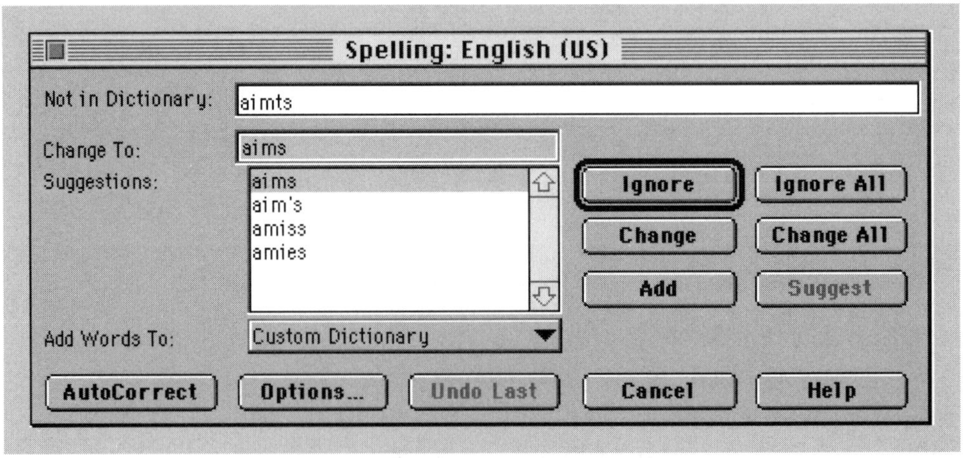

Changing Words

When Word finds a problem word, one of the things you can do is change it in your document. There are several ways you can do this.

Using Word's Suggestions

By default, Word is set to automatically find suggested spellings for a problem word. It displays these suggestions in a scrolling list in the Spelling dialog box. In the previous illustration, Word has come up with four suggestions, including a word I've never heard of: amies.

The Automatic Suggestion feature can be turned on or off in the Options dialog box. If you've got an older Macintosh that tends to be a little slow, you might want to turn this feature off to speed up a spelling check. I'll tell you how to do that in Chapter 23 when I discuss customization.

TIP/TRICK

If the Suggestions scrolling window displays a list of possible suggestions for the problem word, click on the correct one to insert it in the Change To edit box and then click either Change or Change All to change the word and continue the check. Change changes that one occurrence of the misspelling. Change All changes it automatically throughout the rest of the spelling check each time it's spelled wrong. This is handy if you used the word more than once and spelled it incorrectly every time.

If the Suggestions scrolling window does not display a list of possible suggestions for the problem word, click the Suggest button to have Word look for suggestions. If it comes up with any, you can then click one and click Change or Change All to put it in your document and continue the check.

If the Suggestions scrolling window displays only (no suggestions), Word hasn't got the faintest idea what word you're trying to spell. The Suggestion feature won't help you.

For Example: Crossword Puzzle Helper

You can use Word to help you solve crossword puzzles. Really. I know this sounds like a frivolous use for a high-end word processor like Word, but hey, why not?

TIP/TRICK

Continued

Say you need a four letter word for a type of bird. You've got the first and last letters: w and n. You need the middle two letters. Here's what you do. In a Word document window, type in the characters w??n. A question mark is a wildcard character representing one unknown character. (An asterisk is a wildcard character representing any number of unknown characters, in case you ever have a need for that.) Select the four characters and open the Spelling dialog box. If necessary, click the Suggest button to have word come up with suggestions. The answer to the puzzle may appear among them, as my answer did here:

This technique isn't foolproof. For example, Word seems to have trouble if the wildcard is at the beginning or end of a selection — it thinks the wildcard is just regular punctuation it should ignore. But you might find it helpful. I just think it's cool.

Typing a Correction

If you know how the word should be spelled, you can type it into the Change To edit box and click either Change or Change All to change the word and continue the check. Word checks the word you typed. If it doesn't recognize it, it displays a confirmation dialog box like the one shown here. To accept the word and continue checking, click Yes. To change your mind about the word, click No. You'll find that Word has looked it up in its dictionary and may display suggested spellings for it.

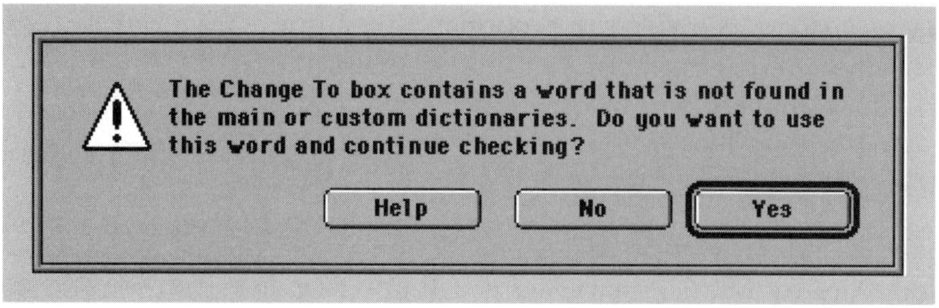

Editing a Problem Word

You can also edit a problem word rather than retyping a correction. In the following illustration, Word has a problem with *inan*. By looking at the document window where the problem word is selected, I can see that it should really be two words, *in an*, which is not one of the suggestions. All I need to do to fix it is insert a space between the first n and the a.

To edit the problem word, click it in the Not in Dictionary edit box to move it into the Change To edit box. Then edit the word in the Change To edit box. When you've got it right, click Change or Change All to change the word and continue the check.

Adding Words

If a word is correctly spelled, you may want to add it to the custom dictionary. By doing this, Word won't stop and bother you the next time it finds the word in one of your documents. This is useful for technical terms and proper names that you often use.

Word does not change its own main dictionary file. Instead, it automatically creates a custom dictionary called Custom Dictionary. (Didn't I tell you that Word doesn't have much of an imagination?) When you add words to the dictionary, that's where they go. You can add other custom dictionaries if you like. I'll tell you how in Chapter 23.

IMPORTANT NOTE

Be careful about adding words to a custom dictionary! If you add an incorrectly spelled word to the dictionary, Word will not alert you if it exists in your document. I'll tell you how to edit the contents of a custom dictionary in Chapter 23.

To add a problem word to a custom dictionary, choose the dictionary from the Add Words To pop-up menu. If you haven't created any additional custom dictionaries, there will be only one choice there: Custom Dictionary. Then click the Add button. Word adds the problem word to the dictionary and continues the check.

Ignoring Words

If a word is correctly spelled but you don't want to add it to the dictionary, you can skip or ignore it. Word offers two buttons for this: Ignore and Ignore All. Ignore skips the word just that one time. Ignore All skips the word each time it appears in any document for the remainder of the Word session.

Handling Repeated Words

In addition to checking the spelling of words, Word's spelling checker also looks for repeated words. In the following illustration, Word has found the word *to* repeated in a sentence. It selects the second occurrence in the document and provides a Delete button to get rid of it. If I want to, however, I can type a new word in the Change To box to replace the second occurrence when it really should have been another word. Then the Delete button turns into a Change button. Of course, I can also use the Ignore button to ignore the repetition.

Adding Words to AutoCorrect

NEW IN WORD 6

The Spelling dialog box also offers an AutoCorrect button which may or may not be available in each problem word situation. Say, for example, that you typed the characters *tyr* when you really meant to type the word *try*. The spelling checker has a problem with *tyr* so it displays the spelling dialog box. The correct word, *try*, is displayed as a suggestion. You can click on *try* to select it and then click the AutoCorrect button. Not only does Word change the error in the document and continue the check, but it creates an AutoCorrect entry that'll make sure the error is corrected as you type it the next time you make it. For more information about Word's new AutoCorrect feature, check Chapter 16.

Undoing the Last Change

NEW IN WORD 6

The Spelling dialog box includes an Undo Last button you can use to undo the last change you made. You might find this useful if your mouse seems to be clicking buttons faster than your mind is processing the spelling check information. When you click Undo Last, Word goes back to the last word it changed, changes it back to what it was, and displays it as the problem word again. You can then change your mind before going on with the check.

Resuming a Check

Although the Spelling dialog box remains on screen throughout the check, there's nothing to stop you from clicking in the document window and making changes there during a check. When you do this, the Spelling dialog box becomes inactive. To make it active again and continue the check, click on it and then click the Start button you'll find inside it. Word continues the check from the insertion point.

The Grammar Checker

If you've always struggled with grammar, you'll definitely want to try Word's grammar checker. It uses grammar and style rules incorporated into a grammar file to find sentences that contain possible errors. You can correct sentences based on Word's suggestions, ignore the problem, or get more information about the rule Word thinks you're breaking. Use it not only to correct your documents but to become a better writer.

In this section, I'll tell you how to use Word's grammar checker to check your document for grammatical or stylistic errors. As you'll see, Word's grammar checker automatically checks for spelling errors, too, so if you plan to use it, don't bother using the spelling checker first. If you want to give the grammar checker a try as you read this, open any document. Word can be very picky about the way you write and can find problems in even your best prose.

NEW IN WORD 6

Word's grammar checker has been revised slightly since previous versions of Word. You can now undo the last change you made. In addition, there are more rules and more ways to customize the grammar checker. I'll tell you all about customization in Chapter 23.

IMPORTANT NOTE

If you did not do a complete installation of Word, the grammar checker may not be available. If the Grammar command does not appear on the Tools menu, you will probably have to install it. Check Appendix A for Word installation information.

Starting the Grammar Checker

The grammar checker works a lot like the spelling checker when it comes to telling Word what to check: what it checks depends on where you position the insertion point or what you select.

- To check the whole document from beginning to end, position the insertion point at the very beginning of the document. When Word is finished checking the document, it tells you.
- To check the document from the insertion point to the end of the document, position the insertion point where you want to begin checking. When Word reaches the end of the document, it offers to continue checking from the beginning.
- To check only a portion of the document, select what you want to check. When Word is finished checking the selection, it offers to check the rest of the document.

Once you've positioned the insertion point or selected text, choose Grammar from the Tools menu. Word begins the grammar check. Before long, it finds a sentence it has a problem with. It selects the sentence in the document window and displays the Grammar dialog box. It might look something like this:

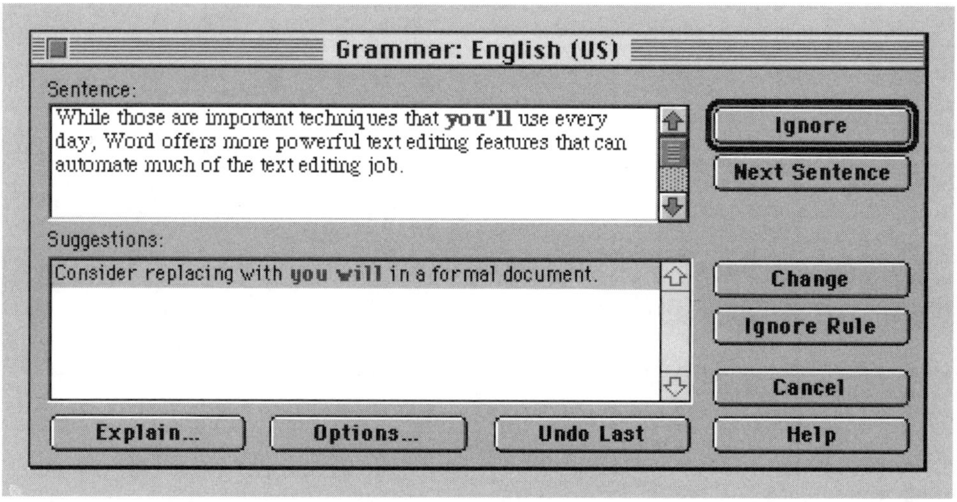

As you'll see as you work with the grammar checker, the options you have depend on the problem Word finds. Let's take a look at some of the options.

Accepting Suggestions

The suggestions scrolling window offers suggestions on how you can fix the problem sentence. In the previous example, Word has a problem with my use of a contraction in a formal document. To change *you'll* to *you will*, all I have to do is click Change. Word makes the change and continues the check.

When the Change button is gray, you can't simply click a button to fix a problem. You have to do a little more work. I'll tell you about editing sentences next.

Editing a Sentence

When you want to edit a sentence, click in the Sentence scrolling window to make it active. Then make whatever changes need to be made and click the Change button. Word makes the change and continues the check.

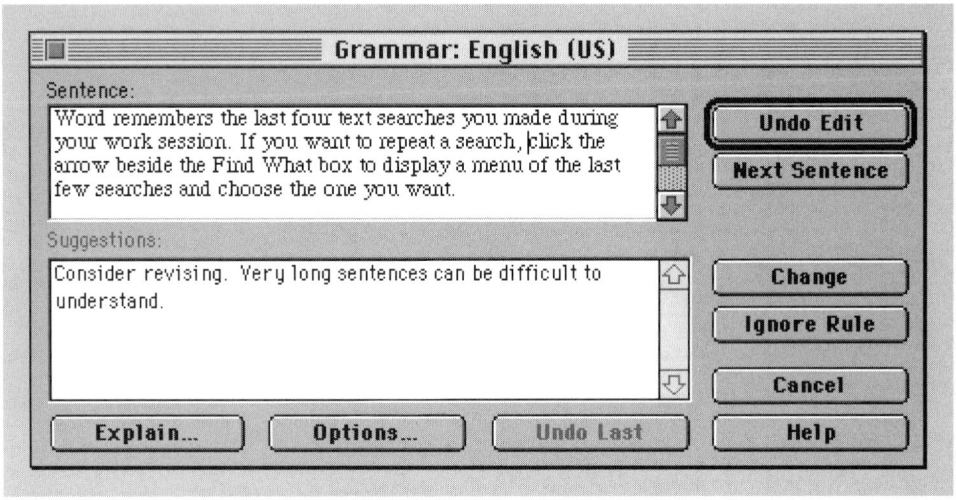

Ignoring Suggestions

There are three ways to ignore Word's suggestions:

- To ignore Word's suggestion about a current problem it has found, click the Ignore button. This tells Word to skip the problem and continue the check. Keep in mind, however, that Word can still find additional problems with the same sentence.

- To ignore any problems Word has with the current sentence, click the Next Sentence button. This tells Word to stop bothering you about the current sentence and move on.
- To tell Word to stop bothering you about a specific rule, click the Ignore Rule button. This tells Word to ignore the current problem and all other problems based on the same rule during the check. This doesn't turn off the rule. I'll tell you how to do that in Chapter 23.

Getting More Information about a Rule

If you don't understand a rule or simply want more information about it, click the Explain button. This displays a scrolling window with additional information about the rule Word thinks you're breaking. Here's what Word has to say about long sentences:

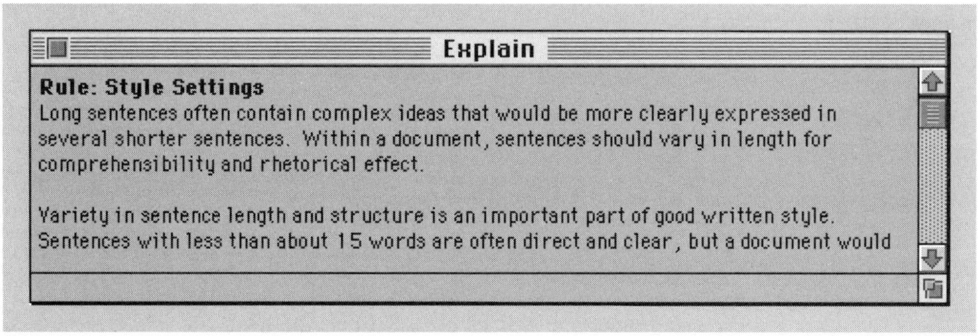

When you're finished reading the information, click in the window's close box to return to the grammar check and its current problem.

Handling Spelling Problems

NEW IN WORD 6

When the grammar checker finds a spelling problem, it displays the Spelling dialog box. Since I already told you about that earlier in this chapter, I won't repeat myself here. Just be aware that when you change, add, or ignore a misspelled word, Word continues the grammar check automatically.

Undoing the Last Change

Like the Spelling dialog box, the Grammar dialog box also includes an Undo Last button to undo the last change you made. When you click Undo Last, Word goes back to the last sentence it changed, changes it back to what it was, and displays it as the problem sentence again.

Resuming a Check

If you click in the document window to make it active or make changes in it during a check, the Grammar dialog box remains on screen but becomes inactive. To make it active and continue the check, click on it and then click the Start button.

Understanding the Reading Statistics

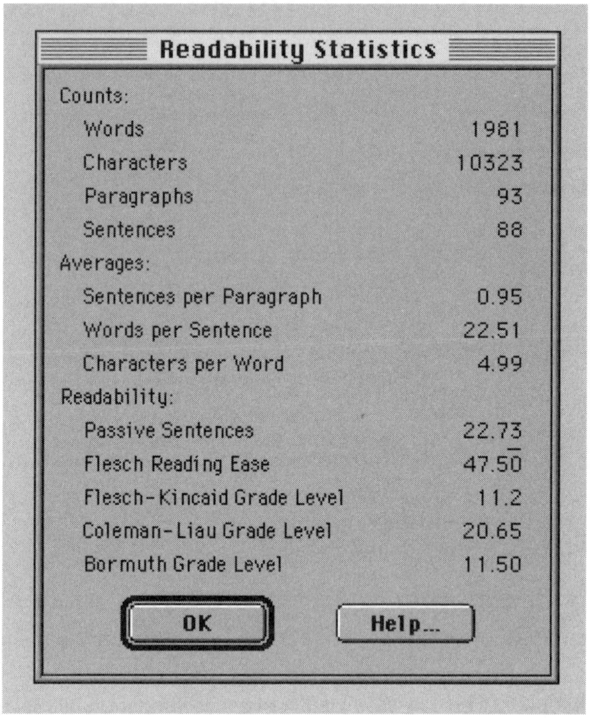

At the end of a grammar check, Word displays readability statistics for the document. Here's what the statistics look like for the Power Macintosh Read Me file that came with my Power Mac.

The first group of numbers are pretty straightforward: word, character, paragraph, and sentence counts. As you'll see later, you can produce the same statistics with Word's Word Count command.

The next group of numbers are averages: Sentences per paragraph, words per sentence, and characters per word. (And I thought *my* sentences were long! Apple definitely needs some new writers!)

The last group of numbers include the percentage of passive sentences and scores for a number of readability indices based on standard formulas. In case you don't remember from high school English class, passive sentences are considered weak and should be avoided. Here's some information about the standard indices:

- **Flesch Reading Ease —** which can range from 0 to 100, is based on the number of syllables per word and words per sentence. Shoot for a score of between 60 and 70. Higher numbers mean that more people should be able to read and understand the text.

- **Flesch-Kincaid Grade Level —** which corresponds to school grade levels, is also based on the number of syllables per word and words per sentence.
- **Coleman-Liau Grade Level —** which also corresponds to school grade levels, is based on the number of characters per word and number of words per sentence.
- **Bormuth Grade Level —** which also corresponds to school grade levels, is also based on the number of characters per word and number of words per sentence.

I find it interesting to see how a document scores. Although many people think they should write to a high school or college grade level, in reality, average writing should score around 7 or 8 on the grade level indices. If your writing falls right in there, you could have a career as a writer! (You might try working for Apple — based on the example above, I think they could use help.)

The Thesaurus

Ever have a problem thinking of just the right word you need? That's what a thesaurus is for: to help you find the perfect word to say what you really mean.

Word's thesaurus makes it easy to look up synonyms for words as you write or proofread your documents. Begin by selecting the word you want to look up. Then choose Thesaurus from the Tools menu or press [⌘][Option][R]. The Thesaurus dialog box appears.

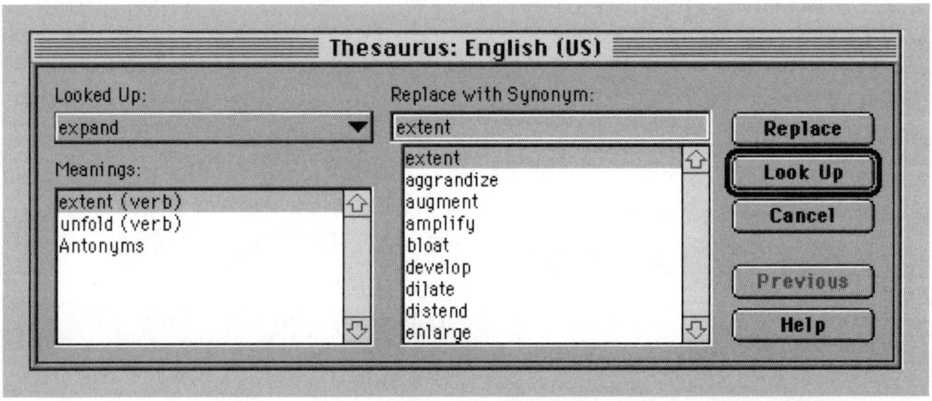

Finding Synonyms, Antonyms, and Related Words

The word you looked up appears in the Looked Up pop-up menu. If you looked up more than one word in a session, all the words you looked up appear in the menu so you can easily go back to one of them.

The Meanings scrolling window displays the different meanings for the word, along with their parts of speech. If opposites or related words are available, you'll see Antonym or Related Words there as well. Click on a word in the Meanings scrolling list to display a list of Replace With words in the right side scrolling window.

- To replace the word you selected in your document, click the word you want to use so it appears in the Replace With edit box and then click Replace. Word puts it in your document.
- To look up one of the Replace With words, click on the word to put it in the Replace With edit box and click Look Up. You can repeat this as many times as you like. Each word you look up is added to the Looked Up pop-up menu.
- To look up a word that doesn't appear on screen, type it into the Replace With edit box and click Look Up.
- To return to the last word you looked up, click the Previous button or choose the word from the Looked Up pop-up menu.

If the Thesaurus Doesn't Know the Word

If the word you looked up is not among those in Word's thesaurus, Word is temporarily stumped. It thinks you've incorrectly spelled the word. In the following example, I've told Word to find a synonym for Macintosh.

Word displays the word you looked up in a Not Found pop-up list. Beneath it, it displays an alphabetical list of all the words in its thesaurus. The selected word is the next closest word to the one it can't find. (Did you ever think of a Macintosh as being close to a mackerel?) Your job is to scroll through the list to find the word you really meant to use, click on it, and then click Look Up. If you don't want to deal with a list containing thousands of words, simply type a new lookup word in the Replace With edit box and click Look Up. Then carry on as instructed above.

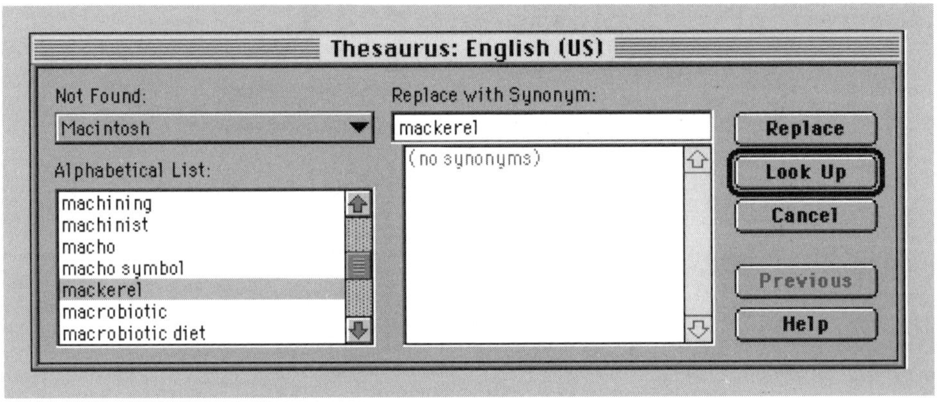

Hyphenation

Hyphenation is more of a formatting tool than a proofing tool. It enables you to automatically or manually insert hyphens to break words that fall at the end of a line. By doing this, the ragged or unjustified side of a block of text appears less ragged. In justified text, hyphenation reduces the amount of space Word needs to insert between words by putting more characters on each line. The end result: the document looks better.

You don't believe me? Look at the illustration shown here. The example on the right has more evenly distributed white space between words. This is especially noticeable in the fifth line down.

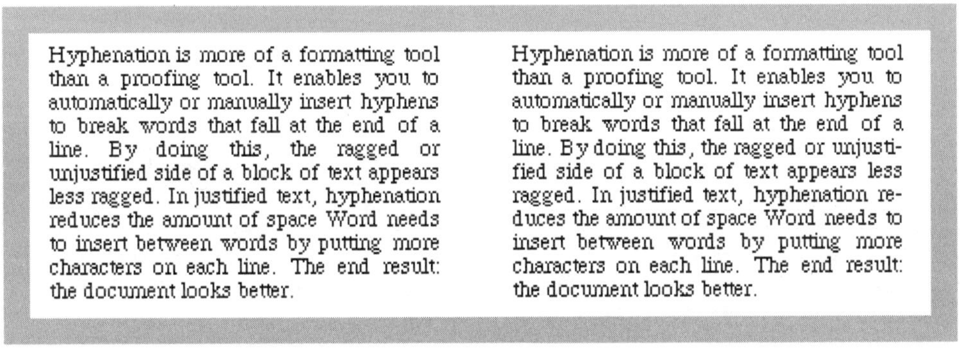

With Word's hyphenation feature you can automatically or manually hyphenate your documents. I'll tell you how in this section. I'll also tell you how you can insert special hyphen and space characters that'll either allow or prevent word splitting.

Automatically Hyphenating Words

To set Word to automatically hyphenate a document, choose Hyphenation from the Tools menu. The Hyphenation dialog box appears.

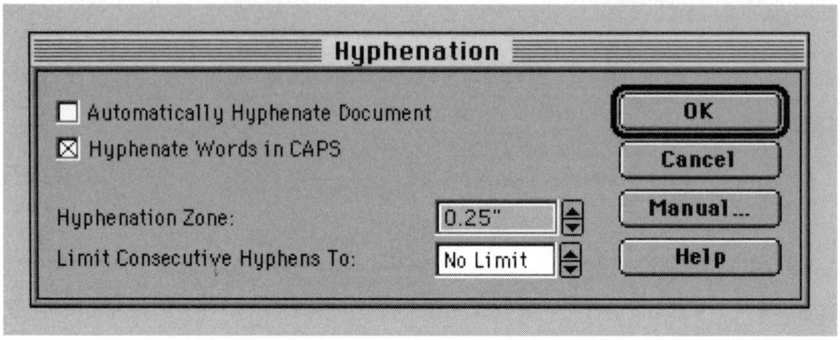

Turn on the check box in front of Automatically Hyphenate Document to tell Word to automatically hyphenate your document either as you type or after it has been typed. Word inserts optional hyphens, which it automatically removes if you edit the text and hyphenation is no longer necessary.

If you don't want words in all uppercase characters hyphenated, turn off the check box for Hyphenate Words in CAPS. This is especially useful if your document includes a lot of long acronyms.

Word uses the values in the Hyphenation Zone and Limit Consecutive Hyphens To edit boxes when determining what it should hyphenate. The hyphenation zone is the distance between the end of the last word in a line and the right indent. For more hyphenation, make this value smaller. For less hyphenation, make it larger. No matter what you set in the Hyphenation Zone edit box, Word will never insert more consecutive hyphens than what you specify in the Limit Consecutive Hyphens To edit box. The default is No Limit.

When you click OK in this dialog box, Word hyphenates any existing text in your document. From then on, everything you type will be hyphenated automatically.

TIP/TRICK

To prevent a paragraph from being automatically hyphenated, select it and then choose Paragraph from the Format menu. Click the Text Flow Tab in the Paragraph dialog box to display its options. Then turn on the check box for Don't Hyphenate and click OK. That paragraph is excluded from the document hyphenation. You can include this option in a paragraph style if you like. I told you about paragraph formatting and styles in Chapters 6 and 7.

Manually Hyphenating Words

If you prefer, you can manually hyphenate a document or selected text. You use the Hyphenate command for that, too. Word hyphenates from the insertion point to the end of the document and then asks if you want to continue from the beginning. If you select text first, Word hyphenates the selection, then offers to hyphenate the rest of the document.

To manually hyphenate a document or selection, position the insertion point or select the text you want to hyphenate. Then choose Hyphenation from the Tools menu. The Hyphenate dialog box appears. Make sure the Automatically Hyphenate Document check box is turned off. Make other settings in the dialog box as I discussed earlier in this section. Then click Manual.

Word starts to examine Words. When it finds one it thinks can be hyphenated, it displays the Manual Hyphenation dialog box. The word in question appears in the Hyphenate At edit box with a hyphen at each position the word can be broken. Word's recommended break is selected with a blinking box. A gray bar marks the last character that could possibly fit on the line — you must break the word at a hyphen before that bar.

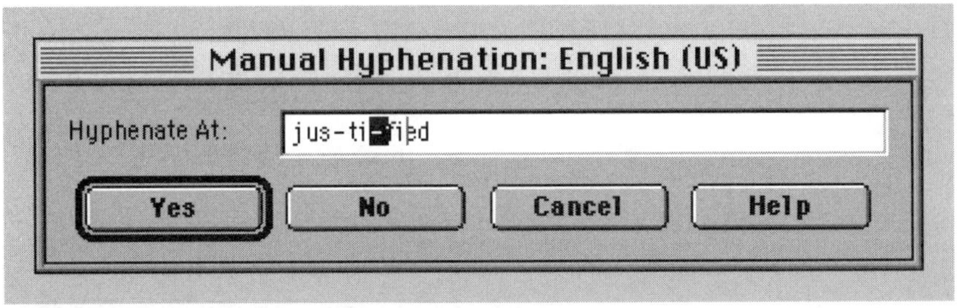

To accept Word's suggestion, just click Yes. To make your own selection, click on the hyphen you want to break at and click Yes. To skip hyphenation for that word, click No. When you click Yes or No, Word either hyphenates or doesn't and moves on to the next word that can be broken.

Special Hyphenation and Space Characters

You can go a step further with manual hyphenation by inserting optional hyphens, nonbreaking hyphens, or nonbreaking spaces. I mentioned these briefly in Chapter 16 when I discussed the Find and Replace commands.

Inserting an Optional Hyphen

An optional hyphen is a special hyphen Word uses if it needs to hyphenate a word. You insert it in the word and it appears on your screen. But if Word doesn't need to break the word, it doesn't print it.

To insert an optional hyphen, position the insertion point where you want the hyphen to appear and press ⌘-. The optional hyphen, which looks like a dotted line, appears in all views except Print Preview, but only if the paragraph marks are displayed. To display paragraph marks, click the Show/Hide ¶ button on the Standard Toolbar.

Inserting a Nonbreaking Hyphen

A nonbreaking hyphen is the opposite of an optional hyphen. It's a hyphen that appears between hyphenated words but never breaks at the end of a line. You might want to use it in proper names that are hyphenated, like *Hastings-on-Hudson* or phone numbers.

To insert a non-breaking hyphen, position the insertion point where you want the hyphen to appear and press ⌘ Shift -. With paragraph marks displayed (click the Show/Hide ¶ button to display them), a nonbreaking hyphen appears as a tilde with a dot beneath it in every view except Print Preview, where it looks like a regular hyphen. With paragraph marks turned off, it looks like a regular hyphen in all views.

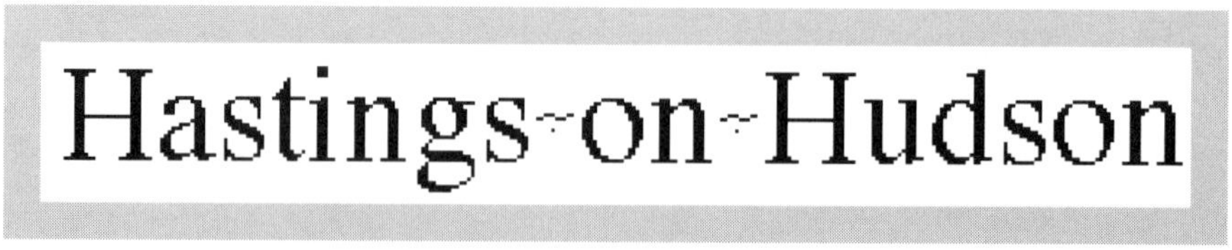

Inserting a Nonbreaking Space

The nonbreaking space is a related character. Although it has nothing to do with hyphens, it does have a lot to do with the way words break at the end of a line. A nonbreaking space is a space that can never come at the end of a line. Use it when you want to keep two words together, like *8:00 A.M.*

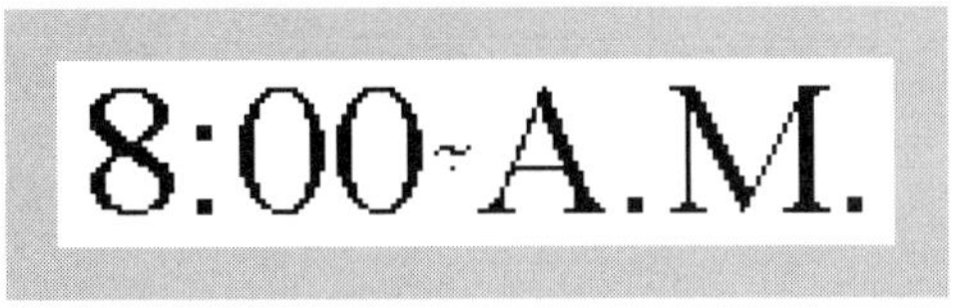

To insert a nonbreaking space, position the insertion point where you want the space to appear and press Control Shift Spacebar. With paragraph marks displayed (remember Show/Hide ¶), a nonbreaking space appears as a short tilde with a dot beneath it in every view except Print Preview where it's invisible (like a space should be). With paragraph marks turned off, it's invisible.

Word Count

If you ever need to know how many pages, words, characters, paragraphs, and lines are in a document, use the Word Count command. It works on either the entire document or any selected text.

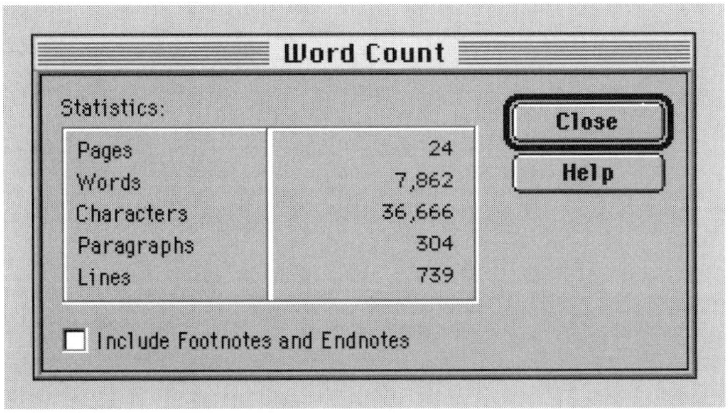

To use Word Count, position the insertion point anywhere within your document or select the portion of the document you want to count. Then choose Word Count from the Tools menu. Word displays the Word Count dialog box, changes the mouse pointer to a watch cursor, and starts counting. You can watch its progress by checking the messages that appear in the Status bar at the bottom of the screen. When it's all finished, the final count appears in the Word Count dialog box. Here's the count for Chapter 16, as I originally wrote it:

If you want Word to also count the text in footnotes and endnotes, turn on the check box for Include Footnotes and Endnotes. Word counts them, too.

Chapter Summary

In this chapter, you learned to use Word's proofing tools: the spelling checker, the grammar checker, the thesaurus, the Hyphenation feature, and finally the Word Count feature. You'll probably use the spelling checker most often in your day to day work, but I hope you'll remember the other tools when you need to perfect an important document prior to printing.

In the next chapter, you'll learn about some other great editing tools: Word's Annotation and new Revision feature. They make it possible for a group of people to work on a document without printing it until it has been finalized and approved by everyone. And if your Macintosh has a microphone, you can use voice annotations to include comments that'll make people sit up and listen.

18

Chapter 18: Annotations and Revisions

In today's business world, it isn't uncommon for a single document to pass through the hands of several authors and reviewers before finalization. Some reviewers attach little notes to document pages, offering suggestions and comments. Other reviewers take out their red pens and mark up the document. By the time the document returns to the person who originally wrote it, it's often a mess. Pity the poor soul who has the job of sorting through the comments and changes to revise the original document. Can you imagine if each reviewer got his own clean copy and marked it up without even knowing what the other reviewers were saying or doing? Do you know what a job it would be to put all those separate revisions into a finalized document? I shudder to even think of it.

NEW IN WORD 6

Word's Annotation and Revision features are designed to make it easier for reviewers to comment on or change a document. The Annotation feature lets you enter text or voice comments into a document so the original author or other reviewers can read or hear what you've got to say. The new Revision feature lets you make changes to a document while marking every single change. The final reviewer then has the option of incorporating or ignoring each revision. To protect the document against unauthorized changes, you can use Word's brand new Protect Document feature to limit changes to annotations or revisions. These features, when used together, can make the document review process quicker and easier while maintaining a complete trail of comments and changes. When used properly, they can also save a heck of a lot of paper, Post-it Notes, and red ink.

In this chapter, you'll learn to use these features to review and revise your documents.

Annotations

What was life like before 3M developed the Post-it note? Can you remember? I can't. It seems like I've been sticking those yellow slips of paper on book pages, memos, and reports since the days of crayons and finger-paint.

Word's Annotation feature is almost like an electronic Post-it note. You insert it where you want to and enter your comment. Anyone reading the document within Word can view the note. Notes can also be printed for later reference. Best of all, notes are not normally printed when you print a document — just like Post-it notes, your comments can be easily removed before the document goes out the door.

NEW IN WORD 6

The Annotation feature is not new to Word version 6. It has changed, however. Rather than use a separate window to display each note one at a time, it now uses a split window similar to the one I showed you when we talked about footnotes and endnotes in Chapter 10. I'll tell you all about Word's Annotation feature in this section.

Adding Annotations

Word offers two kinds of annotations: text and sound.

To add a text annotation, select the document text you want to make a comment about. To add a voice annotation, position the insertion point after the text you want to make a comment about. Then choose Annotation from the Insert menu or press ⌘ Option A. Word inserts your initials and a number between a pair of brackets at the end of the document selection. This is called an annotation mark and it only appears when nonprinting characters like paragraph marks are displayed. Word then splits the document window, as shown here, to display an annotation pane. The annotation pane is where you enter annotations and where other reviewers can read or listen to them. Your initials, between brackets, are there, too.

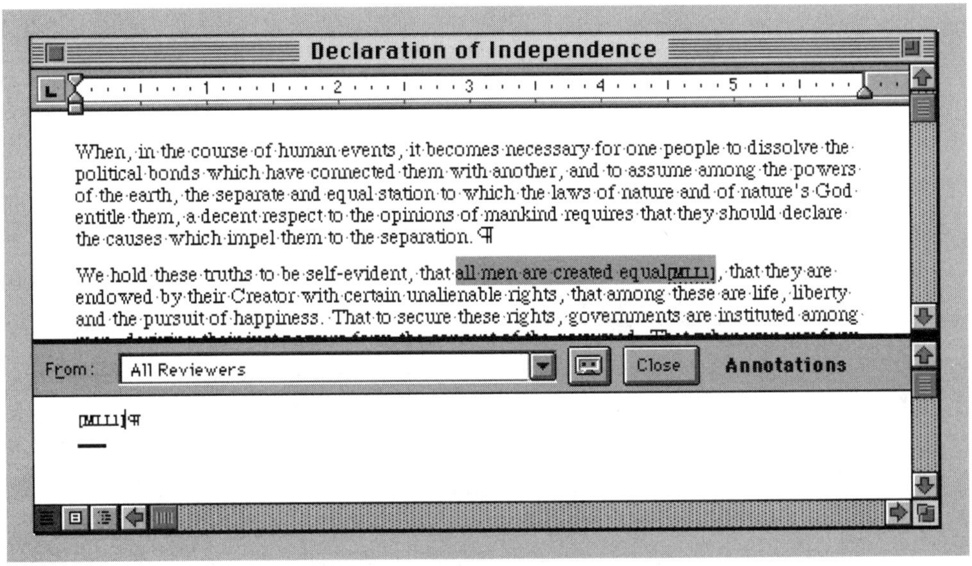

If you don't see your initials in the document window, chances are you've got nonprinting characters turned off. To display the annotation marks in your document, click the Show/Hide ¶ button.

If the initials in the annotation mark are incorrect, that's because they're not set properly in the User Info tab of the Options dialog box. I'll tell you more about the Options dialog box for customizing Word in Chapter 23.

IMPORTANT NOTE

Text Annotations

To add a text annotation, enter your comments after your initials in the Annotation pane. The blinking insertion point should already be there, waiting for you to type. Type in whatever you want to say. Be as verbose as you like. When you're finished entering your annotation, you have two choices:

- Close the annotation pane by clicking the Close button. This hides the annotations from view.
- Add more annotations by clicking in the main document window, selecting the text you want to comment on, and choosing Annotation from the Insert menu again. This adds a new annotation mark in the document and a new entry in the annotation pane.

Voice Annotations

Voice annotations let you add sound to your documents. In order to record a voice annotation, you must have a microphone attached to your Macintosh.

To make a sound or voice annotation, click the Insert Sound Object button in the top of the annotation pane. After a moment, a standard recording dialog box like the one shown here appears.

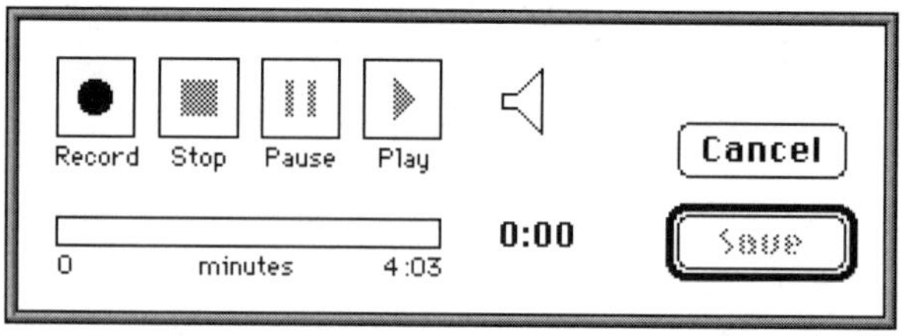

To record a sound, click the Record button and speak into your Macintosh's microphone. The speaker icon within the record dialog box will indicate that it is receiving sound signals by displaying varying waves as you speak. The total length of your message is indicated below this microphone. When you're finished speaking, click Stop. To hear your message before saving it, click Play. To save the message, click Save. Word inserts a sound symbol in the annotation window immediately after your initials. It should look something like this:

TIP/TRICK

There is another way to insert a voice annotation into your document. Position the insertion point in the document where you want the annotation to appear. Then choose Object from the Insert menu. The Object dialog box, which I discussed in Chapter 12 and will discuss again in Chapter 25, appears.

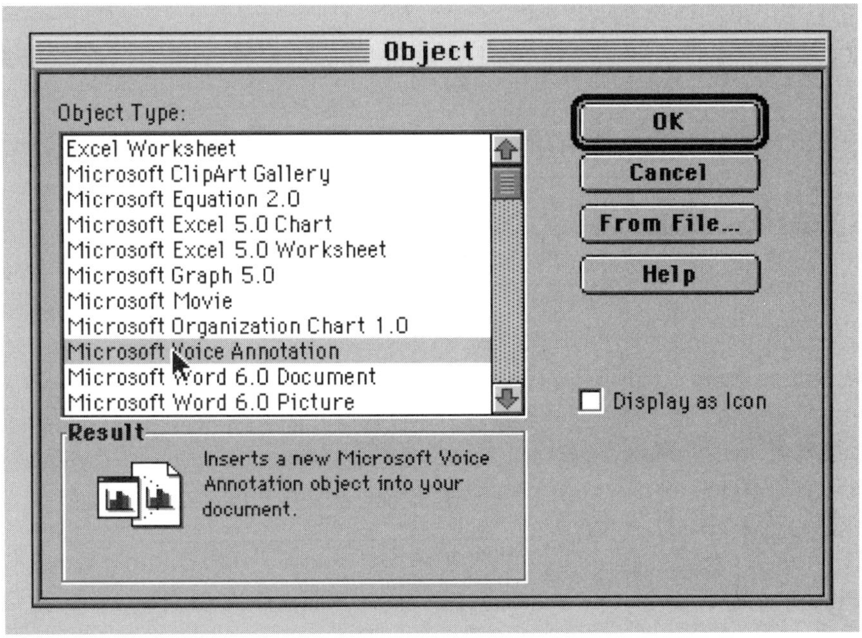

Choose Microsoft Voice Annotation from the Object Type list and click OK. The same recording dialog box I told you about above appears. Record and save your audio comment. Instead of seeing initials in your document to indicate the annotation, the sound symbol appears there. This makes it possible to record and listen to voice annotations without opening the annotation pane.

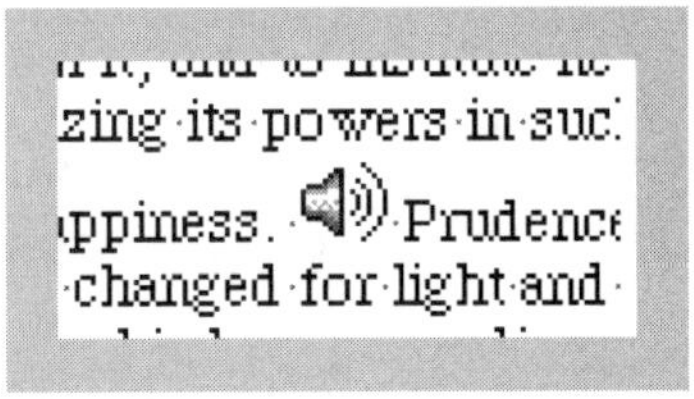

Although it might be a lot of fun to include voice annotations in your documents, recorded sounds take up a lot of disk space, increasing the size of a file. If you record many voice annotations in your document, it could become quite large. Keep this in mind if you need to share your documents with others over network or modem connections.

IMPORTANT NOTE

Text and Sound Together

You can include both a text and sound together in the same annotation. Begin by inserting a text annotation as discussed above. Then click the Insert

Sound Object button to insert a voice annotation immediately after the text annotation. When you're finished, the annotation might look something like this:

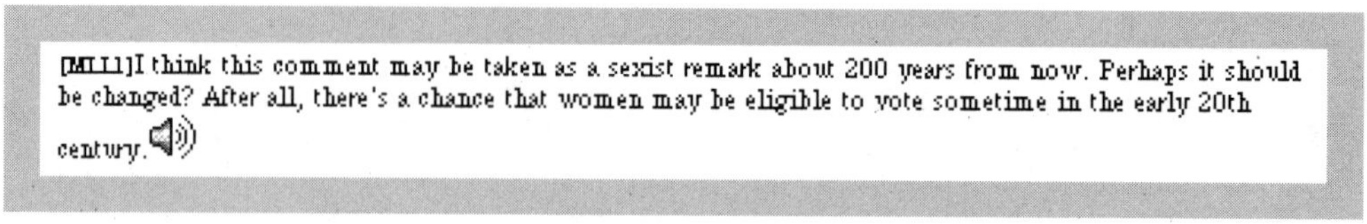

Viewing and Listening to Annotations

You can view and listen to annotations in the annotation pane. If it is not displayed, there are two ways to display it:

- Choose Annotations from the View menu *or*
- Double-click on any annotation note within the document window

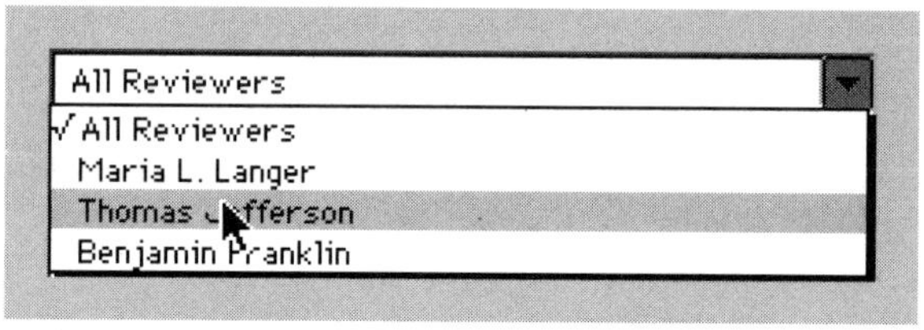

The annotations appear in the order they appear in the main document and are numbered accordingly. This makes them easy to find. By default, the annotation pane displays all the annotations in the document. You can narrow down the display to only one reviewer by choosing the reviewer's name from the Reviewers pop-up menu in the annotation pane.

As you scroll in the document pane, the annotation pane also scrolls to display whatever annotations marks are in view in the document window. As you scroll in the annotation pane, the main document pane scrolls to display whatever annotation marks are in view in the annotation pane. To see an annotation mark and the text immediately before it, click on its annotation mark in the annotation pane. If the reviewer selected text before inserting the annotation, that text appears highlighted (but not selected) in the document window. To quickly select highlighted text in the document window, press Option F11 on an extended keyboard. Otherwise, you can simply drag over the highlighted text to select it.

To listen to a sound annotation, double-click on its sound symbol. Word's Voice Annotation application plays the sound.

TIP/TRICK

You can use Word's Go To command to find annotation marks within your document. Choose Go To from the Edit menu or press ⌘G or F5. The Go To window, which I first discussed in Chapter 2, appears. Select Annotation in the Go To What scrolling list. If desired, choose a reviewer from the Enter Reviewer's name pop-up menu. Then click Previous or Next to scroll through the annotation marks. If the annotation pane is not open, double-click on the annotation mark to open it and read the annotation. When you're finished with the Go To dialog box, click its Close button.

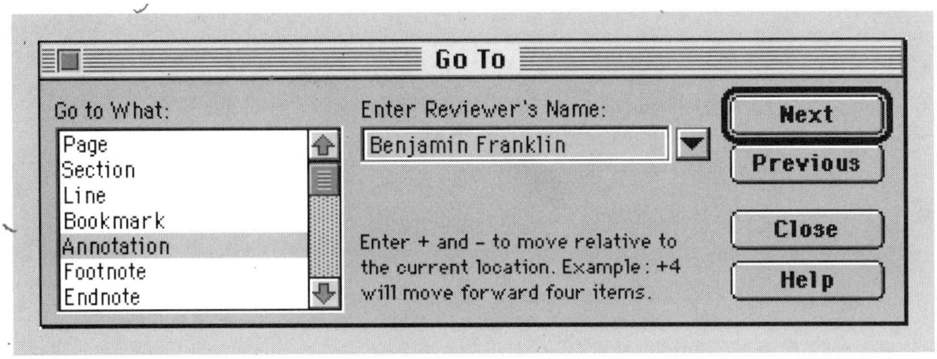

TIP/TRICK

You can also use Word's Find command to find annotation marks in a document. Choose Find from the Edit menu or press ⌘F. The Find dialog box, which I discussed in Chapter 16, appears. Choose Annotation mark from the Special menu/button to insert the annotation mark code (^a) in the Find What edit box. Then click Find Next to scroll through the annotation marks. If the annotation pane is not open, double-click on an annotation mark to open it and read the annotation. When you're finished with the Find dialog box, click its Cancel button or Close box to dismiss it.

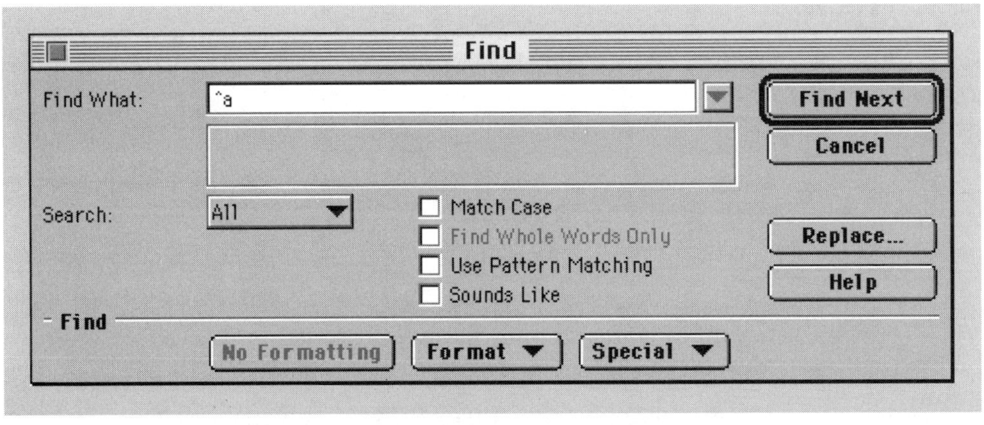

Revising, Formatting, and Deleting Annotations

You can change the contents of an annotation at any time. Simply edit it, using standard editing techniques, in the annotation pane.

You can use the font and paragraph formatting techniques I covered in Chapters 5 and 6 to change the formatting of annotation text. By default, the appearance of the annotation text and annotation marks are determined by the Annotation Text and Annotation Reference styles, which you can modify. I discussed styles in Chapter 7.

You can also delete an annotation if you no longer want it in your document. To do this, click on it in the document window to select it and press [Delete] or [Del]. Both the annotation mark in the document and any annotation mark, text, or sound in the annotation pane disappear. The annotation numbers are adjusted accordingly.

Printing Annotations

NEW IN WORD 6

While you could print annotations in previous versions of Word, you'd first have to export them to a separate document and then print that. As you'll see in a moment, Word version 6 makes it much easier to print annotations by offering a special option in the print dialog box.

Word lets you print annotations either separately or with the document. I discussed printing and the Print dialog box in Chapter 4. Here are the specifics for printing annotations.

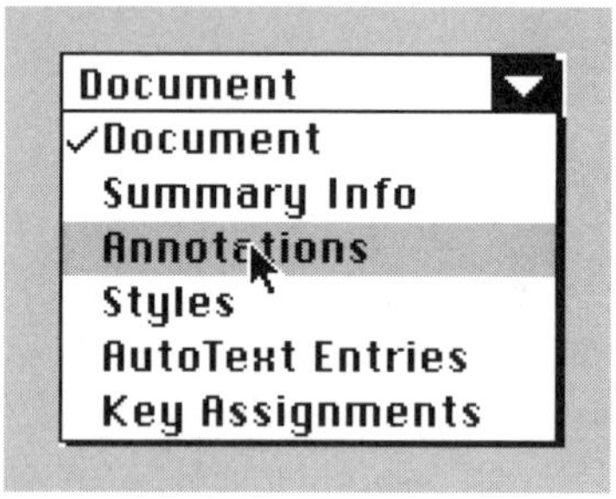

- To print only a document's annotations, choose Print from the File menu or press [⌘][P]. The Print dialog box appears. Choose Annotations from the Print pop-up menu. Then click Print. Word prints the page number the annotation mark appears on, the reviewer's initials with the annotation number, and the text of the annotation. If the annotation is a sound annotation, Word prints the sound symbol.
- To print a document with the annotation marks and annotations, choose Print from the File menu or Press [⌘][P] to display the Print dialog box. Make sure Document is chosen from the What pop-up menu. Then click

the Word Options button. The Options dialog box, which I'll discuss in detail in Chapter 23, appears. Turn on the check box for annotations. (World also turns on the Hidden Text check box.) Click OK. Then click Print back in the Print dialog box. Word prints the text with the annotation marks showing. It then prints all the annotations as discussed above.

IMPORTANT NOTE

After printing a document with annotation marks showing, you may want to turn off the Annotations and Hidden Text check boxes in the Options dialog box so that they do not print the next time you print the document. To do this, choose Options from the Tools menu and click the Print tab. Turn off the Annotations and Hidden Text check boxes and click OK.

Revisions

NEW IN WORD 6

Sometimes a reviewer goes further than simply attaching notes to a document. Sometimes he is authorized to make or suggest actual changes in a document. That's where the red pen normally comes in. When multiple reviewers start marking up a document, it becomes quite a task to figure out who made each change and what those scrawls really mean. That's where Word's Revision feature, which is new in version 6, can help.

When you turn on Word's Revision feature, any changes you make to the document are marked using revision marks and special character formatting like strikethru and underlining. Because the original text of the document remains, you can later decide to accept or reject all or some of the changes. The Revision feature can also keep track of who made each revision and when it was made. You can't get that kind of convenience and detail from red ink on printed pages, can you?

In this section, I'll tell you how you can use Word's Revision feature to review and edit the documents that come across your desk.

For Example: Case in Point

My first job out of college was as an auditor for the New York City Comptroller's Office Bureau of Financial Audit. (No kidding.) I was with "The City" for five years and, during that time, moved up the ranks to the position of Field Audit Supervisor. Part of my job was to edit the audit

Continued

reports my staff members wrote at the conclusion of an audit in preparation for release to the public. The clean copy would come back from the Word Processing Department (we didn't have our own computers in those days) and I'd mark it up. Then back to Word Processing for changes. Then to my boss, Larry, who'd mark it up again. I'd review the changes to make sure his edits hadn't changed the facts, then send it back to Word Processing. The new clean copy would go to Larry's boss, Sylvia, who'd mark it up yet again. Larry and I would both review the changes and send it back to Word Processing. The clean copy (fourth pass, if you've been counting) would go to Sylvia's boss, Frank, who'd (fortunately) make very few changes. Larry and I would review the changes again and send it for its final cleanup in Word Processing.

Meanwhile, I'd have a big, fat folder full of all the markups that had been made since the original handwritten document. Sometimes, if the report needed a lot of work or was particularly sensitive, Larry or Sylvia would review and revise it two or three times. Finally, the final *draft* (no, this wasn't the final report) would be delivered to the Comptroller (Harrison J. Goldin in those days). He'd sign off on it and sometimes parts of it would end up in the newspaper.

The entire process could take from two to eight weeks, depending on the load of the Word Processing Department, vacation schedules, and the importance of the audit. Looking back on this now, I'm amazed at how archaic the whole system was. It was only ten years ago!

There is a point to this story, in case you were wondering. Word's Revision feature, combined with electronic mail, could have made the audit report editing process quicker and easier for all concerned. By routing the report from the auditor's desk to the desks of all four reviewers, all revisions could have been incorporated in the original document without printing a single page. Since all the original text would be there for reviewers to see, there would be less of a chance of getting the facts messed up. There would be no fat folder full of marked up copies and no need for a Word Processing department.

I wonder how they're doing it now in the Bureau of Financial Audit?

Working with the Revision Feature

To work with the Revision feature, choose Revisions from the Tools menu or double-click the MRK indicator in the Status bar. The Revisions dialog box appears.

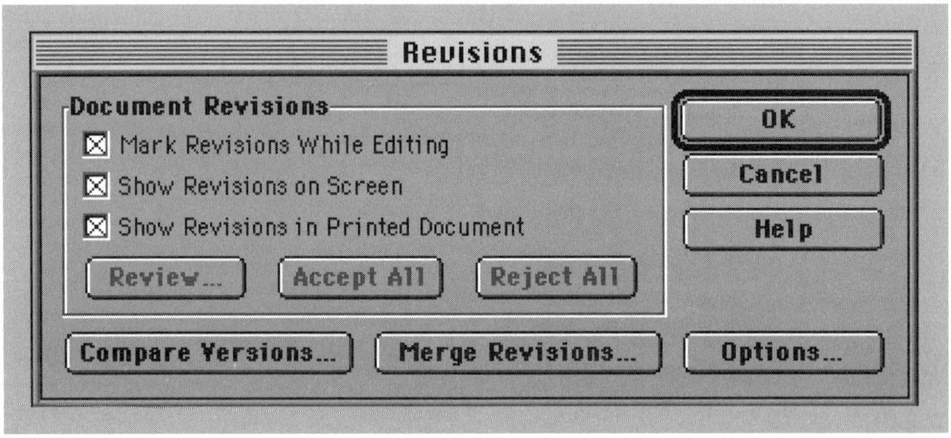

- To turn on the Revision feature, turn on the Mark Revisions While Editing check box. This tells Word to record all the changes you make in the document until the check box is turned off. If this is not turned on, the Revision feature is not activated.
- To see the revision marks on screen, make sure the check box for Show Revisions on Screen is turned on. If this is turned off but the Mark Revisions While Editing check box is turned on, Word will still record document changes, but it will not show them on screen.
- To see revisions in a printout of the document, make sure the check box for Show Revisions in Printed Document is turned on. Whatever revision marks appear on screen will also print out. This may be useful to keep a printed record of document changes.

When you're finished setting these check boxes, click OK to return to the document. You should see the letters MRK in black on the Status bar to indicate that the Revision feature is turned on. When the feature is turned off, this indicator is gray.

Making and Seeing Document Revisions

Once the Revision feature is turned on, every change you make to the contents of the document text is recorded with a variety of colored marks. Let me show you some examples.

In the following illustration, I deleted the words *out of college*. Rather than remove them from the document, Word put a line through them to indicate that they have been deleted. Although you can't see it in the illustration, the text and line through it are blue. Word displays a black vertical bar in the left margin to flag a change in that line.

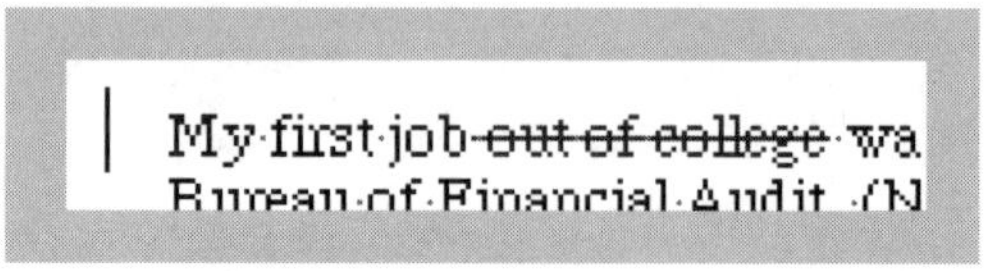

In the next illustration, I replaced the word *clean* with the word *revised*. Word underlined the new word and placed it in front of the old word, which it put a line through. Both words and underlines are blue. A vertical bar appears in the margin.

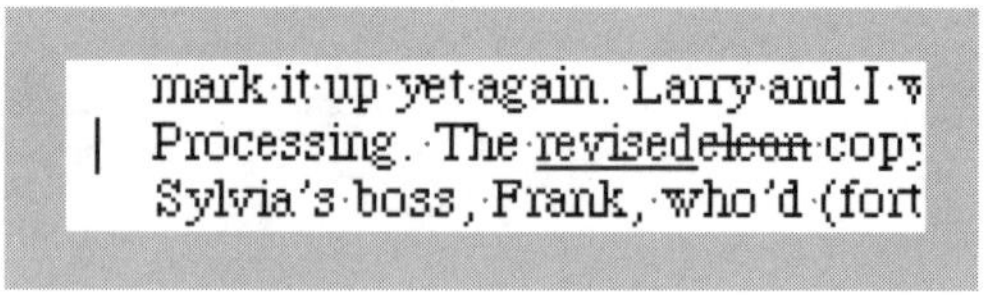

The next thing I tried was using drag and drop text editing to move the sentence *It was only ten years ago!* See how Word marked the change? Remember, everything that has a line through it or underline is colored blue.

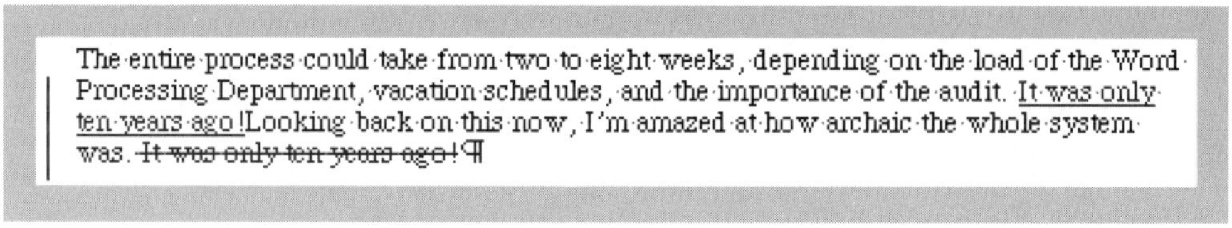

One of the ways Word keeps track of who makes each revision is by color-coding the revisions. By default, the first editor's revisions are blue, the second editor's revisions are green, the third editor's revisions are red, and so on. Up to eight different colors can be used. If there are more than eight editors, Word simply reuses the colors. If one editor edits another editor's work, the color code for the person with the last say is used. Here's an example of text inserted by one editor (underlined) and deleted by another (strikethru).

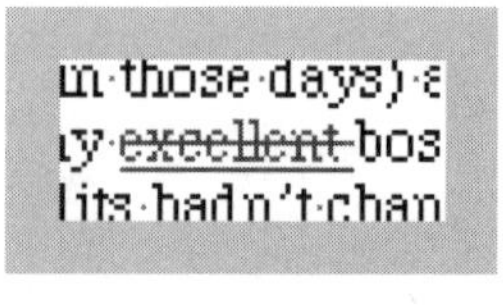

TIP/TRICK

You can customize the way revised text is marked. I'll tell you how in Chapter 23.

Reviewing, Accepting, or Rejecting Revisions

Once a document has been revised, it's up to the person with the final say to incorporate the reviewer's changes into the finished document. The Revision feature makes this easy to do.

Choose Revisions from the Tools menu to open the Revisions dialog box. You have three choices: review the changes one at a time, accept them all, or reject them all.

Reviewing Revisions

To begin reviewing revisions, click the Review button. Word displays the Review Revisions dialog box. To begin the revision process, click the appropriate Find button to move forward or backward in the document.

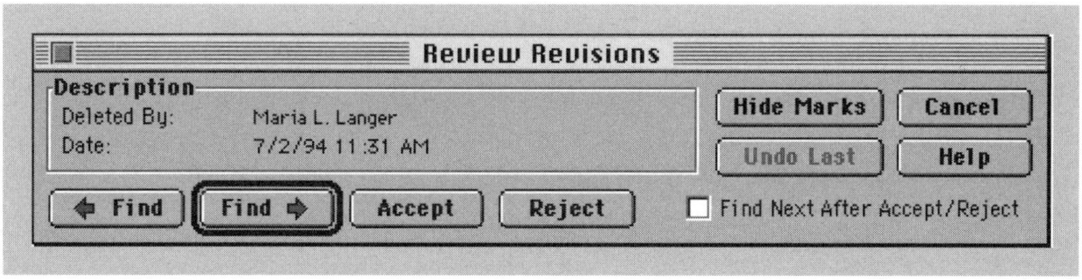

When a revision is selected, the name of the person who made it and the date it was made appears. You can see the revision in the document window behind the dialog box. If the dialog box is in the way, use your mouse pointer to grab it by its title bar and drag it aside.

- To accept a revision, click Accept. The change is made in the document window and the revision marks disappear.
- To reject a revision, click Reject. The text reverts to what it was before the change was made and the revision marks disappear.
- To undo the last change you made, click Undo Last. Whatever you last did — Accept or Reject — is undone so you can decide all over again.

- To hide all revision marks so the document looks like it would with all changes accepted, click Hide Marks. This is very helpful when a sentence contains a lot of revision marks and you can't easily read what the final version would be. To display the marks again, click Show Marks.
- To move to the next or previous revision, click the appropriate Find button.
- To have Word automatically find the next revision when you click Accept or Reject on the current revision, turn on the check box for Find Next After Accept/Reject.

When you're all finished reviewing revisions, click the Close button or Close box to return to the document window.

Accepting All Revisions

If you want to accept all document revisions, click Accept All in the Revisions dialog box. A confirmation dialog box appears, asking if you're sure you want to accept all revisions. Click Yes. All changes to the document are accepted and the revision marks disappear.

TIP/TRICK

If you want to print a copy of the document with revisions accepted but want to keep a record of the revisions, don't accept the revisions. Instead, turn off the Show Revisions in Printed Document check box in the Revisions dialog box. When you print the document, it prints as if all revisions have been accepted, even if the revision marks remain.

Rejecting All Revisions

If you want to reject all document revisions, click Reject All in the Revisions dialog box. A confirmation dialog box appears, asking if you're sure you want to reject all revisions. Click Yes. All changes to the document are removed and the revision marks disappear.

Comparing Document Versions

Another great part of the Revision feature is its ability to compare two documents and record the differences between them. You might find this helpful if you've made changes to both versions and want to review and combine the changes.

To compare two documents, begin by opening one of them with Word and choosing Revisions from the Tools menu. Click the Compare Versions button. A standard Open dialog box appears. Use this dialog box to find and open the other version of the document. If necessary, you can use the Find File button to locate the other document.

As Word conducts the comparison, it displays its progress in the Status bar at the bottom of the document window, as shown below. When it's finished, it displays the document you originally opened with revision marks showing the difference between it and the one you compared it to. You can then review, accept, and reject each revision or all revisions as I instructed above.

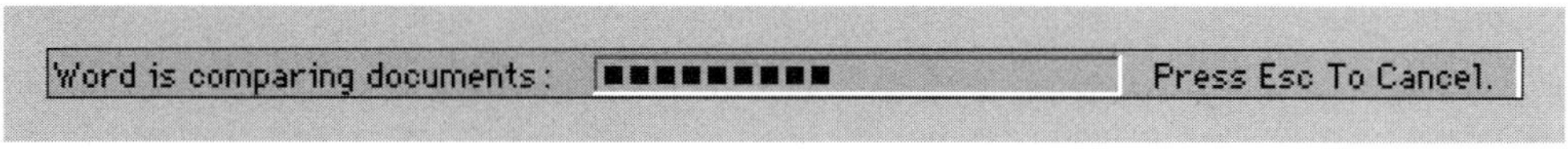

Merging Document Revisions

If the original version of the document was distributed to a number of different reviewers and you got a separate revised copy back from each of them, Word has you covered. The Merge Revisions button in the Revisions dialog box makes it possible to combine separate revisions to a document in one document. This makes it easier to review, accept, or reject changes.

Begin by opening one of the revised documents. Choose Revisions from the Tools menu and click the Merge Revisions button. A standard Open dialog box appears. Use this dialog box to locate and open the original version of the document. Word opens the document and merges the changes into it. Choose Save from the File menu, click the Save button, or press ⌘S to save the revisions in the original document.

If you want to merge another document's revisions into the original document, repeat the procedure in the previous paragraph. You'll see that the second document's revisions appear in a different color. You can repeat this process for as many revised versions as you have. Word assigns a different color to each of the first eight reviewers before it starts reusing colors.

When you're all finished merging revisions, you can use the Review Revisions button in the Revisions dialog box to review revisions one by one as discussed a little earlier in this section.

Preventing Permanent Changes to a Document

I think you'll agree that the Annotation and Revision features of Word can be extremely useful in situations where a single document is reviewed by multiple people. But unless you protect a document, there's nothing to stop a reviewer from making changes rather than annotations or making changes with the Revision feature turned off. In other words, these features aren't useful if they aren't used.

NEW IN WORD 6

Fortunately, Word version 6's Protect Document feature can prevent people who open the document from making changes other than annotations or controlled revisions. Here's how it works.

Protecting a Document

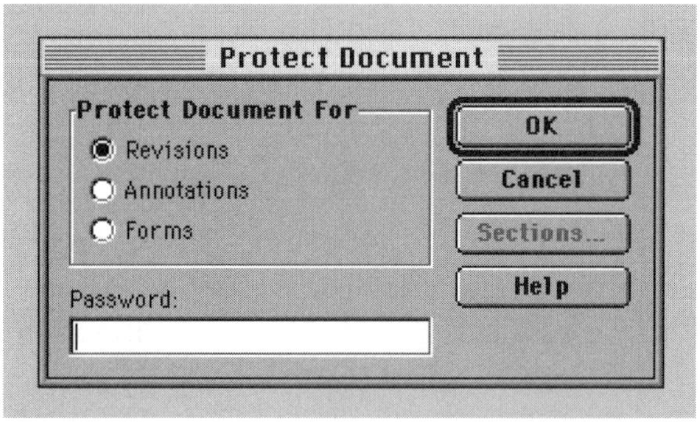

To protect a document, choose Protect Document from the Tools menu. The Protect Document dialog box appears.

- To limit a reviewer to adding or reviewing annotations in the document, choose the Annotations radio button and click OK. Until the document is unprotected, the only thing any reviewer will be able to do is add or review annotations. If a reviewer tries to edit the document, his Macintosh will beep and the following message appears in the Status bar at the bottom of the screen: "This command is not available because the document is locked for edit."

- To limit a reviewer to making revisions with the Revision feature, choose the Revisions radio button and click OK. Until the document is unprotected, a reviewer may make changes to the document, but all changes will be stored by the Revision feature for later acceptance or rejection. The Revision feature cannot be turned off. A reviewer cannot accept or reject revision changes until protection is turned off. A reviewer may still add document annotations, but these are also marked as revisions.

To increase protection, you can assign a password to the Protect Document feature. By doing this, protection can only be turned off after the password is typed in. To assign a password, simply type it into the Password edit box. It will appear as bullet characters on screen to prevent someone from reading the password over your shoulder. Then click OK. Use the Confirm Password dialog box that appears to retype the password for confirmation. Click OK again. Document protection is now password-protected.

IMPORTANT NOTE

If you use password protection, do not forget the password! If you do, you can permanently lose editing capabilities for the document.

TIP/TRICK

The Protect Document dialog box also lets you protect documents that utilize Word's new Forms feature. I'll talk about forms in Chapter 22.

Removing Document Protection

To remove document protection, choose Unprotect Document from the Tools menu.

- If no password was assigned to the document, protection is immediately removed.
- If a password was assigned to the document, the Unprotect Document dialog box appears. Type the password into the Password edit box and click OK to remove document protection.

Chapter Summary

In this chapter, you learned all about Word's Annotation and Revision features. You saw how you can add text and sound notes to documents without changing document text, and how you can keep track of all revisions to a document so they can be reviewed, accepted, or rejected all at once. Finally, you learned to use the Protect Document command to force reviewers to use either the Annotation feature, the Revision feature, or both — thereby protecting the integrity of your original document until a decision-maker decides what to do with reviewers' comments and changes.

In the next chapter, you'll change gears slightly and learn about an improved feature of Microsoft Word: its ability to keep track of addresses and to print envelopes and labels. If you've been using a typewriter to address envelopes and create mailing labels, throw it away! As you'll see in the next chapter, you won't need it anymore.

19

Chapter 19: Envelopes and Labels

ONE OF THE THINGS I HATE TO SEE WHEN I VISIT A CLIENT IN his workplace is a desk with a computer, a printer, *and* a typewriter on it. (I also hate seeing both a computer and a dumb terminal on a desk, but that has nothing to do with Word.) People who keep a typewriter around solely to type addresses on envelopes and create labels are missing out on one of the best features of Word: its ability to print envelopes and labels right on a computer's printer!

NEW IN WORD 6

The ability to print envelopes and mailing labels is not new to Word version 6. This version, however, introduces the Envelopes and Labels command which puts all envelope and label printing settings in one easy-to-find place. In addition, while label printing with Word used to require complex templates and print merge, Word now includes built-in support for popular label sizes, making label printing far easier. I'll tell you about printing labels with mail merge in chapter 21.

In this chapter, you'll learn all about how you can print envelopes and labels with Word. Once you get comfortable using Word and your printer for these tasks, I think you'll give your typewriter to charity — like I did years ago.

FYI: Where's the Addresses Feature?

If you've used previous versions of Word and have developed a certain fondness for the Addresses feature, you may be wondering what happened to it. I'll try to break this to you gently: it's gone.

If you really think about it, though, it really isn't so earth-shattering. After all, what was the Addresses feature anyway? It was a specialized glossary. The Glossary feature is still part of Word, although it's now called AutoText. I told you about it in Chapter 16. You can use the 5.1 Upgrade template that comes with Word version 6 to automatically create AutoText entries for every address in your Word 5.1 address list.

Envelopes

When you send business or personal correspondence, the envelope it's enclosed in is the first thing the recipient sees when he's sorting through his incoming mail. If the postal service hasn't mangled it too badly (I think they've got too many conveyor belts), the envelope's appearance could give the recipient his first real impression of you. If the document you're sending is important, needs immediate attention, or should impress the recipient, would you want to address it by hand or on a typewriter with a faded ribbon? Of course not. You'd want to give it the same attention that you gave the rest of the package. If you're like me (terribly picky), you may even want to match the font and character styles used inside the envelope on the outside of the envelope. To do that, you need to put Word and your printer to work.

You create an envelope for printing by using the Envelopes and Labels command under the Tools menu. Choose this command to display the Envelopes and Labels dialog box. To work with an envelope, click the Envelopes tab to display its options.

Specifying Addresses

An envelope has two addresses: the delivery address (Who is it going to?) and the return address (Who is it coming from?). The Envelopes tab of the Envelopes and Labels dialog box lets you specify both.

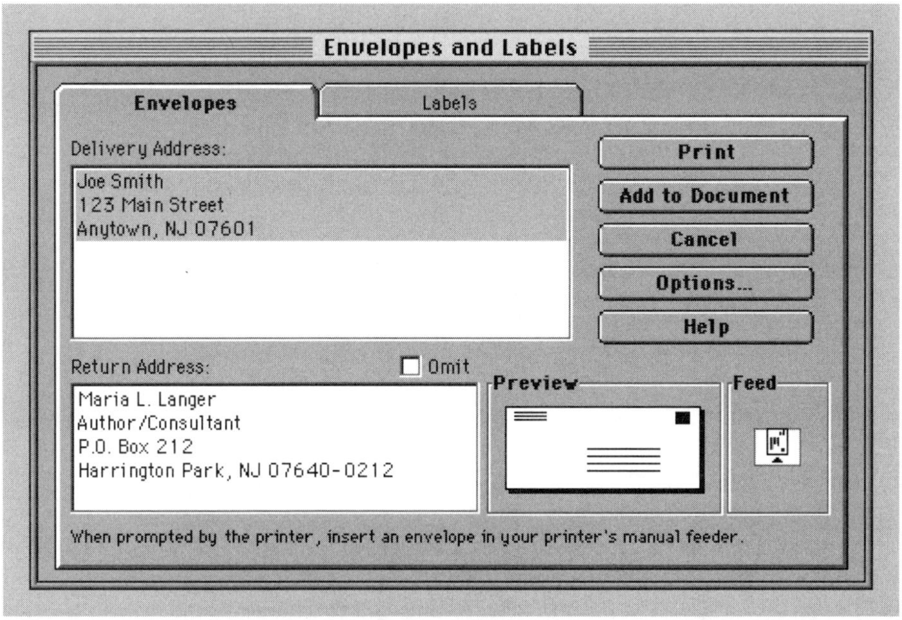

Word is smart. (Haven't I told you that before?) If you have a letter open when you choose Envelopes and Labels from the Tools menu, Word searches for the inside address and uses it as the delivery address for the envelope. You can see that in the previous illustration. I didn't do anything special to get that address in there. I just opened the dialog box with a plain old letter showing.

Of course, if the document you have open contains more than one address, Word might get confused and pick the wrong one. (It's smart, but it's no genius.) You can put the right one in the Delivery Address edit box two ways:

- Select the delivery address within the document window before choosing Envelopes and Labels from the Tools menu. By selecting it first, you tell Word to use it.
- Type whatever address you want to use right into the Delivery Address edit box. Remember to press Return or Shift Return after each line. This is handy if you don't feel like selecting an address first or if the address is not in the currently open document.

Word gets the return address from the entry in the User Info tab of the Options dialog box. I'll tell you more about that in Chapter 23. You can change what's in the Return Address edit box by simply editing it.

TIP/TRICK

If your document has several addresses, you can use Word's Bookmark feature, which I discussed in Chapter 14, to set bookmarks for the delivery and return addresses you want to use. Just name the delivery address *EnvelopeAddress* and the return address *EnvelopeReturn*. Word will automatically use those bookmarks in the Envelopes and Labels dialog box.

Setting Envelope Options

To tell Word what size envelope you want to print on, whether it should include special postal markings, and what fonts it should use for the delivery and return addresses, use the Envelope Options tab of the Envelope Options dialog box. The Envelope Options tab should look like this:

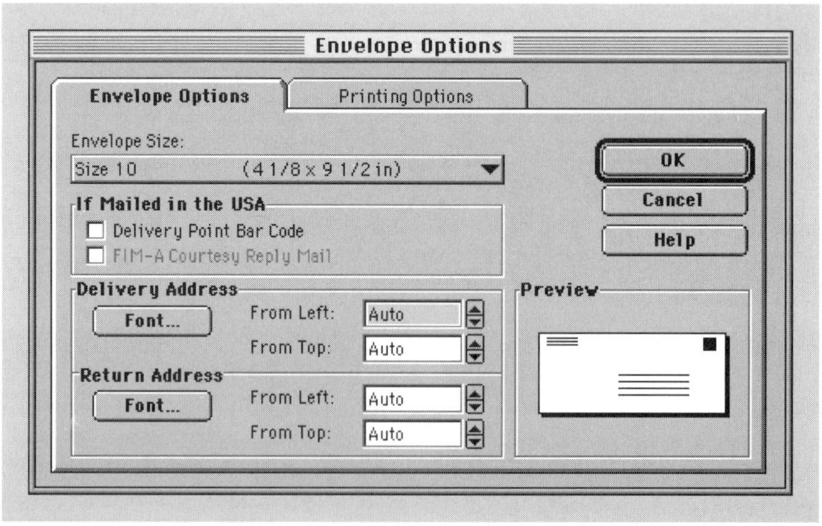

As you make changes, the Preview area in the lower right side of the dialog box changes accordingly. When you're finished making changes, click OK to accept them.

Envelope Size

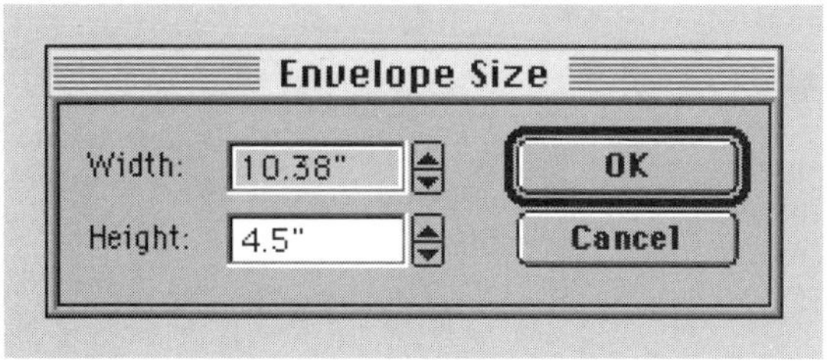

Word provides a handy pop-up menu you can use to choose from among several popular US and European envelope sizes. If you've got an envelope size that isn't on the list, choose Custom Size, the last option on the list. The Envelope Size dialog box appears. Enter the envelope measurements in the Width and Height edit boxes and click OK to create a custom size.

Special Postal Markings

Word supports two kinds of special postal markings that are commonly used in the United States. Use check boxes to turn them on or off.

- **Delivery Point Bar Code** — is the POSTNET bar code that US Postal System equipment can read. This is a series of short lines that appear right above the delivery address. Word draws these lines based on the addressee's zip code.
- **FIM-A Courtesy Reply Mail** — is a series of five vertical bars that identify the front top of the envelope. This is used by US Postal System equipment to correctly position envelopes in the mail sorting machines. In order to turn on this option, you must have the Delivery Point Bar Code option turned on.

Address Positions and Fonts

Although Word automatically positions the return and delivery addresses on an envelope, you can override its options. Simply enter new values in the From Left and From Top edit boxes under Delivery Address and Return Address.

You can also specify a font for the delivery and return addresses. Click the appropriate Font button to display the Envelope Address or Envelope Return

Address dialog box. These two dialog boxes look and work exactly like the Font dialog box I discussed back in Chapter 5. When you're finished making changes in either dialog box, click OK to accept them.

TIP/TRICK

The default settings for the delivery and return addresses on an envelope are determined by two styles: Envelope Address and Envelope Return. You can change the styles for all envelopes you print by modifying these styles and copying them to the Normal template. I told you how to modify styles in Chapter 7 and how to copy styles from documents to templates in Chapter 9.

Setting Printing Options

To tell Word how you plan to feed the envelope into your printer, use the Printing Options tab of the Envelope Options dialog box. If the Envelope Options dialog box is already open, just click the Printing Options tab. If you're looking at the Envelopes and Labels dialog box, click the Options button or Feed illustration. The Printing Options tab looks like this:

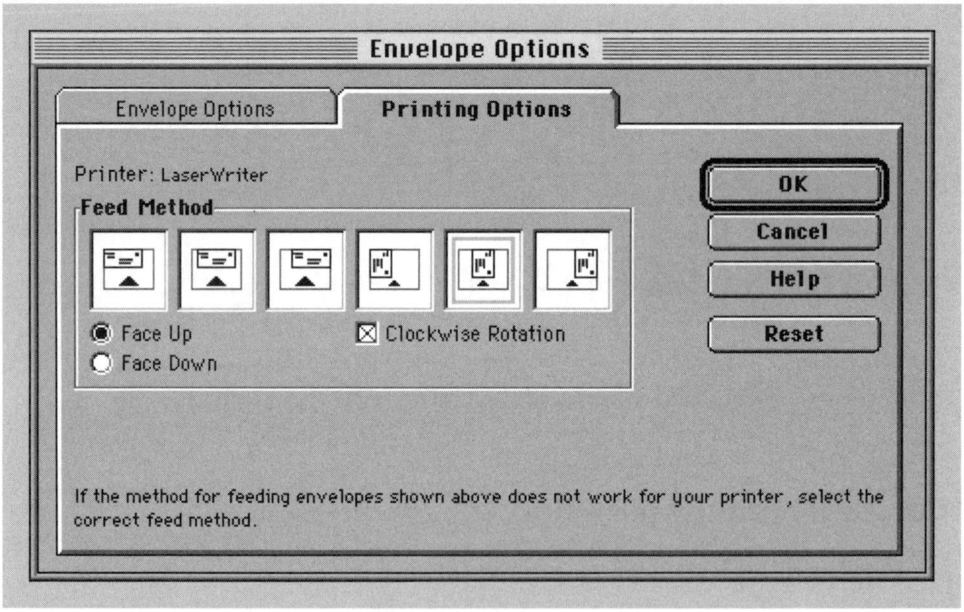

Word knows what printer you'll be printing on based on your selection in Apple's Chooser, which I discussed back in Chapter 4. It offers six feed methods that are illustrated with icons. Click the one that applies to your printer. If necessary, pick the correct radio button for Face Up or Face

Down and turn Clockwise Rotation on or off. The reset button resets the options to the standard for that kind of printer — in most cases, those options will work. When you're finished making changes, click OK to accept them.

TIP/TRICK

If you're not sure how your printer accepts envelopes, print an envelope using the following instructions but print it on plain paper. By examining how the envelope information is positioned on the paper, you should be able to figure out which feed method is correct.

Printing an Envelope

When you've got the envelope information all set up and ready to go, it's time to fire up your printer and print. Insert an envelope into your printer as instructed in its manual. Then click the Print button in the Envelopes and Labels dialog box. A Print dialog box appears. Set the number of copies and paper source, if necessary, and click Print. The envelope prints.

Adding an Envelope to a Document

If you prefer, you can add an envelope to a document. When you click the Add to Document button in the Envelopes and Labels dialog box, Word adds a new section to the beginning of the document, before any of the document text. This section includes all the envelope information: addresses, bar codes, envelope size, and orientation. In Normal view, it might look something like this:

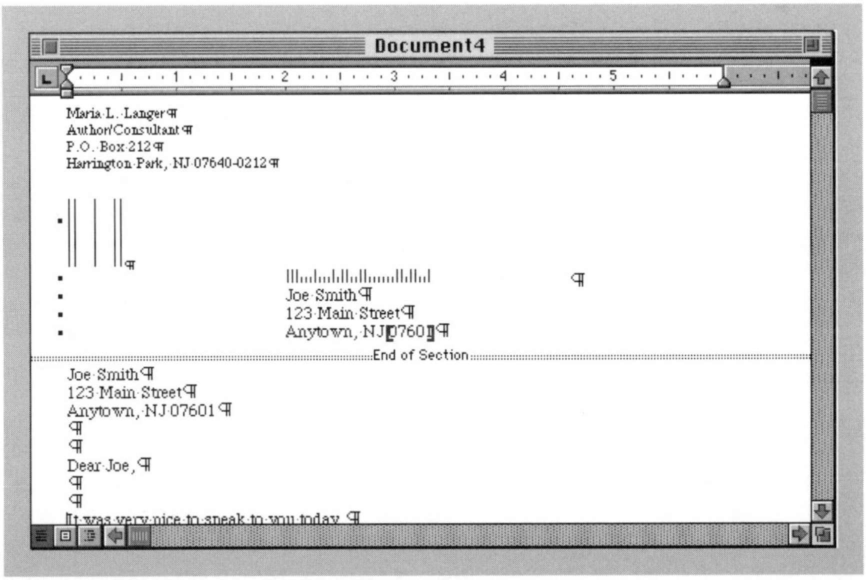

In Page Layout view, however, it looks like this:

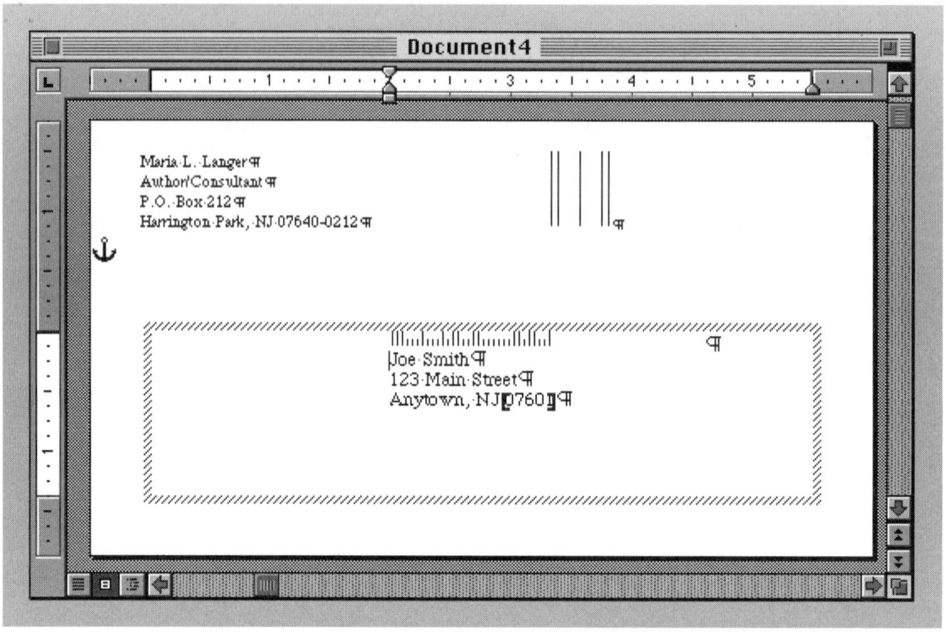

As you can see here, the delivery address and bar code are enclosed in frames so they can be positioned properly on the envelope. So is the FIM-A, if you include one. I told you about frames in Chapter 13.

IMPORTANT NOTE

If an envelope already exists in the document, the Add to Document button changes to a Change Document button. When you click it, Word replaces the original envelope with an envelope created with current settings.

Once your envelope is part of a document, you can add graphics (as I discussed in Chapter 12) or additional text, or you can edit either address. When it comes time to print, choose Print from the File menu or press ⌘P. The document Print dialog box appears. Because the document includes an envelope, Word expands the Print dialog box to show three additional options.

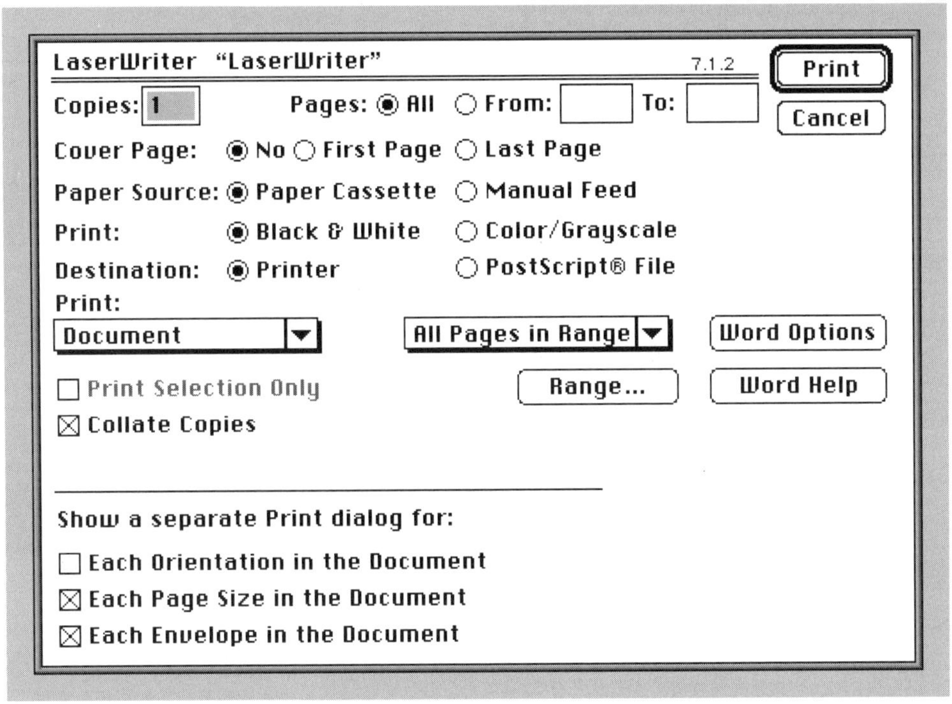

- **Each Orientation in the Document** — when turned on, tells Word to display a Print dialog box before it changes the page orientation.
- **Each Page Size in the Document** — when turned on, tells Word to display a Print dialog box before it changes the paper size. Turning this on is a good idea because it alerts you to insert the correct paper (or envelope) before Word prints.
- **Each Envelope in the Document** — when turned on, tells Word to display a Print dialog box before it prints each envelope in the document. Turning this on is also a good idea because it alerts you to insert an envelope before Word prints.

Choose the appropriate options and click Print to begin printing. If other Print dialog boxes, appear, they will identify the sections they apply to. Click Print to continue printing.

I discussed orientation, paper sizes, and sections in Chapter 8. I discussed the Print dialog box in Chapter 4.

TIP/TRICK

To have Word automatically add custom text or graphics to any envelope you print from a template, create up to two AutoText entries in that template, one for each bit of text or graphic, and name them *EnvelopeExtra1* and *EnvelopeExtra2*. The AutoText entries will include the item's formatting and positioning information. Those entries, as you defined them, will automatically appear on every envelope you print with the template that includes them. To stop printing them, delete or rename the AutoText entries. I told you all about AutoText in Chapter 16.

Labels

NEW IN WORD 6

The label printing capabilities of Word version 6 are greatly improved over previous versions of Word. No more weird, difficult-to-use templates! No more painstakingly defining the size of table cells! Word does almost everything you need to do to print labels — almost any kind of labels! In this section, you'll see for yourself.

You create labels with the Envelopes and Labels command under the Tools menu. Choose this command to display the Envelopes and Labels dialog box. To work with labels, click the Labels tab to display its options.

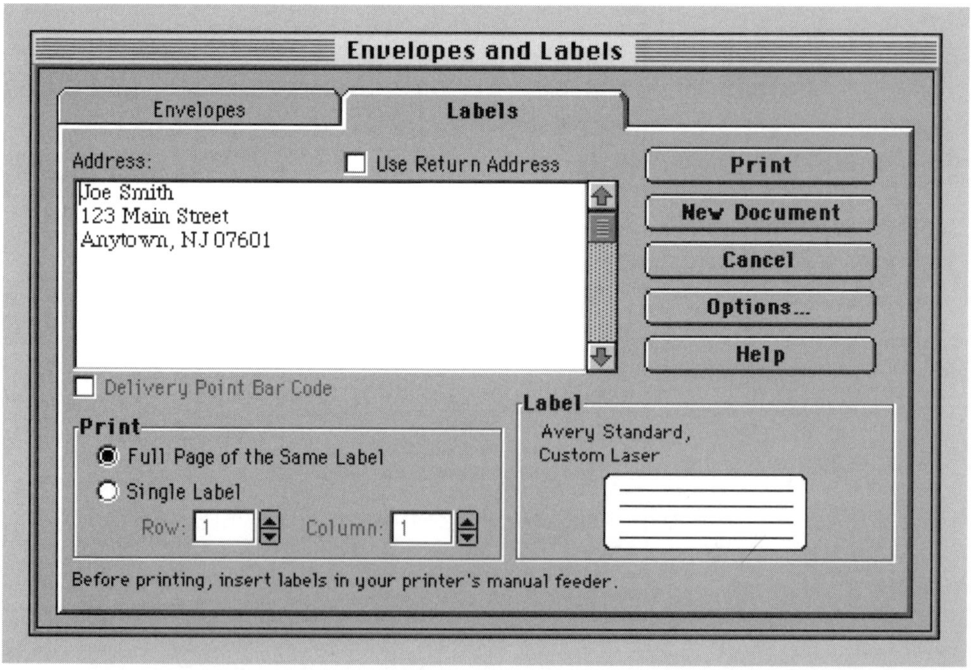

Specifying an Address

When I told you about addressing envelopes, I showed you how smart Word is. It can read the delivery address in a letter and place it in the Envelopes and Labels dialog box. It should come as no surprise, therefore, that it can perform this feat whether you're creating an envelope or a label.

But what if you don't want to use the address it came up with? Or what if you don't want to create a mailing label at all? You can enter new text or edit existing text in the Address edit box of the Labels tab. If you want to create a return address label, turn the Use Return Address check box on. Word inserts the last return address you used or the one set in the User Info tab of the Options dialog box. I'll tell you more about this in Chapter 23.

If you do have a mailing label and you want it to include a POSTNET bar code, turn on the check box for Delivery Point Bar Code. I told you about POSTNET bar codes earlier in this chapter.

Telling Word What to Print

You can print a full page of the same label or a single label. Use radio buttons to choose.

- If you choose the radio button for Full Page of the Same Label, Word fills an entire page of labels with whatever is in the Address box.
- If you choose the radio button for Single Label, the two edit boxes beneath it become active. Choose the label position you want to print by entering row and column numbers in the edit boxes. For example, say you've got a sheet of laser labels that's already half used up. You want to print on the next available label, which is the fourth from the top and the second from the left. Enter 4 in the Row edit box and 2 in the Column edit box to choose that label.

TIP/TRICK

Here's something I've learned from experience. If you're going to print and use laser labels one at a time, start at the *bottom* of the sheet. If you start at the top and peel the labels off as you use them, the thinness of the label backing can make the sheet jam in your printer when it's only half used up. I don't know if you've noticed, but laser labels can be expensive!

Setting Label Options

To choose the proper label size, you'll need to access the Label Options dialog box. Do this by clicking the Options button or the Label illustration in the lower right side of the Envelopes and Labels dialog box.

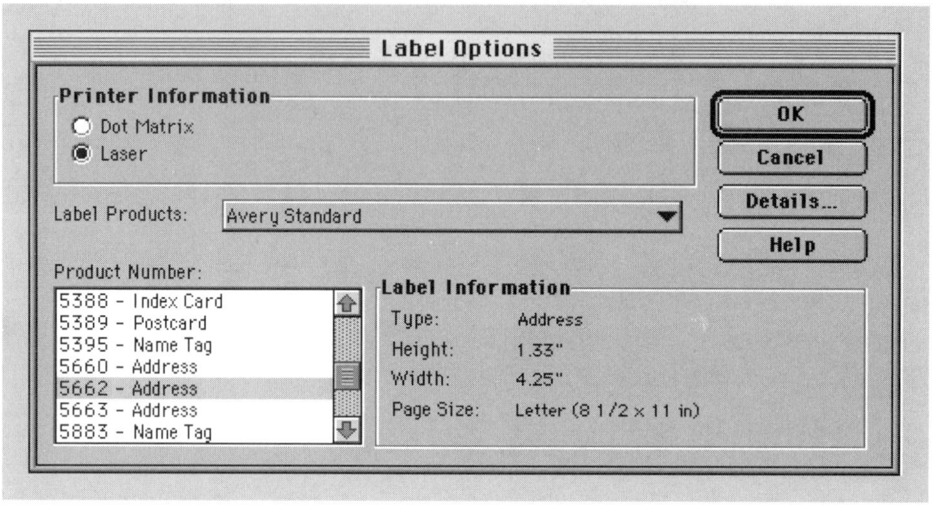

Choosing a Label

To choose a label, begin by telling Word whether your printer is a dot matrix printer like an ImageWriter or a laser printer like a LaserWriter. Then choose the appropriate option from the Label Products pop-up menu. Word supports labels made by Avery, CoStar, and a few other companies. Once you choose a product maker, you can select a Product Number from the scrolling list. You may be surprised by the variety of labels types supported — I certainly was. Word can print address labels, shipping labels, name tags, file folder labels, diskette labels, index cards, post cards, video tape labels, audio tape labels — you name it! All labels are identified with a product number. You can find the product number on the box your labels came in. Once you've selected the label you need, click OK to go back to the Envelopes and Labels dialog box.

Customizing a Label

If your labels aren't included on the list you can create a custom label format. Click the Details button or anywhere within the Label Information area of the Label Options dialog box. The Custom Laser Information or Custom Dot Matrix Information dialog box appears.

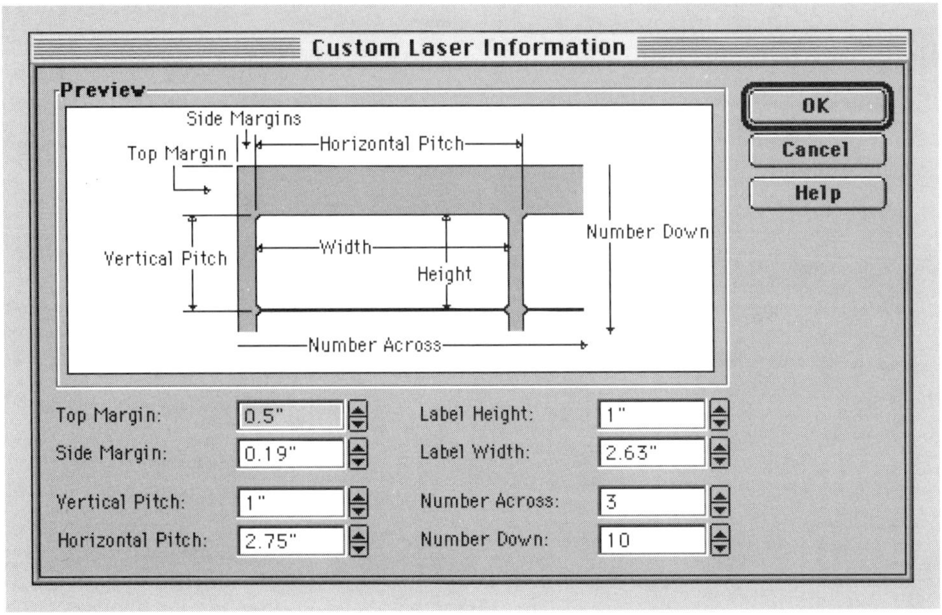

Make appropriate changes in the edit boxes to set the specifications for your labels. Each time you make a change, the Preview area of the dialog box changes accordingly. Each measurement is clearly identified in the Preview so it's not tough to enter the right numbers in the right boxes. When you're all finished, click OK. A confirmation dialog box appears asking if you want to save changes to the custom label information. Click OK to accept your changes and return to the Label Options dialog box.

Printing Labels

To print your labels, click the Print button in the Envelopes and Labels dialog box. A Print dialog box appears. Set the number of copies and paper source, if necessary, and click Print. Word prints the labels.

Creating a Label Document

If you want to create a sheet of labels, each with something different inside them, you can have Word set up a table with cells the same size as your labels. Begin by selecting the proper label size as previously shown. Make sure the Address edit box in the Envelopes and Labels dialog box is empty or contains only the information that you want printed on every label. Select the Full Page of Every Label radio button. Then click the New Document button.

Word creates a full page table with a cell corresponding to each label on the sheet. You can enter information into this template, add graphics to it, format it using standard formatting techniques I discussed in Chapters 5, 6, and 7, and print the labels just as you would any other table. You can even save the document to use the labels again another time. (See Chapter 11 for more information on tables.)

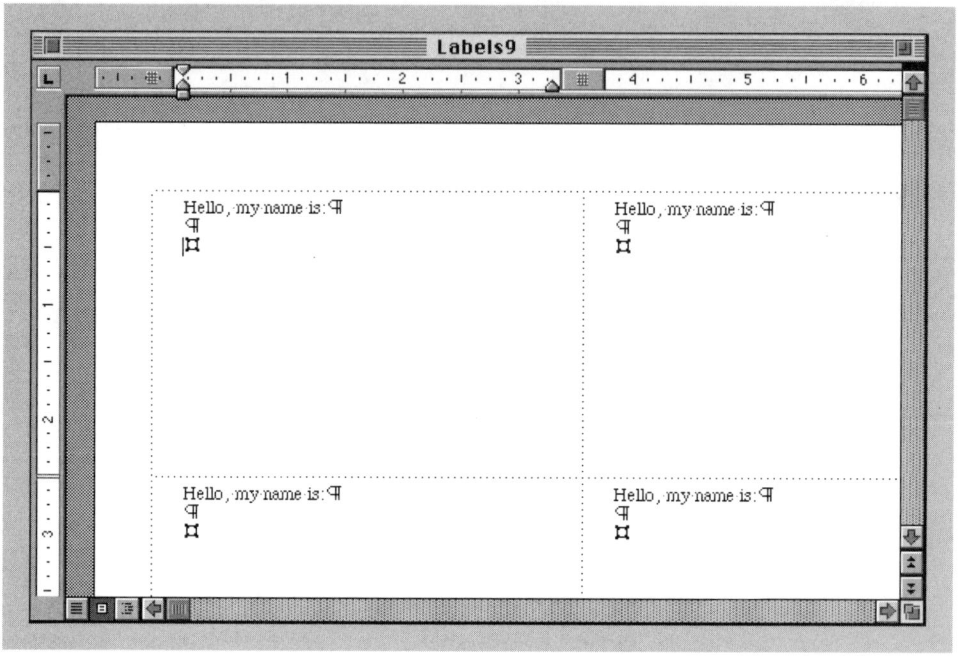

Chapter Summary

In this chapter, you learned how to use Word to create and print envelopes and labels. You saw how Word combines flexibility with ease of use — standard envelope and label sizes are provided, but you can create custom settings. You also learned to add custom text or graphics to envelopes and customize labels before printing. While you might not consider Word the ultimate envelope or label printing utility, it certainly does a fine job handling both tasks.

In the next chapter, you'll tackle Word's new Index and Tables command. You'll see how you can use it to create an index, a table of contents, a table of figures, or a table of authorities. If you create long documents that need these features to help readers find information, read on.

20

Chapter 20: Indexes and Tables of Contents

WOULD YOU BUY A NONFICTION BOOK THAT DIDN'T INCLUDE a table of contents or index? I hope not! Two of the most important parts of any book are the table of contents and index. They make it possible to find information quickly when you need it. But books aren't the only documents that can benefit from a good table of contents and index. Long documents like manuals, legal briefs, reports, and proposals can also be made more reader friendly by the inclusion of either or both of these components.

NEW IN WORD 6

Word's new Index and Tables command takes a lot of the drudgery out of creating complete and accurate indexes, tables of contents, tables of figures, and tables of authorities. With a little preparation beforehand, these features can be added to a document with a few mouse clicks. In this chapter, you'll learn how.

TIP/TRICK

To create an index or table of contents for a book or other very long work, use Word's Master Document feature to organize separate document files into one master document file. Then generate the index or table of contents based on that master document. I told you all about master documents back in Chapter 15.

Creating an Index

An index can improve any long document by making it easy for readers to find specific information in an alphabetical listing of topics along with page references. While a table of contents can point you in the general direction, an index tells you precisely where to go.

Creating an index with Microsoft Word is basically a two-step process. You begin by marking text within the document as index entries. That's the hard part since it'll take time and patience. Once that's finished, you tell Word to compile the index. That's the easy part since Word does all the work. In this section, I'll tell you how to create index entries and how to compile and format an index with Word.

NEW IN WORD 6

Although the Indexing feature in Word is not new to version 6.0, it has changed considerably. It is now more powerful and flexible than ever. If you've used the index feature before, you'll see what I mean as you go through this section of the chapter.

FYI: The Importance of an Index

When I'm browsing the bookstore shelves, the first thing I look at in any nonfiction book is its index. I think of a topic I want to know about and see if there's a listing for it in the index. If there isn't, I put the book down and try another. If there is, I keep browsing. It's for this reason that I think an index is even more important than a table of contents — it's where I look first.

Continued

Creating an index is an art. You need to be familiar with the material you're indexing. You need to know what terms and concepts readers will want to find. Finally, you need to be able to imagine all the different ways readers will look up a complex topic — and provide for all of them.

I admit that I've only had to index an entire book once. Publishers often use professional indexers to index books. After doing one index, I know why — it's tough work that requires a lot of concentration and a "method." If you're good at indexing, you might consider making a career out of it. Think of all you can learn!

Marking Index Entries

In order to create an index, you need to tell Word what you want to include in it. You do this by creating or marking index entries within the document and its footnotes and endnotes. An index entry can be a simple reference to one page, can be a reference spanning multiple pages, or can include cross-references to other index entries. I'll tell you how to create all these kinds of entries in this section.

Creating a Simple Index Entry

To create a simple index entry, begin by finding and selecting text you want to index. The text can be any number of words, but in most cases, you'll want to limit it to a single word or phrase. Once you've got the text selected, press ⌘ Option Shift X. (Don't blame me! I don't make up these shortcut keys!) The Mark Index Entry dialog box appears.

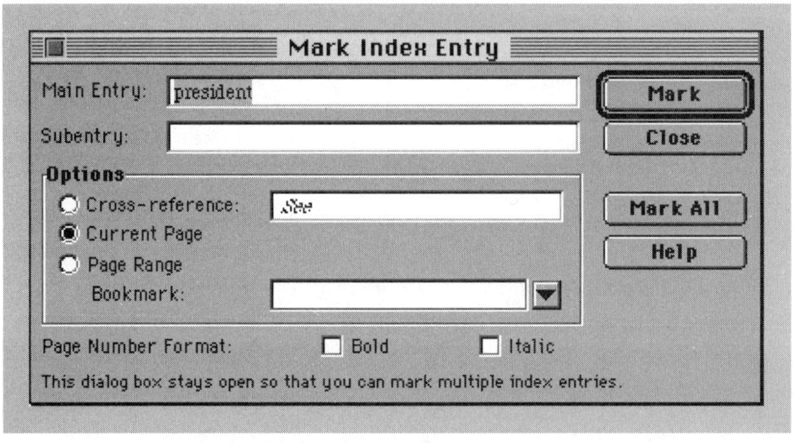

The text you selected appears in the Main Entry edit box. If desired, you can edit the entry text. For example, you might want to change the case to keep it consistent with other entries for the same topic or add additional text to refine the entry.

You can create a subentry for the entry by typing it into the Subentry edit box. This makes it possible to refer to a specific subtopic of the main topic. For example, in my index of the US Constitution, I might want to add a subentry called *commander in chief* to the main entry *president*. You can create another subentry entry if you like by adding a colon (:) after the Subentry text and typing it in.

To apply font formatting like bold or italics to entry or subentry text, select the text and use the appropriate shortcut key. For example, ⌘B makes text bold and ⌘I makes text italic. Don't use the Formatting toolbar buttons — they'll make changes in the document itself. To have the page reference appear in bold or italic (or both), click the Bold or Italic check box beside Page Number Format. I told you all about font formatting back in Chapter 5.

Make sure the radio button beside Current Page is turned on and click either Mark or Mark all to create the entry. The Mark button marks only the single selected occurrence of the word as an index entry. The Mark All button marks the occurrence of the word in any paragraph throughout the document, as long as the entry exactly matches the occurrence — including the use of upper and lowercase characters. This is particularly handy if the word is used often in the document. If you click Mark All, the marking process takes longer to complete since Word has to search the document for every occurrence of the word. A message in the Status bar tells you what Word is doing and indicates how many entries were marked.

When Word is finished marking entries, the Mark Index Entry dialog box remains on your screen so you can use it again. If you look at the document text with nonprinting characters displayed (click Show/Hide ¶ to display them if necessary), you'll see how Word created the index entry. It inserts index codes formatted as hidden text. Here's my simple *president* entry, which included a subentry for *commander in chief*:

To create another entry, simply select the entry text in the document window and click on the Mark Index Entry dialog box to make it active. You'll find that the text you selected is automatically inserted in the Main Entry edit box. Follow the previous procedure to create the new entry.

To create multiple entries for the same text, you don't need to select it each time. Simply position the insertion point right after the text or existing entries for it. Then use the Mark Index Entry dialog box to create and insert the entry.

TIP/TRICK

FYI: What those Codes Mean

In case you're wondering, XE stands for index entry. You'll find those two characters in every index entry you create. Index entries are really fields, but unlike other fields, the index field does not show its results in the document.

The entire index entry appears between curly brackets: {}. Any subentries appear within double quote characters. The main entry comes first followed by a colon and the subentry text. The dotted line you see beneath the text indicates that it's formatted as hidden text. I told you about hidden text in Chapter 5.

In addition to all this, index entries can include "switches" that turn features on or off. You may see these in the entries you create, so here's a list:

Switch	Purpose
\b	Makes the page number for the index entry bold.
\f	Defines an entry type for documents with multiple indexes. The switch would be followed by the entry type code enclosed in double quotes.
\i	Makes the page number for the index entry italic.
\r	Includes the range of pages marked by a bookmark. The switch would be followed by the name of the bookmark enclosed in double quotes.
\t	Inserts text in the entry instead of a page number. The switch would be followed by the desired text enclosed in double quotes.

Creating a Multiple-Page Entry

If you want an entry to refer to multiple pages, you need to mark the page range with a bookmark first. I told you about bookmarks back in Chapter 14. If you skipped over that chapter, you might want to go back and read the Bookmark section now. I'll wait for you here.

You understand bookmarks? Okay, let's move on.

Select the text you want to make an entry for. If the Mark Index Entry dialog box is not open, press ⌘ Option Shift X to open it. If it is open, click on it to make it active. Set the Main Entry and Subentry edit box as I instructed earlier to reflect the desired entry text and formatting. Then click the Page Range radio button under Options to select it. Use the Bookmark pop-up menu to select the bookmark you created for the page range — all the bookmarks in the document are listed. Then click Mark.

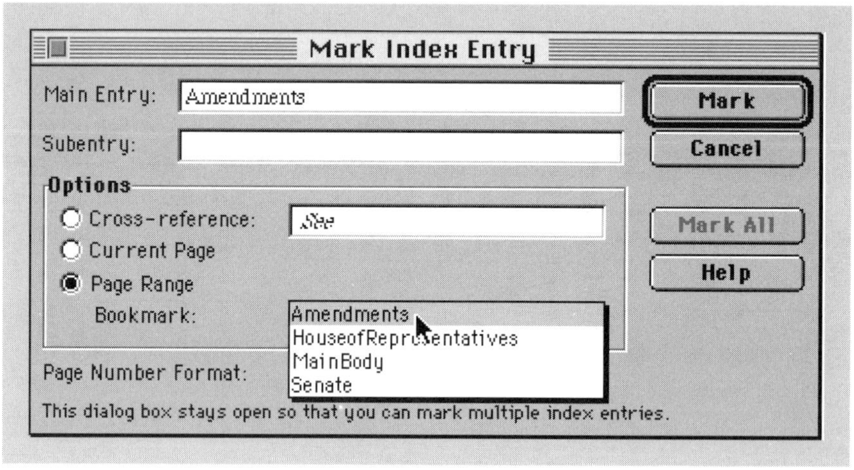

Here's how Word marks the entry in my document:

```
"AMENDMENTS{ XE "Amendments" \r "Amendments" }¶
```

Creating an Entry with a Cross-Reference

You can also create an entry that includes a cross-reference to another entry. This is especially useful if a topic has several different names and you want to guide readers to the name you're using in the index. For example, say I know that some people use the phrase *commander in chief* to refer to the *president*. I might use a cross reference to refer them to *president* entries when they're looking up *commander in chief*. Here's how to do that.

Position the insertion point where you want the entry in your document. Since the entry does not refer to a specific page or print, it doesn't matter where you put it. If the Mark Index Entry dialog box isn't showing, press ⌘ Option Shift X to display it. If it is showing, click it to make it active.

Enter the text you want to use for the entry in the Main Entry edit box. If desired, enter a subentry in the Subentry edit box. Click on the radio button for Cross-reference. Enter the entry you want to refer to in the Cross-reference edit box. You can enter it after the word *see* which is already there by default or remove it and enter your own text. Then click Mark to create the entry.

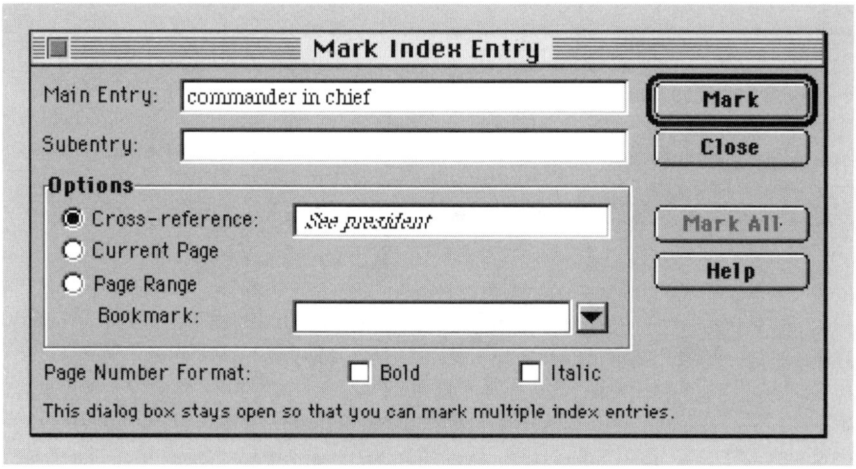

Automatically Adding Index Entries

As you can imagine, marking entries for an index can be very time consuming. If you prefer, you can have Word automatically generate entries based on words you specify in advance. While this is not as flexible or reliable as manually marking entries, it certainly can save time. Here's how you can do it.

I don't think I'd ever depend on automatic entries for an entire index, but I think it would be especially helpful for indexing proper names used throughout a document. Use automatic entries to index the "easy" stuff and then sit down and review the entire document to add or remove entries as you see fit.

TIP/TRICK

Creating a Concordance File

In order for Word to know what words it should index, you need to create a list of them. The list you create is saved in what's called a *concordance file*, which must be specially formatted.

To create a concordance file, create a brand new document and insert a two-column table in it. I told you how to create and work with tables in Chapter 11. In the first column of the table, list the words you want Word to look for in the document, one word per cell. Since Word will perform a case-sensitive search, be sure to list the word twice if some occurrences might be capitalized. In the second column of the document, list the corresponding text you want to use as the main index entry for each word. When you're all finished, save the file.

Marking Index Entries

To use the concordance file to mark index entries, begin by opening the document you want to index. Choose Index and Tables from the Insert menu. The Index and Tables dialog box, which I'll tell you about in more detail in a few minutes, appears. If necessary, click the Index tab to display its options. Then click the AutoMark button. Word displays a standard Open dialog box you can use to find and open the concordance file you created for the index.

When you open the file, Word gets right to work. You can watch its progress by checking the message on the Status bar. When it's finished, your document contains index entries for all the words you listed in the left column of the concordance file, utilizing words you listed in the right column of the file.

IMPORTANT NOTE

Don't depend on this method to create index entries. Word takes you very literally and can include entries you don't want and exclude entries you do want. Check the entries Word created in your document before accepting them. If there's an entry you'd rather not have, delete it before compiling the index.

Compiling an Index

Once you've created index entries, it's time to put Word to work compiling the index. Position the insertion point where you want the index to appear (normally at the end of the document) and choose Index and Tables from the Insert menu. The Index and Tables dialog box appears. If necessary, click the Index tab to display its options.

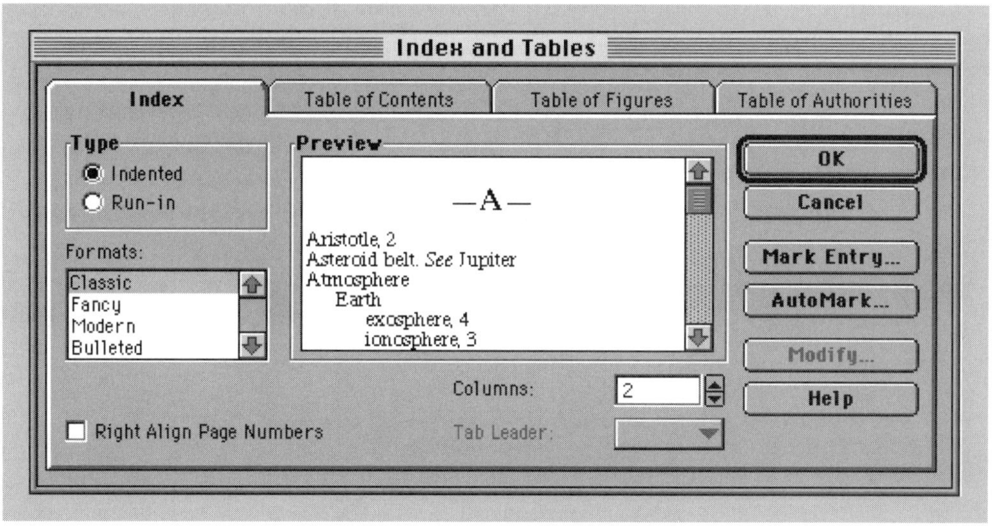

This dialog box lets you choose a format for the index. Several standard formats that you can customize are included. If you prefer, you can create your own custom format — I'll tell you about that near the end of this chapter.

To choose a format, begin by clicking the appropriate type radio button: Indented or Run-in. In an Indented index, each index level and page number in the entry appear on a separate line. In a Run-in index, all index levels and page numbers in the entry appear on the same line, wrapping around to the next line if necessary. Then choose a specific format from the Format scrolling list. If you're not sure which type and format you like, use your mouse to make selections and view them in the Preview window. Call me old fashioned, but my favorite is the Indented Classic, which is shown in the previous illustration.

Once you've selected a type and format, you can customize it with the options on the bottom of the dialog box.

- **Right Align Page Numbers —** when turned on, aligns the page numbers on the right side of the column.
- **Tab Leader —** is a pop-up menu that becomes active only when Right Align Page Numbers is turned on. Use it to pick a tab leader — a character that appears between the index entry text and the page number. I told you about tab leaders in Chapter 6.
- **Columns —** is an edit box you can use to tell Word how many columns to format the index in. The default value is 2, but you might want to change it to 3 if your index contains a lot of short entries and you want to print it on fewer pages.

When you're all finished making formatting selections, click the OK button. Word gets right to work and displays a message about what it's doing in the Status bar. First it repaginates the document. Then it searches for index entries. Finally, it compiles the index and displays it in your document, separating it from the rest of your document with a section break. In Page Layout view, it might look something like this:

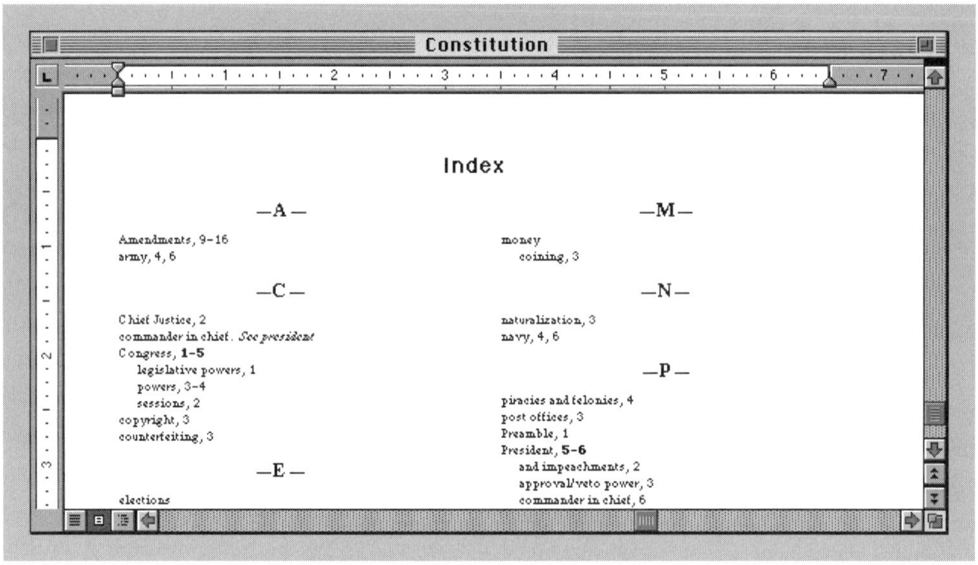

If you already have an index in your document when you click OK, Word will select that index and ask if you want to replace it. Click Yes to replace the existing index with a new index. Click No to create an additional index.

FYI: Fields and the Index and Tables Command

When you insert an index, table of contents, table of figures, or table of authorities in your document, you're really inserting an INDEX, TOC, or TOA field. A *field* is a special code Word uses to show information. XE, TC, and TA are three other fields I discuss throughout this chapter.

If you see weird codes like {INDEX \h "-A-" \c "2"} or {TOC \c "TABLE"} in your document rather than an index or table, you'll need to turn off Field Codes in the View tab of the Options dialog box. You can open the Options dialog box by choosing Options from the Tools menu. I'll tell you more about Options in Chapter 23.

TIP/TRICK

To see a field code rather than its results without turning on the Field Codes option in the Options dialog box, click on the field results to highlight it and press [Shift][F9] (on an extended keyboard). The codes appear for that one field only. To toggle back to view the field results, click on the field and press [Shift][F9] again. You may find that displaying the field codes makes it quicker to scroll in your document than to display the results of the codes.

You can change the appearance of an index or table by modifying the field codes Word inserts. The fields utilize switches that turn certain formatting options on or off. You can learn more about the switches a field uses by choosing Field from the Insert menu to display the Field dialog box and then clicking the Options button.

TIP/TRICK

If you need to, you can convert the results of a field to text to make it easier to edit or work with. Click anywhere on the field and press [⌘][6] or [⌘][Shift][F9] (extended keyboard only). The field is replaced by its results. You can then edit to your heart's content. Just remember that once you convert a field to text, Word no longer recognizes it as a field. It cannot be converted back.

Creating a Table of Contents

A table of contents is a vital component of any long document. It tells readers where they can find discussions of broad topics within the document. Unlike an index, a table of contents is not organized alphabetically. It's organized in the same order as the document itself. In fact, the table of contents usually corresponds to headings used in the document to introduce topics to readers.

Like an index, a table of contents takes two steps to prepare. The first step is to create table of contents entries. If you used Word's outline feature to create your document, you're already done with that step, as you'll see in a moment. If not, you'll have to do a bit more work. The second step is to tell Word to compile the table of contents based on headings, other styles, or table of contents entries. In this section, I'll tell you how to prepare, compile, and format a table of contents with Word.

NEW IN WORD 6

The Table of Contents feature is not new to Word version 6.0, but there are some important changes. I'll do my best to point these out throughout this section.

Based on Built-in Heading Styles

Word builds a table of contents based on table of contents entries you identify within your document. The easiest way to identify a table of contents entry is to format the text with one of Word's built-in heading styles. If you created your document with Word's outlining feature, you've probably already applied the built-in heading styles named Heading 1 through Heading 9 to section headings in your document. I told you about heading styles and hinted about their usefulness for generating a table of contents back in Chapter 15.

If you didn't use Word's outlining feature to create your document, it isn't too late to apply the built-in heading styles. Select a document heading and choose the appropriate heading style from the Style box pop-up menu on the Formatting Toolbar. Apply Heading 1 for a top-level heading, Heading 2 for a second-level heading, Heading 3 for a third-level heading, and so on. If the heading styles are not displayed on the Style box pop-up menu, hold down Shift while pulling the menu down to see them.

TIP/TRICK

If you don't like the appearance of Word's built-in heading styles, you can always change them by modifying the styles. I told you how in Chapter 7.

To have Word compile the table of contents, position the insertion point where you want the table of contents to appear (usually somewhere near the beginning of the document). Choose Index and Tables from the Insert menu. The Index and Tables dialog box appears. If necessary, click the Table of Contents tab to display its options.

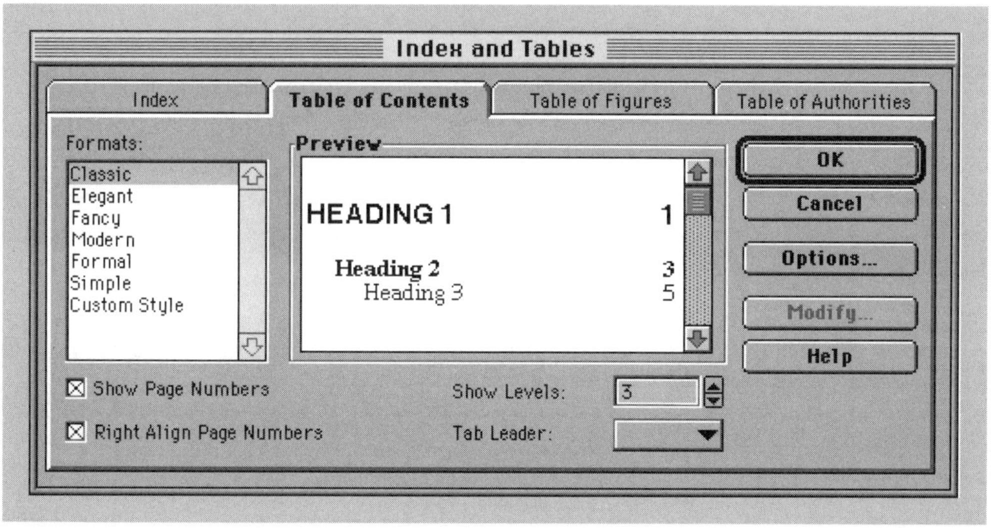

Begin by choosing a format for your table of contents from the Formats scrolling list. The preview window changes each time you click a different option. My favorite is Formal. If you don't like the formats Word offers, you can create your own custom format — I'll tell you how later in this chapter.

Once you've selected a format, you can customize it with the following options:

- **Show Page Numbers** — when turned on, shows the page numbers as part of the table of contents. In most cases, you'll want this turned on. After all, what good is a table of contents if it doesn't show page numbers?

- **Right Align Page Numbers** — when turned on, aligns page numbers against the right side of the page.

- **Show Levels** — is an edit box where you can enter the number of table of contents levels you want to see in the table of contents. Just because you used Heading 1 through Heading 6 in your document, doesn't mean you need to include all those entries in a table of contents. The default value is 3.

- **Tab Leader** — is a pop-up menu you can use to select a tab leader. This option is only available when the Right Align Page Numbers check box is turned on. I told you about tab leaders earlier in this chapter and in Chapter 6.

When you're all finished making formatting selections, click the OK button. Word begins building the table of contents by searching for text formatted with the Heading styles. It then repaginates the document and updates the table of contents entries it finds. You can check Word's progress by monitoring the messages that appear in the status bar. Finally, Word displays the table of contents in your document. Here's part of mine:

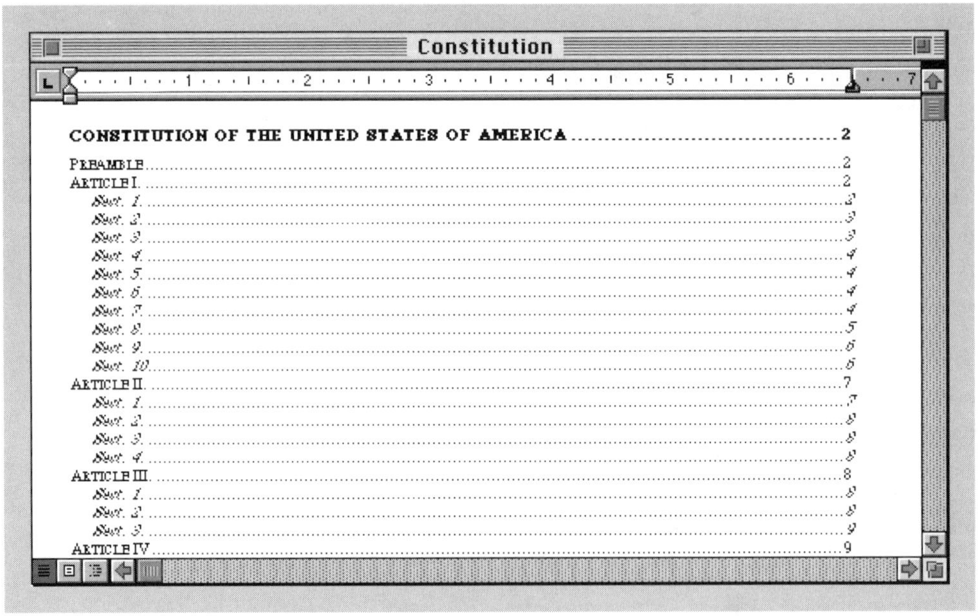

If you already have a table of contents in your document when you click OK, Word will select it and ask if you want to replace it. Click Yes to replace the existing table of contents with a new one. Click No to create an additional table of contents.

Based on Other Styles

NEW IN WORD 6

If you've used styles for headings throughout your document but not Word's built-in styles, don't panic. There's hope for you yet. You can tell Word to use your heading styles rather than Word's when it generates the table of contents. Here's how.

Choose Index and Tables from the Insert menu to open the Index and Tables dialog box. If necessary, click the Table of Contents tab to display its options. Then click the Options button.

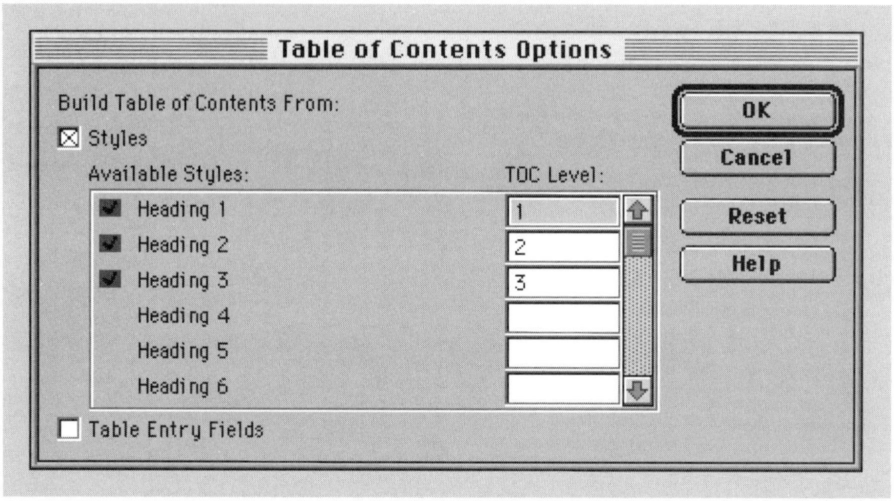

The Table of Contents Options dialog box lets you tell Word what styles you want to use to build a table of contents. By default, the dialog box displays the Heading Styles as TOC Levels 1, 2, and 3. But if you use the Scroll bar to scroll down the list, you'll find the rest of your document's styles listed. Click in the TOC Level edit box beside the style you want to use for a table of contents entry and enter the appropriate level number. When you're finished, it might look something like this:

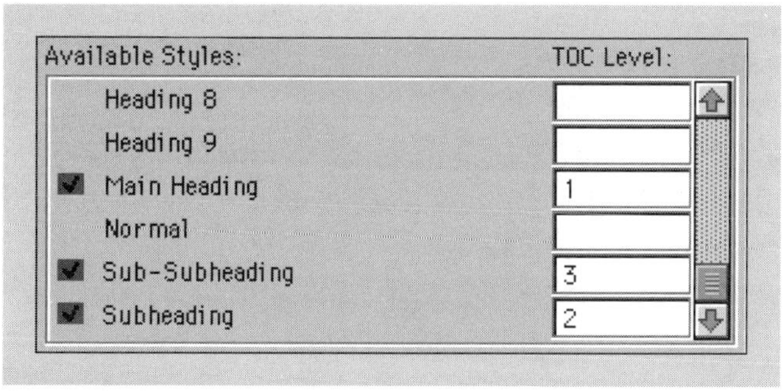

If you want to restore the settings to Word's defaults, click Reset. Otherwise, click OK to accept your changes.

Back in the Index and Tables dialog box, use the previous discussed steps to select the table of contents format. Click OK to compile the table of contents.

Based on TC Entry Fields

There's a third way to identify table of contents entries: by marking them as table of contents (TC) entries. When it's time to compile the table of contents, you tell Word to gather TC field entries rather than headings. Here's how.

Inserting TC Entry Fields

To insert a TC entry in your document, select the text you want to include in the table of contents. Press [⌘][Option][Shift][O] (that's the letter O not a zero). The Mark Table of Contents Entry dialog box appears.

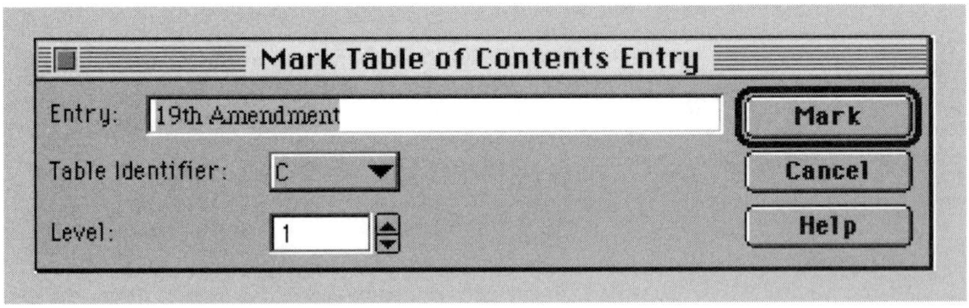

The text you selected appears in the Entry edit box. You can edit it if necessary so it says exactly what you want it to say in the table of contents.

The Table Identifier pop-up menu lets you select a code to apply to the table of contents entry. This makes it possible to have more than one table of contents in a document or to use the Mark Table of Contents Entry dialog box to mark entries for a table of figures (as you'll see in a while). All letters of the alphabet, from A to Z, are included on the menu. The default setting is C (for *contents*) — you don't need to change it unless you want more than one table of contents.

Finally, use the Level edit box to enter a value from 1 to 9 to set the table of contents level for the entry. Then click Mark to mark the entry.

A TC entry field is inserted in your document as hidden text. If nonprinting characters are not displayed, you won't be able to see the field — click the Show/Hide ¶ button to display them. When you're finished, it might look something like this:

19th·Amendment{·TC·"19th·Amendment"·\f·C·\l·"1"·}

The Mark Table of Contents Entry dialog box remains open so you can select and mark other entries. Click in the document window to make it active and select text you want to mark. Then click in the dialog box to make it active, make necessary changes, and mark the entry. You'll need to insert a TC field for every entry you want to include in your document. When you're all finished, click the Close button or the close box to close the Mark Table of Contents Entry dialog box.

FYI: What those Codes Mean

TC stands for table of contents entry. A TC field is a lot like an XE field. It's a special field code you can insert into a document to tell Word that certain text should be used for a table of contents entry. Like XE fields, TC fields can include "switches" that turn features on or off. Here's a list for reference:

Switch	Purpose
\f	Identifies the TC entry for documents with multiple tables. The switch should be followed by an entry identifier letter. When Word generates a table of contents, it can create multiple tables of contents based on the entry identifiers.
\l	Identifies the outline level of the entry. The switch should be followed by a number from 1 to 9.
\n	Turns off page numbering for the entry.

Compiling the Table of Contents

When you're finished marking table of contents entries, you can tell Word to compile the table of contents. Choose Index and Tables from the Insert menu and, if necessary, click the Table of Contents tab to display its options. Then click the Options button to display the Table of Contents Options dialog box. At the bottom of the dialog box is a check box marked Table Entry Fields. Turn this check box on and click OK. This tells Word to create the table of contents based on the TC fields you inserted in your document.

Back in the Index and Tables dialog box, choose the table of contents format you want to use, as discussed earlier in this chapter. Then click OK to generate the table of contents.

Creating a Table of Figures

NEW IN WORD 6

A table of figures is another kind of table you can create with Word. It lets you list and provide page numbers for figures, illustrations, tables, or any other object you identify. The table of figures is brand new and works in conjunction with the new Captions feature, which I discussed in Chapter 14.

As you may have guessed by now, you create a table of figures much like you create an index or table of contents. It's a two step process. The first step is to identify table entries. This is most easily done by using the Caption command on the Insert menu, but Word also lets you create a table of figures based on styles or TC entries. The second step is to tell Word to compile the table of figures. In this section, I'll tell you how to create a table of figures for your documents.

Based on Captions

If you've used Word's Caption feature to add captions to each figure, illustration, table, or other object in your document, you're all set to create your table of figures. I told you about captions in Chapter 14, so if you want more information about creating them, look there.

To compile a table of figures based on captions, begin by positioning the insertion point where you want your table of figures to appear. The usual place is right after the table of contents, if you have one. Then choose Index and Tables from the Insert menu to display the Index and Tables dialog box. If necessary, click the Table of Figures tab to display its options.

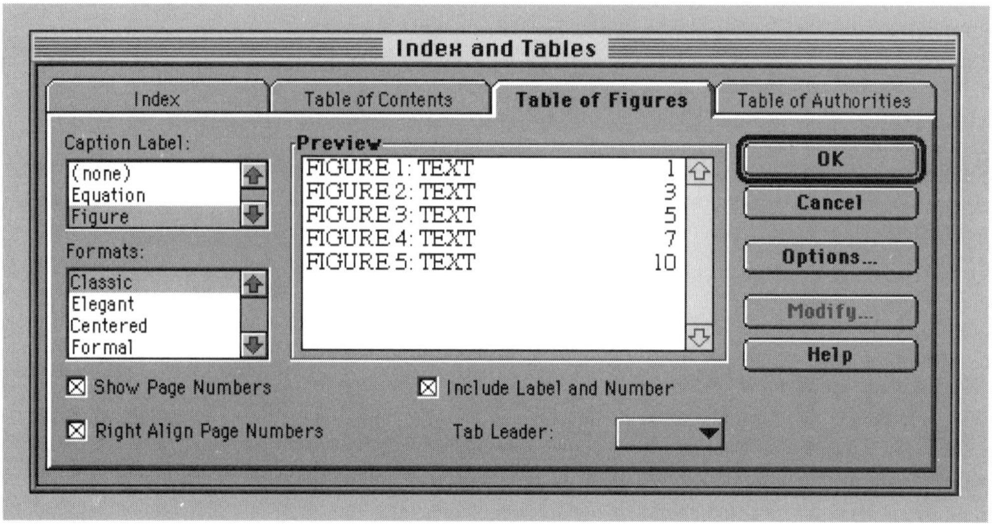

Begin by telling Word what caption labels you want to gather for the table of figures. The Caption Label scrolling list displays a list of all caption labels within the document. Then click on the name of a format in the Formats scrolling list. The contents of the Preview window change depending on the caption label and format you choose. My favorite is Formal. If you don't like the built-in formats, you can create your own custom format. I'll tell you how near the end of this chapter.

Once you've selected a format, you can customize it with options on the bottom of the dialog box.

- **Show Page Numbers** — when turned on, shows the page numbers as part of the table of figures. In most cases, you'll want this turned on.
- **Right Align Page Numbers** — when turned on, aligns page numbers against the right side of the page.
- **Include Label and Number** — when turned on, displays both the caption label and number as part of the entry.
- **Tab Leader** — is a pop-up menu you can use to select a tab leader. This option is only available when the Right Align Page Numbers check box is turned on. I told you about tab leaders earlier in this chapter and in Chapter 6.

When you're all finished making formatting selections, click OK. Word begins building the table of figures by searching for captions. It then repaginates the document and updates the table of figures entries it found. You can check Word's progress by monitoring the messages that appear in the Status bar. Finally, Word displays the table of figures in your document.

You can repeat this process for every caption label in your document. Word is smart enough to generate a different table for each caption, so you don't have to worry about overwriting one table with another. If you already have a table based on a selected caption when you click OK, Word will select it and ask if you want to replace it. Click Yes to replace the existing table with a new one. Click No to create an additional table.

Based on other Styles

If you haven't used captions to identify figures in your document, but you have formatted the names of figures with consistently used styles, you can use those styles to generate a table of figures. While this requires a bit more effort on your part, it isn't tough to do.

Position the insertion point where you want the table of figures to appear. Choose Index and Tables from the Insert menu and, if necessary, click the Table of Figures tab. Click the Options button to display the Table of Figures Options dialog box.

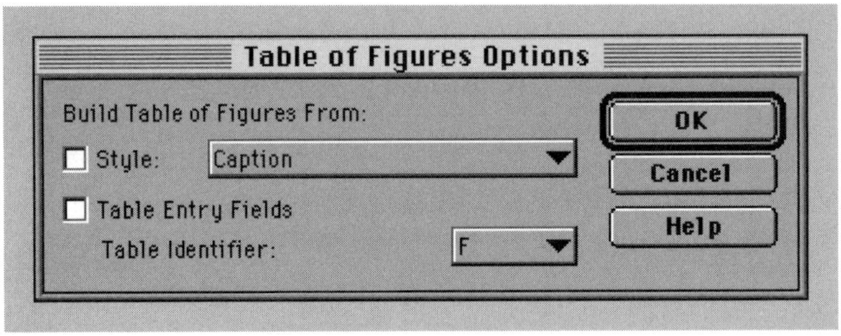

Turn on the Style check box and use the pop-up menu beside it to choose the style you've used to identify figures in your document. Then choose a letter from the Table Identifier pop-up menu. This letter distinguishes one table of figures from another since Word can't use caption labels to make the distinction. For example, if you used a style called Table Heading to identify tables and another called Figure Name to identify figures, you could assign the letter T to the table of tables and the letter F to the table of figures.

When you're all finished making selections, click OK to accept them and dismiss the dialog box. Then choose the table formatting options as previously discussed and click OK to compile the table of figures. You can repeat these steps for each style used to identify objects in your document.

Based on TC Entry Fields

TIP/TRICK

You can also create a table of figures based on TC entry fields. This is where the options under the Table Indentifier pop-up menu come in handy. Assign a different letter to each type of table you want to create. Word can create a separate table for each letter.

When it comes time to compile the table of figures from TC entries, choose Index and Tables from the Insert menu and click the Table of Figures tab to display its options. Then click the Options button to go to the Table of Figures Options dialog box I previously showed you. This time, turn on the check box for Table Entry Fields. Use the Table Identifier pop-up menu to choose the letter corresponding to the one you set with the Table Indentifier pop-up menu. Then click OK to accept the settings and close the dialog box. Choose the table format you want to use in the Index and Tables dialog box and click OK to compile the table of figures.

Creating a Table of Authorities

NEW IN WORD 6

A table of authorities is a special kind of table commonly used in legal documents. It lists citations — references to cases, statutes, rulings, and regulations — in alphabetical order and provides page numbers for each. The table of authorities feature is also new to Word version 6.

Again, creating a table of authorities is a two-step process. The first step is to identify citation entries. The second step is to tell Word to compile the table of authorities. Let's look at the whole process.

Marking Citation Entries

Before you start, you should understand the difference between long and short citation entries. A long citation contains the full text of the citation, like "**Balthauser & Moyer, Inc. v. Hayden**, 59 N.W. 2d. 828 (N.D. 1953)." The long citation is only used once in a document. Subsequent references to the same case can use a short citation, like "**Balthauser & Moyer, Inc. v. Hayden**." You should review the document before marking citation entries and make sure all long citations appear before their corresponding short citations. If you find one that doesn't, move it.

To mark a citation, select the full citation text and press ⌘ Option Shift I. The Mark Citation dialog box appears.

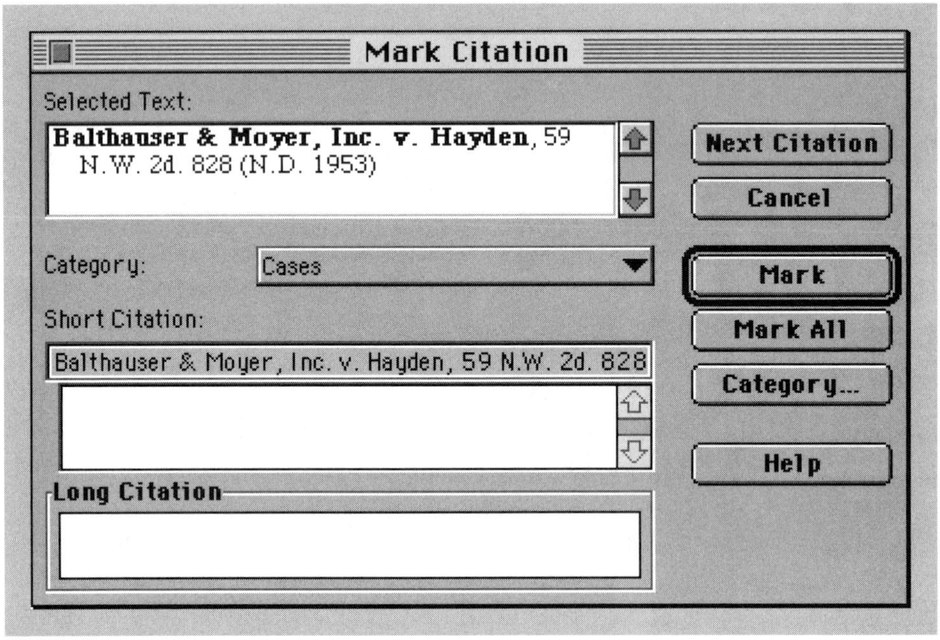

The text you selected appears in the Selected Text and Short Citation edit boxes. Edit the contents of the Selected Text edit box so that it looks the way you want it to appear in the Table of Authorities. You can use standard text editing techniques and apply font formatting with the use of shortcut keys like ⌘ B for bold and ⌘ U for underline.

Choose the citation category from the Category pop-up menu. Word provides 7 commonly-used categories, but you can edit any of them to define a total of 16 custom categories. To modify an existing category or create a new one, click the Category button. The Edit Category dialog box appears. Click the name or number of the category you want to change in the Category scrolling list. Then enter a new name in the Replace With edit box and click Replace. The change you made appears in the Category pop-up menu in the Mark Citation dialog box.

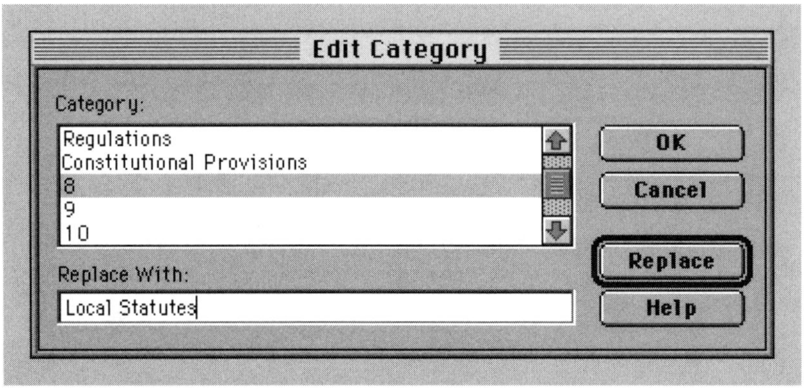

Edit the text in the Short Citation edit box so it matches the short citation you want Word to search for. Then click either the Mark or Mark All button. The Mark button marks only the currently selected citation. The Mark All button marks all citations that match the Selected Text and Short Citation text. Word does a case-sensitive search, so uppercase and lowercase characters must match exactly for text in the document to be marked.

Word marks the entry with special codes it uses to identify entries. You can see this when you look in the document window. If you can't see the codes, that's because nonprinting characters are not displayed — click the Show/Hide ¶ button to display them. The codes are enclosed in curly brackets and formatted as hidden text. This is very similar to the way Word marks index entries. It might look something like this:

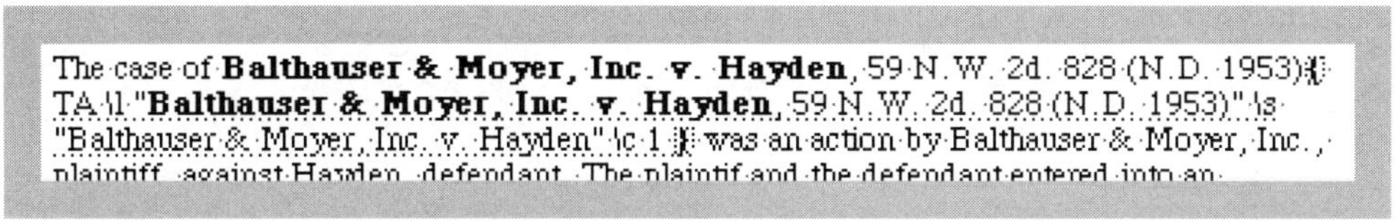
The case of **Balthauser & Moyer, Inc. v. Hayden**, 59 N.W. 2d. 828 (N.D. 1953){ TA \l "**Balthauser & Moyer, Inc. v. Hayden**, 59 N.W. 2d. 828 (N.D. 1953)" \s "Balthauser & Moyer, Inc. v. Hayden" \c 1 } was an action by Balthauser & Moyer, Inc., plaintiff, against Hayden, defendant. The plaintif and the defendant entered into an

The Mark Citation dialog box remains open so you can mark other citations. You can proceed two ways:

- Click in the document window to make it active and select another citation. Then click on the Mark Citation dialog box to make it active and follow the previously detailed steps to mark the entry.

- Click the Next Citation button in the Mark Citation dialog box. Word searches the document for characters normally found in citations, like "v." or "in re." Once Word finds a possible citation, click in the document window to make it active and select the citation. Then click on the Mark Citation dialog box to make it active again and follow the procedures I covered above to mark the entry.

When you're all finished marking citations, click the Cancel button or close box in the Mark Citation dialog box to dismiss it.

FYI: What those Codes Mean

TA stands for table of authorities entry. You'll find those two characters in every table of authorities entry you create. Like index (XE) and table of contents (TC) entries, table of authorities entries are really fields.

In a long citation, the full citation text, enclosed in double quotes, appears right after the \l switch. The short citation, also enclosed in double-quotes, comes next, right after the \s switch. If a short citation is marked, only the short citation appears in the entry.

Here's a list of the possible switches for TA fields:

Switch	Purpose
\b	Makes the page number for the entry bold.
\c	Indicates the category for the citation. The switch is followed by the category number, which corresponds to the order in which categories appear in the Categories pop-up menu. The default is 1 which is Case.
\i	Makes the page number for the entry italic.
\l	Defines the long citation. The switch is followed by the long citation, enclosed in double quotes.
\r	Includes the range of pages marked by a bookmark. The switch is followed by the name of the bookmark enclosed in double quotes.
\s	Defines the short citation. The switch is followed by the short citation, enclosed in double quotes.
\t	Inserts text in the entry instead of a page number. The switch would be followed by the desired text enclosed in double quotes.

Compiling a Table of Authorities

Once you've marked all the citations in your document, you can compile the table of authorities. Position the insertion point where you want the table of authorities to appear. Choose Index and Tables from the Insert menu and, if necessary, click the Table of Authorities tab to display its options.

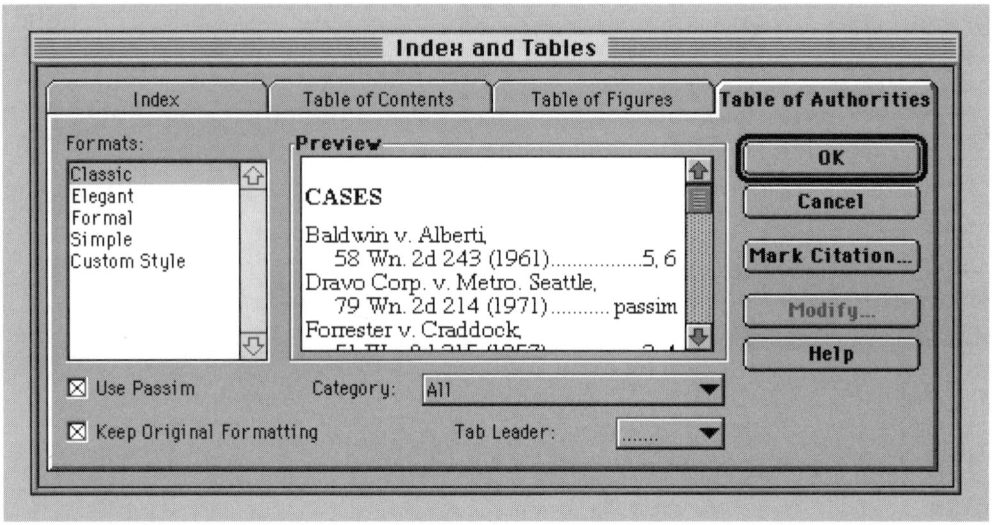

Begin by choosing a format from the Formats scrolling list. The Preview window changes accordingly. My favorite is Classic. If you don't like the formats Word provides, you can create your own custom format. I'll tell you how a little later in this chapter.

Once you've selected a format, you can customize it with the check boxes and pop-up menus at the bottom of the dialog box.

- **Use Passim —** when turned on, replaces five or more references to the same citation with the word *passim*. (I'm no legal eagle and had never heard of this word before I found it in this dialog box, so I looked it up. Passim, which was coined in 1803, means here and there. It has its roots in Latin and French. And you thought you'd only learn about Word in this book.)
- **Keep Original Formatting —** when turned on, tells Word to use the formatting applied to long citations in the Mark Citations dialog box when it compiles the table of citations.

- **Category —** is a pop-up menu you can use to select the citation categories you want to include in the table of authorities. Choose All to include all categories — word creates a complete table of authorities, alphabetizing within each category. If you don't want to include all categories, choose the one you do want from this menu.
- **Tab Leader —** is a pop-up menu you can use to select a tab leader for the space between the entry text and the page number. I told you about tab leaders earlier in this chapter and in Chapter 6.

Once you've made all your formatting selections in the Index and Tables dialog box, click OK. Word collects the table of authorities entries, repaginates the document, and displays the completed table of authorities in your document. You can monitor its progress by watching the messages that appear in the Status bar. If you selected a specific category from the Index and Tables dialog box Category pop-up menu, you can repeat this process for other categories used in your document.

Editing and Deleting XE, TC, and TA Entries

The only ways to change entries created by field codes like XE (index), TC (table of contents or table of figures), and TA (table of authorities) is to edit it in your document or delete it and re-create it.

You can edit an XE, TC, or TA entry the same way you'd edit any other text in your document. To edit it properly, however, you must understand how it works. If you delete a character the entry requires — like a colon, quotation mark, slash, or bracket — you could get unexpected results. Study existing entries in your document to learn more about how they work.

To delete an entry, select the entire entry, from curly bracket to curly bracket and press Delete. The entry disappears. Do not select any text that was originally selected when you created the entry unless you also want to remove that text from your document.

TIP/TRICK

You can delete multiple identical entries with the Replace dialog box. This can be very useful when deleting index or table of authorities entries created with the Mark All button in the Mark Index Entry or Mark Citation dialog box. Select a single entry and use the Cut command to cut it to the clipboard. Choose Replace from the Edit menu to display the Replace dialog box. Click in the Find What edit box to position the insertion point there and use the Paste command to paste the contents of the clipboard into the edit box. Make sure there is nothing (not even a space) in the Replace With edit box. Then click Replace All. Word replaces each occurrence of the entry with nothing, thus deleting it from the document. I explained the Replace feature of Word in detail in Chapter 16.

Creating a Custom Table Format

Word's index and table formats are nice, but they might not be exactly what you want. You can create a custom format by modifying the styles Word uses to prepare the index or table. Here's a list of the styles Word uses:

Style Name	Index and Tables Tab	Purpose
Index 1 through 9	Index	Index entries. There can be up to 9 levels.
Index Heading	Index	Letter headings for an index.
Table of Authorities	Table of Authorities	Table of authorities entries. There is only one level.
Table of Figures	Table of Figures	Table of figures entries. There is only one level.
TOA Heading	Table of Authorities	Category headings for a table of authorities.
TOC 1 through 9	Table of Contents	Table of contents entries. There can be up to 9 levels.

You can modify any of these styles with techniques I told you about in Chapter 7 *after* creating the index or table. You can also modify a style *before* you create the index or table by modifying it from within the Index and Tables dialog box. Choose Custom Style from the Formats scrolling list for the type of index or table you want to create. Then click the Modify button.

A Style dialog box listing each of the styles appears. This dialog box and the Modify Style dialog box that appears when you click the Modify button within it work just like the dialog boxes I told you about in Chapter 7.

Updating Indexes and Tables

As you modify a document, the index or tables you created for it may need to be updated. This will happen when you do any of the following:

- Add or remove text — this can change pagination.
- Add or remove index or table entries — this can change the contents of the index or table.
- Change document layout, page setup, or formatting options — this can change pagination.

In order to make sure the index or table of contents is accurate, you should update it before finalizing your document. Choose Index and Tables from the Insert menu, click on the tab for the item you want to update, check the formatting options, and click OK. If Word asks you if you want to replace the existing index or table, click Yes. Word re-creates the index or table from scratch based on the current pagination and entries.

TIP/TRICK

A quicker way to update an index or table is to click anywhere on it to highlight it and press [⌘] [Option] [Shift] [U] or [F9] (extended keyboard only). You can also hold down [Control] while clicking on the index or table to display the Shortcut menu and choose Update Field. Either way, Word updates the index or table without displaying the Index and Tables dialog box. It may, however, display a dialog box like the one shown here, asking if you want to update only the page numbers or the entire table. Choose the appropriate radio button and click OK.

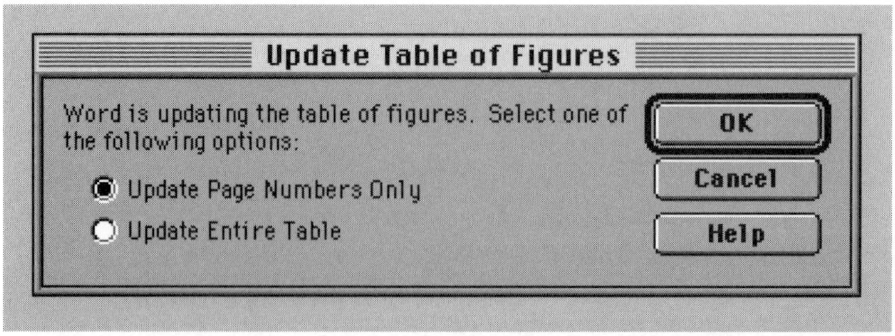

Chapter Summary

In this chapter, you learned to create an index, table of contents, table of figures, and table of authorities. You saw that, in each case, creating the index or table is a two step process. In the first step, you tell Word what to put in the index or table. In the second step, you tell Word to create the index or table. You learned to format and update your indexes and tables, and you also learned more about fields.

In the next chapter, you'll find out about Word's greatly improved mail merge (formerly print merge) feature. You'll see how to create a main document and a data source document and merge the two to create form letters and mailing labels.

21

Chapter 21: Mail Merge

ABOUT NINE YEARS AGO, WHEN MY HOME COMPUTER WAS AN Apple //c running AppleWorks, I marveled at how easy it was to send the same letter to more than one person. I'd write the letter once, addressing it to the first person on my list, and print it. Then I'd delete the first person's name and address, address it to the second person, and print that. I'd do this for every person on my list and consider myself very lucky that I didn't have to type the whole letter over and over.

While you can create form letters this way with Word, there is a much better way: Word's Mail Merge feature. Simply give Word the form document and a list of the information to be included in it, click a few buttons, and let Word create all the final documents automatically. This saves time and effort and makes it easy to reuse the same letter or list of information over and over.

How Mail Merge Works

Word's mail merge feature works by taking two specially-formatted documents and merging them together to create customized letters, envelopes, mailing labels, or catalogs.

- The *main document* contains the text and graphics that will appear in every single completed letter, label, envelope, or catalog page. It also includes the names of *merge fields* that tell Word what information to use and where it should be placed in the document.
- The *data source* contains the raw information to be merged into the main document. The data source is organized into rows with one record per row. The first row is a header row, which provides the names of the merge fields.

Since the merge field names in the main document match those in the data source, Word has no trouble putting the two documents together.

NEW IN WORD 6

If you've used the Print Merge feature in previous Word versions, you'll find that it hasn't only been renamed, but it's been completely reworked. You'll see changes in the Mail Merge Helper and Mail Merge toolbar. Merging form documents with data is now easier than ever.

Using the Mail Merge Helper

Word's Mail Merge Helper makes it easy to create main documents and data sources and merge the two together. As you'll see in a moment, the Mail Merge Helper has three main areas, numbered 1 through 3 — one for each step of the process. I'll take you through each of these areas in this section of the chapter.

As you work with the Mail Merge Helper, keep an eye on the top of the dialog box. That's where you'll find messages that guide you through the mail merge process.

Creating a Main Document

The first step in performing a mail merge is to create or prepare a main document. Remember, the main document is the document that contains text and graphics you want included in every merged item. You can create the main document from scratch with the Print Merge Helper or turn an existing document into a main document.

- To create a main document from scratch, create a new document based on the template you want to use for the form document. I told you about templates in Chapter 9. If desired, you can use the untitled document window that opens automatically when you launch Word. Then choose Mail Merge from the Tools menu to display the Mail Merge Helper.
- To create a main document based on an existing document, open that document first. Then choose Mail Merge from the Tools menu to display the Mail Merge Helper.

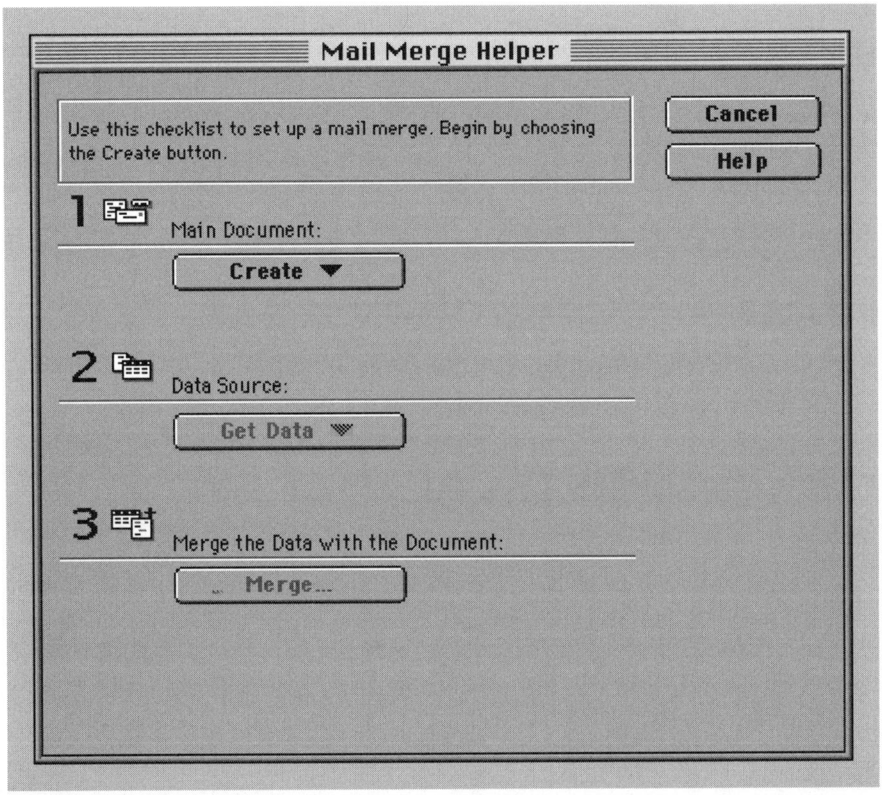

Choosing a Main Document Type

The Mail Merge Helper's Create button/menu lets you choose a type of merged document. Your choices are:

- **Form Letters** — used to send the same basic letter to multiple individuals. Each letter will be printed on a new page. With a little imagination, you can use it to enter data into forms and complete similar tasks. I'll tell you about Word's Form feature in Chapter 22.
- **Mailing Labels** — used to create labels on standard or custom label stock. Completed labels fill a label sheet before starting a new one. I told you about labels in Chapter 19.
- **Envelopes** — used to create standard or custom-sized envelopes. Each envelope will be printed on a new envelope-sized page. I told you about envelopes in Chapter 19, too.
- **Catalog** — used to create catalogs and other lists of information. There are no page breaks between merged items except automatic page breaks.

Whichever one you pick, Word displays a dialog box asking if you want to use the active document window or a new document window. Click whichever button is appropriate: Active Window or New Main Document. If you click New Main Document, Word opens another window based on the normal template. Either way, the merge type and main document name appear in the Mail Merge Helper.

Beginning a Form Letter or Catalog

An Edit button/menu also appears when you create a form letter or catalog. When you use the single command under this menu, the Mail Merge Helper disappears and you can enter the static or non-changing text in the main document window.

To create a form letter or catalog, type the text that you want to appear in every single letter or catalog entry. Leave space for the merge fields you plan to insert in the document. You can also format the text and include graphics if desired. I discussed formatting text in chapters 5 and 6 and working with graphics in Chapter 12. Be sure to save your document when you're finished.

Here's an example of the beginning of a form letter I created. Notice that it does not include any names or addresses.

Here's an example of a catalog I created to list names and addresses. Again, the only thing I entered was the text that doesn't change — in this case, some text that I want before each entry. See how I set up the tabs?

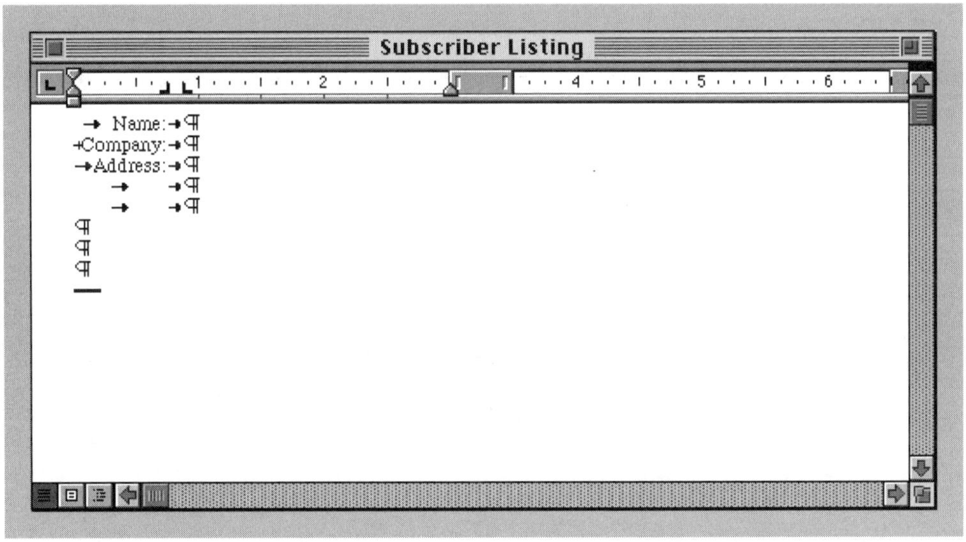

Don't worry about adding fields right now. You'll add them after you create the data source. At that time, you can also add or edit text or graphics, so don't feel as if you've got to get it perfect now.

Returning to the Mail Merge Helper

When you're finished with the document window, click the Mail Merge Helper button on the Mail Merge toolbar to return to the Mail Merge Helper dialog box. I'll tell you more about the buttons on the Mail Merge toolbar a little later.

Creating a Data Source

Once you've created a main document, you need to create a data source. Use the Get Data button/menu in the Mail Merge Helper dialog box to create or open a data source. There are three options to choose from: Create Data Source, Open Data Source, and Header Options.

Create Data Source

Create Data Source lets you create a brand new data source document from scratch. When you choose it, Word displays the Create Data Source dialog box.

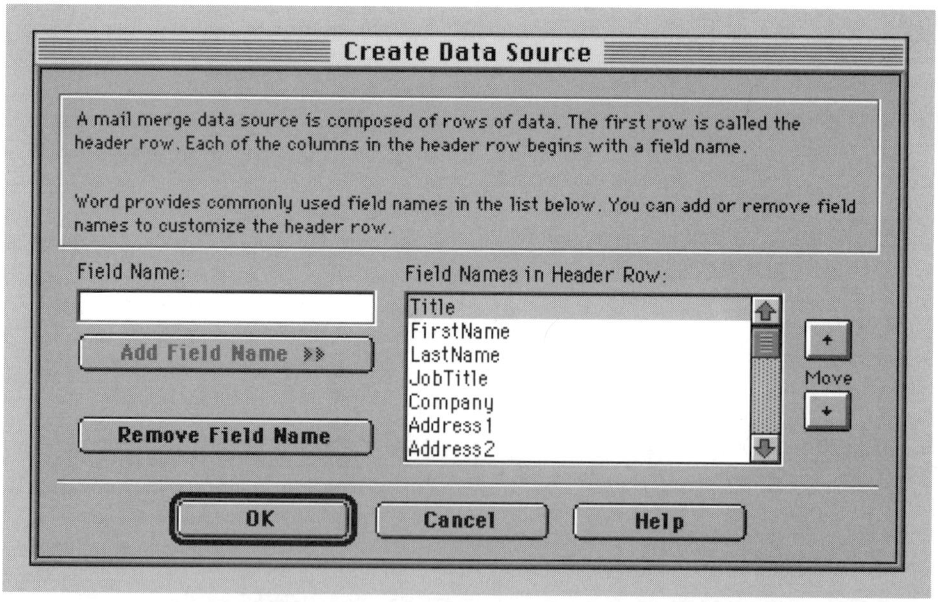

As you can see, this dialog box provides general information about data source documents. It also suggests a list of commonly-used fields in the Field Names in Header Row scrolling list. You can use this list of fields as is or change it.

- To add a field to the scrolling list, enter the name in the Field Name edit box. Field names can be up to 40 characters long, must start with a letter, and cannot include spaces, punctuation, or special characters. You can include the underscore character (_) if you like. When you're finished typing the field name, click the Add Field Name button.
- To remove a field from the scrolling list, click it once to select it and click the Remove Field Name button.
- To rename a field in the scrolling list, remove it from the list and create a new field with the name you want.
- To change the order of field names in the scrolling list, click on the name of a field you want to move and click the up or down Move button to move it up or down in the list. Repeat this for each field you want to move.

When you're finished modifying the field names, click OK to continue. Word presents a standard Save As dialog box you can use to name and save the data source. You may want to save it in the same location you save the main document.

Since you've just created a data source from scratch, it doesn't contain any information. Word displays a dialog box, offering to let you edit the data source or main document. Click Edit Data Source. Word displays a Data Form dialog box with the field names you specified:

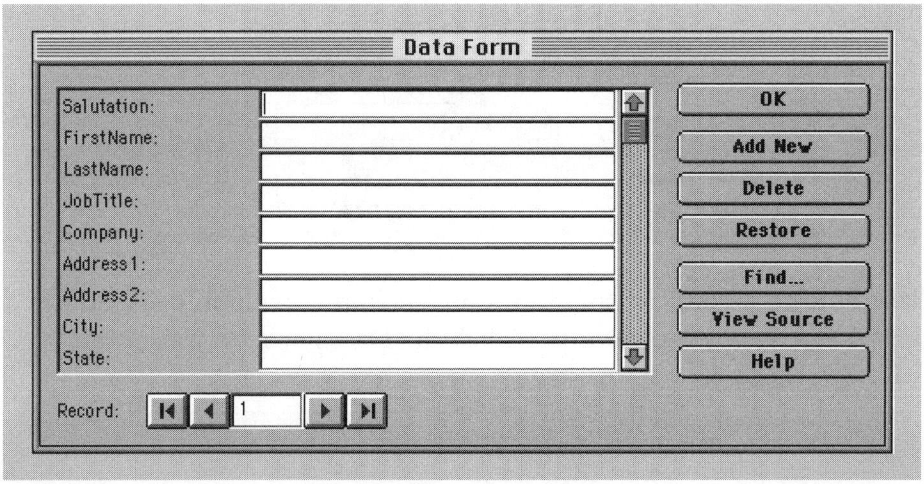

The Data Form dialog box makes it easy to enter data into the data source. Simply type information into each edit box, pressing Tab to move from field to field. If there are more fields than can fit in the window, scroll the contents of the window so you can see each one. When you're finished entering all the information for one record, click the Add New button to create another. The information is cleared from the Data Form dialog box so you can start typing again. Repeat this process for all your records.

As you work with this dialog box, here are a few buttons and other options you might find handy:

- **Record —** displays the current record number as you enter or edit information. To move from record to record, either enter a record number in the Record edit box or use the arrow buttons to move forward and backward. The arrow buttons that include vertical lines bring you to the first or last record.
- **Delete —** deletes the current record.
- **Restore —** removes any changes you may have made to the current record, restoring it to the way it was before you started editing it.
- **Find —** displays a Find in Field dialog box you can use to locate specific records. Enter the text you want to find in the Find What edit box and choose a field name from the In Field pop-up menu. Then click the Find First or Find Next button. Word displays the record containing the text you specified. Click the Close button in the Find in Field dialog box to dismiss it when you're done.

- **View Source —** displays the data source document window. To return to the form from the data source, click the Data Form button in the Print Merge toolbar.

When you're all finished entering and editing information, click the OK button. Word displays the data source — a table of the information you entered. I told you about tables in Chapter 11. If you created more than a handful of fields, you may have to scroll to the right to see the rest of the information. Don't worry about the way the information looks — you probably won't be printing this document. You can edit information in this table just as you would any other table, or you can click the Data Form button to edit with the data form.

Once the data source is completed, you'll be ready to complete the main document by inserting merge fields. If necessary, click the Mail Merge Helper button in the Mail Merge toolbar to display the Mail Merge Helper again.

Open Data Source

If you've already created a data source with the necessary information — perhaps for another mail merge — you can use it with the current mail merge. Choose Open Data Source from the Get Data button/menu. A Standard Open dialog box appears. Use this dialog box to locate and open the data source file you want to use. Then you're ready to complete the main document by inserting merge fields. If a dialog box appears asking if you want to do this, click Edit Main Document. If not, and if the Mail Merge Helper is not showing, click the Mail Merge Helper button in the Mail Merge toolbar to display it again.

Header Options

Header Options, one of the choices on the Get Data button/menu lets you create a separate header source for your data source. This makes it possible to use data available in one document without adding a header row to it or to use the same data with different field names.

To create or open a separate header source, begin by selecting Header Options from the Get Data button/menu in the Mail Merge Helper. The Header Options dialog box appears.

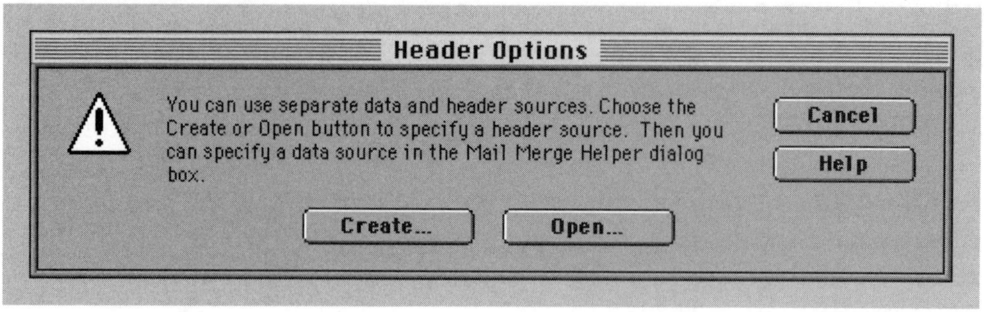

- To create a new header source, click the Create button. The Create Header Source dialog box that appears is virtually identical to the Create Data Source dialog box I discussed earlier. Use this dialog box to add, remove, or rearrange field names.
- To use an existing header source, click the Open button. Use the standard Open dialog box that appears to locate and open a document containing the header source you want to use.

IMPORTANT NOTE

Don't forget to use the Open Data Source command on the Get Data button/menu to locate and open a data source document. Word compares the header source to the data source to determine whether they are compatible. If one of these documents contains more fields than the other, Word displays a dialog box informing you of the problem. You can use the Edit button/menu in the Data Source area of the Mail Merge Helper to edit either the data header or data source to fix the problem.

Once the data source is completed, you'll be ready to complete the main document by inserting merge fields. If a dialog box appears asking if you want to do this, click Edit Main Document. If not, and if the Mail Merge Helper is not showing, click the Mail Merge Helper button in the Mail Merge toolbar to display it again.

FYI: The Relationship between a Main Document and a Data Source

When you use the Mail Merge Helper to create a main document, Word identifies it as a mail merge document. That's why Word always displays the Mail Merge toolbar when a main document is active.

Continued

By creating or identifying a document as a data source for a main document, you establish a relationship between the two documents. When you open a main document, Word automatically searches for the associated data source, looks inside it, and analyzes its data. If it can't find the data source, it displays a dialog box like this:

- Click the Find Data Source button to display a standard Open dialog box you can use to locate and open the data source document.
- Click the Options button to either remove the association between the two documents or convert the main document into a regular Word document.

IMPORTANT NOTE

If you fail to either locate a data source, remove the association between the two documents, or convert the main document to a regular document, Word simply refuses to open the main document. How's that for stubborn?

If you use the Save As command from within Word to rename or move a data source, Word associates the newly saved file to the main document in place of the originally saved data source. This should make you think twice about renaming, moving, or deleting a data source in the Finder.

Converting a Main Document to a Regular Document

TIP/TRICK

You can convert a main document to a regular document at any time with the Mail Merge Helper. With the document active, click the Mail Merge Helper button or choose Mail Merge from the Tools menu. In the Mail Merge Helper that appears, choose Restore to Normal Word Document from the Create button/menu. Word removes the association between the two documents and makes the main document a regular Word document.

Completing the Main Document

Once you've identified a main document or main document type and a data source, you're ready to complete the main document. If you've been following my instructions to create a form letter or catalog, you've already typed in the non-changing text and your document is almost ready to go. If you're creating mailing labels or envelopes, you've still got to provide Word with more information about the labels or envelopes you plan to use.

No matter what kind of document you're creating, you'll have to insert mail merge fields. When Word performs the merge, it will replace each merge field with information from the data source. It's your job to correctly place and format the merge fields.

Inserting Fields in a Form Letter or Catalog

To complete a form letter or catalog you've already begun, the only thing left to do is insert merge fields and fine-tune the text and formatting. Use the Edit button/menu in the Main Document area of the Mail Merge Helper to view and edit the main document. Position the insertion point where you want the first field to go. Then use your mouse to pull down the menu hidden under the Insert Merge Field button on the Mail Merge toolbar. You'll see a list of all the fields included in the data source. Choose the one you want to insert.

Repeat these steps to insert merge fields as necessary throughout your document. If desired, use font and paragraph formatting to change the appearance of text. The way you format a merge field is the way data appears when inserted in its place. I told you about formatting in Chapters 5 and 6.

```
¶
«Salutation» «FirstName» «LastName»¶
«JobTitle»¶
«Company»¶
«Address1»¶
«Address2»¶
«City», «State» «Zip»¶
¶
Dear «Salutation» «LastName»,¶
¶
```

Here's an example of merge fields inserted into a main document to create an inside address and opening for a form letter. Note that spaces and punctuation have been included, wherever necessary, between field names.

FYI: About Merge Fields

NEW IN WORD 6

Normally, each merge field you insert appears in your document between a pair of chevrons (« »). Unlike previous versions of Word, you cannot simply type in a merge field name. That's because each merge field works in conjunction with one of Word's fields, the MERGEFIELD field. In fact, if you have the Field Codes option turned on in the View tab of the Options dialog box, you'll see the word *MERGEFIELD* and the merge field name, enclosed in curly brackets. It might look something like this:

```
{ MERGEFIELD Salutation }
```

TIP/TRICK

If you'd like to show or hide field codes in the current document without opening the Options dialog box, press Option F9 (on an extended keyboard only). I'll tell you about the Options dialog box in Chapter 23.

Setting Up Mailing Labels

To complete a mailing labels main document, you'll need to tell Word what size labels you'll be using and then insert merge fields. Click the Setup button in the Main Document area of the Mail Merge Helper. The Label Options dialog box, which I showed you in Chapter 19, appears. Use this dialog box, and the one that appears when you click the Details button, to specify the correct dimensions for the labels you plan to use. If you're not sure how to use these dialog boxes, read up on them in Chapter 19 where I explained them in detail.

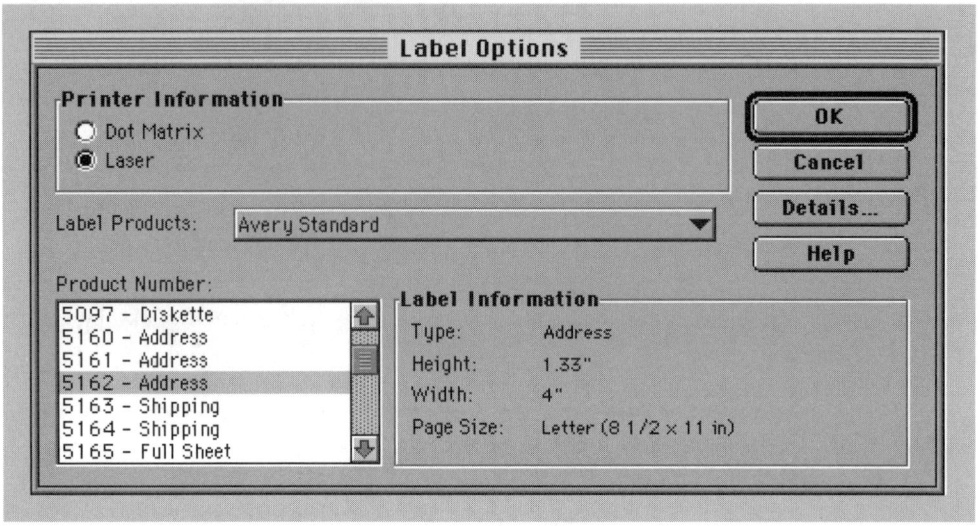

When you're finished specifying label dimensions, click OK in the Label Options dialog box to dismiss it. The Create Labels dialog box appears in its place.

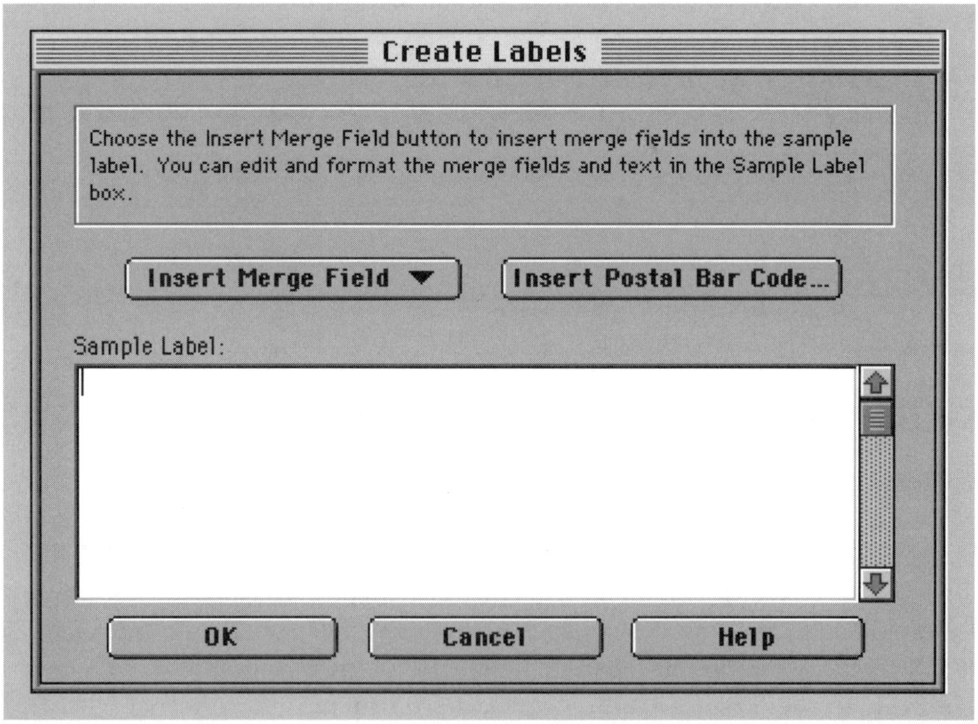

Use the Sample Label scrolling window to enter static text and merge fields to create the label.

- To insert a merge field, position the insertion point where you want the field to go. Then choose a field from the Insert Merge Field button/menu in the dialog box. The list includes all the fields in the data source. Repeat these steps for each field you need to insert. Be sure to include any necessary spaces and punctuation between fields.
- To insert a bar code, click the Insert Postal Bar Code button. The Insert Postal Bar Code dialog box appears. Choose the merge fields containing the zip code and street address from the appropriate pop-up menus. Then click OK. The bar code is inserted at the top of the label.

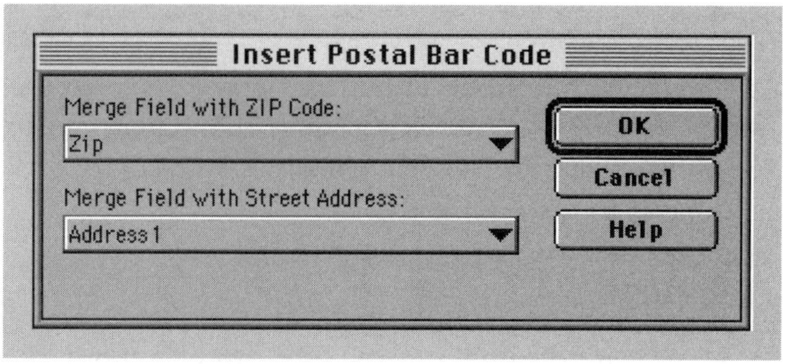

When you're all finished, The Sample Label area of the dialog box might look something like this:

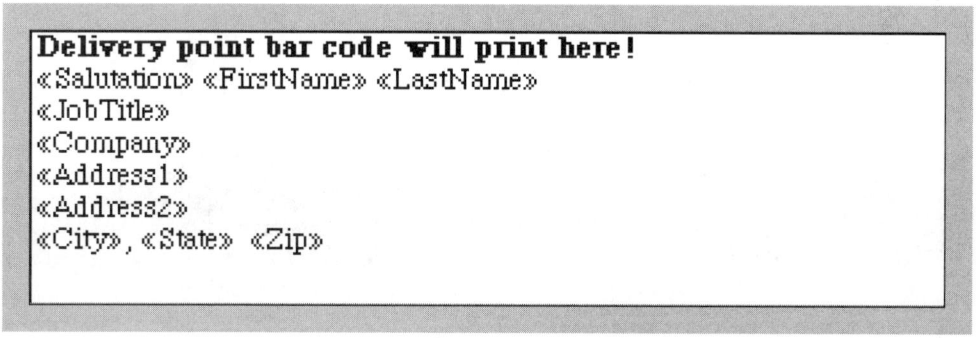

Click OK to continue. Word creates a label document similar to the kind I showed you in Chapter 19. If you want to inspect it and the Mail Merge Helper is in the way, click the Mail Merge Helper's Close button to dismiss it. Here's part of the one I created above:

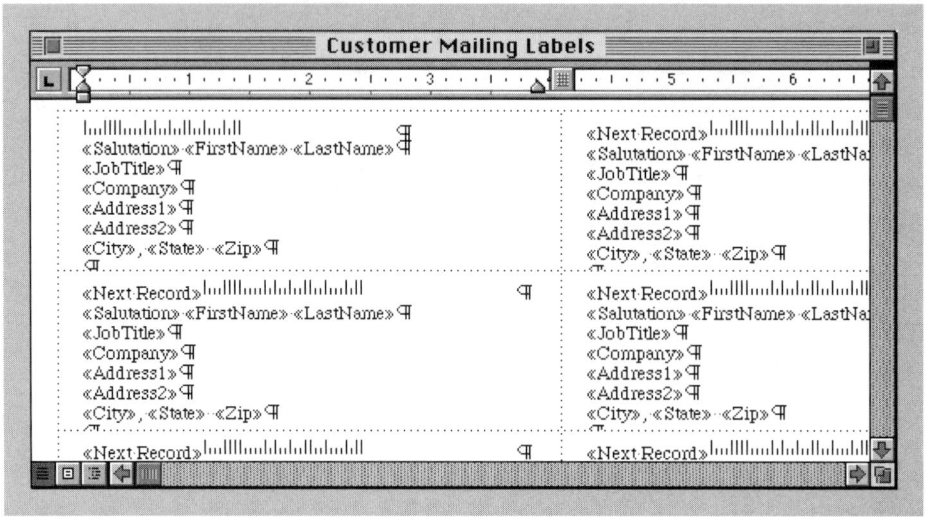

IMPORTANT NOTE

If the field names do not fit within the label boundaries, do not drag the table gridlines to make them fit! Doing so will change the dimensions of the labels — they may no longer fit within the actual labels. Instead, try formatting the fields with a smaller font size.

Setting Up Envelopes

To complete an envelopes main document, you'll need to give Word information about the envelopes you'll be using and then insert merge fields. Click the Setup button in the Main Document area of the Mail Merge Helper. The Envelope Options dialog box, which I showed you in Chapter 19, appears. Use the Envelope Options and Printing Options tabs of this

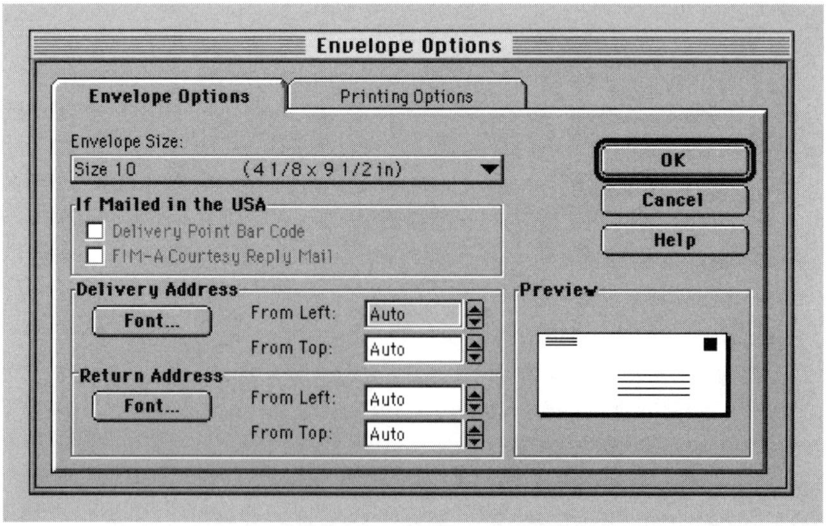

dialog box to specify envelope dimensions, delivery and return address font and position, and printer feed method. If you're not sure how to use this dialog box, read up on it in Chapter 19 where I explained it in detail.

When you're finished specifying envelope options, click OK in the Envelope Options dialog box to dismiss it. Then use the Envelope Address dialog box that appears in its place to insert text and merge fields for the delivery address portion of the envelope. This dialog box looks and works the same way as the Create Labels dialog box I showed you earlier, so consult that section of this chapter for details. If you use the Insert Postal Bar Code button to create a bar code, you'll find that it also includes a check box that will put an FIM-A mark on the envelope. I told you about that in Chapter 19, too.

Click OK to accept the contents of the Envelope Address dialog box. Word positions the return address and merge fields on a document page the same size as the envelope. To view Word's handiwork, you may have to dismiss the Mail Merge Helper by clicking its Close button.

Reviewing and Polishing the Main Document

TIP/TRICK

Before merging the main document and data source, it's a good idea to review the main document carefully and make any last-minute changes that are needed. Here are a few tips.

To see data rather than merge fields in a main document, click the View Merged Data button on the Mail Merge toolbar. Word substitutes actual data source information for the field names. Here's what the inside address and opening of my form letter looks like with data rather than field names.

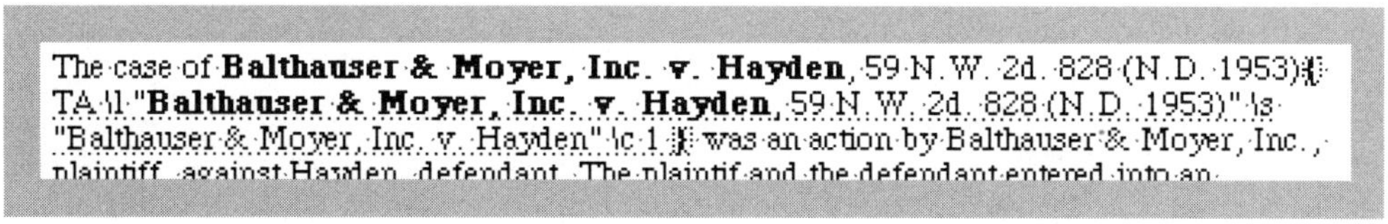

The case of **Balthauser & Moyer, Inc. v. Hayden**, 59 N.W. 2d. 828 (N.D. 1953){ TA \l "**Balthauser & Moyer, Inc. v. Hayden**, 59 N.W. 2d. 828 (N.D. 1953)" \s "Balthauser & Moyer, Inc. v. Hayden" \c 1 } was an action by Balthauser & Moyer, Inc., plaintiff, against Hayden, defendant. The plaintif and the defendant entered into an

The Mail Merge toolbar offers four buttons and an edit box to scroll through the records in the data source once you're viewing data in your main document. Using these buttons makes it possible to check the appearance of every record before performing a merge.

- First Record displays the first record of the data source.

- Previous Record displays the record before the record that is currently showing.

- Next Record displays the record after the record that is currently showing.

- Last Record displays the last record of the data source.

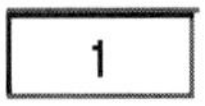

- The Go To Record edit box displays the current record number. You can enter another number in it and press Return to view that record.

You can apply font and paragraph formatting to labels and envelopes as you create them. Select the text you want to change, hold down Control, and click on the selection to display the Shortcut menu. Choose the formatting option you want. I discussed font and paragraph formatting in detail in Chapters 5 and 6.

To see what each page of the merged document will look like when printed, click the View Merged Data button on the Mail Merge tool bar and then switch to Page Layout View or Print Preview. This is especially helpful if you need to confirm that all the information in a label fits inside each label's boundaries.

Merging the Main Document and Data Source

Ready to merge? You are if you've identified the main document and data source and included appropriate merge fields in the main document.

There are two ways to begin the mail merge: from inside the Mail Merge Helper and with tools on the Mail Merge toolbar. Either way, you must begin by making the main document active.

Using the Mail Merge Helper's Merge Button

If the Mail Merge Helper is displayed, you can begin a mail merge by clicking the Merge button. Word displays the Merge dialog box. Make selections within the dialog box and click Merge to begin the merge.

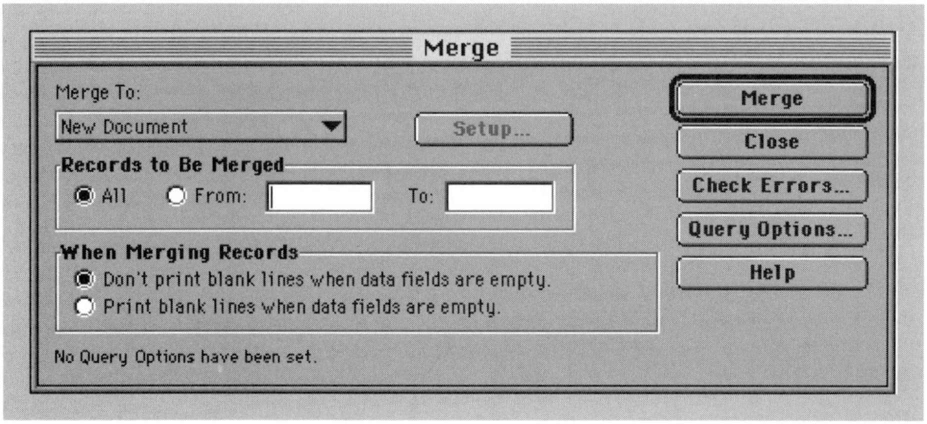

- **Merge To —** a pop-up list that lets you tell Word whether you want to merge the two documents to a New Document, Printer, or Electronic Mail. New Document tells Word to create a document containing the results of the merge. Merged form letters and envelopes are separated by section breaks that begin new pages. Merged label pages are separated by section breaks that begin new pages. Merged catalogs include only automatic page breaks. Printer tells Word to send the results of the merge directly to the printer for printing. Make sure the printer is on and filled with the correct paper, label stock, or envelopes. Electronic Mail tells Word to create electronic mail messages for each merged record. This option is only available if an electronic mail package meets Messaging Application Programming Interface (MAPI) or Vendor-Independent Messaging (VIM) standards. Microsoft Mail is an example of such a package. I'll tell you more about using Word with electronic mail in Chapter 25.
- **Setup —** which is gray unless Electronic Mail is selected in the Merge To pop-up list, identifies the electronic mail address a merged document is sent to.

NEW IN WORD 6

- **Records to Be Merged —** lets you tell Word which records to merge. Click the All or From radio button. If you click the From radio button, enter a starting and ending record number in the From and To edit boxes. Word automatically numbers the data source records sequentially starting at 1.

NEW IN WORD 6

- **When Merging Records —** lets you tell Word how to handle empty fields. The Don't Print Blank Lines when Data Fields are Empty radio button tells word not to print a blank line when a field does not contain data. This is especially helpful when using multiple address merge fields, like there were in the examples in this chapter. When the Don't Print Blank Lines when Data Fields are Empty radio button is selected, Word omits lines that contain only empty fields, most punctuation marks (. ? ! , ; : ¿ ¡), and nonprinting characters like spaces, tabs, and paragraph marks. In previous versions of Word, you had to use complicated If/Then keywords to prevent Word from leaving gaps when fields were empty.

NEW IN WORD 6

- **Check Errors —** displays the Checking and Reporting Errors dialog box, which is shown here. Choose from among three options for checking or merging the document and reporting merge errors. Choose the one you want and click OK. If you choose the first option, Word does not actually complete the merge. If Word finds any errors you can correct them in the main document or data source before merging to a printer.

The Merge dialog box also includes a Query Options button. I'll tell you about that a little later in this chapter.

FYI: More about Checking for Errors

The Check Errors buttons offered in the Merge dialog box and Mail Merge toolbar let you check your mail merge documents for errors without actually performing a merge. This might be helpful if you plan to perform the merge at a later date or hand it off to someone with less experience.

When Word finds an error in a mail merge, it can display a dialog box informing you of the error and offering options to fix it.

Using the Mail Merge Toolbar Buttons

The Mail Merge toolbar offers easy access to merge buttons:

- The Check for Errors button displays the Checking and Reporting Errors dialog box I just told you about. Use it to check the main document and data source for errors. 
- The Merge to New Document button merges the main document and data source to a new document. 
- The Merge to Printer button merges the main document and data source to a printer. 
- The Mail Merge button displays the Merge dialog box. 

Advanced Mail Merge Techniques

Once you've got the basics down pat you may be ready for more advanced techniques — change the contents or record order of a data source, select only specific records for merging, insert database information, or include Word fields to increase the flexibility and power of the Mail Merge feature. That's what this part of the chapter is all about.

Modifying the Data Source

If the data source contains inaccurate, incomplete, or unnecessary information, you can edit it to meet your needs. There are several ways to do this.

NEW IN WORD 6

Previous versions of Word allowed you to edit data documents used in a print merge. In version 6.0, however, Microsoft added buttons, tools, and dialog boxes to simplify the process.

- To use the data form to edit a data source, click the Edit Data Source button (when the main document is active) or the Data Form button (when the data source is active). I told you how to use the data form earlier in this chapter.

- To add a new record when the data source is active, click the Add New Record button. Word adds a row to the bottom of the data source table. Enter information into the new row. I told you how to edit tables back in Chapter 11.

- To delete a record when the data source is active, position the insertion point in the row containing a record you want to delete. Then click the Delete Record button to remove the entire row.

- To add, remove, or rename fields, click the Manage Fields button. The Manage Fields dialog box, which is shown here, appears. To add a field, enter a name in the Field Name edit box and click Add. You can then add data to the field for each record. To delete a field, click the name in the Field Names in Header Row scrolling window and click Remove. A confirmation dialog box appears asking if you're sure you want to delete the field and its data. Click Yes. To rename a field, click the name of the field in the Field Names in Header Row scrolling window and click Rename. Then enter a new name in the Rename Field dialog box that appears and click OK.

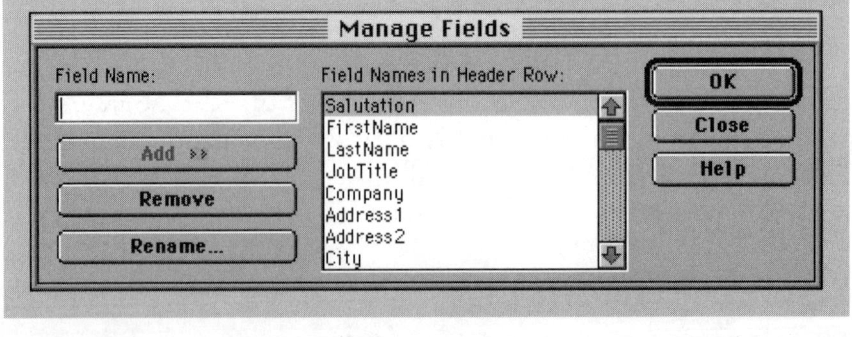

- To locate a record in the data source, click the Find Field button. The Find in Field dialog box, which I illustrated and explained earlier, appears. Use it to locate a record based on the information in a single field.

- To switch from the data source to the main document, click the Mail Merge Main Document button. The main document becomes the active window.

To add, change, or delete information in the data source while its window is active, you can use the standard table editing techniques I told you about in Chapter 11.

Sorting Records

You can sort data source records prior to merging them with the main document. This is especially handy when preparing mailing labels or envelopes that need to be sorted by zip code to get the best postage rates.

The ability to sort mail merge records is not new to Word version 6. It was possible in previous versions of Word through the use of the Sort command on the Tools menu. Version 6, however, adds more flexibility and makes it easier to sort.

NEW IN WORD 6

Using Toolbar Buttons

If you've got the data source displayed, you can use toolbar buttons to sort its records by any field. Position the insertion point in the column you want to sort by and click the Sort Ascending or Sort Descending button. Word performs the sort.

Using Query Options

The Query Options dialog box offers additional sorting options, including the ability to sort by up to three columns, each in ascending or descending order. To open the Query Options dialog box, do one of the following:

- Display the Mail Merge Helper by clicking the Mail Merge Helper button or choosing Mail Merge from the Tools menu. Then click the Query Options button in the Mail Merge Helper. This button will only be active if you've already identified a main document and data source.
- With the main document active, click the Mail Merge button. Then click the Query Options button in the Merge dialog box.

The Query Options dialog box appears. If necessary, click the Sort Records tab to display its options.

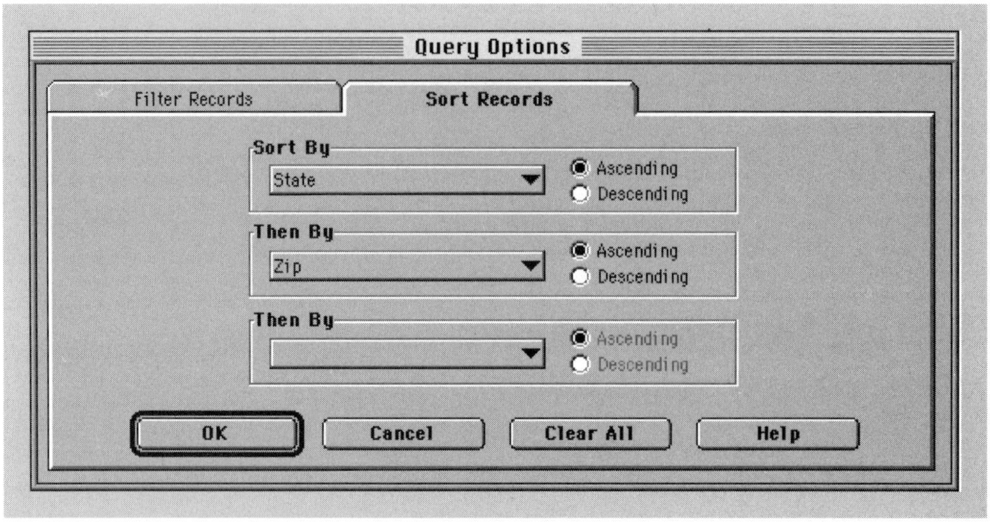

Use the Sort By pop-up menu to choose a field as a primary sort field. All fields in the data source are automatically included. Click the Ascending or Descending radio button to specify the sort order. If desired, you can use the two Then By pop-up menus and their radio buttons to specify secondary and tertiary sorts to be used as "tie breakers" if more than one record contains the same primary sort information. To clear the sort selections, click the Clear All button. To perform the sort, click the OK button and then click the Close button in the Mail Merge Helper or Merge dialog box. The records are sorted.

TIP/TRICK

If you want to sort records as part of a mail merge, you can click the Merge button rather than the Close button in the Mail Merge Helper or Merge dialog box. Word sorts the records before performing the merge.

Selecting Records

NEW IN WORD 6

Word version 6 includes a Filters feature you can use to select specific records based on field contents. To access it, open the Query Options dialog box by clicking the Query Options button in the Mail Merge Helper or Merge dialog box. If necessary, click on the Filter Records tab to view its options.

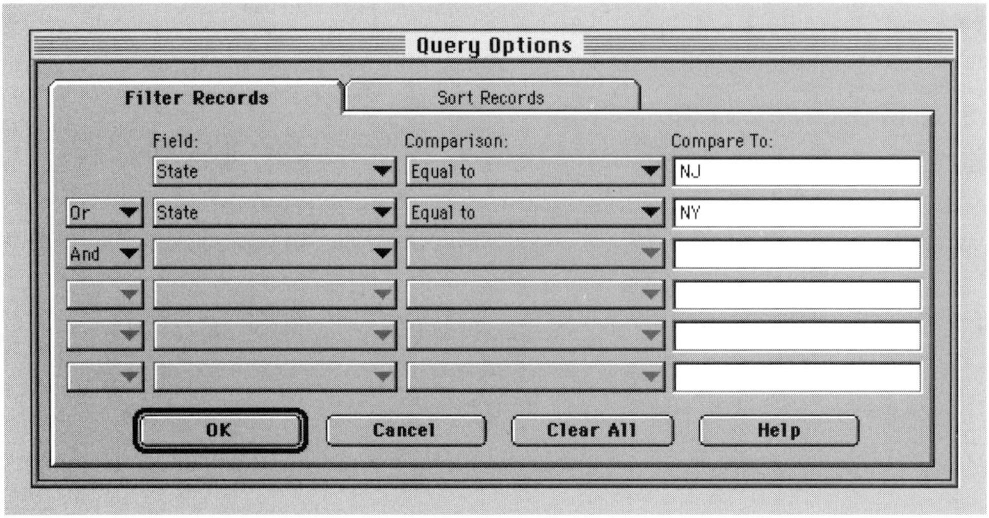

To select only certain records, choose a field name from the first Field pop-up menu. All the field names in the data source are included. Then choose an appropriate comparison phrase from the Comparison pop-up menu on the same line. Your options are Equal To, Not Equal To, Less Than, Greater Than, Less Than or Equal To, Greater Than or Equal To, Is Blank, and Is Not Blank. Finally, enter the comparison information in the Compare To edit box on the same line.

If you want to search for records using multiple filters, choose And or Or from the pop-up menu on the second line and complete that line. *And* tells word to match all or both lines of information. *Or* tells Word to match one line or the other. You can have as many as six filters. In the previous illustration, I told Word to use only the records with State fields containing NY or NJ.

To clear the filter information, click Clear All. To accept it and go back to the Mail Merge Helper or Merge dialog box, click OK. Although the data source document doesn't change, if you perform a merge or use the View Merged Data button to preview the results of a merge, only the records you specified are shown. You'll need to click the Clear All button in the Query Options dialog box to merge all the records.

Inserting a Database

If the records you want to use for a mail merge already exist in another file, you can insert that data into a mail merge source document. The information you insert must be in a format Word can read, like an Excel, Word, or FoxPro file or a tab- or comma-delimited text file. I'll tell you more about sharing files from other applications with Word in Chapter 25.

Begin by making the data source document active. To add new records to the records already in the data source, position the insertion point at the paragraph marker after the last row of the data source table. The new records must have the same number of fields (columns) as the existing data source. To replace existing data source records, position the insertion point anywhere within the data source table. Then either click the Insert Database button or choose Database from the Insert menu. The Database dialog box appears.

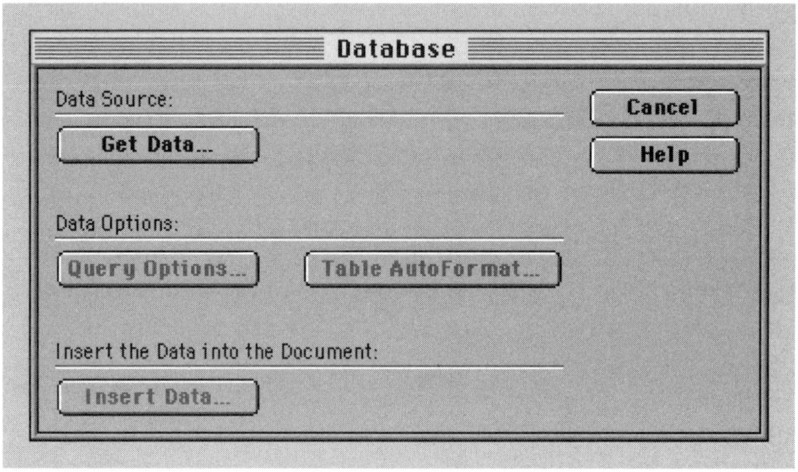

Click the Get Data button. A standard Open dialog box appears. Use this dialog box to locate and open the file containing the database you want to insert. You may need to change the option in the List Files of Type pop-up menu to see the file listed in the directory window. If the file you opened is not a Word file, a Convert File dialog box appears. Choose the appropriate file type from the scrolling list. Then click OK. The name of the file you chose appears under the Get Data button in the Database dialog box.

If you want to include only certain information from the database or you want it inserted in a certain order, click the Query Options button. The Query Options dialog box has three tabs: Filter Records, Sort Records, and Select Fields. I told you about the Sort Records and Filter Records tabs earlier in this chapter, so consult that section for details. The Select Fields tab, however, only appears when inserting a database. It looks like this:

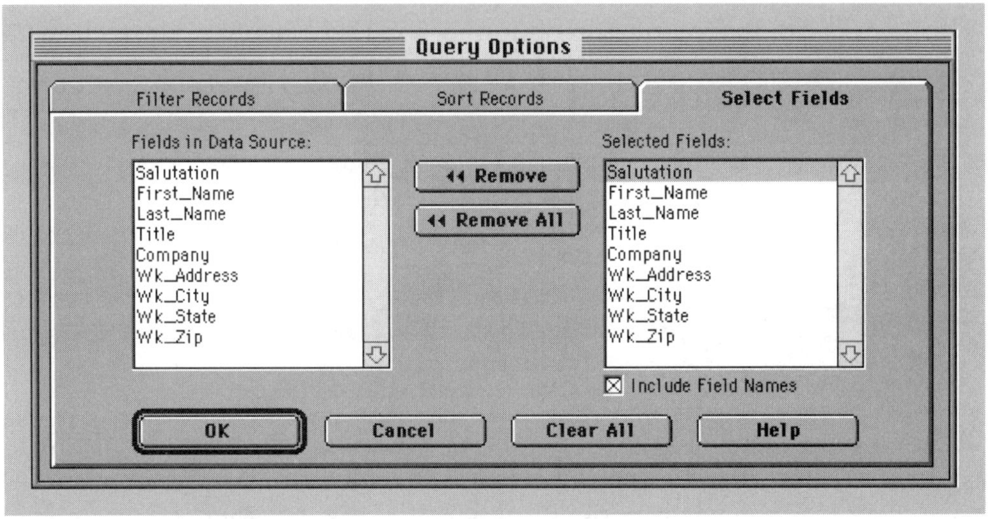

Both the Fields in Data Source and Selected Fields scrolling lists display all the field names in the database. Your job is to make sure the Selected Fields list displays only the fields you want included in the data source file in the correct order.

- To remove a field from the Selected Fields scrolling list, click on it to select it and click Remove. The Remove All and Clear All buttons remove all fields from the Selected Fields list.
- To add a field from the Fields in Data Source scrolling list, click on it to select it and click Select. The Select All button copies all field names to the Selected Fields scrolling list.
- To change the order of field names in the Selected Fields list, remove all the fields, then add them back, one by one, in the order you want them.
- To exclude field names from the data source, turn off the Include Field Names check box. This is helpful if the data source already includes the field names you plan to use or if you plan to use a separate header source.

When you're all finished selecting fields, click OK to return to the Database dialog box.

The Database dialog box also offers a Table AutoFormat button you can use to automatically format the data source table. I told you about Word's new Table AutoFormat feature back in Chapter 11, so you can read up on it there.

When you're all done setting up options in the Database dialog box, click the Insert Data button. The Insert Data dialog box appears.

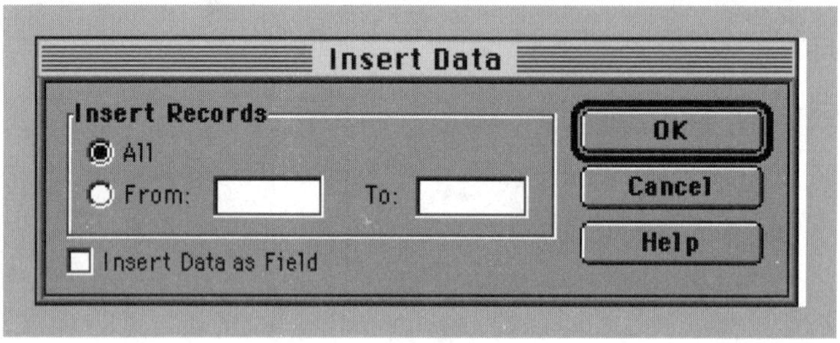

To insert only a range of record numbers, enter values in the From and To edit boxes. If you turn on the Insert Data as Field check box, Word maintains a link between the database document and the data source document. This way, if the database document changes, the data source document will also change when you update fields or perform a mail merge. Click OK to insert the information. The Status bar indicates Word's progress as it creates the database records. If you're replacing existing records with database records, Word displays a confirmation dialog box asking if you really want to replace the records. Click Yes. The records are added.

Including Word Fields

NEW IN WORD 6

Word offers a number of fields that can be used to add power and flexibility to mail merges. Using fields makes it possible to display prompts for information, incorporate if/then logic, and automate certain tasks. You insert a Word mail merge field in a main document by positioning the insertion point where you want the field to appear, and then choosing the field you want from the Insert Word Field button/menu on the Mail Merge toolbar. Word may display the Insert Word Field dialog box asking for more information, depending on the field you chose. When you provide all the information a field needs, Word composes and inserts the complete field in your document.

NEW IN WORD 6

In previous versions of Word, the Print Merge Helper offered a number of keywords you could use to extend the functionality of a print merge. Word version 6 uses fields for the same thing, with some differences in field names and availability.

In this section, I'll provide a brief summary of the mail merge fields so you can see how to use them in your documents.

IMPORTANT NOTE

Remember, if you want to see the complete text of fields you insert in your document, you must set Word to display Field Codes. To do this, choose Options from the Tools menu, click the View tab to display its options, and turn on the check box for Field Codes. You can also use the Shortcut key, [Option][F9]. If you do not do this, only part of the field code displays between mail merge chevron symbols.

TIP/TRICK

To format text that appears as the result of a field, select the entire field and format it so it looks the way you want it to. Or, while using the Insert Word Field dialog box that appears when you insert certain fields, use shortcut keys to format the text you type.

BOOKMARK

NEW IN WORD 6

A BOOKMARK field tells Word where to put the results of an ASK or SET BOOKMARK field in a mail merge. If you plan on using either of these fields in your mail merge, you must insert a BOOKMARK field where you want the variable text to go. Although the BOOKMARK field is similar to the bookmarks I discussed in Chapter 14, you *cannot* use the Bookmark command on the edit menu to insert a BOOKMARK field.

To insert a BOOKMARK field, position the insertion point where you want the field to go and press [⌘][F9] (extended keyboard only). Word inserts an empty pair of field brackets and positions the insertion point between them. Type in the name of the bookmark exactly as you plan to use it. A bookmark name cannot include spaces, punctuation, special characters, or symbols other than the underscore character (_). When you're finished, it might look something like this:

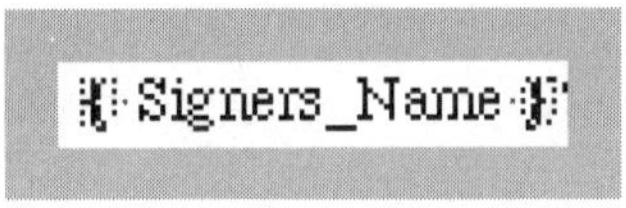

If the bookmark name is exactly the same as another Word field name, type REF before it, like this:

IMPORTANT NOTE

If field codes are not set to display, BOOKMARK fields do not display at all.

ASK

The ASK field tells Word to display a dialog box that requests more information from the person performing the merge. It then puts that information in the specified bookmark throughout the merged documents.

For example, say you've got a form letter that's used by several different people. Since there's no single person signing the letter, you can use the ASK field to get the name of the person who will be signing each letter or the entire batch of letters in the mail merge. That name can then be inserted in a letterhead and in the letter's closing.

To use the ASK field, begin by inserting BOOKMARK fields wherever necessary as discussed above. Then position the insertion point anywhere in your document. I usually insert the ASK field right after the first occurrence of the BOOKMARK field. Choose Ask from the Insert Word Field button/menu. The Insert Word Field: Ask dialog box appears.

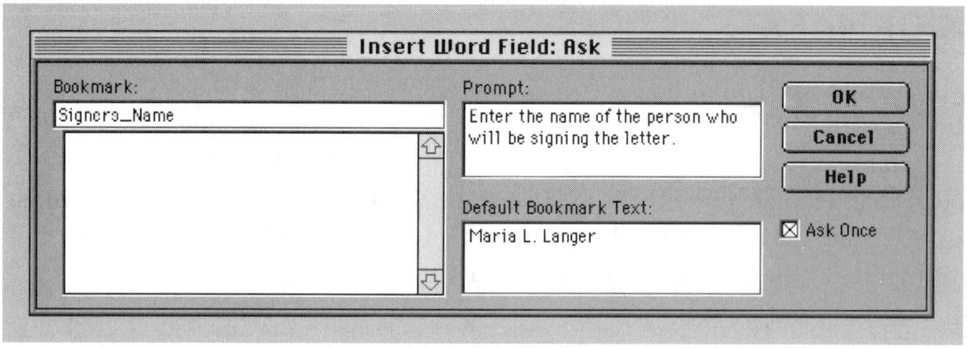

In the Bookmark edit box, type in the name of the BOOKMARK field you inserted. In the Prompt edit box, type in the text you want to use to prompt the user for the correct information. In the Default Bookmark Text edit box, enter any text you want to appear by default in the prompt dialog box. If you only want Word to ask for the information once during the mail merge — in other words, if it doesn't change for all the items in the merge — turn on the Ask Once check box. Then click OK. Word displays an example of the dialog box it will use when performing the merge. Here's what it looks like with the information I provided in the previous illustration:

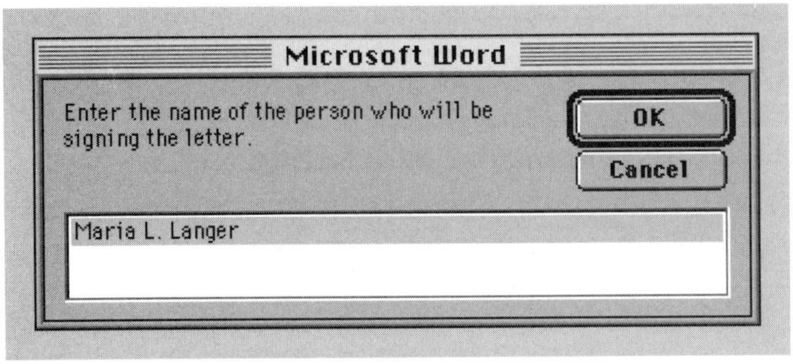

Click OK to dismiss the dialog box. The ASK field is inserted in the document. Now, when you perform the mail merge, Word uses a dialog box to request the information to be inserted in at the bookmark throughout the merge. You enter text into the dialog box (or accept the default text) and click OK.

FILLIN

NEW IN WORD 6

The FILLIN field is similar to the ASK field in that it asks for information to insert into the document. It does not, however, use a bookmark, so there's no need to insert a BOOKMARK field first.

To use the FILLIN field, position the insertion point where you want the user-entered text to appear. Then choose Fill-in from the Insert Word Field button/menu. The Insert Word Field: Fill-in dialog box appears.

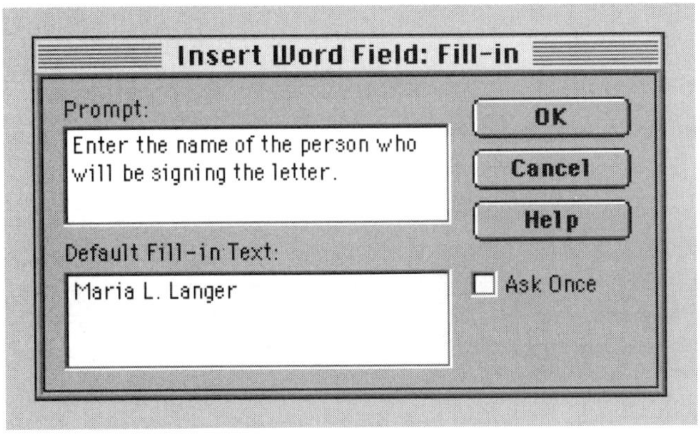

In the Prompt edit box, type in the text you want to use to prompt the user for the correct information. In the Default Fill-in Text edit box, enter any text you want to appear by default in the prompt dialog box. If you only want Word to ask for the information once during the mail merge, turn on the Ask Once check box. Then click OK. Word displays a sample dialog box like the one I showed you for the ASK field. Click OK to dismiss it.

FYI: About ASK and FILLIN Switches

Like the fields I told you about in Chapter 20, Word's ASK and FILLIN mail merge fields also utilize switches to customize the way the field works. Word inserts the switches automatically when you use the Insert Word Field dialog box, but you can change them if you need to.

Switch	Purpose
\d	Appears before the default text assigned to the bookmark. The default text is the text that appears in the edit box of the prompt dialog box.
\o	Tells Word to prompt only once during the mail merge. If this switch is not included, Word prompts for information for each record.

SET

Like the ASK field, the SET field sets the value of a bookmark. It does not, however, display a prompt. The SET field is particularly useful when inserted within an IF field since you can use it to change a bookmark based on an evaluation of other fields. I'll tell you more about the IF field in a moment.

To use the SET field, begin by inserting one or more bookmarks as discussed above. Position the insertion point where you want the SET field to go. If you're setting a bookmark for the entire document, you may want to include the SET field at the beginning where it's easy to find and change. If you're including the SET field within an IF field, you must position it properly within the IF field. Then choose Set Bookmark from the Insert Word Field button/menu. The Insert Word Field: Set dialog box appears.

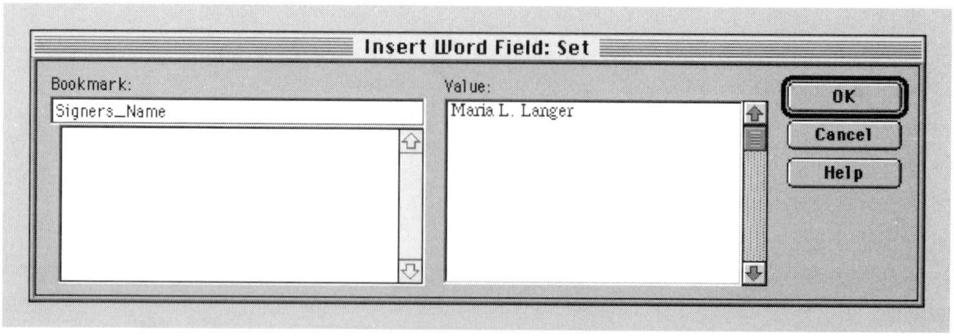

In the Bookmark edit box, type in the name of the bookmark. In the Value edit box, type in the information you want to set the bookmark to. Then click OK. When you perform the merge, Word uses the contents of the Value edit box in the BOOKMARK field.

IF

An IF field makes it possible to include if/then logic in a mail merge. Use this to provide different pieces of information depending on the value in another field.

For example, say you've got two phone numbers you want to provide in a form letter. One number is for out-of-state callers while the other is for in-state callers. You can use an IF field to evaluate the contents of a State field and act on it.

To use the IF field, position the insertion point where you want the outcome of the evaluation to go. Then choose IF...Then...Else from the Insert Word Field button/menu. The Insert Word Field: IF dialog box appears.

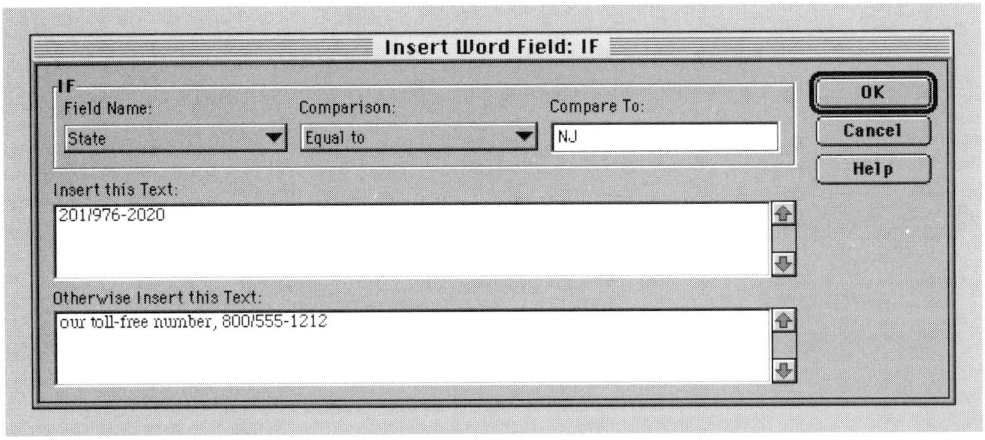

Choose the field you want to evaluate from the Field Name pop-up menu. All the merge fields included in the main document automatically appear. Choose an operator from the Comparison pop-up menu. The options are Equal To, Not Equal To, Less Than, Greater Than, Less Than or Equal To, Greater Than or Equal To, Is Blank, and Is Not Blank. Type the text you want to match in the Compare to Edit Box. In the Insert this Text edit box, type in the text you want to insert if the evaluation is true — that is, if the comparison matches. In the Otherwise Insert this Text edit box, type in the text you want to insert if the evaluation is false. In the previous example, Word will insert the local (201) phone number for any record with an address in New Jersey and the 800 phone number for all the other records. Here's an example of what it might look like:

```
If·you·have·any·questions,·don't·hesitate·to·call·us·at·{·IF·{·MERGEFIELD·State·}·=·"NJ"·
"201/976-2020"·"our·toll-free·number,·800/555-1212"·}.·Our·representatives·are·standing·
by·to·assist·you.¶
```

This is a very simple example of an IF field. With a little imagination, you can get an IF field to do all kinds of customizations based on the contents of merge fields in the data source.

FYI: IF Field Switches

The IF field can also accept switches, although they are not automatically inserted by the Insert Word Field dialog box. The switches specify how Word should consider the case of text when it makes the comparison. By default, Word's IF field makes a case-sensitive comparison. That means the case of the text you type in the Compare To edit box must exactly match the case of the text in the data source. By using one of these four switches, you can force Word to convert the data source text to a specific case prior to making the comparison. The text is not actually converted in the document.

To use one of the IF switches, insert it immediately after the MERGE-FIELD name in the beginning of the IF field. In the following example, Word will convert the contents of the City field to all uppercase letters and compare it to the text NEW YORK to determine the outcome of the IF field.

```
{·IF·{·MERGEFIELD·City·\*·upper·}·=·"NEW·YORK"·"We·offer·free·same-day·courier·
delivery·to·shipping·addresses·in·New·York·City."·"There·is·a·10%·shipping·charge·for·
overnight·delivery."·}¶
```

Continued

Switch	Purpose
* upper	converts the text to all uppercase for comparison purposes: NEW YORK.
* lower	converts the text to all lowercase for comparison purposes: new york.
* firstcap	converts only the first letter of the text to uppercase for comparison purposes: New york.
* caps	converts the text to initial caps for comparison purposes: New York.

MERGEREC

NEW IN WORD 6

The MERGEREC field inserts the number of the current data record. This can be useful if you want to keep track of the record numbers in a merge.

To use the MERGEREC field, position the insertion point where you want the record number to go. Then choose Merge Record # from the Insert Word Field button/menu. The field is inserted in the document.

MERGESEQ

NEW IN WORD 6

The MERGESEQ field inserts the sequence number of the current data record. This differs from the MERGEREC number in that it always starts at 1, no matter what range of records you're merging.

To use the MERGESEQ field, position the insertion point where you want the record number to go. Then choose Merge Sequence # from the Insert Word Field button/menu. The field is inserted in the document.

NEXT

The NEXT field tells Word to print information for the next record without creating a new merge document. Word inserts this field automatically when it creates labels. It also uses this technique without inserting the field when you choose Catalog as the type of mail merge.

To use the NEXT field, position the insertion point where you want the next record to go. Then choose Next Record from the Insert Word Field button/menu. The field is inserted in the document. If there is no next record, Word prints nothing.

NEXTIF

The NEXTIF field uses if/then logic to determine whether the current record should be merged into the current merge document or into a new merge document. If the comparison criteria you specify matches, Word uses information from the next record in the current merged document.

To use the NEXTIF field, position the insertion point where you want the next record to go. Then choose Next Record If from the Insert Word Field button/menu. The Insert Word Field: Next Record If dialog box appears.

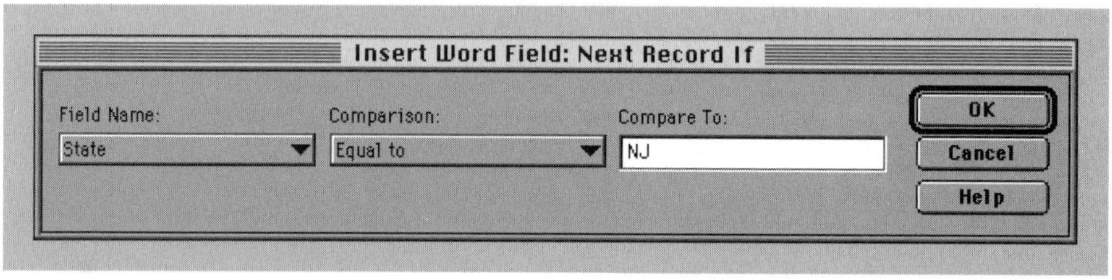

Use the Field Name pop-up menu to choose a field to evaluate. Use the Comparison pop-up menu to choose a comparison operator. The choices are the same as those for the IF field I previously discussed. Finally, enter the comparison text in the Compare To edit box. When you click OK, Word inserts the completed field into the document.

NEW IN WORD 6

In previous versions of Word for Windows, the NEXTIF field was used to specify how data was merged into a Word document. This field was not available in previous versions of Word for Macintosh.

SKIPIF

NEW IN WORD 6

The SKIPIF field is another holdover from Word for Windows that did not appear in previous Macintosh versions. It works much like the NEXTIF field, except it completely skips over the current record if it matches the comparison criteria you specify. You can get the same kind of functionality as this field by using the Filter Records tab options in the Query Options dialog box. I told you about that earlier in this chapter.

You insert the SKIPIF field the same way you insert the NEXTIF field. The dialog boxes are identical.

Other Fields

TIP/TRICK

You can use other Word fields within a mail merge. Word fields are particularly useful when used in conjunction with IF and SET fields. To access all of Word's fields, choose Field from the Insert menu. The Field dialog box appears.

Click on the field category in the Category scrolling list to narrow down the contents of the Field Name list. Click on a field name to select it and provide additional information in the Field Codes edit box by typing it in or using the Field Options dialog box that appears when you click the Options button. When you're all finished, click OK to insert the field.

Chapter Summary

In this chapter, you learned to use Word's powerful Mail Merge feature to create form letters, labels, envelopes, and catalogs. You saw how to use the Mail Merge Helper to create the two documents needed for a mail merge: the main document and the data source. You also saw how to insert mail merge fields into the main document and perform the merge. You learned about Word's new Query Options dialog box and the sorting and filtering features it provides. Finally, you learned about Word's other mail merge fields and how you can use them in your mail merges to add power and flexibility.

In the next chapter, you'll learn about Word's new Form Feature. You'll see how you can create database forms that you and others can use to enter, store, and print information. You'll also see how you can create special form fields that can give your documents a polished look.

22

Chapter 22: Forms

IN VERSION 6 OF WORD, MICROSOFT ADDED A NEW FORM feature. With it, you can create forms that can be filled out within Microsoft Word. You can then print or save either the entire form or just the form's data. If you save only the form's data, you can then import it into a database created with Microsoft FoxPro or Claris FileMaker Pro, or add it to a data source document for a mail merge. I'll tell you about exchanging information with other applications in Chapter 25. I told you about mail merge in Chapter 21.

NEW IN WORD 6

Word's Form feature is a great way to collect information electronically. Distribute blank forms via network to other Word 6 users and collect them via network once they're

TIP/TRICK

completed. The result: information formatted to your specifications, all ready to be imported into a database. Best of all, you won't have any trouble reading the responses (typing beats handwriting for legibility), you won't have to type in a single piece of information manually, and you don't have to print.

In this chapter, you'll learn how to create a form. You'll see how to insert and modify fields for user-entered information, and how to add online help to guide users filling out the form. You'll also learn to protect a form to prevent changes, and how to fill in a form, taking advantage of all the features it has to offer.

Creating a Form

Before you begin creating a form, it's helpful to have a general idea of what it will look like when completed. Just as artists begin with a sketch of their subject before putting a brush to canvas, you should begin with a rough draft of your form before creating it in Word. If you're copying an existing form, you're all ready to go. But if the form is just an idea drifting around in your mind, use an old fashioned word processor (pencil and paper) to sketch it out.

There are two basic kinds of forms. A *text form* consists primarily of text with spaces within the text for user-entered information. An example would be a lease agreement. A *grid form* consists primarily of boxes with form labels and spaces for user-entered information. An example would be your tax return. Of course, there's nothing preventing you from creating a form that combines flowing text with one or more grids.

No matter what kind of form you create, it's important that you begin by creating a template so that AutoText entries and macros stored in your Normal template are available to anyone who fills out the form. I told you about templates in Chapter 9 and about AutoText in Chapter 16. I'll tell you about macros in Chapter 26.

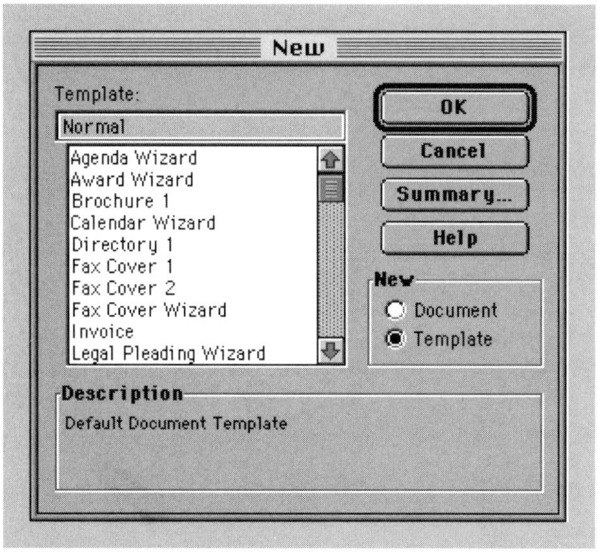

Select New from the File menu to display the New dialog box shown here. Click the Template radio button and click OK. A blank document called Template1 appears. You're all ready to create your form.

Text Forms

For a text form, enter the text that will appear in every form. In a way, this is very similar to creating a mail merge main document. For now, do not include spaces or blanks for user-entered information — I'll show you how to insert fields in a little while. You can format the text using the formatting techniques I covered in Chapters 5 and 6 and insert graphics and frames using techniques I covered in Chapters 12 and 13.

Grid Forms

For a grid form, use Word's Table feature to create a framework for the form. I told you how to create tables back in Chapter 11, so if you skipped that chapter, it's time to go back and read it. Remember to include cells for the form label text as well as the places where user-entered text will appear. Don't put anything in the cells for user-entered text — I'll show you how to insert form fields in the next section. You can include text formatting, graphics, borders, and shading to give your forms a professional look. I covered all that in Chapters 5, 6, 11, 12, and 13.

Saving a Form

If you're like me, you like to save your documents periodically as you work with them. When you save a form, it's a good idea to save it in the same folder as the rest of Word's templates. This way, when you need to fill in the form, it will appear with the other available templates in the template list of the New dialog box. Be sure to give the form file an appropriate name so you know what it's for. I discussed saving files in Chapter 3.

Using the Form Field Dialog Box

Throughout this book, I've been discussing fields. A field is a special code that Word uses to insert specific information. A form field is similar, but different. It's a code that you define for the collection of information on a form. As you'll see in this section, Word offers many options that let you customize the way a form field looks and works.

To insert a form field, begin by positioning the insertion point where you want the field to go — the same place you want to accept user-entered data. Then choose Form Field from the Insert menu. The Form Field dialog box appears.

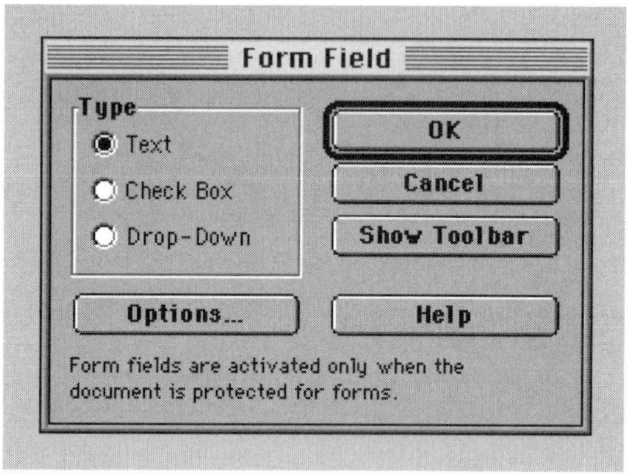

The Form Field dialog box lets you choose from three types of form fields: text, check box, or drop-down.

Text Form Fields

A text form field is probably the most commonly used field type. Use it for fields in which you want users to type text.

To insert a text form field, make sure the Text radio button is selected in the Form Field dialog box. Then click Options to set specifications for the text field. The Text Form Field Options dialog box appears. This is where you give Word all the information it needs to insert and format the field.

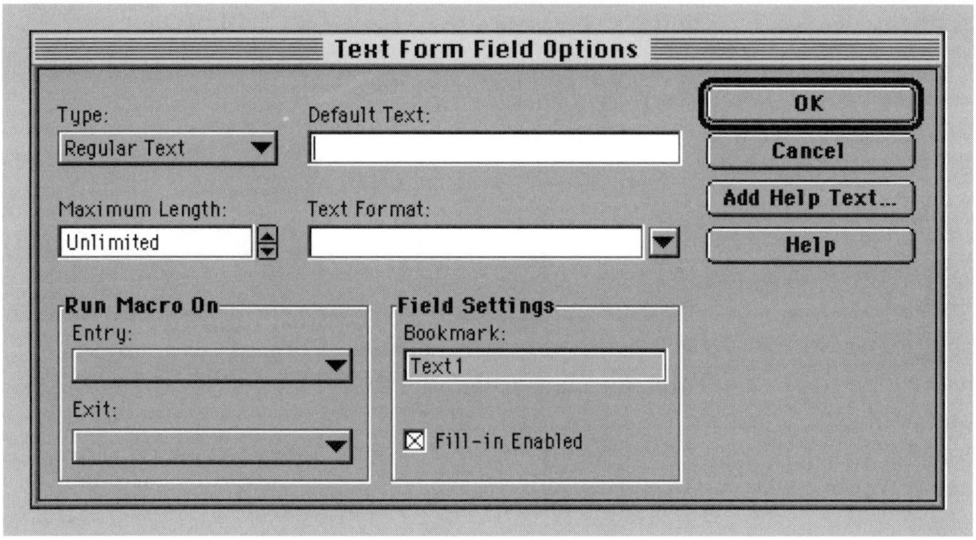

Field Types

The first thing you need to specify is the type of text form field. Use the Type pop-up menu to choose from among six options:

- **Regular Text —** is for the entry of any kind of typed data, including text, numbers, dates, or times.
- **Number —** is for the entry of numerical data. When you use a Number field, Word checks to make sure the user enters a number before letting him continue to fill out the form.
- **Date —** is for the entry of a date or a time. When you use a Date field, Word checks to make sure the user entered a valid date or time before letting him continue to fill out the form.
- **Current Date —** enters the current date.
- **Current Time —** enters the current time.
- **Calculation —** instructs Word to perform a calculation based on numbers in the document.

IMPORTANT NOTE

Word does not automatically update the contents of the Current Date, Current Time, or Calculation field when you print unless the Update Fields check box is turned on in the Print tab of the Options dialog box. I'll tell you more about the Options dialog box in Chapter 23. You can manually update any selected field by pressing [⌘ Option Shift U] or [F9]. If the field cannot be selected in the form because it has not been enabled (like a calculation field), consider using an exit macro to perform the update automatically. I'll tell you more about macros later in this chapter and again in Chapter 26.

Default Values and Expressions

If you choose a Regular Text, Number, or Date field, Word lets you enter a default value for that field in an edit box beside the Type pop-up menu. How that edit box is labeled depends on which kind of text field you selected: default text, default number, or default date. The default value you enter will appear in the form automatically. This is useful if a field normally contains a specific value, but can sometimes contain other values. The user can change the value if he wants to as he enters information into the form.

If you choose a Calculation field, you must enter a mathematical expression in the Expression edit box beside the Type pop-up menu. Expressions begin with an equals sign (=) and can contain references to any cell or bookmark in the document. I explained Word's formula field in Chapter 11 when I told you about tables.

Maximum Length

Use the Maximum Length edit box to specify a maximum length in characters for field contents. The width of the field in the form will be adjusted up to the value you enter. *Unlimited* means the contents of the field can be any length at all.

Format

The Format edit box lets you specify the format of the text, number, date, or time entered in the field. The options displayed by the pop-up menu vary depending on the type of field you choose from the Type pop-up menu:

- **Text Format:** Options offered for Text fields include Uppercase, Lower Case, First Capital, and Title Case.
- **Number Format:** Options offered for Number and Calculation fields can specify the number of decimal places and the inclusion of commas and currency symbols. I discussed number formats in Chapter 11 when I explained formulas.

- **Date Format:** Options offered for Date and Current Date fields can specify the way days, months, dates, and years appear. There are 13 formats to choose from:

Format	Example
M/d/yy	10/31/94
dddd, MMMM dd, yyyy	Monday, October 31, 1994
d MMMM, yyyy	31 October, 1994
MMMM d, yyyy	October 31, 1994
d-MMMM-yy	31-October-94
MMMM, yy	October, 94
MMM-yy	Oct-94
M/d/yy hh:mm AM/PM	10/31/94 2:15 PM
M/d/yy hh:mm:ss AM/PM	10/31/94 2:15:23 PM
hh:mm AM/PM	2:15 PM
hh:mm:ss AM/PM	2:15:23 PM
H:mm	14:15
H:mm:ss	14:15:23

- **Time Format:** Options offered for Time fields can specify whether the time includes seconds or is on a 24-hour clock. The four formats to choose from are the same as the last four options in the Date Format pop-up menu.

To format the overall appearance of the contents of a field, use the font and paragraph formatting techniques I covered in Chapters 5 and 6 to format the field itself.

TIP/TRICK

Check Box Fields

A Check Box field displays a check box the user can click to turn a value on or off. This is commonly used for yes or no responses: an X in the box indicates Yes while an empty box indicates No.

To insert a Check Box form field, click the Check Box radio button in the Form Field dialog box. Then click Options to set specifications for the Check Box field. The Check Box Form Field Options dialog box appears.

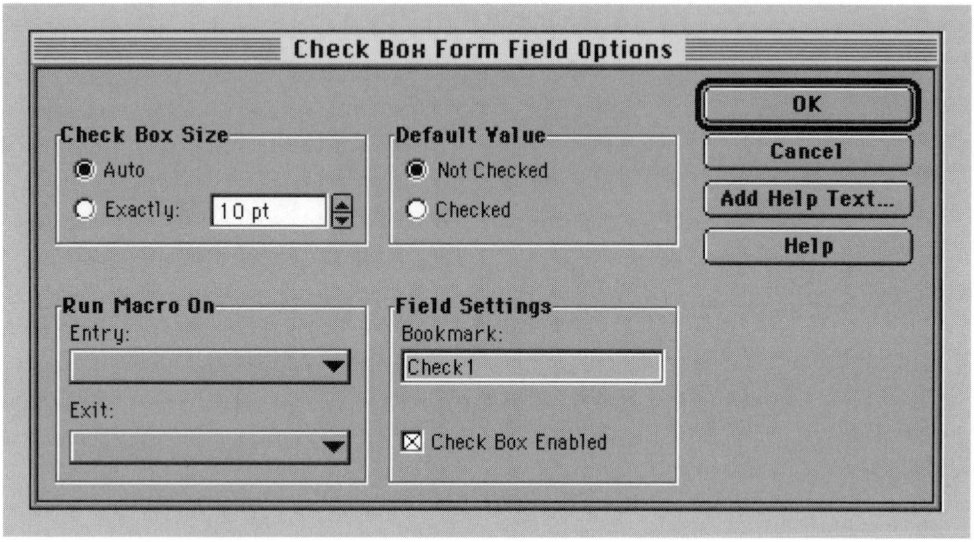

Check Box Size

The Check Box Size area lets you tell Word how big to make the check box. Click the Auto radio button to have Word automatically size the check box according to the text around it. Click the Exactly radio button and enter a value in points in the edit box beside it to specify an exact size for the check box.

Default Value

Use the Default Value area to determine whether the check box is turned on or off by default. As long as the check box is enabled, the user will be able to override whatever default value — not checked or checked — you choose.

Drop-Down Fields

A drop-down field displays a drop-down or pop-up list of valid field values. The user selects from among the values to enter data in the field. Drop-down fields are best used for fields that can contain a limited number of values. An example might be a Marital Status check box field which can contain values for married, single, divorced, or widowed.

To insert a drop-down form field, click the Drop-Down radio button in the Form Field dialog box. Then click Options to set specifications for the drop-down field. The Drop-Down Form Field Options dialog box appears.

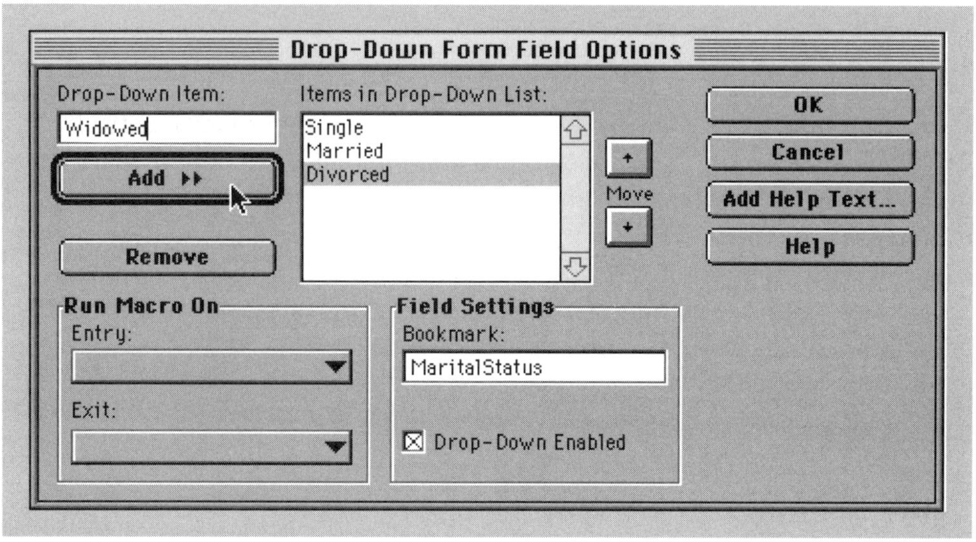

Adding Drop-Down Items

To add an item to the drop-down list that appears in the form, enter the item test in the Drop-Down Item edit box. Be sure to enter it exactly the way you want it to appear in the form. Then click the Add button. The item is added to the Items in Drop-Down List scrolling window. Repeat this process for each item you want to add.

Removing Drop-Down Items

To remove an item from the drop-down list that appears in the form, click on the item in the Items in Drop-Down List scrolling window to select it and click the Remove button. The item is removed.

Changing the Order of Drop-Down Items

You can also change the order items appear in the drop-down list in the form. Click on an item you want to move in the Items in Drop-Down List scrolling window to select it. Then click the up or down Move Arrow buttons to change its order. The order items appear in this scrolling list is the same order they will appear in the form.

Additional Options

In addition to the field-specific options I've discussed, each Field Options dialog box offers two other options.

Run Macro On

If the form document contains Macros, you can have Word automatically run a macro when the insertion point enters the field, exits the field, or both. Use the Entry pop-up menu to choose the macro to run when the insertion point enters the field. Use the Exit pop-up menu to choose the macro to run when the insertion point exits the field. Only the macros in the current document template are listed for use on these two menus. I'll tell you about macros in Chapter 26.

TIP/TRICK

To ensure that the contents of any calculation fields are updated properly, use an exit macro to update all fields.

Field Settings

The Field Settings dialog box lets you name the field with a bookmark and specify whether the user should be able to fill in the field. To give the field a name, enter a field name in the Bookmark edit box. Bookmark names must begin with a letter, cannot contain punctuation, symbols, or spaces, and have no more than 40 characters. I told you about bookmarks in Chapter 14. To enable the field for user entry, confirm that the Fill-in Enabled check box is turned on. This check box is only active for Regular Text, Number, and Date fields.

Using the Forms Toolbar

Word version 6 includes a Forms toolbar you can display and use to make inserting Form fields and other form features easier. To display it, do one of the following:

- Choose Form Field from the Insert menu and click the Show Toolbar button.

- Choose Toolbars from the View menu, click on the Forms check box to turn it on, and click OK.
- Hold down the Control key while clicking a toolbar to display the Toolbars shortcut menu. Choose Forms from the menu.

The Text Form Field button inserts a Text form field.

The Check Box Form Field button inserts a Check Box form field.

The Drop-Down Form Field button inserts a Drop-Down form field.

The Form Field Options button opens the Form Field Options dialog box for a selected field.

The Insert Table inserts a Word table. It works just like the Insert Table button on the Standard Toolbar, which I discussed in detail back in Chapter 11.

The Insert Frame button inserts a frame around selected text or objects. It works just like the Insert Frame button I discussed in Chapter 12. I also discussed frames in Chapter 13.

FYI: How Form Fields Look On Screen

The way a form field appears on screen depends on the field options you included. Here's the scoop:

- By default, all form fields appear with shading around them; you can turn shading on or off with the Form Field Shading button, as I'll discuss in a moment.
- If a form field has a default value, that value appears in the field.
- If a form field does not have a default value, the field appears as a series of small circles, one per character. If you set the field's Maximum Length, there's one circle per character you specified. If you didn't set the field's Maximum Length, only five circles appear. This expands as you fill out the form.

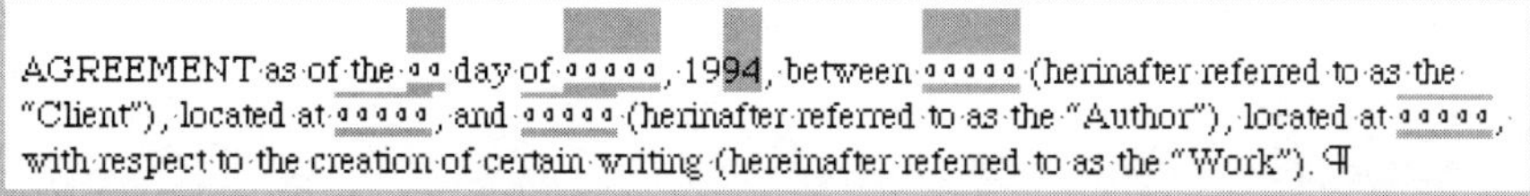
AGREEMENT as of the ◦◦ day of ◦◦◦◦◦, 1994, between ◦◦◦◦◦ (herinafter referred to as the "Client"), located at ◦◦◦◦◦, and ◦◦◦◦◦ (herinafter referred to as the "Author"), located at ◦◦◦◦◦, with respect to the creation of certain writing (hereinafter referred to as the "Work"). ¶

Continued

- If a form field is formatted as a check box, the check box appears. It may or may not have an X in it depending on how you set the Default Value.

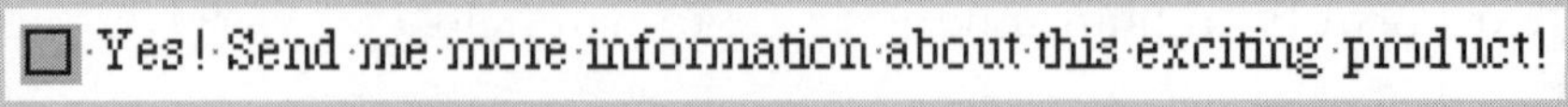

- If a form field is formatted as a drop-down list, the first value in the list appears in the field. When the field is protected for forms (which I'll discuss later in this chapter), a tiny arrow appears beside the field. Users click this arrow to display the drop-down list.

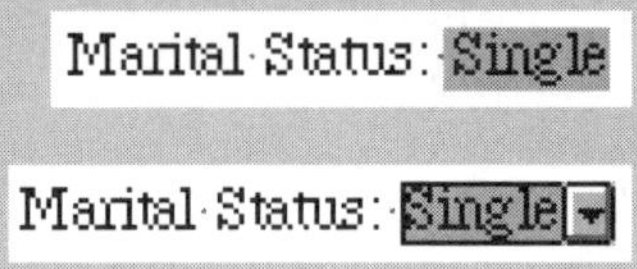

Modifying and Formatting Form Fields

Once you've inserted a form field, you can modify it to include shading, format text, or change field options.

Shading Form Fields

By default, form fields are shaded so they stand out from the other text in the document. You can turn shading on or off by clicking the Form Field Shading button on the Forms toolbar.

Form field shading does not print. If you want form fields to be shaded in a printed document, use the shading options for table cells or paragraphs. I covered tables and shading in Chapters 11 and 13.

Formatting Text

To specify how entered text appears in the document, apply font or paragraph formatting to the field itself. For example, if you want an underline to appear under the data entered into a form, select the field and use the appropriate toolbar button, menu command, or shortcut key to make it underlined. When the form is completed, the field text has the formatting you specified.

Changing Form Field Options

To change the options you specified for a form field, click the field to select it and click the Form Field Options button on the Forms toolbar, or simply double-click the field. The appropriate Form Field Options dialog box appears. Make any necessary changes and click the OK button.

Deleting a Form Field

You can also remove a form field from the document if you decide you don't really need it. Select the entire field and press Delete or Del, or choose Clear from the Edit menu.

Adding Form Field Help

No matter how straightforward your form design is, there's always a few users who can't figure out what information goes into certain form fields. Word lets you communicate exactly what you want the user to enter through the use of Form Field help. You can define a message that appears in the Status bar when the insertion point enters the field or define a message that appears in Word's help window when the user presses Help or ⌘ /.

To add help to a form field, display the Form Field Options dialog box for the field by double-clicking it or by selecting it and clicking the Form Field Options button on the Forms toolbar. Then click the Add Help Text button. The Form Field Help Text dialog box appears.

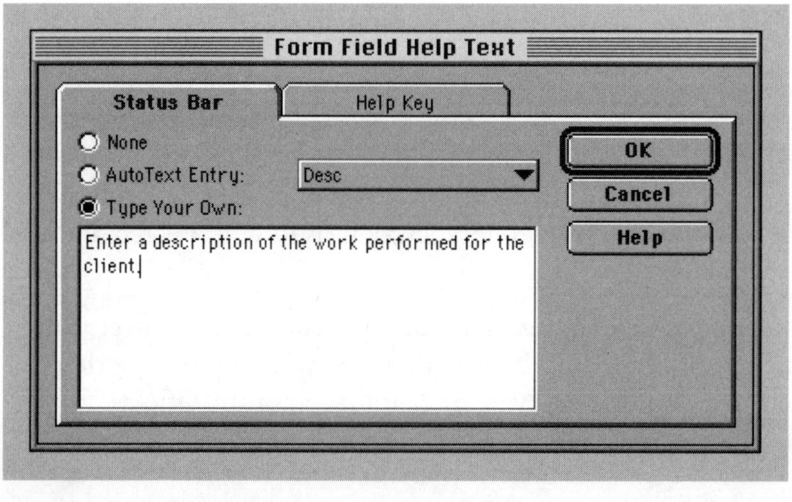

The Form Field Help Text dialog box has two tabs: Status Bar and Help Key. The tabs are virtually identical. Click the tab corresponding to the placement of the help text — you can add both kinds of help text if you like. To add text that already exists in the template as an AutoText entry, click the AutoText Entry radio button and choose an entry from the pop-up list beside it. To enter other text, click the Type Your Own radio button and enter text in the edit box below it.

When you're all finished entering help text, click OK to dismiss the Form Field Help Text dialog box. Then click OK again to dismiss the Form Field Options dialog box.

IMPORTANT NOTE

You can only view form field help after the document has been protected for forms. I'll discuss that next.

Protecting a Form

A form doesn't really act like a form until it has been protected. I first discussed protection back in Chapter 18 when I discussed revisions and annotations. Protecting a document for a form prevents users from changing anything other than what's inside the form fields. It also enables fields for entry, disables certain Word menu commands, and activates form field help.

IMPORTANT NOTE

You must save the document with protection enabled in order to use the document as a form. The last two steps for form creation should always be:

1. Protect the document and
2. Save the document.

Protecting an Entire Document for a Form

To protect an entire document for a form, choose Protect Document from the Tools menu. The Protect Document dialog box appears. Click the radio button beside Forms and click OK. The document is now protected and has been converted into a Word form.

To unprotect a form for further editing before use, choose Unprotect from the Tools menu. You can then edit the document as you would any other Word document. You cannot, however, enter information into fields.

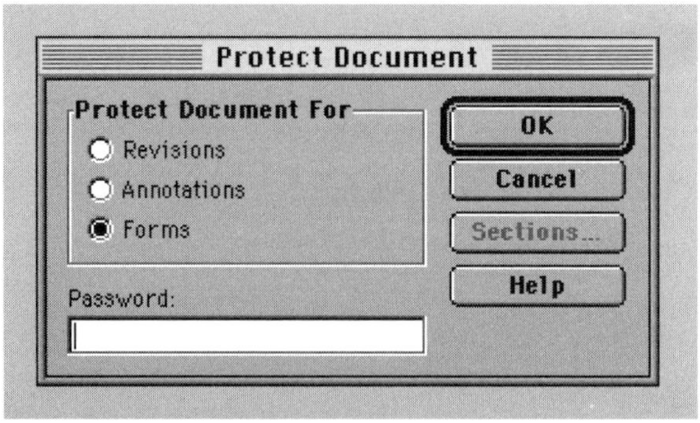

If the Forms toolbar is displayed, you can click the Protect Form button to quickly toggle protection on or off.

You can prevent others from unprotecting a form by entering a password in the Protect Document dialog box. I discussed this in detail back in Chapter 18.

TIP/TRICK

Protecting Specific Sections of a Document for a Form

If your form document consists of multiple sections, you can protect specific sections of it for a form. I discussed sections in Chapter 8.

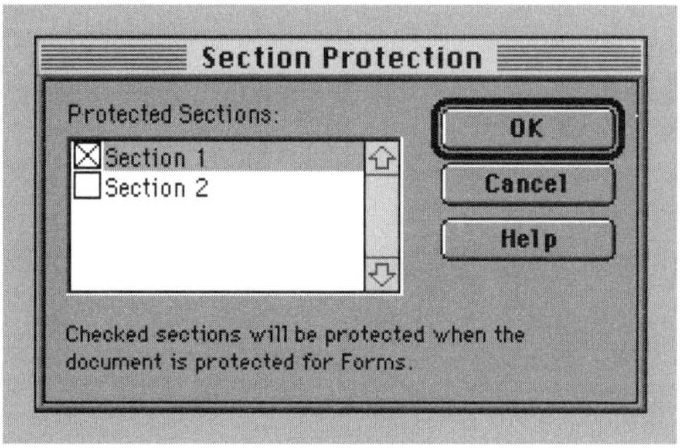

To protect specific sections for a form, choose Protect Document from the Tools menu to display the Protect Document dialog box. Click the radio button beside Forms. Then click the Sections button. The Section Protection dialog box appears. Click the check boxes beside a section number to turn section protection on or off. Click OK when you're finished and click OK again in the Protect Document dialog box to complete the protection. Only the sections you chose are protected and converted into a Word form.

Working with Forms

Once a form has been created and saved to disk, it can be used to collect information. In this section, I'll tell you how to open a form, enter and edit data, view form field help, and save and print the completed form.

Opening a Form

To open a form, choose New from the File menu. The New dialog box appears. Use the scrolling list to find the form template you want to open. Click it once to select it and click OK to create a new document based on that form. An untitled document window appears with all the text, fields, and formatting of the form template.

Entering Data

If the entire document is protected as a form, the first field in the form will be selected when you open it. Enter the appropriate text in that field. To move to the next field, press Tab or Return. Repeat this process until you have entered information into all of the fields. Word skips over any fields that are not enabled for entry, like calculation fields.

To enter information into a drop-down list, click the arrow beside the list to display a menu of options, and then choose the value you want. To turn a check box on or off, click it. To move backward from field to field, press Shift Tab or Shift Return.

If only part of the document is protected as a form, you'll have to locate that section in order to complete it. Use the Scroll bar to scroll through the document until you find the section(s) containing the form. Then click on a field to select it and begin entering information. Pressing Tab or Return when the insertion point is in an unprotected area of the document will insert tab or return characters.

Editing Data

You can edit the contents of any field using the standard text editing techniques I covered in Chapter 2. You can insert or delete characters or copy and paste all or part of a field's contents. The only two things you won't be able to do is format text or edit text outside a field.

Viewing Help

If a form field includes help, you can display it one of two ways:

- To display Status bar help, click in a field to make it active and look in the Status bar at the bottom of the screen. If Status bar help has been defined, it appears there.

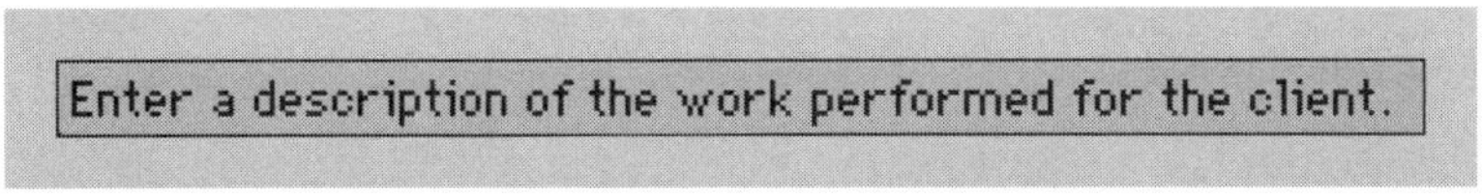

- To display help, click in a field to make it active and press Help or ⌘/. A Help dialog box appears. When you are finished with it, click OK to dismiss it.

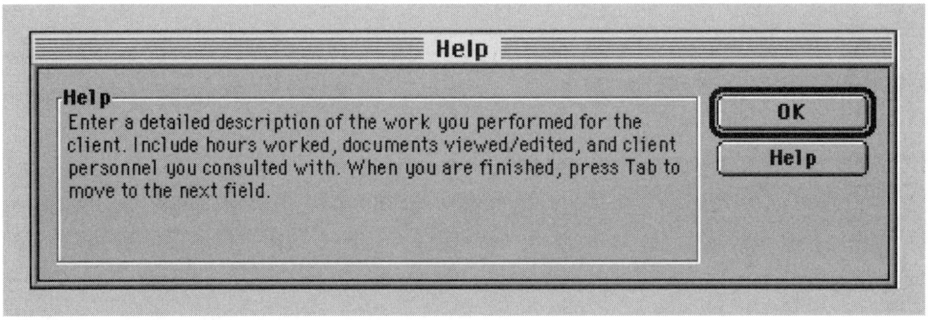

If you try to view help for a field that does not have form field help specified, nothing happens: the Status bar displays normal Status bar information and a Help dialog box does not appear.

Saving a Completed Form

When it's time to save the completed form, you have two options.

- To save the entire form as a Word document, choose Save or Save As from the File menu, give the document a name, specify a disk location, and click Save. In other words, don't do anything special — just save it. I discussed saving documents in Chapter 3.
- To save only the data entered into the form, begin by choosing Save or Save As from the File menu. Click the Options button to display the Save tab of the Options dialog box. Turn on the check box for Save Data Only for Forms and click OK. Then give the document a name and specify a disk location. If you expect to import the data into a program other than Word, use the Save File as Type pop-up menu to choose an appropriate file type — Text Only is a safe bet since all programs can read plain text files. Then click Save to save the text.

FYI: Saving Data Only for Forms

When you save only the data in a form, Word creates a new document containing just the contents of the fields. Each field's contents are enclosed in double quotes and separated by a comma. There's a paragraph mark at the end of the document. Here's an example:

```
"Maria·Langer","P.O.·Box·212","Harrington·Park","NJ","07640-0212"¶
```

This format is easily understandable by Word and other applications. Saving only the data makes it easy to import form field contents into a data source for a mail merge or into a database document created with another application. I discussed mail merge in Chapter 21 and will discuss exchanging information with other applications in Chapter 25.

Printing a Completed Form

You have two options when you want to print a completed form.

- To print the entire form, choose Print from the File menu, set appropriate options in the Print dialog box, and click the print button. I discussed printing in Chapter 4.
- To print only the contents of form fields, choose Print from the File menu to display the Print dialog box. Click the Word Options button to display the Print tab of the Options dialog box. Turn on the check box for Print Data Only for Forms and click OK. Then set appropriate options in the Print dialog box and click Print. Word prints the contents of form fields the way they appear on the page. If your form closely matched a preprinted form, you could use this feature to have Word fill the form out. I'll tell you more about the Options dialog box in Chapter 23.

TIP/TRICK

If you always want just the form data to print when you print a specific form, turn on the check box for Print Data Only for Forms before saving the finalized template. This way, the option is turned on by default for any new document created from that template file.

Chapter Summary

In this chapter, you learned to use Word's new Forms feature to create your own custom forms. You saw how to create form template files and insert form fields. You learned about the different kinds of form fields and how they can be used to create professional-looking forms. You also learned to open, fill out, edit, save, and print the forms you and others create with Word.

The next chapter begins the final section of the book, which covers advanced features of Word. In Chapter 23, you'll begin by learning some of Word's customization options. You'll find out about the Options dialog box I've mentioned throughout the book and you'll see how you can use it to customize the way Word looks and works.

P A R T

5

Applying Word's Advanced Features

THIS PART OF THE BOOK WILL INTRODUCE YOU TO THE advanced features of Microsoft Word, including customizing Word, exchanging information with other documents and applications, and using Word's new macro feature.

23

Chapter 23: Customizing Word Options

NEW IN WORD 6

WORD HAS ALWAYS BEEN HIGHLY USER-CONFIGURABLE, BUT version 6 adds even more preference settings. The Options dialog box, which replaces and expands the Preferences dialog box in previous versions, gives you access to most configuration settings. I've mentioned the Options dialog box throughout this book. Now it's time to take a close look at it. Open it by choosing Options from the Tools menu. You'll see that it has a total of 12 tabs. I'll tell you about them one by one.

User Info Tab Options

The User Info tab is where you introduce yourself to Word. Word automatically uses the name and company name you provided when you installed it and can figure out your initials based on your name.

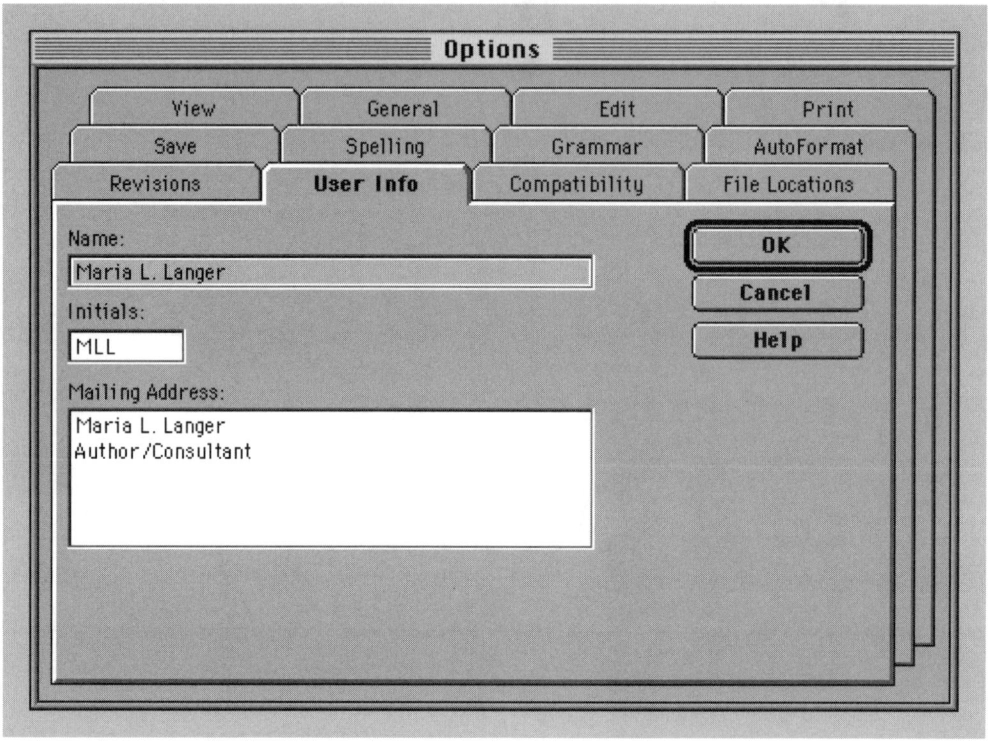

Name

The name you enter in the Name edit box is the name Word uses in a variety of places throughout Word:

- In the Author field of the Summary Info dialog box I told you about in Chapter 3.
- In the Reviewer pop-up menu of the annotations pane I told you about in Chapter 18.
- In the Review Revisions dialog box I told you about in Chapter 18.

Initials

The initials you enter in the Initials edit box are used by Word's Annotation feature, which I told you about in Chapter 18.

Mailing Address

The name, company name (or title), and address you enter in the Mailing Address edit box is used as the return address by the Envelope and Labels feature.

NEW IN WORD 6

General Tab Options

The General tab lets you set miscellaneous Word preferences that affect the way Word looks and works.

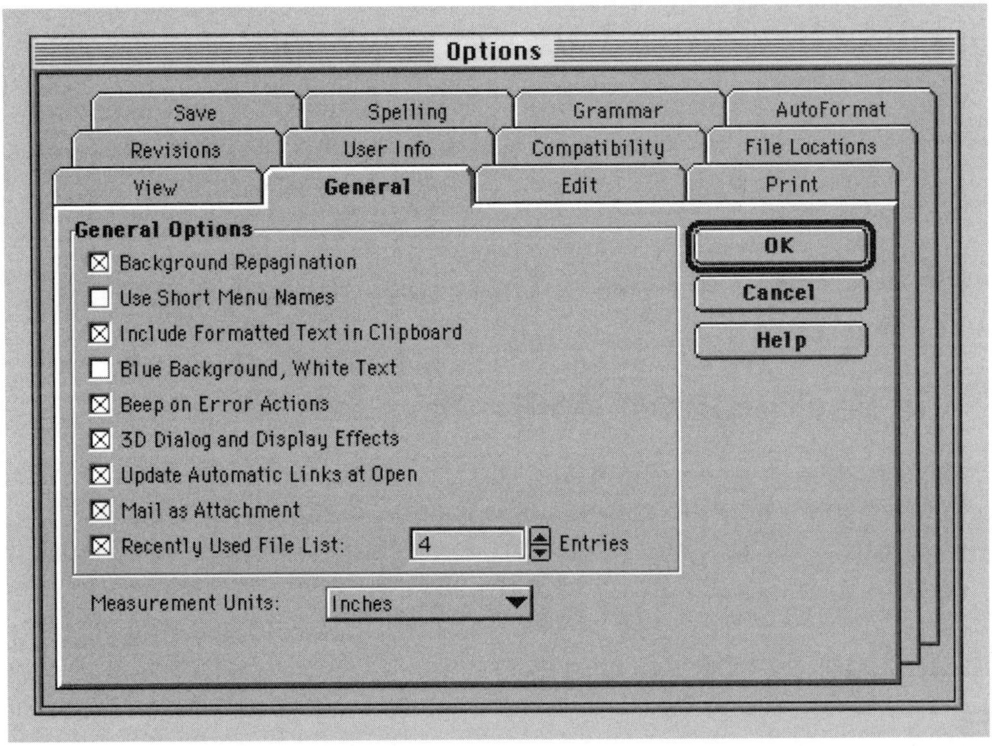

Background Repagination

When the Background Repagination checkbox is turned on, Word automatically repaginates documents in the background while you Work. I told you about pagination in Chapter 8. By default, this option is turned on.

Use Short Menu Names

When the Use Short Menu Names check box is turned on, Word uses abbreviated menu names in the Menu bar, like this:

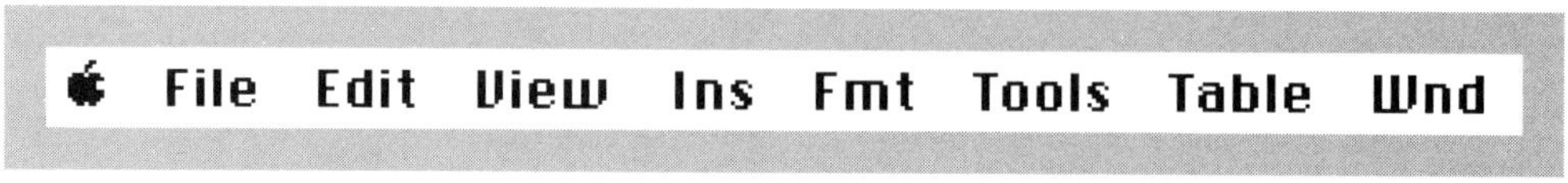

This may be helpful if you're using Word on a small-screen Macintosh. By default, this option is turned off.

Include Formatted Text in Clipboard

When the Include Formatted Text in Clipboard check box is turned on, Word includes font and paragraph formatting in text you copy to the Clipboard with the Copy or Cut commands, toolbar buttons, or shortcut keys. This means formatted text can be copied and pasted or cut and pasted without losing formatting. I told you about font and paragraph formatting in Chapters 5 and 6 and about the Clipboard in Chapter 2. By default, this option is turned on.

Blue Background, White Text

NEW IN WORD 6

When the Blue Background, White Text check box is turned on, Word displays text in white on a blue background. This makes Word look like WordPerfect for DOS. Why you'd want to do that is beyond me — I think WordPerfect for DOS is pretty ugly. By default, this option is turned off.

Beep on Error Actions

NEW IN WORD 6

When the Beep on Error Actions check box is turned on, Word uses the System alert sound to tell you you've done something wrong. You can set the System alert sound with the Sounds control panel that came with your Macintosh. By default, this option is turned on.

3D Dialog and Display Effects

When the 3D Dialog and Display Effects check box is turned on, Word displays dialog boxes and other screen elements with a three-dimensional effect and in color. This makes Word more aesthetically pleasing. By default, this option is turned on. If you're using Word on a black and white monitor, you may want to turn it off.

Update Automatic Links at Open

NEW IN WORD 6

When the Update Automatic Links at Open check box is turned on, when you open a file, Word automatically updates information in it that is linked to another file. I'll tell you about linking files in Chapter 25. By default, this option is turned on.

Mail as Attachment

NEW IN WORD 6

When the Mail as Attachment check box is turned on, Word can attach documents to an electronic mail message if an electronic mail program like Microsoft Mail is installed on your Macintosh. I'll tell you about attaching documents to Microsoft Mail messages in Chapter 25. By default, this option is turned on.

Recently Used File List

When the Recently Used File List check box is turned on, Word includes a list of the most recently closed files near the bottom of the File menu, making them quick and easy to reopen. When this check box is turned on, you can enter a value from 1 to 9 in the Entries edit box. By default, this option is turned on with 4 entries.

Measurement Units

Use the Measurement Units pop-up menu to choose the measurement unit you prefer to work with. This unit will appear in most dialog boxes requiring a measurement entry and on the rulers. I told you about measurement units in Chapter 1. The choices are inches, centimeters, points, and picas. The default measurement unit is inches.

View Tab Options

The View tab lets you specify what screen elements Word should display in each of Word's working views: Normal, Page Layout, and Outline or Master Document. There are options under Show, Window, and Nonprinting Characters. The following illustration shows what this tab looks like for Normal view, but it changes for Page Layout and Outline views. I'll discuss all the options here.

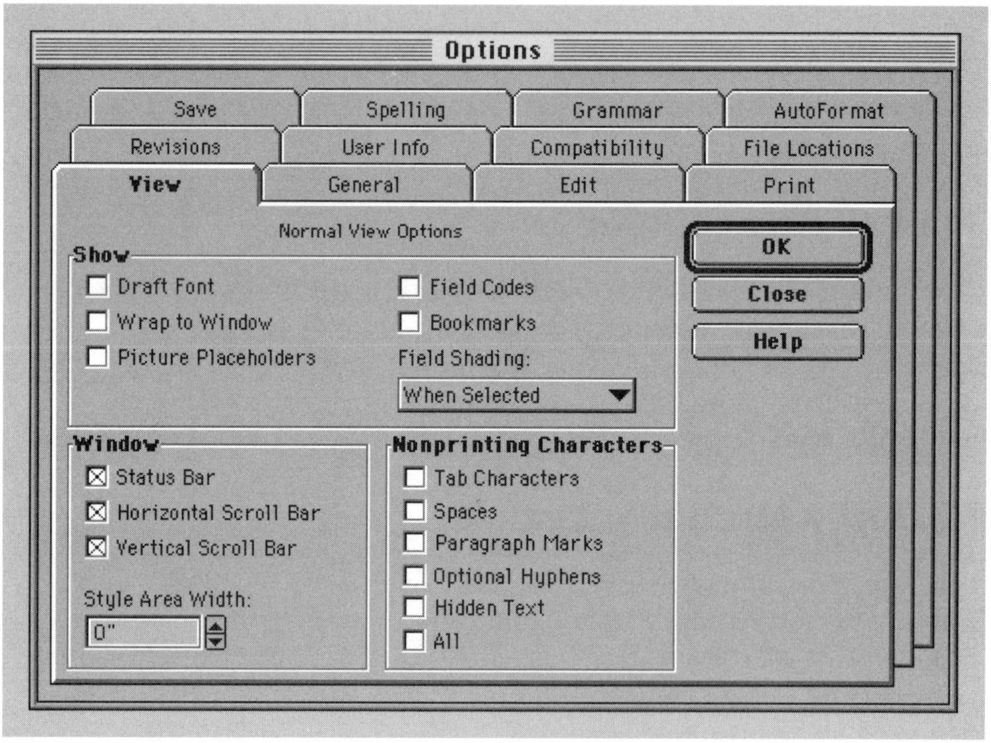

Draft Font

NEW IN WORD 6

The Draft Font option appears in Normal and Outline views. When the check box is turned on, Word displays any font formatting as underlined and bold rather than as actual (WYSIWYG) formatting. In addition, it displays graphics as empty boxes. I told you about font formatting in Chapter 5. Depending on the speed of your computer and the complexity of your document design, turning on this option could speed up screen display. By default, this option is turned off in both views.

Drawings

NEW IN WORD 6

The Drawings option appears in Page Layout view only. When the check box is turned on, Word displays Word drawing objects on the document page. I told you about drawings in Chapter 12. By default, this option is turned on.

Wrap to Window

NEW IN WORD 6

The Wrap to Window option appears in Normal and Outline views. When the check box is turned on, Word wraps text from one line to the next based on the width of the window rather than margin and indent settings. I told you about margins in Chapter 8 and indents in Chapter 6. By default, this option is turned off in both views.

Object Anchors

NEW IN WORD 6

The Object Anchors option appears in Page Layout view only. When the check box is turned on, Word displays an anchor symbol when you click on a drawing object or frame. The anchor indicates that the object is attached to a paragraph. I told you about the anchor in Chapters 12 and 13. By default, this option is turned off.

Text Boundaries

The Text Boundaries option appears in Page Layout view only. When the check box is turned on, Word displays dotted lines around page margins, text columns, objects, and frames. I told you about margins and columns in Chapter 8, and about objects and frames in Chapters 12 and 13. By default, this option is turned off.

Picture Placeholders

The Picture Placeholders option appears in all views. When the check box is turned on, Word displays a box the size of a graphic rather than the actual graphic. I told you about graphics in Chapter 12. Turning this option on can speed up scrolling and screen display. By default, this option is turned off in all views.

Field Codes

NEW IN WORD 6

The Field Codes option appears in all views. When the check box is turned on, Word displays field codes rather than field results. I told you about fields in Chapters 20 and 22. By default, this option is turned off in all views.

Bookmarks

NEW IN WORD 6

The Bookmarks option appears in all views. When the check box is turned on, Word displays bookmarks and linked objects by enclosing them in gray bracket characters: [ ]. I told you about bookmarks in Chapter 14 and will tell you about linked documents in Chapter 25. By default, this option is turned off in all views.

Field Shading

NEW IN WORD 6

The Field Shading option appears in all views. Use the pop-up menu to choose from among three field shading options: Never, Always, and When Selected. I told you about fields in Chapters 20 and 22. The default setting for all views is When Selected, meaning that Word shades a field when you click on it. Field shading does not print, no matter how it is set here.

Status Bar

NEW IN WORD 6

The Status Bar option appears in all views. When the check box is turned on, Word displays the Status bar at the bottom of the screen. I told you about the Status bar in Chapter 1. By default, this option is turned on in all views.

Horizontal Scroll Bar

NEW IN WORD 6

The Horizontal Scroll Bar option appears in all views. When the check box is turned on, Word displays a Horizontal Scroll bar along the bottom of the document window. I told you about the Horizontal Scroll bar in Chapter 1. By default, this option is turned on in all views.

Vertical Scroll Bar

NEW IN WORD 6

The Vertical Scroll Bar option appears in all views. When the check box is turned on, Word displays a Vertical Scroll bar along the right side of the document window. I told you about the Vertical Scroll bar in Chapter 1. By default, this option is turned on in all views.

Style Area Width

The Style Area Width option appears in Normal and Outline views. Use the edit box to enter a width from 0 to 3.89" for the style area. I told you about the style area in Chapters 7 and 15. By default, this option is set to 0, thus hiding the style area.

NEW IN WORD 6

Vertical Ruler

The Vertical Ruler option appears in Page Layout view only. When the check box is turned on, Word displays a vertical ruler along the left side of the document window in Page Layout view when Ruler under the View menu is turned on. By default, this option is turned on.

NEW IN WORD 6

Tab Characters

The Tab Characters option appears in all views. When the check box is turned on, Word displays tab characters as right-pointing arrows. By default, this option is turned off in all views.

NEW IN WORD 6

Spaces

The Spaces option appears in all views. When the check box is turned on, Word displays space characters as gray dots between words. By default, this option is turned off in all views.

NEW IN WORD 6

Paragraph Marks

The Paragraph Marks option appears in all views. When the check box is turned on, Word displays return characters as backwards Ps like this: ¶. By default, this option is turned off in all views.

NEW IN WORD 6

Optional Hyphens

The Optional Hyphen option appears in all views. When the check box is turned on, Word displays optional hyphen characters as dotted lines between words. By default, this option is turned off in all views.

NEW IN WORD 6

Hidden Text

NEW IN WORD 6

The Hidden Text option appears in all views. When the check box is turned on, Word displays hidden text characters with dotted lines beneath them. By default, this option is turned off in all views.

All

NEW IN WORD 6

The All option appears in all views. When the check box is turned on, Word displays all nonprinting characters, including the ones listed separately above. In order to display all nonprinting characters, you must turn on the Show/Hide ¶ button in the Standard Toolbar. By default, this option is turned off in all views.

File Locations Tab Options

NEW IN WORD 6

The File Locations tab lets you set the default file locations for Word files. By setting these correctly, Word knows where to look for and save files. The file locations are automatically set by Word when you install it, but you can modify file locations with the options under this tab. This makes it possible to set default file locations for your document, templates, and other files.

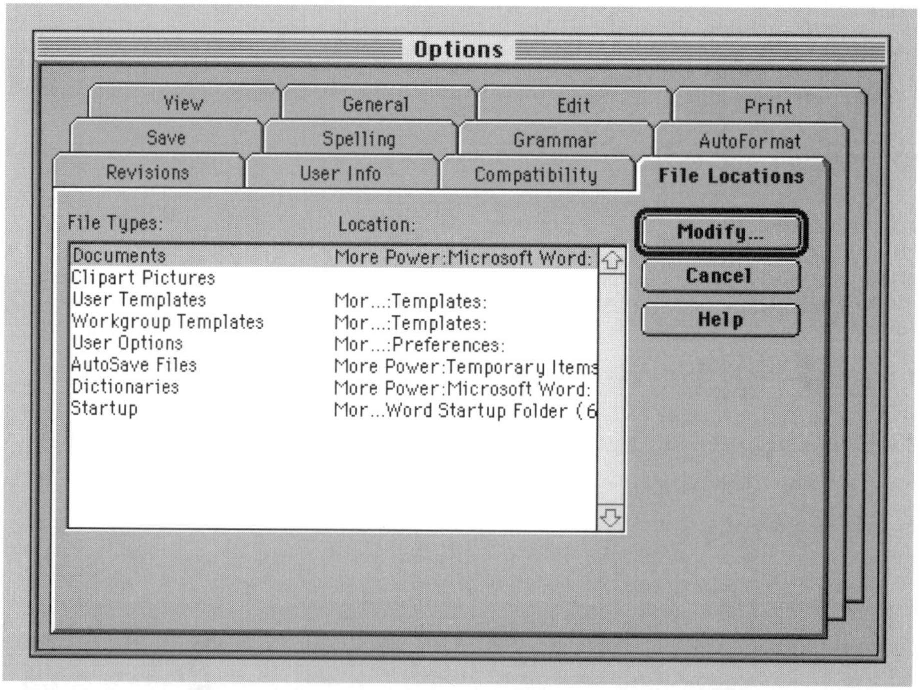

To change a file location, click on the name of a file type in the scrolling list and click the Modify button. A standard Open dialog box appears. Use the directory portion of the window to locate and open the folder where Word can find that file type and click Use Selected Folder. The dialog box disappears, returning you to the Options dialog box. The pathname under Location changes to what you just specified.

Save Tab Options

The Save tab lets you set preferences for saving files. Options in this dialog box can be global, affecting all documents, or for the document that is active when you open the dialog box. I told you about saving documents in Chapter 3.

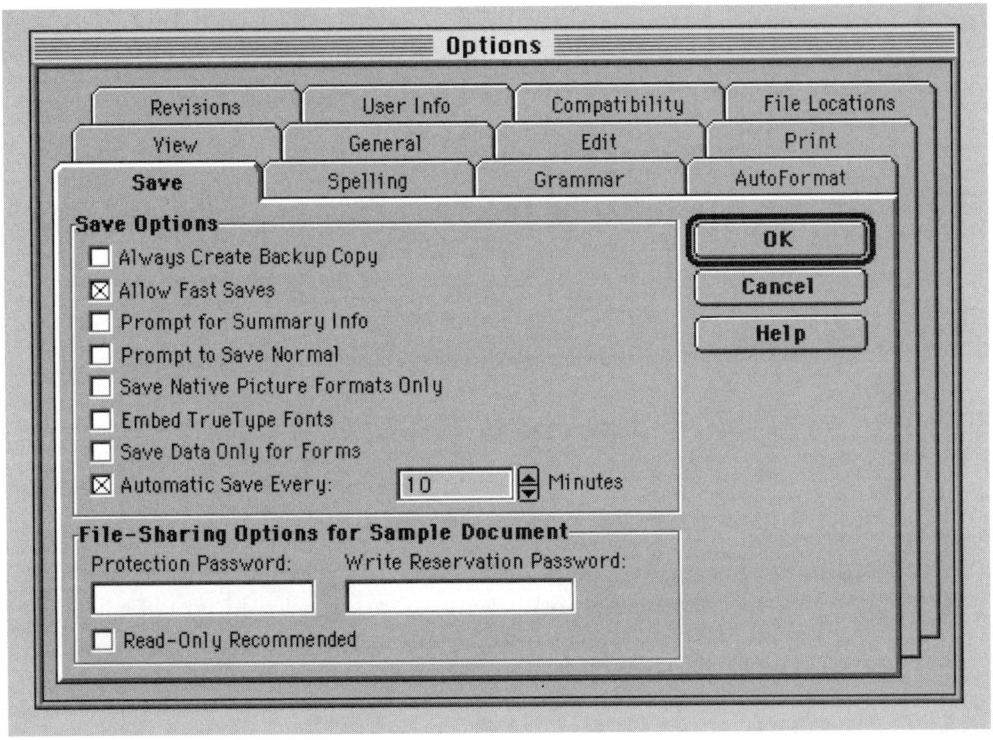

Always Create Backup Copy

When the Always Create Backup Copy check box is turned on, each time you save a file, Word first copies the last saved version of it, giving it the name Backup of *Document* (where *Document* is the original document name). If necessary, Word truncates the file name so it does not exceed 31 characters, the maximum file name length. If a backup file already exists, Word replaces it with the new backup. Word then saves the current file. As a result, you always have two versions of each file — the last saved version and the previously saved version. By default, this option is turned off.

Allow Fast Saves

When the Allow Fast Saves check box is turned on, Word saves only changes to a file, appending them to the last saved version on disk. This greatly increases the speed at which Word saves files, especially long ones. You may notice that a fast saved file may take up more space on disk than the same file saved with the fast save feature turned off. By default, this option is turned on.

Prompt for Summary Info

When the Prompt for Summary Info check box is turned on, Word automatically displays the Summary Info dialog box whenever you save a document for the first time. By default, this option is turned off.

Prompt to Save Normal

NEW IN WORD 6

When the Prompt to Save Normal check box is turned on, when you quit Word, it displays a dialog box asking if you want to save changes to the Normal template. When this check box is turned off, Word automatically saves changes to the Normal template without asking. I told you about templates in Chapter 9. By default, this option is turned off.

Save Native Picture Formats Only

NEW IN WORD 6

When the Save Native Picture Formats Only check box is turned on, Word saves imported graphics as Macintosh graphics, no matter what computer platform (DOS, Windows, etc.) they were created on. This can save disk space. I told you about graphics in Chapter 12 and will tell you about importing graphics in Chapter 25. By default, this option is turned off.

Embed TrueType Fonts

NEW IN WORD 6

When the Embed TrueType Fonts check box is turned on, Word saves the TrueType fonts used to create the document as part of the document so others who open the document file without the specific fonts installed can view the document the way it was created. By default, this option is turned off.

Save Data Only for Forms

NEW IN WORD 6

When the Save Data Only for Forms check box is turned on, Word saves the information entered into a form as a record that can be used in a database or mail merge. I told you about mail merge in Chapter 21 and about forms in Chapter 22. By default, this option is turned off.

Automatic Save

When the Automatic Save check box is turned on, Word automatically saves open documents as you work. Enter a value from 1 to 120 in the Minutes edit box to tell Word how often to save. By default, this option is turned on and set to 10 minutes.

NEW IN WORD 6

In previous versions of Word, the Save Reminder option let you tell Word how often it should remind you to save the file. The Automatic Save feature in version 6 doesn't bother you with reminders — it just saves the file.

Protection Password

NEW IN WORD 6

The Protection Password option can be used to assign a password to the document that is active when you open the Options dialog box. Enter up to 15 characters in the Protection Password edit box. A password is case sensitive — it distinguishes between uppercase and lowercase characters — can include any combination of characters, including numbers, symbols, and spaces. As you type, Word displays bullet (•) characters in place of the password to prevent someone from seeing the password as you enter it. When you click OK after entering the password, Word displays a confirmation dialog box like the one shown here so you can confirm the password you entered. Type it again in this dialog box and click OK to complete the protection.

When you try to open the file, Word displays the Password dialog box. You'll have to enter the password correctly and click OK to open the file.

To remove a password from a file, delete the password in the Protection Password edit box, click OK to close the Options dialog box, and save the document.

IMPORTANT NOTE

If you assign a password to a file, do not lose it! Otherwise, you may never be able to open the file again!

Write Reservation Password

NEW IN WORD 6

The Write Reservation Password option can be used to assign a "read-only" password to the document that is active when you open the Options dialog box. You enter the password the same way you enter the Protection Password I just told you about. When you open a document that has a Write Reservation Password, you get a Password dialog box like this:

If you know the password, type it in and click OK to get full access to the document. If you don't know the password, click Read Only. The document opens and the words *Read-Only* appear in its Title bar. You'll be able to make changes to the document, but when you try to save your changes, Word reminds you that the document is read-only. The only way you can save changes is to save the document with a different name or in a different disk location using the Save As dialog box.

Read Only Recommended

The Read Only Recommended option works for the document that is active when you open the Options dialog box. When you turn this check box on, it displays a dialog box like this every time someone opens the file:

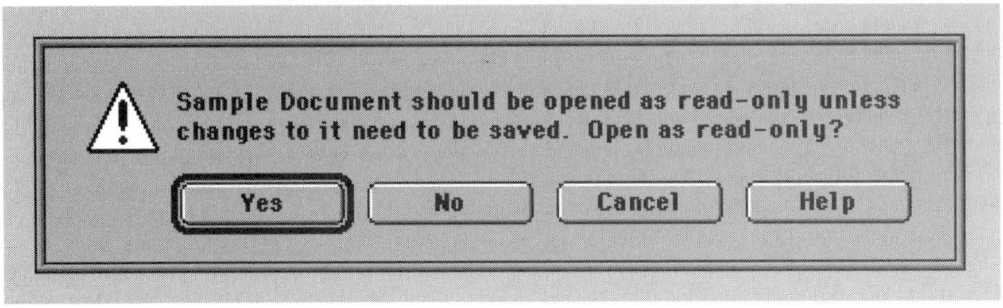

To open the file as a read-only file, click Yes. To open the file as a regular file, click No. By default, this option is turned off.

Edit Tab Options

The Edit tab lets you set preferences for editing Word documents. I discussed editing in Chapter 2.

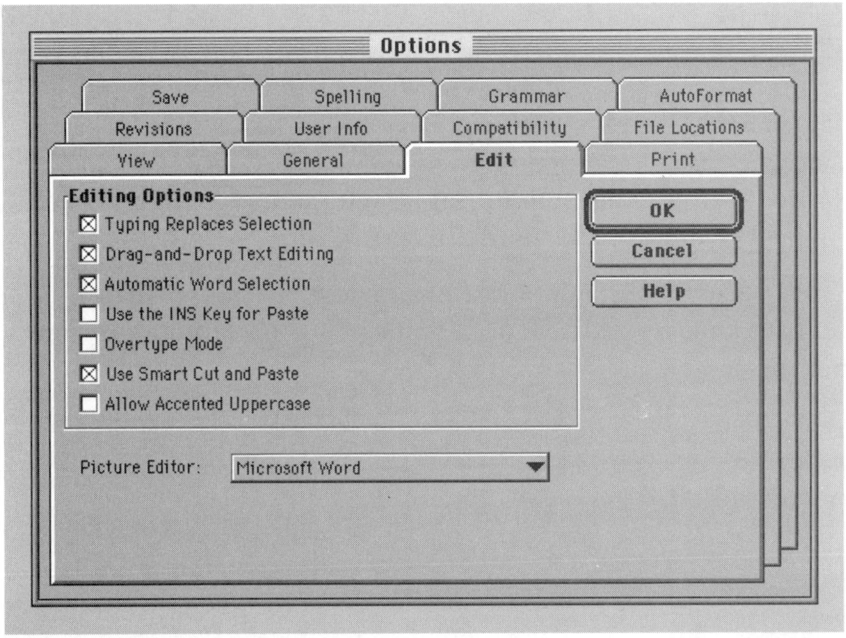

Typing Replaces Selection

NEW IN WORD 6

When the Typing Replaces Selection check box is turned on, Word deletes any selected text as soon as you begin typing. This is the way most Macintosh programs work. By default, this option is turned on.

Drag and Drop Text Editing

When the Drag and Drop Text editing check box is turned on, Word lets you move or copy selected text by dragging it to a new location (move) or holding down Option while dragging it to a new location (copy). This makes it possible to move or copy text without using the Cut, Copy, and Paste commands, toolbar buttons, or shortcut keys. By default, this option is turned on.

Automatic Word Selection

NEW IN WORD 6

When the Automatic Word Selection check box is turned on, Word automatically selects an entire Word when part of the word is selected. By default, this option is turned on. I personally find this very annoying since I often want to select only part of a word, so I keep it turned off.

Use the INS Key for Paste

NEW IN WORD 6

When the Use the INS Key for Paste check box is turned on, Word lets you paste the contents of the clipboard into your document by pressing Ins on an extended keyboard. There's a catch to this. The Ins key is also the Help key, so pressing it by itself will open Word's Help feature, which I told you about in Chapter 1. To use this option, you have to press Shift Help, which is the same as Ins. By default, this option is turned off.

TIP/TRICK

The Use the INS Key for Paste option seems to be more trouble than it's worth. If you have an extended keyboard, you can use F4 to do the same thing without turning on any other options.

Overtype Mode

NEW IN WORD 6

When the Overtype Mode check box is turned on, Word's insertion point cursor changes to an overtype cursor. Instead of inserting text as you type, you'll replace text as you type. By default, this option is turned off.

TIP/TRICK

Turning on this option is the same as double-clicking the OVR indicator in the Status bar.

Use Smart Cut and Paste

NEW IN WORD 6

When the Use Smart Cut and Paste check box is turned on, Word automatically removes unneeded spaces or adds needed spaces when you delete or insert text. By default, this option is turned on.

Allow Accented Uppercase

NEW IN WORD 6

When the Allow Accented Uppercase check box is turned on, Word's proofing tools and the Change Case feature suggest the inclusion of an accent mark over text formatted as French. I told you about the proofing tools and the Language feature in Chapter 17. By default, this option is turned off.

Picture Editor

NEW IN WORD 6

The Picture Editor pop-up menu lets you choose an application to edit pictures in Word. The default setting is Microsoft Word.

Print Tab Options

The Print tab lets you set preferences for printing word documents. Options in this dialog box can be global, affecting all documents, or for the document that is active when you open the dialog box. I discussed printing in Chapter 4.

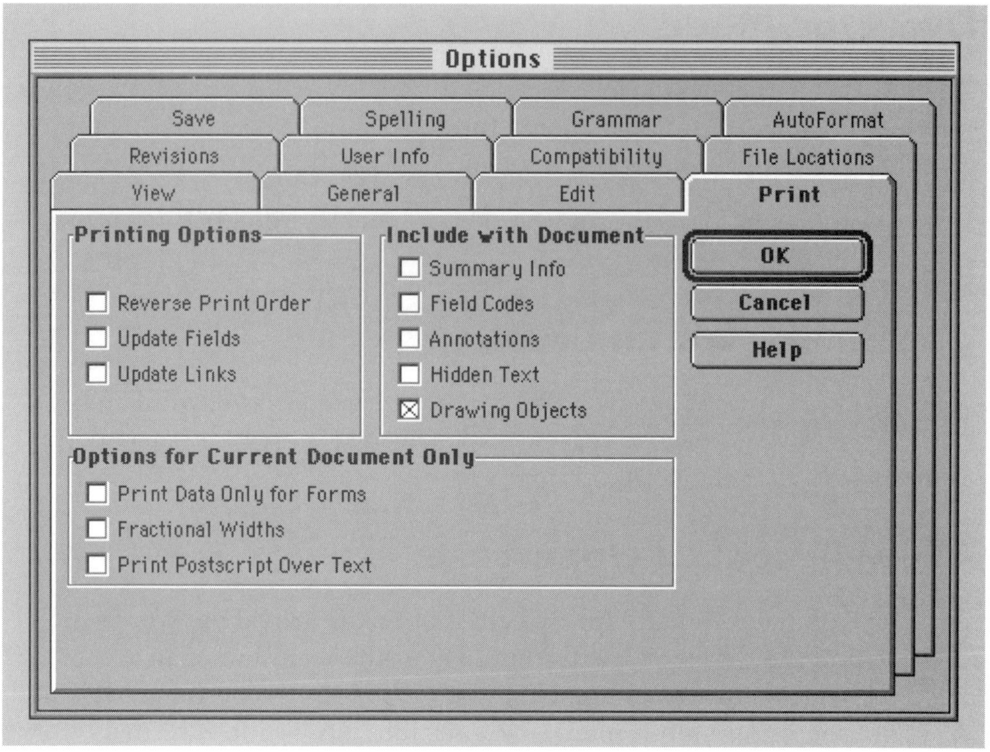

Reverse Print Order

When the Reverse Print Order check box is turned on, Word prints the last page of the print range first. By default, this check box is turned off.

This option is handy for two things:

TIP/TRICK

- If your printer leaves paper face up in the output tray rather than face down, you probably spend a lot of time shuffling through pages to put them in the right order. Turn on this option to have Word do it for you automatically.
- If you want to print a document double-sided, print all the odd pages first, then take the stack of pages and put them back in the paper tray or cassette face down, turn on this option, and print the even pages. Be careful, though — if your document has an odd number of pages, keep the last odd page out of the tray when printing the even pages. Otherwise, page 2 might print on the back of page 3 rather than page 1.

Update Fields

NEW IN WORD 6

When the Update Fields check box is turned on, Word automatically updates the results of all fields included in the document before printing. This includes a table of contents, index, date fields, etc. I told you about fields in Chapters 20 and 22. By default, this option is turned off.

Update Links

NEW IN WORD 6

When the Update Links check box is turned on, Word automatically updates links between the document being printed and any other documents before printing. I'll tell you about linking documents in Chapter 25. By default, this option is turned off.

Summary Info

When the Summary Info check box is turned on, Word prints the Summary Info for the file on a separate page at the end of the document. I told you about Summary Info in Chapter 3. By default, this option is turned off.

Field Codes

NEW IN WORD 6

When the Field Codes check box is turned on, Word prints field codes rather than field results in the document. I told you about field codes throughout this book, but especially in Chapters 20 and 21. By default, this option is turned off.

Annotations

NEW IN WORD 6

When the Annotations check box is turned on, Word prints any document annotations on a separate page at the end of the document. I told you about annotations in Chapter 18. By default, this option is turned off.

Hidden Text

When the Hidden Text check box is turned on, Word prints text formatted as hidden. When printing, Word does not include the dotted line under hidden text that appears on screen. I told you about hidden text in Chapter 5. By default, this option is turned off.

Drawing Objects

NEW IN WORD 6

When the Drawing Objects check box is turned on, Word prints objects you drew in the document with Word's Drawing feature. I told you about the Drawing feature and graphics in Chapter 12. By default, this option is turned on.

Print Data Only for Forms

NEW IN WORD 6

The Print Data Only for Forms option applies only to the document that was active when you opened the Options dialog box. When this check box is turned on, Word prints only the data or information entered into a Word form rather than the entire form. I told you about forms in Chapter 22. By default, this check box is turned off.

Fractional Widths

The Fractional Widths option applies only to the document that was active when you opened the Options dialog box. When this check box is turned on, Word adjusts the spacing of proportionally spaced fonts like Helvetica and Times. This can make your document look better when printed. In general, you should not use this option with monospaced fonts like Courier and Monaco. I talked about Fonts in Chapter 5. By default, this option is turned off.

Print PostScript Over Text

NEW IN WORD 6

The Print PostScript Over Text option applies only to the document that was active when you opened the Options dialog box. When this check box is turned on, Word can print PostScript-generated text or graphics over other text and graphics on the document page. This option will only work if you have a PostScript printer. By default, this option is turned off.

AutoFormat Tab Options

NEW IN WORD 6

The AutoFormat tab lets you set preferences for Word's AutoFormat feature. I told you about AutoFormat in Chapter 9 and about styles, which AutoFormat can affect, in Chapter 7. Because the AutoFormat feature of Word is brand new in version 6, all of these options are also new to Word. By default, all of these options are turned on.

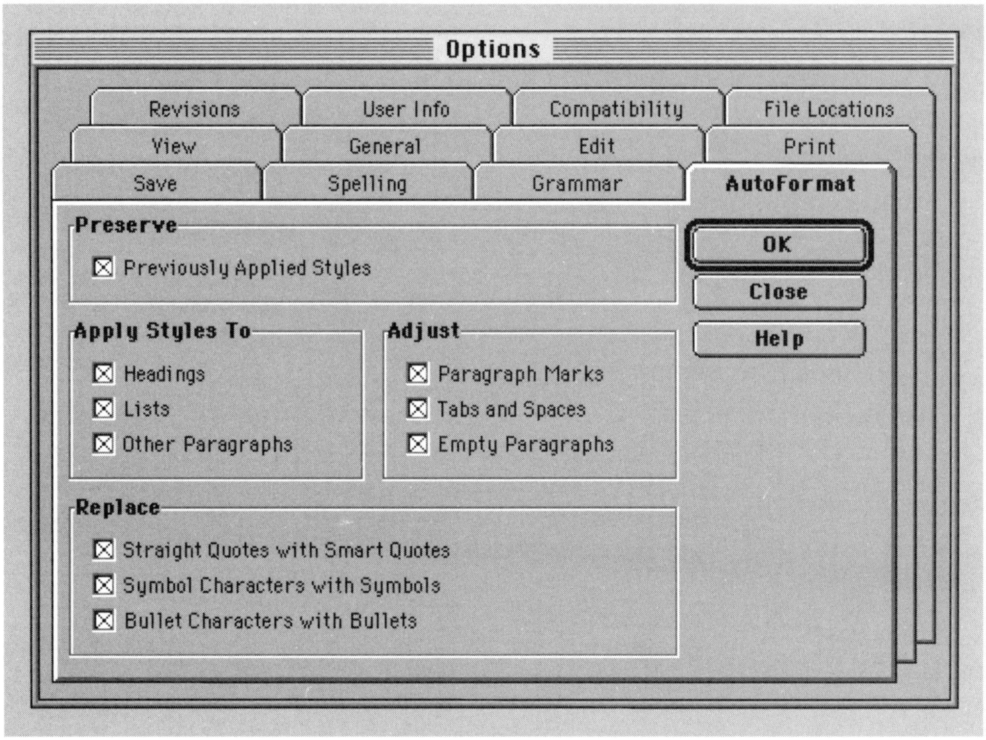

Previously Applied Styles

When the Previously Applied Styles check box is turned on, Word keeps styles you applied to text.

Headings

When the Headings check box is turned on, Word applies its built-in heading styles (Heading 1, Heading 2, ... Heading 9) to the headings in outlines and other appropriate text.

Lists

When the Lists check box is turned on, Word applies list and bullet styles to list text. Word also removes any manual numbering or bullet characters. I told you about lists in Chapter 15.

Other Paragraphs

When the Other Paragraphs check box is turned on, Word applies styles like its built-in Body Text and Inside Address styles to text other than headings and lists.

Paragraph Marks

When the Paragraph Marks check box is turned on, Word adds or removes Return characters as needed. This makes it possible to automatically remove paragraph marks inserted in error at the end of each line.

Tabs and Empty Spaces

When the Tabs and Empty Spaces check box is turned on, Word replaces multiple consecutive spaces with tab characters and removes unnecessary tab and space characters.

Empty Paragraphs

When the Empty Paragraphs check box is turned on, Word removes blank lines between paragraphs and uses paragraph spacing to add space between them. I told you about paragraph spacing in Chapter 6.

Straight Quotes with Smart Quotes

When the Straight Quotes to Smart Quotes check box is turned on, Word replaces standard straight quote characters with curly quote characters. I told you about smart or curly quotes in Chapter 4.

Symbol Characters with Symbols

When the Symbol Characters with Symbols check box is turned on, Word replaces commonly used symbol abbreviations like (R) and (TM) with the proper symbols, like ® and ™. I told you about symbols in Chapter 4.

Bullet Characters with Bullets

When the Bullet Characters with Bullets check box is turned on, Word replaces commonly used bullet characters like a dash (-), an asterisk (*), or a plus (+) with a regular bullet character (•). I told you about bullets in Chapter 4.

Revisions Tab Options

The Revisions tab lets you set preferences for Word's Revisions feature. I told you about revisions in Chapter 18. Because the Revisions feature of Word is new in version 6, all of these options are also new to Word.

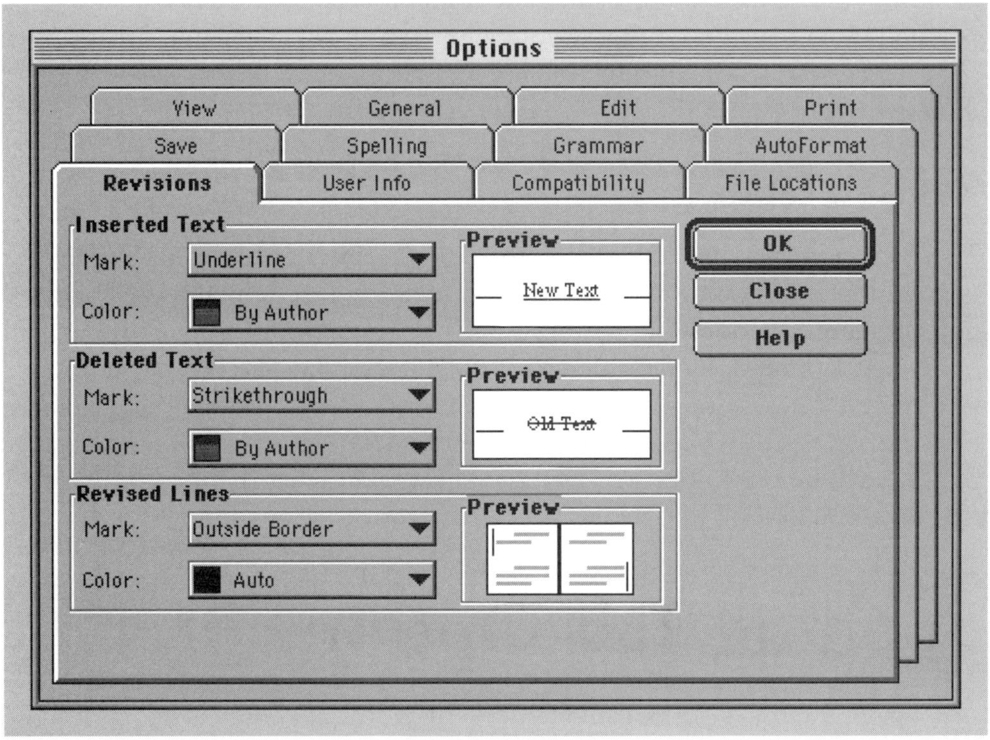

Inserted Text

The Inserted Text area lets you set the appearance for text inserted with the Revision feature turned on. Use the Mark pop-up menu to choose among different formatting options for inserted text: none, Bold, Italic, Underline, or Double Underline. The default setting is Underline. Use the Color pop-up menu to choose from among different colors for inserted text. There are sixteen colors to choose from. If you choose Author, which is the default setting, each reviewer is automatically assigned a different color. The Preview area shows you what inserted text will look like.

Deleted Text

The Deleted Text area lets you set the appearance for text deleted with the Revision feature turned on. Use the Mark pop-up menu to choose from among two different formatting options for deleted text: Hidden and Strikethrough. The default setting is Strikethrough. Use the Color pop-up menu to choose from among different colors for deleted text. There are sixteen colors to choose from. If you choose Author, the default setting, each reviewer is automatically assigned a different color. The Preview area shows you what deleted text will look like.

Revised Lines

The Revised Lines area lets you set the margin appearance for lines of text that have been revised with the Revision feature turned on. Use the Mark pop-up menu to choose from among formatting options for revised lines: none, Left Border, Right Border, and Outside Border. The default setting is Outside border. Use the Color pop-up menu to choose from among different colors for the revised line mark. If you choose Auto, which is the default, the line will be black. The Preview area shows you what the margins beside revised text will look like.

Spelling Tab Options

The Spelling tab lets you set preferences for Word's spelling checker. I told you about the spelling checker in Chapter 17.

Always Suggest

When the Always Suggest check box is turned on, Word always tries to suggest possible spellings for words it does not recognize. By default, this option is turned on.

TIP/TRICK

If you're using Word on an older, slower Macintosh model, you may want to turn off this option. It could speed up the spell check. You can always click the Suggest button in the Spelling dialog box to have Word look up a word when you need it to.

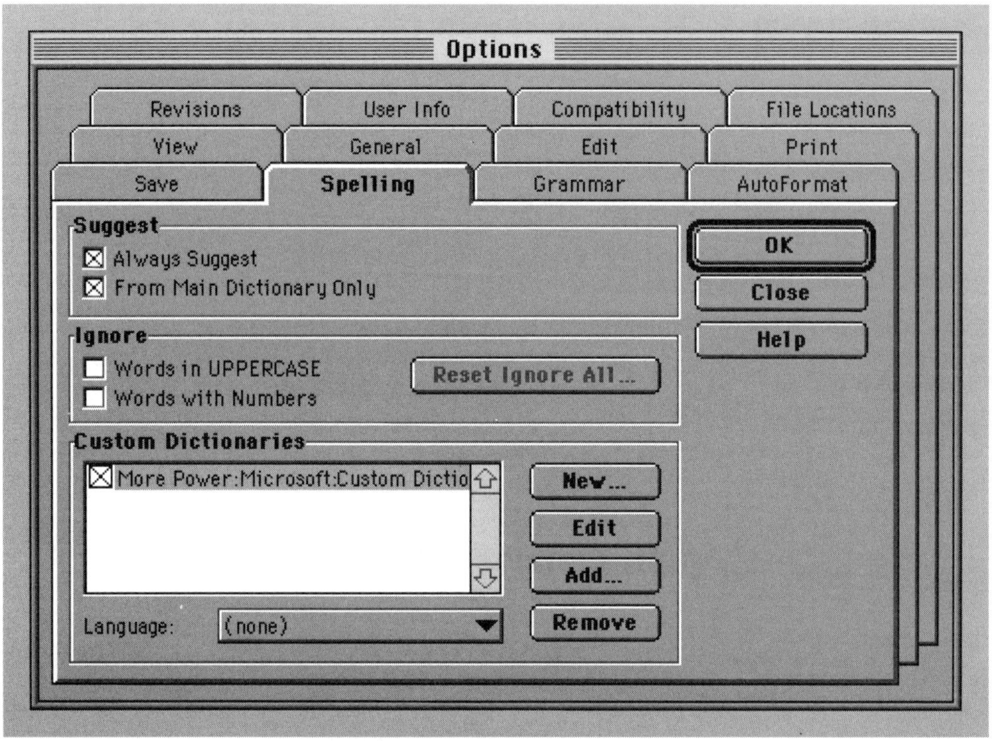

From Main Dictionary Only

NEW IN WORD 6

When the From Main Dictionary Only check box is turned on, Word only suggests words that are in the main dictionary file — not in custom dictionaries. By default, this option is turned on.

Words in UPPERCASE

When the Words in UPPERCASE check box is turned on, Word ignores words in all uppercase letters, like acronyms. By default, this check box is turned off.

Words with Numbers

When the Words with Numbers check box is turned on, Word ignores any word that includes a number, like 2nd or 16th. By default, this option is turned off.

Reset Ignore All

The Reset Ignore All button clears the list of words you told Word to ignore during the current session by clicking the Ignore All button in the Spelling dialog box. After clicking this button, if Word encounters any of the words you previously told it to ignore during a spelling check, it will show the word as an unknown.

Custom Dictionaries

The Custom dictionaries area of the Spelling tab lets you turn on up to 10 custom dictionaries. The available dictionaries appear in the Custom Dictionaries scrolling list. To turn one on or off, click the check box before the dictionary name.

- **New** — lets you create a new dictionary. Click the New button to display a standard Save As dialog box. Enter a new name in the Save Current Document As edit box and click Save. If you save it with the name Custom Dictionary, it will overwrite the existing custom dictionary, so be sure to give it a new name. The new dictionary appears in the Custom Dictionaries scrolling list with its check box turned on.

TIP/TRICK

You can also create a new dictionary by opening a Word document file and typing in the words you want to include in the dictionary. Be sure to press Return after each word. Choose Save As from the File menu to display the Save As dialog box. Choose Speller Custom Dictionary from the Save File as Type pop-up menu, give the dictionary a name, and save it in the Microsoft folder. Then use the Add button to add it to the list of Custom Dictionaries.

- **Edit** — lets you edit a custom dictionary. Select the dictionary you want to edit in the Custom Dictionaries scrolling list and click the Edit button. A dialog box appears, telling you that you'll be able to edit the custom dictionary as a Word document. Click Yes to continue. Click the Close button to dismiss the Options dialog box. Your dictionary appears in an open document window. Edit it as necessary to add or remove words. When you're finished, save and close it.

- **Add** — lets you add a custom dictionary. Click the Add button to display a standard Open dialog box. Make sure the List Files of Type pop-up menu at the bottom of the dialog box says Speller Custom Dictionary. Then locate and open the dictionary file you want to add. It appears in the Custom Dictionaries scrolling list.

TIP/TRICK

If someone in your workplace has built up a large custom dictionary of technical terms you use every day, you can benefit from all their hard work. Put a copy of their custom dictionary file in the Microsoft folder of your Macintosh and use the Add button to add it to the dictionaries your copy of Word uses.

NEW IN WORD 6

- **Remove** — lets you remove a dictionary from the Custom Dictionaries scrolling list. Click on the dictionary name to select it and click Remove. The dictionary disappears.

IMPORTANT NOTE

The Remove button does not delete the dictionary file. It simply removes it from the list of dictionaries Word is aware of.

Language

The Language pop-up menu lets you assign a specific language to a custom dictionary file. Click on the name of the dictionary in the Custom Dictionaries scrolling list and then choose a language from the Language pop-up menu. From then on, Word uses that dictionary when checking the spelling of text formatted in that language. If you choose none, which is the default setting, Word uses the custom dictionary for all documents it checks.

Grammar Tab Options

The Grammar tab lets you set preferences for Word's grammar checker. I told you about the grammar checker in Chapter 17.

Use Grammar and Style Rules

The Use Grammar and Style Rules scrolling list lets you choose from among sets of rules settings. The three built-in sets are:

- **Strictly (all rules)** — sets Word to enforce all grammar and style rules in the grammar checker.
- **For Business Writing** — sets Word to enforce only those grammar and style rules that are appropriate for formal or business documents.
- **For Casual Writing** — sets Word to enforce only those grammar and style rules that are appropriate for informal or casual documents.

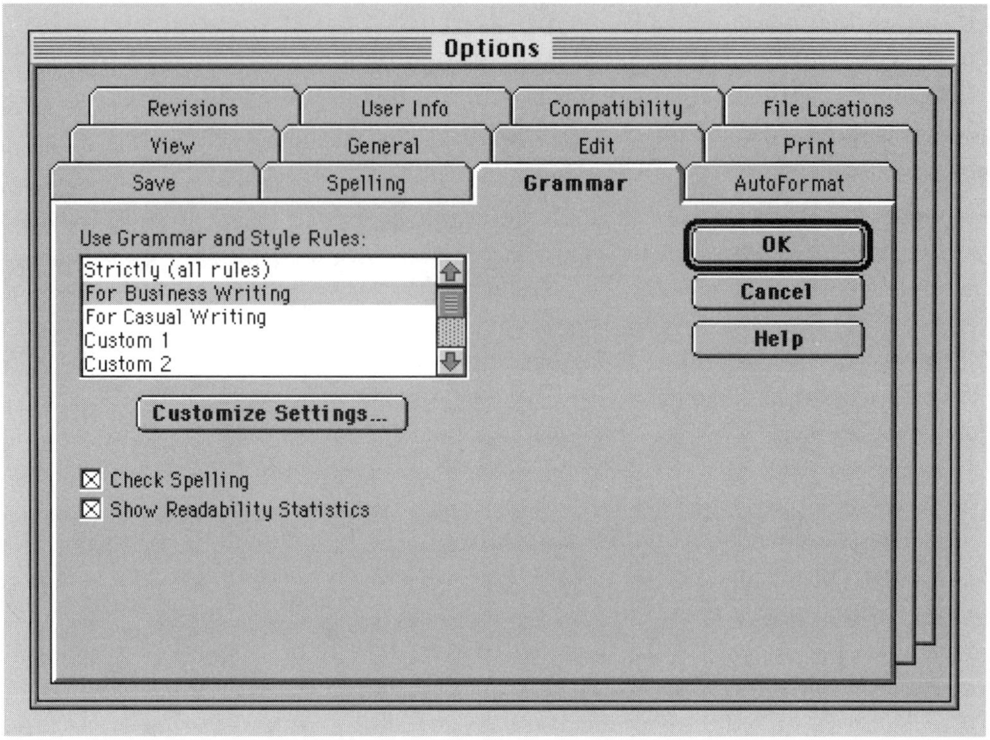

You can customize the built-in or custom sets with the Customize Settings button, which I'll discuss next. By default, this option is set to For Business Writing.

Customize Settings

The Customize Settings button lets you specify which rules should be included in each rule set. Click on the set you want to change in the scrolling list and click the Customize Settings button. The Customize Grammar Settings dialog box appears.

The Use Grammar and Style Rules pop-up menu lists all the rule sets. If you haven't already done so, choose the one you want to customize. Then click the Grammar or Style radio button to display the grammar or styles rules in the scrolling window. Click on the check mark in front of a rule to turn it off. Click on the blank area in front of a rule to turn it on. For more information about a rule, click it to select it and click the Explain button. A window appears with an explanation of the rule. When you're finished reading it, click on its close box to dismiss it.

The Catch area at the bottom of the window offers pop-up menus to set how Word should search for and flag split infinitives, consecutive nouns, and prepositional phrases. Use the Sentences Containing More Words Than edit box to tell Word how long a long sentence really is.

At any time during customization, you can click the Reset All button to reset the rule set to defaults. Once you've finished making changes in the dialog box, click OK to accept them.

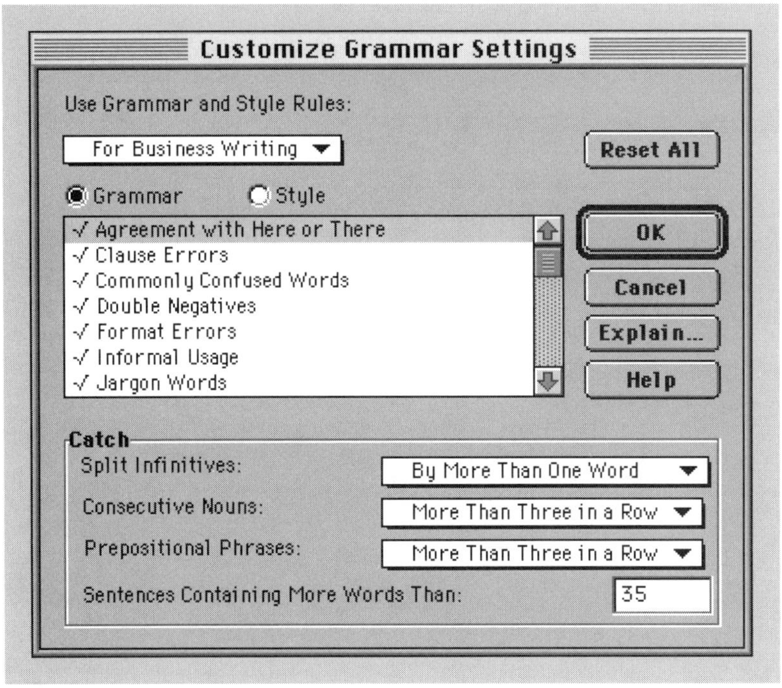

Check Spelling

When you turn on the Check Spelling check box, Word includes a spelling check as part of its grammar check. Whenever Word finds an unrecognized word during a grammar check, it displays the Spelling dialog box. This makes it possible to check grammar and spelling all at once. By default, this option is turned on.

Show Readability Statistics

When you turn on the Show Readability Statistics check box, at the end of a grammar check, Word displays a dialog box containing statistics about the text it checked. By default, this option is turned on.

Compatibility Tab Options

NEW IN WORD 6

The Compatibility tab lets you set options that determine how Word displays the current document. This is useful if the document was created in another program and you want it to look and work like the original document. The changes you make affect the document only while you work with it in Word and do not become part of the document. I'll tell you more about working with non-Word documents in Word in Chapter 25.

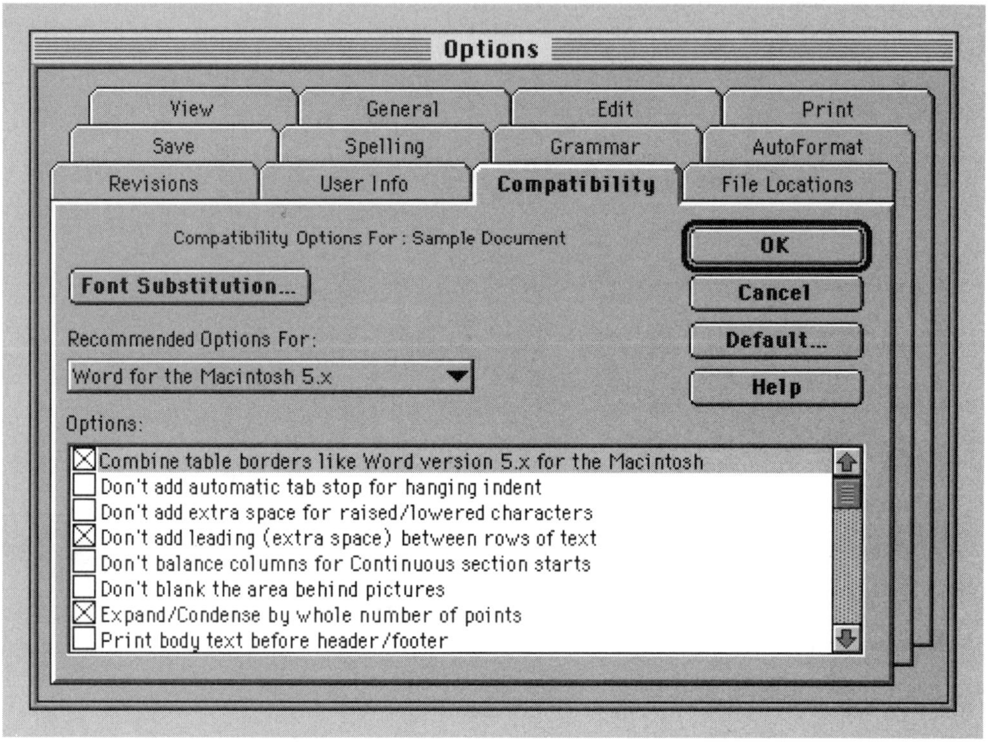

Font Substitution

The Font Substitution button lets you specify fonts available in your system for those in the document that are not available. This button only works if the document was created with fonts you don't have.

Recommended Options For

The Recommended Options For pop-up menu displays a list of programs that create word processing documents. Among them are: Word for Windows 6.0, 2.0, and 1.0; Word for Macintosh 5.x; Word for MS-DOS; and WordPerfect. There's also an option called Custom that you can use to create your own custom settings for documents created by other word processors. When you choose one of these programs, the Options scrolling list displays checks in the boxes in front of some of the options. These are recommended settings and can be changed.

Options

The Options scrolling list can be used to customize compatibility settings. Click in the check box before an option to turn it on or off. Here's a brief summary of the options:

- **Combine Table Borders Like Word Version 5.x for Macintosh —** tells Word to uses the border of the rightmost cell when two adjoining cells have different border settings applied to their common border. I told you about table borders in Chapter 11.
- **Don't Add Automatic Tab Stop for Hanging Indent —** tells Word to ignore the automatic tab stop it normally uses for a hanging indent. I told you about hanging indents and tab stops in Chapter 6.
- **Don't Add Extra Space for Raised/Lowered Characters —** tells Word not to insert additional space between lines for superscript or subscript characters. I told you about superscripts and subscripts in Chapter 5.
- **Don't Add Leading (Extra Space) between Rows of Text —** tells Word not to include leading between lines of text. I told you about line spacing in Chapter 6.
- **Don't Balance Columns for Continuous Section Starts —** tells Word not to make column lengths even at the end of a section or the document. I told you about multiple column text and sections in Chapter 8.
- **Don't Blank the Area Behind Pictures —** tells Word not to hide any text or graphics surrounding an inserted picture. I told you about graphics in Chapter 12.

- **Expand/Condense by Whole Number of Points** — tells Word to use a whole (not fractional) number of points when applying Expand or Condense font formatting. I told you about expanding and condensing font characters in Chapter 5.
- **Print Body Text before Header/Footer** — tells Word to print the body text before it prints the header or footer. I told you about headers and footers in Chapter 10.
- **Print Colors as Black on Noncolor Printers** — tells Word to print all colors as black rather than as shades of gray on noncolor printers. I told you about printing in Chapter 4.
- **Show Hard Page or Column Breaks in Frames** — tells Word to display any manual page or column breaks in the middle of a frame. I told you about manual page and column breaks in Chapter 8.
- **Suppress Extra Line Spacing at Top of Page** — tells Word to ignore Line Spacing settings greater than one line for lines at the top of a page. I told you about line spacing in Chapter 6.
- **Suppress Extra Line Spacing at Top of Page like Mac Word 5.x** — tells Word to ignore Line Spacing settings greater than one line for lines at the top of a page. I told you about line spacing in Chapter 6.
- **Suppress Space Before After a Hard Page or Column Break** — tells Word to ignore Space Before settings for paragraphs following a manual page or column break. I told you about paragraph spacing in Chapter 6 and about page and column breaks in Chapter 8.
- **Swap Left and Right Borders on Odd Facing Pages** — tells Word to print a left side paragraph border on the right side of a paragraph on an odd numbered page when the Different Odd/Even Headers or Mirror Margins check box is turned on in the Document Layout dialog box. I told you about paragraph borders in Chapter 13 and about the Document Layout dialog box in Chapter 8.
- **Treat \" as "" in Mail Merge Data Sources** — tells Word to convert a data delimiter of a slash and a quotation mark to a pair of quotation marks so Word can recognize them. I told you about mail merge in Chapter 21.
- **Use Larger Small Caps like Mac Word 5.x** — tells Word to use larger small caps characters like it does in Word version 5.0 and 5.1. I told you about small caps in Chapter 4.

- **Wrap Trailing Spaces to Next Line** — tells Word to move any space characters that appear in the margin after a word to the beginning of the next line of text. I told you about word wrap in Chapter 2 and about margins in Chapter 8.

Default

Clicking the Default button sets the current option settings as the default in the template the current document is based on. Each time you create a new document with that template, the settings you made the defaults will be used.

Resetting All Options to Word's Defaults

Most of the settings in the Options dialog box are stored in a file called Word Settings (6). This is a special preferences file Word stores in the Preferences folder inside the System folder.

To reset Options to Word's default or "factory" settings, drag the Word Settings (6) file out of the Preferences folder. You can delete it if you no longer want to use the settings at all. The next time you launch Word, it creates a brand new settings file with its defaults.

Chapter Summary

In this chapter, you learned everything you could ever want to know about the options Word offers in its Options dialog box. You've seen how you can use it to customize the way Word looks and works for you.

In the next chapter, you'll learn more about customizing Word. You'll see how you can customize Word's toolbars, menus, and shortcut keys. These change can make put the commands you use most often at your fingertips, making the time you spend with Word more productive.

24

Chapter 24: Customizing Toolbars, Menus, and Shortcut Keys

NEW IN WORD 6

IF YOU'RE LOOKING FOR MORE WAYS TO CUSTOMIZE THE WAY Word works, consider its toolbars, menus, and shortcut keys. You can add, remove, and rearrange toolbar buttons and menu commands; rename and add menus; and add, remove, and change shortcut keys. The greatly improved Toolbars and Customize dialog boxes, with a little imagination, allow you to make Word look and work exactly the way you want it to.

For Example: Making Word 6 Look and Work Like Word 5.1

I love Word version 6 and look forward to taking advantage of as many of its features as possible. But it wasn't always like that. When I first started using it, I was frustrated by the differences between it and Word version 5.1. Toolbar, ruler, and ribbon buttons I'd grown to depend on were missing. Menu commands I used every day were gone or relocated. Shortcut keys embedded in my brain no longer worked — or, worse yet, did things they never did before. If you're switching from Word 5.1 to Word 6.0, you'll know exactly what I mean as you also struggle to change the way you work to fit the new Word.

Here's a little project for you. Use the techniques in this chapter to change Word's toolbars, menus, and shortcut keys to more closely resemble those you know and love from Word version 5.1. You'll find that Microsoft has already helped you perform this task by providing a Word for the Macintosh 5.1 toolbar in its Toolbars dialog box. While I don't recommend cloning Word 5.1 with Word 6.0, I do admit that it's a great way to learn more about customizing Word. If you attach your changes to a special template (rather than to the Normal template) you can relive the days of Word 5.1 any time — just create a new document based on that template.

Toolbars

NEW IN WORD 6

The first Word toolbar appeared in Word 5.1. There was only one toolbar and it was somewhat customizable — you could replace existing buttons with buttons that performed other tasks. You could not, however, add buttons, remove buttons, or create custom toolbars. Word version 6 adds these capabilities, making the toolbar feature of Word more powerful than ever.

Let's take a look at how you can display multiple toolbars, customize existing toolbars, and create your own toolbars from scratch.

Displaying Different Toolbars

Throughout this book, you've seen that certain toolbars appear automatically as you work with Word. The Standard and Formatting toolbars display by default when you start Word. The Drawing toolbar, which I told you about in Chapter 12, displays when you click the Drawing button on the Standard Toolbar and doesn't disappear until you click it again. There are also toolbars for Print Preview, Outlining, Master Document view, Borders, Mail Merge, Forms, and other features.

You can determine which toolbars are displayed at any time. The Toolbars dialog box lets you turn toolbars on or off, customize the way they look and work, and create and delete custom toolbars. Choose Toolbars from the View menu. The Toolbars dialog box appears.

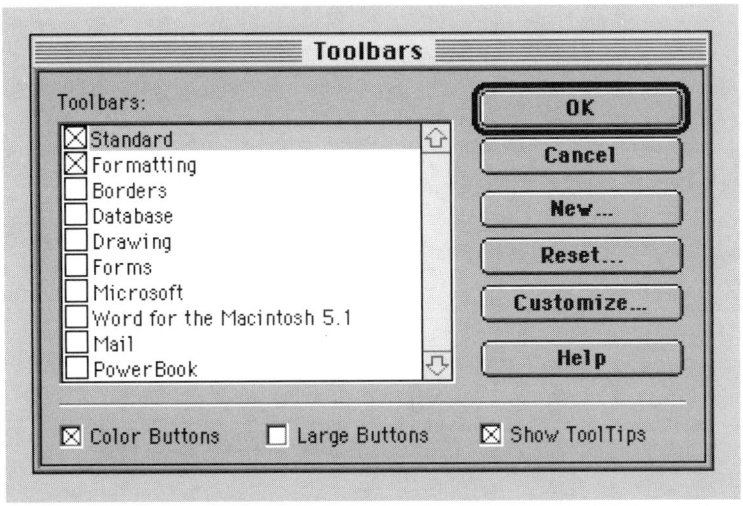

- To display a toolbar, turn on the check box to the left of the toolbar name. When you click OK, the toolbar appears on your screen.
- To hide a toolbar, turn off the check box to the left of the toolbar name. When you click OK, the toolbar disappears.

- To customize the way a toolbar looks and works, use the check boxes at the bottom of the Toolbars dialog box. Color Buttons displays toolbar buttons in color. You might want to turn this off if you have a black and white monitor. Large Buttons enlarges the size of the toolbar buttons, making them roughly twice the size of regular buttons. The problem with this, however, is that fewer buttons fit on screen. Show ToolTips displays the name of the button when you point to it. I told you about ToolTips in Chapter 1.

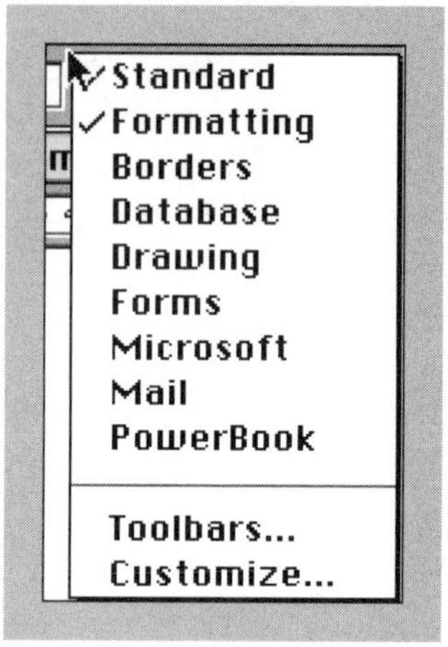

TIP/TRICK

You can also turn toolbars on or off with the Toolbars shortcut menu. Hold down Control and click on the gray area of a toolbar between or under its buttons. The Toolbars shortcut menu appears. Choose the menu you want to hide or display.

FYI: Floating a Toolbar

Toolbars, when displayed, can be either *anchored* or *floating*. The Standard and Formatting toolbars are good examples of anchored toolbars — by default, they're snapped in place at the top of the screen. A floating toolbar, however, can be positioned anywhere you like on the screen. It has a tiny title bar, close box, and size box you can use to move, close, and resize it.

- To float a toolbar, double-click the gray area between its buttons. It becomes detached from its anchored position on the screen.

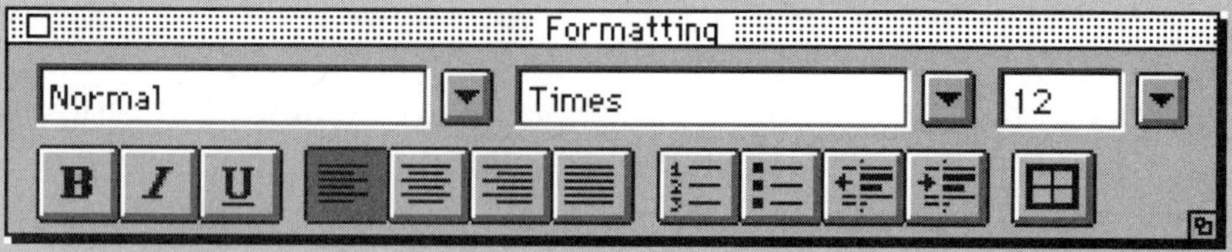

- To move a floating toolbar, drag its title bar.
- To resize and reshape a floating toolbar, drag its size box.

Continued

- To close a floating toolbar, click its close box.
- To anchor a floating toolbar to its previously anchored position, double-click its title bar or the gray area between its buttons.
- To anchor a floating toolbar to the side or bottom of the screen, drag it to the desired position. If a side-anchored toolbar is long, you may not see all of its buttons, depending on the size of your screen.

Adding, Removing, and Rearranging Toolbar Buttons

To add, remove, or rearrange toolbar buttons, begin by displaying the toolbar you want to change. Then do one of the following:

- Choose Toolbars from the View menu and click the Customize button *or*
- Choose Customize from the Toolbars shortcut menu *or*
- Choose Customize from the Tools menu

Either way, the Customize dialog box appears. If necessary click on the Toolbars button to display its options.

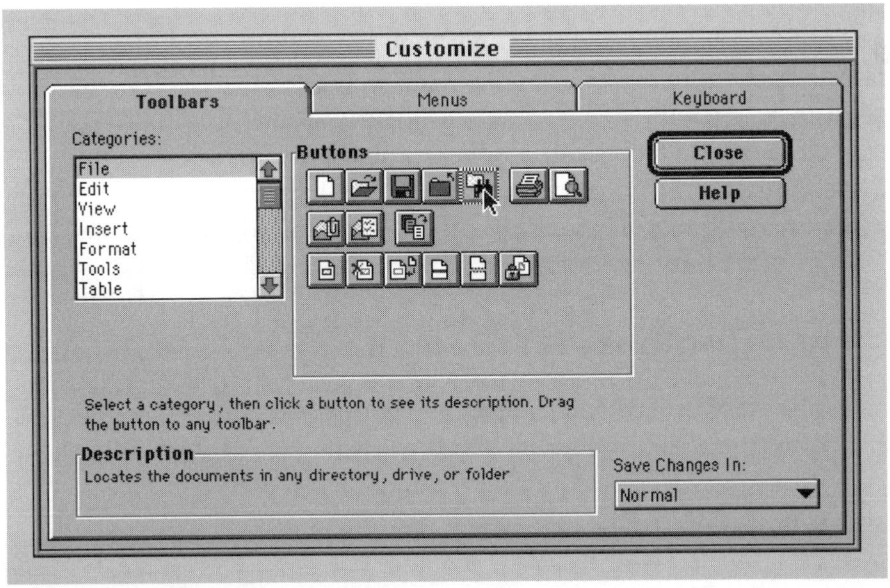

Toolbar buttons are separated into categories that roughly correspond to Word's menus. Select a category from the scrolling list and the appropriate buttons or other items appear in the Buttons area. Click on a button or other item to see a description in the Description area.

- To add a button to a toolbar, drag it from the Buttons area of the Customize dialog box to the toolbar you want to add it to.
- To remove a button from a toolbar, drag it off the toolbar.
- To move a toolbar button, drag it into a new position on the toolbar.

When you add, remove, or reposition toolbar buttons, all other buttons on the toolbar shift accordingly. If you add more toolbar buttons than can be displayed on an anchored toolbar, the ones on the end will not be displayed.

When you make changes to a toolbar, your changes are recorded in a template file. If you have a document based on a template other than Normal open in your document, you can use the Save Changes In pop-up menu at the bottom of the Customize dialog box to choose a template to save the toolbar changes in. If the only open documents are based on the Normal template, All Documents (Normal) will be the only choice. Changes will be saved to the Normal template and your customized toolbar will be available in every document.

When you're all finished making toolbar changes, click the Close button in the Customize dialog box.

TIP/TRICK

You can also move, delete, or copy a toolbar button without using the Customize dialog box. To move a toolbar button, hold down [⌘] while dragging it to a new position. To delete a toolbar button, hold down [⌘] while dragging it off the toolbar. To copy a toolbar button, hold down [Option] while dragging it into place on a second toolbar. If you hold down [Option] while dragging a toolbar button off a toolbar, Word creates a custom toolbar with just that button on it.

Resetting a Toolbar

To reset a toolbar to Word's defaults, open the Toolbars dialog box by choosing Toolbars from the View or Toolbar shortcut menu. Select the toolbar you want to reset from the Toolbars scrolling list and click Reset. The Reset Toolbar dialog box appears.

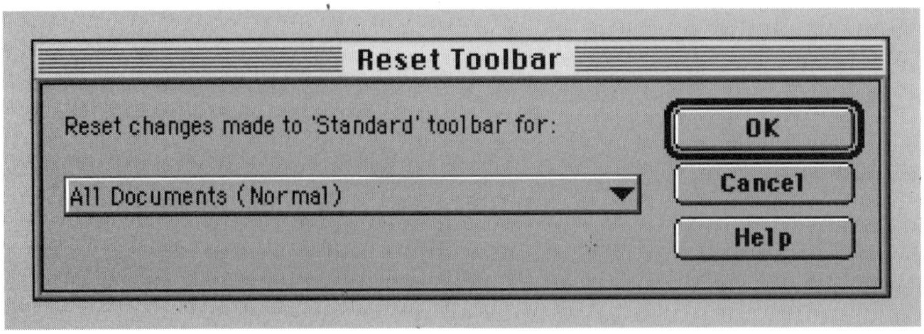

The pop-up menu lets you select the template you want to reset the toolbar in. For example, if you have documents based on Normal and on Letter 1 open, you can choose to reset normal for only one of the templates by choosing it from the pop-up menu. If the only open documents are based on the Normal template, All Documents (Normal) will be the only choice.

Creating a Custom Toolbar

Word version 6 also lets you create custom toolbars from scratch. Open the Toolbars dialog box by choosing Toolbars from the View or Toolbar shortcut menu. Then click the New button. The New Toolbar dialog box appears.

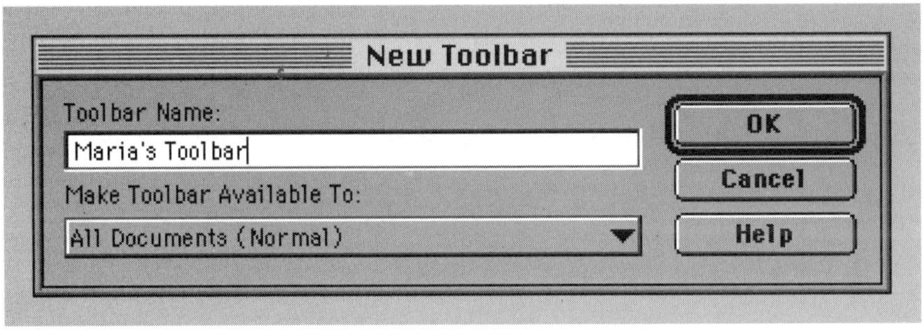

Enter a name for the toolbar in the Toolbar name edit box. If documents based on templates other than Normal are open, you can choose a template from the Make Toolbar Available To pop-up menu so the toolbar becomes part of that template. Otherwise, the toolbar becomes part of the Normal Template and is available in all documents. Click OK to create the toolbar. It appears in the upper left side of your screen as a tiny, buttonless toolbar, like the one shown here, and the Customize dialog box appears.

Use the previously discussed techniques to add, remove, and reposition buttons on your new toolbar. You'll find that it grows to accommodate all the buttons you place on it. When you're all finished, click Close in the Customize dialog box.

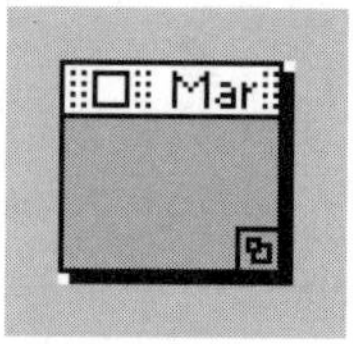

Your custom toolbar is listed among the available toolbars in the Toolbars dialog box. It can be displayed, hidden, or anchored just like any other toolbar. You can create as many custom toolbars as you like.

Deleting a Custom Toolbar

Although you cannot delete Word's built-in toolbars, you can delete toolbars you create. To delete a custom toolbar, open the Toolbars dialog box by selecting Toolbars from the View or Toolbar shortcut menu. Scroll down in the Toolbars scrolling list to display the custom toolbar you want to delete, select it, and click the Delete button. A confirmation dialog box appears. Click Yes to complete the deletion.

Creating a Custom Button

You can also create a custom button to put on a toolbar. A custom button can activate a command or macro that does not have a button assigned to it. I'll tell you more about macros in Chapter 26.

Begin by displaying the toolbar you want to add the button to. Then open the Customize dialog box by clicking the Customize button in the Toolbars dialog box or choosing Customize from the Tools or Toolbar shortcut menu. Make sure the Toolbars tab is selected.

Scroll down in the Categories scrolling list until you see All Commands and the four options below the dashed line. These are commands that do not have buttons assigned to them. Choose one of these five categories to display a list of related items in a scrolling window beside the

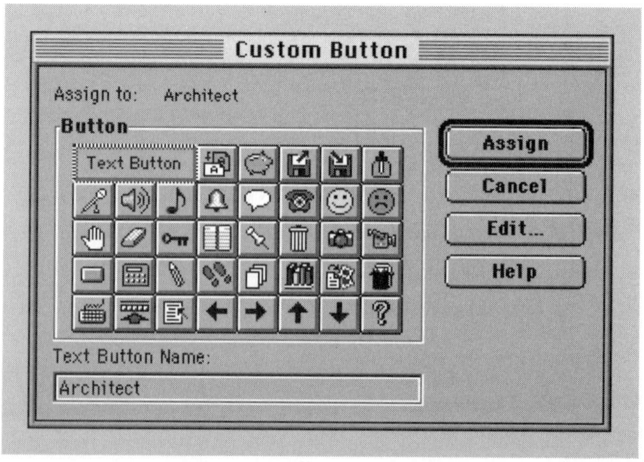

Categories window. Scroll in the list to find the item you want to add and drag it to a toolbar. When you release the mouse button, a blank button is added to the toolbar and the Custom Button dialog box appears.

In this illustration, I've assigned a Font called Architect to a button. I now need to choose a button to represent that font on the toolbar. Here are the options:

- To create a text button (a button with words on it rather than pictures), click on Text Button to select it, enter a name in the Text Button Name edit box, and click Assign.
- To use one of Word's built-in button icons, click the icon you like and click Assign.
- To create your own custom button icon based on one of Word's built-in button icons, click the icon you want to edit and click the Edit button. The button editor appears. You can then edit the contents of the Picture window by choosing a color from the Colors area and clicking on pixels to turn them on or off. If you have any artistic abilities, you can do quite a nice job. The Move arrows let you nudge your button icon within the Picture space to better center it. When you're finished, click OK to accept the custom button.

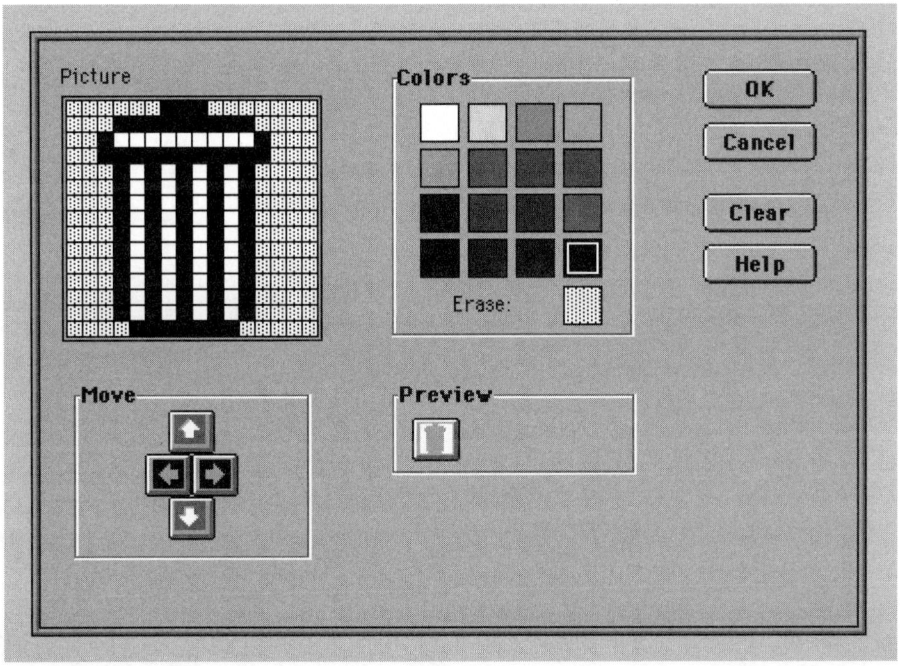

Because custom toolbar buttons are stored on the toolbar and not in Word's customize dialog box, if you delete a custom toolbar button as instructed earlier in this section, it's gone for good.

Copying a Custom Toolbar from One Template to Another

Each time you create or change a toolbar, Word lets you pick a template to assign it to. But what if you want to copy a toolbar to another template? That's where the Organizer, which I first discussed in Chapter 9, comes in.

Choose Templates from the File menu to open the Templates and Add-ins dialog box. I discussed this dialog box back in Chapter 9, so I won't talk about it again here. Click the Organizer button to open the Organizer dialog box. If necessary, click the Toolbars tab to display its options.

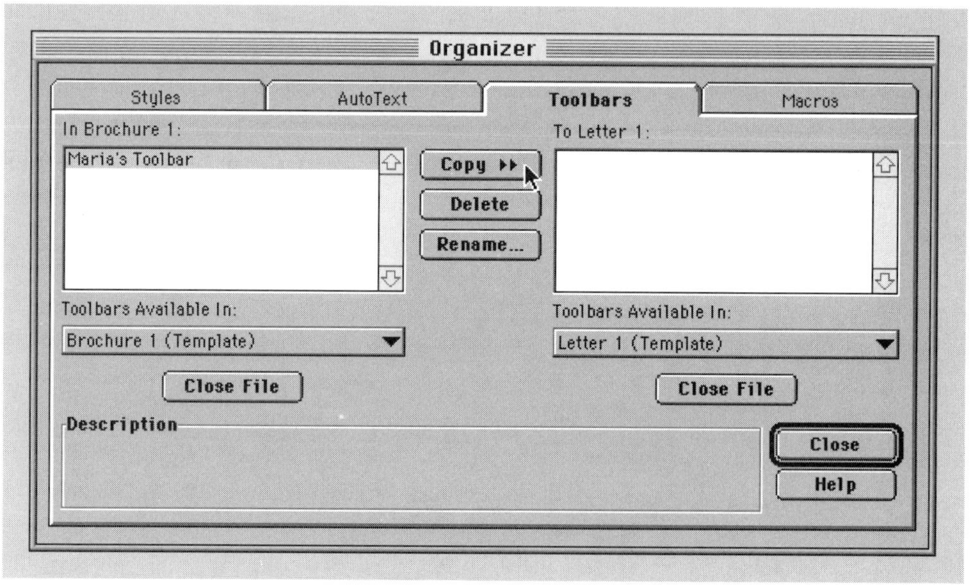

Use the Close File and Open File buttons at the bottom of each window to display the templates you want to copy a toolbar from and to. In the illustration shown here, there's a toolbar named Maria's Toolbar in the Brochure 1 template (on the left) that I want to copy to the Letter 1 template (on the right). Click on the name of the toolbar you want to copy and click the Copy button. The toolbar is copied. You can also use this dialog box to delete or rename toolbars by selecting a toolbar and clicking the Delete or Rename button. When you're all finished making changes, click the Close button.

Menus

NEW IN WORD 6

The ability to customize menus has been part of Word for quite a while now. This feature enables you to add, remove, or rearrange menu commands and add custom menus. What's new in Word version 6, however, is the ability to save menu modifications to specific templates and rename menus. I'll tell you about all of these things now.

Adding Menu Commands

To add commands to an existing menu, choose Customize from the Tools menu to display the Customize dialog box. Click the Menus tab to display its options.

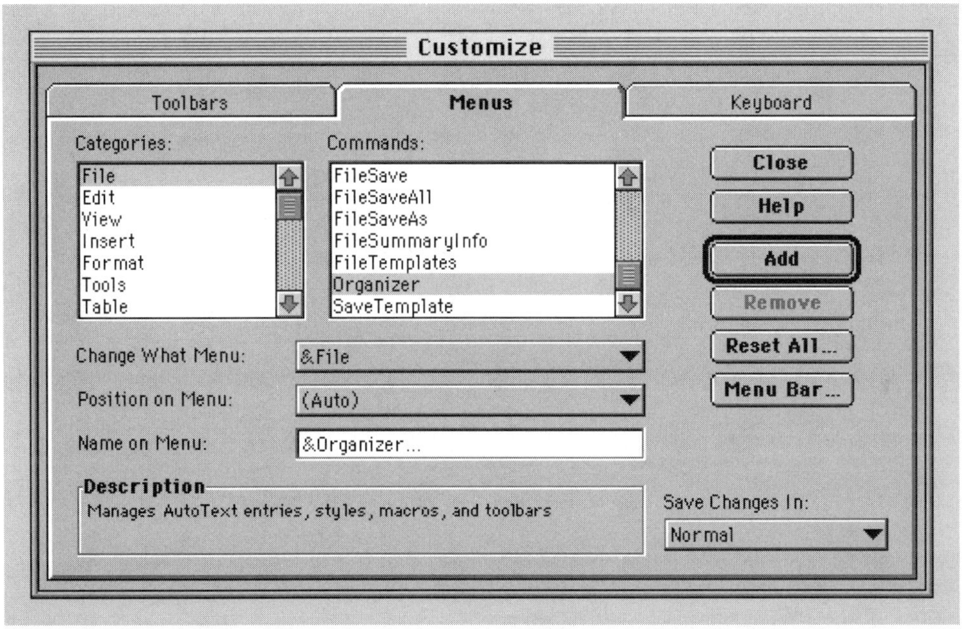

The dialog box has two scrolling windows. Categories is a list of categories that roughly corresponds to Word's menus. When you choose a category, the list of items to the right of it changes accordingly. The right side scrolling list can be named Commands, Macros, Fonts, AutoText, or Styles, depending on which category you select. You can choose a template to incorporate the changes into the Save Changes In pop-up list.

To add a command to a menu, choose the command category from the Categories list and then choose the item from the scrolling list to its right. Use the Change What Menu pop-up menu to pick a regular or shortcut menu to modify. Use the Position on Menu pop-up menu to select a position for the command. If you choose an existing command or separator from that menu, the new item will be added below it. Finally, enter a name for the command in the Name on Menu edit box. Then click Add or Add Below (whichever appears) to add the item to the selected menu. When you're all finished adding commands, click the Close button to close the Customize dialog box.

FYI: About those Ampersands

As I discussed way back in Chapter 1, it's possible to activate Word's menu commands without using your mouse. When you press [⌘][Tab] or [F10] (on an extended keyboard), Word activates the Menu bar. Each menu has an underscore under one letter of its name. By pressing this letter on your keyboard, you can open the menu. Once the menu is open, you'll see underscores under command name letters. Pressing a letter chooses the command.

You can include the underscored character in commands you add to Word's menus too. When you include an ampersand character (&) in a command name, the letter immediately after the ampersand will have an underscore beneath it when you activate Word's mouseless menus. So if you were wondering why there were ampersands in menu and command names in the Customize dialog box, wonder no more. They mark the mouseless menu keys Word uses or recommends. You can override whatever Word suggests in the Name on Menu edit box by typing in the name (including or excluding an ampersand) the way you want it to appear.

Removing a Menu Command

If you think Word's menus have more commands than you need, you can remove a few to lighten them up. Begin by choosing Customize from the Tools menu to open the Customize dialog box. If necessary, click the Menus tab.

Choose the menu containing the command you want to remove from the Change What Menu pop-up menu. Choose the command you want to remove from the Position on Menu pop-up menu. Then click Remove. The command is removed from the menu.

TIP/TRICK

You can also remove a command from a menu without opening the Customize dialog box. Press [⌘] [Option] [-]. The mouse pointer turns into a bold minus sign. Use this pointer to choose the command you want to remove from its menu. The command is instantly removed and the mouse pointer returns to normal.

Rearranging Menu Commands

To rearrange the order that commands appear on a menu, use the previously outlined procedures to remove a command from a menu and add it back in a new position. This makes it possible to have commands appear in any order you like.

Resetting Menus

If you decide you don't like the changes you made to Word's menus, you can restore them to the original defaults. Choose Customize from the Tools menu to open the Customize dialog box and click the Menus tab, if necessary, to display its options. Then click the Reset All button. A confirmation dialog box appears. Click Yes to restore them to default settings.

Renaming Commands

You can also rename commands already on menus. Open the Customize dialog box by choosing Customize from the Tools menu. Click the Menus tab to display its options. Choose a menu from the Categories scrolling list and then choose the command you want to rename from the Commands scrolling list beside it. The Add button should change to a Rename button if the command is included on the menu. Type a new name into the Name on Menu edit box and click Rename. Word renames the menu command.

Adding, Removing, and Renaming Menus

Fans of the Work menu in previous versions of Word will be glad to know that Word version 6 also enables them to create a Work menu. In fact, you can add as many custom menus as you like — just remember that only the ones that fit on your Menu bar will be displayed on screen. You can also remove and re-name existing menus. Here's how.

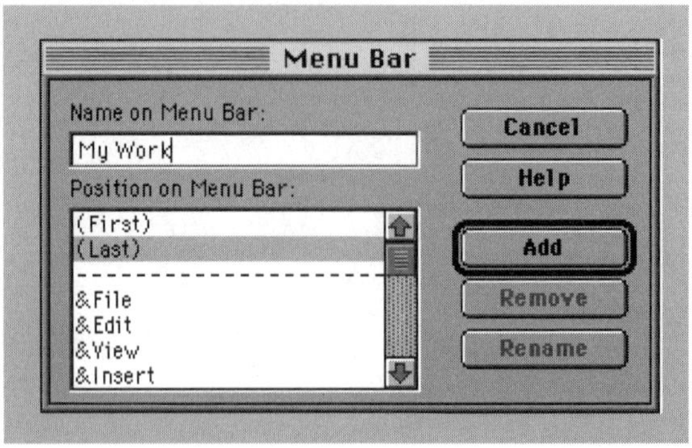

Choose Customize from the Tools menu to display the Customize dialog box. If necessary, click the Menus tab. Then click the Menu Bar button. The Menu Bar dialog box appears.

- To add a new menu, enter a menu name in the Name on Menu Bar edit box and choose a position from the Position on Menu Bar scrolling list. If you choose the name of an existing menu, your menu will be placed after it. Then click Add or Add After (whichever button appears). Click Close to close the dialog box and use the Customize dialog box to add commands and other items to your new menu. The menu does not appear on the Menu bar until you click the Close button in the Customize dialog box.
- To remove an existing menu, choose a menu from the Position on Menu Bar scrolling list. Click the Remove button. A confirmation dialog box appears. Click Yes to remove the menu and any commands assigned to it. The menu does not disappear until you click Close in the Menu Bar and Customize dialog boxes.
- To rename an existing menu, enter a new name for the menu in the Name on Menu Bar edit box and choose the current menu name from the Position on Menu Bar scrolling list. Click Rename. The menu name does not change until you click Close in the Menu Bar and Customize dialog boxes.

Shortcut Keys

To me, the most timesaving feature of any Macintosh application is its shortcut keys. I find it much quicker to type a keystroke for a command I use often than to reach for the mouse, move it up to the menu bar, pull down the right menu, and choose the desired command. I can't remember the last time I choose Save from the File menu to save a file — I always use the universal shortcut, [⌘][S]. The same goes for many menu commands.

Appendix C lists the shortcut keys built into Word. Those are the commands that are ready to use right now. But if you don't like a shortcut key assignment or a command you often use doesn't have one, you can change or add them. That's what I'll tell you about in this section of the chapter.

Adding Shortcut Keys

You add shortcut keys with the Customize dialog box. Choose Customize from the Tools menu to display the dialog box. If necessary, click the Keyboard tab.

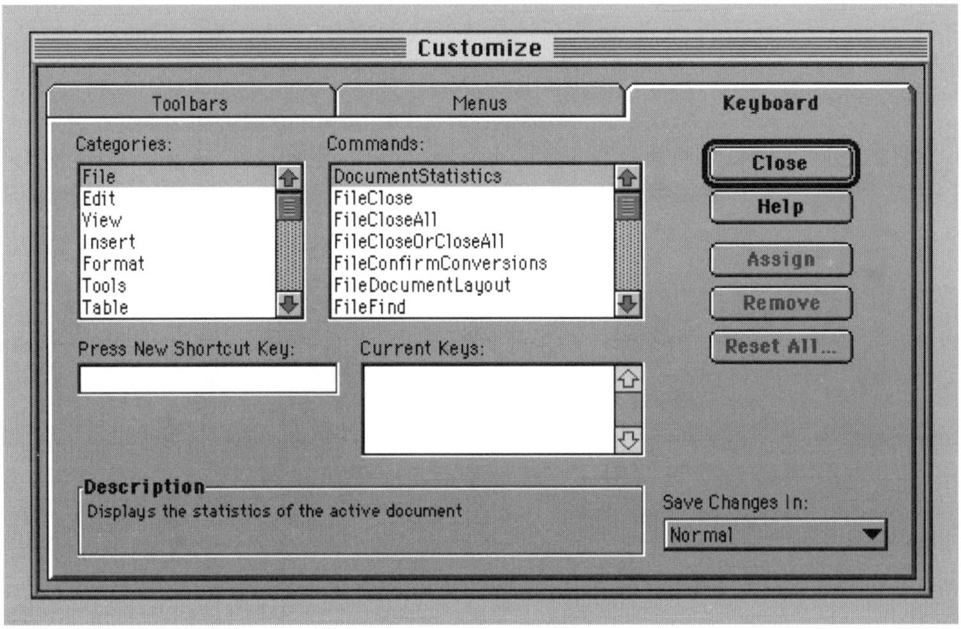

Like the other tabs on the Customize dialog box, the Keyboard tab displays two scrolling windows. Categories is a list of categories that roughly corresponds to Word's menus. When you choose a category, the list of items to the right of it changes accordingly. The right side scrolling list can be named Commands, Macros, Fonts, AutoText, Styles, or Common Symbols, depending on which category you select. You can choose a template to incorporate the changes into the Save Changes In pop-up list.

To add a shortcut key to an item, choose the appropriate category from the Categories scrolling list and then choose the command or other item from the scrolling list to the right. If the item already has a shortcut key, it appears in the Current Keys scrolling list. Click in the Press New Shortcut Key edit box to make it active and type a shortcut key. You can use almost any combination of ⌘, Option, Shift, Control, and other keys that doesn't produce a character on screen. For example, Option 2 would not be a good choice because it produces the ™ character, which you might need to type into documents. Control 2 or ⌘ Option 2 might be better. Whatever keys you type appear in the Press New Shortcut key edit box. Any current assignments appear as a message beneath the edit box, like this:

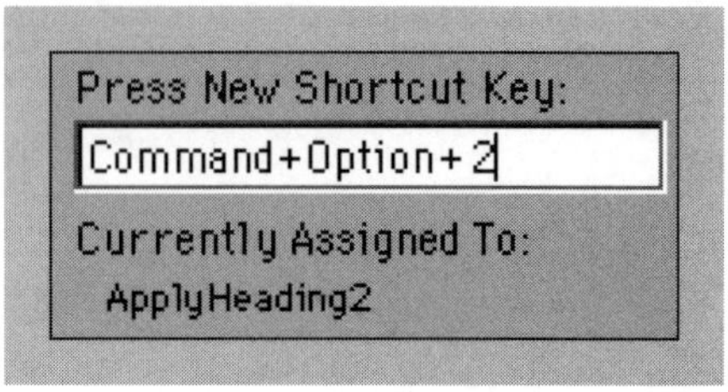

Click Assign to assign the shortcut key to the command. The new shortcut key appears in the Current Keys scrolling list. If the shortcut key was already assigned to another command, it is automatically removed from that other command.

TIP/TRICK

You can quickly select the menu command you want to assign a shortcut key to by pressing ⌘ Option + (use the + on the numeric keypad). The mouse pointer turns into a cloverleaf, like the one on the ⌘ key. Use this pointer to select the menu command you want to add a shortcut key to. The Customize dialog box appears with the command already displayed. Follow the previously outlined procedures to add a shortcut key.

TIP/TRICK

If desired, you can create a two-part shortcut key like ⌘ Shift Q and then 1. With the insertion point in the Press New Shortcut Key edit box, press a key combination for the first part of the shortcut key and then press a single key or Shift with a single key for the second part. Each part appears, separated by a comma. This increases the number of shortcut keys you can use.

Removing Shortcut Keys

You can also remove shortcut key assignments from commands and other items. Open the Customize dialog box by choosing Customize from the Tools menu. If necessary, click the Keyboard tab to display its options. Then select the item's category from the Categories scrolling list and select the item name from the list on the right. In the Current Keys scrolling list, select the shortcut key you want to remove and click the Remove button. Word instantly removes the shortcut key. If the key was previously assigned to another command or item, Word reassigns it.

Resetting Shortcut Keys

You can restore all shortcut key assignments to default settings for a template with the Customize dialog box. Choose Customize from the Tools menu to display the dialog box and, if necessary, click the Keyboard tab. Then click the Reset All button. A confirmation dialog box appears. Click Yes to reset the shortcut keys to default settings.

TIP/TRICK

Try This! Listing All Commands

Although I tried throughout this book to list shortcut keys for each of the commands I told you about, listing them all in the book's text would have been impossible. That's what Appendix C is for. Here's a secret: I created Appendix C by using Word's List Commands command and editing, sorting, and reformatting the result.

If you need a list of all commands Word has to offer, you can use the List Commands command to create one. Here's how.

1. Choose Customize from the Tools menu to display the Customize dialog box.
2. In order to use the List Commands command, you must assign it to a toolbar, menu, or shortcut key. Click the tab corresponding to the type of item you want to customize.
3. In the Categories scrolling window, choose All Commands.
4. In the Commands scrolling window, choose ListCommands. The commands will be in alphabetical order, so you'll have to scroll about halfway through them to find ListCommands.
5. Follow the appropriate procedures discussed above to assign the command to a toolbar, menu, or shortcut key.
6. When you're all finished, click the Close, Add, or Assign button (whichever applies) to dismiss the Customize dialog box.
7. Click the toolbar button, choose the menu command, or press the shortcut key you created. The List Commands dialog box appears.

Continued

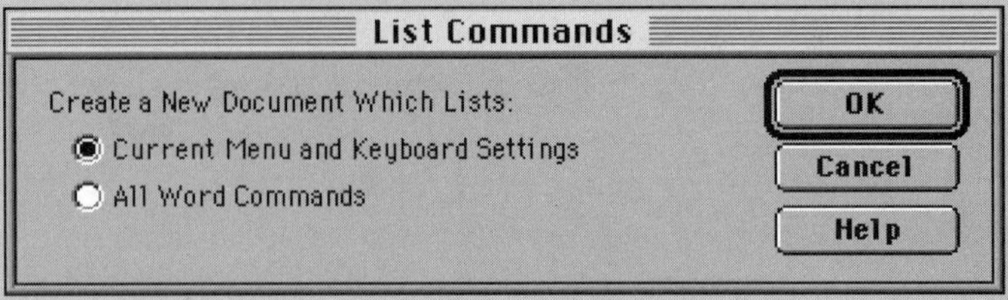

8. Click the radio button for Current Menu and Keyboard Settings or All Word Commands to choose what you want listed. Then click OK. Word creates the table of commands. You can monitor its progress in the Status bar. When it's finished, you'll have a new document that contains a table listing the commands you specified.

This is a good example of the kinds of commands Word has but doesn't normally make available. With a table of commands, you can find the commands you want to use and add them to Word with the techniques discussed throughout this chapter.

Chapter Summary

In this chapter, you learned to customize Word's toolbars, menus, and shortcut keys. This powerful feature can help make you more productive by putting the commands and features you use most at your fingertips.

In the next chapter, you'll see how you can exchange information between Word and some other popular applications. You'll also learn to use Object Linking and Embedding and Publish and Subscribe to link information from one document to another, thus ensuring that both documents contain the most up to date information available.

25

Chapter 25: Sharing Information

SCENARIO 1: YOU'VE JUST CREATED A CHART WITH MICROSOFT Excel that perfectly illustrates a point you're trying to make in a Microsoft Word document. Scenario 2: You've been accumulating data in a Claris FileMaker Pro database for the past six months and now need to use it in a Microsoft Word mail merge. Scenario 3: You've used Microsoft Word's outline feature to put together a business plan and now your boss wants you to create a Microsoft PowerPoint presentation with the same information.

What do all these scenarios have in common? They require you to take information that exists in a document created with one application and use it in a document created with another application. While the thought of doing something like this might seem mind-boggling at first, not only is it possible, but it's easy. That's what this chapter is all about: sharing information between documents and applications.

This chapter provides you with a brief refresher course on copying and pasting information between documents, then moves on to more advanced topics like Apple's Publish and Subscribe and Microsoft's Object Linking and Embedding. You'll learn how you can open documents created in other applications from within Word and save Word documents in a format other applications can read. If you find yourself juggling applications and entering the same information over and over, this chapter is for you.

"Advanced" Copy and Paste

Sharing information among documents has always been a Macintosh feature. From the day the first Macintosh appeared, Macintosh users have been able to copy information from one document and paste it into another. When the same information is needed over and over, this can be a real time-saver.

In this section, I'll review the techniques for copying and pasting between documents — including documents that weren't even created with Word. If the Copy and Paste commands are new to you, go back and read about them in Chapter 2 before continuing.

Between Word Documents

Copying information from one Word document to another is easy since anyone can have more than one Word document open at the same time. Open the source document — the document containing the information you want to copy. Select the information and choose Copy from the Edit menu, press ⌘C, or click the Copy button on the Standard Toolbar.

Now open the other Word document, or, if it's already open, use the Window menu to make it active. Position the insertion point where you want the copied information to appear. Choose Paste from the Edit menu, press ⌘V, or click the Paste button to paste it in. It's as simple as that.

Between Word and Another Application

Copying information from a Word document to a document created in another application — or vice versa — is almost as easy. The only problem you might encounter deals with RAM constraints. If you don't have enough RAM in your Macintosh to open Word and the other application at the same time, you'll have to open the documents one at a time.

Follow the procedures outlined in the first part of this section to open the source document, select the information you want to copy, and copy it to the Clipboard. Then open the other application's document, position the insertion point, and paste.

If, when trying to open the other document, you get a message telling you that there isn't enough memory to open the application, click OK to dismiss the dialog box. Then save all your open documents and quit the currently open application. If you're using a Microsoft product like Word or Excel, you might get a dialog box asking if you want to save the contents of the Clipboard for use in other applications.

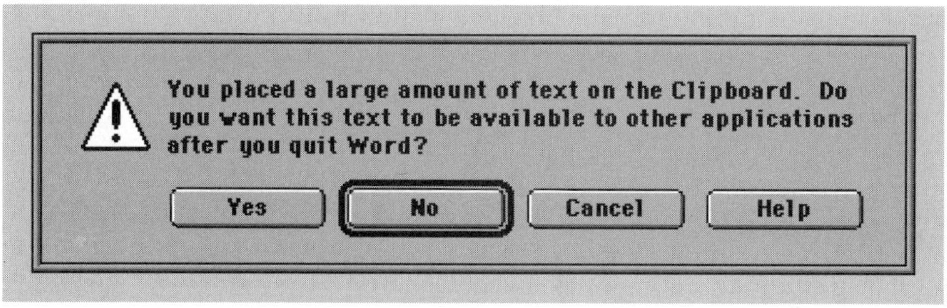

It's important that you click Yes in this dialog box. Then, when the application quits, open the other application's document, position the insertion point, and paste. If you're pasting a large amount of information into a Microsoft application's document, you might see a message telling you that Word is reading from a large external Clipboard. That's fine.

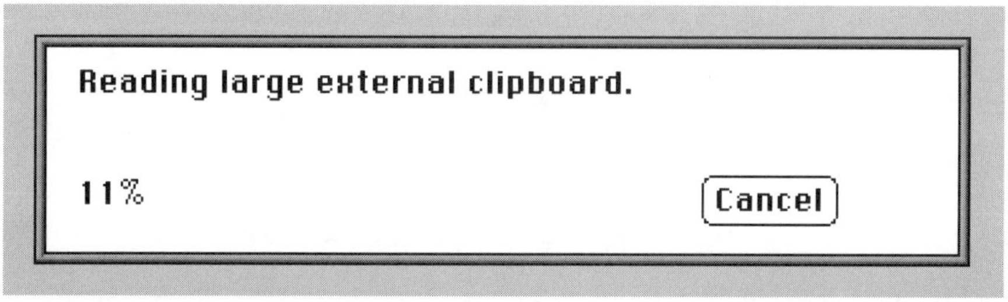

TIP/TRICK

Remember, any information that can be selected can be copied and pasted. This means you can paste an Excel worksheet or chart into a Word document or paste text written in Word into a MacDraw Pro document. The possibilities are endless. If you're not sure if copy and paste works, try it. You may be pleasantly surprised by the results. (Remember the Undo command if you're not!)

FYI: Why an External Clipboard?

In case you're wondering why Microsoft products ask you if you want to save the contents of the Clipboard, here's the answer. Microsoft products do not use Apple's Clipboard. They have their own internal Clipboard. When you quit a Microsoft application or switch from it to another active application like the Finder, it transfers the Clipboard contents to Apple's Clipboard. If you quit without switching first and there's a lot of information on the Clipboard, the program asks you whether you want to save the Clipboard contents — after all, why bother transferring a lot of information if it isn't really needed? That also explains the "reading large external Clipboard" message you get when you paste something from another application into a Microsoft applications' document.

TIP/TRICK

When a Microsoft application asks whether you want to save the contents of the Clipboard and you don't need to save it, say No. This reduces the amount of RAM used up by Apple's Clipboard, making more RAM available for other things.

TIP/TRICK

If you want to copy or move a selection from one Microsoft Office (Word, Excel, or PowerPoint) document to another, you can simply drag the selection from one application's document window to the other's. Dragging moves the selection. Holding down Option while dragging copies the selection. This only works if you have the latest version of Microsoft Office installed.

Publish and Subscribe

With System 7 came Publish and Subscribe. Publish and Subscribe takes copy and paste a step further by enabling you to "publish" all or part of a document. Other documents, including those created by other users on a network, can then "subscribe" to the published edition to include its information. Because there's a link between the documents, if the information in one document changes, the same information in the other document changes.

In this section, I'll tell you how you can use Publish and Subscribe to share information between documents of one or more applications. Although the instructions I'll provide here apply specifically to Word, the concepts and techniques apply to any program that supports Publish and Subscribe. With these instructions and a little Macintosh know-how, you should be able to use Publish and Subscribe in almost any application.

Publishing an Edition

To make all or part of a document available for use by other documents, you must create a *publisher*. A publisher is the part of the document that includes information you want to share. When you create a publisher, Word saves an *edition* file on disk. Other documents use the contents of the edition file, which is linked to the publisher.

To create a publisher and save an edition file, begin by selecting the information you want to share. Choose Create Publisher from the Publishing submenu under the Edit menu. A dialog box like the one shown here appears.

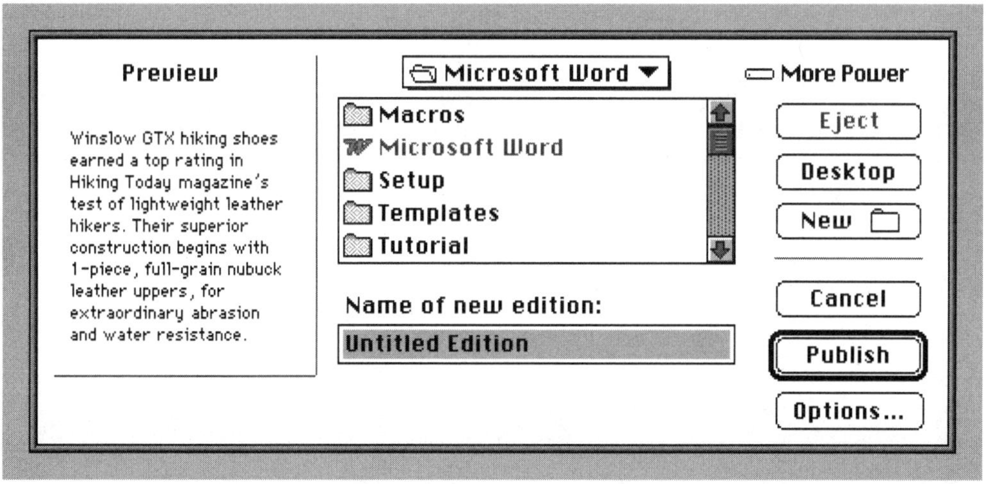

Use this dialog box to choose a disk location and enter a name for the edition file. The disk location can be in any folder or disk mounted on your Macintosh. Just remember that any document that subscribes to the edition must be able to find it.

If desired, you can click the Options button to display the Publisher Options dialog box. It lets you specify the format in which the edition is saved. Options include RTF or Rich Text Format (which includes character formatting), Text, and PICT. You can decrease the size of the file by turning off one or more of the check boxes. For example, if you know you're going to use the edition in another word processing document, you don't need the PICT format, so you can turn it off. When you're finished with the Publisher Options dialog box, click OK to dismiss it.

Click Publish in the Create Publisher dialog box. Word saves the edition file on disk. It also creates a bookmark in the source document called INTERN_LINK1. You can see the bookmark brackets in the source document if you turn on the Bookmarks check box in the View tab of the Options dialog box. I told you about bookmarks in Chapter 14 and about the Options dialog box in Chapter 23.

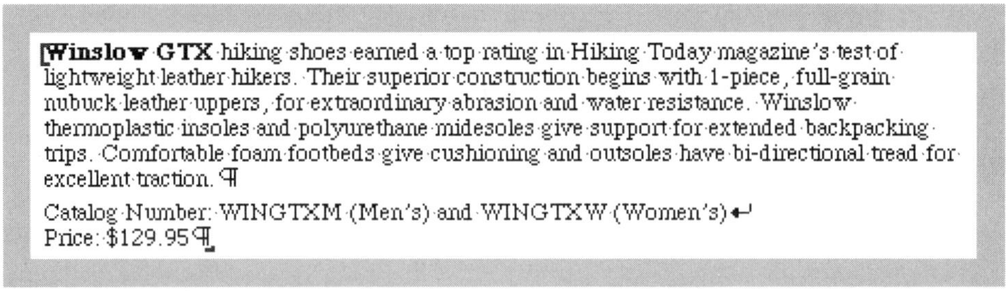
[Winslow GTX hiking shoes earned a top rating in Hiking Today magazine's test of lightweight leather hikers. Their superior construction begins with 1-piece, full-grain nubuck leather uppers, for extraordinary abrasion and water resistance. Winslow thermoplastic insoles and polyurethane midesoles give support for extended backpacking trips. Comfortable foam footbeds give cushioning and outsoles have bi-directional tread for excellent traction. ¶

Catalog Number: WINGTXM (Men's) and WINGTXW (Women's)↵
Price: $129.95¶]

You can create as many edition files as you want from one source document. Just follow the previous steps and make sure you give each edition a unique name if saving them in the same disk location.

Subscribing to an Edition

Once an edition exists, a document can become a *subscriber* to it and include its information. By subscribing to an edition, the document can get up-to-date information as soon as the edition changes — something that isn't possible with a simple copy and paste operation.

Position the insertion point where you want the information to appear. Choose Subscribe To from the Publishing submenu under the Edit menu. The Subscribe To dialog box appears.

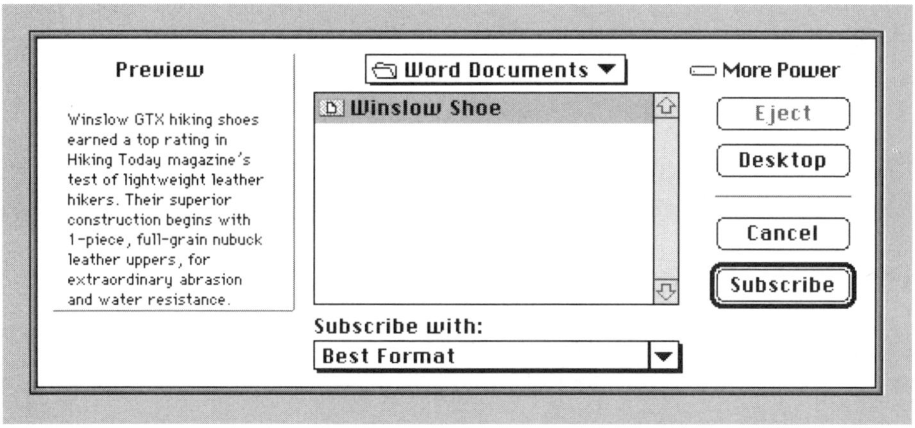

Use this dialog box to locate the edition file you want to use. Only edition files appear in the directory window. If desired, use the Subscribe With pop-up menu to choose a format. Your options are Best Format, Formatted Text (RTF), Unformatted Text, or Picture. Then click Subscribe. The information appears in the document. Here's an example:

FYI: Links and Fields

An edition is placed in a Word file as a field. The field code Word automatically inserts when you subscribe to an edition gives Word the information it needs to find and display the edition in the document. This is also true for a link and an embedded object, as you'll see later in this chapter. All links are described to Word in terms of fields.

If unusual codes appear in the document rather than the information you subscribed to, it's because you've got field codes set to display in the document. Turn off the Field Codes check box in the View tab of the Options dialog box. I told you about the Options dialog box in Chapter 23.

Controlling Updates

By default, Word updates an edition each time the publisher is saved. You can change this frequency by setting Publisher Options.

Click in or select the publisher. Choose Publisher Options from the Publishing submenu under the Edit menu. The Publisher Options dialog box appears.

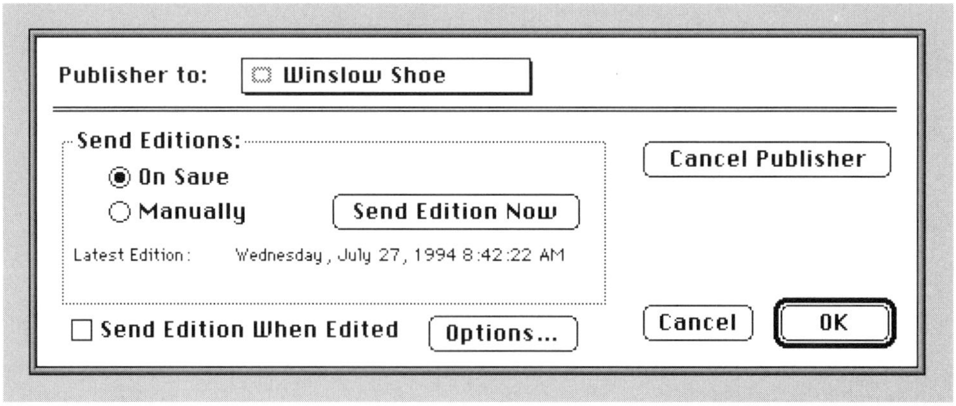

- To update the edition each time the publisher is saved, click the On Save radio button.

- To update the edition each time the publisher is edited, click the On Save radio button and turn on the Send Edition when Edited check box.
- To update the edition manually, click the Manually radio button and make sure the Send Edition when Edited check box is turned off. To manually update an edition, you'll have to open this dialog box and click the Send Edition Now button.

By default, Word also updates a subscriber each time the publisher sends new information to the edition. This is especially handy when the publisher and subscriber documents are maintained by two different users on a network. If you don't want Word to update the subscriber so frequently, you can change the subscriber options.

Click in or select the subscriber and choose Subscriber Options from the Publishing submenu under the Edit menu. The Subscriber Options dialog box appears.

- To update the subscriber each time the edition changes, click the Automatically radio button.

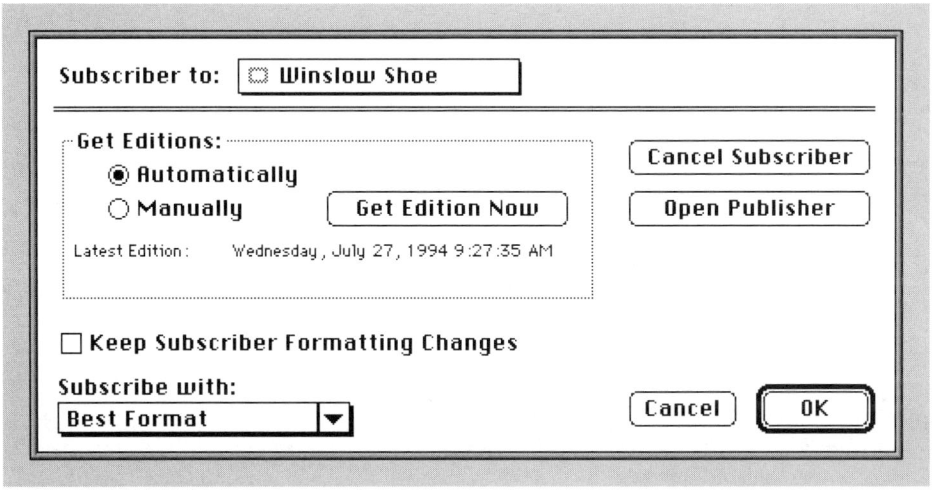

- To update the subscriber manually, click the Manually radio button. To manually update the subscriber, you'll have to open this dialog box and click the Get Edition Now button.
- To prevent Word from changing the formatting of the subscriber when it updates it, turn on the Keep Subscriber Formatting Changes check box.

IMPORTANT NOTE

If Word can't find an edition when it needs to update the subscriber, it displays a straightforward dialog box telling you about the problem. Your only choice is to click OK. Although the text remains in the document, it will never be updated again. You can cancel the subscriber, as discussed later in this chapter to prevent further appearances of the error dialog.

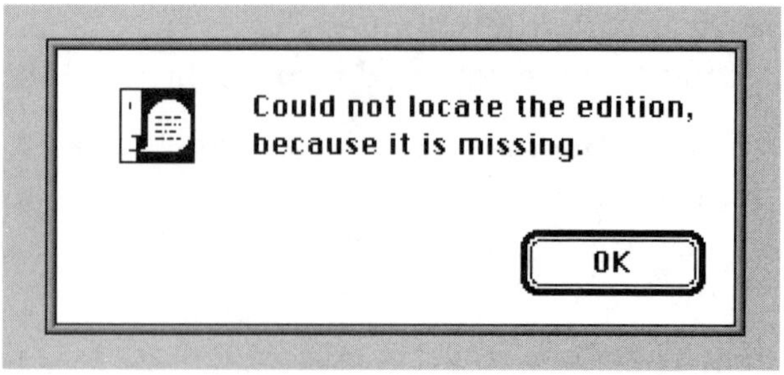

Switching from Subscriber to Publisher

Sometimes, while working with a subscriber, you might need to open its publisher. Word's Subscriber Options dialog box, which I just showed you, offers an Open Publisher button. Click this button to open the edition's publisher. If the publisher is an application other than Word, you'll need to have enough RAM to open both Word and the other application at the same time.

Canceling a Publisher or Subscriber

You can cancel a publisher or subscriber at any time. When you cancel a publisher, the text remains in the source document, but the edition, which remains on disk, is no longer updated. You can delete the edition file in the Finder if desired. When you cancel a subscriber, the text remains in the subscribing document but is no longer updated. You can edit it like any other text.

- To cancel a publisher, click on or select the publisher and choose Publisher Options from the Publishing submenu under the Edit menu. Then click the Cancel Publisher button. When the confirmation dialog box appears, click Yes.

- To cancel a subscriber, click on or select the subscriber and choose Subscriber Options from the Publishing submenu under the Edit menu. Then click the Cancel Subscriber button. When the confirmation dialog box appears, click Yes.

Object Linking and Embedding

Microsoft has its own brand of Publish and Subscribe, which it calls Object Linking and Embedding or OLE. When you *link* information in one Microsoft document to another, the information is maintained in the source document. The destination document merely contains the instructions it needs to find and display the linked information. You specify how often the link should be updated and whether the information should be displayed in the destination document. Sound familiar? It's very similar to Publish and Subscribe.

When you *embed* an object, the object is inserted in the destination document and becomes part of it. Double-clicking the embedded object launches the application that created it so you can edit it. There's no link.

In this section, I'll tell you how you can use linking and embedding to share information between Microsoft documents. Again, I'll concentrate on the instructions you'll use within a Word document. Once you can link documents to Word documents, I'm sure you'll be able to link from Word documents to other Microsoft documents. The commands are very similar.

FYI: Moving from One Microsoft Application to Another

NEW IN WORD 6

If you've got several Microsoft applications installed on your Macintosh and find yourself switching among them throughout the day, Word's new Microsoft toolbar can help. Choose Toolbars from the View menu, turn on the check box beside Microsoft in the scrolling list, and click OK. The Microsoft toolbar, which contains only five buttons, appears.

The Microsoft Excel button launches Excel or switches to it if it's already active. Excel is Microsoft's spreadsheet application.

The Microsoft PowerPoint button launches PowerPoint or switches to it if it's already active. PowerPoint is Microsoft's presentation software application.

Continued

The Microsoft Mail button launches Microsoft Mail or switches to it if it's already active. Microsoft Mail is Microsoft's electronic mail software application.

The Microsoft FoxPro button launches FoxPro or switches to it if it's already active. FoxPro is Microsoft's database application.

The Microsoft Project button launches Project or switches to it if it's already active. Project is Microsoft's project management software application.

Creating Links with the Paste Special Command

To create a link between two documents, begin by opening the source document and selecting the information you want to include in the destination document. Copy the information to the Clipboard using the Edit menu's Copy command, the ⌘C shortcut key, or the Copy button on the Standard Toolbar. Then switch to or open the Word document, position the insertion point where you want the information to appear, and choose Paste Special from the Edit menu. The Paste Special dialog box appears.

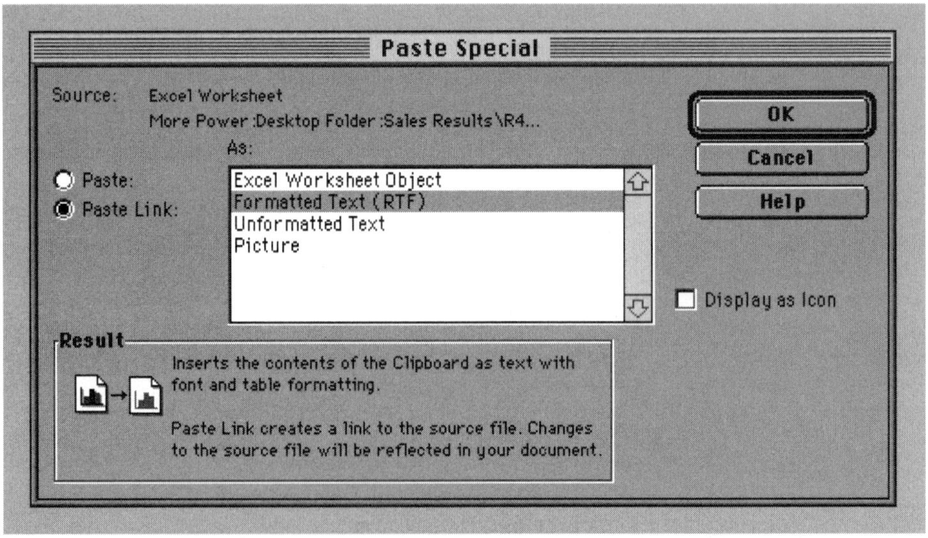

The options offered in this dialog box vary slightly depending on the application that created the original document. The name and path to the source document appears at the top of the window. There are two paste options: Paste and Paste Link. Paste pastes without a link — very much like the Paste command would. Paste Link creates the link so make sure you click its radio button if you want to link the two documents. The As scrolling list offers format options. This is a lot like the Subscribe With pop-up menu I showed you in the Subscribe To dialog box earlier in this chapter. If you choose Object, you'll embed the information as an object rather than link to it. I'll tell you more about embedding objects a little later.

As you make changes in the dialog box, the Result area explains exactly what will happen when you click OK. If you turn on the Display as Icon check box, the selected information appears as an icon in the Word document. When you're finished setting options, click OK.

After a moment, Word displays the document with the linked information. In the following example, I linked an Excel spreadsheet file as Formatted Text (RTF). It appears as a Word table, complete with all the borders and other formatting options I set in Excel. I told you about Word tables back in Chapter 11.

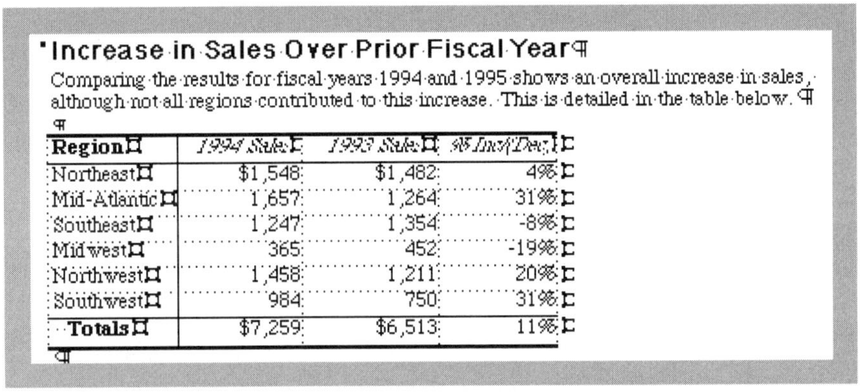

Increase in Sales Over Prior Fiscal Year

Comparing the results for fiscal years 1994 and 1995 shows an overall increase in sales, although not all regions contributed to this increase. This is detailed in the table below.

Region	*1994 Sales*	*1995 Sales*	*% Inc/(Dec)*
Northeast	$1,548	$1,482	4%
Mid-Atlantic	1,657	1,264	31%
Southeast	1,247	1,354	-8%
Midwest	365	452	-19%
Northwest	1,458	1,211	20%
Southwest	984	750	31%
Totals	$7,259	$6,513	11%

Creating Links with Insert Menu Commands

You can also create a link to a file by inserting a file or picture into the Word document.

- To link an entire file, position the insertion point where you want the file to appear and choose File from the Insert menu. Use the Insert File dialog box that appears to locate and open a file to insert. If you turn on the Link to File check box, a link is established between the two files.

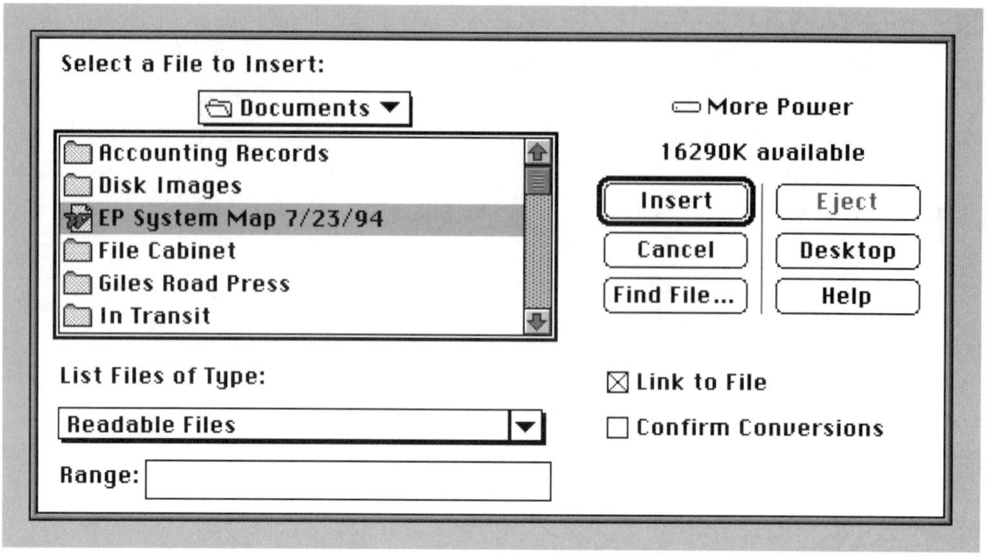

- To link a graphic file, position the insertion point where you want the graphic to appear and choose Picture from the Insert menu. The Insert Picture dialog box, which is very similar to the Insert File dialog box, lets you locate and open a picture. Turn on the Link to File check box to establish a link between the two files.

Updating, Changing, or Breaking Links

By default, Word automatically updates links to source documents when it opens a document containing one or more links. It also updates links automatically if the source document changes while the document containing the links is open. You can change the way Word updates links, manually update links, and make other changes to links.

Choose Links from the Edit menu to display the Links dialog box.

This dialog box lists all the links for the active document and lets you change the ones you select. Click on a link to select it or hold down [⌘] and click multiple links to select more than one.

- To automatically update links when new information is available in the source document, click the Automatic radio button.
- To manually update links, click the Manual radio button. In order to update links once you've set Manual updating, you can click the Update Now button in this dialog box or click on the linked item in the document window and press [F9].

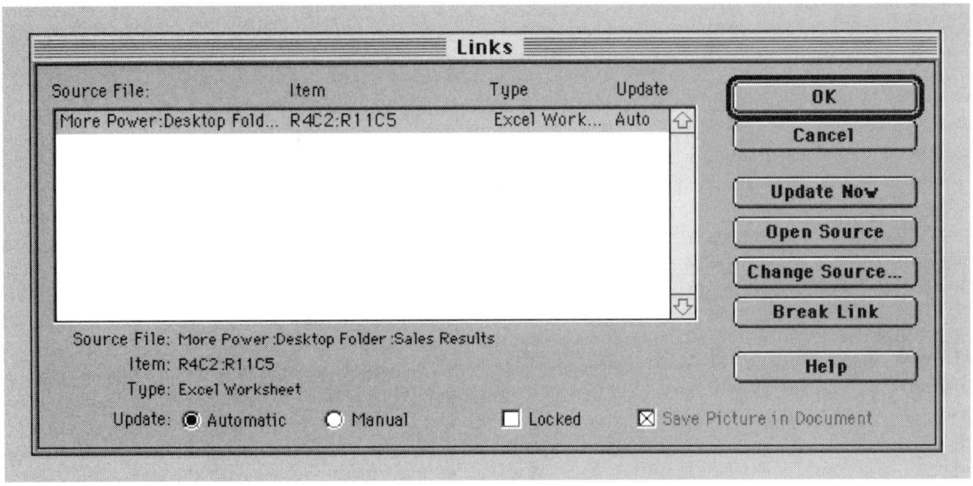

- To prevent a link from being updated, turn on the Lock Link check box. The Update Now button turns gray and cannot be used.
- To open the source document, click Open Source. The document is opened in its application. You can then edit and re-save it.
- To change the source document, click Change Source. The Change Source dialog box, which looks and works much like a standard Open dialog box, appears. Use it to select a new source document, change the item linked within the document, or both.
- To break a link, click the Break Link button. In the confirmation dialog box that appears, click Yes. If you break a link, the linked information remains in the document, but the link can't be updated.
- If the linked item is a graphic object, you can reduce the amount of disk space the destination document requires by turning off the Save Picture in Document check box. This way Word stores only the link data in the file, not the entire graphic. This check box is also available in the Insert Picture dialog box I discussed previously.

TIP/TRICK

Embedding Objects with the Object Command

Back in Chapter 12, I told you how to insert graphic objects into Word documents. In that chapter, I showed you how to insert pictures and objects created with WordArt, Equation Editor, and Microsoft Graph. You may not have realized it then, but you were actually embedding objects into your document. Although the object was created with another application, it became part of the Word document. Double-clicking the object launched the creating application so you could edit the object.

To embed an object, position the insertion point where you want the object to appear and choose Object from the Insert menu. The Object dialog box appears.

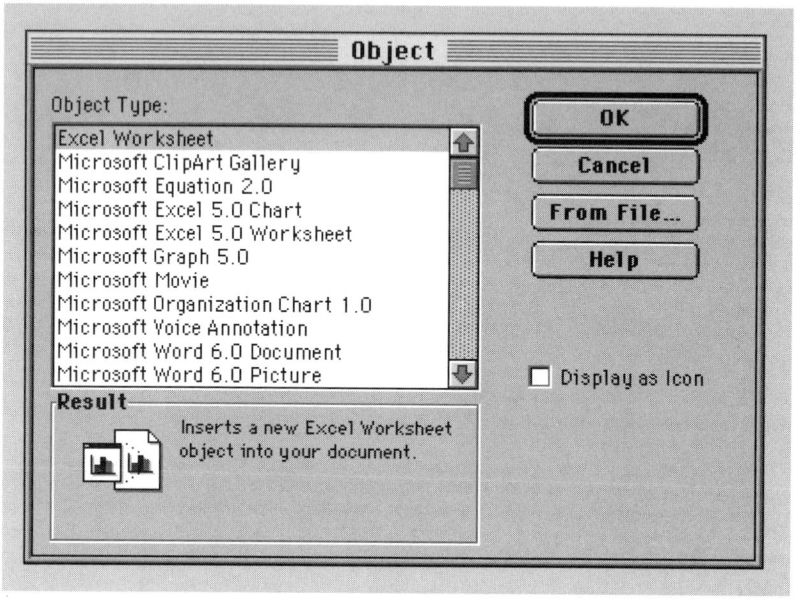

- To embed a new object, select the type of object to embed from the Object Type scrolling list. Word launches the appropriate application so you can create the file to embed. To insert the object and return to the Word document, choose Quit from the application's File menu. A dialog box appears like the one shown here, asking if you want to update the file in the destination document. Click Yes. The application quits and the file is inserted into the Word document.

TIP/TRICK

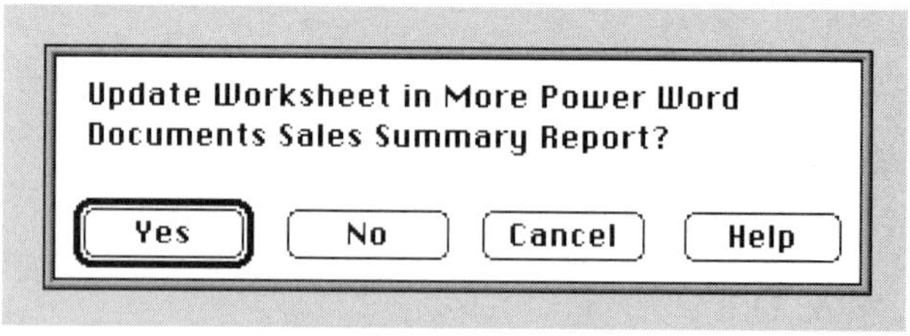

To quickly embed a new Microsoft Excel worksheet or Microsoft Graph Chart, click the Insert Excel Worksheet or Insert Chart button on the Standard Toolbar. These buttons launch the appropriate application and open a new document window so you can create the new worksheet or chart.

- To embed an existing object, click the From File button. A standard Open dialog box appears. Use it to locate and insert a file. By default, the file is inserted as an embedded object, but if you turn on the Link to File check box, Word creates a link between the source and destination documents.
- To display an embedded object as an icon, turn on the Display as Icon check box you'll find in the Object or From File dialog box.

Embedding Objects with the Paste Special Command

Earlier in this chapter, I showed you the Paste Special dialog box and how you can use it to paste links to documents. You can also use it to embed objects.

Open the source document, select the information you want to embed, and copy it to the Clipboard. Switch to the destination document and position the insertion point where you want the information to be embedded. Then choose Paste Special from the Edit menu. Make sure the Paste (not Paste Link) radio button is selected. In the As scrolling list, choose the item with the word "Object" in its name — options in this list vary depending on what is selected. Click OK to paste it as an object.

Editing Embedded Objects

Editing an embedded object is easy. Select the object in the destination document and choose Edit from the Object submenu under the Edit menu. (The exact name of the submenu varies depending on the kind of object you've selected.) Or simply double-click on the object. Word launches the application that created the object and displays it in a window for editing. When you're finished making changes, quit the application and click Yes when Word asks whether you want to update the file.

Converting Embedded Objects

You can convert the file format of an embedded object three different ways:

- To permanently convert the file format of an embedded object, select the object and choose Convert from the Object submenu under the Edit menu. (The Exact name of the submenu varies depending on the kind of object you've selected.) Click the Convert To radio button and choose an Object Type from the scrolling list. Click OK to complete the conversion.

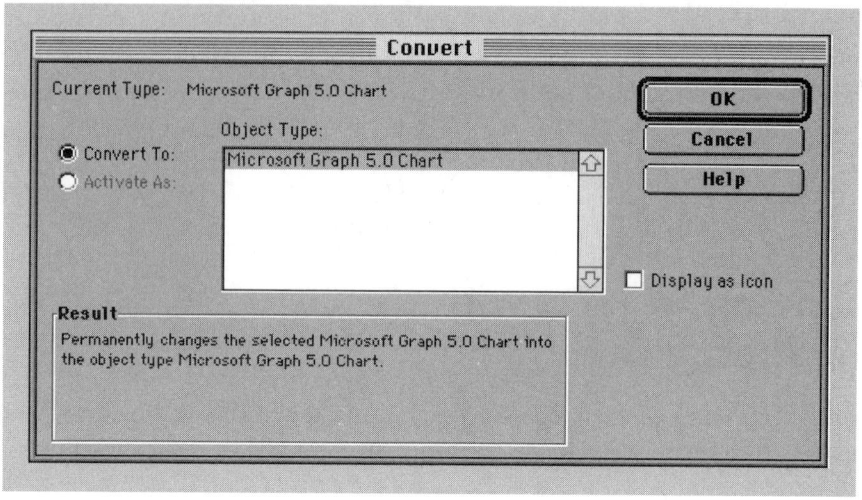

- To temporarily convert the file format of an embedded object, select the object and choose Convert from the Object submenu under the Edit menu. Click the Activate As radio button and choose an Object Type from the scrolling list. Click OK to complete the conversion. When you double-click the object to edit it, it opens in the newly selected application. But when you save the Word document containing the object, the object reverts back to its original file format.

IMPORTANT NOTE

The Object Types Word offers in this dialog box depend on the compatible programs Word recognizes. The Activate As radio button will not work if only one Object Type is listed.

- To convert an embedded object to a graphic, click it to select it and press ⌘ Shift F9. The object is converted to an editable Word drawing object. This can reduce the size of the file containing the embedded object. I discussed drawing objects in Chapter 12.

Distributing Word Files with Microsoft Mail

If you use Microsoft Mail, you can send documents directly from Microsoft Word to other people on the Microsoft Mail server. You can also create routing slips for documents you want reviewed by other Word users and use Word's Mail Merge feature to merge documents directly to electronic mail. I'll explain briefly how to do all these things in this section.

Sending Word Documents as Mail Attachments

To send a Word document as an attachment to a Microsoft Mail message, open the document and choose Send from the File menu. (This option only appears if you have Microsoft Mail installed.) If you are not already signed on to the Microsoft Mail server, a sign-on screen appears — use it to sign on. Use the Microsoft Mail Address Mail dialog box that appears to address the message to one or more recipients and click Close. Then enter a Subject and message in the Send Document message form. You can use the Options button to set other Mail options as you can with any other Microsoft Mail message. Finally, click the Send button to send the message.

Creating Routing Slips

A routing slip is designed to work with Word's Annotation, Review, and Forms features, which I covered in Chapters 18 and 22. By creating and using a routing slip, you determine who gets to see the document and what order it is distributed in.

Open the document you want to distribute and choose Add Routing Slip from the File menu. (This option only appears if you have Microsoft Mail installed.) If you are not already signed on to the Microsoft Mail server, use the sign-on screen that appears to sign on. The Routing Slip dialog box appears.

Use the Address button to display Microsoft Mail's Address Mail dialog box and select message recipients. You can change the order of recipients in the To scrolling list by selecting a recipient and clicking the up or down Move button. You can remove a recipient by selecting one and clicking Remove. Enter an optional subject and message text in the appropriate areas of the dialog box. Click the One After Another or All at Once radio button under Route to Recipients to determine how the document is routed. Turn on the Return When Done check box to have the document returned to you when the last recipient is finished reviewing the document. Turn on the Track Status check box to have Word automatically send you a message each time the document is routed to another reviewer. Finally choose the appropriate Protect For option from the pop-up menu: none, Annotations, Revisions, or Forms. I discussed protection for annotations and revisions in Chapter 18 and for forms in Chapter 22.

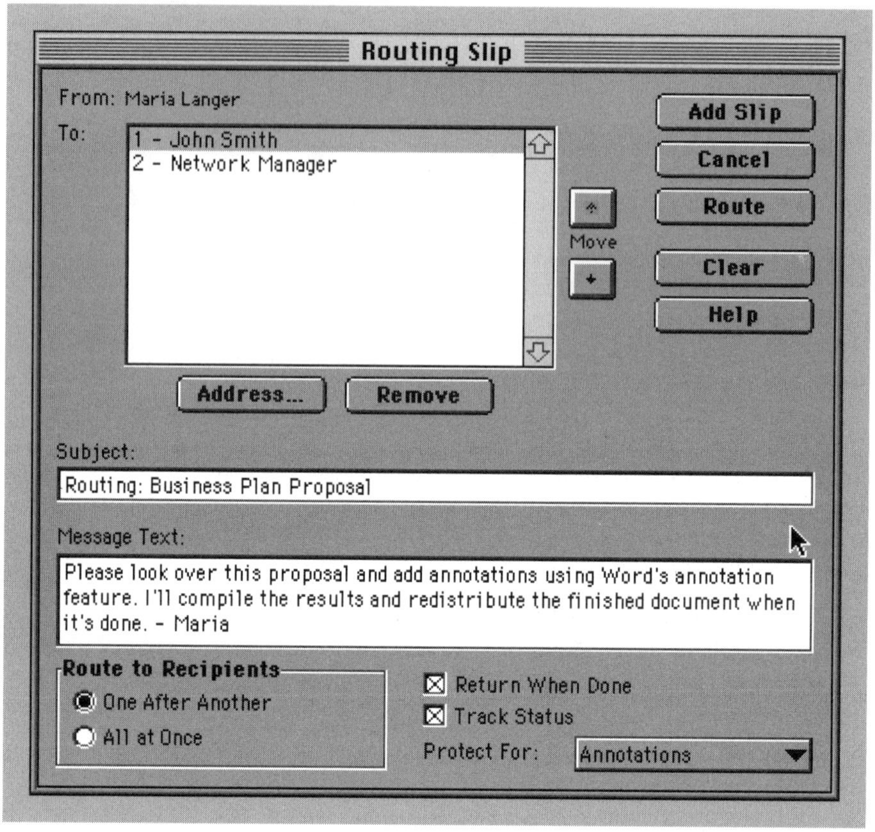

After setting all these options, click the Route button to send the document and routing slip to the names on the list via Microsoft Mail. The Add Slip button merely adds the routing slip to the document — you'll need to choose Send from the File menu to send the document on its way.

When a recipient gets the document, it comes as an attachment to a Microsoft Mail message containing the text of the message you entered in the Routing Slip dialog box. At the bottom of the message are instructions for sending the document and routing slip to the next person on the slip: "When you are done reviewing this document, choose Send from the Word File menu to continue the routing."

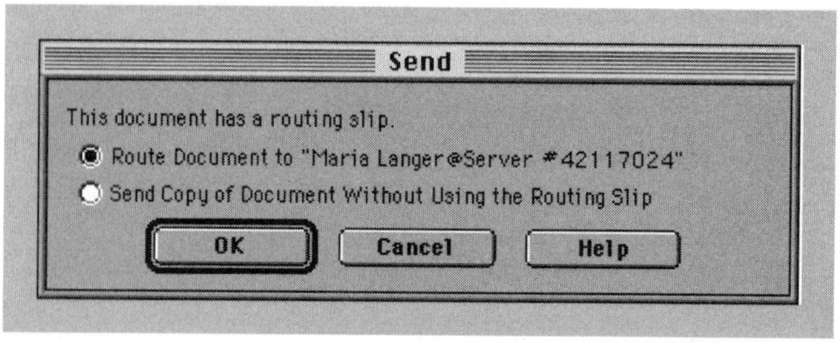

When the recipient chooses Send as instructed, a dialog box like the one illustrated here appears. The recipient then has the option of routing the document to the next person on the routing slip or sending the document without the routing slip.

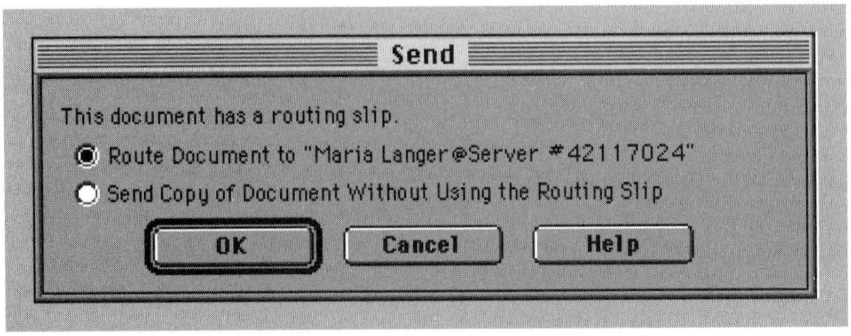

Merging to Electronic Mail

Word's much improved Mail Merge feature, which I discussed in Chapter 21, also has the ability to merge documents to Microsoft Mail. For the merge to work, however, you must include the Microsoft Mail addresses of each of the recipients in one of the data source's fields. And, of course, you must be logged on to the Microsoft Mail server.

When you're all ready to merge the main document and data source document, click the Merge button on the Mail Merge toolbar to display the Merge dialog box. Choose Electronic Mail from the Merge To pop-up menu. (This option only appears if you have Microsoft Mail or another MAPI- or VIM-standard electronic mail package installed.) Click the Setup button. The Merge To Setup dialog box appears.

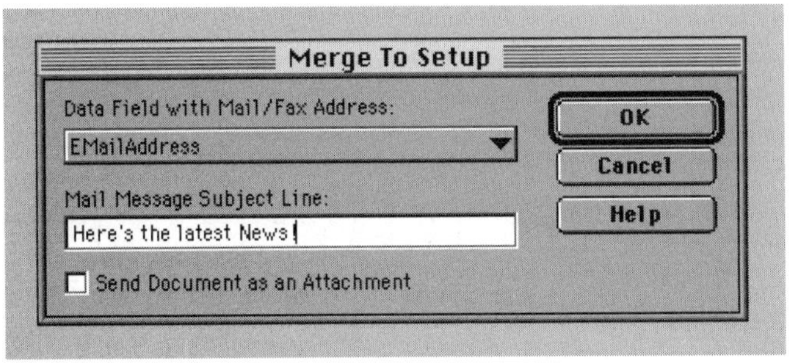

Use the Data Field with Mail/Fax Address pop-up menu to select the field containing the electronic mail addresses of the recipients. Enter subject text in the Mail Message Subject Line edit box. Then click OK. Make any other necessary settings changes in the Merge dialog box and click the Merge button. Word merges the document right to electronic mail.

Importing and Exporting Text

The old fashioned way of sharing information between applications involves importing and exporting. When you import, you take information created and maintained in another file format and use it in Microsoft Word. Once in Word, you can save it as a Word document. When you export, you take information created and maintained in Word and save it in a format other programs can read. This is usually some form of plain text, but as you'll see in this section, Word can save in other file formats, too.

In many applications, you import and export text through the use of Import and Export commands. Not so with Word. To bring external information into a Word document, you simply open that document with the Open command on the File menu or the File or Picture commands on the Insert menu. To save Word information in a format other programs can use, you simply save it in the appropriate format.

In this section, I'll tell you more about exchanging information with files in different formats.

Opening and Inserting Documents Created with Other Applications

To open a document created with an application other than Word, begin by choosing Open from the File menu. The standard Open dialog box, which I covered in some detail in Chapter 3, appears.

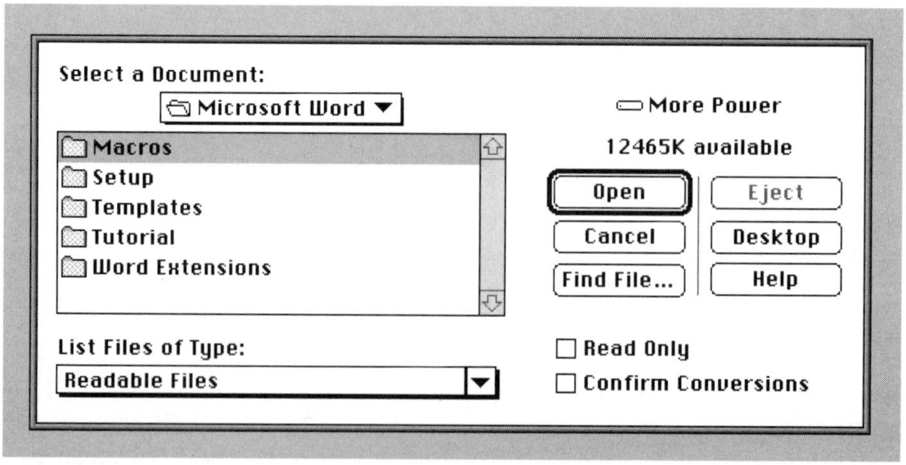

To insert a document created with an application other than Word, position the insertion point where you want the file to appear and choose either File (for a text-type file) or Picture (for a graphic file) from the Insert menu. The Insert File or Insert Picture dialog box appears. Both dialog boxes bear a striking resemblance to the Open dialog box. I showed you the Insert File dialog box earlier in this chapter, so you can see for yourself.

Word's Converters

The directory list window displays all files in the current folder of the type indicated in the List Files of Type pop-up menu. By default, Word searches for Readable Files in the Open and Insert File dialog boxes and All Graphic Files in the Insert Picture dialog box. You can use the List Files of Type pop-up menu to broaden or narrow the list of files Word displays. Word uses converters to read and display files. Some converters are built into Word while others come with Word and can be installed as part of the Word installation. I'll discuss installation in Appendix A.

Here's a quick list of the options on the List Files of Type pop-up menu that appears in the Open and Insert File dialog boxes with all converters installed. I told you about the graphic formats you'll find in the Insert Picture dialog box back in Chapter 12.

- **All Files** — lists every single file, no matter what it is. It'll even list applications. If you use All Files to display and open a file, be prepared for unexpected results.

TIP/TRICK

If you want to see a secret message from prisoners held in a software factory, use Word to open your System file. You'll see a list of Blue Meanies, too. *Just don't save the file when you're finished!*

- **Readable Files** — are what Word looks for by default. A readable file is any file Word can read with its converters.
- **Word Documents** — are documents saved in Word format.
- **Document Templates** — are documents saved as Word template files.
- **Rich Text Format (RTF)** — are files that contain special formatting codes that Word and other word processing applications can read.
- **Text Files** — are files saved in plain text format. Just about every application can read files saved in plain text, even Apple's lowly TeachText and SimpleText freebie word processors.

- **Word 3.x for the Macintosh** — are files saved by a very, very old version of Word. Word 6.0 does not need converters to open files saved in Word 4.0 or 5.x formats.
- **Microsoft Excel 3.x Worksheet, Microsoft Excel 4.x Worksheet, Microsoft 5.x Worksheet** — are files saved in those versions of Microsoft Excel. When you open a worksheet file in Word, it opens as a cell table. I told you about tables in Chapter 11.
- **Text with Layout** — are text files that have been saved in such a way to preserve page formatting. When you save a file as a Text with Layout type, Word converts the file so that the overall appearance of the text looks the same, even when opened with a very basic word processor.
- **Works 4.0 for the Macintosh** — are files saved by Microsoft Works version 4.0.

Once you've located, selected, and opened a document with any of these dialog boxes, Word may have additional questions for you before it finally displays it. For example, when you have All Files selected and try to open an Excel 4.0 document, Word displays the Open Worksheet dialog box, letting you select a specific document in an Excel workbook or a specific range within the worksheet. You can even turn on a Format for Mail Merge button to have Word automatically turn the file into a data source document for mail merge. I told you about mail merge in Chapter 21.

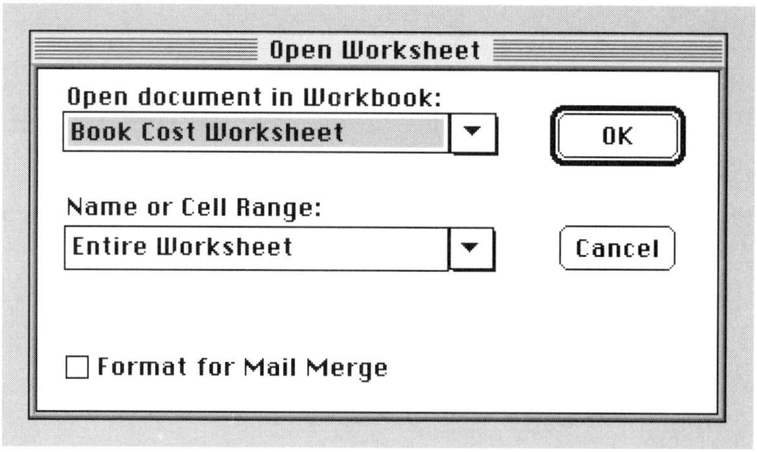

Word may also display the Convert File dialog box. Click an option in the Convert File From scrolling list and click the OK button to complete the conversion. If Word can open the file, it will. If it can't, it'll tell you so.

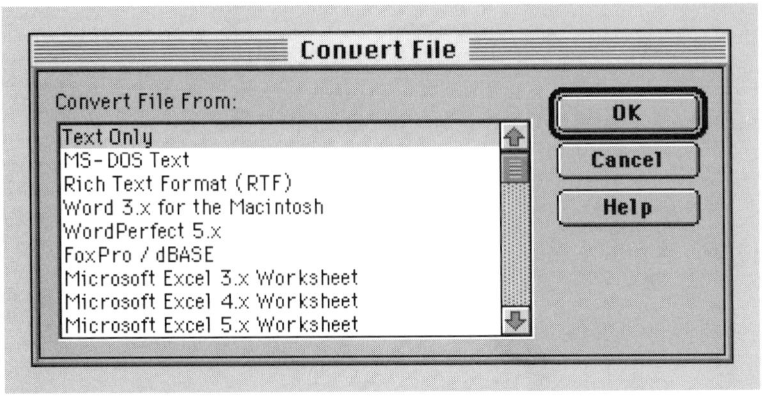

Saving Files in Non-Word Formats

You can also save files in non-Word formats. Choose Save As from the File menu to display the Save As dialog box. Then pull down the Save File as Type pop-up menu to see what formats are available. Word uses converters to save in all the formats I listed above, as well as these additional formats:

- **MS-DOS Text Only** — converts files to plain text, utilizing the extended ASCII character set which is standard for MS-DOS compatible files.
- **Text Only with Line Breaks, MS-DOS Text with Line Breaks** — converts all line breaks, section breaks, and page breaks to paragraph marks. The MS-DOS option uses the extended ASCII character set.
- **Stationery** — saves as a System 7 stationery file. I explained stationery documents in Chapter 9.
- **Speller Custom Dictionary, Speller Exclude Dictionary** — are two kinds of dictionary files for Word's Spelling checker. I told you about them in Chapter 23.
- **WordPerfect** — formats include a variety of WordPerfect versions for Macintosh, MS-DOS, and Windows.
- **Word for Windows** — saves as Word for Windows-compatible files.

- **Word for Macintosh 4.0, 5.0, 5.1** — saves in the three most recent versions of Word for Macintosh. Be sure to save in version 5.1 or 5.0 when sending a Word file to someone who has not yet upgraded to Word 6.0

TIP/TRICK

If you want to use information stored in a Word table in a database program, save the file as Text Only. Word converts the table to tab-delimited (or separated) text. This format is easy for database programs like Claris FileMaker Pro and Microsoft FoxPro to read and import.

TIP/TRICK

If you want to use a Word outline as the basis for a PowerPoint 4.0 presentation, save the file in Word Document format. If you're still using PowerPoint 3.0, save the file in Word 5.1 format. PowerPoint has no trouble reading outlines in Word files. It will create a slide for each Heading 1 item. I told you about outlines in Chapter 15.

Chapter Summary

In this chapter, you learned all kinds of things about sharing information between documents and applications — starting with "advanced" copy and paste and moving on to Publish and Subscribe, and Object Linking and Embedding. You learned how you can send Word files via Microsoft Mail without even opening Microsoft Mail, and how you can import (open or insert) and export (save) in a variety of file formats.

In the next and final chapter, you'll learn about two of Word's automation features: Wizards and macros. You'll see how these two new features can help make your life easier by eliminating tedious tasks.

26

Chapter 26: Automation with Wizards and Macros

NEW IN WORD 6

Word version 6 offers two ways to automate tasks. Its new Wizard feature guides you step by step through the creation of a formatted document, like a résumé, a business letter, or a table. The Macro feature lets you combine commands and keystrokes so you can perform a number of tasks by issuing only one command. Both of these features can help you be more productive.

In this chapter, you'll learn about wizards and macros and how you can use them in your day to day work with Word.

Wizards

As I mentioned in Chapter 2 when I discussed new documents, and again in Chapter 9 when I discussed templates, Word's New dialog box lets you create a new document with a wizard. A wizard uses dialog boxes to ask you questions about the information you include in a specific type of document. Once it's finished asking questions, it prepares a finished document that you can use as-is or fine-tune using standard editing techniques. Word includes wizards for the following kinds of documents: agenda, award, calendar, fax cover, legal pleading, letter, memo, newsletter, résumé, and table.

In this section, I'll show you how to use one of Word's wizards to create a new document. Fire up your Macintosh, launch Microsoft Word, and follow along with me.

Creating a New Document with a Wizard

To create a new document with a wizard, choose New from the File menu to display the New dialog box. Use the scrolling list of templates and wizards to find the wizard you want to use. For my example, I'll use the Letter wizard. Click on it to select it and click OK.

Responding to Wizard Questions

After a few moments, Word displays the first Wizard dialog box on top of a brand new document window. (Be patient — this can take a while. The Status bar tells you what Word is up to while you wait.) For the Letter wizard, Word begins by asking what kind of letter you want to write.

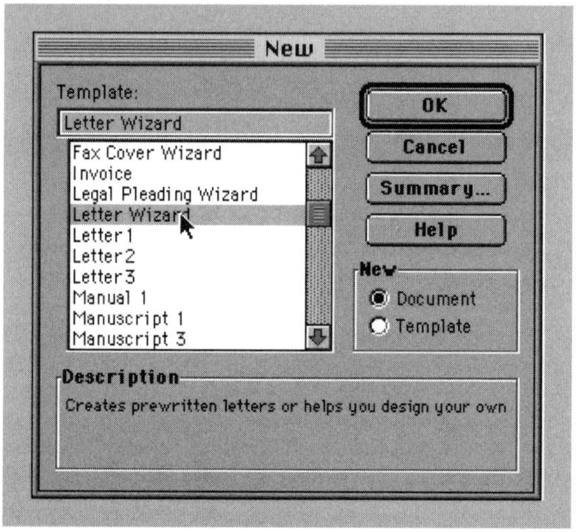

As you can see, you have three choices:

- **Select a Prewritten Business Letter** — lets you choose among a list of standard letters written by professional writers. If you choose this option, the list appears when you click Next.
- **Write a Business Letter** — lets you compose your own business letter.
- **Write a Personal Letter** — lets you compose your own personal letter.

Choose the option you want by clicking its radio button. For my example, I'll write my own business letter. Then click Next to move on to the next dialog box, where Word asks what items you want to include in your letter.

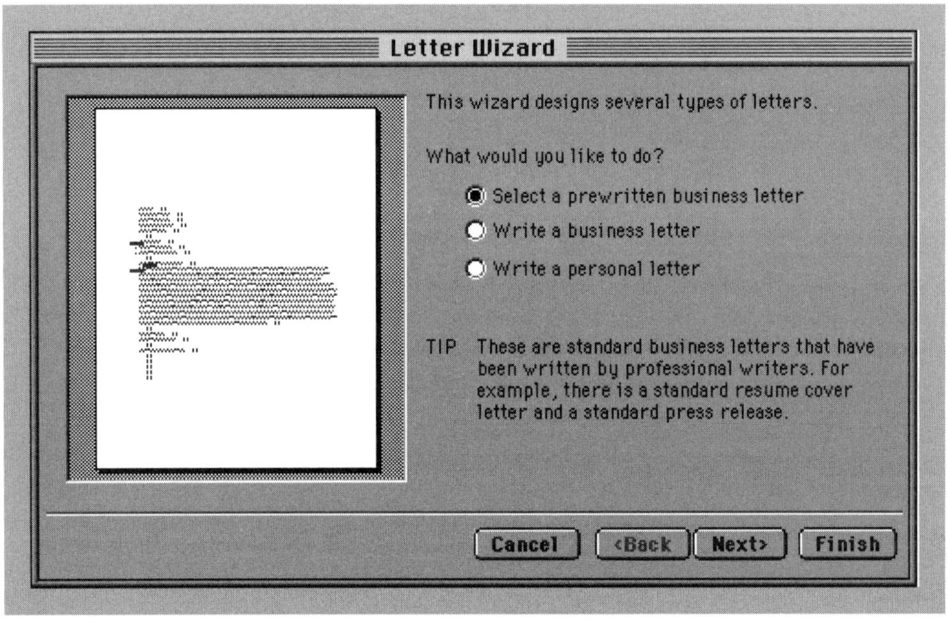

Use the check box to turn the different options on or off. They're self-explanatory so I won't bother listing them here. For my business letter, I want to include page numbers, date, writer's initials, and enclosures, so I'll turn them all on. Then click Next to move to the next dialog box, where Word asks what kind of paper you will print on.

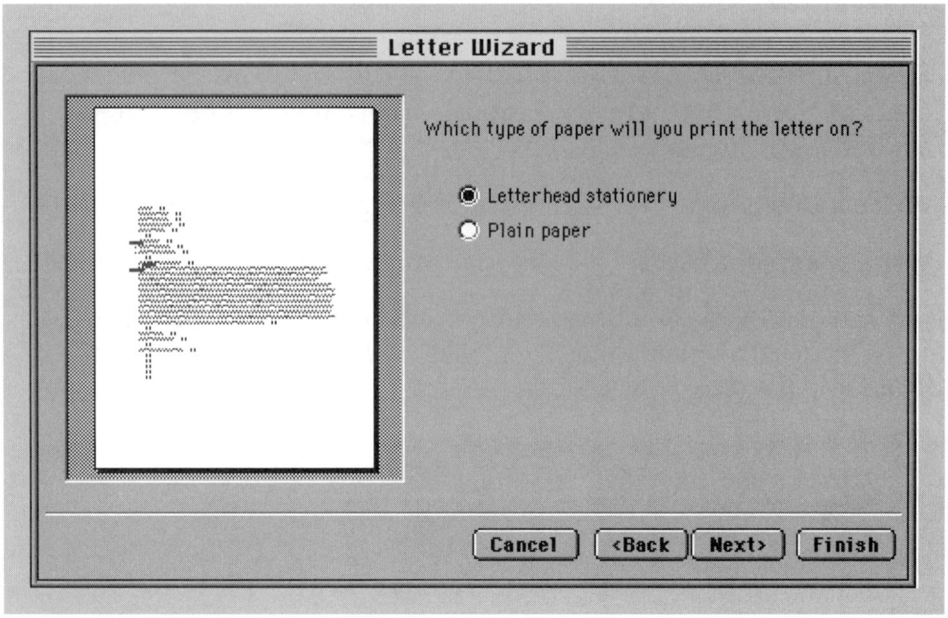

Your choices are:

- **Letterhead Stationery** — tells Word you plan to print on letterhead. If you choose this option, Word displays another dialog box asking for information about the position of the letterhead design.
- **Plain Paper** — tells Word you plan to print on plain paper.

Choose the option you want by clicking its radio button. If you change the option that's already selected, the letter preview on the left side of the dialog box will change. For my example, I'll be printing on letterhead, so I'll leave that selected. Then click Next to continue working with the wizard. In the next dialog box, Word asks for specifics about the letterhead design position and size.

The letterhead design is the printed part of the letterhead. Click the appropriate radio button for its position: At the Top, On the Left, or On the Right. Then measure the distance between the top, left, or right margin and the inside edge of the letterhead design and enter that measurement in the edit box. My letterhead is on the left and takes up 1½ inches of space, so I'll click On the Left and enter 1.5. Then click Next to continue.

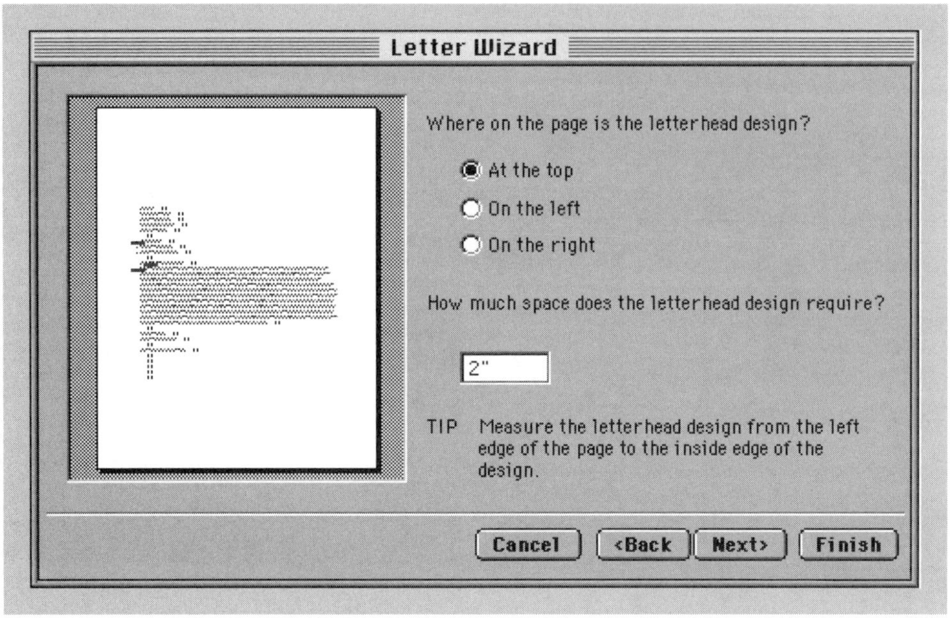

Next, Word asks for the names and addresses to go on the letter. Enter the name, title, company, and address of the recipient. Type it in exactly the way it appears in the letter. Word already knows your name and address. How? You told it in the User Info tab of the Options dialog box. I told you about the Options dialog box in Chapter 23. You can change what appears in the dialog box with standard editing techniques.

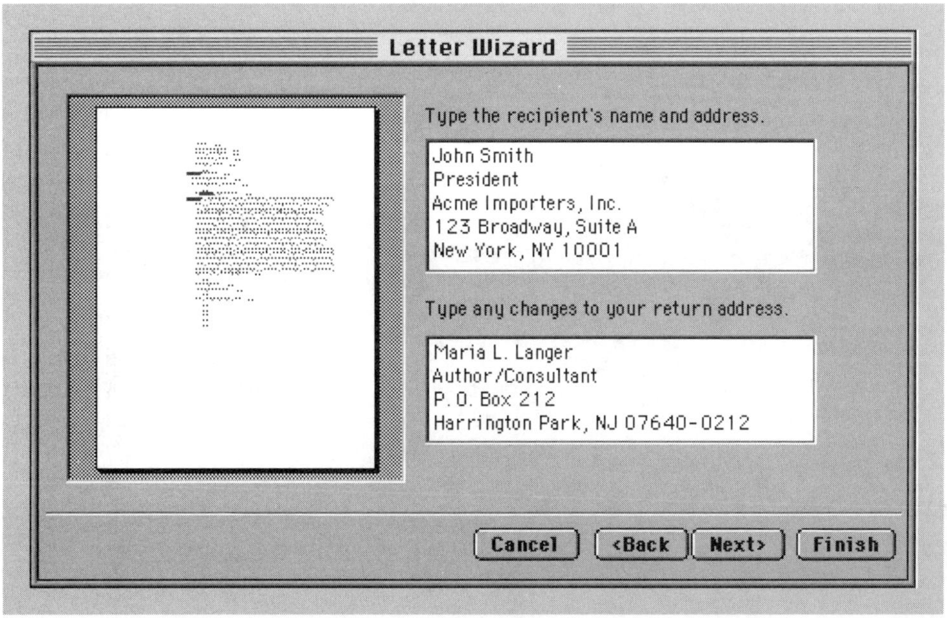

When you're finished, click Next to go to the next dialog box. Now Word wants to know what style letter you want to use. I told you about template styles in Chapter 9. Your choices are Classic, Contemporary, and Typewriter.

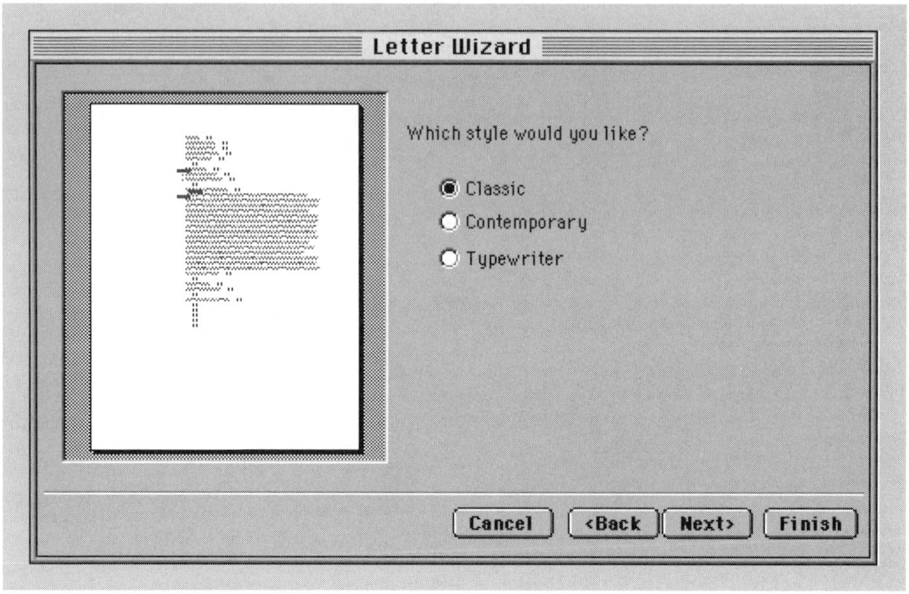

Click the radio button for the one you want. For my example, I'll choose Contemporary. If you change the current setting, Word changes the preview on the left side of the dialog box. Click Next to display the last dialog box, the one with the checkered flag.

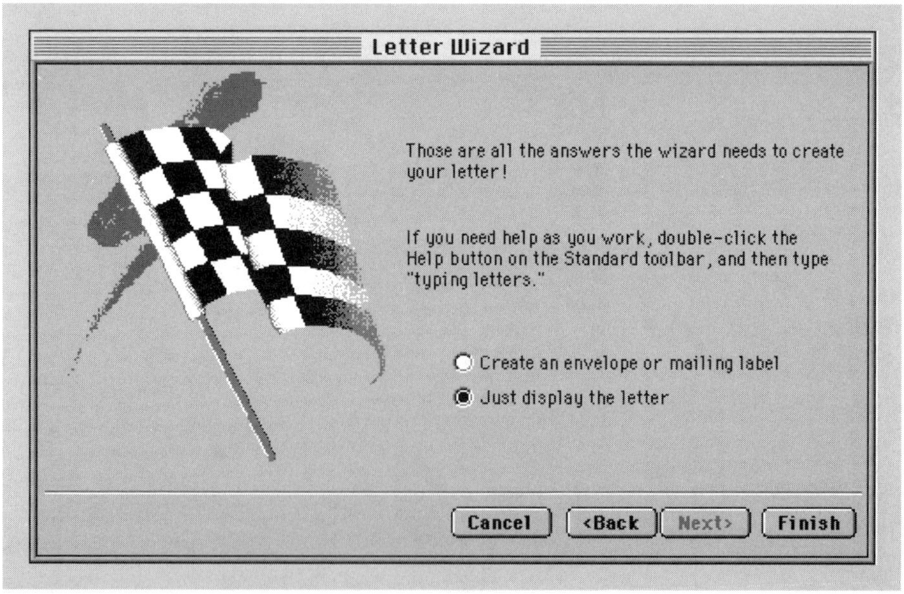

Word offers two more options:

- **Create an Envelope or Mailing Label** — tells Word to create an envelope or mailing label for the letter. If you choose this option, Word creates the letter and displays the Envelopes and Labels dialog box so you can set up the envelope or label you want.
- **Just Display the Letter** — tells Word to create and display the letter on screen so you can complete it.

Click the appropriate radio button. For my example, I just want the letter. Then click Finish.

Modifying the Document

After a few moments, Word displays the completed document in an untitled document window. It shows the document in Page Layout view. You'll see all the information you entered, as well as some other text Word put in automatically. Bookmarks, which I discussed in Chapter 14, have been inserted throughout the document. You'll also see that Word applied styles from the Normal template to the document. I told you about styles in Chapter 7 and about templates in Chapter 9. Here's the top of my letter:

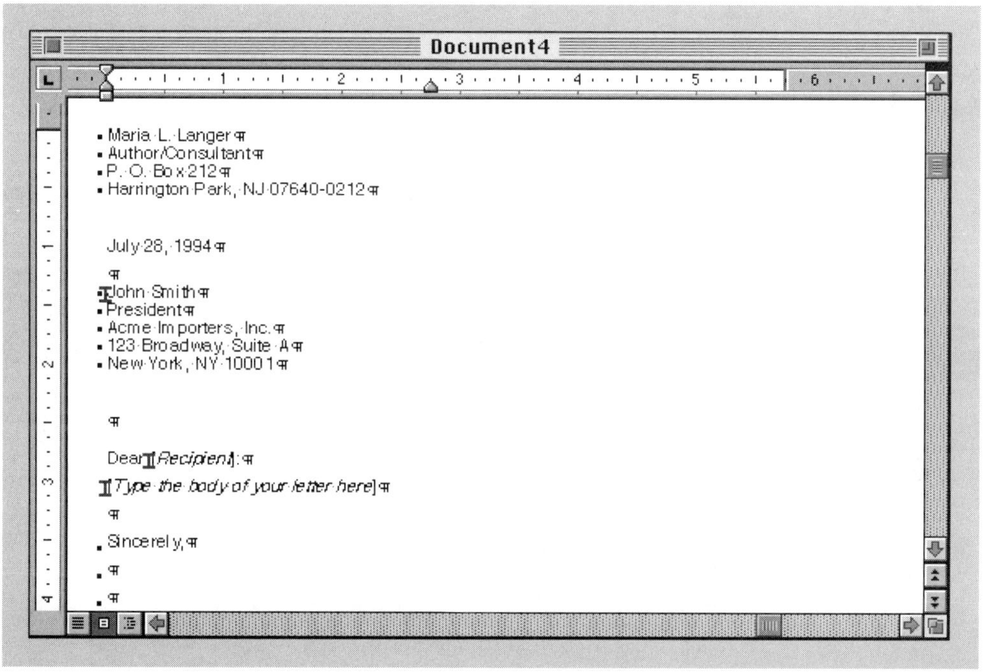

The wizard didn't write the whole letter for you. You'll need to provide some additional information. Begin by selecting the word *Recipient*, along with the brackets that surround it, in the salutation of the letter.

Then type in the name of the person the way you want to address him. If I'm on friendly terms with John Smith, I might just type in *John*. If I've never met the man before, I might want to be more formal and type in *Mr. Smith*.

Next, select the text *Type the body of your letter here* and the brackets that enclose it. Type in the body of your letter. Write as much or as little as you like. Word inserts the body above the closing.

Continue reviewing the document. Select and replace any italicized text Word puts in brackets in the document. That's Word's way of saying that you need to put in your own information. You can also add text, remove unwanted text or empty paragraphs, and change styles assigned to the document. When you're all finished, you can save and print the letter just as if you'd typed it from scratch yourself.

More about Wizards

Here are some additional things to keep in mind when working with wizards:

- Each wizard is different and will ask different questions. Your responses to a wizard's questions may determine what question the wizard asks next and what options are available. It would be impossible for me to walk you through every possible combination within the pages of this book. I don't think you'll need my help, anyway. As my Letter wizard example shows, wizards are straightforward and relatively easy to use.

- Some wizards, like the Fax Cover wizard, prepare a protected form. This may limit the information you can change. You'll have to unprotect the form to make any major changes. I told you about forms in Chapter 22.

- Don't be afraid to experiment with answers to wizard questions. You can always use the Back button in a wizard dialog box to backtrack through your responses and change them. Or, if the final product of a wizard isn't what you intended, start over by creating a new document from the wizard.

- A wizard remembers your answers to questions, making it easy for you to re-create the same kinds of documents over and over with the same settings. Use the Finish button in a wizard to complete the document without going through all the steps.

Macros

Word's powerful new macro feature makes it possible to automate many of the routine tasks you perform with Word. Here are some examples:

- What are the last three commands you often use when creating a letter or other document? For me, it's usually Save, Print, and Close, in that order. You can create a macro that issues all three commands.
- Do you often find yourself digging around in dialog boxes to turn an option on or off? If so, you can create a macro that automates the whole task for you.
- Ever use information created in another application, like a database, in a mail merge? If so, you might be familiar with the multitude of steps it takes to get the data ready and perform the merge. A macro can do it all for you automatically.

These are just three examples. I'm sure you can come up with many more. Best of all, not only can a macro perform a set of tasks you specify, but it can do it far faster and more accurately than you can. That in itself is a good reason to use macros.

In this section, I'll tell you how you can record, use, and modify a macro. I'll also tell you a little about WordBasic and how you can copy macros from one template to another. As I did in the previous section, I'll show you with actual examples, so you might want to launch Word and follow along with me.

Recording a Macro

The way I see it, there are three main steps to recording a macro: getting ready; assigning the macro to a toolbar, menu, or shortcut key; and recording. I'll go through each of these steps here.

Getting Ready to Record

Before you start recording a macro, it's a good idea to have a clear idea of what you want the macro to do. This way, you can perform the macro steps smoothly, anticipating any of Word's prompts for information. You should also prepare by having an appropriate document window open and active.

In my example, I'll create the Save/Print/Close macro I mentioned a moment ago. The steps I'll want to perform include using the Save command, using the Print command and clicking the Print button in the Print dialog box, and using the Close command. To record the macro smoothly, I want to make sure I've got a document open and ready to save, print, and close. The document should already have a name so the Save As dialog box does not appear when I use the Save command.

Starting the Macro Recorder

Word gives you two ways to start the macro recorder:

- Double-click the REC indicator in the Status bar. Word displays the Record Macro dialog box.
- Choose Macro from the Tools menu. Word displays the Macro dialog box, which I'll tell you about a little later. Click the Record button to display the Record Macro dialog box.

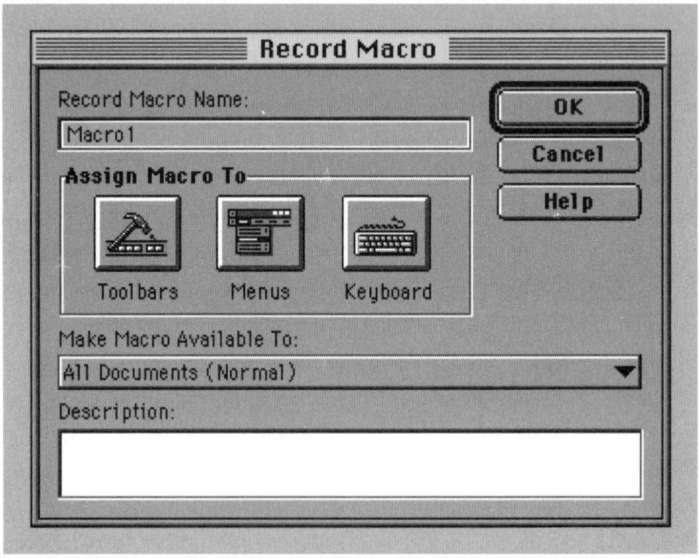

Enter a name for the macro in the Record Macro Name edit box. A macro name can be up to 36 characters in length and cannot contain spaces, commas, or periods. For my example, I'll use the name SavePrintClose, since this describes what my macro will do.

Use the Make Macro Available To pop-up menu to select a template to include the macro in. The pop-up menu will only display the names of templates used to create currently open documents. I'll tell you later how you can copy macros from one template to another. If you choose All Documents (Normal), the macro will be available in all documents.

If desired, enter a description of up to 255 characters in the Description edit box. If you assign the macro to a toolbar button or menu item (which I'll discuss in a moment), the first 100 characters or so of the description appears in the Status bar when you choose the menu item or position your mouse pointer over the toolbar button.

Assigning a Macro to a Toolbar, Menu, or Shortcut Key

The Record Macro dialog box also gives you the option of assigning the macro to a toolbar button, menu item, or shortcut key. To do this, click the Toolbars, Menus, or Keyboard button. Word displays the Customize dialog box, which I discussed in detail in Chapter 24. Since I clicked the Menus button, Word displays the Menus tab.

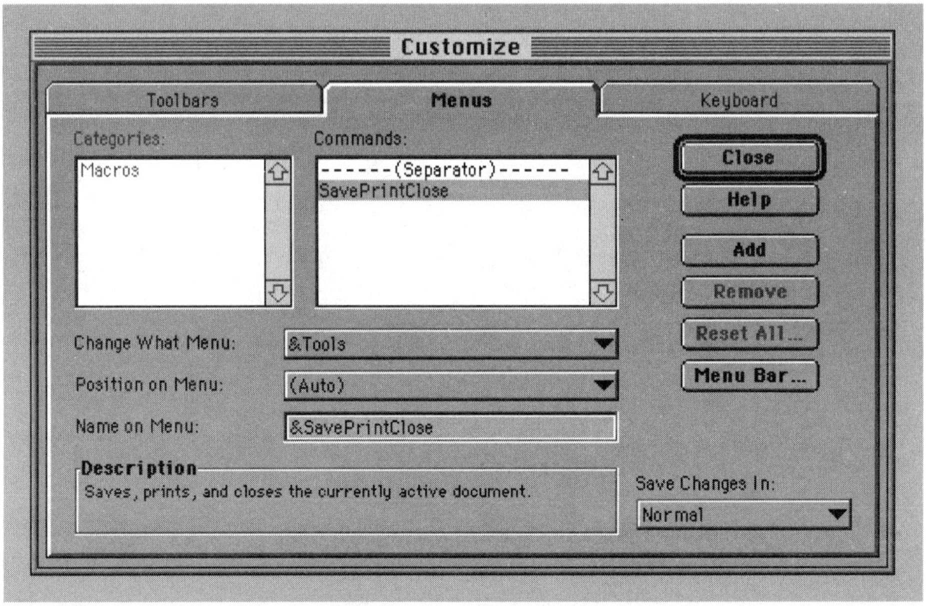

Use this dialog box to assign the macro to a toolbar, menu, or shortcut key. In my example, I want to assign my macro to the File menu under the Save All command, so I set the pop-up menus and edit box as illustrated here and clicked Add Below. If you're not sure how to use this dialog box, read about it in Chapter 24.

After assigning the macro to a toolbar, menu, or keyboard shortcut, click the Close button to dismiss the Customize dialog box.

Recording, Pausing, and Stopping

Word begins recording the macro. You can tell when Word is recording in the following ways:

- The REC indicator in the Status bar is black instead of gray *and*
- Word displays the tiny Record Macro toolbar *and*
- The mouse pointer turns white when positioned in the document window

Perform the steps you want to include in your macro. Take your time and work carefully. Word is taking notes of everything you do. If you need to pause in the recording process, click the Pause button on the Record Macro toolbar. To continue, just click it again. To stop recording, click the Stop button.

Here are my steps and Word's reactions to them:

What I Do	What Word Does
Press ⌘S to save the file.	Since the file already has a name, Word saves it with its current name and disk location without displaying a dialog box. I discussed saving files in Chapter 3.
Press ⌘P to print the file.	Word displays the Print dialog box for the printer I selected in the Chooser. I discussed the Print dialog box and Chooser in Chapter 4.
Click the Print button in the Print dialog box.	Word accepts the settings in the dialog box and sends the document to be printed.
Press ⌘W to close the file.	Word closes the document window. Since it has already been saved, Word does not display a dialog box asking me if I want to save changes.
Click the Stop button on the Record Macro toolbar.	Word stops recording the macro. REC in the Status bar turns gray, the Record Macro toolbar disappears, and the mouse pointer returns to normal.

I could have used menu commands rather than shortcut keys to perform all my steps. No matter how you issue a command, Word records it properly.

If You Mess Up

If you mess up while recording a macro, don't panic. Click the Stop button to stop recording and start all over again from scratch. I'll tell you how to delete a macro a little later.

FYI: When a Macro is Saved

Since a macro is added to a template file, it isn't saved until the template is saved. This is normally when you quit Word, but you can force Word to save all files, including templates, by choosing Save All from the File menu.

TIP/TRICK

Using a Macro

The way you use a macro depends on whether you assigned it to a toolbar, menu, or keyboard shortcut.

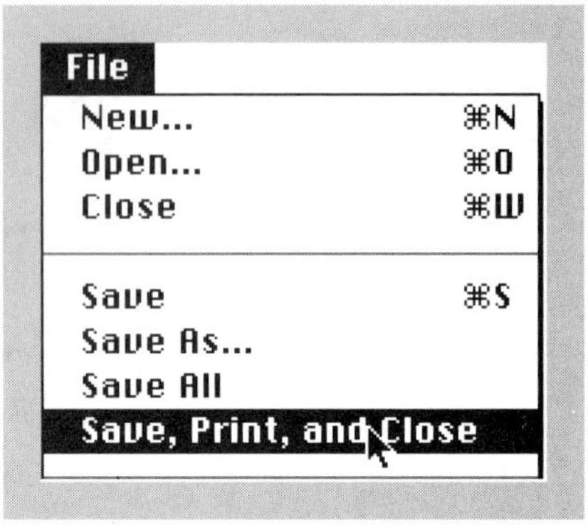

- If your macro was assigned to the toolbar, click its toolbar button. If its toolbar is not displayed, choose Toolbars from the View menu, turn on the check box for the appropriate toolbar, and click OK. I told you about toolbars in Chapter 24.
- If your macro was assigned to a menu (like mine was), pull down the menu and choose the command.
- If your macro was assigned to a shortcut key, press the appropriate key combination.
- If your macro wasn't assigned to a toolbar, menu, or shortcut key, choose Macro from the Tools menu to display the Macro dialog box. Click once on the macro name in the scrolling list to select it and click the Run button.

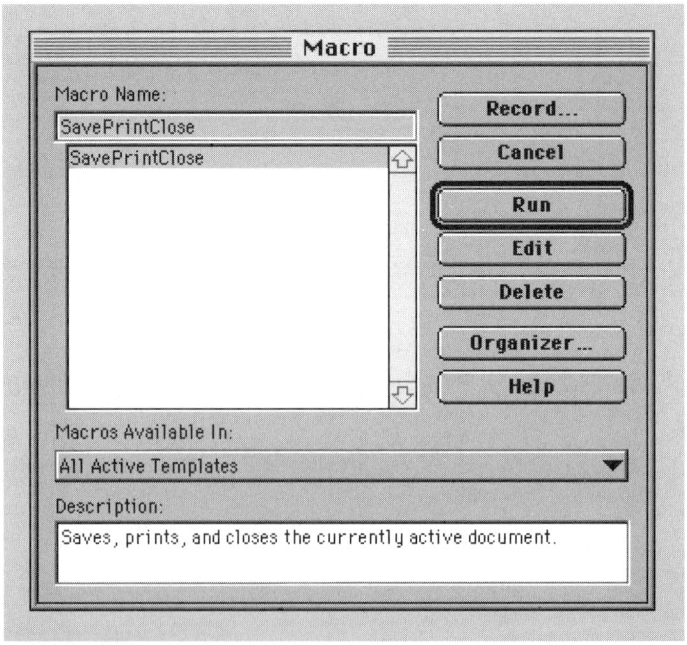

Word performs all the steps in the macro to the best of its abilities. A watch cursor appears while it's working. You'll see how fast it can work. When it's all done, you can continue working with Word.

If a macro step displays a dialog box or other prompt you didn't account for when recording the macro, one of two things may happen. Word could pause, wait for you to respond to the dialog box, and continue running the macro when you click OK. This is what happens when I run my SavePrint-Close macro on a file that has not been named and the Save As dialog box appears. Otherwise, Word could display an error message telling you it couldn't perform a command in the macro and why. In the following example, a macro step tells Word to delete a table column, but when the macro was run, no column was selected so it couldn't perform that step.

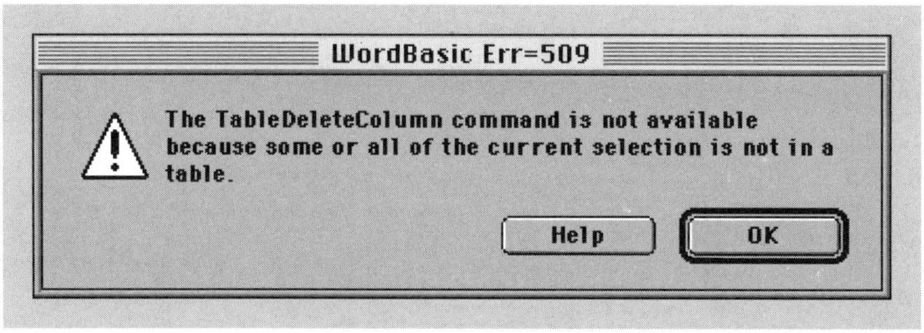

Don't get frustrated if your macros don't work properly the first few times you try writing them. Instead, try to understand why the macro didn't work so you can prevent the problem from happening in the future.

Deleting Macros

You can delete a macro with the Macro dialog box. Choose Macro from the Tools menu. If necessary, use the Macros Available In pop-up menu to change the contents of the scrolling list of macro names. Click on the name of the macro you want to delete and click the Delete button. When Word displays a confirmation dialog box, click Yes. The macro is removed from the list.

Renaming and Copying Macros

The Organizer dialog box, which I discussed in Chapters 9 and 17, lets you rename, delete, or copy macros. There are two ways to open it:

- Choose Macro from the Tools menu to display the Macro dialog box and click its Organizer button.
- Choose Templates from the File menu to display the Templates and Add-ins dialog box and click its Organizer button. Then click the Macros tab.

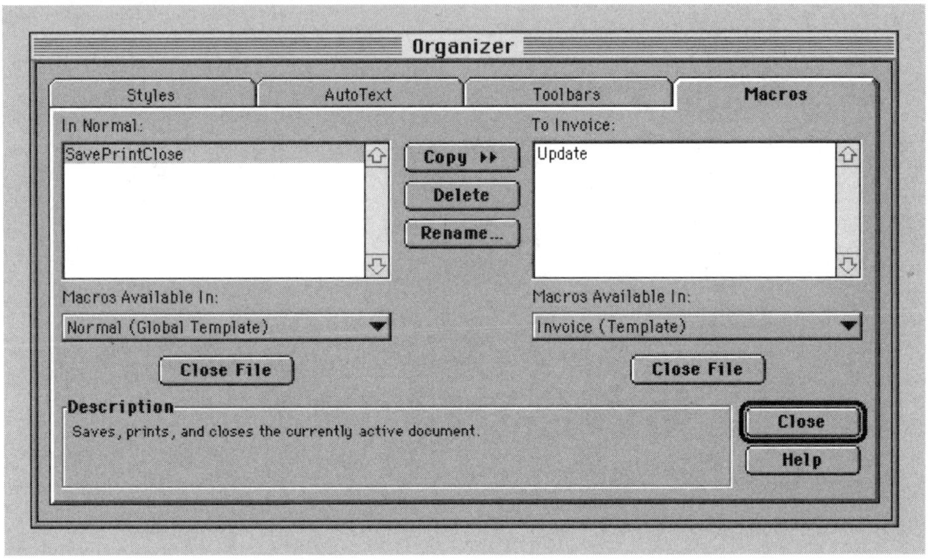

Use the Close File and Open File buttons on either side of the dialog box to close or open template files. A list of macros within a file appears in the scrolling list on its side of the dialog box.

- To rename a macro, click on the macro name to select it and click the Rename button. A Rename dialog box appears. Type in a new name for the macro. Remember the macro naming rules I discussed earlier. Then click OK.
- To delete a macro, click on the macro name to select it and click the Delete button. A confirmation dialog box appears. Click Yes to delete the macro or Yes to All to delete all the selected macros if more than one is selected.

- To copy a macro from one template to another, make sure both the source and destination templates are open and displayed in the dialog box. Then click the name of the macro you want to copy to select it and click the Copy button. It's copied to the other template. It is not necessary to copy macros from the Normal template to other templates since macros in the Normal template are automatically available to all templates.

Modifying a Macro

You can edit an existing macro or write one from scratch. To do so, you'll need a good understanding of WordBasic, the language that macros are written in. While the intricacies of WordBasic are beyond the scope of this book, I can show you how to get started reading and understanding macros.

To open a macro for editing, choose Macro from the Tools menu to display the Macro dialog box. Click on the name of the macro you want to edit and click the Edit button. Word opens a window that contains the instructions in the macro. It also displays the Macro toolbar, which includes buttons you can use to edit and debug (or fix) macros.

My SavePrintClose macro looks like this:

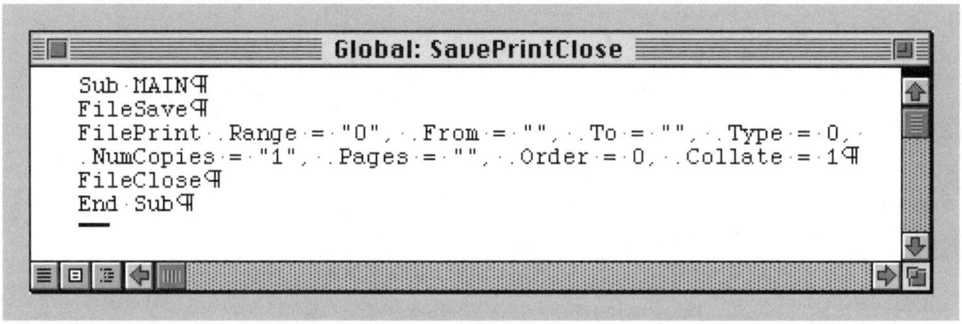

If you look closely, you can see all the commands I issued to create my macro:

- **FileSave** — tells Word to choose Save from the File menu.
- **FilePrint** — tells Word to choose Print from the File menu. The information after FilePrint gives Word all the information it would find in the Print dialog box.
- **FileClose** — tells Word to close the file.

Each of these commands is written in a separate paragraph. Sub MAIN, at the beginning of the macro, names the main subroutine. End Sub, at the end of the macro, ends the subroutine and the macro.

If you know what commands you want to add, remove, or delete from a macro, you can edit the macro right inside this window using standard text editing techniques. When you close the window, Word asks if you want to save changes to the macro. Click Yes.

TIP/TRICK

You can also use the Macro dialog box to write a macro from scratch. Choose Macro from the Tools menu to display the Macro dialog box. Enter a name in the Macro Name edit box, and then click Create. Word displays an empty document window for your macro, as well as the Macro toolbar. Use the window and toolbar to type in and record a macro. When you close the window, click Yes to save the changes.

If you don't know WordBasic, you're better off recording macros using the techniques I discussed earlier in this chapter. This will prevent mistakes and eliminate a lot of debugging.

FYI: About WordBasic

If you're wondering what WordBasic is all about, it's a programming language developed by Microsoft specifically for Word. With it, you can create simple macros like the one I recorded here or custom Word applications, complete with their own dialog boxes. You can even write your own wizards.

Word's online Help feature includes a complete reference guide for WordBasic. To access it, do one of the following:

- Choose Microsoft Word Help from the Help menu. Scroll down in the Contents list until you see the topic Programming with Microsoft Word and click the icon beside it.
- Choose Search For Help On from the Help menu. Type WordBasic into the edit box at the top of the Search Help dialog box and press Return. Then click WordBasic Help in the bottom part of the window and click Go To or press Return.

Continued

WordBasic isn't for the average user. It isn't even for the power user. It's for someone who wants to squeeze more out of Microsoft Word than it already offers. I think Word offers an awful lot already. If you don't think it's enough, maybe WordBasic is something you should look into.

Chapter Summary

In this chapter, you learned about two new automation features in Word: wizards and macros. You learned how to create a document with a wizard, and how to record your own time-saving macros, which you can attach to toolbars, menus, or shortcut keys.

In the final pages of this book, you'll find three appendices: Appendix A provides general information about installing Microsoft Word. Appendix B presents some cross-platform considerations you should bear in mind when exchanging Word files between Macintosh and Windows users. Appendix C provides a list of standard shortcut keys you can use to access Word commands.

Appendix A: Installing Microsoft Word

Microsoft Word includes an installer application called Microsoft Setup that makes it easy to install and deinstall Word components. In this Appendix, I'll tell you all about the options Word's setup program offers.

Before You Start

Before installing Word, it's a good idea to restart your Macintosh with all extensions and control panels turned off. This will prevent problems caused by virus protection software and init conflicts and ensure that your Word installation is completed correctly the first time around.

To disable extensions and control panels, simply hold down the Shift key while restarting (or starting) your Macintosh. When the Welcome to Macintosh (or Welcome to Power Macintosh) window appears, the additional message "Extensions Off" should appear within it. Release the Shift key and let your Macintosh finish starting. Now you're ready to use the setup program.

Starting the Setup Process

1. Insert Disk 1 of the Microsoft Word application disk set in your disk drive. The disk icon appears on your desktop and its window opens on your Macintosh screen.

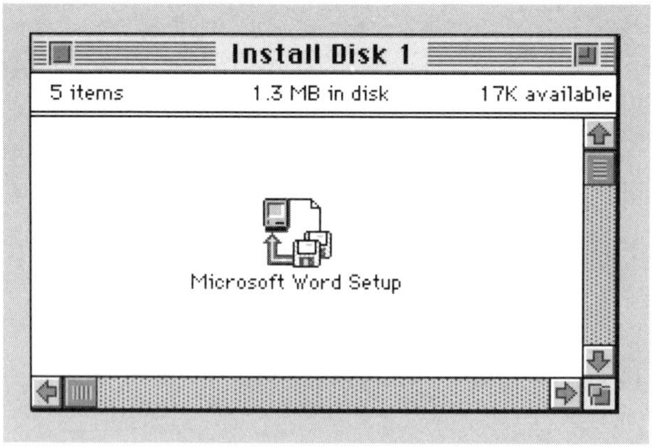

2. Double-click the Microsoft Word Setup icon to launch Microsoft Setup and open the Microsoft Word Setup document. A gray window appears, telling you that your computer is starting Word Setup and that you need to wait.

3. When the first Microsoft Word 6.0 Setup window appears, click OK to continue using Setup.

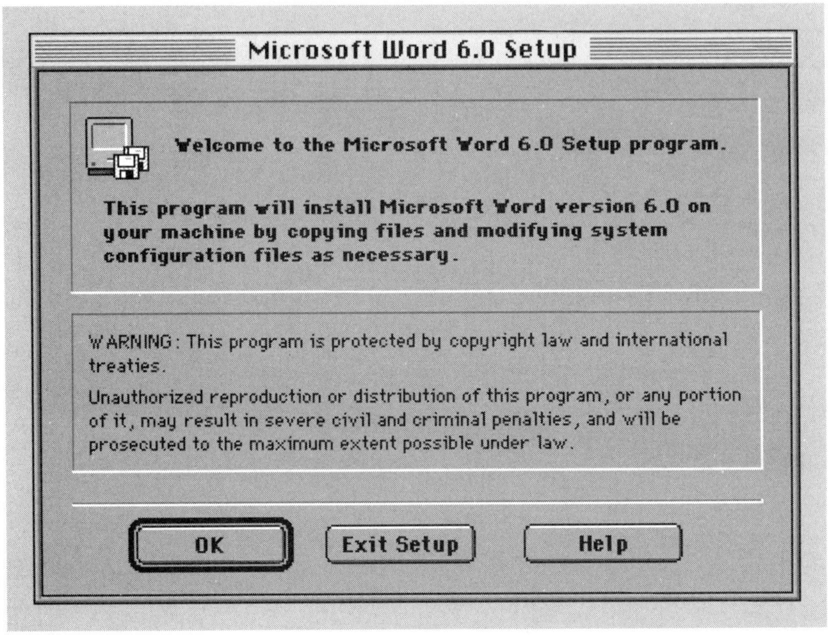

4. Setup prompts you to enter your name and organization. Type the information into the edit boxes. You can press Tab to move from one edit box to the other. Then click OK.

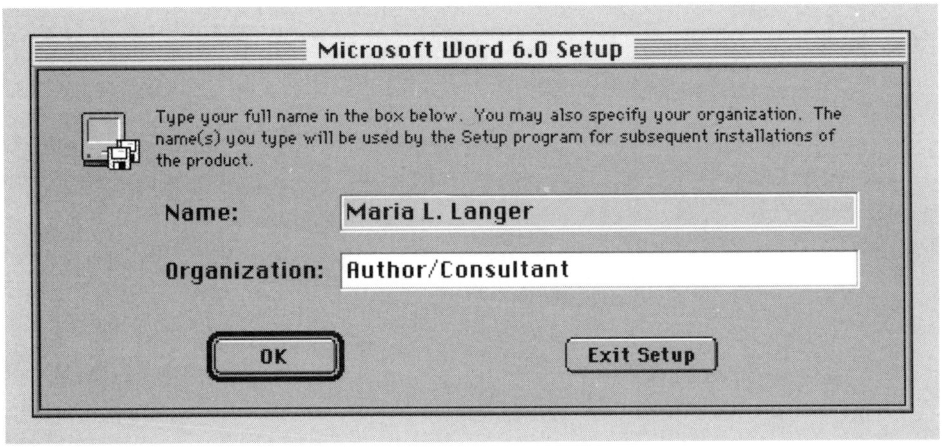

5. Setup asks you to confirm the information you entered. If there's an error, you can click Change to correct it. If everything is entered correctly, click OK.

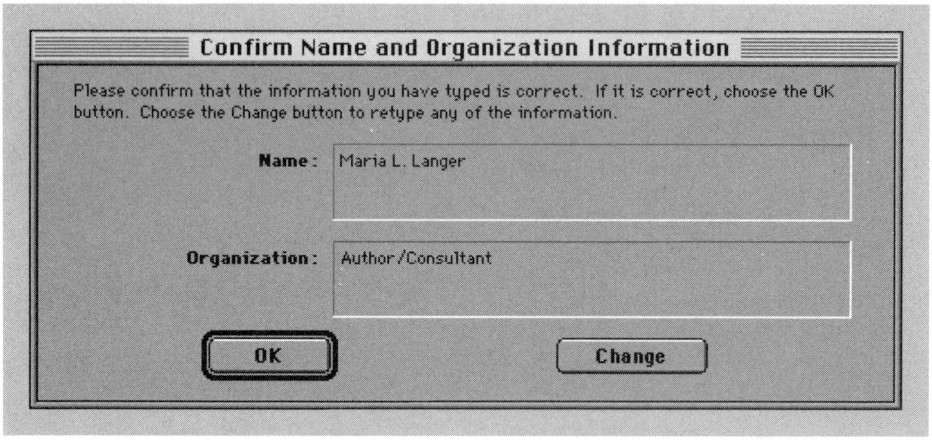

6. Setup displays a large dialog box with a lengthy number at the top. Write the number on your registration card as instructed in the dialog box. If you need to change this number, you can click the Change button. Otherwise, click OK.

7. After a moment, a directory dialog box similar to the standard Save As dialog box appears. If a previous version of Word (like 5.0 or 5.1) exists on your hard disk, its folder will be selected in the directory scrolling window and a message at the bottom of the window tells you that you can install over it. This will, in effect, "update" that version of Word to the new version by replacing its files. To do this, click Setup while the Word folder is selected.

   To install Word 6.0 in a different folder, use the directory portion of the window to open the folder you want Word's folder installed into. Then click the New Folder button to create a folder for Word. Accept the default new folder name (Microsoft Word) or change it. Then click OK. The folder is created and becomes selected. Click Setup to continue.

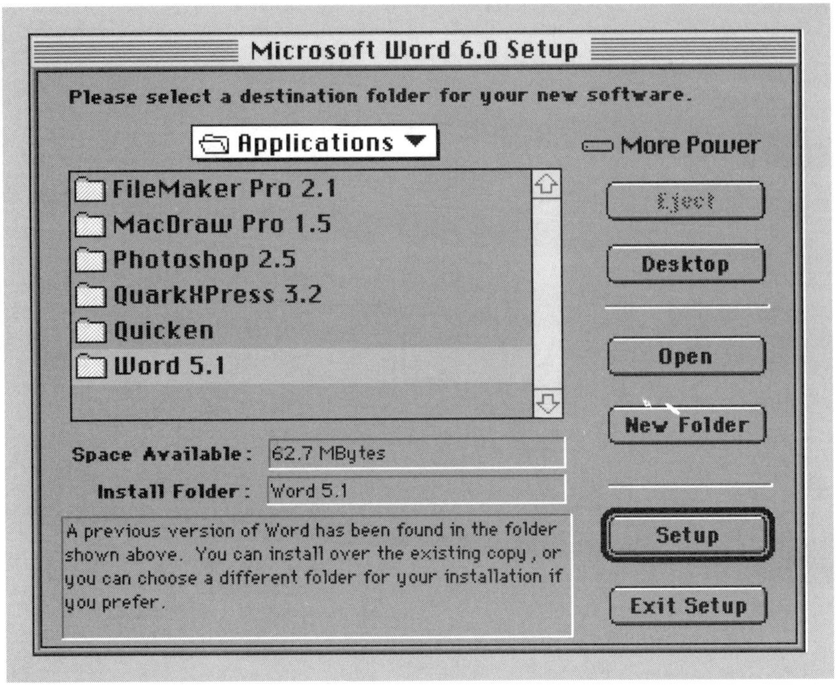

Choosing Setup Options

Setup offers three installation options. Typical, Complete/Custom, and Minimum.

If you click the Typical or Minimum button, Setup immediately begins installing Word. As it copies information from disk, it displays windows with Word information, as well as a Setup status window. When Setup finishes reading a disk, it ejects it and asks for another. When it's all done, it tells you and offers a chance to restart your Macintosh. Click Restart to complete the installation, restart your Macintosh, and begin using your new software.

Here are some additional details for each type of installation.

Typical

Typical installs Word with only the most commonly used options. When you choose Typical, Setup installs the Microsoft Word application and Object Linking and Embedding extension, as well as these components:

Accessories

- Movie

Proofing Tools

- Spelling
- Thesaurus

Converters and Filters

- Filters

Online Help

- Word Help
- Technical Support Help

Tools

- Microsoft System Information
- Setup

Complete/Custom

Complete/Custom installs Word with options you select. You can select any combination of options — even all of them. Your choices are:

Microsoft Word

Object Linking and Embedding

Cross-Platform Fonts

Accessories

- Graph
- Equation Editor
- WordArt
- WordArt Fonts
- Movie
- Voice Annotation

Proofing Tools

- Spelling
- Hyphenation
- Thesaurus
- Grammar

Converters and Filters

- Converters
- Filters

Online Help

- Word Help
- Examples and Demos
- WordBasic Help
- Technical Support Help
- Word Readme Help

Wizards, Templates, and Letters

- Templates and Wizards
- Letters
- Macro Templates

Tools

- Dialog Editor
- Microsoft System Information
- Setup

When you choose Complete/Custom, Setup displays a dialog box that lets you choose the options to install. By default, all options are selected.

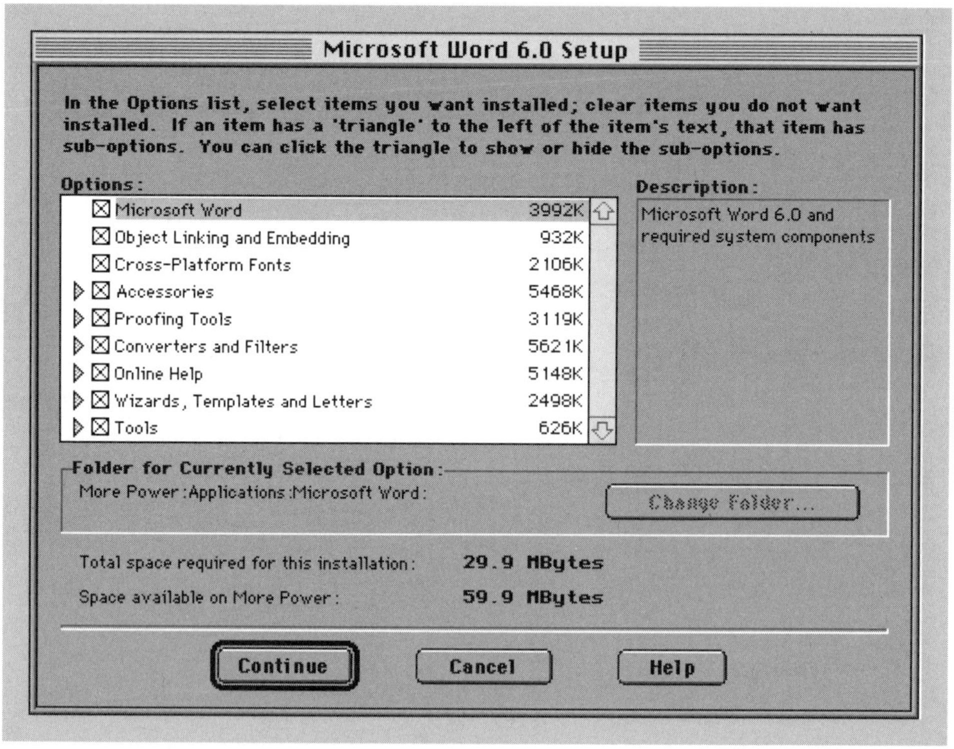

You can turn an option off by clicking in the check box before it to remove the X. If an item has a triangle before it, you can click the triangle to display the components of that item and turn various components on or off. By doing this, you can select exactly what you want to install. The total amount of hard disk space the installation requires is indicated near the bottom of the dialog box. To begin the installation, click Continue.

Minimum

Minimum installs Word with only the options absolutely necessary to use Word. This is particularly useful if you've got limited disk space.

When you choose minimum, Setup installs the Microsoft Word application, as well as these components:

Proofing Tools

- Spelling

Converters and Filters

- Filters

Tools

- Microsoft System Information

Installation Results

Setup installs two folders on your hard disk: Microsoft and Microsoft Word (or the folder name you specified). The Microsoft folder contains files and utilities used by Microsoft applications, including Word. The Microsoft Word folder contains the Word application, help files, and folders for additional items you may have installed. Setup may also install various items in your System folder, depending on the options installed.

Adding/Removing Word Components

The Setup program also lets you add or remove Word options at any time. Insert Disk 1 in your disk drive. When the Install Disk 1 window appears, double-click Microsoft Word Setup to launch Microsoft Setup and open the Microsoft Word setup file. After a few moments, the installation maintenance program window appears. It offers three options: Add/Remove, Reinstall, and Remove All.

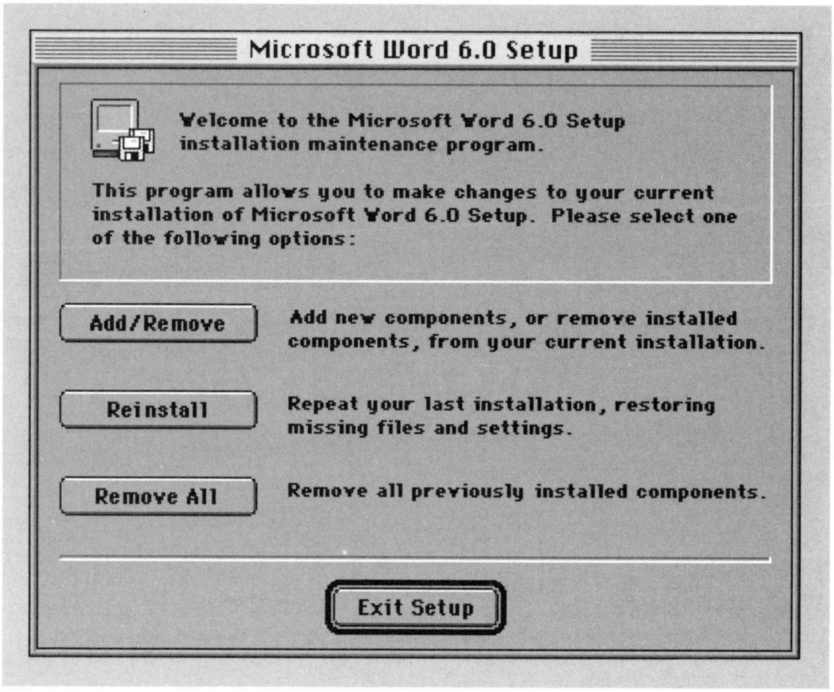

Add/Remove

Add/Remove lets you install additional components or remove components you no longer want installed. When you click the Add/Remove button, Setup displays a dialog box with two lists. On the left is a list of the items that have not been installed. On the right is a list of the items that have been installed. These lists work just like the one in the Complete/Custom install window I discussed above.

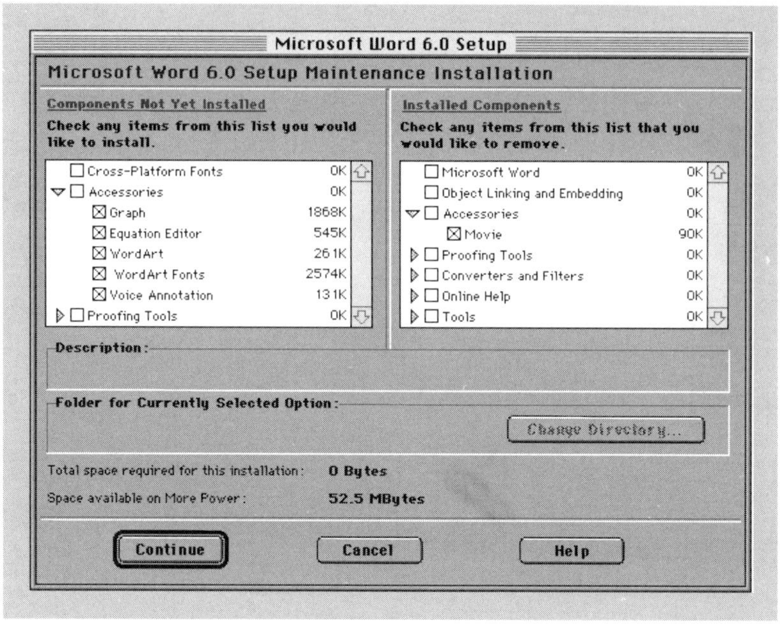

- To install additional items, click the check box before the item category you want to install on the left side list to turn it on. Then click the triangle beside the item and click the check boxes before individual items to turn them on or off. The total space required for the installation appears near the bottom of the dialog box.
- To deinstall items, click the check box before the item category you want to deinstall on the right side list to turn it on. Then click the triangle beside the item and click the check boxes before individual items to turn them on or off. The total space freed up by the deinstallation appears near the bottom of the dialog box.

When you're finished turning options on or off, click Continue. Word prompts you for necessary disks and tells you when installation is done.

Reinstall

Reinstall repeats the last installation. You might find this useful if files were not installed properly because setup was interrupted.

Remove All

Remove All removes all installed components of Word. This is a quick way to remove Word from a computer.

Appendix B: Cross-platform Considerations

As Macintosh users, we've always been faced with the problem that only 15 to 25 percent of personal computer users use Macintoshes. As a result, exchanging files with other computer users isn't always as easy as sticking a floppy disk into a Macintosh disk drive. (Ever try to stick a 5¼ inch disk in a 3½ inch drive?) In a business environment with a mix of computer platforms — Macintosh, DOS, and Windows — it's important to be able to exchange files between different systems.

In this Appendix, I'll discuss the four main considerations for exchanging files between different platforms: fonts, file names, file formats, and disk formats.

FYI: What is Windows?

Windows is an operating system that works with DOS (Disk Operating System) to give IBM-compatible computers a graphical user interface. It does not replace DOS. Instead, it's an application that runs under DOS, much like Word is an application that runs under System 7. When a DOS user launches Windows, he sees a Finder-like desktop with icons and windows. He can then double-click on icons to launch Windows-compatible programs.

I've used Windows on several occasions (usually under duress) and have been very frustrated by it. It might look like a Mac, but it isn't. Deleting icons doesn't delete files. Inserting a disk doesn't make the disk's icon appear on the desktop. To get Windows to recognize that a file or program exists, you have to enter DOS pathnames in a dialog box. If you type them in wrong, Windows can't find the file. To make things worse, because all the graphical elements in Windows are software based rather than ROM-based like in a Macintosh, Windows can be very slow, depending on the speed of the computer it runs on.

Future versions of Windows may replace DOS. That'll be great for IBM-compatible computer users — they won't be faced with an unfriendly *C-prompt* (C:\>) when they start their computers in the morning. But they still won't have Macs.

Fonts

As I discussed in Chapter 5, Macintosh users have had the luxury of multiple fonts since the very first Macintosh model appeared. DOS users, on the other hand, have only recently gained the ability to change fonts within a document. The ability to use a variety of fonts depends on the user's printer and its installed fonts, the fonts installed in DOS, and the fonts the user's applications recognize. Even if the DOS user's system can support multiple fonts, there's a chance he might not have the same fonts you do.

What it all boils down to is this: if you're converting a Word file to a non-Macintosh format, there's a chance that the font information will be lost. In that case a default font may be used by the DOS application to display the document. It'll look different than the way you created it.

Microsoft helps us get around this problem when exchanging files with Word for Windows users. It provides a number of cross-platform TrueType fonts with both versions of Word. If you use these fonts, the font information is retained when the file is opened on a Windows computer, as long as the same fonts have been installed by the Word for Windows user.

Here's a list of the cross-platform fonts Microsoft includes with Word 6.0:

- **Arial** — a sans serif font similar to Helvetica
- **Courier New** — a cross-platform version of Courier
- **Times New Roman** — a cross-platform version of Times
- **Wingdings** — a dingbats font similar to Zapf Dingbats

File Names

Macintosh users are spoiled. We can use up to 31 characters in file names and can include any character except the colon (:). DOS and Windows users aren't so lucky. They're limited to 8-character file names followed by a period (which they call a "dot") and a 3-character extension. DOS and Windows applications often use the file name extension to determine what type of file it is and what application created it. (Macintosh computers use a file type and creator code we don't normally see to do this.)

When saving a file you will pass along to a DOS or Windows user, try to remember to give the file a DOS-like name. Otherwise, when the file is read on a DOS computer, the file name will be truncated. "My Letter to Bob" may become "!MYLETTE.RTO". Not very descriptive, is it?

File Formats

When you save a Microsoft Word file as a Word Document — the default option in the Save As dialog box, which I told you about in Chapter 3 — that file contains certain formatting information that Word 6.0 understands. If you try to open that file with, say, WordPerfect for DOS, you may get a screen full of gibberish. At the very least, you'll get the document's text with a lot of unwanted characters thrown in.

As I discussed in Chapters 3 and 25, Word 6.0 includes translators that make it easy to save Word files to a wide variety of popular Macintosh, DOS, and Windows formats. If you know the file you've created will be opened by a WordPerfect for Windows user, choose WordPerfect 5.x for Windows from the Save File as Type pop-up menu in the Save As dialog box. This automatically converts Word's formatting information to a format that WordPerfect can read and understand. There will be no gibberish and the file should retain most of its formatting.

If the document you've created will be read by a Word 6.0 for Windows user, you don't need to use any of Word's built-in translators. Instead, save the file as a plain Word Document. The file formats of Word 6.0 for Macintosh and Word 6.0 for Windows are virtually identical so no translation is necessary.

One more thing: if you don't know what kind of computer will eventually read your file, you can always save it as Text Only. This creates a plain ASCII file which can be read by any computer — and I do mean *any* computer. Just keep in mind that any font or paragraph formatting included in the file will be lost when you save it as Text Only. Text only is just that: only text.

Disk Formats

The final consideration in getting a Word for Macintosh file into the hands of a DOS or Windows user is disk format. You're probably aware that Macintosh disks have a different format than DOS disks. If you stick a Macintosh disk in a DOS computer, you'll get the very unfriendly message:

```
Not ready reading drive A
Abort, Retry, Fail?_
```

If you stick a DOS disk into a Macintosh computer which isn't prepared to read it, your Mac will kindly offer to initialize or format the disk for you. This is not what you want to do when the disk contains data — initializing a disk erases it!

Apple has given us all kinds of hardware and software tools to help us deal with disk compatibility issues. SuperDrives, which have been standard in all new Macintosh models since 1989, make it possible for a Macintosh to read and write to DOS disks. Apple File Exchange, a utility that is part of the System software, works with a SuperDrive to copy files between disks of different formats. With System 7.5, Apple includes Macintosh PC Exchange, a control panel that lets you read DOS disks without having to launch special utilities. If you need to save files onto DOS disks, consult the documentation that came with your Macintosh for information on either of these utilities. One thing you won't be able to do without special hardware: save files onto 5¼ inch disks.

If your Macintosh is on a network of Macintosh and DOS-based machines, you probably won't have to deal with floppy disks to share files with a co-worker. Simply send the file to him via electronic mail or save it to the server in a folder he can access. If you need more information about doing either of these things, contact your network administrator.

Another way you can get a Macintosh file onto a DOS disk is via modem. A modem is a device that lets two computers talk to each other over phone lines. Modems don't care what kind of computers are doing the talking. As long as both computers have appropriate telecommunications software and can connect, the modem can exchange any kind of information, including files. If you're using Word on a Macintosh without a SuperDrive that isn't connected to a network, this might be the only way you can exchange files with an IBM-compatible computer.

Appendix C: Shortcut Keys for Word 6

Command Name	Shortcut Key
All Caps	⌘ Shift A
Annotation	⌘ Option A
Apply Heading1	⌘ Option 1
Apply Heading2	⌘ Option 2
Apply Heading3	⌘ Option 3
Apply List Bullet	⌘ Shift L
Auto Format	⌘ K
Auto Text	⌘ Option V
Bold	⌘ B
Bold	⌘ Shift B
Bookmark	⌘ Shift F5
Cancel	⌘ .
Cancel	Esc
Center Para or Pa	⌘ E pref. 1. Beside, near 2. Beyond 3. Subsidiary
Change Case	⌘ Option C
Change Case	Shift F3
Char Left	←
Char Left Extend	Shift ←
Char Right	→
Char Right Extend	Shift →
Clear	Clear
Clear	Del
Close or Close All	⌘ W
Close Pane	Control Shift C
Column Break	⌘ Shift Return

Continued

Command Name	Shortcut Key
Column Select	⌘ Shift F8
Copy	⌘ C
Copy	F3
Copy As Picture	⌘ Option D
Copy Format	⌘ Shift C
Copy Text	Shift F2
Customize Add Menu Shortcut	⌘ Option =
Customize Keyboard	⌘ Option ▦ −
Customize Keyboard Shortcut	⌘ Option ▦ +
Customize Remove Menu Shortcut	⌘ Option −
Cut	⌘ X
Cut	F2
Date Field	Control Shift D
Delete Back Word	⌘ Delete
Delete Row	⌘ Control X
Delete Word	⌘ Del
Delete Word	⌘ Option G
Demote to Body Text	⌘ Shift N
Do Field Click	Option Shift F9
Doc Close	⌘ F4
Doc Restore	⌘ F5
Doc Restore	Control F5

Continued

Command Name	Shortcut Key
Doc Split	⌘ Option S
Double Underline	⌘ Shift D
End of Column	Option Pg Dn
End of Column	Option Shift Pg Dn
End of Doc Extend	⌘ Shift End
End of Document	⌘ End
End of Line	Control ↓
End of Line	End
End of Line Extend	Shift End
End of Row	Option End
End of Row	Option Shift End
End of Window	⌘ Pg Dn
End of Window Extend	⌘ Shift Pg Dn
Endnote Now	⌘ Option E
Extend Selection	F8
Field Chars	⌘ F9
Field Codes	Option F9
Find	⌘ F
Font	⌘ D
Font	⌘ Shift F
Font Size Select	⌘ Shift P
Footnote Now	⌘ Option F
Go Back	⌘ Option Z
Go Back	Shift F5

Continued

Command Name	Shortcut Key
Go To	⌘ G
Go To	F5
Go to Next Page	⌘ Option Pg Dn
Go to Previous Page	⌘ Option Pg Up
Goto Annotation Scope	Option F11
Grow Font	⌘ Shift .
Grow Font One Point	⌘]
Hanging Indent	⌘ T
Header Footer Link	Control Shift R
Help	⌘ /
Help	Help
Hidden	⌘ Shift H
Indent	⌘ M
Insert Row	⌘ Control V
Italic	⌘ I
Italic	⌘ Shift I
Justify Para	⌘ J
Left Para	⌘ L
Line Down	↓
Line Down Extend	Shift ↓
Line Up	↑
Line Up Extend	Shift ↑
List Commands	Control =
Lock Fields	⌘ 3
Lock Fields	⌘ F11

Continued

Command Name	Shortcut Key
Mail Merge Check	Control Shift K
Mail Merge Edit Data Source	Control Shift E
Mail Merge to Doc	Control Shift N
Mail Merge to Printer	Control Shift M
Mark Citation	⌘ Option Shift I
Mark Index Entry	⌘ Option Shift X
Mark Table of Contents Entry	⌘ Option Shift O
Menu Mode	⌘ Tab
Menu Mode	F10
Menu Mode	▦ +
Merge Field	Control Shift F
Microsoft System Info	⌘ Option Help
New	⌘ N
Next Field	F11
Next Object	Option ↓
Next Window	⌘ F6
Next Window	Option F6
Normal	⌘ Option N
Normal Style	⌘ Shift N
Normal Style	Option Shift Clear
Open	⌘ O
Open or Close Up Para	⌘ 0

Continued

Command Name	Shortcut Key
Other Pane	F6
Other Pane	Shift F6
Outline	⌘ Option O
Outline Collapse	Control Shift −
Outline Demote	Option Shift →
Outline Expand	Control Shift =
Outline Move Down	Option Shift ↓
Outline Move Up	Option Shift ↑
Outline Promote	Option Shift ←
Outline Show First Line	Control Shift L
Overtype	Control Help
Page	⌘ Option P
Page Break	Shift Enter
Page Down	Pg Dn
Page Down Extend	Shift Pg Dn
Page Field	Control Shift P
Page Up	Pg Up
Page Up Extend	Shift Pg Up
Para Down	⌘ ↓
Para Down Extend	⌘ Shift ↓
Para Up	⌘ ↑
Para Up Extend	⌘ Shift ↑
Paste	⌘ V
Paste	F4

Continued

Command Name	Shortcut Key
Paste Format	⌘ Shift V
Prev Field	Shift F11
Prev Object	Option ↑
Prev Window	Option Shift F6
Print	⌘ P
Print Preview	⌘ F2
Print Preview	⌘ Option I
Quit	⌘ Q
Redo	Option Shift Delete
Redo or Repeat	⌘ Y
Redo or Repeat	Option Return
Repeat Find	⌘ Option Y
Repeat Find	⌘ Shift F4
Repeat Find	Shift F4
Replace	⌘ H
Reset Char	⌘ Shift Z
Reset Char	⌘ Spacebar
Reset Para	⌘ Option Q
Right Para	⌘ R
Save	⌘ S
Save As	Cmd 20
Section Break	⌘ Enter
Select All	⌘ A
Select Table	⌘ Option T
Select Table	Option Clear

Continued

Command Name	Shortcut Key
Show All	⌘ 8
Show All	▦ F8
Show All Headings	Control Shift A
Show Heading1	Control Shift 1
Show Heading2	Control Shift 2
Show Heading3	Control Shift 3
Show Heading4	Control Shift 4
Show Heading5	Control Shift 5
Show Heading6	Control Shift 6
Show Heading7	Control Shift 7
Show Heading8	Control Shift 8
Show Heading9	Control Shift 9
Shrink Font	⌘ Shift ,
Shrink Font One Point	⌘ [
Shrink Selection	Shift F8
Small Caps	⌘ Shift K
Space Para1	⌘ 1
Space Para1	⌘ 1
Space Para15	⌘ 5
Space Para15	⌘ 5
Space Para2	⌘ 2
Space Para2	⌘ 2
Spelling	⌘ Option L
Spelling	F7

Continued

Command Name	Shortcut Key
Spike	⌘ F3
Spike	⌘ Shift F3
Start of Column	Option Pg Up
Start of Column	Option Shift Pg Up
Start of Doc Extend	⌘ Shift Home
Start of Document	⌘ Home
Start of Line	Control ↑
Start of Line	Home
Start of Line Extend	Shift Home
Start of Row	Option Home
Start of Row	Option Shift Home
Start of Window	⌘ Pg Up
Start of Window Extend	⌘ Shift Pg Up
Style	⌘ Shift S
Subscript	⌘ =
Superscript	⌘ Shift =
Symbol Font	⌘ Shift Q
Thesaurus	⌘ Option R
Thesaurus	Shift F7
Time Field	Control Shift T
Toggle Field Display	Shift F9
Tool	⌘ ▦ /
Tool	⌘ Shift /
Tool	Shift Ins

Continued

Command Name	Shortcut Key
Un Hang	⌘ Shift T
Un Indent	⌘ Shift M
Underline	⌘ Shift U
Underline	⌘ U
Undo	⌘ Z
Undo	F1
Undo	Option Delete
Unlink Fields	⌘ 6
Unlink Fields	⌘ Shift F9
Unlock Fields	⌘ 4
Unlock Fields	⌘ Shift F11
Update Auto Format	⌘ Option U
Update Fields	⌘ Option Shift U
Update Fields	F9
Update Source	⌘ Shift F7
Word Left	⌘ ←
Word Left	Option ←
Word Left Extend	⌘ Shift ←
Word Right	⌘ →
Word Right	Option →
Word Right Extend	⌘ Shift →
Word Underline	⌘ Shift W

Index

B

C

D

E

F

G

H

I

J

K

L

M

N

O

P

Q

R

S

T

V

W

X

Z

Word 6 Template Disk Offer

As you learned in this book, Word 6's greatly improved template feature lets you include your own style sheets, AutoText entries, macros, toolbars, shortcut keys, and menus in template files. You can use this feature to create custom applications for specific types of documents.

The Word 6 Templates Disk, which was created by the author of this book, Maria Langer, contains 50 fully documented, customizable Word 6 templates that include:

- *Practical* styles for letters, reports, and other common documents.
- AutoText entries for commonly used boilerplate text.
- Toolbars buttons and shortcut keys to invoke macros and activate commands.
- Headers for printing page layout registration marks and watermarks on document pages.
- Standard business forms for gathering information.
- Macros for commonly repeated tasks and more advanced applications.
- Toolbar buttons, menu commands, and settings to emulate Word 5.1.

The Word 6 Templates Disk is available in Macintosh or Windows format for $19.95 (US) or $21.95 (outside US). These prices include postage. NJ residents must add 6% sales tax.

To order, complete the form below and send it, with payment or credit card information, to: Giles Road Press, P.O. Box 212, Harrington Park, NJ 07640-0212. Credit card orders may be faxed to 201/767-7457. You can also use this order form to request a free sample issue of ***Macintosh Tips & Tricks***, the *affordable* news and productivity newsletter for Macintosh users, even if you're not ordering a disk. Please print neatly!

- - - - - - - - ✂ - ✂ - - - - - - - - - -

Order Form

Name: Ryuji TSUKISE

Company: ____________________

Address: ____________________

____

____

Day Phone: ____________________ E-Mail: ____________________

❑ Please send _____ copies of ***The Word 6 Templates Disk*** at $19.95 (US) or $21.95 (outside US) for a total of $________. Format: ___ Macintosh ___ Windows

❑ Please send a free sample issue of ***Macintosh Tips & Tricks***.

Payment by: Check Money Order MasterCard Visa American Express Discover

If paying by credit card, you *must* provide the following information:

Card Number: ____________________

Expires: ____________ Signature: ____________________